CD START INSTRUCTIONS

1 Place the CD-ROM in your CD-ROM drive.

2 Launch your Web browser. *See below if you do not have a Web browser.

3 From your Web browser, select Open File from the File menu. Select the CD-ROM (usually drive D for PCs and the Desktop for Macs), then select the file called Welcome.htm.

* We have included the Microsoft Web browser Internet Explorer on this CD in case you do not have a browser or would like to upgrade or change your browser. Please review the CD-ROM appendix of this book for more information on this software as well as other software on this CD.

MINIMUM SYSTEM REQUIREMENTS

Designed to work on both Macintosh and Windows operating systems

Macintosh

- Computer: 68030
- Memory: 8MB of RAM
- Platform: System 7.0 or higher
- Software: Web browser
- Hardware: 2X CD-ROM Drive

Windows

- Computer: 386 IBM PC-compatible
- Memory: 8MB of RAM
- Platform: Windows 3.1, NT or 95
- Software: Web browser
- Hardware: 2X CD-ROM Drive

Women's Wire WEB Directory

PLEASE NOTE—USE OF THE CD-ROM AND THE PROGRAMS INCLUDED ON THE CD-ROM PACKAGED WITH THIS BOOK IS SUBJECT TO AN END-USER LICENSE AGREEMENT (THE "AGREEMENT") FOUND AT THE BACK OF THE BOOK. PLEASE READ THE AGREEMENT CAREFULLY BEFORE MAKING YOUR PURCHASE DECISION. PURCHASE OF THE BOOK AND USE OF THE CD-ROM , PROGRAMS, WILL CONSTITUTE ACCEPTANCE OF THE AGREEMENT.

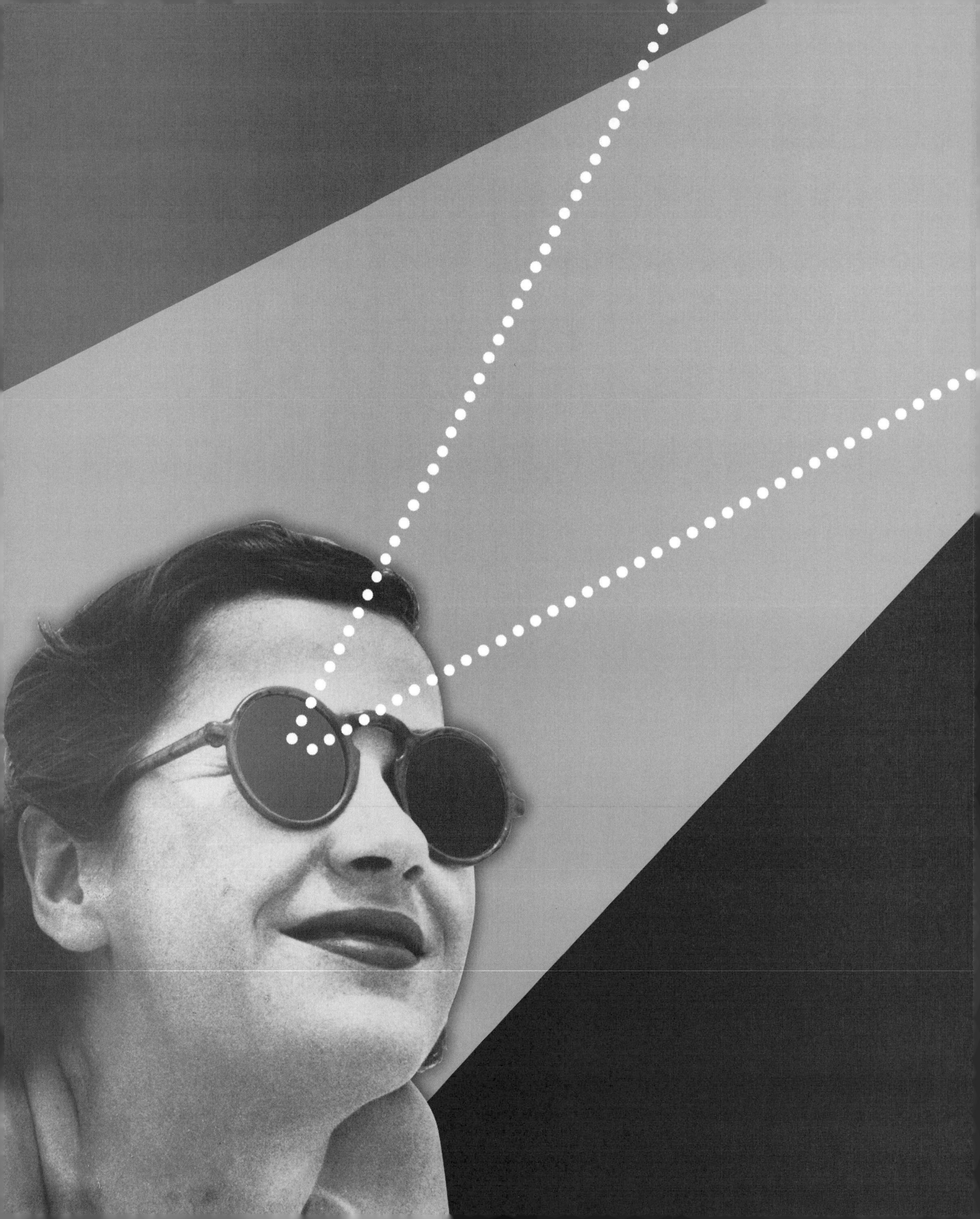

Women's Wire WEB Directory

ELLEN PACK

Lycos Press
An imprint of Macmillan Computer Publishing USA
Emeryville, California

Publisher	**Joe Wikert**
Associate Publisher	**Juliet Langley**
Publishing Director	**Cheryl Applewood**
Acquisitions Editor	**Kenyon Brown**
Development Editor	**Renee Wilmeth**
Copy Editor	**Debi Anker**
Production Editor	**Barbara Dahl**
Proofreaders	**Barbara Dahl and Jeff Barash**
Cover Design	**Bay Graphics**
Book Design and Layout	**Bruce Lundquist**

Lycos Press books are developed as a joint effort of Lycos and Que. They are published by Macmillan Computer Publishing USA, a Simon & Schuster Company.

Lycos Press imprint books are produced on a Macintosh computer system with the following applications: FrameMaker®, Microsoft® Word, QuarkXPress®, Adobe Illustrator®, Adobe Photoshop®, Adobe Streamline™, MacLink®*Plus*, Aldus® FreeHand™, Collage Plus™.

Lycos Press, an imprint of
Macmillan Computer Publishing USA
5903 Christie Avenue
Emeryville, CA 94608

ISBN 0-78971-068-4

Manufactured in the United States of America

10 9 8 7 6 5 4 3 2 1

TABLE OF CONTENTS

FOREWORD xi

ACKNOWLEGDEMENTS xiii

ABOUT LYCOS, INC xv

INTRODUCTION xvii

Chapter 1:
GETTING STARTED 1

What Is the World Wide Web and Why Should I Care? 1

Benefits of Being Online 1

So, What's the Difference between the Internet and the Web? 2

The Parts of the Web 3

What Will I Find on the Web? 3

Web Addressing 5

What Do I Need to Get on the Web? 5

The Hardware 5

The Software 6

What's an Internet Service Provider? 6

How to Find an Internet Service Provider 7

Great, but How Much Does All This Stuff Cost? 8

Now Where To? 8

What about Multimedia? 9

Women on the Net 10

Who Are They? 10

If You Build It, They Will Come 10

The Culture of the Internet 11

So, Who's Watching Me? (Safety and Privacy on the Web) 12

Is the Internet Okay for My Kids? 12

What Else Is in the Book? 12

Chime In! 13

Chapter 2:
MIND AND BODY 14

General Health 16

Pharmaceuticals 23

Illness and Conditions 24

Aging 30

Recovery and Abuse 31

Sports and Fitness 32

Nutrition 36

Alternative Medicine 38

Spirituality 40

Sexuality and Reproductive Health 42

Mental Health 44

Chapter 3:
CAREERS AND NETWORKING 50

Job Search 52

Regional and Specialty Employment Resources 60

Career Issues 65

Career Development 68

Entrepreneurship 74

Professional Organizations and Networking 77

Chapter 4: ENTERTAINMENT AND LEISURE 84

Museums 86

Humanities 87

Dance 88

Theater 89

Books 90

Movies 92

Listings and Events 94

Celebrities 94

Television 95

The Cybersoap Uberlist 95

Travel 99

Hobbies 101

Mags and 'Zines 103

Dining 106

Music 107

Comics and Cartoons 108

Astrology and Mysticism 110

Humor 110

Fun and Games 112

Pop Culture 113

Chapter 5: NEWS, POLITICS, AND THE LAW 116

General News 118

News Magazines 120

Television and Radio News 122

Newspapers and Newswires 124

Weather 128

Facts and Figures 130

The Law 131

Political Media 137

Public Policy and Organizations 140

Chapter 6: FAMILY 144

Pregnancy and Childbirth 146

Parenting 148

Children with Disabilities 152

Family Education 153

Games 157

Places To Go 158

Family Entertainment 160

Holiday Goodies 165

Teens 165

Family Issues 166

Adoption 169

Divorce 169

Caring for Elder Parents 170

Chapter 7:
RELATIONSHIPS 172

Dating and Romance 174

Matchmaking and Personals 182

Gay and Lesbian 185

Single Life 187

Friendship 189

Wedding Planning and Marriage 190

Chapter 8:
FASHION AND BEAUTY 196

Fashion Media 198

Fashion Designers 204

Apparel and Accessories 208

Shoes 210

Models and Modeling Agencies 212

Beauty 214

Cosmetics 217

Informational 219

Institutes and Organizations 219

Chapter 9:
EDUCATION 226

Early Childhood Resources 228

K through 12 Resources 231

College and Post Graduate 237

Women's Studies 241

Financial Aid, Scholarships, and Loans 243

Libraries 246

Teachers and Scholars 248

Educational Services and Resources 252

Chapter 10:
PERSONAL FINANCE AND BUSINESS 258

Investing 260

Financial Markets 266

Stocks 267

Mutual Funds 270

Tax Preparation 272

Personal Finance 273

Financial Advice 277

Home Banking 278

Saving 278

Retirement Planning 280

Real Estate 280

Real Estate Listings 281

Business and Small Business 282

Business News 285

Chapter 11: HABITAT 290

Home Improvement 292

Decor 294

Auctions, Classifieds, and Real Estate Listings 298

Entertaining 299

Cooking 302

Gardening and Horticulture 309

Hobbies and Collecting 315

Pet Care 317

Chapter 12: TECHNOLOGY AND THE INTERNET 322

Computer Hardware and Software 324

- PCs 324
- Macintosh 326
- Cross Platform 328

Internet Access and Help 331

Netiquette 335

Cool Site Pages 336

Web Publishing and HTML 339

Security 345

Industry News 346

Chapter 13: SHOPPING 352

Designers and Retailers 354

Apparel 356

Virtual Malls 358

Automotive 366

Books 369

Food and Drink 372

Music and Video 375

Flowers and Gifts 376

Sales and Bargains 378

Hobbies 379

Travel 380

Chapter 14: COMMUNITY AND SOCIAL SERVICE 384

Charities 386

Activism, Advocacy, and Support 387

General Nonprofits 393

Minorities 397

Gay and Lesbian Rights 399

Seniors 400

Environmental and Animal Rights 401

Government Related 404

Crime and Fraud Prevention 405

Chapter 15:
SEARCH AND REFERENCE 408

Search Engines, Directories, and Guides 410

Some Well-Known Directories 412

Examples of Search Engines 412

People and Business Directories 414

Dictionaries, Translators, and Grammar References 419

Encyclopedias and Quotations 423

Miscellaneous Reference 424

Calendar and Time Reference 428

Government References and Statistics 429

Professional Reference 431

Libraries 431

Statistics 433

Postal and Geographic Reference 434

Genealogical Reference 437

APPENDIX A: Tips for Using Lycos to Search the Web 440

APPENDIX B: Using the CD-ROM 444

GLOSSARY OF INTERNET LINGO 448

CREDITS 452

INDEX OF SITE NAMES 454

FOREWORD

When I was approached by Lycos Press to write a Web directory for women, the decision was a no-brainer. The idea represented exactly what I believe in and enjoy doing—helping more women get online, sharing my opinion about what constitutes a great Web site, and ushering in the new medium that is changing our lives.

Since I first went online back in 1992, I have been enamored with the possibilities of creating content and communities on the Internet of special interest to women. Having spent a fair amount of time getting friends and family members online, I am occasionally frustrated that it is still not as easy to use as it will be one day. I enjoy introducing people to the Web for the first time—and watching their expressions as the possibilities of its uses sink in. When I started out, I was repeatedly told women wouldn't use the Web. I knew that if there were worthwhile information and real benefits, women would be there—in fact, there'd be no stopping them.

This book was designed to be used by people of all "surfing" abilities. It's an introduction for beginners as well as a resource for those who already know what they are doing. The people who have worked on putting the directory together—all Web-savvy—have also learned during the process. Such is the medium—constantly changing and wowing its audience.

It is somewhat ironic that I have written a book and founded a company based on providing information and services to women. I have never believed that women need or want special treatment. Nor do I believe that women have a set of interests that can be easily defined. Of course we're all different, are in various stages of life, and have varied family situations. Some of us have careers, some do not. Some use the Internet for work, others as a hobby. Many are deeply involved in politics, others could care less. Some live for fashion, others resent it. Yet we have been shaped by historic events, role models, and prevailing attitudes that have given us a common way to approach life, an attitude, a collective sense of humor.

It is with this in mind that I dare to create a directory to the Web for women, one that demystifies the technology, helps women discern the most useful and entertaining sites on the Web, and tosses stereotypes to the wind.

Ellen Pack
Founder, Women's Wire

ACKNOWLEDGMENTS

This book reflects the work of many creative minds and avid surfers. Contributing writers took on a chapter or more and scoured thousands of sites to find the very best ones in each category. They described the site and highlighted important features. They uncovered practical ways to use the Internet, and found entertaining, off-the-wall sites. The book could never have happened without their conscientious work and speedy turnaround.

Thanks especially to the following writers for their hard work and belief in the project: John Flanders, "Getting Started" and the "Glossary" (he has a real knack for explaining a difficult subject in an approachable way); Michelle Cohen, "Mind and Body," "Careers and Networking," "Entertainment," "Relationships," "Personal Finance and Business," and "Technology and the Internet" (this woman knows the Web); Helen Lee and Elizabeth Collins, "Entertainment;" Alice Rhee, "News and Politics;" Alison Woo, "Family;" Tricia Nelson, "Fashion & Beauty" and "Shopping;" Brad Kloza, "Education;" Ann Sample, "Habitat;" Andrea Kowalski, "Community and Social Services;" and Colin Hendricks, "Search & Reference."

Also, thanks to Marny Requa for helping to organize and edit much of the material in this book. And many thanks to David Lehmer, whose tireless production efforts including screen shots, permissions, and formatting helped bring this book to life.

I am grateful to the entire team at Lycos Press and particularly to Ken Brown for asking us to write this directory, and to Renee Wilmeth and Barbara Dahl at Lycos for pulling it all together under incredible time pressure.

A special thanks to Women's Wire editors, designers, and writers Laurie Kretchmar, Katharine Mieszkowski, Tam Putnam, Barbara Moffatt, Margo Carn, Deborah Russell, Lourdes Livingston, Sarah Stillpass, Susan Adrian, and Andy Erdman, who have created and produced the editorial features that you see every day on Women's Wire and throughout the pages of this book.

Finally, I also very much appreciate Marleen McDaniel and the investors in Wire Networks who have believed in Women's Wire from the very early days and whose vision has helped make Women's Wire what it is today.

ABOUT LYCOS, INC.

In the brief time since the world has had point-and-click access to the multigraphic, multimedia World Wide Web, the number of people going on-line has exploded to 30 million at last count, all roaming about the tens of millions of places to visit in Cyberspace.

As the Web makes its way into our everyday lives, the kinds of people logging on are changing. Today, there are as many Webmasters as novices, or newbies, and all are struggling to get the most from the vast wells of information scattered about the Web. Even well-prepared surfers stumble aimlessly through cyberspace using hit-or-miss methods in search of useful information, with few results, little substance, and a lot of frustration.

In 1994, the Lycos technology was created by a scientist at Carnegie Mellon University to help those on the Web regain control of the Web. The company's powerful technology is the bedrock underlying a family of guides that untangle the Web, offering a simple and intuitive interface for all types of Web surfers, from GenXers to seniors, from Net vets to newbies.

Lycos (http://www.lycos.com) is a premium navigation tool for cyberspace, providing not just searches but unique editorial content and Web reviews that all draw on the company's extensive catalog of over 60 million Web sites (and growing).

DESTINATION, LYCOS

Lycos designed its home base on the premise that people want to experience the Web in three fundamentally different ways: They want to search for specific subjects or destinations, they want to browse interesting categories, or they want recommendations on sites that have been reviewed for quality of their content and graphics. Traditionally, Internet companies have provided part of this solution, but none has offered a finding tool that accommodates all degrees and types of curiosity. Lycos has.

Lycos utilizes its CentiSpeed spider technology as the foundation for finding and cataloging the vast variety of content on the World Wide Web. CentiSpeed processes a search faster than earlier technologies, featuring Virtual Memory Control, User-Level Handling and Algorithmic Word Compaction. This advanced technology allows the engine to execute more than 4,000 queries per second. CentiSpeed provides faster search results and unparalleled power to search the most comprehensive catalog of the World Wide Web. Lycos uses statistical word calculations and avoids full-word indexing, which helps provide the most relevant search results available on the Web.

In mid 1995, Lycos acquired Point Communications, widely recognized by Web veterans for its collection of critical reviews of the Web. Now an integrated part on the Lycos service, Point continues to provide thousands of in-depth site reviews and a thorough rating of the top Web sites throughout the world. The reviews are conducted by professional reviewers and editors who rate sites according to content, presentation, and overall experience on a scale of 1 to 50. Reviews are presented as comprehensive abstracts that truly provide the user with subjective critiques widely heralded for their accuracy and perceptiveness. In addition, Point's top five percent ratings for Web sites receive a special "Top 5% Badge" icon, the Web's equivalent to the famed consumer "Good Housekeeping Seal."

And for Web browsers who don't need a touring list of well-reviewed sites but who may not be destination-specific, Lycos offers its Sites by Subject. Organizing thousands of Web sites into subject categories, Lycos Sites by Subject gives the cybersurfer at-a-glance Web browsing, including sports, entertainment, social issues, and children's sites. A compilation of the most popular sites on the Internet by the Lycos standard—those with the greatest number of links from other sites—the directory provides Web travelers with a more organized approach to finding worthwhile places to visit on the Web.

Spiders on Steroids

Lycos was originally developed at Carnegie Mellon University by Dr. Michael "Fuzzy" Mauldin, who holds a Ph.D. in conceptual information retrieval. Now chief scientist at the company, Dr. Mauldin continues to expand the unique exploration and indexing technology. Utilizing this technology, Lycos strives to deliver a family of guides to the Internet that are unparalleled for their accuracy, relevance, and comprehensiveness. Lycos is one of the most frequently visited sites on the Web and is one of the leading sites for advertisers.

The Lycos database is constantly being refined by dozens of software robots, or agents, called "spiders." These spiders roam the Web endlessly, finding and downloading Web pages. Once a page is found, the spiders create abstracts which consist of the title, headings and subheading, 100 most weighty words, first 20 lines, size in bytes, and number of words. Heuristic (self-teaching) software looks at where the words appear in the document, their proximity to other words, frequency, and site popularity to determine relevance.

Lycos eliminates extraneous words like "the," "a," "and," "or," and "it" that add no value and slow down finding capabilities. The resulting abstracts are merged, older versions discarded, and a new, up-to-date database is distributed to all Lycos servers and licensees. This process is repeated continuously, resulting in a depth and comprehensiveness that makes Lycos a top information guide company.

Online providers or software makers can license Lycos—the spider, search engine, catalog, directory, and Point reviews—to make them available to users.

Lycos, Inc., an Internet exploration company, was founded specifically to find, index, and filter information on the Internet and World Wide Web. CMG Information Services, Inc. (NASDAQ: CMGI) is a majority shareholder in Lycos, Inc. through its strategic investment and development business unit, CMG@Ventures. CMGI is a leading provider of direct marketing services investing in and integrating advanced Internet, interactive media, and database management technologies.

INTRODUCTION

At first, getting online may make you feel like you've been let loose in an unfamiliar city without a map—you're sure there are interesting sites to see, but the road signs are few and far between. You start exploring, but you have this uncomfortable feeling that just around the corner there might be something big you're missing.

At Women's Wire, we spend a lot of time checking out other Web sites and we like to share what we've learned. That's the spirit of this book. Let the book be your guide as you explore the diverse sites on the World Wide Web. Like a descriptive city map—full of fun and historic landmarks—it will help you get your bearings online, tell you about the sites worth catching, and give you the tools you need to set out on your own. Chapter 1 explains how to get online and what to expect from the Web. The remaining chapters introduce you to some of the best sites on the Web—they are organized into subject areas to allow you to follow your interests. The listings are in random order within each subtopic—kind of like the Web itself.

Along the way, we provide some tips to optimize your experience, and some local color to make your journey more interesting. Finally, a glossary at the back helps you decipher some of the lingo you will encounter along the way.

Throughout the chapters, you will see these graphic seals highlighting particular sites:

Women's Wire Surfer Pick: The favorite sites of staffers at Women's Wire.

100 Best Web Sites: If you've only got time to check out a few, look through our top recommendations.

International Appeal: These sites are global in their approach—some are offered in multiple languages, others include resources about several countries or an international perspective.

Kid Appeal: Sites to check out if you are surfing with children.

Also look for these hands-on features in every chapter:

- 10 Useful Things: At the beginning of each chapter is a list of 10 practical things you can do on the Web. Everyone has heard about the vast amounts of information available on the Internet—we aim to show you some of the down-to-earth ways you can use it in everyday life.
- Internet Minute: A brief explanation of how to do something techy, these tips and tricks should make navigating the Web quicker and easier.
- Where They Surf: Bookmarks of cyber celebs offering insight into how others are using the Net for work and play.
- Overheard on Women's Wire: Words of wisdom taken directly from live chat guests and exclusive interviews on Women's Wire.
- Spotlight: A special look at different topics, telling you essential facts and sites where you can find out more.
- Just for Fun: Pointers for amusing yourself on the Web.

If, in your travels, you find fabulous sites that you think should be included in our next edition, please let us know. Also, we'd love to hear your suggestions and comments, particularly about how you have used this book personally and professionally. You can send e-mail to directory@women.com.

Bon Voyage.

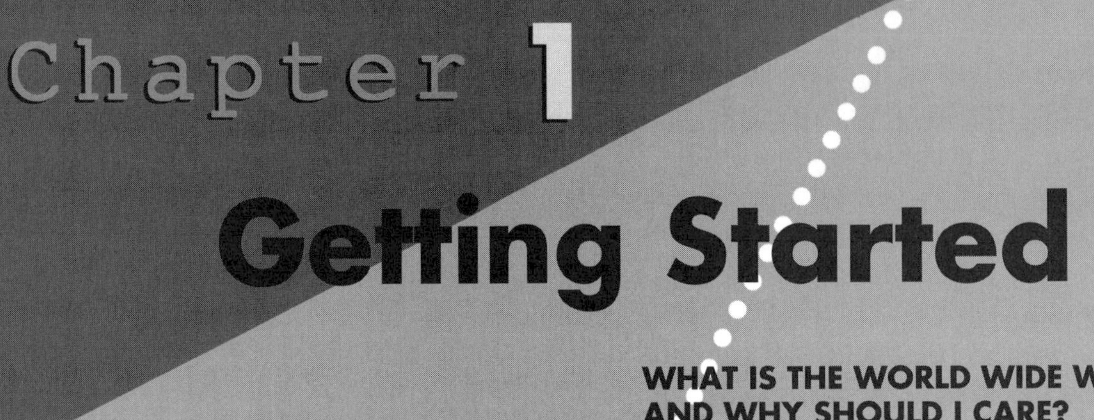

Chapter 1

Getting Started

- WHAT IS THE WORLD WIDE WEB AND WHY SHOULD I CARE?
- WHAT WILL I FIND ON THE WEB?
- WHAT DO I NEED TO GET ON THE WEB?
- WOMEN ON THE NET
- THE CULTURE OF THE INTERNET
- SO, WHO'S WATCHING ME? (SAFETY AND PRIVACY ON THE WEB)
- WHAT ELSE IS IN THE BOOK?

The World Wide Web is a vast sea of information and entertainment accessible from your personal computer. It is a shared resource based on open standards enabling anyone to search its vast offerings and contribute content in the form of Web pages. Picking up where television, radio, and print leave off, it is a global publishing platform featuring a huge amount of diverse multimedia content from individuals, corporations, nonprofits, and government organizations. In this new media where anyone can be a publisher, irreverent, "way-new" journalism is available just a click away from traditional information sources like newswires and magazines, and the sheer magnitude of it all can be overwhelming.

This book will help demystify the Web and show you how to get the most from your Web travels. It will explain a bit about the technology and translate some of the jargon that pervades the medium, though you really don't have to understand it all to begin to take advantage of the Web.

This first chapter tells you everything you need to know to get online for the first time and begin to explore. If you are already online and you are the type who doesn't need to know what an acronym stands for in order to use it, then skip ahead to the next chapter to begin the tour.

The remaining chapters will take you on a journey to some of the best resources that the Web has to offer. This book and CD-ROM package has almost everything you need to explore the Web. The only other thing you'll need to bring along is your sense of adventure.

WHAT IS THE WORLD WIDE WEB AND WHY SHOULD I CARE?

The World Wide Web is the multimedia portion of the Internet. It's the convergence of many forms of media and communications including sound, video, and text.

Information on the Web is arranged in "pages"—so called because photos and illustrations, headlines and text, maps and graphics are combined on screen in what look like the pages of a magazine (see Figure 1.1). Groups of linked pages from the same individual or organization make up a Web site. The first page of a Web site, or the entry point, is referred to as the home page. There are more than 400,000 Web sites featuring more than 75 million Web pages and the number continues to grow daily.

One of the main strengths of the Web is that it's easy to get around. By clicking with your mouse on highlighted or underlined text, you can instantly jump to a related page from the same service—or to a related topic on a computer thousands of miles away. This "hypertext" linking makes Web surfing a snap, allowing users to follow a thread of thought through all kinds of information around the world.

Benefits of Being Online

Women are busier than ever managing that balancing act called life. So you might be wondering if surfing

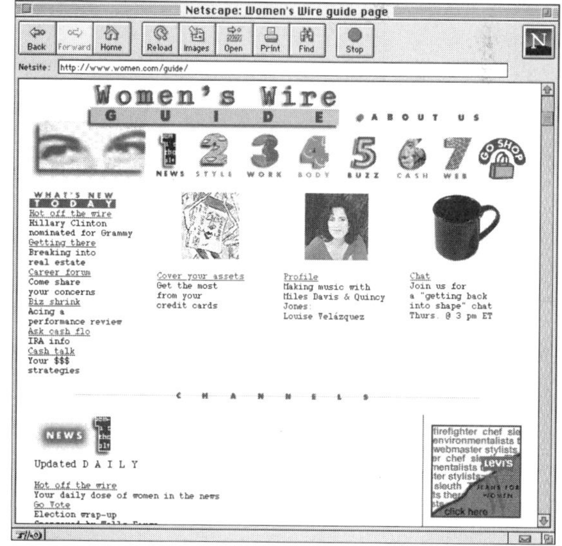

Figure 1.1

The Women's Wire Web site, *http://www.women.com*

400,000 Web sites is really going to save you time. Probably not right away, but don't let that stop you.

The Internet is changing the way people work and live. It makes working from home feasible, talking to people in other countries an everyday event, and gives a whole new dimension to information overload.

Up-to-the-instant news is available from major news purveyors like CNN and NBC as well as from specialized Web stops like Women's Wire offering the world's only "Women in the News" and Family Planet's "Parent's Daily." And rather than making you wait until the story you care about is broadcast, the Web lets you select the stories that you are interested in and follow them 24 hours a day.

The Internet is about quick and easy communicating. Faster than a speeding FedEx®, e-mail makes sending documents around the world an instant affair. But there's more to communicating on the Internet than personal e-mail. Groups of people interested in the same topic can form electronic mailings lists to easily discuss and disseminate information amongst a larger audience. The Internet also supports public discussion areas called "newsgroups." These public conversation areas are used for everything from fan clubs to support groups and they are the foundation for the many virtual communities created on the Internet.

Information resources you used to have to leave home to find are now easily accessible on the Web. You can perform trademark searches, look up a word in a French-English dictionary, or check the traffic conditions on the Los Angeles freeways…all from the comfort of your PC. And these are just a few examples. The Web offers instant access to experts online, from the National Women's Health Resource Center *(http://www.women.com/body/ qa.bod.html)* to Heloise's Household Hints *(http://homearts.com/gh/advice/08helof1.htm).* Stock quotes, in-depth health information, fashion trends, classified ads, and kids resources are all just a few clicks away.

Many people are using the Web to find jobs, keep in touch with family and friends, and promote businesses and nonprofit organizations. Aside from being truly useful, the Web can be downright entertaining.

So, What's the Difference between the Internet and the Web?

The Internet is the backbone—it is a network of data phone lines connecting to computers which in turn are connected to other networks of computers. Thousands of computer networks at businesses, universities, government agencies, and libraries are connected via phone lines. Most of the Internet remains text based. The Web is the graphical portion of the Internet. It is colorful, illustrative, and where most of the growth and commercial interests are aiming. The Web is actually a subset of the Internet though people commonly use the terms Web, Internet, and the Net interchangeably.

Individuals hook up to the Internet by making a connection with a computer system that's on the Net—through an online service at their work or school, a local Internet Service Provider (ISP), or a library or government agency that offers connections.

The Internet is constructed so that you can access computer systems from Poland to South Africa to Japan to the Americas, all in seconds. And all without incurring long distance phone charges other than at most a call (usually local) into a connected computer. That makes it especially valuable for researchers and businesses that need to share information.

The World Wide Web is a graphical interface that runs over the Internet making it easy to navigate and colorful to look at. Documents are created using a Hypertext Markup Language (HTML) and viewed with a Web browser. The Web was conceived as a way to make scientific information more accessible to more people through the use of linked hypertext documents on the Internet. A formal way to make these hyperlinks and hypertext documents more functional was then established throughout the Internet community, and the World Wide Web was born.

Technically speaking, the Web is a communications protocol that transmits over the Internet, much like telephone voice conversations are just one protocol traveling over voice phone lines which may also carry fax transmissions, modem signals, etc. On the Web, the protocols and conventions make it easy for anyone to browse and contribute to the Internet.

The Parts of the Web

The World Wide Web is made up of two major components: (1) hypertext documents with hyperlinks; and (2) the Internet and its communications network.

In simple terms the Internet is the newspaper and the hypertext documents are the ink or content. The newspaper carries the content. With the help of browser software providing easy to use, friendly interfaces the Web comes alive, and otherwise boring text documents are able to take on a new dimension. You can click on words that are "hot" (usually displayed in a different color or underlined—see Figure 1.2) to reach a new page that is linked to the previous page, navigating a web of inter-linked documents.

A special Hypertext Markup Language (HTML) is used to create hypertext documents. Creators of Web sites use HTML to designate which words on the page they want to make "hot" and which Web pages they want to hyperlink to from the selected word or phrase. HTML is also used to display text, graphics, audio, and full motion video clips in Web pages.

WHAT WILL I FIND ON THE WEB?

There are more than 400,000 Web sites out there to explore, and the number keeps growing every day. The original members of the Internet are still there: universities, scientific and research agencies, and the government. But with the Web's flood of popularity, a commercial environment has emerged. Though subscription services are starting to appear, the vast

HOW DID THIS INTERNET THING GET STARTED?

The Internet was devised by the U. S. military as a dedicated communications network between military operations groups. The military, in the midst of the cold war, wanted to protect vital defense communications in the event of a nuclear attack. The Internet was established between three sites in the early 1960s. The original network was named ARPAnet after the Advanced Research Projects Agency. The Internet expanded as computer technology advanced and in 1980 the National Science Foundation established the NSFnet which replaced ARPAnet. The NFSnet later became known as the Internet. During the 80s, the NSFnet's use was restricted to research institutes and universities. By the end of the 80s the military had moved to their own networks and the Internet was the domain of the university community.

One of the most significant developments to the Internet occurred in 1991. That year the National Research and Education Network (NREN) was established. This network's goals were to develop and maintain high speed, high capacity research and educational networks and to help develop commercial uses of the Internet. The NREN eliminated restrictions to access and use of the Internet which prompted the blossoming of the World Wide Web.

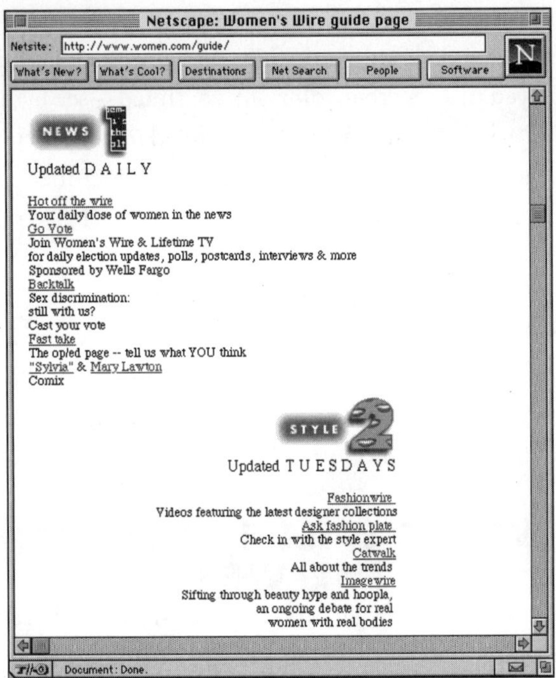

Figure 1.2
An example of hyperlinks from the Women's Wire guide page, *http://www.women.com/guide*

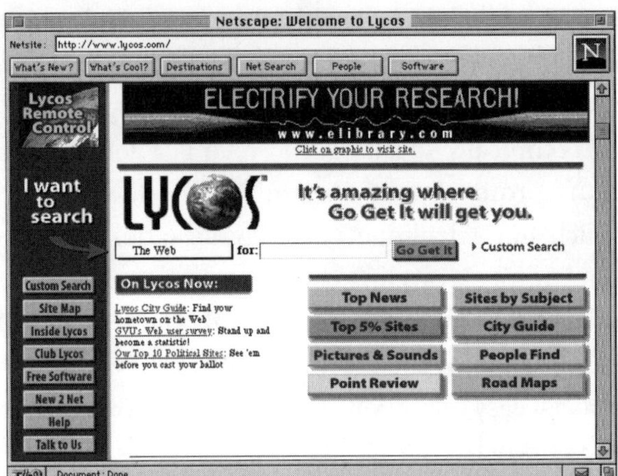

Figure 1.3
The Lycos search engine, *http://www.lycos.com*

majority of the information and sites on the Net are still free of charge and open to anyone who comes across them. The general categories of sites you will tend to see include:

Search engines and directories: These sites are designed to help you find other sites of interest on the Web. In addition to offering keyword searching of the entire Web, many of them organize sites on the Web into subject categories for organized browsing (see Figure 1.3).

Corporate sites: Companies promoting and selling products like bookstores, banks, clothing manufacturers, cosmetics companies, and software developers to name a few. These sites can be like interactive brochures offering detailed product information and sometimes offer the ability to contact people at the company directly.

Nonprofit organization sites: Nonprofit organizations and associations create Web sites to educate the world about their missions and disseminate information about various issues and causes.

Media sites: Media organizations create sites that provide all kinds of news, entertainment, stock quotes, sports scores, opinion columns, and video clips.

Personal home pages: Individuals create sites featuring information about themselves and their interests including photographs and artwork. Personal Web pages can be used as resumes or to share family photos and information.

University sites: Schools have sites which provide access to research papers, libraries, curricula, and alumni information (see Figure 1.4).

Government sites: Government agencies have sites which provide access to public information and records. For example, the Library of Congress and the IRS have Web sites. Also, many state and local governments are putting public information online—such as court records and parking violations.

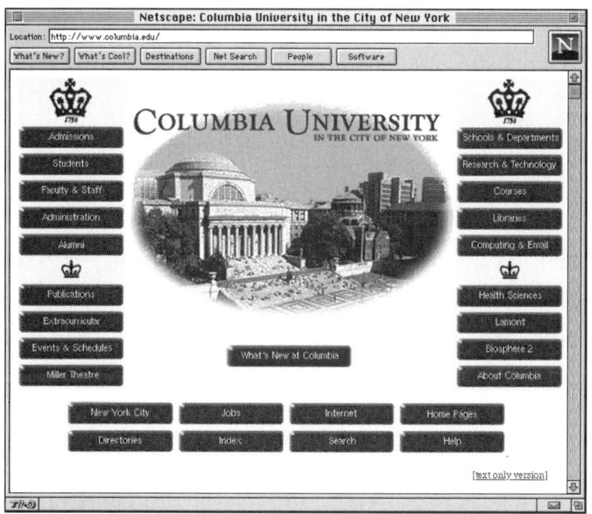

Figure 1.4
Columbia University's home page, *http://www.columbia.edu*

Web Addressing

By now you probably have seen Web addresses appear on everything from the evening news to cereal boxes. The Internet's domain name system (DNS) makes it easy to find a particular site if you have its Uniform Resource Locator (URL) or address. Think of a URL as a pointer to a particular Web site. When you type a URL into the appropriate location in your Web browser, it will take you to the Web site at that address.

WHAT DO I NEED TO GET ON THE WEB?

The first thing to know is that getting online for the first time is usually the most difficult part of using the Web. Expect to spend some time setting up your computer and Internet connection. To surf the Web, you will need a computer (hardware), a browser (software), and an account with an Internet Service Provider (ISP).

KEY TERMS

Hyperlink (or Link): A point and click button, icon, or text link that jumps to another page on the Web in the same or a different Web site anywhere in the world.

Hypertext Markup Language (HTML): HTML is the programming language of the Internet. This allows Web surfers to click on words and graphics to link to other pages on the Web.

Browser: Software that allows you to navigate ("browse") the Web. The most popular brand names are Netscape Navigator and Microsoft Internet Explorer.

Interface: The text, menus, or graphics a computer or online service uses to organize information or communicate.

Multimedia: A catch-all phrase that mainly means the convergence of many kinds of media including sound, video, text, graphics, and animation.

The Hardware

To take full advantage of software to access the Web, you need at least a PC with a 25mhz 486 with 8MB (megabytes) of RAM (16MB is better), or a Mac with a 68040 or PowerPC processor with the same amount of memory.

A Must: Go for the fastest modem you can buy, one that runs at 33,600 (look for a common standard called V.42). Slower modems like 28,800bps or 14,400bps can seem to take forever to load a Web page, particularly the ones with lots of multimedia or graphics. You don't need a CD-ROM to surf the Net; a sound card for your PC is optional, but nice to have.

Modems operate over regular phone lines. If you find yourself spending a lot of time on the Internet, a second phone line might be helpful—and your friends will not get frustrated because your line is constantly busy. Another alternative is voice mail systems offered by phone companies. With these systems, when you are online and someone calls your number they will automatically be forwarded to your voice mail. If you are planning to spend a lot of time online for work, you might want to consider getting digital phone lines called ISDN, which many regional telephone companies are starting to offer to consumers. They're several time faster than the fastest standard modem; but the ISDN modem can cost $500.00, and the monthly line fees are more expensive than regular lines.

Remember, you can find lots of advice about systems on the Web at sites such as c|net (http://www.cnet.com).

The Software

The software you will need depends on how you are planning to hook up to the Net. Netscape Navigator and Internet Explorer are the most common graphical software or Web browsers. This Internet software is smart enough to handle more than just the Web; browsers can give users the same point and click access to e-mail, newsgroups, FTP, Gopher, and other Net services that once needed special software to run.

It is a good idea to keep up with the latest versions of browsers in order to have all of the bells and whistles. You can do this by periodically checking in to the Web site of the company that develops the browser you are using. For example, to reach Netscape (see Figure 1.5), go to *http://www.netscape.com* and for Internet Explorer, go to *http://www.microsoft.com/ie.* Most of these browsers, such as the one in this book, are free or on a try-before-you-buy basis.

What's an Internet Service Provider?

ISP stands for Internet Service Provider, a company that provides you with the ability to connect to the Internet. An ISP is a company that allows users to dial into a local modem bank, connect to their high speed Internet pipelines, and thereby access the

ANATOMY OF A WEB ADDRESS

The first thing you will notice is that every address starts with the protocol *http://*, which stands for hypertext transfer protocol. The most popular browsers are set up so that you don't have to enter the http each time and can just enter the remainder of the address. Following the protocol is the host name, *www*. Typically a Web address starts with the letters *www,* though it is not required. It is followed by the domain. Domains have two parts—the unique domain registered by a company, organization, or individual and the top level domain which comes last. Top-level domains are a way to classify sites, much like an area code classifies a telephone number to what state and/or area of the state it is physically located in.

Example: **http://www.women.com**

http:// = hypertext tranfer protocol

www. = host name

women.com = domain name

/news = the directory or subsection of the site where the particular page is located

Sometimes you will see longer Web addresses that have a lot of slashes (/) in them. These represent subdirectories on the computer where the site is housed and will take you directly to specific parts of a site. For example, *http://www.women.com/body* will take you directly to the body channel or section on the Women's Wire Web site.

Figure 1.5

Netscape's home page, *http://www.netscape.com*

Internet. Most ISPs include or make available other services such as e-mail and Web site hosting for businesses and individuals. The core business for most of these folks is connecting users to the Internet via local points of presence (POPs).

Online services are a little different. Users of America Online (AOL) and CompuServe dial into a proprietary network and access information maintained by the online service. The online services provide a gateway for their members to access the rest of the Internet.

For the most part online services are easier to set up accounts with and friendlier to navigate. However, the content is usually limited in comparison to the Web and performance when you go out on the Web is noticeably slower. Most Internet newbies tend to start off on an online service and upgrade to a direct connect ISP within months.

Both ISPs and Online Services provide Internet e-mail capabilities.

How to Find an Internet Service Provider

A good source for local Internet service providers, which are most likely to have local, non-toll phone numbers for access, is in the computer classifieds, your local Yellow Pages, or weekly business section of the local newspaper. National providers often advertise in *Internet World, NetGuide,* and other PC magazines.

Following is a list of common top-level domain names and their meanings:

.com One of the most common domains found on the Internet. It identifies a site as a commercial site, usually produced by a for-profit company. For example, *http://www.ticketmaster.com*.

.org This domain is most commonly found at non profit association Web sites and traditional social organizations. For example, *http://ca.lwv.org* is the California League of Women Voters.

.gov Found at notable sites like the White House *(http://www.whitehouse.gov)* and the Library of Congress *(http://www.loc.gov)*, this domain is used for U. S. government organizations.

.edu This domain identifies the site as an educational organization. Colleges, high schools, and elementary schools usually have ".edu" within their domain name. For example, *www.columbia.edu*.

.net This domain is typically used by networks, such as Internet service providers.

.us and others Many countries, including the United States, have domains that end with a country code. Countries like Austria with country code ".at" or the U.S. with the extension ".us" help Web surfers identify which shores they have landed on.

When selecting an ISP, check on the following:

Local access phone numbers. Toll charges or surcharges for long distance calls or Internet services providing 800 numbers become very costly very quickly.

Speed of access. Make sure 33,600bps connection is offered, and see what percentage of their modems is below 28.8kbps. Just because you're using a fast modem, doesn't mean you have connected at the same speed. A good rule to remember is you are only as quick as the slowest link. Don't let that be your ISP.

Hours allowed. Most Net providers offer a healthy dose of free hours per month. After your number of hours are used up, you are charged per hour. It is best to find the provider with the most free hours or unlimited time. If you are using your Internet account for business or research, plan on spending lots of time online.

Quality of service. Before you sign up, call the service provider or send an e-mail or two. See how knowledgeable and responsive they are, and use that as an indicator of how responsive they may be when you run into problems. Also, ask for a copy of the set-up instructions they supply. They may read like Greek since much of an Internet set-up is technical. But are they simply stated, detailed, and easy to follow? Typically, the easier the instructions, the more user-friendly the software.

THE WEB ON TV

It's no longer a requirement to have an expensive PC to surf the Web. There are several companies creating services that give you the ability to view the Web from your television set. For example, a set-top box from Palo Alto-based WebTV Networks transforms your television into a Web browser and lets you navigate the Web with a remote control. A small box that sits on top of your television connects to the Web using a standard phone line and is available in computer and electronic stores for about $300.00. While this technology seems promising, it is still very new and will only be successful if it is widely adopted. You will want to do some additional research before buying TV-based Internet services.

Great, but How Much Does All This Stuff Cost?

If you're starting from square one, use the following figures as a guide, not the final word, and you should do just fine. For a good Pentium computer, with printer, modem, and monitor, plan to spend between $1,300.00 and $1,800.00. Browser software is included in this book, but if you decide to buy another browser package to receive additional features, plan on spending another $39.00.

Before you buy software, check with your Internet Service Provider to (1) make sure it is compatible, and (2) to see if they already have a licensed copy for free or deep discount. This should be enough to get you on the World Wide Web and allow you to send and receive e-mail. Look for flat-fee accounts with a large or unlimited number of hours and that let your computer communicate directly to the Internet. They average from $14.95 per month to $24.95 per month. Once you are on the Web, most of the content is free.

Now Where To?

Congratulations, you've made the leap to the Internet. You might be glad to learn that getting online for the first time is actually the most difficult part. Now, where do you go? A good place for "newbies" to go is a search engine or index, such as Lycos or Yahoo! (see Figure 1.6), to get a sense of what the Web has to offer. However, an easier way is to find a chapter in this book that interests you, look for a site that you want to browse, find the URL beginning with

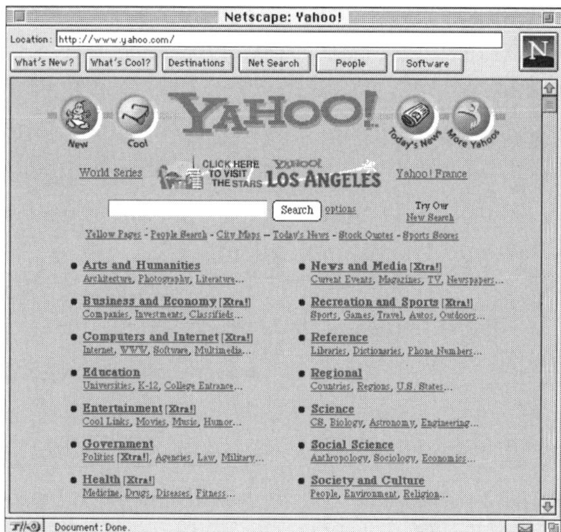

Figure 1.6
The Yahoo! Directory, *http://www.yahoo.com*

"http://," and type it in the location box located about 1 inch from the top of your screen inside your Web browser software. Once you reach a site, just click on the underlined hypertext or graphic buttons and start exploring.

When you find sites that you like and think you might want to return to, you can add them to your list of bookmarks. Simply choose to add a site to bookmarks from the bookmark menu in your browser. Next time you want to visit the site, you won't have to type in the URL.

What about Multimedia?

Multimedia—namely video, sound, and graphics—can enrich any online experience. The Internet can give you access to videoconferencing, voice e-mails, and the sending of pictures or electronic images to friends and relatives. You can also listen to live concerts or radio stations around the world, take a virtual trip to Antarctica, or view an expedition to the top of Mt. Everest—all at little to no cost.

When considering whether or not to start venturing into multimedia on the Internet there are five key things to remember:

1 **Bandwidth**—The single most frustrating part of the Internet is download time. Most multimedia files transmitted across the Internet are large files. Long download times, unfortunately, should be expected. If you're attempting to use multimedia over the Internet, you should be running at the highest bandwidth possible, a modem speed of at least 28.8kbps and preferably 33.6kbps.

2 **Tolerance**—This medium is still in its infancy. Two years ago audio and video files were just starting to appear in archaic forms with download times that gave the user an opportunity to make dinner or clean the house. Now live video and audio can stream across modem lines with-

CHANGING YOUR DEFAULT HOME PAGE

When you first open your browser software it will be preset to open to a particular Web page, usually your ISP or the software company that wrote the browser. Most people don't realize that they can change the default page that the browser opens to. If you are using Netscape Navigator, go to the Preferences Menu in your browser software and you will see a place to type in your favorite Web address. If you are using Internet Explorer, go to the View Menu and select Options and you will be able to do the same thing. Now, each time you connect to the Web, your favorite site will automatically open first. Some good starting pages are:

Women's Wire *(http://www.women.com)*

Lycos *(http://www.lycos.com)*

Yahoo! *(http://www.yahoo.com)*

out any wait at all. (This is called streaming.) This live stream is not exactly the best quality, but as this technology matures, so will the quality.

3 **Hardware**—When you talk multimedia, whether it's on the Internet or on a CD ROM, a Pentium Processor machine with at least 8MB of RAM or a high end Macintosh is the only way to go. When you buy a computer, just ask the salesperson if the computer meets these minimum requirements. If the computer doesn't meet the minimum requirements, don't expect superb multimedia experiences.

4 **Plug-Ins**—Plug-ins are programs that run inside of your Web browser. These plug-ins will help you view multimedia files or run special programs. They are available on the Internet from many different software developers. Unfortunately, they are not built in to your browser and so you must download them in order to use them. Good sites will walk you through this process step by step.

5 **Java**—Java is a programming language which can be used to create interactive multimedia content on the Web such as tickertapes, sounds, and animations. You will need to have a Java-capable browser, such as Netscape 3.0 or Internet Explorer 3.0 or later, in order to see Java applications.

WOMEN ON THE NET

Today there are many sites of interest to women. This book will introduce you to hundreds of sites in a wide variety of topical areas from parenting to education. The best sites in each category have been selected to save you time. In the early days of the Internet, women were pretty scarce online. When Women's Wire first went online in 1994, women represented about one in ten people online and the industry pundits were filled with skepticism. They thought women would never go online in big numbers. Today women represent 37% of the online population and are the fastest growing segment on the Internet. It is estimated that there will be 40 million women online by the year 2000.

Who Are They?

Women online reflect the women you see every day and some that you don't. They are workers, students, jocks, executives, spouses, singles, soccer moms, young girls, and seniors. In a typical month, Women's Wire has visitors from 85 countries, from Australia to Venezuela.

Women are surfing the Web for news, academic research, sports scores, career networking, entertainment, and personal finance. They are using the Web to run businesses, to raise families, to communicate with others, and just to surf.

If You Build It, They Will Come

That was the radical notion that gave birth to Women's Wire way back a couple of years ago when people wondered why more women weren't online. Today Women's Wire is the home of original feature stories, news, live chats, interactive polls, cool resources, and hot links to a wide range of Web sites. The site has different channels, or content areas, that focus on news, style, work, health, entertainment, cash, and the Web.

Each week in BackTalk, Women's Wire asks the women of the Web to voice their opinions on topics from Barbie to Bosnia (see Figure 1.7). The wide range of resulting comments is weekly proof that just like in the real world not all women on the Web think alike.

THE CULTURE OF THE INTERNET

Most new mediums start off as a fad among a few early adopters. As time goes by and the medium matures, and if it's lucky, the fad turns into a lasting trend and catches on with a much larger group of people. And so it's been with the Web. The pop culture status for the Internet was ushered in by the university society and catapulted into a phenomenon with a lot of help from the press.

The growth of the Internet is radical—it has reached critical mass. It's not just here in the United States. Global adoption of the Internet has made the world a whole lot smaller, and the concept of a global town square is at the fingertips of most computer users. Although English is certainly the predominant language on the Internet, many sites can be found in different languages. Greek, Spanish, German, and Japanese are all common languages on the Internet. In fact, if you don't know these languages already, you could learn them on the Internet.

The Internet has a unique language and culture with its own vocabulary and an endless supply of acronyms. But there is no need to be intimidated, yesterday's "newbie" (newcomer) is today's "netizen" (online citizen). There are a few tricks you can easily learn about this new culture. LIKE WHEN YOU TYPE IN ALL CAPS IT IS CONSIDERED YELLING! So it's best to use lower case, unless of course, you want to yell. Here are a few other tips.

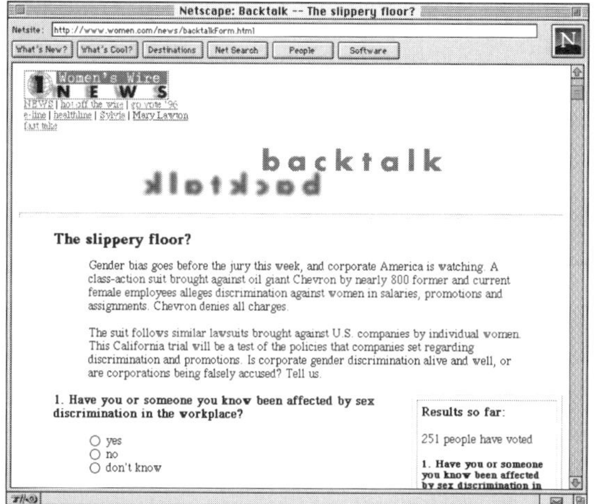

Figure 1.7
Women's Wire's BackTalk Poll,
http://www.women.com/news/backtalkForm.html

As people were sending out text based e-mail, the need to convey emotion to illustrate their statements was crucial. An "emoticon" (emotion + icon) is a group of letters or symbols that form a picture when viewed from a certain angle. These pictures are usually of faces and they are used as a way of representing feeling in an otherwise emotion-free zone.

Turn your head to the side to view:

:-) smile

;-) wink

:-(sad

:-o awe

o:-) angelic

Freedom of speech reigns on the Internet, and people sometimes use public forums for their own personal soapbox.

Usenet Newsgroups are public bulletin boards on a part of the Internet called Usenet. Readers can post, read, and reply to messages from other Internet users in any particular group. There are currently more than 14,000 newsgroups on the Web and the topics vary wildly. Whether your interests are spirituality or sports, there is a newsgroup for you. In addition many Web sites offer discussion areas and live chat rooms where you can talk with others. Even if a government were to regulate content on the Internet, it would be next to impossible to enforce. Since Web surfers can access computers outside of the country, non-regulated information could be stored there. It is truly a global network!

SO, WHO'S WATCHING ME? (SAFETY AND PRIVACY ON THE WEB)

For the most part, nobody is "watching you." In most cases you are anonymous. Although, most Internet computers can track what region you are coming from, what browser you are using, and how much time you are spending on their site, there is little else they can recognize.

Some sites will ask you to register and fill out a questionnaire. Most sites are looking for basic information so that they can customize their content offerings and attract appropriate advertisers that match your demographic profile and interests. As a rule, the Internet is no more or less safe than giving vital statistics to a data entry person at the other end of an 800 telephone number.

Is the Internet Okay for My Kids?

It's not only appropriate, some say, it's imperative. Schools are getting "wired" and kids must have access to the Internet. There is so much out there relevant to them—the Library of Congress, NASA, travel pages to anywhere in the world, political ideas and commentary, schools and educational site—and it will continue to grow.

Like any community, the Internet has its bad neighborhoods. On the Internet there are forums for pornography, fetishes, and racism. When an adult area is a click away there tends to be a lot of warnings posted. It is unlikely that you will just stumble upon such areas unless you go looking for them. It's a small part, and as the Internet becomes more popular for business and families, it will, some hope, become even less prevalent.

But steering children away from trouble is an acknowledged Net problem. Some suggestions if you have young children:

Don't let them register to enter sites. As an adult, you know what information should be given out. Don't allow children to give that information to unknown entities. Simply instruct your children to call you when they need to enter a registration site.

Keep an eye on young users in newsgroups. There are a number of newsgroups dedicated to school children and many that are geared toward older children. However, there are also some that cater to fringe tastes. Since most newsgroups are unmediated, people can and *do* say anything on and off the topic. It is a good idea for parents to be aware of which newsgroups their children are frequenting.

Use a software blocker. These are relatively new products designed to restrict access to certain areas. Examples include SurfWatch *(http://www.surfwatch.com)*, which blocks 1,000 explicit Net newsgroups, and Net Nanny which is available at *http://www.netnanny.com.*

This can be family time. It beats the TV. Browsing with your children can be fun and entertaining. Spend some time with them finding the wonders of the Web.

WHAT ELSE IS IN THE BOOK?

This book is designed to be the ultimate site-seeing guide—highlighting the most useful and interesting sites and helping you navigate during your journey. Each chapter is chock full o' tips and listings of useful things you can do on the Web right now. Look for the *Internet Minute* in each chapter which will explain a new aspect of surfing the Web. *Where They Surf* highlights the favorite sites of well-known people and *Overheard* features quotable quotes from Women's Wire guests. And be sure to check out Women's Wire's take on the 100 best sites out there for women—look for the seal throughout the book.

Contained herein are enough links to enticing content on the World Wide Web to keep anyone busy for days and to make each online experience a new and exciting one. Once you find your favorite sites, you will probably want to visit them regularly. The Web is constantly changing and evolving. Sites that don't change often, simply don't last.

Chime In!

One of the greatest aspects of the Web is its interactivity. There are many opportunitics to voice your opinion, offer feedback, send a letter to the editor, or write in for customer support. More often than not, the people behind the Web sites are thrilled to hear from you. The more interactive you get, the more the Web will become a place that reflects your tastes and opinions.

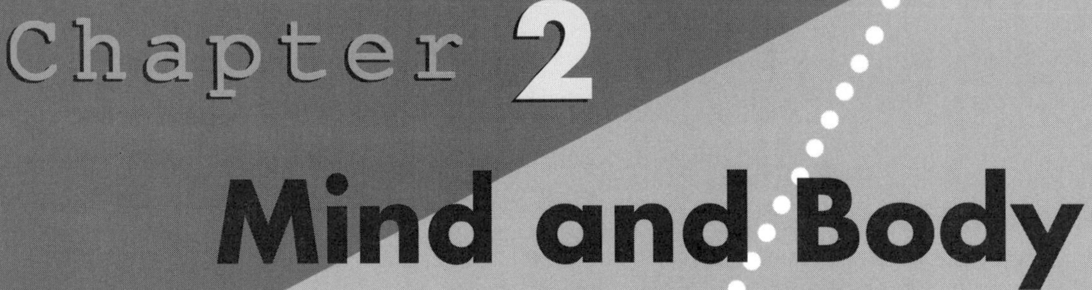

Chapter 2

Mind and Body

GENERAL HEALTH

PHARMACEUTICALS

ILLNESS AND CONDITIONS

AGING

RECOVERY AND ABUSE

SPORTS AND FITNESS

NUTRITION

ALTERNATIVE MEDICINE

SPIRITUALITY

SEXUALITY AND REPRODUCTIVE HEALTH

MENTAL HEALTH

10 THINGS YOU CAN DO FOR YOUR MIND AND BODY *RIGHT NOW*

1 Use Thrive's U.S. Pollen Map to find out what pollens are in the air in your region at different times of the year.

http://pathfinder.com/thrive/health/pollen.map.html

2 Get a nutritional profile customized for your height, weight, and frame size detailing your daily caloric needs, vitamin and mineral needs, cholesterol and fat limitations.

http://www.cyberdiet.com

3 Check the description, side effects, and dosage of more than 4,000 prescription and over the counter drugs.

http://www.rxlist.com

4 Find the most effective vitamin and mineral treatments for everyday health problems from asthma to yeast infections in Prevention's Vitamin Dispenser.

http://www.womensedge.com/house/vitamin_dispenser/index.html

5 Ask the Bod Squad (aka The National Women's Health Resource Center) for answers to your health questions about everything from pap smears to uterine fibroids.

http://www.women.com/body/qa.bod.html

6 Look up common childhood illnesses and read up on signs, symptoms, prevention, home treatment, duration, and contagiousness in this easy-to-navigate and easy-to-understand resource.

http://www.kidshealth.org

7 Go Ask Alice your questions about sexuality, sexual health, relationships, drugs, and emotional well-being…or just read through the well-organized archived material for bold answers to uninhibited questions from the Health Education division of Columbia University Health Services.

http://www.columbia.edu/cu/healthwise

8 Read Healthline every week to tap into the latest health news. Short, informative dispatches deliver useful information about complex medical discoveries and the latest scientific news.

http://www.women.com/body/healthline.html

9 Calculate the dates when you are ovulating (your most fertile days) and the corresponding due dates for your baby if you become pregnant during those dates using an online ovulation calculator.

http://homearts.com/depts/health/fetal/calculator.html

10 Plug in to Sportzone for the latest statistics, rankings, scores, and schedules for the women's college basketball season.

http://espnet.sportszone.com/ncw

A health question left unanswered by a visit to the doctor used to mean going to the library to pore over stacks of thick medical volumes, sifting through the well-meaning but often inaccurate advice of friends and relatives, and waiting by the mailbox for a deluge of cheerful pamphlets. Today, a growing number of people are turning to the World Wide Web as a painless way to research their health and body concerns. From the most technical medical journal to the advice of those who have "been there," the Web puts a treasure trove of health information at your fingertips.

Concerned about a medication you're taking? Searchable databases give you the low-down on drug interactions, dosages, side effects, and more. Overwhelmed by conflicting advice on your pregnancy? Get the facts you're looking for, in the privacy of your home or office. Follow lively discussions on the benefits of herbal medicine, get the latest news on immunization for kids, even find the perfect diet for your lifestyle and body type.

Find a supportive community during times of crisis. From breast cancer to drug abuse to mental illness, individuals and groups throughout the world go online to share their common experiences and establish networks of information and emotional support.

GENERAL HEALTH

Women's Wire Body Channel

http://www.women.com/body

Eye-catching graphics make this handy site a pleasure to visit (see Figure 2.1). Keep up with the latest health news for women, get answers from resident experts (Bod Squad and Sexpert)...or read what others are asking, and find useful information and facts on everything from quitting smoking to dealing with menopause. Test your knowledge with personalized health quizzes covering stress, skin care, STDs, and more. And read the athlete profiles, product reviews, and fitness reports from *Women's Sports+Fitness* magazine.

Good Health Web

http://www.social.com/health

The Good Health Web isn't much to look at, but it can be incredibly useful for tracking down hard-to-find health information—like where to sign up for the bed-wetting, breast cancer, and ovarian cancer mailing lists. It includes an organized database of 1,000 U.S. health organizations, a collection of health-related FAQs, a list of Internet mailing lists and newsgroups on health-related topics, as well as links to other health sites on the Web.

KidsHealth

http://www.kidshealth.org

The Nemours Foundation, which funds children's medical institutions across the country, has created KidsHealth.org to spread the word about childhood and teen health topics. This site is a boon for parents, with tips on treating bug bites, interactive polls, and in-depth articles on everything from childhood obesity to Rocky Mountain Spotted Fever. Some of the articles on KidsHealth seem too wordy for children to understand, but they're sure to love the choo-choos.

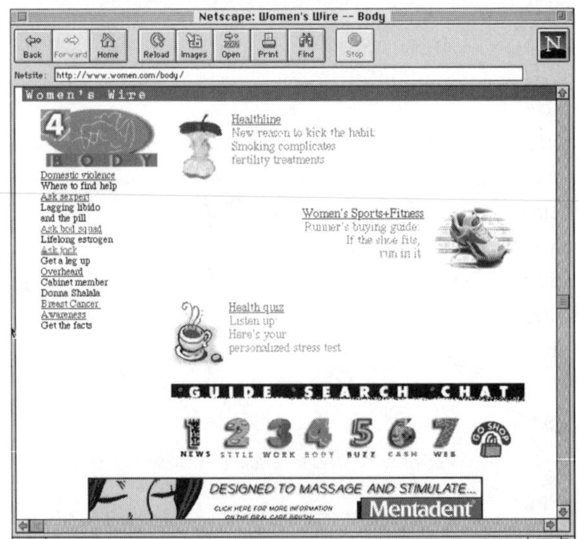

Figure 2.1

Women's Wire Body Channel,

http://www.women.com/body

WellnessWeb

http://www.wellweb.com

If you can stomach its commercial side (the medical professionals and patients behind the site are collecting a catalog of unconventional health products, including nutriceuticals), Wellness Web is worth a visit. Don't miss the "Women and Health" section featuring information on medical tests, menopause, and various illnesses. Or, if you want to kick the habit, stop by the "Smoker's Clinic." And since they say laughter is the best medicine, there's even a Be Happy Be Well area, with links to games, newspapers, and other fun sites to take your mind off your ills.

All About Health Magazine

http://www.allabouthealth.com

All About Health Magazine, an Rx of a 'zine if ever there was one, mixes consumer health information with the latest in medical news. The site includes sections covering the special concerns of women, men, parents, and teens. Organized into topics ranging from abortion to yoga, HealthLinx, the site's main feature, is a promising wellspring of medical information. The Toronto-based site's vibrant graphics and breadth of material make it a good bookmark.

Tom's Guide to Good Livin'

http://www.teleport.com/~heston/index.html

Dr. Tom Heston offers up the Top Ten U.S. Leading Causes of Death at his Guide to Good Livin' site, and though some are expected (Heart Disease tops the charts), others are surprising. These are just some of the fascinating health factoids at Dr. Tom's site, which serves as a sort of medical multivitamin, giving you tiny doses of important info as well as tidbits of recent research on various ailments and issues ranging from cancer to preventive medicine.

INTERNATIONAL APPEAL

GlobalMedic

http://www.globalmedic.com

This terrific all-in-one resource comes from a Montreal-based health information company, and is offered in both English and French. It's sort of an online encyclopedia (in fact, it includes a medical encyclopedia). At the Check Up area, you're asked "What is the reason for your consultation?" You can then choose from a list of common complaints, and are asked a series of questions until the site comes up with possible causes for your discomfort (the results are linked to the encyclopedia).

Ask an Oral Maxillofacial Surgeon

http://www.calweb.com/~goldman/unframedaskomfs.html

The first thing you might ask about oral maxillofacial surgery is, "What is it?" (Think wisdom teeth, chin augmentation, and so forth.) Dr. Kim E. Goldman adds one new question a week to this simple Q&A page. The site offers clear explanations, drawings, and color photos. You can also read about orthognathic surgery (for underbites or overbites) and pulling wisdom teeth at an early age. Ouch.

INTERNATIONAL APPEAL

Ask NOAH About Health

http://www.noah.cuny.edu

If NOAH doesn't know everything, he'll at least point you in the right direction for info on AIDS, cancer, pregnancy, and more. NOAH has a good-sized database of medical articles, aimed at regular folks as well as medical professionals. A click on "Nutrition," for example, pops up articles ranging from "A Consumer's Guide to Fats," to a link to an online "Personal Food Analyst." NOAH speaks Spanish, too. Muy bueno!

Healthline Publishing, Inc.

http://www.health-line.com

Healthline Publishing puts much of its editorial content online, and despite a dearth of graphics, the site has worthwhile info about asthma, skin disorders, and myriad other ailments. Three publications are online, all written by physicians and health care professionals, including the complete contents of two specialty newsletters—"Allergy & Asthma" and "Skin Care Today."

100 BEST SITES

Women's Edge

http://www.womensedge.com

Brought to you by *Prevention Magazine,* this women's resource features timely articles like FoodScanner (nutritionally analyzes over 400 foods), and a reassuring piece on how to deal with abnormal Pap smear results. Regular featured topics include natural healing, weight loss, children's issues, and nutrition, with an emphasis, of course, on prevention (see Figure 2.2). An ounce is worth a pound of cure, and you'll find at least that much here.

Dr. Frank Boehm's Essays

http://www.dr-boehm.com

Dr. Frank Boehm, a Professor of OB/GYN and Director of Obstetrics at Vanderbilt University Medical School, is the author of a series of essays called "Doctors Cry, Too," excerpted here. In "Can We Talk," for example, he discusses his fears about whether his teenage daughter's high school sex ed classes are adequately preparing her for the pressures of puberty. In a world where medicine has become a cold, distant technology, these essays remind us of the humanity behind the clipboard.

Healthwise

http://www.columbia.edu/cu/healthwise

Healthwise, the health education program of Columbia University Health Services lives up to its name. Helpful features include a trove of smartly written stories and tips (see Figure 2.3). A recent article on sleep deprivation included a wide-awake analysis of insomnia and other sleep disorders, and offered suggestions for coping with a chronic lack of zzzzs. Students (and Internauts) can turn to Go Ask Alice, where one can anonymously ask questions about anything from snoring to sex. Alice's answers are archived, and it's easy to get hooked on browsing these very honest questions and forthright responses, organized into general sections like "Fitness and Nutrition," or "Sexual Health and Relationships."

INTERNATIONAL APPEAL

Cyberspace Hospital

http://CH.nus.sg/CH/ch.html

Patients and practitioners alike will want to admit themselves to the Cyberspace Hospital to browse its collection of worldwide health links and resources (see Figure 2.4). Created by the National University of Singapore, the site resembles a hospital structure—you can almost hear the elevator "ding." Each area has links to sites in that field: Visit ICU (Level 3), for instance, and you'll find the Australian and New Zealand Intensive Care Society. You'll be discharged with a dose of healthful resources.

INTERNATIONAL APPEAL

Travel Health Online

http://www.tripprep.com/index.html

Travel health information publisher Shoreland, Inc. has put its worldly wellness wisdom online. Here,

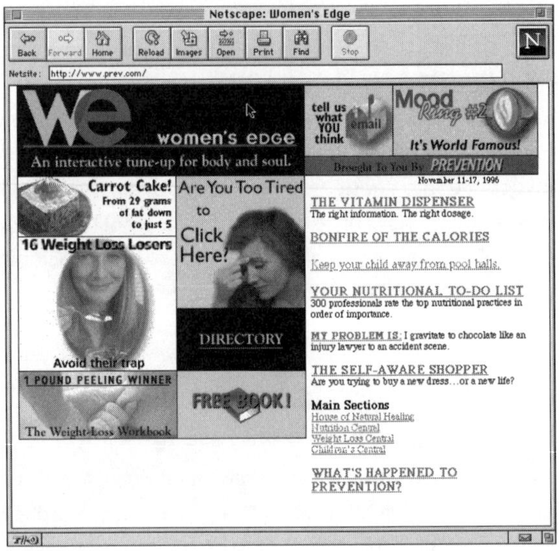

Figure 2.2

Women's Edge from *Prevention Magazine*, *http://www.womensedge.com*

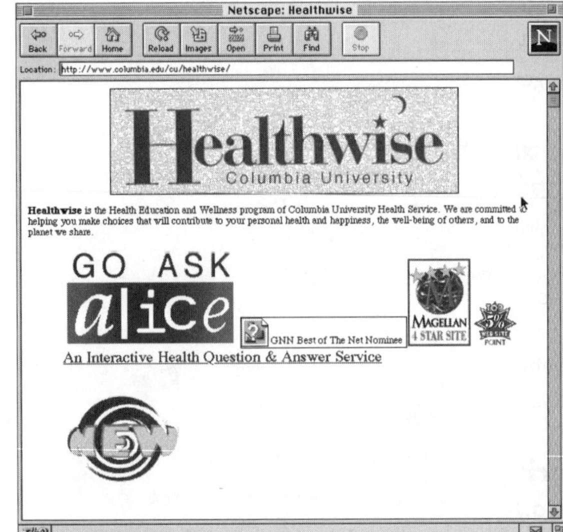

Figure 2.3

Healthwise from Columbia University, *http://www.columbia.edu/cu/healthwise*

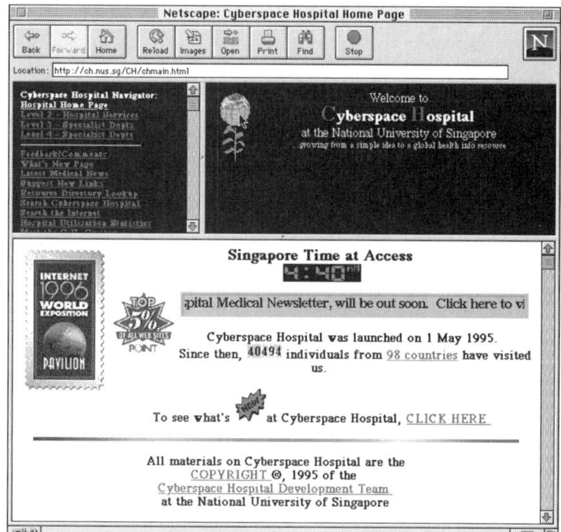

Figure 2.4
Cyberspace Hospital,
http://ch.nus.sg/CH/ch.html

you'll find Country Summary Profiles alerting travelers to health dangers that lie in wait in dozens of nations, from Afghanistan to Zimbabwe. Profiles include summaries of disease risks and recommended or required vaccinations. You'll also find a section summarizing the causes, symptoms, and treatments for illnesses that can vex or even kill travelers. Stop here to steel yourself against the dangers of the road.

HealthAtoZ

http://www.healthatoz.com

HealthAtoZ, from the Medical Network, is a solid index for both consumer and professional medicinal matters. This mega links collection is easy to use, with creative categorization that massages it into accessibility. Each link is briefly described, so you know whether it's worth the click, and a search engine lets you hunt for specific terms.

Thrive

http://pathfinder.com/thrive

Part of Time Inc.'s huge Pathfinder site, Thrive has loads of useful health and fitness information (see Figure 2.5). Its five sections (eats, health, sex, shape, and newsstand) present voluminous amounts of health news, with some straight from the pages of *Health* magazine. Kudos for the interactive U.S. pollen map, stress test, vitamin and mineral guide, as well as the downloadable, er, advice on a better, safer sex life.

Healthy Flying with Diana Fairechild

http://www.maui.net/~diana

Diana Fairechild, a former flight attendant, has created this innovative site to help you fly with ease. Bet you didn't know your captain gets ten times more air than you do (you get the recycled stuff). Don't worry: Fairechild recommends you request "full utilization of air" if you start to feel clammy or faint. You'll find lots of help with time changes, too. A great find for frequent travelers.

Online Health Network

http://www.healthnet.ivi.com

The Online Health Network, from the Mayo Clinic, is a great collection of health info. Visit the Newsstand to browse the Mayo Online Health Magazine, which covers a menagerie of medical issues. Hit the Library for Health Education Topics. A daily HealthTip administers a dose of preventive care. Since this is a commercial site,

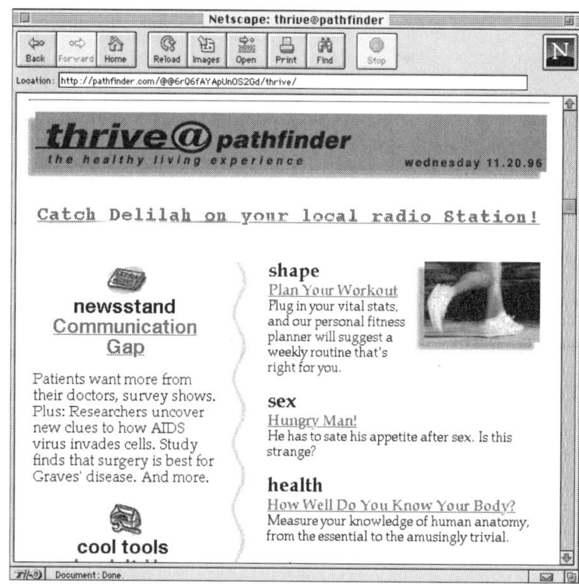

Figure 2.5
Pathfinder's Thrive,
http://pathfinder.com/thrive

you'll also find ordering info for products like the "Safety Monkey" CD-ROM, which "shows young children that safety isn't something to monkey around with."

Healthtouch

http://www.healthtouch.com

Healthtouch, a consumer health info compendium available at pharmacies, now makes its content available online. Search the drug database for info on side effects and missed dosage instructions. The Health Information collection includes articles like "Holiday Stress: Asthma & Allergies." Most of this info comes from non-profit or government health agencies: The Health Resource Directory gives brief descriptions of each institution and lists contact info.

Health Ink

http://www.healthink.com

Health Ink, which features stories from managed care publications, is awash in seemingly silly but actually serious features about health and fitness. Wander into the Health & You section for articles such as, "Is Your Nose

I·N·T·E·R·N·E·T M·I·N·U·T·E

E-MAIL LISTS

One of the best things you can do with e-mail, besides keeping up with friends and conducting long-distance flirtations, is to subscribe to e-mail lists, a misleading name but an easy concept. There are two kinds of e-mail lists—read-only lists and read/write lists:

1 The read-only variety is very much like a print newsletter or magazine distributed to subscribers. The differences are that e-mail newsletters come to your e-mailbox not your snail mailbox and most of them are free.

2 The read/write variety creates an interactive, asynchronous group communication environment. In an "unmoderated" list, whatever a subscriber posts to the list gets distributed to all list subscribers. Some lists are "moderated" which means that the person managing the list reviews the comments and decides whether to distribute them to the mailing list or not. It's sort of like a chain letter but better because a discussion list can function as a brain pool, a community, a mentoring/support system, a hangout. There are thousands of discussion lists and many on health-related topics: FOODTALK—Read it...Do it: Food, Nutrition, Food Safety; EAT-DIS—Eating Disorders List; GENDIS-J—Jewish Genetic Diseases Discussion; YEAST-L—Yeast-Related Medical Discussion List

There are a number of places on the Web where you can get a list of lists and where you can subscribe to lists quickly and easily if your browser has mail capabilities. Try:

http://tile.net

http://www.neosoft.com/internet/paml

http://www.liszt.com

Look for information about how to subscribe to mailing lists on these sites and others which will provide step-by-step instructions for beginners. A couple of caveats, however: Some lists are high volume and can deposit a hundred or more messages into your e-mailbox every day, so add subscriptions slowly. Keep the instructions for unsubscribing, because you don't send comments to the same address as you send administrative requests, and you don't want to look like a rank newbie to everyone on the list.

Getting Bigger?" (about the natural expansion of the proboscis with age) and, "Beans—Up Close and Personal." Browsing the online offerings proves that a dose of levity goes a long way.

Medical Mall

http://www.rain.org/~medmall

Families everywhere will want to bookmark Medical Mall, created by Dr. Chris Landon's Pediatric Foundation, for its well-stocked collection of pediatric health care information. One highlight is the Ask Dr. Landon Page, where you can leave questions for Dr. Landon to answer online or read through replies to FAQs on childhood health issues. Medical Mall has a strong commitment to public health, offering downloadable immunization guides and schedules to educate parents.

Achoo

http://www.achoo.com/

Achoo is nothing to sneeze at—it's a new and potentially comprehensive healthcare site index. Listings are divvied up into three areas—Human Life (the body, diseases, general health), the Practice of Medicine (professional medical sites), and the Business of Health (products and services). Already listing more than 5,000 health resources, and adding features like real-time discussion groups and marketing services, Achoo delivers a well-organized filter for the thousands of health sites piling up online.

First Aid Online

http://www2.vivid.net/~cicely/safety

First Aid Online helps us handle the minor emergencies of everyday life. The simple, mostly text site, created by Andrea Foster, includes detailed descriptions of how to identify and treat the most common injuries. Entries are thorough and, where necessary, linked to related pages on subjects such as CPR. You'll also find a list of suggested supplies for equipping the home medicine chest. With First Aid Online, you'll wish you could stuff your computer in there, too.

MedSurf

http://www.medsurf.com

No matter your level of knowledge, MedSurf has a wellness wave worth catching. You can use the site's search engine or browse the categorized listings. Some listings fit into the broader scope of mental health. The Support Groups page includes listings for the SNAP: Survivors Network of those Abused by Priests, The Single Parent Project, along with sites for groups such as Heart Link Support Group for heart patients.

Safety Link

http://www.safetylink.com/

Safety Link is a production of International Product Safety News, a publication devoted to product safety. On its Web pages, you won't find the newsletter itself—instead, you see a comprehensive list of links to product- and workplace-safety resources across the Net. Webmaster Arthur Michael has tracked down germane pages from sources worldwide.

Cyberspace TeleMedical Office

http://www.telemedical.com

Here's a virtual medical center filled with consumer and practitioner information, advice, and product ads. Other sites feature similar resources, but the TeleMedical Office has an interesting mix of consumer and professional information, putting a lot of good material at your fingertips. You can view the contents based on your level of expertise or just wander through the site's mixed resources.

MedicineNet Medical Dictionary

http://www.medicinenet.com/MAINMENU/GLOSSARY/Gloss_A.htm

MedicineNet's Medical Dictionary helps cure the textbook-term blues. Its simple A-to-Z listing offers brief, basic definitions for seemingly complex terms, from Achlorhydria to Zygote.

Your Health Daily

http://nytsyn.com/live/Lead

This New York Times Syndicate creation dispenses health news on a variety of topics every day. Set up like a newsletter, the past few days of stories are at the top, with common topics below. Each of the common topics (including asthma, depression, and smoking) has a short archive of stories featured on the page. Note: Most of the material comes from medical and business news services, not doctors.

Duke University Healthy Devil On-Line

http://gilligan.mc.duke.edu/h-devil

This site is a campus healthcare answer zone offering friendly advice on serious issues. Designed for the college community, its point-and-click home page is an amusingly drawn, devilish dorm room with links to write-ups on modern healthcare topics (see Figure 2.6). Today's toughest issues, including drug abuse, unwanted pregnancy, and suicide are handled with honesty and sensitivity. But non-college users shouldn't be turned off: some of the advice could be a real life-saver.

The Longevity Game

http://www.northwesternmutual.com/games/longevity/longevity-main.html

Those cut-ups at Northwestern Mutual Life have come up with an online quiz-o-rama that calculates your life expectancy based on your risk factors. The Longevity Game is sort of an underwriter's version of The Game of Life. You start out with an average life span of 73 years, then the "game" adds or subtracts years based on your habits and genetics. Then, presumably, you'll buy insurance accordingly.

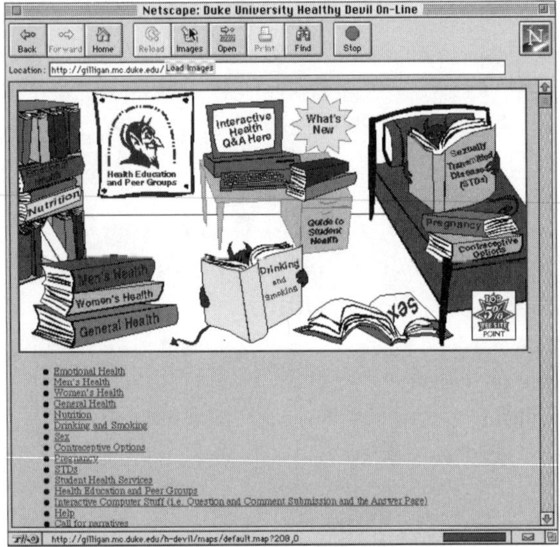

Figure 2.6

Duke University's Healthy Devil Online, *http://gilligan.mc.duke.edu/h-devil*

Medicine Box

http://www.medicinebox.com/medbox

Designed to disseminate pharmaceutical company info, this site features consumer education and illness information. The Remedy Corner includes pamphlets on various medications, while The Ailment Center tackles the conditions that require such medications, drawing on a variety of references to provide information. Consumers can also join the "Coupon Club" to hear about drug discounts, and the Animal Health Center offers info on common pet diseases.

PEDINFO Home Page

http://www.uab.edu/pedinfo

The University of Alabama at Birmingham's PEDINFO site offers a good dose of links and material for parents and medical professionals seeking pediatric information. Though as young as the patients it helps, PEDINFO is already a healthy source of resources on subspecialties such as injury prevention and dentistry, as well as for finding online pediatrics publications, medical software, and education information.

Dear Doc...

http://www.deardoc.artifex.net

INTERNATIONAL APPEAL

Those of us too shy to actually go to see a physician will enjoy this site. It's a philanthropic idea: inviting medical questions and then answering them on this page, with complete anonymity promised. Backed by the credentials of McGill University medical school, membership in the Canadian College of Family Physicians, etc., the "doc" goes by the pen name "Dr. Verde." It's up to you whether you'd like to follow the advice posted here.

The Progress of Nations 1996

http://www.unicef.org/pon96

INTERNATIONAL APPEAL

This "state of the world" report from UNICEF, issued every year, is both a social and medical scorecard, and a compendium of odd facts and stats (example: Finland has the highest percentage of 15-year-olds who smoke). This wide-ranging document covers everything from teen birth rates in Japan (they're the lowest ever), to the shocking statistic that 65 women die each day in the Americas due to pregnancy or childbirth problems.

Pediatric Points of Interest

http://www.med.jhu.edu/peds/neonatology/

From Baltimore's Johns Hopkins University, this site gives parents and professionals alike plenty of sites worth exploring (see Figure 2.7). With more than 700 links, and growing faster than a 12-year-old, it's a kid's health index that covers all the bases. You'll also find fun and games for kids, and other non-technical stuff. And for those with specific questions: The Electronic Consultations page.

Women's Health Hot Line

http://www.soft-design.com/softinfo/womens-health.html

Edited by medical journalist Charlotte Libov, this online newsletter addresses women's health concerns frankly and with authority. Among the topics Libov addresses: the physiological and emotional consequences of heart disease, the risks of smoking, and how best to evaluate medical news from today's confusing media sources. A super and long-overdue reference for women of all ages.

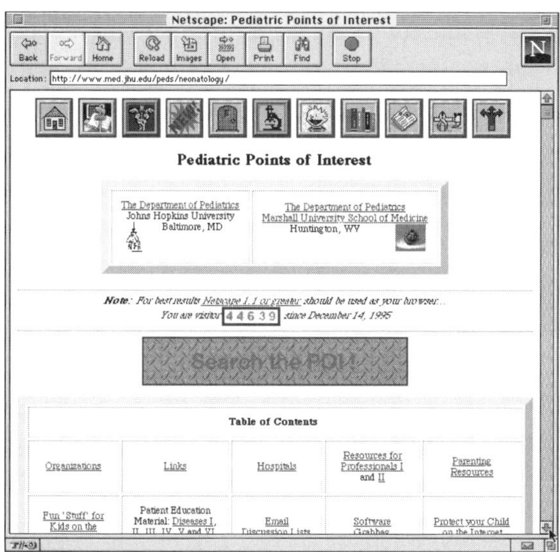

Figure 2.7

Johns Hopkins' Pediatric Points of Interest, *http://www.med.jhu.edu/peds/neonatology/*

PHARMACEUTICALS

RxList—The Internet Drug Index

http://www.rxlist.com

This searchable database of 4,000 prescription, over the counter and soon-to-be FDA-approved drugs is a good resource for anyone concerned about side effects, dosage, or adverse reactions. Type in the name of the pill or potion in question; it then searches its database and cross-references findings by commercial and generic name and drug group. A plus: The engine has fuzzy logic, so misspellings won't deter its path.

MedicineNet

http://www.medicinenet.com

MedicineNet offers comprehensive, easy-to-understand information on everything from common ailments to prescription drugs. Diseases and Treatments features a listing of health problems and solutions, from "Acne" to "Warts, Genital," each described in detail, with key points outlined right up top. There's even an online Medical Dictionary that explains the lingo. The Pharmacy pages include backgrounders on brand-name and prescription drugs.

Pharmaceutical Information Network Home Page

http://pharminfo.com/cgi-bin/print_hit_bold.pl/pin_hp.html

It's a mouthful, but it's the place to go for info on any pill or potion you could ever imagine. Search the PharmInfo database by keyword, or learn more by checking out FAQs, forums, articles, news groups, and, of course, zillions of links to other pharmaceutical and medical Web sites.

MAPS

http://www.maps.org

The Multidisciplinary Association for Psychedelic Research wants you. You may want to consider signing up if you believe that psychedelic drugs such as psilobycin, LSD, ketamine, and marijuana can be used in legitimate medical therapy for certain physical and mental disorders. The MAPS newsletter details efforts to use marijuana in combating the severe weight loss associated with AIDS, Russian research into ketamine as a treatment for alcoholism, and similar projects.

ILLNESS AND CONDITIONS

Diseases & Disorders

http://www.mic.ki.se/Diseases/index.html

This page, part of the Karolinska Institute's Biomedical Resources index, is a handy disease guide for doctors and patients. It's mostly a collection of links, but what links! The amazing array of Web sites around the world range from a USDA site that helps us "Outsmart E. Coli," to a study from Iceland about the "Occupational Hazards of Piano Playing." If you think you've got it, chances are this server does, too.

Sudden Infant Death Syndrome Network

http://q.continuum.net/~sidsnet

Sudden Infant Death Syndrome kills 7,000 babies a year. The SIDS Network established a home page to distribute information about this medical phenomenon which cannot yet be explained. It tells you what SIDS is not: contagious, predictable or, thankfully, painful to the victim. Visitors can check out research updates and a touching section written by relatives who have lost babies to SIDS.

The Tourette Syndrome Home Page

http://www.umd.umich.edu/~infinit/tourette.html

Tourette Syndrome has long been treated as a "fringe disease." It's a mysterious neurological disorder that is sometimes dismissed as hyperactivity. This page helps people understand Tourette Syndrome and cope with it. Besides a no-nonsense explanation, this page includes links to other Tourette pages and resources, like the Tourette support newsgroup.

Repetitive Strain Injury Page

http://engr-www.unl.edu/ee/eeshop/rsi.html

This page by Paul Marxhausen explores Repetitive Strain Injury (RSI), a common and disabling ailment that hits computing professionals the hardest. (The most publicized form of RSI is Carpal Tunnel Syndrome.) The site offers tips on how to prevent RSI, movies of exercises you can do, and a list of doctors who may understand and diagnose RSI ailments.

The Diabetes Homepage

http://www.nd.edu/~hhowisen/diabetes.html

This is the single best spot for diabetes information on the Web. Not only does it have detailed information for the layperson, but it's presented in an entertaining graphical format. The offbeat tone takes a little getting used to, but the well-organized links to the world's major diabetes sites are worth hunting for. This comprehensive site even offers links to data on diabetes in cats.

OncoLink: U. of Pennsylvania Cancer Resource

http://point.lycos.com/reviews/database/zzhmc006.html

This frequently updated online clearinghouse from the University of Pennsylvania Hospital provides excellent education and support resources for cancer patients, professionals, and families. It's a large but well-organized site where meetings are announced, Neoplasma and other journals are offered, there's a keyword search, and items are arranged by medical specialties. You'll find a fine balance between docspeak and ordinary layman's interests, like a gallery of children's art.

Children with Diabetes

http://www.castleweb.com/diabetes

Meet Philippa, a 3-year-old who helps do her own blood tests. Or Daniel, 15, who was diagnosed with juvenile diabetes in July 1995. Children with Diabetes gives them an online meeting place and gives their parents and others dozens of tips on coping with the disease, and they're constantly adding new people and news. You can find a camp in the United States that caters to kids with diabetes, or even trade recipes. A wonderfully friendly source.

Asperger's Syndrome Resources

http://www.udel.edu/bkirby/asperger

Asperger's Syndrome is an autism-related disorder that can produce many symptoms but is often characterized by brilliance and a need for routines. This page, maintained by the parents of an AS child, should be a routine destination for anyone who is touched by autism. Reader-friendly and very helpful, it has an enormous collection of links that should answer just about any question from someone studying AS to how to live with it.

The Parkinson's Web

http://neuro-chief e.mgh.harvard.edu/parkinsonsweb/Main/PDmain.html

This page from Massachusetts General Hospital offers information to people with Parkinson's Disease, their families, and caregivers. If you're just learning about the disease, the online primer provides an easy-to-understand introduction. The directory of support organizations is comprehensive, and a link to the MGH NeuroWebForum allows you to post questions to moderated discussion groups.

The Prostate Cancer InfoLink

http://www.comed.com/prostate

This well-designed site contains a lot of good information, including "Ask Arthur," a series of questions from patients and family members about the disease and its treatment. Or visit the Prostate Cancer Experience, where patients share their battles with the cancer. Other sections have useful definitions of the many acronyms associated with prostate cancer. This is definitely a layperson's site, and a good one at that.

National Psoriasis Foundation

http://www.psoriasis.org

Like every good disease site, this one gives you the facts: psoriasis can't be cured, but it can't be transmitted, either. Nobody knows how (or why) it shows up. The NPF covers all the bases from treatment techniques (with before and after photos) and calls for research volunteers. Easily the best psoriasis resource out there.

Sleep Medicine Home Page

http://www.cloud9.net/~thorpy/

A collection of sleep-related sites, with information on the sleep disorders that plague some 40 million Americans. Professional groups, sleep research centers, and a variety of support groups cover narcolepsy, enuresis, apnea, and Restless Legs Syndrome. Even if you think sleep is a waste of time, the sections on caffeine (complete with estimates of what a fatal overdose would be) may give you a jolt.

Children and Adults with Attention Deficit Disorders

http://www.chadd.org

Attention Deficit Disorder, once thought to affect only kids, remains with 70 percent of patients as they continue into adulthood. That's the word from this home page of ADD advocates, which covers political, medical, and social issues of the disease. One of the best resources here is the list of local chapters nationwide, with meeting times and contact numbers and addresses. CHADD's dedication to patients and its members is easily visible here.

Heart Information Network

http://www.heartinfo.com

Get heart disease information—and win $5,000.00! First recognize that the Heart Information Network wants to send you stuff—but this site has tons of information to offer. Like the section on determining your own heart disease risk. And just so you won't feel alone, HeartInfo stacks up several stories from other patients, like how Richard Hughes lost more than 100 pounds after a triple bypass surgery. Some inspirational stuff here.

The World of Multiple Sclerosis

http://www.ifmss.org.uk

An estimated 3 million people worldwide have MS, according to this British site that serves as a clearinghouse of information. Learn about the newest medicines and use a nifty database to check on past and present research. It's equally useful for doctors wanting to stay in touch and for patients or relatives wishing to learn more about the disease. And many sections are multilingual.

American Cancer Society

http://www.cancer.org

The ACS is one of the best-known groups fighting the disease through research and education. Visitors will find informative and entertaining material, especially in the section on the Great American SmokeScream. The more studious will find the facts on breast cancer, plus links to other cancer sites. And, in keeping with the "political" theme, the ACS urges you to support the Food and Drug Administration's proposed regulation of tobacco.

Centers for Disease Control National AIDS Clearinghouse

http://cdcnac.aspensys.com

The Centers for Disease Control have set up this (very thorough) central repository for AIDS information. In addition to offering help on getting into the big databases of AIDS-related information (like the Culturally-Specific Educational Materials), they provide daily summaries of AIDS articles in major news publications, addresses for a mailing list, and an FTP site for AIDS-related documents. They also point you to reference specialists for further help.

National Alliance of Breast Cancer Organizations

http://www.nabco.org

This site, created by the National Alliance of Breast Cancer Organizations, dispenses valuable information on mammograms, new treatments, and the latest research. Click on Trail News to access descriptions of the latest clinical trials produced in conjunction with the National Cancer Institute. You will find solid suggestions for finding a low cost mammogram and a listing of support groups across the United States. There's also a good section entitled, "Myths & Facts" that dispels some of the hype surrounding breast cancer.

The Breast Cancer Roundtable

http://www.seas.gwu.edu/student/tlooms/MGT243/breast_cancer_roundtable.html

Breast cancer used to be a hush-hush thing. No more, thanks to efforts like this one by George Washington University student Thelma Looms. Each month, a different issue is held up for discussion (example: is there a link between abortion and breast cancer?). Then visitors weigh in on the topic, trading theories, and suggestions. The growing resource section delivers some statistics on the disease, and the creators offer links to mammography databases and other sites of interest.

The HIV InfoWeb

http://carebase2.jri.org/infoweb

This Massachusetts-based site is one of the better clearinghouses for AIDS and HIV-related information. Find dozens of newsletters like AIDS Treatment News (all reproduced on this server—you won't have to leave) and even more sources of federal, state, and local news. There's a search engine here, making access to info relatively painless. Also included: an AIDS discrimination self-help manual and a list of clinical trials in the Massachusetts area.

Harvard AIDS Institute

http://www.hsph.harvard.edu/Organizations/hai/home_pg.html

Harvard has an excellent research institute that tracks and reports on new findings and case studies as well as providing usual links to top AIDS sites. In HAI's AIDS Review, you can read a startling account of the disease's spread in India, where many simply dismiss the virus. Find out about research seminars or grab a copy of one of the institute's reports. A useful tool in the spread of AIDS awareness.

SPOTLIGHT ON BREAST CANCER AWARENESS

In 1996, 46,000 women in the U.S. alone will die from breast cancer. The best tool to fight breast cancer is a simple one: knowledge.

Five Facts

1 The overall breast cancer death rate dropped 5% between 1989 and 1993 in the U.S., reversing a 10-year trend in the opposite direction. But the rate is still rising among black women, according to the National Cancer Institute.

2 Our best line of defense is early detection: self-exams, mammography (X-rays of the breast), and breast exams done by health professionals.

3 Age is the single most important risk factor for breast cancer for most women. Two-thirds of all cases occur among women over age 50.

4 Approximately 10% of breast cancers are considered to be inherited through the genes BRCA1 and BRCA2, the so-called "breast cancer genes." Testing for BRCA1 is available.

5 The most recent research (published June 22, 1996, in the journal, *The Lancet)* indicates that taking the Pill puts women at a slightly higher risk for breast cancer. But 10 years after women stop taking the Pill, they are no more likely to get breast cancer than those who never took the Pill.

Five Sites

The Y-ME National Breast Cancer Organization
http://www.yme.org
The Y-ME National Breast Cancer Organization breast self-examination page provides step-by-step instructions and illustrations on one of the most important things you can do for yourself.

Survivors, In Search of a Voice
http://aorta.library.mun.ca/bc/survivor
Survivors, In Search of a Voice takes you on a journey through 100 compelling pages of personal essays, photographs, and artwork by women stricken with breast cancer.

National Breast Cancer Coalition
http://www.natlbcc.org
Flex your political muscle and join the National Breast Cancer Coalition to get Washington to appropriate more money for research and treatment.

The Breast Cancer Information Clearinghouse
http://nysernet.org/breast/Default.html
The Breast Cancer Information Clearinghouse has details on subscribing to breast cancer mailing lists.

Harvard Medical School Department of Radiology
http://www.bih.harvard.edu/radiology/Modalities/Mammo/mammo.html#mammo
Harvard Medical School and Beth Israel Hospital's Department of Radiology explain the ins and outs of mammography.

The Congenital Heart Disease Resource Page

http://www.csun.edu/~hfmth006/sheri/heart.html

California State University-Northridge math specialist Sheri Berger has put together a list of resources especially for parents of children with congenital heart disease. Parents can find information about a support group and the addresses of several e-mail discussion lists. Otherwise this is mainly a batch of links, but a good batch, offering heart-related pages from Israel to Iowa.

National Organization for Rare Disorders

http://www.pcnet.com/~orphan

Diseases that strike a relatively small number of people can mystify and isolate their victims in a cloud of ignorance and pain. But NORD's Web site can clear up misconceptions and questions with detailed information on more than 1,000 rare disorders. Each entry describes symptoms, typical population affected, and possible avenues of treatment. And the terminology isn't too bad.

The Names Project

http://www.aidsquilt.org

There are 32,000 panels of what has been called "the largest on-going community arts project in the world." From this site, you'll learn about the project, how to make a panel and where portions of the quilt will be on display (see Figure 2.8). You also can see a selection of panels and find out about events. This sobering and dignified site gives you the numbers behind AIDS, but it also offers something more valuable: the people.

International Myeloma Foundation

http://www.comed.com/IMF/imf.html

Multiple myeloma is a deadly cancer of the bone marrow that currently has no cure. This worldwide group is seeking, ultimately, a cure to myeloma, but is primarily concerned with making life with the disease more comfortable. Visitors can get answers to their questions about myeloma. There's also a newsletter with articles by physicians and patients, or you can join a patients' network.

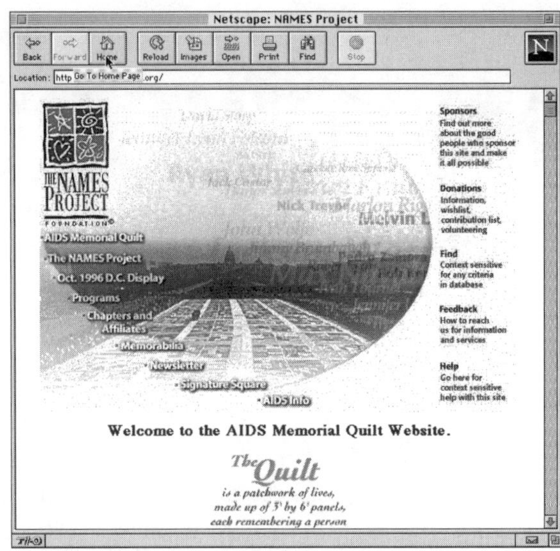

Figure 2.8

The Names Project for the AIDS Quilt, *http://www.aidsquilt.org.*

AIDS in Mexico

http://jeff.dca.udg.mx/sida/Ingles/aids.html

Credit the University of Guadalajara for expanding its reach. The collection of AIDS-related materials here, in English and Spanish, is a practical and handy index to the disease and how it affects Mexicans. Besides Spanish-language articles on the spread of AIDS (known as SIDA south of the border), this site provides tips on dealing with food at home and in restaurants as well as several publications.

CancerGuide

http://cancerguide.org

This is a hopeful, folksy guide to fighting cancer. Creator Steve Dunn starts with a neophyte-friendly essay on cancer fundamentals, and then goes on to show how to plug into the big-time medical databases. Includes useful tools like the highly recommended "The Median Isn't the Message" by Stephen Jay Gould, for those with difficult prognoses, and lots more. "Steve's Guide to Clinical Trials" discusses Interleukin-2, the drug that saved his life.

The Alzheimer Page

http://www.biostat.wustl.edu/alzheimer

The Washington University School of Medicine serves as host for this digest and guide to an Alzheimer e-mail discussion group. All sorts, from physicians to students to patients—contribute to the conversation, and each posting is automatically transferred onto the Web site. Most are thoughtful, compassionate messages on dealing with the disease and caring for loved ones. For those affected by Alzheimer's, this can be a valuable resource.

Caregiver Survivor Resources

http://www.geocities.com/Athens/1330

Jim and Merlene Sherman introduce themselves at their Caregiver Survivor Resources page thus: "We have been married for 38 years. For over 13 years we were caregivers to both sets of parents, now deceased." Here, they seek to pass along some of their painfully achieved expertise by providing links to Internet resources for caregivers.

Glaucoma Research Foundation

http://www.glaucoma.org

Until multimedia allows us to hear Web pages, you'll be wanting to protect your eyesight. That's the goal of the GRF, a non-profit group dedicated to combating the second-leading cause of blindness. GRF's site tells you about research underway and describes how you can leave your eyes to research—and maybe pass on the gift of sight.

The RenalNet Information Service

http://ns.gamewood.net/renalnet.html

Kidney disease is what this site is all about. Two Virginia nephrologists (that's, uh, kidney specialists) created RenalNet, a great guide to the Web's kidney sites, case reviews, and tutorials. This place has loads of links which will be most useful to doctors and med students. For patients, there's a search engine that can help locate dialysis units around the country.

Endometriosis Information and Links

http://www.frii.com/~geomanda/endo

Amanda (of Amanda's Spot on the Web) has created a very comprehensive, link-rich resource on the painful disease endometriosis. In addition to an explanation and possible causes, you'll find very practical tips here, such as a section on "communicating effectively with your doctors." For the strong, there are photos. And, there are links to lots of additional resources. If you suffer from endometriosis, you'll want to bookmark this site.

The Body Electric

http://www.surgery.com

Probably the most well-known plastic and reconstructive surgery site on the Web, The Body Electric provides detailed information on a broad range of cosmetic surgery options, from breast implants to liposculpture. Also, check out "what's new," or locate other plastic surgery locations on the Web. You can also browse their Physician Locator, but beware: Surgeons pay to be listed here, so you probably don't want to consider this a recommendation.

INTERNATIONAL APPEAL

P-Link, The Plastic Surgery Link

http://www.nvpc.nl/plink

Brought to you by the Dutch Society of Plastic Surgery, this is probably the most thorough compendium of plastic surgery resources on the Web. You can track down subjects like Hand Surgery and Microsurgery, browse through surgeons' home pages, or get up-to-date on the latest News. There's something here for the professional, the patient, and the merely curious.

Chronic Illnet

http://www.calypte.com/ci_home.html

Chronic Illnet is a funky-looking site that provides research news about diseases like chronic fatigue syndrome, AIDS, and cancer (see Figure 2.9). The authors try to reach a wide audience, but still offer technical information in reports with titles like "Immunosuppresive Retrovirus Peptides." At the other end of the spectrum is the still-developing community page, with stories (for instance) written by AIDS patients.

National Stroke Association

http://www.stroke.org

This Colorado group is fighting this debilitating condition through research and education. Visitors can order NSA materials for teaching or browse the monthly newsletter. The NSA encourages visitors to set up screening programs using free materials. It's a good idea,

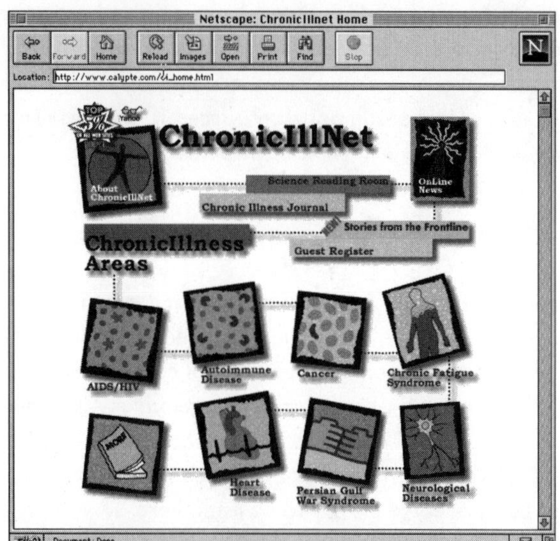

Figure 2.9
Chronic Illnet Web site,
http://www.callypte.com/ci_home.html

especially when you consider that a stroke occurs every minute in America.

Blind Links

http://seidata.com/~marriage/rblind.html

Blind Links is a collection of pointers to resources for the blind. These links will send you to areas of the Web with the visually impaired in mind. For example, a link to the University of Missouri-Columbia gives tips on how to design Web pages that are accessible to blind people using adaptive technology. Many of the resources listed are gopher sites, so don't expect a lot of flashy formatting.

Deaf World Web

http://deafworldweb.org/dww

This Web features an interactive finger spelling guide (and quiz), a list of 10 commandments ("I am a proud Deaf Being who brought you out of pure oralism, out of oppression."), "DEAFinitions of wit," and more. The site is still growing, but already there are plenty of links to "Deaf History," job postings, and more. Try "jumplinks" for readiest access to these very helpful resources.

College and Career Programs for Deaf Students

http://www.gallaudet.edu/~cadsweb/ccg/credits.html

This is the online version of the book, College and Career Programs for Deaf Students, and includes most of the information of the printed text. The Q&A section answers several questions aspiring deaf students may have. The pages list national programs, as well as programs in specific schools, organized by region. This site proves that, just because you can't hear, doesn't mean you can't be a successful student.

Disability Resources from Evan Kemp Associates

http://disability.com

This commercial site offers tips, products, and services to disabled Net surfers. In its monthly tips section, they show how handicapped drivers can overcome obstacles at self-serve gas stations. And in a reprinted speech by Evan J. Kemp, former chair of the Equal Employment Opportunity Commission and overseer of this site, you can read his take on affirmative action: "Monetary reparations might be far less costly to society than racial preferences."

AGING

The Health and Retirement Study (HRS)

http://www.umich.edu/~hrswww

The University of Michigan sponsors this page tracking the results of its health and retirement study, conducted to explore factors leading to retirement, as well as seniors' continued health and economic well-being afterwards. The site includes a Fact Sheet from the National Institute on Aging, and pointers to reference materials compiled by the study's research groups.

INTERNATIONAL APPEAL

World Health Network

http://www.worldhealth.net

The WHN's member organizations—the American Academy of Anti-Aging Medicine, the National Academy of Sports Medicine, and the Longevity Institute

International among them—put their long-lived research, info, news, and publications online here. A highlight: the Longevity Test, which poses genetic and lifestyle questions to determine your life expectancy.

GeroWeb

http://www.iog.wayne.edu/GeroWeb.html

The Institute of Gerontology at Wayne State University supports this center for links and resources on aging. Easy on the eyes, with annotated link lists separated into categories for universities, government agencies, private organizations, health and biomedical research sources, and more. Whether you're a senior looking for activities, or a researcher looking for raw materials, GeroWeb is a good place to start.

Menopause: Another Change in Life

http://www.ppfa.org/ppfa/menopub.html

This site, brought to you by Planned Parenthood, identifies menopause for the major turning point that it is, yet seeks to de-mystify "the change" as much as possible. What you'll find here: a very matter-of-fact explanation of body changes, touching on areas like Osteoporosis, Hormone Replacement Therapy and Sex Life, an extensive bibliography, and lots of good advice.

PowerSurge

http://members.aol.com/dearest/index.html

This site was created by Alice Lotto Stamm as an online community "for women on the pause" as a way to help move the topic of menopause "out of the closet" (see Figure 2.10). Power Surge is not only empowering its message, but crackles visually as well. Weekly live chats feature celebrity guests such as Gail Sheehy, author of *Passages,* as well as noted physicians and other experts. A great place to re-energize.

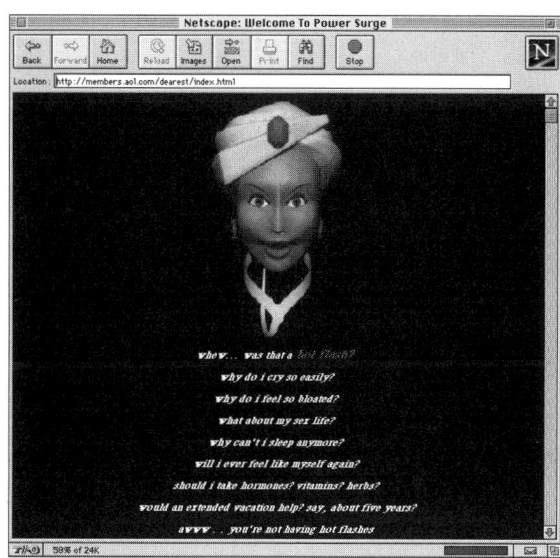

Figure 2.10

PowerSurge—a site about menopause, *http://members.aol.com/dearest/index.html*

RECOVERY AND ABUSE

Web of Addictions

http://www.well.com/user/woa

Andrew L. Homer Ph.D. and Dick Dillon put together this recovery resource site because of their concern "about the appalling extent of misinformation about drugs on the Internet." You'll find government policy criticism from former San Jose police chief Joe McNamara, links to organizations such as Indiana U.'s Alcohol and Drug Info. Center, instructions for participating in an online 12-step meeting, and more.

The Wounded Healer Journal

http://idealist.com/wounded_healer

This is a resource which focuses on the needs of psychotherapists and people who have survived child abuse, and provides resources for victims of abuse in general. You can find relevant news and point-of-view pieces, treatment resources, and other interesting links, along with chats and forums. If you don't have the time to check back frequently (and items are added often), there's a weekly e-mail service available to keep you updated.

SafetyNet Domestic Violence Resources

http://www.cybergrrl.com/dv.html

This valuable reference on domestic violence issues is maintained by a former director of the Domestic Abuse Awareness Project in New York City. The site features alarming statistics on domestic abuse, as well as pointers to shelters for battered women and children throughout the U.S. and the U.K. The complete Domestic Violence Handbook is also here, a potential life-saver for anyone in an abusive situation.

Sexual Assault Information Page

http://www.cs.utk.edu/~bartley/salnfoPage.html

This powerful resource from University of Tennessee student Chris Bartley offers tips on prevention and links to assault survivors' networks. A superb discussion of "date rape" examines the problem of miscommunication between friends, and how to understand when "no" really means "no." Those seeking immediate help can jump to a rape crisis center for counseling and advice.

National Women's Resource Center

http://www.nwrc.org

The goal of the NWRC is to develop policy and provide education in the areas of alcohol, tobacco and drug abuse, and mental illness among women. Their eye-pleasing and well-organized Web page serves as a Meta-resource for anyone seeking information on the aforementioned topics by providing a vast collection of documents, events calendars, forums, and other resources.

SPORTS AND FITNESS

Schneid's Volleyball Page

http://www.xnet.com/~schneid/vball.shtml

With text links listed over blue background, it's not fancy, but talk about extensive! Here are enough diagrammed offensive and defensive schemes, and skill primers to turn a novice Web surfer into a wise old coach. Check out reviews of the best balls, ankle supports, and other equipment. Then it's back to business with more nutrition, fitness, and sports medicine than a body has a right to, free of charge.

Gymn Forum

INTERNATIONAL APPEAL

http://gymn.digiweb.com/gymn

From site manager Rachele Harless, here's a well-balanced view of the gymnastics world. Woven into the text are links to the likes of Romanian National Championships results, a press release on '96 U.S. Olympics coach Peter Kormann, and (yikes!) a response to the Female Triad (disordered eating, amenorrhea, and osteoporosis). Just getting to read names like Svetlana Khorkina is also a bonus.

Women's Sports Page

http://fiat.gslis.utexas.edu/~lewisa/womsprt.htm

This no-frills index offers a terrific collection of links to everything from women's soccer to gender equity discussions to track and field. You'll also find plenty of rugby, karate, weightlifting, and other formerly "unladylike" sports. Compiled by citizen Amy Lewis, this is a great resource for anyone excited to know that team handball isn't just for men anymore.

Golf Online

http://www.golfonline.com

The editors of *Golf Magazine* bring you this daily updated window onto the professional tours, with articles, instruction, and features galore. Standout feature: The Private Lesson allows you to fill out a "personal profiler" (surveying trouble spots in all aspects of your game), and then returns specific tips to help you bring that score down. With reviews of the latest equipment as well, GolfOnline is right on time with the sport's recent wave of trendiness.

International Paralympic Committee

INTERNATIONAL APPEAL

http://info.lut.ac.uk/research/paad/ipc/ipc.html

To further its mission of promoting sports for athletes with disabilities, the IPC organizes and sanctions championship events and games throughout the world. Their home page offers resources on individual sports ranging from alpine skiing to sailing, plus links to related organizations (like

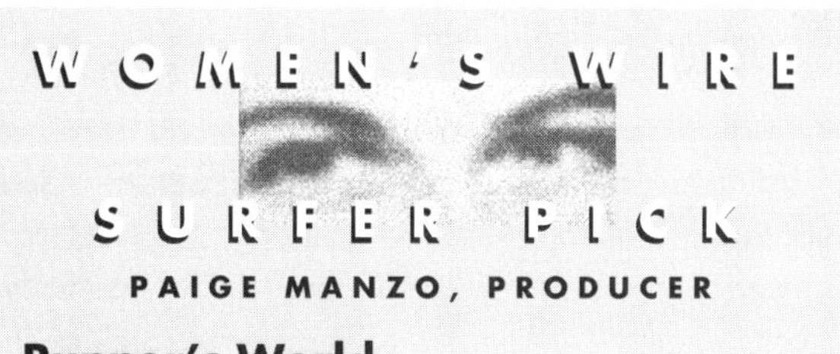

PAIGE MANZO, PRODUCER

Runner's World

http://www.runnersworld.com

The excellent electronic edition of Runner's World is great for pertinent daily news updates, resources on running products/gear, nutrition, injury prevention and recovery, and more. Features include a shoe buyer's guide (where you can determine your foot type), training tips such as "Fat-Burning Workouts," and interesting nutrition advice. There's a Women's Running section and an interactive forum for sounding off on everything from Olympic Gold Races to how many miles your pair of Nikes lasted before the heel blew out. Competition info, first steps for new runners, and a directory of related sites make this a complete resource for running enthusiasts of all levels of ability.

Four Sites Worth Running To:

Internet Resources for Runners is a nicely designed, not-to-be-missed resource—books, clubs, races—for runners of all levels.
http://irfr.com

Dr. Pritbut's Running Injuries Page lists common running ailments, risk factors, and self-treatment advice.
http://www.cark.net/pub/pribut/spsport.html

The Running Page is a good index of publications and clubs, plus lists of upcoming races and race results.
http://sunsite.unc.edu/drears/running/running.html

USA Track & Field provides interesting tidbits, such as how U.S. women pulled in $1.15 million in winnings vs. the men's $744K.
http://www.usaldr.org/money95.htm

the Wheelchair Chicago Bulls basketball team). Athletes and anyone else interested in disability sports and issues will find plenty here.

United States Swimming

http://www.usswim.org

USS, Inc. is the sanctioned governing body for competitive swimming in the United States. Their (mostly text) home page is a wealth of swimming information, including a history of the sport, diaries of U.S. Olympians, meet results, qualifying standards and more. There's a special Kid Pool here for the tadpoles, a searchable swim club listing, and a primer on "What to Watch in a Swim Meet." This is a good resource for athletes, coaches, and parents.

USA Track & Field

http://www.doitsports.com/usatf/index.html

In support of the USATF's mission to provide athletes of all ages with opportunities to pursue track, field, and distance running excellence, this page offers athletics news, event schedules, and other resources like a directory of member associations, coaching education programs, and local road races (listed via a clickable U.S. map). Bio files on "Today's Stars," are available as well. A great read for athletes and fans alike.

Female Bodybuilders

http://www.slip.net/~frs/femuscle

This page, from Web-ster Marc Meloon, is an honest-to-goodness tribute to female bodybuilders. Meloon gives some "House Recommendations" for contenders to follow. Besides top names like Cory Everson, Lenda Murray, and Bev Francis, dozens of competitors can be seen here, and audio files allow you to hear interviews with his favorites: sometimes sexy, sometimes scary, always sculpted and strong.

MARGO CARN, EDITOR

Women's Rugby

http://vail.al.arizona.edu/rugby

Yes, women do play rugby, tackling and all! And here's the site to prove it—with info for the player, the diehard fan, or anyone who just wants to know. Read about scrums, rucks, and mauls; see scores, match schedules, and rules; contact women's teams around the world.

Hiking and Walking Homepage

http://elaine.teleport.com/~walking/hiking.html

Here's a fine guide and info index for those who put one foot in front of the other for the pure joy of it. Via newsgroups and club links, it'll hook you up with walkers and hikers around the world. For psychological insights, click on Connecting With Nature; and should the kids not share your enthusiasm, read "Walking Without Whining," among other articles. An excellent resource for pedestrians.

The Body Project

http://www.bodyzine.com

With an eye toward foiling health industry hucksters, this 'zine offers articles and features on physical fitness and overall wellness. A recent issue included food facts from consumer activist/nutritionist Keith Klein, an interactive Fat Loss Forum, Phil Kaplan's guide to cycle training, and a photo gallery featuring Arnold Schwarzenegger and other "fitness models." A generous read, with past issue archives, "FitLinks," and desktop shopping, too.

Fitness Partner Connection Jumpsite

http://www.cdc.net/~primus/fpc/fpchome.html

Two personal trainers and a Web page expert created this index of over 450 links to exercise and wellness sites, which are categorized under Training & Sports, Nutrition & Health, Publications, etc. A Plyometric FAQ (under Strength & Bodybuilding), for instance, included exercises for increasing vertical leaping ability, and there's even a link to the Skydive Archive. A fine bookmark for fitness buffs.

Balance Fitness Magazine

http://hyperlink.com/balance

This is a fine resource for diet and fitness, with back issues well-organized by subject. Graphics are limited, content is

[OVERHEARD ON WOMEN'S WIRE]

http://chat.women.com

"Women are getting more recognition. I had to run against boys in high school because there was no girls' team. In the 1996 Olympics, the women athletes are getting a lot of publicity. They are great role models."

—Olympian Evelyn Ashford live from Atlanta in a chat on Women's Wire. A four-time Olympic gold medalist, Ashford attended the games as spectator for the first time, 20 years after she won her first gold.

up and down: an article on stomach exercises was full of good info; and the "Adventures of Garfield the Glucose Molecule" was funny and educational; but "How to Relax" merely suggested one breathe slowly and take relaxation classes. Still, well worth the visit for the fitness-minded.

Mirkin Report

http://www.wdn.com/mirkin/

Each month, sports-medicine expert and fat-free guru Dr. Gabe Mirkin combs medical journals for fitness and health breakthroughs, reporting his findings in the Mirkin Report newsletter. Subscriptions are offered on his Web site, but so are a host of free reports, recipes, and other info for the health conscious. Dieters, fitness buffs, and those looking for a lean, mean way to cook Shrimp Jambalaya can find plenty of ideas.

Dr. Pribut's Running Injuries Page

http://www.clark.net/pub/pribut/spsport.html

Runners suffering maladies from plantar fasciitis to simple overtraining will appreciate the insights offered in this virtual diagnosis/treatment manual. Author Stephen M. Pribut is a podiatrist, so feet get lots of the attention, but a quick once over of the HTML home page should point you toward pertinent information on common running ailments in the knees, ankles, and other areas.

Aerobics!

http://grove.ufl.edu/~evilgreg/Aerobics

Don your spandex and leggings and surf on over to this aerobic dance page for access to a library of basic patterns, FAQs, and pertinent newsgroups. And if you're not fully satisfied with the moves already archived here,

[OVERHEARD ON WOMEN'S WIRE]

http://chat.women.com

"All evidence shows that the people who exercise hard can eat almost anything."

THINK YOU'RE FAT?

"Get your percentage body fat checked. Especially women, when they think they should lose the last five pounds, they are often below their allotted body fat. Let's say that a woman is 18% body fat, when we normally recommend 22% body fat. Then, her target weight is unrealistic. It is based on a dream instead of physiology."

MAKING YOUR WORKOUT MORE EFFICIENT:

"Wind sprints are like magic. The secret is to put a little intense sprint in the middle of your gentle aerobic exercise. It's a way of adding intensity without getting hurt. In a half hour of jogging, for example, I would add six wind sprints, 20 seconds long. The secret is not to run super hard during the sprint. Just get a little out of breath. Your body tries hard to recover and that's when the miraculous changes in metabolism take place."

—Covert Bailey, fitness guru and author of "Smart Eating: Choosing Wisely, Living Lean," in a live chat on Women's Wire.

provisions are made for contributing your own favorites. A burgeoning fitness resource with plans to expand into boxerobics, water aerobics, and more.

NUTRITION

Cyberdiet

http://www.cyberdiet.com

Dietician Timi Gustafson had never been on the Web when she decided to take her business to the Net last summer. It didn't matter. "I was such a newbie that I didn't know enough to be scared or intimidated," she says. With a little technological coaching and a lot of vision, she's created a highly interactive, resourceful site. Calculate your recommended daily caloric and vitamin needs, read health articles, and browse healthy meal plans.

The Training-Nutrition Home Page

http://www.dgsys.com/~trnutr/index.html

This nutritional-information site is geared mainly toward bodybuilders and revolves around building up one's muscles sans steroids. The FAQ list includes sensible-sounding recipes and snack suggestions. There are plenty of dietary specifics on calorie counts and electrolytes, plus instructions on when to eat what. This should be a fun site for those in the target audience: "hardcore natural bodybuilders and other serious amateur athletes."

The Science of Obesity and Weight Control

http://www.loop.com/~bkrentzman

Dr. Ben Krentzman's Science of Obesity and Weight Control offers info on current obesity treatments, especially the increasingly popular phentermine and fenfluramine (phen/fen) medication combo. Krentzman includes lively discourse on topics ranging from the role of genetics to the effects of yo-yo dieting. Though this site focuses heavily on weight control, Krentzman also serves up a fat collection of links to low-fat recipes, diet plans, and fitness information.

Arbor Communications—Guide to Nutrition Resources

http://netspace.net.au/%7Ehelmant/nutid.htm

This comprehensive directory of Net nutrition resources comes courtesy of Australia's Arbor Communications. The site features listings organized into two main categories—Applied Nutrition (clinical nutrition, dietetics, nutrition journals, and multimedia) and Food ("for resources concerning food composition, food science, and food safety.") Each category is bursting with good-for-you sites, and if you still can't find what you want, the Search page lists even more.

where they surf

Surfer: Timi Gustafson

Registered dietition and co-creator of CyberDiet *(http://www.cyberdiet.com)*, a highly trafficked comprehensive, interactive site about nutrition.

Her favorite sites of the moment:

Sportszone

http://espnet.sportszone.com

"Sportszone provides the latest scores and daily recaps about my favorite sports: tennis, golf, skiing, and track and field events. It also offers human interest stories about individual athletes."

Silicon Investor

http://www.techstocks.com

"This is a nifty site for both the casual and serious investor. It provides stock news and trends, quotes, charts, and a place to ask and receive responses to my many questions."

Food and Nutrition Information Center

http://www.nalusda.gov/fnic

Operated as part of the USDA's National Agricultural Library (NAL), the FNIC is a clearinghouse of food and nutrition-related information; its Web site is the center's online outlet for spreading the word on healthy eating (see Figure 2.11). The home page is as crisp-looking as the red apple icons used for bullets, with links galore. Just the thing to keep the doctor away!

Nutritionist's ToolBox

http://www.fsci.umn.edu/tools.htp

The Nutritionist's Tool Box is a handy collection of nutritional know-how. The site, courtesy of the University of Minnesota's Department of Food Science and Nutrition, includes nutritional breakdowns on more than 1,170 standard foods, plus the kCal-culator, which calculates your energy needs, so you can match your caloric intake to your activity output. To help kids learn good-food basics, the page links to K-12 resources for teaching healthy eating habits.

World Guide to Vegetarianism

http://www.veg.org/veg/Guide/

The World Guide to Vegetarianism is a geographical listing of restaurants, organizations, and services of interest to vegetarians (see Figure 2.12). So, if you're a vegetarian in Lancaster, Pennsylvania or Tasmania, Australia, you'll know to check out Lanvina or Mimosa Whole Foods (respectively). Also: lists of airlines and cruise lines that cater to herbivores. And, if your favorite store or restaurant isn't listed here, your additions are cheerfully welcomed.

Nutri Link

http://www.cyberg8t.com/morfin56/index.htm

Hosted by Oscar M. Guevara, a dietetic tech student, Nutri Link serves as a clearinghouse for users to share their nutritionally sound information, ideas, stories, and links. Users can sign in as participants to add to the site; or just browse what's been added so far. The pantry is still relatively bare, but then again as of this writing, the site had just launched. There are lots of links to other sites, along with requests for participation from users.

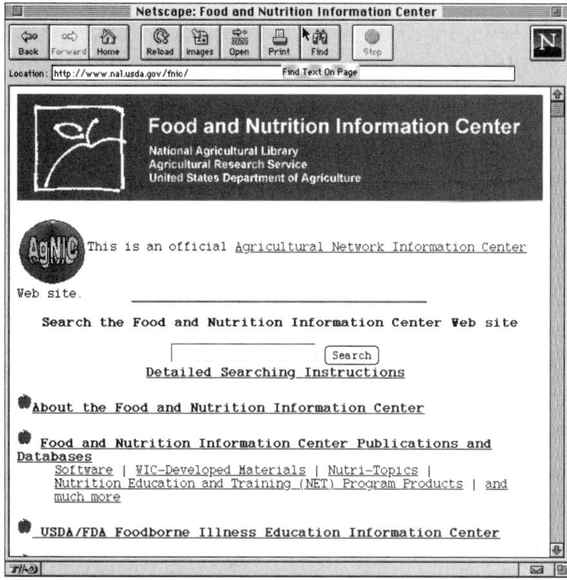

Figure 2.11
The USDA's Food and Nutrition Center, *http://www.nal.usda.gov/fnic*

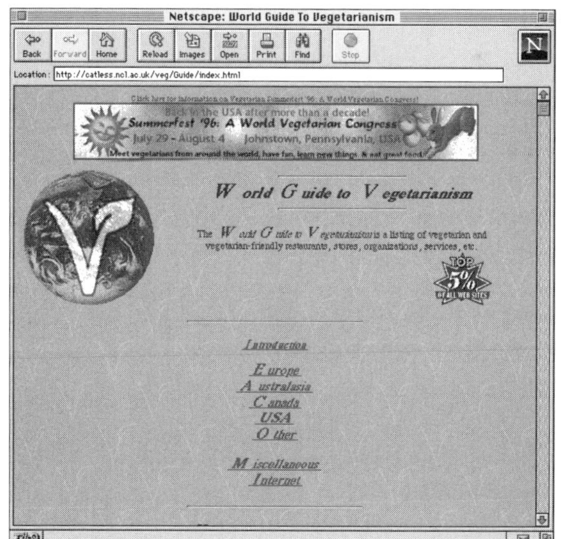

Figure 2.12
The World Guide to Vegetarianism, *http://www.veg.org/veg/Guide/*

The Nutrition Pages

http://deja-vu.oldiron.cornell.edu/~jabbo/index.html

Basically, this site (also known as "Sweet Sweetback's Badass Nutrition Page") is a compendium of FAQs answered by nutrition student Tim Triche, Jr., who covers topics like cholesterol, alternative health practices, and sports nutrition (see Figure 2.13). The standard exhortations to eat better are presented with funky grafix in no-nonsense fashion, and an open forum invites readers to submit their own essays on nutrition and wellness.

American Institute for Cancer Research

http://www.aicr.org

It's not often that you find the words "Poached Pears with Chocolate Sauce" mentioned at a cancer site. But that's just one of the recipes recommended by this national leader in diet, nutrition, and cancer. For patients and their families, there's a great FAQ ("Eggs—good or bad for you?") and a rotating list of recipes.

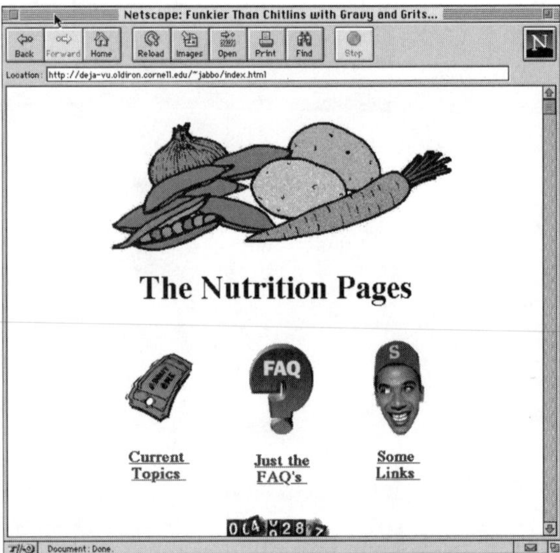

Figure 2.13
The Nutrition Pages,
http://deja-vu.oldiron.cornell.edu/~jabbo/index.html

Eating Disorders Shared Awareness

http://www.mirror-mirror.com/eatdis.htm

This attractive, well-stocked site is the cooperative effort of two women who have been there. You can read up on Anorexia, Bulimia, and Compulsive Overeating, including Signs and Symptoms, Getting Help, and various factors involved in these disorders (for example: eating disorders in relation to sexual abuse, older women, and societal pressures). In addition to helpful and inspirational materials, you'll find lots of links to other information sources (see Figure 2.14).

ALTERNATIVE MEDICINE

Homeopathy Home Page

http://www.dungeon.com/~cam/homeo.html

Homeopathy, a medical treatment practice based on the "law of similars," and emphasizing the whole person, is gaining in popularity. You can find out more on this page

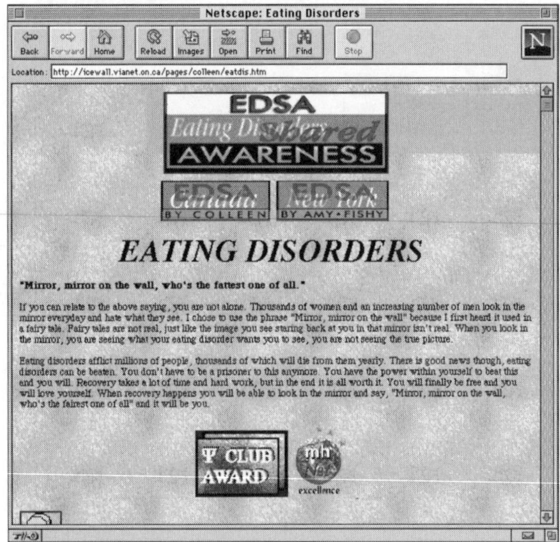

Figure 2.14
Eating Disorders Shared Awareness
http://www.mirror-mirror.com/eatdis.htm

from Briton Nick Haworth, who offers links to databases and Web pages devoted to the healing art. Lovers of body manipulation can link to the osteopathic page. Worldwide addresses for consultations, too.

Chiropractic Online Today

http://www.panix.com/~tonto1/dc.html

Help celebrate the 100th anniversary of the chiropractic profession by perusing this online magazine dedicated to healthy backs and necks. Features include history, a brief summary of medical news, and a growing referral list for chiropractors (Dr. Paul J. Vaillancourt is your man in Kittery, Maine). The information here is well split between public and professional use.

HerbNET

http://www.herbnet.com

HerbNET, from the Herb Growing and Marketing Network, offers a homegrown collection of resources and info. Check out the Magazine for updates on herbal news and happenings, as well as recipes and other goodies. Herbalists, or those just curious about the powers of plants, will be impressed by the resources, recipes, and references that have taken root at HerbNET.

HealthCraze!

http://www.newhope.com/hcz

Looking for an herbal headache cure or the latest nutrient news? HealthCraze! has it all, in a selection of areas devoted to alternative health care (see Figure 2.15). The site, from New Hope Communications, covers a healthy range of subjects. High points: the Nutrition Advisor, where you'll find write-ups on topics such as Low-Fat Living, and Cancer Fighting Vegetables; and the VitaMan section, covering impact of vitamins and minerals on Depression, Fertility, and more.

Acupuncture.com

http://acupuncture.com

Here you'll find plenty of information about this increasingly popular alternative therapy, along with coverage of other Oriental treatments such as herbology and massage (see Figure 2.16). Click on topics to access consumer, student, and practitioner-level texts. Practitioner referral and student information pages are also included. Lovely to look at—the site has serene graphics reminiscent of stained glass and watercolors—and intriguing to read, Acupuncture.com pricks the imagination without overselling the subject.

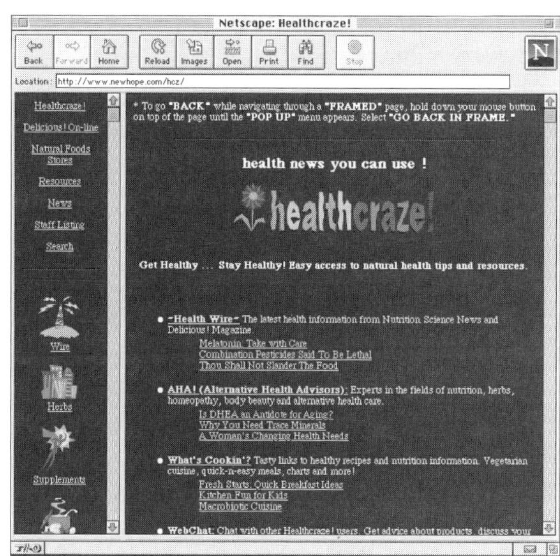

Figure 2.15
HealthCraze Web site, *http://www.newhope.com/hcz*

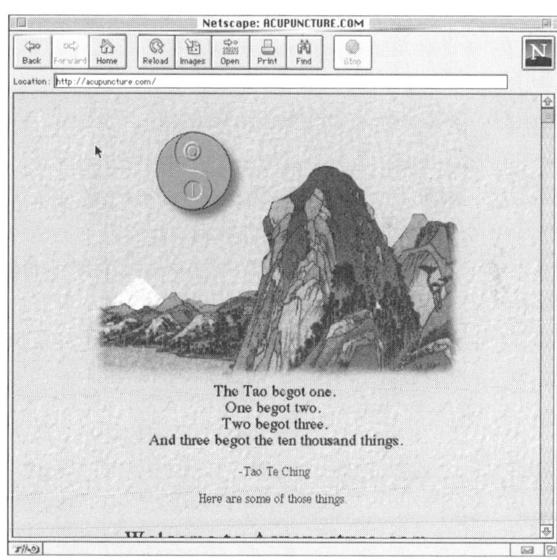

Figure 2.16
Acupuncture.com home page, *http://acupuncture.com*

Holistic Internet Resources

http://www.hir.com

Holistic Internet Resources (HIR) is aiming to put the entire holistic world at your feet. More than an index of sites, HIR also includes listings of events, seminars, and workshops on- and off-line, and a great collection of articles and book reviews submitted by users. In addition, HIR includes the small but growing Guide to Practitioners and Schools (a fee is charged for inclusion), where you can read about alternative pros.

Institute of Chinese Medicine

http://www.wp.com/icm

The Web site for the Institute of Chinese Medicine (ICM) in Wheaton, Maryland promotes the institute's methods of acupuncture, herbal treatments, and other techniques. Ancient Chinese secrets have evolved with the times, though—at the Modern Technologies pages you'll find out about some more newfangled treatments like Auricular (Ear) Therapies for pain and infection.

AMMA Therapy

http://www.newcenter.edu/amma

Looking to get the kinks out? Try AMMA Therapy. A history page explains that "AMMA, the oldest Chinese word to describe massage, is an ancient healing system dating back about 5,000 years to the period of the Yellow Emperor." Other pages offer tips on finding an AMMA Therapist and what to expect during a massage session. The site's clean text design is consistent with the simplicity of the information.

Wellness World

http://wellness-world.com

Wellness World is an online marketplace for good-for-you goods, services, and information. The Seattle-based site offers a directory that reads like a what's what of alternative therapies and non-traditional treatments, from acupressure to yoga. Each entry has a brief description, as well as links to related Wellness World pages, such as chat areas. The site also features the Intelligent Health site, where a homeopathic practitioner offers advice, recipes, and news.

SPIRITUALITY

New Age Journal Online

http://www.newage.com/

This site, the online version of the magazine, is anchored by articles on the health of the mind AND the body, from practical tips on diets to borderline government conspiracies about artificial sweeteners. The New Age Forum allows open discussion about alternative healing, spiritual health, the role of technology, and other Web sites. Also here: the Holistic Health Directory, a U.S. database of alternative practitioners.

The I Ching

http://websites.earthlink.net/~wuwei

Here is noted scholar and author wu wei's interpretation of "The Book of Changes." Would-be diviners of wisdom and the future (in other words, you) may find this I Ching primer worth the while. An HTML introduction and history provide proper background, while "Using..." and "Interpreting..." offer help on everything from Phrasing Questions to the Meaning of the Kua. For other essential info, you can order various books and products from here.

Kabbalah Now

http://www.cyborganic.com/People/ovid/kbl.html

Kabbalah student Ovid Jacob has melded technology and spirituality in this Kabbal-links site, dedicated to the explanation and study of this ancient Jewish mysticism. Included are his interpretations of various scholarly works ranging from the basic to the esoteric, as well as the intricate paintings and drawings that accompany them. For those who wish to explore further, there's a very comprehensive list of links to other Kabbalistic pages.

Angelnet

http://skywebs.com/angelnet.html

Celestial souls will want to hover over this page of cherub chat, spiritually hosted by the cleverly titled EcoCre8ive Community (see Figure 2.17). Seraphs can visit an Angelic Virtual Altar or embark on "an alchemical interactive journey" in the labyrinth of the Secret

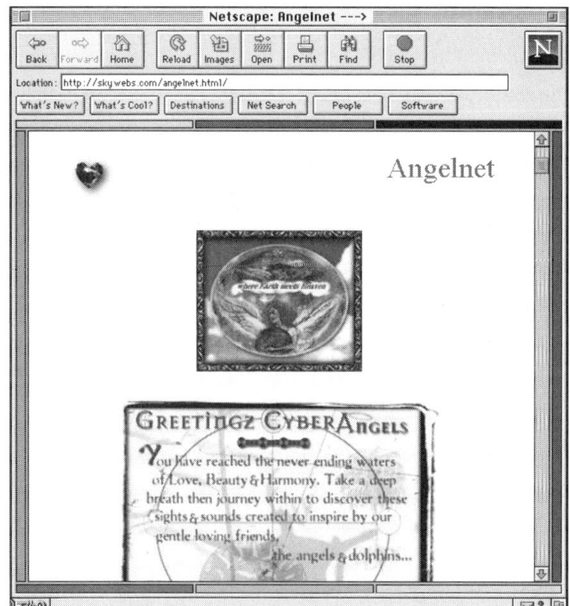

Figure 2.17
Angelnet Web Site,
http://skywebs.com/angelnet.html

Mystery, where discovering the lost treasure of Atlantis could result in some heavenly prizes. Stellar animation and clever interactivity.

How To Talk New Age

http://www.well.com/user/mick/newagept.html

With all this talk of New Age religions, lifestyles, and music, it's handy to have a guide to help you sort through it all. That's where Mick Winter's Dictionary for the New Age comes in. The illustrated glossary explains everything from acupuncture to zen. Now if he can just explain the popularity of Yanni.

Mysticism in World Religions

http://www.realtime.net/~rlp/dwp/mystic

Web page designer Deb Platt maintains this compare/contrast resource on the mystical teachings of prominent world religions. A simple interface allows browsing of topics such as ego vs. soul, detachment and renunciation and union, from the Christian, Buddhist, and Hindu traditions. Source materials range from the writings of an anonymous English monk to the Bible and the Bhagavad Gita. A nice overview for the mystically inclined.

Vodoun (Voodoo) Information Pages

http://www.vmedia.com/shannon/voodoo/voodoo.html

This is a serious and extensive resource on the spiritual practice of Vodoun, commonly called voodoo. Webmistress Shannon Turlington Settle has obviously done her homework, hoping to put to rest popular "misconceptions" about cannibalism, zombification, and other alleged practices. Visitors can read about ritual fundamentals such as "Feeding the Loa," and then consider "The Role of Black Magic," among other voodoo facets.

INTERNATIONAL APPEAL

Spirit-WWW

http://www.spiritweb.org

Spiritual seekers may well find they've hit the motherlode at this site, which is a virtual encyclopedia of strange phenomena and alternative realities. Selections available on this home page include channeling, astrology, faith healing, meditation, and UFOs. Contortionists will enjoy the Yoga page, which provides an overview of the different practices. Plus New Age art, movies, audio clips, and more.

Yoga Paths

http://www.spiritweb.org/Spirit/Yoga/Overview.html

As a collection of variously authored resources, this subsite of Spirit-WWW aims to offer a comprehensive overview of yoga's many schools and traditions. There's plenty here to occupy, inform, and perhaps enlighten those in search of the supreme godhead within themselves. Links to The Integral Yoga Web Site and more, make an already dense grid of Yoga Paths well worth exploring.

SEXUALITY AND REPRODUCTIVE HEALTH

Safer Sex Page

http://www.safersex.org

This is a very blunt page on the serious subject of safe sex. Don't expect cybersmut: the multimedia here is in the range of how to put on a condom, not Porky's. Plenty of HIV/AIDS data, including downloadable QuickTime movies and discussion of frightening topics you may not have even considered, like needle-sharing during steroid use.

Coalition for Positive Sexuality—Sex-Education for Teens

http://www.webcom.com/~cps

This funky and colorful site addresses the realities of human sexuality to a teen audience that must face those realities in their lives (see Figure 2.18). Dedicated to "having a positive attitude about sexuality—gay, straight, or bi," these educators refuse to put their heads in the proverbial sand. Topics ranging from Respect to STDs are covered, and the message is: Inform yourself, then make wise choices.

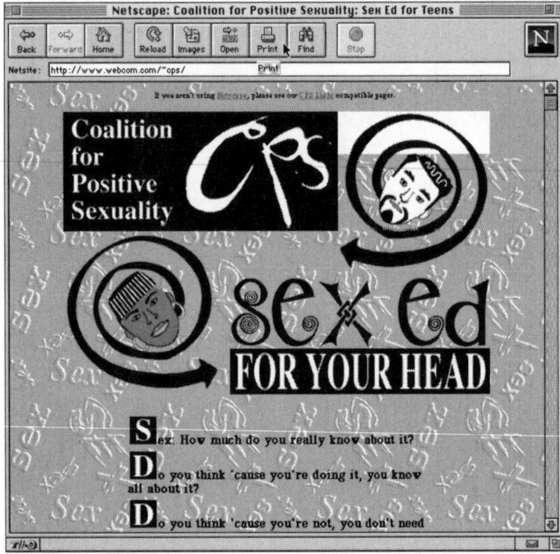

Figure 2.18
The Web site of the Coalition for Positive Sexuality, *http://www.webcom.com/~cps*

Dr. Ruth's SexNet

http://www.drruth.com

The diminutive sexpert is at it again. This colorful, fun, and helpful site aims to help clear up the mysteries surrounding sexuality in typical Ruthian style (see Figure 2.19). Great for teens or grownups, with the Daily Sex Tip (example: The All Important Kiss), Ask Dr. Ruth (of course), and more. You'll find an important resource list here that's missing from other sexuality sites: Romantic Getaways.

Atlanta Reproductive Health Center

http://www.ivf.com/index.html

With gems like Internet radio broadcasts and links to all things reproductive on the Web (the water births home page will get your attention), an Atlanta doctor turned cyberhealth guru has arguably amassed the most comprehensive women's health site. Especially helpful was the easy-to-navigate picture index dividing featured subjects from endometriosis to STD's.

Obstetric Ultrasound

http://www.hkstar.com/~joewoo/joewoo2.html

Here Dr. Joseph Woo offers a straightforward lesson on ultrasound scanning, which enables doctors (and families)

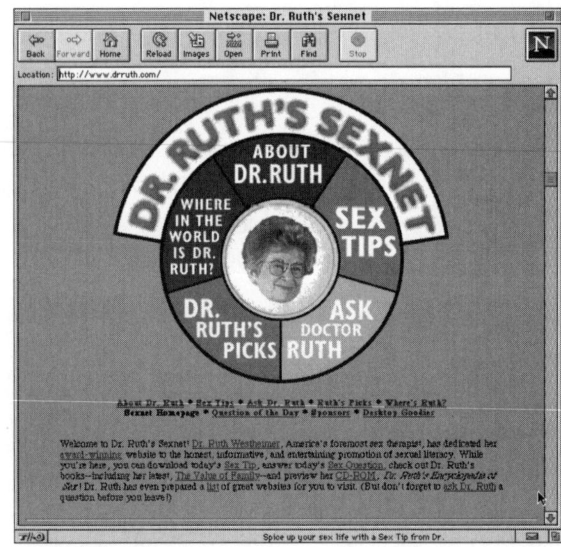

Figure 2.19
Dr. Ruth's SexNet, *http://www.drruth.com*

to check the development of their soon-to-be newest member of the family. The explanation of ultrasound comes first—why it's used, how it works, etc.—followed by the pictures, which are really amazing. The scans represent several periods of development, from five weeks to nearly five months.

FERTILITEXT

http://www.fertilitext.org

Created by a coalition of fertility specialists, FERTILITEXT answers questions on a variety of fertility issues. It's dense with information, including the Specific Topics area, and the glossary of fertility terms is a must-see. Bonus: a membership listing with descriptions of practitioner's training and treatment specialties. Heavy on info, light on looks; but for couples struggling with infertility, this site offers straightforward answers.

Online Birth Center

http://www.efn.org/~djz/birth/birthindex.html

Donna Dolezal Zelzer maintains this online library of articles, reviews, and other information about pregnancy, midwifery, and breastfeeding. The site is a good introduction to one midwife's outlook on mainstream medicine. Visitors to this page can also explore the "HomeBirth Choice," get information on becoming a midwife themselves, or find out "What midwives want from their clients."

Abortion & Reproductive Rights Internet Resources

http://www.caral.org/abortion.html

This well-balanced site from The California Abortion and Reproductive Rights Action League (CARAL) offers more than one political position on abortion. The links are divided into "Pro-Choice" and "Anti-Choice," and include such odd bedfellows as ProLife News and a "Guide for Active Feminists." Visitors can also link directly to CARAL's home page for pro-choice news.

La Leche League International Home Page

http://www.prairienet.org/llli

The La Leche League is an international, nonprofit breastfeeding support organization. In addition to general information about the group, this official Web site provides answers to frequently asked breastfeeding questions, links to other breastfeeding-related pages, and information about local groups. Especially interesting (and useful) is the organization's 1996 catalog. Here, you'll find topics ranging from advocacy to childbirth to mothers' choices.

where they surf

Surfer: Dr. Ruth Westheimer

The nation's foremost sex therapist and TV personality, Dr. Ruth, recently launched her own Web site at http://www.drruth.com

Her favorite sites of the moment:

Sexuality Bytes

http://www.sexualitybytes.com.au

"This 'on-line encyclopedia of sex and sexual health' covers a broad range of sexual topics: Sexuality Bytes for Adults and The Sex Files for Teenagers. From the Australian organization NSW Family Planning. Not for the euphemistically inclined."

The Coalition for Positive Sexuality

http://www.positive.org/cps

"A graphically-appealing safer sex site aimed at teenagers. The Coalition's goal is to help prevent teens from making life-threatening choices about sex and to expand their notions of healthy, normal sexuality."

The Planned Parenthood National Site

http://www.igc.apc.org/ppfa

The experts in all things reproductive have done it again (or, still), providing a one-stop resource to answer your questions and provide you with online informational pamphlets on sexual and reproductive health, including contraception, pregnancy, STDs, sexuality, abortion, reproductive rights, and related topics (see Figure 2.20). You'll also find mailing lists, tons of Internet links, news articles, and more. Save time. Stop here first.

The Visible Embryo

http://www.visembryo.ucsf.edu

This medical tutorial—all about the first four weeks of pregnancy—was developed for first-year med students at the University of California at San Francisco. Replete with images, diagrams, and explanations you can understand (most of the time), the Visible Embryo does a good job with a rather large amount of information (who knew all this stuff happened in four weeks?).

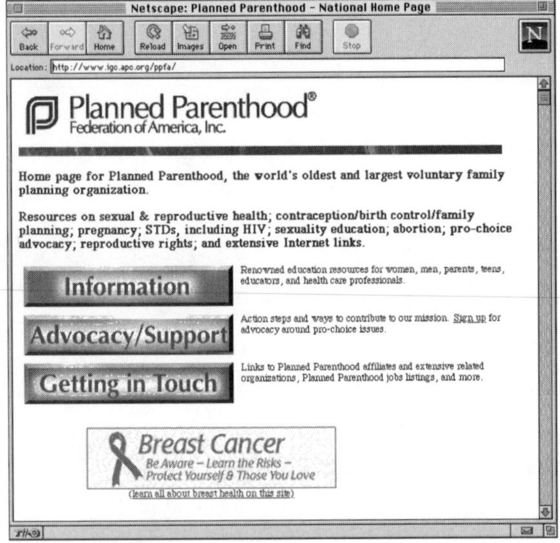

Figure 2.20
Planned Parenthood's National Web Site, *http://www.igc.apc.org/ppfa*

MENTAL HEALTH

Bipolar Disorders: Pendulum Resources

http://www.trenton.edu/~ellisles/dek

Bipolar disorder is perhaps more commonly known as manic depression. This page from Pendulum (a support group for sufferers) offers e-mail lists, articles like "Long Term Effects of Lithium Therapy," and access to pharmacological Web pages. Many bibliographic references can be found here as well. Those dealing with bipolar maladies may also want to check out the more comprehensive GROHOL Mental Health Page.

Dr. Grohol's Mental Health Page

http://www.coil.com/~grohol

Dr. Grohol's site is a one-stop index for explanation, support, and resources on psychology and mental health issues. Check out newsgroups, mailing lists, and live interactive chats, and read editorials by the good Doctor that have appeared in various major publications. Especially helpful links: the FAQ on an incredibly broad range of topics and the Suicide Helpline.

The Arc

http://TheArc.org/welcome.html

Formerly the Association for Retarded Citizens, the volunteer corps presents this thorough elaboration on a disability affecting some 2.5 percent of Americans. Essential stuff for the mental-health advocate.

Mental Health Net

http://www.cmhcsys.com/mhn.htm

John Grohol, the founder of Psych Central, has compiled this index totaling more than 3,500 individual resources, including the Self-Help Sourcebook, a gopher site describing the types of headaches and tips on beating shyness, and an enormous database of mental health conferences and programs.

David Baldwin's Trauma Info Pages

http://gladstone.uoregon.edu/~dvb/trauma.htm

Psychologist David Baldwin has compiled a fascinating guide to the subject of emotional trauma (including Post-Traumatic Stress Disorder), whether it be an individual traumatic experience or a large-scale disaster. Baldwin's pages are aimed at clinicians and researchers, but victims and their families will also find support information, including links to other Web sources.

Dr. Bob's Virtual En-psych-lopedia

http://uhs.bsd.uchicago.edu/~bhsiung/tips/tips.html

This site is like sitting amongst a group of doctors while they talk "shop." Part of a resource-and-cool-stuff-packed home page, the Virtual En-psych-lopedia collects doctors' tips on mental health medications from a discussion list and presents them in an edited and indexed form that's easy to use. From fatigue to depression to addictions, this is one place to find out what doctors are saying about the latest research and techniques.

[OVERHEARD ON WOMEN'S WIRE]

http://chat.women.com

ON WHAT BEING DEPRESSED FEELS LIKE:

"In the midst of a major episode, it was hard to finish reading a paragraph, much less write a paragraph. It was excruciating. I felt like I'd lost about 60 IQ points. And on top of that, there was this absolutely intense sense of being defective, worthless, ugly—you name it. I felt I did not deserve to breathe air on this planet.

ON WHAT CAUSES DEPRESSIVE EPISODES:

"Stress of any kind—even good stress, like getting married—can trigger mood disorders in susceptible people. It's called 'kindling.' My episodes of depression have always been pretty clearly linked to loss—loss of a boyfriend, moving to a new city, my father's death."

ON ACCEPTING THE CONCEPT OF MENTAL ILLNESS:

"It took me a long time to really wrap my mind around the fact that I had a bona fide mental illness. Even now I am sometimes reluctant to use that term, even though intellectually I know it's correct."

—Washington Post reporter Tracy Thompson, author of "The Beast: A Reckoning with Depression," in a live conference on Women's Wire.

Real World: Suicide

http://www.paranoia.com/~real/suicide

Real World: Suicide addresses this painful subject with honesty and openness. The site features Suicide Resources with links to online assistance such as the Suicide Prevention Mailing List; but its main event is the Official Suicide FAQ, which covers basics such as warning signs, and ways friends and family can help depressed individuals. Can mere FAQs on this taboo subject help save lives? They certainly can't hurt.

INTERNATIONAL APPEAL

The American Academy of Child & Adolescent Psychiatry

http://www.aacap.org/web/aacap

Getting help can be as easy as reading one of the award-winning "Facts for Families" sheets produced by AACAP. In "Making Day Care A Good Experience," you'll learn that a high turnover rate in day care employees can be stressful for a child. All 51 documents come in English, French, and Spanish and help guide a parent through difficult (and maybe unfamiliar) topics, like lead exposure and psychiatric medicine for kids.

Depression

http://www.duke.edu/~ntd/depression.html

For this uncommon page, the moderators of the alt.support.depression news group have extracted the best items from their Frequently Asked Questions files, and distilled them into a "Depression Primer." Are you persistently anxious or having difficulty concentrating? Here, you can hunt up news groups where you can discuss your concerns with others, or connect to The Option Institute, a teaching center offering programs to help overcome depression.

The Recovery Home Page

http://www1.shore.net/~tcfraser/recovery.htm

This highly organized collection of information is for anyone suffering from the maladies addressed by 12-step recovery programs. T. C. Fraser starts off with selections from the AA Big Book, but quickly broadens his scope to include addictions like cocaine, sex, and overeating. You'll also get instructions for using other electronic recovery media, like UseNet, Internet Relay Chat, and BBSs. Very strong coverage of a serious subject, without ever becoming preachy or pompous.

In Loving Memory

http://home.earthlink.net/~jimncarol/ilm.htm

This bittersweet site is the online version of a Washington State-based newsletter for parents who have lost their only or all children. Grieving parents will find some solace here in the sad reality of their shared experience with other such families. The site includes submitted poetry, a monthly anniversaries page, and columns written by members. The site carries the spirit of intermingled pain and remembrance.

Specifica

http://www.realtime.net/~mmjw/

Maintained by Texas psychologist Jeanine Wade, this offbeat site offers hearty links and info on the medical and mental health scene (see Figure 2.21). Some of the sites merely seem strange, like "Noodles' Panic-Anxiety Page" (it's the unsettling color scheme), but others are actively odd, like the Obsessive-Compulsive Disorder link. Great links to AIDS and HIV resources around the world, too.

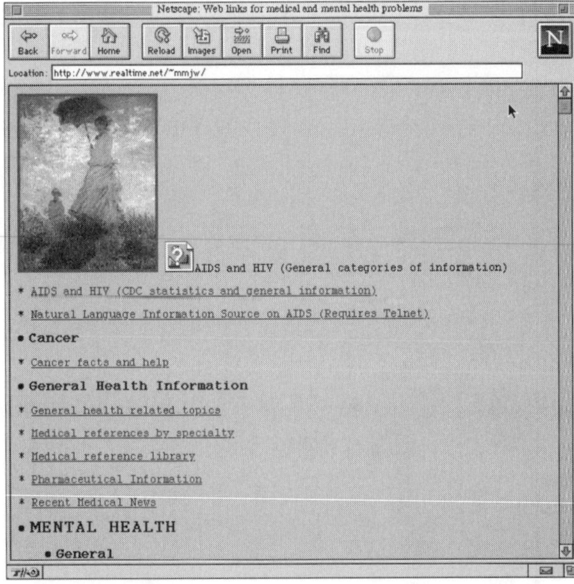

Figure 2.21

The Specifica Web site, *http://www.realtime.net/~mmjw/*

Noodles' Panic-Anxiety Page

http://www.algy.com/anxiety/anxiety.html

Anxiety and Panic disorders are the subject of this quirky site (see Figure 2.22), maintained by someone who himself suffered the disorders and was frustrated by the lack of information and understanding among the public at large. Here, you'll find news articles, support groups, and relaxation techniques, in addition to definitions and clarification of symptoms and causes of Anxiety, Panic, and related disorders.

Figure 2.22
Noodles' Panic-Anxiety Web Page, *http://www.algy.com/anxiety/anxiety.html*

Depression FAQ

http://www.psych.helsinki.fi/~janne/asdfaq/index.html

Brought to you by Janne Sinkkonen, a graduate student in Helsinki, this site is just as the title promises: simple. No graphics, yet everything you need to know on the subject of depression MUST be somewhere on this site. From the comprehensive Depression Primer, to thought-provoking FAQ items like "Are Antidepressants just 'happy pills?'" this is a good first stop in your depression research.

DreamLink

http://www.iag.net/~hutchib/.dream

Utilize your dreams as keys to better self-understanding. That's the advice from this page hosted by avid dream watchers, who provide great info on dream analysis. Jung said it was important to focus on feelings generated by a dream; Freud felt they were carriers of repressed wishes. Whatever the theory, you can send your own dreams to DreamLink and they'll return their own stellar spin on the story (see Figure 2.23). Or, simply read the dreams of others online.

Figure 2.23
DreamLink, *http://www.iag.net/~hutchib/.dream*

Self-Help Psychology Magazine

http://www.cybertowers.com/selfhelp

"Is Your Relationship Stuck?" and "12 Suggestions for Taking Care of Yourself" are two of the articles available at this e-zine on self-analysis and popular psychology. The site also advertises and reviews books on self-help topics and provides a "Professional's Corner" for therapists to exchange views and information.

Jane's Brain Page

http://maui.net/~jms

This slightly wacky amateur guide to brain chemistry provides a glossary to some technical terminology, running down a list of neurotransmitters like norepinephrine and serotonin, then discussing the supposed effects of the stuff as it all courses across your synapses. Personality disorders and their possible biochemical origins are also discussed. This isn't so academic as it is intriguingly weird.

Hypnotica Home Page

http://www.servtech.com/public/hypnotica

Charles E. Henderson offers a folksy walk-through on the benefits of self-hypnosis, using techniques that he has taught over the years to help people lose weight, stop smoking, or guide themselves to a better life. His presentation is easy to understand and less dopey than cynics would expect, with a sly sense of humor and an effective anecdotal approach.

The Cyber Psychic

http://www.hollys.com/cyber-psychic/

You don't have to call the Psychic Friends Network to make an extrasensory connection. Instead, elevate yourself to this page from Holly Sumner, a North Carolina psychic and astrologer (she's a certified hypnotherapist, too) for tips and info on the predictable world (see Figure 2.24). An entry on meditation suggests anyone can learn the art, which is not "some magical state" but rather the ability to produce alpha brainwaves on demand.

Figure 2.24
The Cyber Psychic,
http://www.hollys.com/cyber-psychic/

If you have a burning question about your future, why not see what Tarot cards have to say. This site provides free readings.

http://www.facade.com/attraction/tarot/

Wondering how your day is going to go? Check in with Antoinette, Women's Wire's star diva, for a sign.

http://www.women.com/buzz/horoscope.html

Play The Longevity Game and find out how long you can expect to live based on life insurance industry research from Northwestern Mutual Life.

http://www.northwesternmutual.com/games/longevity

☞ KEYWORDS

For more information on topics in this chapter, start your Web search with these keywords.

Health, illness, and conditions: menopause, cancer, heart desease, sexually transmitted diseases, hysterectomy, endometriosis, osteoporosis, HIV and AIDS, fertility, plastic surgery, disabilities, arthritis

Recovery and abuse: associations and organizations, alcoholism, rape, sexual abuse, addiction, child abuse, domestic violence

Fitness: body shaping, exercise, aerobics

Nutrition: eating disorders, food safety, diets, weight control, vitamins

Sports: tennis, gymnastics, ice skating, women's volleyball, swimming, women's basketball

Alternative medicine: associations and organizations, herbal remedies, chiropractic, massage therapy

Spirituality: spiritual leaders, new age, mysticism, meditation

Human sexuality: birth control

Pregnancy and childbirth: childbirth, birth methods, birth defects

Mental health: emotional health, depression, stress, anxiety, grief, jealousy, self-esteem, body image, hypnosis, psychics

Chapter 3

Careers and Networking

JOB SEARCH

REGIONAL AND SPECIALTY EMPLOYMENT RESOURCES

CAREER ISSUES

CAREER DEVELOPMENT

ENTREPRENEURSHIP

PROFESSIONAL ORGANIZATIONS AND NETWORKING

10 THINGS YOU CAN DO FOR YOUR CAREER *RIGHT NOW*

1 Get professional help from the Women's Wire Biz Shrink.

http://www.women.com/work/qa.biz.html

2 Complete the Self-Assessment Exercises courtesy of Bowling Green State University to help you make important decisions about what you really want out of your career.

http://www.bgsu.edu/offices/careers/process/step1.html

3 Try out a new field: search for internships in everything from Accounting to Zoology in Tripod's Internship Database.

http://www.tripod.com/work/internships

4 Zoology it is? Find out how much you can expect to be paid, working conditions, and how hard you'll have to work to find a job in the years to come in the Occupational Outlook Handbook.

http://stats.bls.gov/ocohome.htm

5 Join a live chat with a career expert.

http://www.aboutwork.com/chat

6 Use the Salary Calculator to figure out how much dough to ask for so you can pay the rent if you relocate from your job in Iowa to that new one in New York City. Hint: Are you sitting down?

http://www.homefair.com/homefair/cmr/salcalc.html

7 Brush up on your resume skills with this Quick Guide to Resume Writing.

http://www.wm.edu/csrv/career/stualum/guidjob.html

8 Send your resume and cover letter out to some hot companies, painlessly, at the Extreme Resume Drop.

http://www.mainquad.com/theQuad/wich/introPages/lo/erd.html

9 Quitting that old job? Fired? Make sure you know Your Rights in the Workplace.

http://140.174.208.58/yrw/toc.html

10 Want to improve on the job? Play Stump the Mentor at Hard@work.

http://www.hardatwork.com/Stump/Stump.html#play

Changing jobs or hunting for that first job can almost be a career in itself. Resume after resume, interviews if you're lucky, endless networking. (Who was it that said the job search goes like this: "no no no no no no no no no no YES"?) The resources available on the Internet can make your search a little—possibly a lot—easier. With well-organized listings of plum jobs in every field, you can tap into sources much more quickly, and thanks to a nifty little thing called a search engine, you can hunt down leads you may never have found at all.

How can you be so sure that quality employers are posting their job openings online? The word from companies—from startups who love the low-cost nature of the Net, to major corporations—is that the applicants they get from their online postings tend to be smart, ambitious, and highly qualified. Recruiters say that the new medium is a terrific cost-efficient way to reach good people.

Starting your own business, or just want to grow further in your present career? The Web is a natural for networking. From professional groups to career consultants, you can get advice, support, and innumerable resources to help you along your way.

Whether you're a college senior contemplating your first real job, a busy executive who wants to avoid the "glass ceiling," or a mom running your own enterprise from home, find out how you can get plugged into a non-stop resource for success.

JOB SEARCH

The Monster Board

http://www.monster.com

Few endeavors in life are as overwhelming as a job search, and few Web resources are as beneficial to job seekers as The Monster Board (see Figure 3.1). Post your resume, search the gargantuan job database, apply for work online, and get outstanding advice on networking, calculating your salary, and, of course, interviewing. Staffer Thom Guertin says, "Our in-house mantra here at The Monster Board is 'Functional, Fast, Fun,' in that order." Our sentiments exactly.

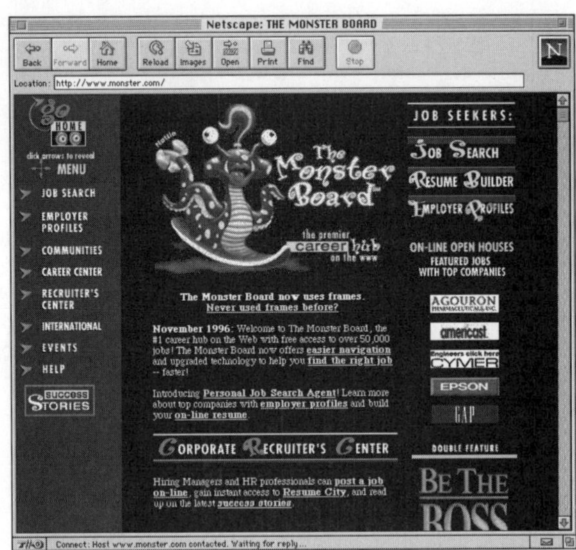

Figure 3.1

The Monster Board, *http://www.monster.com*

The Riley Guide

http://www.jobtrak.com/jobguide

Margaret Riley, author of *The Guide to Internet Job Searching* and columnist for the *National Business Employment Weekly*, has produced a comprehensive site with lists of links to job sites, all neatly categorized by type, and an insightful overview of the job-searching process.

Career Mosaic

http://www.careermosaic.com

Put all the pieces together and what do you get? One incredibly detailed job-search site, which includes a special "College Connection" and sections on jobs in Canada, Japan, and the U.K. You name it, it's there, from specific fields to high-profile employers to advice on how to write that winning resume.

BAMTA Job Bank

http://www.bamta.org/BAMTAJB

The name stands for Broad Alliance for Multimedia Technology and Applications, and this Web site features job openings in multimedia related areas. Companies and organizations can submit their job openings to be posted and individuals can browse through job lists check. Job searchers should read carefully—an individual who is not an employer, but has dreamed of being one or, has a job idea, can make up an opening and post it under the job classification of "My Dream Job."

Online Career Center

http://www.occ.com/occ

OCC accesses a huge collection of job listings, mainly culled from Internet newsgroups (and many posted by recruiters), which you can sift through by state, by industry, or alphabetically. Here, as with other mega-compendiums, you can post your resume or study up on graduate and professional schools. A unique feature: The "HyperResume" service, which creates hypertext resumes, then generates a resume URL just for you.

America's Job Bank

http://www.ajb.dni.us

Linking 1,800 state employment-service offices in the United States, America's Job Bank lists upwards of 100,000 jobs at any given time—probably the largest source for job postings on the Net. And we're not talking just technical jobs.

JobHunt

http://rescomp.stanford.edu/jobs

This isn't a place to send your resume—it's an extensive listing of job-hunting resources on the Web and elsewhere. Sure, you've probably heard about Career Mosaic, but did you know about Dynamic Resource, Resumes On-Line, and World Job Seekers? They're among the over 100 useful resources listed here, including newsgroups, classified ads from major newspapers, and sites which will help you polish your interview skills. (So far, no sites to help you polish your shoes.)

America's Employers

http://www.americasemployers.com

The good news is that all kinds of companies are advertising job openings on their corporate Web sites. The bad news is that you could spend the rest of your career

where they surf

Surfer: Margaret F. Riley

Creator of the Riley Guide *(http://www.jobtrak.com/jobguide)*, an online resource for job hunting, and author of the book, *The Guide to Internet Job Searching.*

Her favorite sites of the moment:

Yahoo

http://www.yahoo.com

I love Yahoo for lots of reasons. It's a great directory of Internet information, it's well organized (and I really appreciate organization), and the content is not limited by any boundaries. What do you want to know? It's here somewhere.

Pathfinder

http://www.pathfinder.com

Money and *Fortune Magazines,* sports, entertainment, current news and information, and even my horoscope. It's definitely not like your standard *Time Magazine* on the newsstand.

just finding them. America's Employers aims to help by providing an extensive collection of links directly to the recruitment pitches of U.S. businesses with Web sites. America's Employers also serves up a corporate database of company contact information to help you track down those positions that aren't advertised (the "hidden" job market).

The Catapult

http://www.wm.edu/catapult/catapult.html

This College of William and Mary career-center page has plenty of job-seeking advice for grads. Among several helpful articles, site organizer Leo Charette's "Tips On Interviewing" includes more than 50 questions often popped on prospective employees. Still, the links are this site's pot o' gold. If you've ever considered a career in dentistry, zookeeping, or investment banking, you can access backgrounders here. Lacks glamour, but very newsy.

Best Bets from the Net

http://asa.ugl.lib.umich.edu/chdocs/employment

Before you dive into the Monster Board or any of the slew of other job search clearinghouses on the Net, you may want to check here (see Figure 3.2). The draw: this site organizes the resources by particular need, which can be especially helpful if you're in a specialized field, such as academia or Government. Also, Best Bets rates the resources within each field. A good place to start to make your search seem less bewildering.

The Virtual Press Job Information

http://www.aloha.com/~william/vpjic.html

Yet another place to start your job search. A huge compendium of job listings, career aids, and related links. Low on frills, this site is well organized with categories that run from Job Banks and Databases, to more specific professions, to the less commonly seen Jobs for Differently Abled Persons. Spend some time here, and you may walk away with a job. Or at least a lead or two.

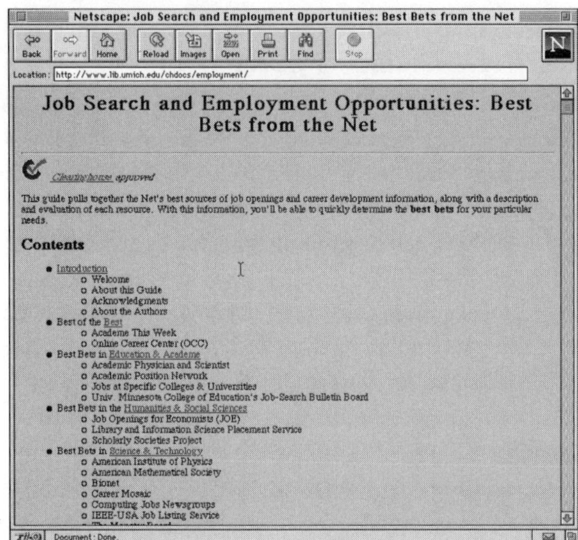

Figure 3.2
Best Bets from the Net, *http://asa.ugl.lib.umich.edu/chdocs/employment*

Career Search-Jobs Online

http://greatinfo.com/business_cntr/career.html

Yet another huge (and we mean HUGE it took a good while to scroll to the bottom of the home page) directory of directories of job search resources. What the heck, while you're here you might as well hit 'em all, right? And here they are. All of them.

Archeus-Work search resources

http://www.golden.net/~archeus/worksrch.htm

Links to a HUGE treasure chest of useful articles on how to write a resume/cover letter and breeze through an interview (see Figure 3.3). Articles are rated for quality using a one- to five-star rating system and organized in a sharp-looking, easy-to-navigate manner. The site is maintained by Gary Will, and he REALLY wants to help you succeed.

Interbiznet

http://www.interbiznet.com/ibn/top25.html

The place for career advancement advice, with articles like "The First Steps in Your Hunt." Their top 25 electronic

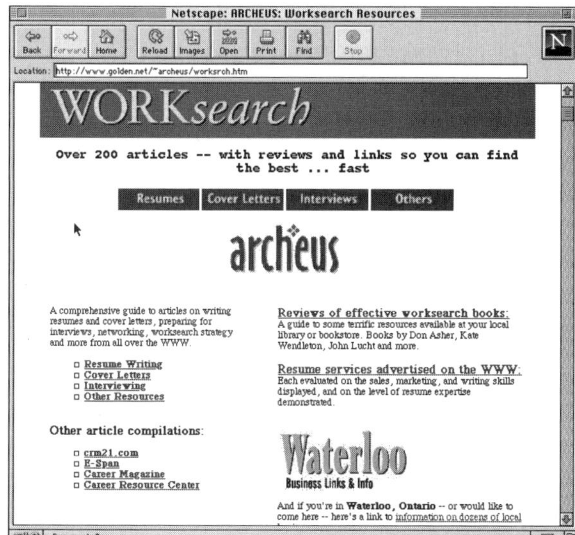

Figure 3.3

Archeus Work Web site, *http://www.golden.net/~archeus/worksrch.htm*

recruiters resource collection *(www.interbiznet.com/ibn/top25.html)* is like a one-stop shopping spree. For your search, you can choose between many of the top job sites as well as databases of Internships, volunteer positions, positions at the U.S. Department of Labor, and more. If it's not here, does it exist??

The Job Search Process

http://www.jobtrak.com/jobsearch_docs/pointers.html

Once again, those terrific JobTrak folks have stepped in to provide easy-to-follow guidance up the slippery slope of career development. These tips (courtesy of the George Washington University Career Center) could tilt the balance in your job search, so do yourself a favor and scrutinize this motherlode of information from top to bottom.

Career and Resume Management for the 21st Century

http://crm21.com

Career and Resume Management for the 21st Century provides professional career and resume services, not only for job seekers, but for employers and recruiters, as well. Features include the Internet Resume Registry, on-line employment ads, an archive of resume databases on the Web, and much more. Links to recruiting, contract and consulting firms, publications, and career transition specialists are also featured.

CareerNet's Career Resource Center

http://www.careers.org

This site provides a job resource center with links to more than 15,000 jobs and pointers to other career-related Web sites. Visitors will find links to associations, franchising opportunities and library resources as well as the usual huge job-and-resume databases.

Jobtrak

http://www.jobtrak.com

In partnership with hundreds of colleges and graduate schools, Jobtrak offers juicy job listings, job search tips, and access to top recruiters to Alumnae, students, and former students (see Figure 3.4). It's considered a great resource for employers to find terrific people, and it's probably the career resource most frequently linked to by other career sites. And for those who aren't quite ready for the real world: a comprehensive guide to graduate schools.

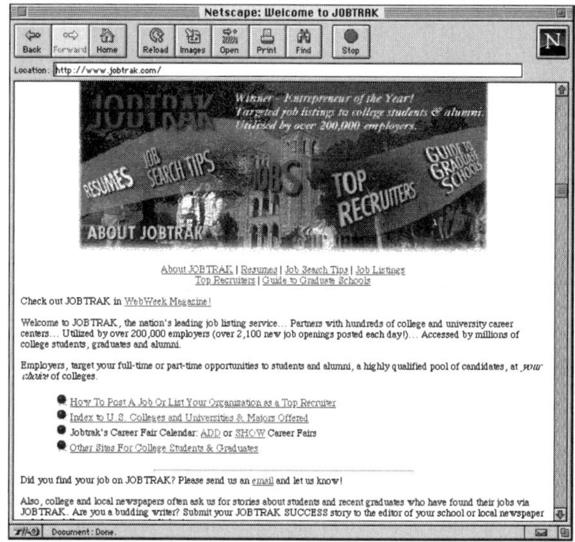

Figure 3.4

Jobtrak, *http://www.jobtrak.com*

E-Span

http://www.espan.com

You can search for job opportunities in Internet newsgroups and on the Web, as well as check out employer profiles of the companies you're interested in. Listings are up to date and somewhat varied, though they tend to lean toward the technical side. Also includes the Career Companion, a convenient "briefcase" of resources to enhance, or even change, your present career.

NCS Career Magazine

http://www.careermag.com

This cyber-publication goes a long way toward being "a comprehensive online resource for job seekers, human resource managers, and career-minded professionals." On our last visit we saw a multitude of want-ads for software engineers, nurses, and one for "NATO Scientist (Italy)." Stanford U.'s online job service index is accessible, and "Be Your Own Headhunter" is just one of many career-related articles archived here.

Best Jobs USA

http://www.bestjobsusa.com/

Job seekers and employers alike get a good shot at finding what they're looking for at this simple, resource-laden site. Search the RCI best jobs database, or throw your resume onto the pile (free) at the resume pavilion. Plus, you can read through timely articles in *Employment Review Magazine* to get you in the mood.

Careers—Where to Go to Make Your Dough

http://www.internetuniv.com/career/index.html

The folks at Internet University use eye-popping grafix (see Figure 3.5) and lots of cool links in their attempt to answer that big question: What To Do? Find The Right City (often ignored in career search sites), and hunt for The Right Job. Great advice on Research, Interviewing, and Salary, as well as the prerequisite job search database (via the ubiquitous Intellimatch service). Great for recent grads or anyone sick of the same old runaround.

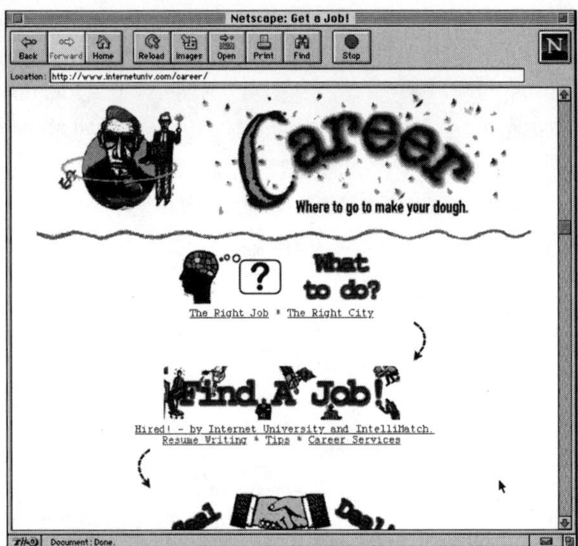

Figure 3.5
Internet University,
http://www.internetuniv.com/career/index.html

Turbo-Charge Your Job Search

http://hbs-chicago.org/int1.html

Stop off here before you bring your career search online! Jon Paul, a member of the Harvard Business School Club of Chicago, put this site together to help people realize how much value the Internet could add to their career search. Check out the no-nonsense facts on why the Internet is a good addition to your job hunt, then move on to the well-organized resources to help you in your search.

BSA CareerMart

http://208.193.201.5

With its "virtual marketplace" interface and lots of hi-tech bells and whistles (including the Virtual Conference Center, where you can participate in real-time job fairs and chats), this might be a fun place even if you weren't looking for a job. As it turns out, CareerMart is a one-stop shop for most of your career search needs as well. Browse job listings, post your resume, or stop by the Advice Tent for useful info and reports from the front.

CareerWeb

http://www.cweb.com

Job-hunters can search listings by category and location, as well as post their resumes and receive e-mail about new job listings. The entrepreneurial center offers information on small business services and valuable resources in the form of articles and information on a variety of entrepreneurship issues. CareerWeb is also home to a quarterly newsletter for job-hunters and employers alike, featuring articles by employment experts, covering topics such as resume savvy and online recruiting.

IntelliMatch Online Career Services

http://www.intellimatch.com/index.html

IntelliMatch offers one of the most extensive resume and employer match-ups on the Net. Job-seekers fill out lengthy forms to create a specific skills inventory. The idea is to create a "structured resume" that becomes part of Intellimatch's database, from which employers can get your address and contact you. The jobs are mostly technical ones, and it naturally takes quite a bit of time to fill out the forms—but hey, you don't have to dress up!

INTERNATIONAL APPEAL

University of Waterloo Career Development Manual

http://www.adm.uwaterloo.ca/infocecs/CRC/manual-home.html

This manual offers a five-step process to finding the career that's right for you. You begin by filling in forms to assess personal skills (sorry, hackey-sack excellence doesn't count). Next, you'll learn how to research career options and specific firms. And finally, you'll find tips on getting and keeping that right job. For example: Once hired, "Do not make criticisms about the job or other employers in public."

JobCenter

http://www.jobcenter.com

JobCenter is one of the myriad Web spots that posts employers' help wanted ads and jobseekers' resumes—also, it offers a matching service that will e-mail postings of likely prospects right to you. The fee to post a resume includes the job-matching and a resume-critiquing service. Some general job-hunting advice is available for free. A highlight of this site is its design; there are only three forms users might need ("Post," "Edit," or "Search"), and links are clearly marked.

CareerPath

http://www.careerpath.com

An amazingly useful service whose resource base consists of the Help Wanted ads in most major urban newspapers, including the *New York Times, LA Times, Washington Post,* and more (see Figure 3.6). Narrow your search by selecting your chosen fields from a surprisingly diverse list, then view the current week's listings in each category. Now you can search the classifieds without having to scan through pages of "Driver...Dentist...Domino's..." to find what you're after.

Virtual Job Fair

http://www.careerexpo.com

WestTech Career Expo plans job fairs in real life, and it maintains this site to bridge the gap between job seekers and employers. The site makes a pitch for WestTech's job expos, but it also offers visitors a fill-in-the-blanks resume form to advertise their skills. In the job-search section, we found nearly a dozen "technical writer" and

Figure 3.6

CareerPath, *http://www.careerpath.com*

many more "programmer" positions. The site also offers a library of articles and essays on topics like career trends and job burnout.

Heart

http://www.career.com

In the growing field of online job services, Heart differentiates itself by offering a direct relationship between job-seeker and job-offerer. With the basics down, it has developed e-mail and FTP links with prospective employers that will channel your resume to the right person. And through its occasional CyberFairs (via telnet), qualified job-seekers can have "virtual interviews" with hiring firms. Though still light on listings, this innovative site shows potential.

Quick Guide to Resume Writing

http://www.wm.edu/csrv/career/stualum/guidjob.html

This page on creating snappy resumes isn't the best, but it's probably the snappiest. Kristin Smith Guenov (of the University of Maine career center) provides a sample resume (do her bosses know it's hers?) that links key points—name, education, references, etc.—to explanations of those points. Guenov's unintended gift: she accidentally demonstrates the potential of a colorful online resume—still rare on the Web.

Sharp Placement Professionals Inc.

http://www.liglobal.com/B_C/Career

The people at Sharp Placement Professionals of Westbury, NY say they know a thing or two about applying for a job, and they're willing to share it with you here. The online tutorial takes a sample resume, then dissects it to reveal the powerful phrases that might breathe life into your career. This is a practical site that could prove even more useful if Sharp keeps stockpiling the tips.

Recruiters OnLine Network

http://www.onramp.net/ron

Geared to its roughly 1,000 members, this network has one major advantage over other job-seeking sites: the address and e-mail list of member recruiter firms across the United States. Need a headhunter in Pennsylvania? There are several (and 10 times as many in California). Additionally, non-members can read Joyce Lain Kennedy columns ("Interviewing Well is the Best Revenge"), post their resumes, and, if all other careers seem a dead-end, learn to become a head-hunter!

Getting Past Go: A Survival Guide for College Graduates

http://ignatius.lattanze.loyola.edu/MonGen/home.html

College grads can enroll here to learn what wasn't taught in school: how to land a job. When composing your resume, "Be honest and accurate! Employers do check, and people who make false claims get fired." Then sponsor Monumental General Insurance Group slyly brings up the question of insurance: no longer under mom and pop's roof, are you still covered? Sign up now, before tragedy strikes! Link-laden, shallow but helpful, this is intelligent Webvertising.

Feminist Career Center

http://www.feminist.org/911/911jobs.html

Brought to you by the Feminist Majority, this is the place where progressive job-seekers and employers can find one another without abandoning their feminist ideals (see Figure 3.7). Jobs posted actually seemed quite interesting for anyone with a bit of an activist bent. Other offerings include internships, and information on woman-oriented career expos. Do good work and still be employed!

Workplace at Galaxy

http://lmc.tradewave.com/galaxy/Community/Workplace.html

The Workplace pages at this commercial "everything" magazine offer some valuable job and career search tools. A sampling: The Entry Level Job Seeker Homepage ("Welcome...Assistant!"), a collection of guides and articles, and a resource list of job search directories which includes many specialized fields within the arts, academia, medicine, science, and more! Warning: Some of the linked resources are quite outdated.

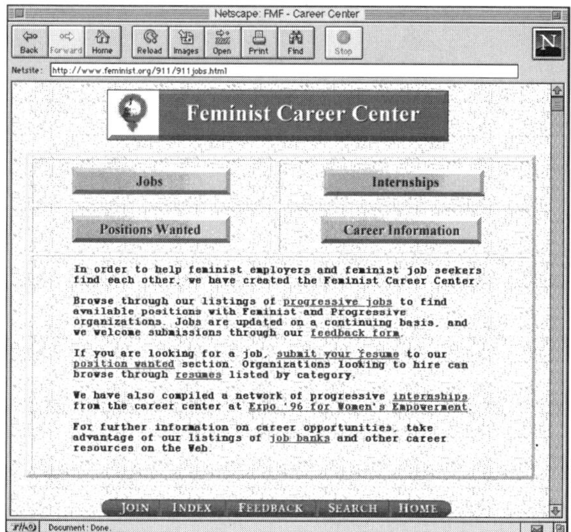

Figure 3.7
Feminist Career Center, *http://www.feminist.org/911/911jobs.html*

Careers On Line
http://www.disserv.stu.umn.edu/TC/Grants/COL/aboutCOL.html

A real find for individuals with disabilities, this service provided by the University of Minnesota offers career links and advice to differently abled individuals. Here, also, is a collection of Adaptive Technology Products and Resources to make information more accessible to people with disabilities. You can also check out the Job Accommodation Handbook and Network for tips for employers, disability accommodation, and much more. What the information highway *should* be all about.

Job Seekers Go Online for an Edge on the Competition
http://bcn.boulder.co.us/business/BCBR/august/onlinjob.html

As a part of a Boulder, CO community network, this link is merely one article: No links, no graphics, nothing for the kids...However, it does concisely state the reasons why you should add the Web to your job search. Follow along while individuals test out various online resources, get the verdict and recommendations. Get the site as a bonus if you live in Boulder, CO.

Exec-u-Net
http://www.clickit.com/touch/execunet/execunet.htm

Sponsored by Access Business Online, a commercial firm, this service is best known for placement of high-level executives. They try to tease you into buying membership with lo-info listings, but with a bit of digging, nonmembers can find some resources they can use to climb a few rungs on the corporate ladder.

where they surf

Surfer: Yana Parker

Author of *The Damn Good Resume Guide, The Resume Catalog,* and *Resume Pro: The Professional's Guide.*

Her favorite sites of the moment:

JobSmart
http://www.jobsmart.org

"Probably the classiest, most useful site for top caliber career and jobs information in Northern California, with lots of goodies for anybody anywhere. Created with taste by Mary-Ellen Mort, the bay area librarian-with-an-attitude. TIP: Check out 'Ask Electra' thoroughly."

Excite
http://www.excite.com

"I use this a lot because it finds what I want, but best of all it displays the information in a very sophisticated yet accessible way—so I don't have to pick through a mile-long list of garbage."

Help Wanted

http://www.helpwanted.com/

With such an encouraging name, the folks at Recruitment Online, Inc. should have no trouble getting hits at this site. You can find a recruiter to help you in your search, post your resume free, or check out the Job of the Day, and Job of the Week. Be warned: The majority of these leads are in the technical fields.

GlobalNet's Latin American Career Center

http://www.globalnt.com/bolsa/

Resumes and job offers are posted in Spanish; a boon to Spanish-speaking job seekers worldwide. Like other sites, opportunities are divided into fields of interest, except, of course, they're in Spanish.

The Job-Banker

http://www.nmaa.org/jobbank.htm

Brought to you by the National Multimedia Association of America, this is a free service, and you can post your resume and search for jobs by state, category, or commitment (part-time, full-time, contract). Listings are up to date and somewhat varied, though most do have something to do with—you guessed it—multimedia.

SkillSearch

http://www.internet-is.com/skillsearch/index.html

SkillSearch is a professional membership organization linking individuals with 2 to 30 years of experience in the workplace to organizations that need their talents. Services enable members to network with active employers online. You can test out the service before you sign on as a member.

Extreme Resume Drop

http://www.mainquad.com/resumedrop.html

Housed at Extreme Quad, a site catering to you-know-the-type college students, Resume Drop (see Figure 3.8) is a gnaarly way to send your resume off to hundreds of companies electronically. You can also browse through their career advice, resume tips, and job listings for college grads. Duude!

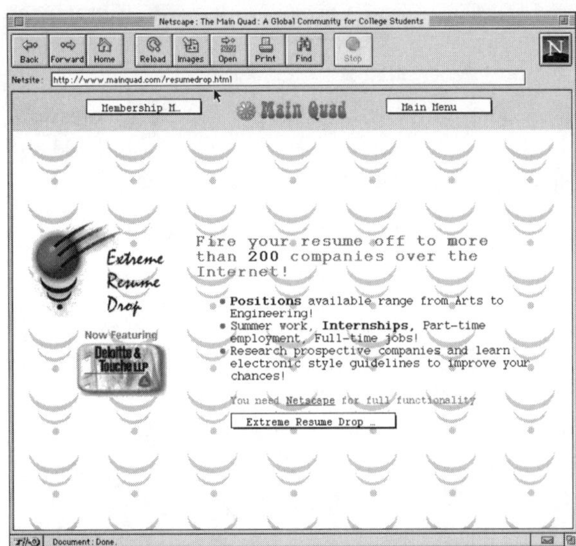

Figure 3.8

Extreme Resume Drop, *http://www.mainquad.com/resumedrop.html*

Career Toolbox

http://www.careertoolbox.com/

Brought to you by the folks at Chivas Regal (you'd BETTER be working so you can afford the stuff). Funky image maps guide you down the career path of your choice (i.e., be your own boss, improve your performance at your present job, etc.), providing facts and resources along the way. Great feature: the Tool of the Week. Downside: annoying over-use of frames.

REGIONAL AND SPECIALTY EMPLOYMENT RESOURCES

FedWorld via Telnet

telnet://fedworld.gov

It's a pain to telnet into—access is menu driven (via telnet)—and you've got to sit through terminal configuration questions, but once you're there you'll find a healthy list of job listings from the federal government's Office of Personnel Management. You can search by choosing from a selective list of agencies, by broad geographic region or center, or by individual state. Job openings can be keyword searched on a local or national level and the positions posted seem to represent all lines of professional endeavor. Job postings provide contact, salary, and classification information.

Advertising and Media Jobs Page

http://www.nationjob.com/media

Housed in the NationJob career search site, this is a comprehensive collection of job listings in magazines, TV, marketing, and other media-related fields. The words "editor" and "writer" appear enough times to make any media job-seeker drool, and it's a welcome relief from the "All Tech All The Time" job search sites.

Scholarly Societies Project

http://asa.ugl.lib.umich.edu/chdocs/employment/job-guide.humanities.html#4

Not an employment service per se, but job seekers can find some serious leads, since many of the societies provide employment listings as well as information. Provides generous offerings for scientists, social scientists, and business majors; but arts and humanities majors should find this site of special interest, especially if their interests lean towards the esoteric—you'll find the Czech and Slovak Simulation Society (CSSS) Web page here.

Careerfile

http://www.careerfile.com/index.html

An efficient job-search and matching site dedicated to the New England area. It's free for job-seekers and there is a small fee for employers. Features informative articles on topics such as the art of finding outstanding employees.

Jobs in Academe

http://www.chronicle.merit.edu/

Boost your chances of finding your way into a field that's growing tougher and more competitive daily. Puts you on the trail of academic and related positions all around the nation. Also provides up-to-the-minute news of the week and interesting items such as "Finance and Personal

[OVERHEARD ON WOMEN'S WIRE]

http://chat.women.com

"Some women see competitive women as 'unfeminine' and worthy objects for attack."

ON COMPETITION:

"The ambivalence many women feel around competition causes some of us to go about it indirectly, even covertly. If you can't compete with your friends—or 'shouldn't,' you can compete with an enemy!"

ON NETWORKING:

"I believe we are creating our own networks. Not the 'consciousness raising' sessions of the past, but networks where women talk honestly and openly about career issues. Kodak in Rochester, NY, for example, has a very active women's network with hundreds of women belonging."

—Carolyn Duff, author of "When Women Work Together" in a chat on Women's Wire.

Planning" and a guide to alternative journalism, plus more. Be an academic, or just surf like one!

TechWeb

http://www.techweb.com

You have to sign into this CMP Publication's Web site, but its employment-resource page is worth it. The online home to Communications Week, Home PC, and others, Techweb reprints articles on employment—many worthwhile. And the site is fully searchable. Good news from Information Week: "Recruiters who use the Net generally give it high grades." Sparse job listings, quality links, but overall: a good job!

High Technology Careers Magazine

http://www.hightechcareers.com

The online face of a magazine that keeps high-tech career-hoppers up to date on job trends and opportunities and offers how-to pieces like "The Secrets of Great Resumes" or advice on matching career with personality. Something different: an online resume-posting service that Webmasters say will get a description of your skills in front of potential employers while preserving your anonymity until you reply to a response.

Cool Works

http://www.coolworks.com/showme

Here's a way to see the world: seasonal jobs are advertised at this site by park services, ranches, and hotels when the tourist traffic increases. If you're willing to pick up and move for a few months, there seem to be plenty of employers in exotic locales who'll hire you (see Figure 3.9). Webmaster Bill Berg recommends seasonal employment as a way of broadening one's experience. Some employers listed even seem to suggest that working for them is practically a free vacation: you can get "ski breaks arranged whenever possible."

Freelance On-line

http://haven.ios.com/~freelans/index2.html

A directory and resource center for freelancers in the communication fields (i.e., editors, writers, designers, artists). Membership is free, and you can browse through the directory for contracts and positions offered in your

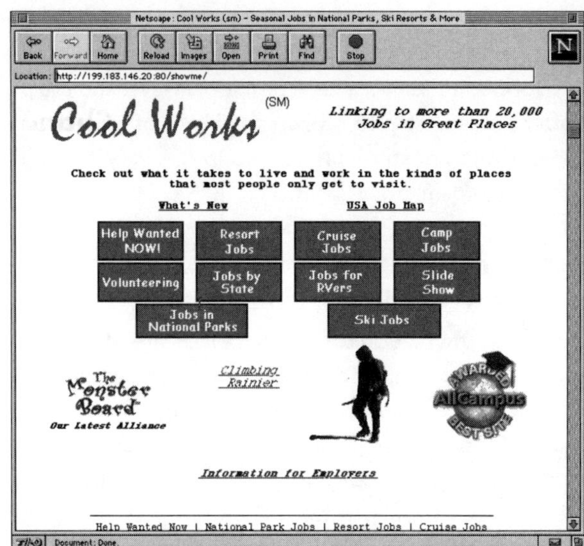

Figure 3.9

Coolworks, *http://www.coolworks.com/showme*

chosen field. You can also advertise your availability by answering a series of questions about your skills, location, and salary expectations.

The Virtual Headbook

http://www.xmission.com/~wintrnx/vh/virtual.htm

This casting-agent resource is also a great place for job-seeking models and actors to place their resumes and headshots. (There is a fee.) Material is categorized according to age, sex, ethnic look, and location. If you place your resume and photo online, Virtual Headbook will even give you access to The Actor's Trunk, an archive of theater, agency, and union contacts.

AJR JobLink

http://www.newslink.org/joblink.html

A service of the American Journalism Review, this site is a great resource for job-seeking journalists, as well as prospective employers. Their specialty is the customized approach they offer to both job-seekers and prospective employers: You get a free hyperlink for your resume, clippings, or any other personal information to set you apart in a notoriously competitive field. Recent graduates can skip right to the special category for entry-level positions. A smart way to get a jump on the competition.

Good Works—A Guide to Social Change Careers

http://www.essential.org/goodworks/

A good resource for seekers of a career alternative to the corporate world. Subscribe to the directory ($24.00) or job-search online for free, with a clickable map of states to narrow your search. We turned up some interesting listings, though we did do our searching in California.

INTERNATIONAL APPEAL

Aupair JobMatch Service

http://www.ipl.co.uk/cgi-bin/forum/aupairs/sublist.html

This U.K.-based information exchange company provides this service as a preliminary step to matching up nannies with families. Choose one of five languages, then register (it's free) yourself as an au pair looking for employment. Or, search the database (you can narrow your search by specifying preferred nationality of the family, preferred location of the position, etc.). See the world, and get paid to do it!

American Physiological Society Job Listings

gopher://oac.hsc.uth.tmc.edu:3300/11/employ

If you're looking for opportunities in the fields of Exercise Science, Physical Therapy, or the Biomedical field in general, this gopher menu provides a handful of up-to-date job listings. Add it to your list of job search tools.

Telecommuting Jobs

http://www.tjobs.com/

Interested in career opportunities that will allow you to work from home at least part of the time? This site lets you narrow your job search by providing telecommuter job listings. You can also post your resume and "job seeker" status for prospective employers to see. Job listings are divided into several categories (example: Artists, Engineers, Writers), and all have a healthy number of listings. A great feature: a big "position filled" sign by positions that have been filled.

Medsearch America

http://www.medsearch.com/

This directory/job resource is directed toward those with an interest in the health care field as well as environmental science, biology, and chemistry. The service is free for job seekers, and it offers a shot at some interesting job opportunities nationwide. The listings are up to date, and you can be reassured by the comments of apparently pleased regulars.

Contract Employment Weekly

http://www.ceweekly.wa.com/

This site, devoted to those seeking contract employment, charges a fee of $33.00 for access to full job listings, but you can check out a portion of the listings free, as a guest. Most jobs listed here are in the technical field. A plus: listings are updated very frequently.

INTERNATIONAL APPEAL

CyberDyne CS Limited

http://www.demon.co.uk/cyberdyne/cyber.html

Search for a new opportunity internationally at this U.K.-based site. Oriented toward contract workers, with a strong technical emphasis, the CyberDyne folks allow you to search for job listings by desired country, as well as provide links to newsgroups in nearly every international job-related category imaginable.

Hotflash Jobs!

http://iquest.com/~ntes/jobslist.html

Brought to you by National Technical Employment Services, this site features job listings in the technical and engineering fields, all free, and updated daily (you can avoid cold leads by browsing just this week's new jobs)! You can also find a recruiter by state, or upload your resume. What more could you need?

Employment Opportunities in Wildlife and Fisheries Science

http://wfscnet.tamu.edu/jobs.html

Despite the catchy-sounding name, this is a worthwhile place to search for jobs and internships in the natural resources field. Originating at Texas A & M University, there's a real variety of jobs posted here, including seasonal, academic and non-academic, government, and private sector. If you want to swim with dolphins, run with wolves, or just shuffle papers, add this site to your search.

Business Job Finder

http://www.cob.ohio-state.edu/dept/fin/osujobs.htm

This Ohio State University-based job search site focuses on resources for finding that great job in the business world (i.e., finance, accounting, and management). Thinking of going for the MBA instead? The MBA Page at this site is a really good place to start (it gives you the real low-down on B-school), and there are links to other MBA resources as well.

Get a Job!

http://sensemedia.net/getajob

The folks at SenseMedia who bring you this site will post your resume in HTML format free of charge, as they're trying to get their site established as a place for employers in the hypermedia field to look when they're seeking good people. In addition, there are the usual links to

[OVERHEARD ON WOMEN'S WIRE]

http://chat.women.com

SET GOALS:

"Try to set goals for yourself every day. They are your road map. They tell you which way you should go when faced with competing priorities.

Also, without goals, when unexpected things come up, it's hard to tell what is most important—what you really want or need to have done by the end of the day."

TAKE BREAKS:

"Often we think we're getting more done when we take no breaks. But we are actually losing some of our mental sharpness because we haven't given our brains a chance to focus on other things. Another very important thing you might be missing out on…is interaction with people outside of your direct work space…You don't want to be one of those people who suddenly finds herself facing an unexpected career challenge and realizing that she has cultivated no associates or outside associates who can help."

IDENTIFY TIME-SUCKS:

"One question to ask yourself in this regard is: 'Does this contribute to my success? Or, the success of my organization? Or, the success of my family?' If it doesn't, why are you spending time on it?"

—Paula Ancona, author of the syndicated biz column "Working Smarter" and the book *SuccessAbilities*, on time management in a live chat on Women's Wire.

zillions of job search sites. If you're a spinner of Webs, it can't hurt to stop by here.

Jobs.cz

INTERNATIONAL APPEAL

http://www.jobs.cz/english_welcome.html

The first job server in the Czech republic. Want to hang out in Prague with the rest of the international set? "Czech" out this collection of job listings. You can post your resume, learn a bit about the Czech labor market (nearly 0% unemployment rate!), and look through some jobs that would be relevant to the international community. Keep in mind that if you don't know the Czech language, teaching English is your best career bet.

Entertainment Recruiting Network

http://www.showbizjobs.com/

Say hello to Hollywood with this resource brought to you by recruitment managers for leading companies in the film, TV, recording and other entertainment industries. The bulletin board is free for job-seekers (recruiters pay a fee). The listings are up to date and interesting, and the presence of Big Names (i.e., Disney, E!, Spelling, Sony Pictures, etc.) is enough to make anyone see stars.

Online Sports

http://www.onlinesports.com/pages/CareerCenter.html

Sponsored by a professional search firm for the sporting goods industry, this is a sports-related job and resume resource for those with an interest in a career in sports management, marketing, or similar fields. Browse through available positions or post your resume. Now you know where to turn if three seasons on TV just aren't enough.

MMWire Classifieds

http://www.mmwire.com/classifieds.html

A smart place to search for jobs in mulitmedia, video games, interactive entertainment, and online services throughout the U.S. A great feature: the MM Scoreboard, which provides the latest numbers in the hardware, software, online, and game markets, so you know which star to hitch your wagon to.

Job Hunt

http://www.taos.com/resume/index.html

Produced by Taos Mountain Software, this site's got hip visuals and good advice for the job-seeking techie (uh, yeah). Their Top Ten Tips for writing a technical resume is especially informative and helpful.

CAREER ISSUES

Center for Labor Research and Education Gopher Menu

gopher://violet.berkeley.edu:2521/1

The Center for Labor Research and Education produces educational programs, publications, research, and materials on issues that are relevant to organized labor and the workforce. Visitors to its gopher menu will find topical reports, project details, and other labor information.

Hard@Work

http://www.hardatwork.com

Hard@Work's mission, they say, "is to reduce the oversupply of fear and alienation in the workplace." You're invited to play "Stump the Mentor," and if the computer can't solve your difficulties motivating employees or managing the boss, it's time to create an original solution and add it to the database. News-reader technology enables interactive discussion forums, such as the Water Cooler.

Employee Relations Web Picks

http://www.webcom.com/garnet/labor

Employee Relations Web Picks is a treasure trove of all things legally binding in the human resources game. Although the original content and off-site links frequently have a New York State focus, you'll find plenty of information in the section "Lawsuits you should know about." This is a top-notch resource for employers hoping to keep up to date in the field (and for employees who want to be as up to date as their bosses).

AFL-CIO

http://www.aflcio.org

America's largest labor organization has worked its way into cyberspace, offering a series of policy statements, press releases, and tips on how to unionize. You can find out about the AFL-CIO's stance on affirmative action, or read the *AFL-CIO News*. Elsewhere, its boycott list included R.J. Reynolds Tobacco Co. and Tyson/Holly Farms Chicken on our last visit. Salty stuff for workers, with one caveat: Don't visit the "How To Organize a Union" section with your boss in the room.

Psychology.Com

www.psychology.com

This site promotes an organization called Integrated EAP Inc., a network of health care pros specializing in psychological services. The emphasis is on the workplace, and some of the information is aimed at employers who might be seeking support services for employees. The site includes a listing of licensed psychiatrists, psychologists, and social workers across the U.S. and links to related Web sites. Probably the best place to find the 12 step program for workaholics.

NewWork News

www.newwork.com/Today's_news.html

The job of the New Work Corporation is, well, work. Each day, this California-based corporation tracks down newspaper stories about labor and the workplace—like a feature on a successful Massachusetts temp agency and the return of 30,000 striking New York janitors. Not all the stories can be accessed online, but you'll find a brief description of each item. The focus includes the American and world economy and job cutbacks around the globe. For students of the workplace, it's like having a news filter.

Bureau of Labor Statistics home page

http://stats.bls.gov

One of those rare things in life that turns out to be exactly what it says it is. Your resource for all data, publications, and other forms of information on the phenomenon of Work. Beware, though—the amount of information can be daunting. You can conduct a search by keyword, so choose your keywords carefully.

9to5: What every woman needs to know about sexual harassment

http://www.cs.utk.edu/~bartley/other/9to5.html

9to5 is an advocacy organization dedicated to addressing the issue of sexual harassment of women in the workplace. This site identifies the problem, explains the laws, and clearly illuminates the steps you can take to prevent and end harassment on the job. Read It, Print It, Post It over the water cooler.

Satore Township (a Retreat on the Shores of the Internet...)

http://www.crl.com/~mikekell/viw.html

File this one under D for Different. This site is devoted to the study of violence in the workplace. You can link to lists of books on the subject, get general facts on workplace violence, or read articles on subjects like Death in the Office. This is the place to find a wealth of resources—online and otherwise—to turn to for help or information on this very real concern.

National Center for Employee Ownership

http://www.nceo.org

This is run by a private nonprofit organization dedicated to providing info on Employee Stock Ownership Plans (ESOPs) and other forms of employee ownership. The site itself is attractive, colorful, well organized, and jam-packed with useful info on employee ownership. You can become a member, but there's plenty here for non-members, too.

Legal Information Institute

http://www.law.cornell.edu/topical.html

Maintained by Cornell University Law School, this site contains valuable information for the entrepreneur or small business owner, as well as anyone with questions on employment law. With topics such as Law of Commercial Transactions and Taxation, here's where you'll find out if you can sue Microsoft for stealing your new product idea. Bookmark the Employment Law section and refer to it next time your boss tells you that 2.5 minutes is more than enough time for lunch.

Business and Workplace Briefs—Nolo Press

http://140.174.208.58/bus.html#3

This well-known legal self-help firm has brought their good advice online. This fact-packed site covers workplace issues from discrimination and disability, to hiring and firing, and many in between. Read it before you go to work.

INTERNATIONAL APPEAL

Worklife

http://www.ozemail.com.au/~worklife

This site, from an Australia-based consulting and counseling company, seeks to address worklife as a whole life process, rather than "just a job." The newsletter, which you can read online, addresses career and life management issues and contains links to other valuable resources in those areas. The organization has offices throughout the world if you like what you see.

Working Together Listserv (mailing list)

http://www.west.net/~bpbooks/wtlsta.html

This is an mailing list/forum dedicated to the subject of gender issues in the workplace. The goal is to discuss these issues to reach a common goal of diversity and productivity. The issues addressed in the list are thought provoking, and the site features an equally interesting question of the week, such as, "What do we call each other at work?" Subscribe (it's free) and get involved!

INTERNATIONAL APPEAL

Upjohn Institute for Employment Research

http://www.upjohninst.org

The W.E. Upjohn Institute is a nonprofit organization devoted to finding, evaluating, and promoting solutions to

---

[OVERHEARD ON WOMEN'S WIRE]

http://chat.women.com

"My suggestion is to seek out line management assignments and high risk projects. Then perform beyond expectations, and keep your sense of humor!"

ON GETTING $$$ FOR A NEW BIZ:

"One of the biggest problems for women is that you need to have credit to get credit. And frequently married women will have credit in their husband's name on their car loans, home loans, or their credit cards."

WHAT YOU SHOULD DO:

"One of the most important things that women of any age can do is to begin to build a good credit record by purchasing the next car in their name and a credit card in their own name."

—Kathleen Brown, on what women can do to break the glass ceiling, in a live chat on Women's Wire. Brown, a former treasurer of California, is a Senior VP at Bank of America.

---

employment-related problems. And we've all got a few of those. The Web site is a great place to read about the latest in employment-related research and pilot projects for schools, international issues, and labor/political issues. Of particular interest: studies involving the labor and economic changes in Eastern Europe.

The Economic Conversion Information Exchange

http://netsite.esa.doc.gov/oeci

Created by the U.S. Department of Commerce and the Department of Defense, this site is an information clearinghouse assisting communities, industries, and their workers affected by defense downsizing. Among its press releases (mostly via gopher), you can read the list of DOD proposed closures. Also here: employment and wage figures for communities across the United States. Not pretty. But then, neither are base closures.

My Boss Is a

http://www.myboss.com

Lots of people think their boss is the worst there is, but a quick survey of the stories posted at this just-for-fun site might change a few minds. Some submissions are serious and some are downright sad, but the real goal here is to let off some steam and commiserate with your fellow sufferers. Readers are invited to vote for their favorite each week, which should give you an idea just how many people feel moved to submit their stories. You know you have a bad boss when "he visits you in the hospital and brings you work, not flowers."

CAREER DEVELOPMENT

Women's Wire Work Channel

http://www.women.com/work

This isn't a "Thank God it's Friday" site. It's a place where people who love their jobs (or would like to) talk about getting ahead and having a life in the work world (see Figure 3.10). Find out what it's really like to have a dream job like TV writer, Webmaster, or chef, and hear what it really takes to break into these hot fields. Have your own unique career situation addressed by the resident Biz Shrink. And get a little inspiration from exceptional women who've truly made their mark, such as Maya Lin, designer of the Vietnam Veterans Memorial and Judy McGrath, president of MTV. It's a combination of useful tips and real-world insights for everyone from the college senior to the small business owner.

Advancing Women

http://www.advancingwomen.com/workplace.phtml

Whether you're in search of a job or comfortably established in your position, a visit to Advancing Women may put you a step ahead. Articles and links covering everything from entrepreneurship and small business to "Grrls" and "Latinas on the rise" make this a site you shouldn't miss.

California School-to-Career Information System

http://wwwstc.cahwnet.gov

The California School-to-Career Information System is a joint project of the state's public school system and local business partners. This home page tells about the system's

Figure 3.10

Women's Wire Work Channel, *http://www.women.com/work*

career guidance activities, aimed at helping students move easily from school into employment.

Saludos Web

http://www.wenet.net/saludos

Saludos Web promotes Hispanic careers and education with links to job listings, internships, and scholarships. Includes articles from *Saludos Hispanos Magazine*, resume postings, and a variety of Hispanic-related Web links.

Women's Business Resource Site

http://www.athenet.net/~ccain

A terrific resource for providing information on available business opportunities, as well as thought-provoking articles on topics such as the glass ceiling, employee issues, and the viability of doing business on the Web. Comprehensive, easy-to-follow advice on how to start, grow, and maintain your business, with links to the best resources around. There's also market news, tax tidbits, and a chance to hook up with the Good Ole Girls Network. If it's not on every woman business dynamo's bookmark list, it should be!

Women's Web/BizNet

http://www.womweb.com/index.html

Do you know what the top 25 jobs for women in 1995 were? If not, you can find them here, along with offerings from magazines such as *Working Woman* and *Working Mother*. A great source of information and discourse on issues such as child care, equality in the workplace, and emerging technology. An easy way to stay on top of the latest news on gender in the workplace.

Academic Careers Information Database

http://www.acm.org/member_services/career

The Association for Computing Machinery maintains this site for pointers to online information about academic careers. They provide a graduate assistantship directory, as well as lists of resources for obtaining academic funding and grants, along with a resume referral service and articles of interest. Very useful: CareerLine, a personal "help desk" service, where you can ask career-related questions.

About Work

http://www.aboutwork.com

Ready for your first job? Changing careers? Maybe you just want to find a way to work from home or get ahead in your present career. About Work is just that, and you can find both visually delicious and useful advice on all of the above (see Figure 3.11). Join a resume chat, swap office stories, or let the Career Switch section give you the guts—and the information—to make the change.

Job Web

http://www.jobweb.com

Another huge resource for your job search. The listings here are more likely to be in the technology field, but a few surprises can be found (Scholastic, Inc. needs a CD-Rom producer, for example). Here also lives a decent-sized library of the career development materials that used to require one to take up temporary residence in the local library, such as lists of graduate and professional schools and info on career choices from aquatic science to zookeeping.

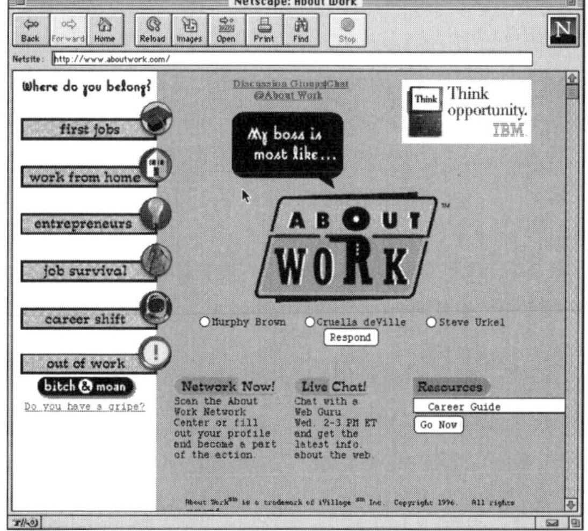

Figure 3.11

About Work, *http://www.aboutwork.com*

Harvard Business School

http://www.hbs.harvard.edu

"Understanding the art of profitability" is the key to this overview of Harvard Business School's MBA and Executive Education programs. Courses such as "Data Decisions and Negotiations" are described, along with admissions and financial aid procedures, desired characteristics of program graduates, and so on. A bonus: Marr's Official Rating Guide to Business School Webs.

Careers in Architecture

http://www.aia.org/career.htm

Aspiring Frank Lloyd Wrights can plug into the American Institute of Architects Careers in Architecture page to learn about the trade, where to study it, and the possibilities of practicing it. Architecture, it explains, "is the imaginative blend of art and science in the design of environments for people." Lists include accredited universities and available scholarships. Spartan, clean, and fully functional, this page does Wright proud.

Exploring Your Future in Math and Science

http://www.cs.wisc.edu/~karavan/afl/home.html

"Girls say they enjoy math in earlier grades, but tend to shy away in adolescence," claim these University of Wisconsin students, who created this page to help reverse the trend. Here's some encouragement: chief engineers earn an average of $79,998, and retail brokers break in at $90,000. Critical thinking for classroom projects and links to Caltech's "Women's Center" add to this resource for pre-college females who'd put pi into an equation before the oven.

Kansas Mentor Project

www.ksu.edu/~dangle

From "Kansas Careers" at Kansas State University, this page is chock full of career development resources for women. Particularly valuable (though still under construction on our last visit) is the "Interest Assessment for Women," a tool which helps women identify possible careers based on real-life interests and experiences. Good links to college financial aid info and job search networks, too.

1996-97 Occupational Outlook Handbook

http://stats.bls.gov/ocohome.htm

Now you don't have to go to the library and fight with the college kids over it anymore. If you're not familiar with this job-hunter's bible, it's often the first stop on the career research journey (see Figure 3.12). You'll find a diverse list of occupations, each with average salaries, working conditions, education/experience required, and outlook for the future, as well as lists of relevant resources.

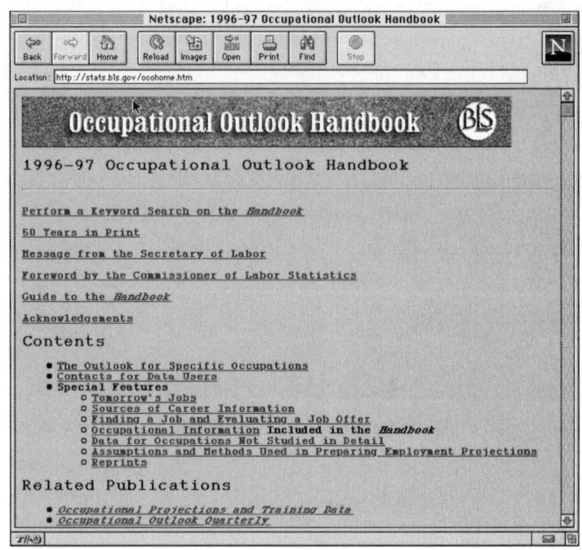

Figure 3.12
Occupational Outlook Handbook, *http://stats.bls.gov/ocohome.htm*

Business Questions and Answers

http://www.summary.com/qanda.htm

Sponsored by Soundview, this site is basically a bulletin board where you can post your work-related questions and the site's editors as well as outsiders will answer them as best they can. Some questions were quite thought-provoking, and the answers pointed us toward some valuable contacts and resources. Some sample topics: how to start a mentoring program, conducting customer satisfaction surveys, changing one's image in the corporate world, and how managers interact with "virtual employees."

Career Alternatives for Art Historians

http://www.nd.edu/~crosenbe/jobs.html

A very useful site for those individuals with a background in Art History who want some ideas on the career options available to them. There's an easy-to-navigate table divided into job categories as diverse as "Art Law" and "Independent Producer: Film and TV." Goes on to list positions often open to Art Historians, and provides links to more job listings.

CareersNet

INTERNATIONAL APPEAL

http://www.careersnet.com

An open door on the front page invites us to begin our step-by-step career search process. From skills assessment to networking, each phase is addressed in a "big picture" way. So what if the listed resources are all located in the U.K., and they really just want you to use their consulting services. There's enough encouragement here to push the job hunter or career changer just a little further up that steep and slippery slope.

The Insurance Career Center

http://www.connectyou.com/talent

You'll find this site packed full of information and resources for insurance industry professionals. Search hundreds of jobs at top companies, or post and edit your resume, or check out a collection of other resources. If you're working in the insurance industry, or would like to, this would be a good one to bookmark.

The Environmental Careers Organization

http://www.eco.org

ECO is a nonprofit organization dedicated to the development of individuals' environmental careers. You can search environmental placement services specializing in paid internships or network with alumni of past ECO internship programs online or face-to-face at any of the organization's many networking events. Also, check out career fairs, job listings, or related Hot Web Sites. If you're interested in a career with an environmental focus, here's a good place to start.

Career Plan for Fiction Writers

http://www.crayne.com/victory/carrplan.html

The aspiring fiction writer has a hard road ahead. Victory Crayne's Web site seeks to make it a little easier by providing both motivational and practical aid to the aspiring wordsmith. After checking out some useful advice (how to find an agent, for example), inspirational words, and a good list of resources for writers, you may even think twice before you take that boring day job.

The Writer's Edge

http://www.nashville.net/~edge

Screenwriter? Playwright? Novelist? Here's a monster collection of resources for writers, including categories for Web authoring and info for young writers. There's also a bulletin board, a classified link, and more. Search here to find writing positions (some for artists and illustrators as well), internships, and other opportunities throughout the world.

Scrivenery: A Writer's Journal

http://www.lit-arts.com/scriven/scriven.htm

The Scrivenery, maintained by Ed Williams, is a monthly online publication for writers. It features prose exercises in technique and structure, as well as samples of the fiction submitted in response to the exercises, essays on the writing life, a calendar of literary birthdays, bits of news from the publishing biz, market information, and links to over 200 other writing-related resources.

Writers Resource Center

http://www.azstarnet.com/~poewar/writer/writer.html

Site "Curator" John Hewitt has put together a compendium of useful articles, market links, and educational resources. Well organized to cover the writing craft from Tech Writing to Poetry, the site also includes a link to a powerful search engine. A great bookmark for one-stop research on your writing career.

Telecommuting and Telework Resource Page

http://grove.ufl.edu/~pflewis/commute.html

Here's a directory for the '90s and beyond: a collection of resources for the telecommuter. Includes lists of organizations and associations, programs and initiatives, conferences you may want to attend, as well as books, newsletters, and articles on the subject. Site publisher Patty Lewis has added a new segment: The academic discussion of telecommuting as a social and economic phenomenon. Stuff to remember next time you're stuck on the bridge at rush hour!

Smart Valley Inc.'s Telecommuting Web Pages

http://www.svi.org/PROJECTS/TCOMMUTE/webguide

A comprehensive guide that you can download which covers all facets of telecommuting, including Basics of Telecommuting, a plan for implementation that you can configure for your own office, discussion of lifestyle changes, as well as a place for those who have experienced this "virtual office" environment to share their experiences. Discuss this site at your next tele-video-conference!

Center on Education and Work

http://www.cew.wisc.edu

Sponsored by the University of Wisconsin School of Education, this site focuses on the implications of education and work in society, and provides opportunities to seek both. You'll find notices for a variety of related conferences and events to be held throughout the nation in the coming year, background information, plus related links. Updated conscientiously and regularly.

Science's Next Wave

http://www.nextwave.org

Dedicated to the future of science, this e-zine emphasizes resources for the next generation of scientists. Check out: New Niches, the section on alternative and new science careers. Current issue featured six Role Models who made the transition from scientist to entrepreneur.

College Grad Job Hunter

http://www.collegegrad.com

Your online key to professional life *aprés* college. In addition to job postings, check out the valuable info on resumes, interviews and negotiations, and some words of wisdom on what to do once you've actually got that new job (see Figure 3.13). Eye-catching and well-organized, this site is a painless way to help the transition to the real world.

Law Employment Center

http://www.lawjobs.com

A great site for the wannabe lawyer or those considering the field. Search legal job listings and salary averages by region or check out legal recruiters. Cool feature: Asked & Answered—Ask law firm prez Ann Israel questions about the law employment marketplace, or browse through others' questions and her answers to them.

It's My Future

http://www.myfuture.com/OUTPUT/career.htm

Aimed mainly at teens about to put their high school days behind them, this site is clever, funny, useful, and packed

Figure 3.13

College Grad Job Hunter, *http://www.collegegrad.com*

SPOTLIGHT ON ENTREPRENEURS

Women are making their presence felt in the U.S. economy. Women-owned businesses are growing in number and range, and as women business owners expand their companies, they add to the growth of the national economy as well.

Five Facts

1 Women-owned businesses contribute more than $1.6 trillion annually in revenues to the economy, more than the gross domestic product of most countries.

2 The latest U.S. Census data indicates women owned 6.4 million businesses in 1992; current calculations indicate that women now own almost 8 million firms.

3 Employment growth in women-owned businesses exceeds the national average in nearly every region of the country and in nearly every major industry. Women-owned businesses employ one out of every five U.S. workers with a total of 18.5 million employees.

4 Women-owned businesses are more likely to remain in business than the average U.S. firm. Nearly three-quarters of women-owned firms in business in 1991 were still in business three years later, compared to two-thirds of all U.S. firms.

5 Home-based businesses owned by women are making a substantial economic contribution. These businesses provide full or part-time employment for 14 million people.

Five Sites

SBA's Women's Business Ownership Page
http://www.sbaonline.sba.gov/womeninbusiness
Dedicated to providing women business owners with a network of training, counseling, and mentoring services.

MoneyHunter
http://www.moneyhunter.com
Get the scoop on who's on top in the investor/entrepreneur world and great advice from leading business experts, then download their business plan template.

Idea Cafe
http://www.ideacafe.com
Search for ways to finance your business. Network away at CyberSchmooze. Then unwind with a coffee break.

Herring.com
http://www.herring.com
Search the Entrepreneur's Resource Center, an on-line workshop for entrepreneurs.

SOHO central
http://www.hoaa.com
They'll show you lots of reasons why home-based businesses are one of the fastest growing business trends of the '90s.

with good advice and resources. Fresh career tips include, The Industrial Strength Toolkit, Create a Highly Effective Resume, and even Military Opportunities. And the rest of the site, with lifestyle pointers and radical grafix, is definitely worth a look.

Pencom Interactive Salary Survey

http://www.pencomsi.com/industry.html

Though it's geared to individuals in the computer biz (who we all know are overpaid anyway), this is a fun little exercise: You enter your location, the field you work in, and any additional skills, then ask the magic question—What Am I Worth?

Career Atlas for the Road

http://isdn.net/nis

Sponsored by a professional recruiting and career achievement consulting firm, this site addresses more than just, "Which job do you want?"—but rather, "What career are you PASSIONATE about?" They present some very interesting questions to ask yourself, and things to think about, before settling for a job, plus links to cool job sites. Or, you can buy the book.

Planning Your Future

http://safetynet.doleta.gov

Aimed at Federal employees facing downsizing, this site is a good stop for anyone facing a career change, voluntary or involuntary. Contains useful information on beginning a job search, and figuring out your options. (For example: Should you go back to school?) Includes a huge collection of internet resources, with an emphasis on the fact that the career change is a step-by-step process.

ENTREPRENEURSHIP

The VINE™ Entrepreneur Mall

http://www.thevine.com/vine-f.htm

The VINE is a great destination for the hardcore inventor or entrepreneur. You'll find the products and services of innovative (sometimes frighteningly so) entrepreneurs and emerging growth companies, and you can contact the VINE folks to advertise your own. You can also read up on the success stories and case studies of those who came before you. And where else can you order the GoBabies Diaper Changing Kit?

THE VIRTUAL WATERCOOLER

Whether you are working from home or taking a break at the office, chat rooms on the Net can provide a great place to shmooze, network, or just hang out.

Women's Wire Chat

http://www.women.com/chat

Any time of day you will find people getting to know each other in the Women's Wire chat rooms. Watch for announcements of chats with career experts.

Talk Shop

http://www.aboutwork.com/chat

Vent your work frustrations and get job advice from experts in the About Work chat room.

Yahoo Net Events

http://events.yahoo.com

Check in daily to Yahoo's chat schedule for the latest listings and direct links to the many and varied live events taking place on the Net.

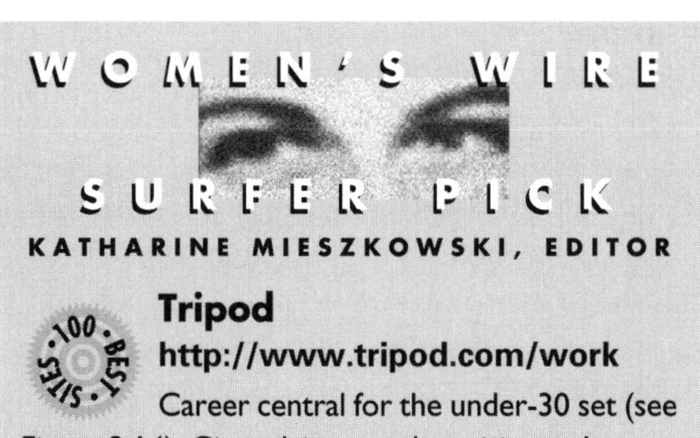

KATHARINE MIESZKOWSKI, EDITOR

Tripod

http://www.tripod.com/work

Career central for the under-30 set (see Figure 3.14). Give advice to other visitors about their work worries in the Dilemma section. Build your online resume, post it, and search through other people's. Good voyeurism opportunities. The best way to figure out if you're interested in a particular field is to work as an intern, and this site can help you snag that internship—you can search their internship database by location or subject. Even though it is geared towards the recent grad, there's something useful for just about everyone who lives in the "real world" of work.

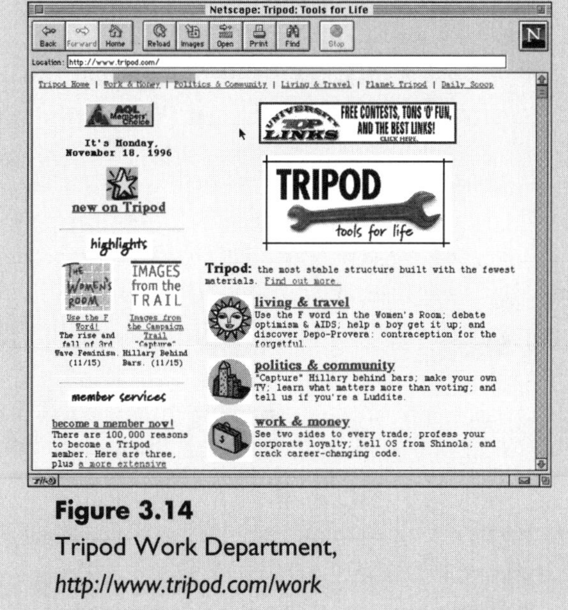

Figure 3.14
Tripod Work Department,
http://www.tripod.com/work

SOHO Central

http://www.hoaa.com

The name stands for Small Office/Home Office and the site is the online headquarters of the Home Office Association of America, the national organization for full-time, home-based professionals. They'll show you lots of reasons why home-based businesses are one of the fastest growing business trends of the '90s. Includes updates on news and new products, links to home-office related sites, and benefits of membership in the Association (which include such useful perks as airline discounts, free tax/accounting checkup, and newsletter subscription).

Idea Cafe

http://www.ideacafe.com

A place for great business ideas to meet in a colorful, friendly atmosphere (see Figure 3.15). Search for ways to finance your business, network away at CyberSchmooze, check out hot new products and services in TechnoTapas, and click your way through a tasty menu of resources, forums, and articles. Then unwind with a coffee break: go to Lite Bytes for a cartoon, a quote, and your latest biz horoscope.

MoneyHunter

http://www.moneyhunter.com

MoneyHunter is a great resource for entrepreneurs seeking funding, and it's even fun to navigate (see Figure 3.16). Baffled by what those venture capital folks were saying? Whip out the handy Investorspeak decoder, and you're nearly a pro. Get the scoop on who's

Figure 3.15
The Idea Cafe, *http://www.ideacafe.com*

on top in the investor/entrepreneur world and advice from leading business experts...even download "the Internet's most popular business plan template." The Web site will be joined by The MoneyHunt Show on PBS beginning in January 1997.

Working Solo

http://www.workingsolo.com

A searchable guide to more than 1200 valuable business resources for the small business entrepreneur. They've gathered news, marketing tips, legal and tax information, and tons of hot links for the solo businessperson. So, they plug their own go-for-it books and tapes here, but if

I·N·T·E·R·N·E·T M·I·N·U·T·E

USING THE WEB TO LOCATE PEOPLE

Looking for a long-lost love, a childhood friend, or a business contact whose card you've lost? The Web can help. You can track down phone numbers, addresses, personal Web pages and e-mail addresses. No more operator charges, you can search all of the U.S. white and yellow pages in seconds for free.

There are lots of people-finder resources on the Web. Once you find the one you like, the process is usually straightforward: Just fill in the fields where you know the information such as first name, last name, state. If your first search does not return the results you want, try entering less specific information. For example, the initial of the person's first name rather than the full name, or a state rather than a city.

Four 11

http://www.four11.com

Search for e-mail addresses and telephone numbers with a special section on searching for government officials and celebrities.

Infospace

http://www.infospace.com

Access to U.S. and Canada telephone directories, a worldwide e-mail search, business listings, and a toll-free directory.

Switchboard

http://www.swithboard.com

A searchable directory of people and businesses—also an area called Switchboard stories with tales of people finding each other using the Switchboard service.

WhoWhere

http://www.whowhere.com

E-mail, personal home pages, phone numbers and addresses, and business information. Plus Who Where Communities helps you locate people who belong to specific affinity groups or who have particular interests.

While centralized directory information is great, there has been concern raised that privacy is potentially threatened by the accessibility of personal information on the Internet. Generally this information is being taken from other public sources of information such as the telephone book. So if you take precautions with listing this information (for example, not listing your street address or listing only the first initial of your name) it should generally appear the same way on the Internet.

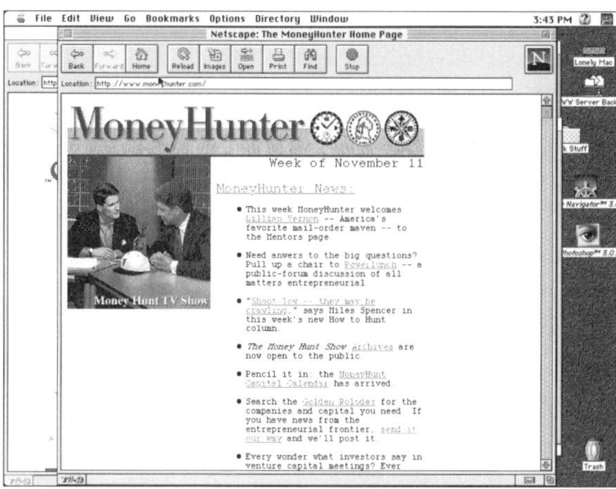

Figure 3.16

MoneyHunter, *http://www.moneyhunter.com*

you can stand that, they've also got a good sampling of what's out there.

Enterprise Profit Ability

http://www.profitability.com

This site is dedicated to explaining the board simulation "game" Profit Ability, which tests business and entrepreneurial skills of up to six people. While the simulation looks fun and interesting, the online quiz was insightful, and we could read the glowing praise of those who had experienced it; how to obtain the thing remains shrouded in mystery. Is this a consulting group? A secret cult? A scam? Let us know if you find out.

Business Plan

http://web.bu.edu/SMGMIS/mba/is823/pseudo/pres.htm

Elegantly named, this page is nothing more than a sample business plan for a product called, fittingly, Pseudo. Organized into sections, follow along and learn the ropes as you go. This particular specimen is thoroughly modern, including such strategies as using a Web page for marketing, linking to as many search engines as possible, and opening "storefronts" in virtual shopping malls.

The Franchise Handbook

http://www.franchise1.com

The online version of the magazine of the same name, this is a good info resource if you're into setting up a franchise of your own. Get help selecting a franchise, take a look at associations nationwide, browse the featured franchise, or scroll through a directory of franchise opportunities. However, before you decide to open up a Mickey D's on your block, better check with the neighbors.

Business Incorporating Guide

http://www.corporate.com

Sponsored by Corporate Agents Inc., an incorporation consulting firm, this site features an up-to-date guide to the information you need to incorporate your business in any state. Gives you in plain English the advantages of incorporating, types of corporations, how to incorporate, and even gives you the opportunity to Incorporate Online. While you're here, check out more small biz-related online resources.

PROFESSIONAL ORGANIZATIONS AND NETWORKING

Feminist.com career page

http://www.feminist.com/career.html

Links for everything from the Association of Women Industrial Designers to the Glass Ceiling Commission. Whether your profession is Mathematics or Film and Television, you've got a great info resource here at your fingertips. Also check out: lots of resources on issues such as sexual harassment, and parenting, children, and community.

HR Headquarters

http://www.hrhq.com

Mounted by the magazine *Personnel Journal,* HR Headquarters is jam-packed with news and advice for people in the human resources game. The centerpiece of the site is the database of articles from the magazine itself. Visitors can sort this information by category, then select, say, "Alternative work schedules." The "Recruiting" section includes tips on how headhunters can bag the prize specimens lurking on today's college campuses.

BizWomen

http://www.bizwomen.com

BizWomen bills itself as an online "interactive community for successful women in business" who want to use a computer network to network professionally. BizWomen mixes links to business news and information sources with opportunities for women to have an online presence. Founder Marianne Babiera-Krammel's remedy for what she felt was a shortage of Web sites for women seems like a good idea, but it could use some more depth in the coverage of business issues specific to women.

The Ada Project

http://www.cs.yale.edu/HTML/YALE/CS/HyPlans/tap

Women have traditionally had a tough time making inroads into the computer science boys' club, and a site like The Ada Project can help level the CS playing field. Based at Yale University, TAP is a collection of resources that will interest any woman who works with computers. Home to lists of computer conferences for women, reviews of pertinent books, even a link to photos of Sandra Bullock in the movie "The Net."

Association of Women Industrial Designers

http://www.core77.com/AWID

Industrial design has been traditionally the domain of men, but more and more women are entering the field. This site serves as their forum, and as a "network for developing...collaborative resources." The group is sponsored by Pratt Institute's Industrial Design Department in Brooklyn, NY. AWID provides a link to the Industrial Design Network, where valuable resources include a job bank, recent industry news, and a comprehensive worldwide design firm listing.

National Organization for Women

http://now.org/now/home.html

Women, it is reported here, still earn on average only 75 cents for every dollar earned by men. NOW's online page is dedicated to bringing readers the latest information on this and other issues, and to bringing readers up to speed on the organization and its ongoing projects. Read the full text of the Equal Rights Amendment, a proposal that has been causing a brouhaha in the U.S. since 1921. Thank heavens it made it to the Internet Age. Now if everyone could just get it by Jesse Helms...

Web-grrl

http://www.webgrrls.com

The by-now famous networking group comprised of women (and grrlz!) in the new media biz, or those who are just interested. With chapters worldwide, Webgrrls provides a forum for women to exchange information, find job and business leads, learn about new technologies, mentor, intern, train, and more. At the site, you can find out about upcoming face-to-face gatherings in a city near you.

Women in Technology International (WITI)

http://www.witi.com

Motivated by the dearth of women in high-level positions, Carolyn Leighton founded WITI "to increase the number of women promoted to key areas of responsibility in technology." This virtual campus (see Figure 3.17), complete with career center, well-being center, networking cafe, technology center, and "off campus shuttle," is set to raise the net-ucation level of women of all ages. Look for special projects, like Take Your Children on the Internet Week (October 25–November 1).

International Directory of Women Web Designers

http://www.primenet.com/~shauna/women.html

Organized by country and by state, this is reportedly the Web's only comprehensive international directory of woman-owned and -operated Web design and Internet consulting companies.

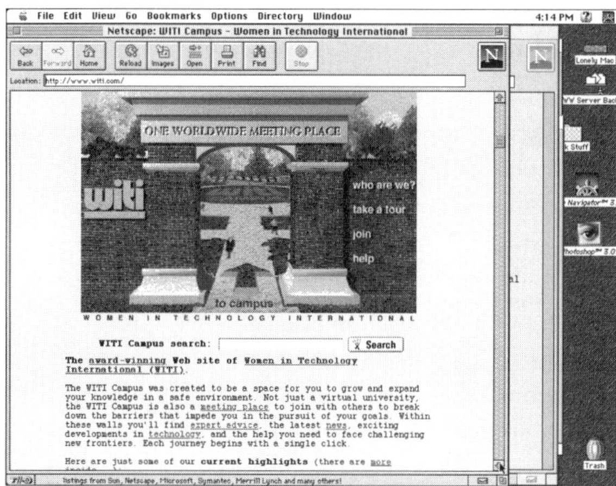

Figure 3.17
Women in Technology International,
http://www.witi.com

Women's Studio Workshop
http://www.webmark.com/wsw/wswhome.htm

This site from the Hudson River Valley artists' collective promotes its programs for women, including grants, internships, and exhibition opportunities. The group describes its artist-in-residence programs which include studio space and technical support. Also, get info on *The Binnewater Tides,* an arts journal addressing issues not covered by the mainstream arts press. An informative page that could use a boost.

The Business Women's Network
http://www.tpag.com/BWN/BWN.html

A division of Public Affairs Group, Inc., BWN was designed to provide communication and networking between top women's business organizations. The site is the home of the Business Women's Network Directory, a compilation of information profiling over 500 of the top business women's organizations in the U.S., as well as a stack of articles and reports covering the progress of women in corporate America. Who needs the old boys anyway?

National Association of Female Executives
http://www.nafe.com

The Web site of the largest business women's association in the country. Eye-pleasing and well-organized, this site helps achieve the NAFE goal, " to empower its members to achieve career success and financial security" by providing information, job resources, networking events, and more. Even if you're not a member, you can use the impressive collection of on- and off-line resources for women on the move.

SBA's Women's Business Ownership page
http://www.sbaonline.sba.gov/womeninbusiness

Their mission is to provide current and future women business owners with a network of training, counseling, and mentoring services. The site provides some seriously useful information on funding sources. You'll also find links to various free publications, a roundup of news and statistics, and a list of woman-owned enterprises, with an emphasis on fields traditionally occupied by men, such as construction. Definitely stop here if you're trying to scrape up funding for your budding business.

Women in Higher Education
http://www.itis.com/wihe

Aimed at women who hold administrative jobs on campus, and women who would like to. You have to subscribe to the (paper) newsletter to view full monthly issues, but you don't have to be a subscriber to browse through Career Connections, where you'll find job listings at universities nationwide.

WAHM—The Online Magazine for Work-At-Home Moms
http://www.maricle.com/wahm

Dedicated to the unique concerns of the mom who works from home. Cute graphics point to topics such as Advice and Business Opportunities. The Question of the Month addresses a relevant topic like, "Did you suffer loss of identity when you left the traditional working world?"...then opens up the discussion, bulletin board-style. A long-awaited resource for those among us who grapple with the three-peanut-butter-sandwich lunch.

Pharmacy Week

http://pharminfo.com/pharmmall/PharmWeek/pharmweek.html

Weekly newsletter for health systems pharmacists. Features pharmacy job openings throughout the world, and you can subscribe via e-mail to receive your weekly listings. The newsletter is free, but they do ask, albeit very nicely, for a voluntary $19.95 lifetime subscription to help them offset costs. A small price to pay for opportunity.

Inkspot

http://www.inkspot.com/~ohi/inkspot

A career and networking resource for writers, Inkspot provides useful resources like market info and classifieds, as well as sound career advice and inspiration. There's also list of links to everything from agents to networking info. Also organized by genre, so if you're a Horror scribe, you won't have to scroll through info on Children's markets. Don't miss the Writer's Block bulletin board—find out what works for others, or post your own remedy.

Herring.com

http://www.herring.com

If you're in the Technology or Entertainment business, bookmark this! The online sibling of *Red Herring Magazine,* this site dishes out up-to-the-minute industry news and job listings with tasty graphics for your viewing pleasure (see Figure 3.18). From here, visitors can search the Entrepreneur's Resource Center, an online workshop for entrepreneurs.

Le Tip

http://www.letip.org

Here's a way to network shamelessly, provided you're prepared to admit that that's what you're doing. Attend regional meetings of this business networking organization and hand out lots of business cards, or pass along your tip online. What qualifies as a "tip"? "...A company or person who is interested in a specific service or product and is expecting a call from a LeTip member." Spread the Wealth!

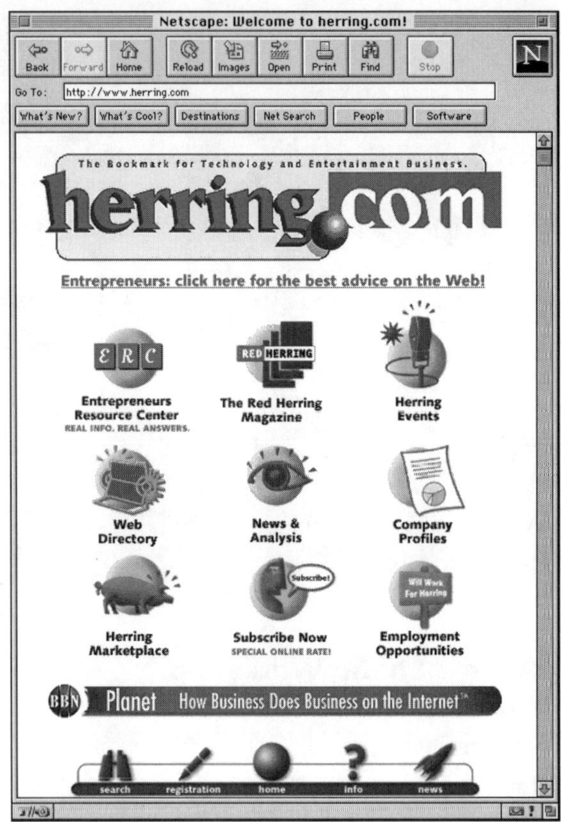

Figure 3.18
Herring.com, *http://www.herring.com*

Amazon City Professional District

http://www.amazoncity.com/professional/index.html

Though Amazon City itself, the new kid on the women's Web block is a bit skimpy on the content, we found some useful stuff in the professional district, dedicated to women who want to advance their careers or search for new ones. The networking center is buzzing with activity, from job seekers to those offering their services, to women who just want to hook up with similar professionals. Check out: The Entrepreneur of the Month section. Go girl!!

Hospitality Net Virtual Job Exchange

http://www.hospitalitynet.nl/job

Ground Zero for anyone seeking opportunities in the hospitality industry (i.e., hotels and restaurants), Hospitality Net has positioned itself as an information and communication source for the industry, and the Job Exchange is a well-known part of it. Listings are fairly up to date, and represent a pretty broad spectrum of jobs within the industry.

Society for Human Resource Management

http://www.shrm.org/

The Society for Human Resource Management home page offers information about the group along with industry news and access to articles in the society's *HR Magazine*. Includes a Frequently Asked Questions (FAQ) file that provides legal information for human resources professionals.

Web-sters' Net-Work: Women in Info Technology

http://lucien.berkeley.edu/women_in_it.html

The Women in Information Technology site features links to bibliographies, directories, papers, organizations, career information, and a host of other resources concerning women in the fields of technology and computer science.

The Training.net

http://www.trainingnet.com

The Training.net, a Web resource for training, human resources (HR), and management development, features a trade directory, employment database, daily news service, chat area, events calendar, and more. The Training.net also features a database of information from solution providers in the areas of training, HR, and development.

SCORE home page

http://www.sbaonline.sba.gov/SCORE

The Service Corps of Retired Executives is a nonprofit association consisting of retired business professionals who volunteer their service as business consultants. These great folks put years of success and knowledge to work counseling and training small business owners and others free of charge. Here's where you can find out what they're all about, and how you can get in touch with them—there are chapters in nearly every state.

Having trouble finishing that cover letter? Check what the pros do, on the Writers Block Bulletin Board at Inkspot.

http://www.interlog.com/~ohi/ink/poll1results.html

Your scary boss will seem like a real pussycat when you check out some true boss horror stories in My Boss Is a.

http://www.myboss.com

Get your latest biz horoscope at Idea Cafe.

http://www.IdeaCafe.com:80/LB/lbstars.html

Try out some choices as a recent grad just entering the world of work. Play The Money Game at **http://www.myfuture.com/OUTPUT/score.htm**. Go for the high score!

WomenBiz

http://www.frsa.com/womenbiz

With a home page that crackles with three-deck headlines proclaiming victory for womankind (see Figure 3.19), who wouldn't be inspired by this resource exchange site for the woman business owner? Technology, money, networking, advice—they've got it covered. The Money Matters section was especially useful, offering timely articles on investing and taxes, with plenty of room for you to add your own two cents!

Cyberspace Field of Dreams

http://www.gridley.org/~imaging/links1.html

Gives the term "leveling the playing field" new meaning! This site is dedicated to helping women in business get past first base with resources, articles, advice, news, and freebies. Read "How to Network," then join the e-mail discussion group for support in achieving your dreams.

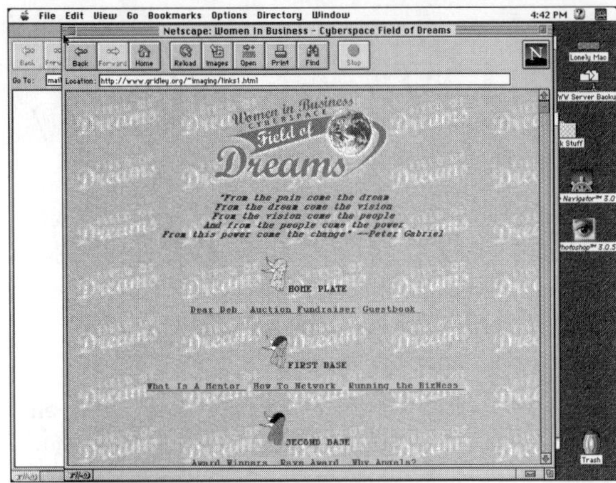

Figure 3.19
WomenBiz, *http://www.frsa.com/womenbiz*

☞ KEYWORDS

For more information on topics in this chapter, start your Web search with these keywords.

Careers and networking: professional groups, organizations, associations

Job search: resumes, employment resources, employment directories

Career issues: sexual harassment, discrimination, career development, mentors, role models

Chapter 4

Entertainment and Leisure

MUSEUMS

HUMANITIES

DANCE

THEATER

BOOKS

MOVIES

LISTINGS AND EVENTS

CELEBRITIES

TELEVISION

TRAVEL

HOBBIES

MAGS AND 'ZINES

DINING

MUSIC

COMICS AND CARTOONS

ASTROLOGY AND MYSTICISM

HUMOR

FUN AND GAMES

POP CULTURE

10 ENTERTAINING THINGS TO DO *RIGHT NOW*

1 See the movie trailers from the latest flicks before splurging for the ticket.

http://www.hollywood.com

2 Check in to "The Ultimate Band List" to find out who's playing in your town.

http://www.ubl.com

3 Look up cocktail recipes to serve the right potion at your next party. (Non-alcoholic libations also available.)

http://www.hotwired.com/cocktail

4 Check out what's on the tube tonight and chat about your favorite shows.

http://www.tvnet.com

5 Plan a trip to an art opening. The City of Women provides a list of times and dates of art festivals all over the world.

http://www.sigov.si/uzp/city

6 Research the best new restaurants in your area. Complete dining information—including reviews of old and new restaurants, with special categories for vegetarians and the kosher-conscious.

http://www.ird.net/diningout.html

7 Find out what you should read offline with these punchy reviews of the latest books and mags.

http://www.women.com/buzz/books.html

8 Get the most up-to-date info on your favorite soaps and their stars. The Soap Opera List has show-by-show listings, reviews, discussion groups, and more.

http://198.147.102.253/UTVL/soa_list.html

9 Learn a new game—one to play at a party, or to play with your family—at the Social Recreation Resources page (remember to type a space before "shaffer").

http://pacifier.com/ shaffer/games/games.html

10 Find out which Broadway, off-Broadway, and other theater productions are coming to your area on the Playbill Online page.

http://piano.symgrp.com/playbill

From Hollywood to the East Village, the Web is bringing the latest and greatest in entertainment to your desktop. And you don't have to stand in line for a ticket.

Film buffs can get the latest news on the stars and dish with other fans from around the world about the latest flicks. Collect pictures of your favorites, or check out online videos and film clips. If you love daytime dramas, don't miss cybersoaps and serials which are like online shows with all the intrigue of "Melrose Place." Many are interactive, so you can actually influence the plot.

The online music scene is also a buzzing, expanding area of the Web. You can listen to a few tracks before you buy the CD, or send a favorite tune to a friend. Bands reach ears they never would have before, and audiences can get a jump on great new sounds. Live concerts are even being broadcast over the Web.

Mags and 'zines have gone online in a big way, too. You can browse the latest issue of your favorite magazine or experience the eye candy and smart writing of cool new Webzines. A little surfing can dig up a gold mine of fiction, art, photography, and humor.

The Web is quickly becoming *the* place to go for entertainment. Expand your horizons, keep up on what's new, and share your favorites with fans around the world. Come check out the virtual attractions.

MUSEUMS

WebMuseum

http://sunsite.unc.edu/louvre

The WebMuseum is exactly what it sounds like—a virtual gallery full of paintings from around the world and throughout history (er, after 1280), including special exhibits like a recent one featuring post-Impressionist Paul Cezanne. It's more convenient than a real museum, allows you to take the pictures with you (by downloading them), and is open all year round.

A Docent's Tour of Salvador Dali Resources

http://www.empower.net/dali/dalimain.html

Fans of this revolutionary painter will find his paintings, biography, and information about surrealism and Dadaism at this site. There are few better places to find information on a single artist.

The Smithsonian Institute

http://www.si.edu/newstart.htm

Museum-lovers should pay a visit to this site which contains all the Smithsonian institutions, including the National Air and Space Museum, the Cooper-Hewitt National Design Museum, and the National Portrait Gallery. Not all the museums are content-rich, but one of the best places to go is the National Zoo, where users can view slide shows and Webcams of cute baby animals.

Art Crimes

http://www.graffiti.org/index.html

Some may think of graffiti as the work of hooligans maligning public spaces, but it is a growing art form that's becoming more and more accepted and widespread. Those who still aren't convinced should visit the online exhibitions at Art Crimes, and then try creating some graffiti of their own at the site's World Wide Wall.

Asian Arts

http://www.webart.com/asianart/splendors/index.html

Asian art history spans millenia and covers many different countries and even philosophies of life. This online journal (see Figure 4.1) from the Asian Art Museum in San Francisco presents the area's rich cultural heritage beautifully by featuring online exhibitions and photographs from different galleries, along with articles, a forum, and other useful information for those interested in non-Western creativity.

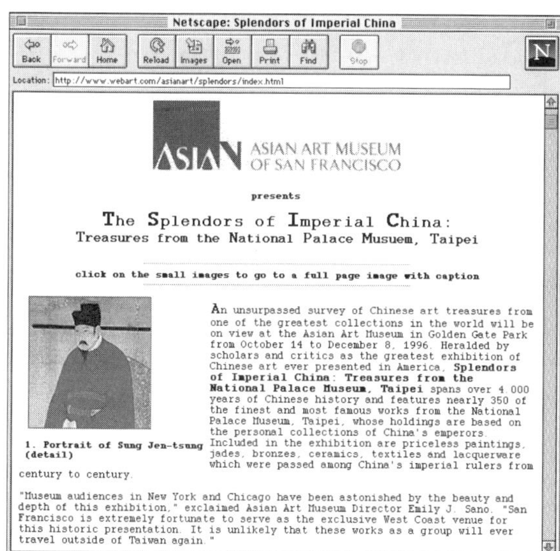

Figure 4.1
Asian Arts,
http://www.webart.com/asianart/splendors/index.html

the blue dot
http://www.razorfish.com/bluedot

the blue dot is an original online space for exhibits of all types: photography, art, experimental film, poetry—plus some fun treks and experiences as well. For instance, users can follow a hunt for gargoyles, take a sanity quiz, or view a collection of unauthorized postage stamps.

PhotArchipelago
http://www.webcom.com/cityg/resource/pa/Explorer.html

This is the gateway to photography exhibits and literature around the Web, organized like a sea-going exploration of a group of scattered islands. There's no better page to start browsing, since PhotArchipelago provides users with both a list of links and reviews of all the exhibits listed.

Natural History Museum of Los Angeles County
http://www.lam.mus.ca.us/lacmnh

Users can view exhibits at the museum or find out information about visiting, then start a tour of thousands of exhibits around the Web. The best thing at this site is the Guide to Museums and Cultural Resources, which has descriptions and links to just about every cultural center both in cyberspace and out.

HUMANITIES

alt.culture
http://www.altculture.com

This giant encyclopedia is a wonderful pop culture source for those who want to know the cultural significance of Birkenstocks or the meaning of the term "slash lit" (homosexual fantasies written by women about Kirk and Spock of *Star Trek*). Based on a book of the same name, this site is the A–Z of the 1990s, complete with a random function so users can find out the meanings of terms they didn't even know existed.

Bjorn's Guide to Philosophy
http://www.knuten.liu.se/~bjoch509

For anyone who's ever pondered about God, existence, natural laws, or the self, this is the site to visit. Mainly concentrated on Western philosophy, this is a page that actually holds a great deal of useful information (biographies, links, books, and papers) on about 30 important philosophers and their ideas.

Isis
http://www.netdiva.com/isisplus.html

The contributions of women of African descent have long been overlooked in society, but Isis actively seeks to remedy that. The site provides links to Internet sources about black female writers, artists, musicians, and others, along with places of interest to black women interested in culture and the arts.

Native Sources
http://indy4.fdl.cc.mn.us/~isk

This is a wonderful place for anyone interested in the sciences, arts, and cultures of Native American tribes—not just the totem poles or the feathered headdresses, but the history and knowledge of a proud and spiritual people. Users will find book reviews, educational resources, myths, comprehensive information on Native foods and astronomy, and much more.

Pantheon.org

http://www.pantheon.org

Located on these user-friendly pages are two incredibly extensive and highly useful encyclopedias, The Encyclopedia Mythica and The Encyclopedia Mystica. Visit here to find out about concepts and characters in Norse, Mayan, Chinese, and Etruscan mythologies; great mysteries like Atlantis and Stonehenge; and different kinds of religions—including voodoo and Shamanism.

Zuzu's Petals Literary Resource

http://www.lehigh.net/zuzu/zu-link.htm

Zuzu's Petals, named after Jimmy Stewart's daughter in *It's a Wonderful Life,* is a critically acclaimed journal that publishes essays, poetry, fiction, and reviews. Its online companion aims to present the best resources for creative people on the Internet (see Figure 4.2). You can access issues of the print journal here and discover places to foster your creativity.

Figure 4.2

Zuzu's Petals Literary Resource, *http://www.lehigh.net/zuzu/zu-link.htm*

China the Beautiful

http://www.chinapage.com/china.html

This is a place dedicated to the arts, literature, poetry, history, and culture of a vast and ancient country. Users can learn about the art of seal carving, the significance of dragons, Chinese calligraphy, or sayings from Chinese scholars such as Confucius, Mencius, or Chuang Tze. It's a great site to browse and learn from.

INTERNATIONAL APPEAL

Diotima

http://www.uky.edu/ArtsSciences/Classics/gender.html

Named after the woman who reportedly taught Socrates about love, Diotima is the Internet resource for women in antiquity. If you are interested in the representation of women in Greek culture, the Bible, or other ancient cultures, you will find this a useful resource. Much of the site consists of lists of where to find scholarship on such women on the Web, but original materials can also be found.

The English Server

http://english-server.hss.cmu.edu

This site at Carnegie Mellon University has been publishing humanities texts for years and currently includes thousands of them on varied topics from poetry and software to race and recipes. Some are links, but much of the information is contained at the server—and all of it is worthy of perusal.

DANCE

Henry Neeman's Dance Hotlist

http://zeus.ncsa.uiuc.edu:8080/~hneeman/dance_hotlist.html

No graphics or real content here, just a long, long resource list with more than 500 dancing links—er, links to sites about dancing—that will take the curious to Web sites covering every conceivable form of participatory dance from the flamenco and country line dancing to Victorian and Cajun/Zydeco.

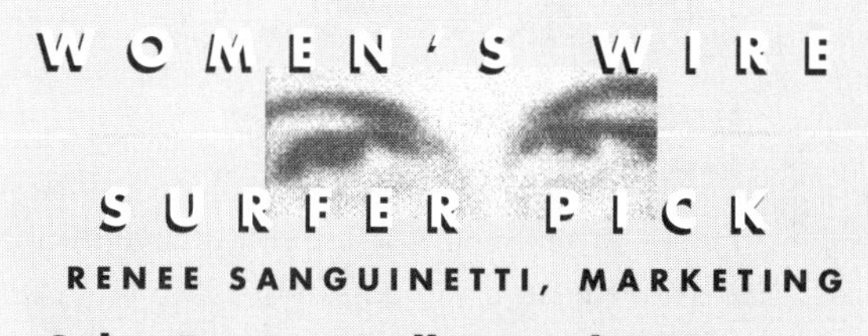

RENEE SANGUINETTI, MARKETING

CyberDance: Ballet on the Net

http://www.thepoint.net/~raw/dance.htm

This list of over 2,000 links to different ballet and modern dance sites includes companies, organizations, news and information, 'zines, newsgroups, dance education, people, and chats—it's all here. Cyberdance is a great place for those just beginning a dance adventure on the Web, but the sheer amount of information can seem a bit intimidating at first.

Middle Eastern Dance Reference Guide

http://www.lpl.arizona.edu/~kimberly/medance/medance.html

This type of dance, perhaps more commonly known as belly dancing, is featured at an attractive site that includes information on names, costuming, music, a dancer's directory, and where to find belly dancing in the mainstream media (including episodes of *The Simpsons*). This guide is mainly aimed at dancers, but is interesting for others, too.

DanceScape

http://wchat.on.ca/dance/pages/dscape1.htm

This may not be the kind of ballroom dancing older members of society are used to—but the Web site that covers it is a great resource for competitive ballroom dancers everywhere. With news on events, publications, organizations, places to dance, and links to images, plus a personals section for those in need, this site is proof that the music can't be stopped.

Dance Online

http://www.danceonline.com

This is what every dance magazine should be like: elegant, fluid, graceful (see Figure 4.3). With features, interviews,

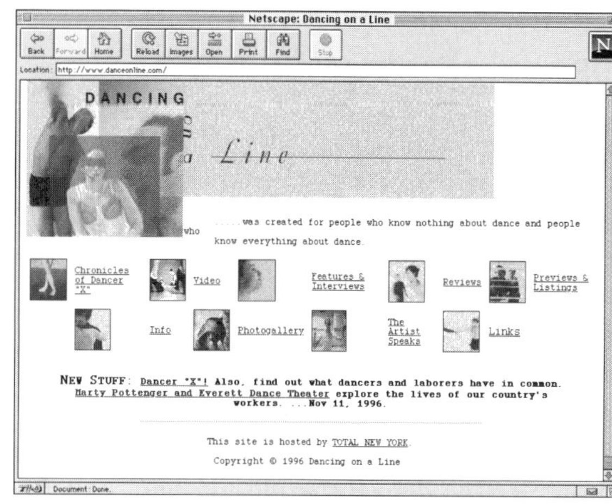

Figure 4.3

Dance Online, *http://www.danceonline.com*

videos, and listings for the dance world, it's a treasure. A section called The Artist Speaks allows dancers to discuss their ideas and works, and The Chronicles of Dancer X is a continuing story.

THEATER

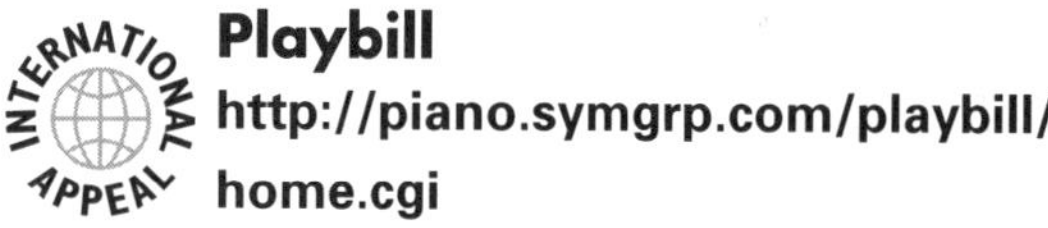

Playbill

http://piano.symgrp.com/playbill/home.cgi

Theater lovers will be thrilled with the Playbill Web site. It provides excellent content about theatrical and musical productions around the world, including features and complete listings.

Aisle Say

http://www.escape.com/~theanet/AisleSay.html

This weekly updated theater e-zine has a fresh, professional voice. The reviewers know what they're talking about, and they'll give theater lovers extensive, critical reviews of plays around the globe. The site consists mostly of reviews, although some special features and other sections can be found.

Theatre Central (International)

http://www.theatre-central.com

Although as of press time this site hadn't yet added some of its listings, what it already had available was very impressive. Theater resources from around the country have found a place here, including links to Web resources and professionals. Theater Central also has a journal section that spotlights different theater scenes, shows, and reviews.

Jogle's Favorite Theatre Related Resources

http://pscinfo.psc.edu/~geigel/menus/Theatre.html

Okay, okay, it's a list of links to other Web sites. But even so, this site does stand out because there are so many theater links on the Web and not nearly as many good ways to find them. From stagecraft to ticket sales to college and children's groups, Jogle's has got a link to it.

INTERNATIONAL APPEAL

Kabuki for Everyone

http://www.fix.co.jp/kabuki/kabuki.html

Websurfers who would like to understand this traditional form of Japanese theater should visit here. They'll learn that kabuki was created by a shrine maiden and then taken over by men in drag, called "onnagata." They'll watch an onnagata transform himself into a female character, discover the instruments used in kabuki, and find out about new performances.

The Really Useful Company Presents...

http://www.reallyuseful.com

Even those who don't believe Andrew Lloyd Webber is a musical genius will enjoy this site, which features all of his shows complete with graphics and sound. Current news on productions, where they're playing, and samples of the music are available—the site will have users involuntarily humming "Memory" from *Cats* or *Sunset Boulevard*'s "With One Look."

BOOKS

100 BEST SITES

Book Wire

http://www.bookwire.com

Bookworms will find a fine resource in Book Wire, a site that lists literary events, best-seller lists and thousands of links to publishers, booksellers, and libraries. This is definitely a good place to start your Internet exploration of literature and foster a love of the written word.

Book Stacks Unlimited, Inc.

http://www.books.com/scripts/news.exe

This is a virtual bookstore with a cafe for conferences and author interviews, a spoken word section, the latest news in the literary world, exhibits, and a daily poem. It's a great place to find out about recently published books. Kudos to the editors for maintaining the Author's Pen, a list of over 550 writers, both classic and popular, from Albert Camus to Douglas Adams.

100 BEST SITES

Amazon Books

http://www.amazon.com

There's nothing in the world like browsing through a well-stocked bookstore, but Amazon Books is the next best thing (see Figure 4.4). Here, users can search for over a million titles, read interviews with authors, check out reviews, view best-seller lists, buy books, or just find out about the Book of the Day.

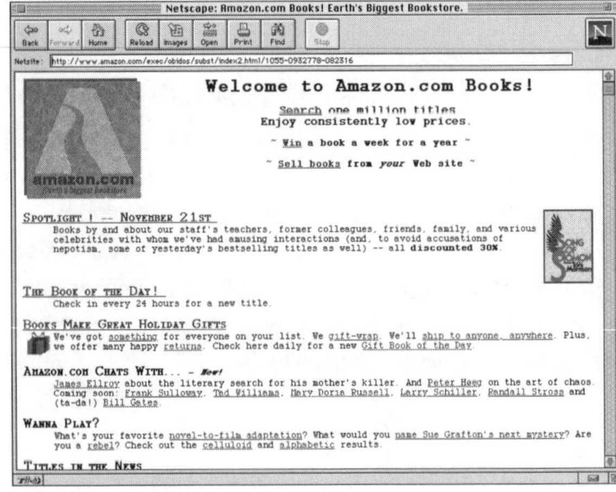

Figure 4.4

Amazon Books, *http://www.amazon.com*

Objectivism (and Ayn Rand) Web Service

http://www.vix.com/pub/objectivism

This site is dedicated to writer Ayn Rand and the philosophy of objectivism—a view of rationality and intellectual independence. Users will find writings, including poetry and movie reviews, all from an objectivist perspective. Anyone who found something to agree with in Rand's novels should find this useful.

Dorothy Parker Page

http://www.users.interport.net/~eppie/parker/parker.html

When Dorothy Parker started writing in the 1920s, her witty prose was considered cynical, slightly licentious, and unwomanly. This site, which isn't very graphically sophisticated, has three books' worth of Parker's writings available for readers to discover for themselves.

Jane Austen Information Page

http://uts.cc.utexas.edu/~churchh/janeinfo.html

It's easy to get lost in a book, and it's also easy to get lost at this Web site for Jane Austen—but in both cases, this is a good thing. Here, readers will find full texts of many of Austen's novels, along with biographical information. For those into literary humor, there are even a few top 10 lists.

Zora Neale Hurston Home Page

http://pages.prodigy.com/zora

This tribute to one of the Harlem Renaissance's respected authors includes interesting photographs, essays, bibliographies, and a few excerpts from her stories. There are also details of the Webmaster's visit to Hurston's gravesite, an account of her induction into the Women's Hall of Fame, and a chronology of her life.

19th Century American Women Writers Web

http://www.clever.net/19cwww

This library focuses on women like Harriet Beecher Stowe and Rebecca Harding Davis, with some biographical information as well as electronic texts, RealAudio lectures, and a message board. The site is graphics-heavy and a bit sparse, but has great potential to be a valuable service for anyone interested in women who were both writing and being written about in 19th Century literature.

Project Bartleby

http://www.cc.columbia.edu/acis/bartleby

Bartleby Library at Columbia University makes available accurate, extensive texts of some major works of poetry, all of which are either in the public domain or under Columbia license. For instance, interested surfers can find over 100 poems by Emily Dickinson, along with the entire contents of *Bartlett's Familiar Quotations*. The site is constantly growing, too.

[OVERHEARD ON WOMEN'S WIRE]

http://chat.women.com

"I believe that most readers, and buyers, of fiction, are women. I think my books are mostly ABOUT women, but I don't think of them as exclusively FOR women. We women have been learning what it's like to be a man for our whole lives, through our reading. Seems like men would want to cop the same advantage, no?"

—Novelist, Barbara Kingsolver, in a live chat on Women's Wire.

The Complete Works of William Shakespeare

http://the-tech.mit.edu/Shakespeare/works.html

This is the place to find all of the Bard's writings on the Web, with full texts. What makes reading Shakespeare through the Internet more interesting than in print is that one can participate in discussions, search the text, or click on hyperlinks that lead from those more difficult words to a glossary.

Ton Cremers and Marian Beereboom's Book Information Web site

http://www.xs4all.nl/~cremers

Bibliophiles will enjoy roaming this site, which features hundreds of links to sites on the Web devoted to topics like printing presses, rare books, and the art of making books and paper. The maintainers of the site do not include sites for new books, so if one is looking for modern fiction this isn't the place to go.

Literary Kicks

http://www.charm.net/~brooklyn/LitKicks.html

Many young people of the 1950s weren't fooled by the era's complacency and patriotic optimism—they were rebels and hipsters, and their influence on American culture can't be denied. This site is a tribute to them, containing many pages of information about individuals like Allen Ginsberg and Jack Kerouac, their contributions to creativity, Beat events, and much more.

MOVIES

The Internet Movie Database

http://us.imdb.com

If the Internet Movie Database doesn't have it, it's probably not worth knowing. This fan-based site (see Figure 4.5) contains extensive information on films and television shows plus their casts and crews, including filmographies for anyone who's ever been involved with a movie. This is truly one of the most useful entertainment sites to ever exist on the Web.

[OVERHEARD ON WOMEN'S WIRE]

http://chat.women.com

"I was stunned because I had no idea the book was nominated. I think I probably thought (the Pulitzer) had been awarded already. I woke up the next day and thought that it must have been a mistake."

ON HER WRITING CAREER:

"I married quite young and had five children. So, for maybe 12

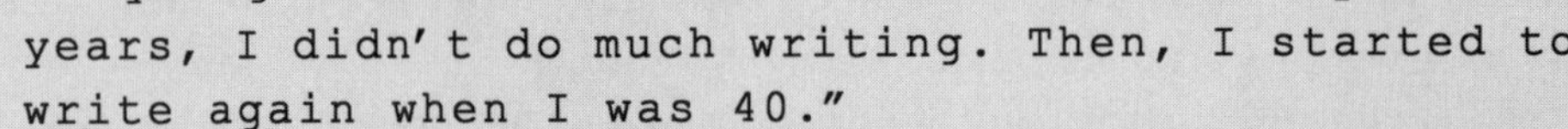

years, I didn't do much writing. Then, I started to write again when I was 40."

—Carol Shields, author and guest on Women's Wire on winning the Pulitzer Prize for fiction for *The Stone Diaries*.

Figure 4.5

The Internet Movie Database, *http://us.imdb.com*

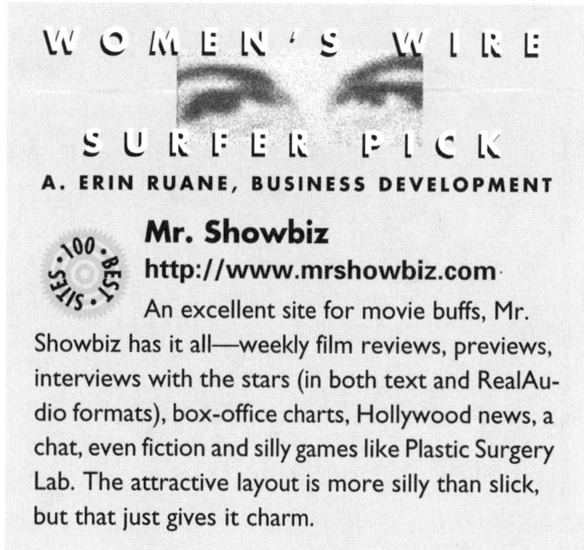

A. ERIN RUANE, BUSINESS DEVELOPMENT

Mr. Showbiz

http://www.mrshowbiz.com

An excellent site for movie buffs, Mr. Showbiz has it all—weekly film reviews, previews, interviews with the stars (in both text and RealAudio formats), box-office charts, Hollywood news, a chat, even fiction and silly games like Plastic Surgery Lab. The attractive layout is more silly than slick, but that just gives it charm.

cludes interesting features and hourly updated news from *Variety/Reuters,* along with all the usual trappings of movie magazines.

FilmZone

http://www.filmzone.com

Those who'd rather see *Welcome to the Dollhouse* than the next Arnold Schwarzenegger action extravaganza might want to visit these pages, at which foreign and independent films receive higher billing than their Hollywood counterparts. There are few places better to get information on films of all kinds—besides, the predict-o-scripts are hilarious.

Film.com

http://www.film.com

This glossy movie site doesn't just feature the usual—reviews, news, release dates, features—it also offers television listings for movies and a section called Cinecism, where editors get to go at the industry in a cutting and funny way. Also check out the useful Film Festivals listing here.

The Biz

http://pathfinder.com/bizmag

There are so many entertainment sites on the Web, it's hard to know which ones are worth the time to surf. The Biz, however, stands out because of its content, which in-

Hollywood Online

http://www.hollywood.com

Slick, glossy movie sites are not exactly scarce on the Web, but Hollywood Online is one of the better ones. It uses the online medium to spotlight movies and in an exhaustive way, including reviews, trailers, sound bites, and synopses. Television is also covered, but less comprehensively.

Secrets and Whispers: Daughters of the Dust home page

http://www.pacificnet.net/geechee/Daughter1.html

This page pays tribute to a film, *Daughters of the Dust,* which lovingly portrays the spirit of women of color in a Gullah community on the Sea Islands of the South. As a result, it's not just a Web site about one film, but an entire (usually overlooked) diaspora. And it's a celebration of black women filmmakers as well.

Girls on Film

http://www.girlsonfilm.com

This site features fresh and funny takes on recent films from four New York City girls (see Figure 4.6). Lise,

Figure 4.6
Girls on Film, *http://www.girlsonfilm.com*

Sibyl, Andrea, and Clare write features and reviews and foster discussion on topics such as rape scenes in movies. They do a great job of maintaining a Web site that isn't just a movie review site with attitude, it's a whole new perspective.

LISTINGS AND EVENTS

MovieLink and Moviefone
http://web4.movielink.com

The only thing missing from this site is the familiar Moviefone announcer's voice: "If you know the name of the movie you'd like to see, please press 1." Like the national phone service, the Web site provides users with local showtimes and tickets, but it also includes previews, posters, trailers, a chat, and new release dates. For truly useful film information, MovieLink can't be beat.

The Film Festivals Server
http://www.filmfestivals.com

Whether it's the Cannes Film Festival, the Flanders International Film Festival in Ghent, or the 20th Montreal World Film Festival, the Film Festivals server has information on it. This site contains complete news from every film festival around the world, including awards, interviews, daily coverage, and guides to cities and different events.

CELEBRITIES

People Magazine Online
http://www.people.com

A slick online version of one of America's favorite fluff magazines, plus cool stuff added on for Internet junkies. For news on celebrities, gossip, and best-dressed lists, no other publication compares. The only possible beef is that the site, for whatever reason, doesn't use as many pictures as the magazine does.

Faces
http://www.web-usa.com/faces

This isn't so much a celebrity site as it is a game, but it's still fascinating. You will learn, for instance, that combining Ronald Reagan's head with George Clooney's eyes and Bill Clinton's nose and chin produces a creature that looks much like Elvis Presley. It must be seen to believed. Weird, but very cool.

RuPaul's House of Love
http://www.teleport.com/~rupaul

She's beautiful, she's witty, she's famous, she's...a man. Full of RuPaul's attitude and spunk, this site tells all about everyone's favorite transvestite and you can even send him letters soliciting advice. This is the definitive source for all things RuPaul, complete with images, sound, and, of course, info on how to buy RuPaul merchandise.

Supermodel.com

http://www.supermodel.com

Unlike many other supermodel sites on the Web, this one isn't just geared to the drooling boys online. Pictures of the biggest names in modeling and rising stars exist here, along with often updated news, fashion features, chats with talent scouts, interviews, and a featured model of the month.

Internet Crime Archives

http://mayhem.net/Crime

Celebrities aren't always movie stars, and this site is dedicated to a different kind of famous person—infamous, really. Cannibals, serial killers, the Jeffrey Dahmers and David Koreshes of the world are all here at the Internet Crime Archives. You will get the shivers from all the fascinating—and frightening—information here.

TELEVISION

The Ultimate Television List

http://tvnet.com

For many TV watchers, the Ultimate Television List is a utopia: a huge site containing links to every American TV show from the *A-Team* to the *X-Files,* news, TV listings, and ways to contact TV stations around the world.

Soap Links

http://members.aol.com/soaplinks/index.html

With a name like Soap Links, this site could only be dedicated to everyone's closet obsession, soap operas. Of course, many soap fans work during the day, which is where Web-based soap sites come in. For information and updates on all the daytime soaps, a few nighttime soaps, and non-U.S. dramas as well, this is a good starting point.

The Cybersoap Uberlist

If daytime TV doesn't fit into your schedule or you can't get the 24-hour sci-fi channel, never fear! The Web has plenty of its own steamy soaps, twisted mysteries, and chilling thrillers.

20something Hipsters Hanging Out in a Cool Place

101 Hollywood Blvd.
http://home.navisoft.com/brewpubclub/101.htm
Young, funky filmmakers frolic in LA (isn't that what they always do?). This site is great for those who are crazy about the movie biz or brewpubs—for some reason, both figure prominently.

The East Village
http://www.eastvillage.com
Enter the last bastion of Bohemia through the trials and tribulations of 20something Manhattan hipsters living the life.

Geek Cereal
http://www.geekcereal.com
Lose yourself in someone else's drama through these short glimpses of San Francisco life. Sometimes truth is duller than fiction.

MelrosEast
http://www.inx.net/~mvo/MelrosEast.html
Get past the unimaginative name, and find a funky, funny, well-written cybersoap about young hipsters in NYC that's a bit more—well—personal, with the characters' journal entries as narrative.

The Spot
http://www.thespot.com
Sexy babes of both genders living in a Hollywood beach house tell their tales of tangled affairs, failed careers, deceit, and treachery.

Gay 20something Hipsters Hanging Out in a Cool Place

770 Oceanwalk
http://www.newyorkmetro.com/ocean.html
You, too, could become a character at the Fire Island timeshare that houses this gay-themed drama. Send your comments, and get your beach clothes ready!

Dyke Street: A Soap
http://www.demon.co.uk/world/ukgay/ukg000f.html
Dyke drama meets the cyberworld.

Gay Daze
http://www.gaydaze.com
We're here, we're queer, and we're fa-ha-habulous! See the saga of a doctor, a dancer, a lover, a loser, a father, and a "natural" woman unfold in gay LA.

Java Jabber
http://www.buffalopride.com/jabber/jabber.html
Follow the drama of three gay guys and one straight girl living in a house in the suburbs with only one bathroom.

As the Office Turns

475 Madison Avenue
http://475Madison.msn.com
Word on the Ave. has it that the goings-on at this supposedly fictional Manhattan ad agency are on-target enough to have some *real* Madison Avenue players squirming and others snickering in amusement.

Cretins, Inc.
http://www.nembley.com
Giggle fiendishly as you find your way around the stunningly incompetent corporate headquarters of BilgeCorp.

Journal of a Short-Timer
http://www.ccnet.com/~kharb/jst/journalwelcome.html
Read the weekly journal of a disillusioned teacher in a hard-knock high school.

So@pNet
http://www.soapnet.com
Real events allegedly influence the dramas that unfold at a fictional software company.

Sci-fi/Cyberthriller

Above the Unicorn
http://www.chiweb.com/entertainment/unicorn
Be part of a group that's genetically creating superhumans to replace corporate employees.

Brentwood
http://www.hallucinet.com/brentwood
This Real Audio techno-murder mystery generously includes a script-like text version. (That way, your boss won't know you're catching up on the action at work!)

Generation War
http://www.webmovie.com/ffwd/genwar.htm
This cyberpunk sci-fi drama set in the very scary future, filled with live actors, digital sets, and special effects has been called the first made-on-a-PC movie.

The Lurker Files
http://www.yahooligans.com/content/rh
The Lurker controls the minds of college students in an online chat room. Beware!

Media Secrets
http://www.bluepearl.com/ms
A male/female team of reporters uses hackers to get info to create breaking headlines.

Root
http://www.libertynet.org/~openeye/root/html/root1-p1.html
An artificial life form who's been around for four millennia plays at games of chance as multimedia pushes his sci-fi adventures.

Techno3
http://www.bluepearl.com/entertainment/soap/techno3text.html
Could this techno-thriller featuring three hot babes and the evil cyberlord who controls them be the *Charlie's Angels* of tomorrow?

Traditional Mystery/Detective Drama

Cracks in the Web
http://www.directnet.com/~gmorris/title.html
Follow Flap Jack through this well-written, detail-driven, weekly spy thriller.

The Heart Hotel
http://www.itp.tsoa.nyu.edu/~student/yorbClass/Web/hotel
Enter different rooms of the VRML whodunit hotel.

Kapow
http://www.kapow.com
Snoop around the Web and greater LA solving nutty mysteries with bumbling super sleuth Mace Broade and his sidekicks.

Letters from Abroad
http://www.actual-reality.co.uk/abroad/abroad.htm
Online crime-solvers get a shot at a London vacation.

Scrolling Mystery Theater
http://www.fiction.com
Creative use of frames showcases detective fiction and thrillers.

Strange Case of the Lost Elvis Diaries, The
http://home.mem.net/~welk/elvisdiaries.html
Get your online comic mystery with overtones of *The Maltese Falcon.*

Traditional Soap Opera

Affairs of the Net
http://www.chiweb.com/entertainment/affairs
Intercept the e-mail messages of a couple in love.

ALT.DAYS
http://www.io.com/~jlc/alt_days
The storylines of the online, alternate version of *Days of Our Lives,* have nothing to do with the TV drama, though some of the characters are the same.

As the Web Turns
http://www.metzger.com/soap/index.html
Get your online dose of an old-fashioned style soap.

Chiphead Harry Daily Soap
http://exp1.mobius.net/baudeville/html/Chiphead.html
The bizarre murder (or maybe not) of cybermillionaire Chiphead Harry grips techno-town.

Crescendo Cove
http://www.kw.igs.net/CrescendoCove
Enter the Lois-Lane-and-Clark-Kent-like saga of Bolt Fastener magnate Steel Bolt and the women who love him. This larger-than-life story is a fresh breath among the 20something neighbor and cyberspy clones.

Ferndale
http://www.ferndale.com
Four people open their lives to the public as they share their problems over the Internet.

FollyWorld
http://members.aol.com/follyworld/index.html
Follow the characters of *Guiding Light* as they romp through alternative storylines.

Moms' Night Out
http://www.nocalshopper.com/mom.html
Three best friends in northern California live their "Only In Marin" lives.

O'Brien's Cafe
http://dowling.tcimet.net
Rumors fly about the staff and regulars at O'Brien's Cafe, as the cat in the corner bums a cigarette.

Oakdale 2
http://members.aol.com/oakdaletwo/index.html
See the characters of *As the World Turns* in situations you won't find on TV.

The Southerners
http://www.ex.ac.uk/~jpgoss/southerners
Follow the lives of downmarket urban Londoners around their favorite hangouts.

St. Cyberburg
http://www.stcyberburg.com
A virtual city is the setting for this interactive cyberdrama.

Stepstones
http://www.stepstones.com
Take an intriguing, intimate look at the lives of the Stepstones Family of Long Island, NY, and their friends.

Something Different

Diary of a Madwoman in the Attic
http://www.chiweb.com/entertainment/madwoman
Read the diary entries of a woman delving into her own mind.

Food Tales
http://www.bpe.com/fun/fiction/index.html
At last, something different! It's a creative interactive drama that features a different recipe in each chapter, Wine Valley Radio, and dozens of tasty food links.

GrapeJam
http://www.grapejam.com
Join the Grapes, an interactive comedy troupe, as they unfurl their Southern California yarn.

The Loser Living Upstairs
http://www.calpoly.edu/~ttokuuke/loser.html
Get bizarre updates on the guy in the upstairs apartment.

Maintenance Men's Lounge
http://www.thunk.com/thunktv.htm
You might not be able to follow the story, but you'll have fun trying to sort through this chaotic sitcom environment with its grainy, stammering streaming video, and mumbled audio.

Mudders
http://newyorkmetro.com/mudders.html
A transplanted New Yorker/single mom finds herself in the southern world of Monster Trucks.

Rhino Beach
http://www.e-cafe.com/rhinobeach
In this *Animal Farm*-esque serial, the characters—all members of the animal kingdom—romp around the Rhino Beach Club in a tropical island setting

The Squat

http://www.thesquat.com

Sick of the slick sophisticates inhabiting the Spot? Sneak a peak at the squalid squatmates in this trailer park parody.

Shakespeare's Diary

http://home.navisoft.com/brewpubclub/first.htm

Visit the Renaissance Faire that never ends.

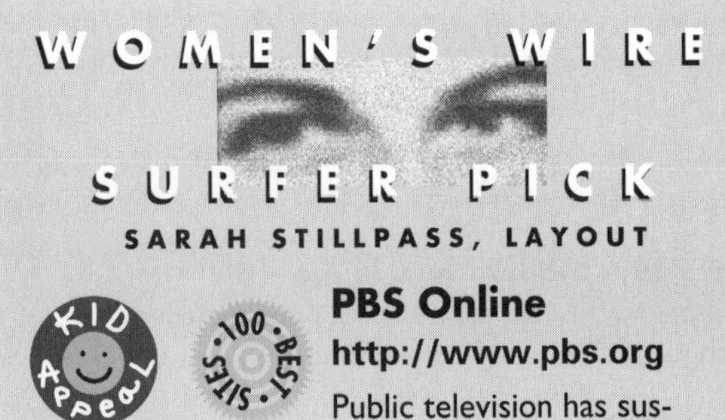

PBS Online

http://www.pbs.org

Public television has sustained some direct attacks from parts of the government in recent years, but that hasn't stopped it from putting out an excellent Web site (see Figure 4.7). PBS Online covers all the quality shows that have made it a valuable part of today's culture in a comprehensive way, from *Mr. Roger's Neighborhood* to daily news summaries on Newshour.

Figure 4.7

PBS Online, *http://www.pbs.org*

Discovery Channel Online

http://www.discovery.com

Surfers can immerse themselves for hours at the Discovery Channel's official site. Sure, it has TV listings and a place to buy CD-ROMs, but this site is so much more than that. You can watch Keiko the whale through the whimsical Keiko Cam, travel to the outback, or find out about the origin of the bikini through the many interesting articles found here.

Lifetime Online

http://www.lifetimetv.com

The cable channel for women has a Web site that not only gives TV viewers a program guide, but includes video and audio on Lifetime specials about remarkable women (see Figure 4.8). It has sections on parenting, relationships, recipes, and sports and fitness—this section includes some fascinating features about female athletes, like the women of the Colorado Silver Bullets professional baseball team.

The Sci-Fi Channel: The Dominion

http://www.scifi.com

The Dominion is a place for fans of science fiction to find out what the Sci-Fi Channel has in store this month, but it is much more than that. They can buy merchandise from different science fiction shows, chat, download free stuff, or find out about the channel's original programming. The Orbit section offers links out to other science fiction sites.

NBC Online

http://www.nbc.com

This site excels because it offers so much to the viewers of shows like *Mad About You, Seinfeld, Days of Our Lives,* and all the other NBC hits. You can find bios, news, and info on how to get tickets to filmings. Other features include the history of the network's peacock logo, RealAudio greetings from stars, and frequent chats with actors and actresses of NBC programs.

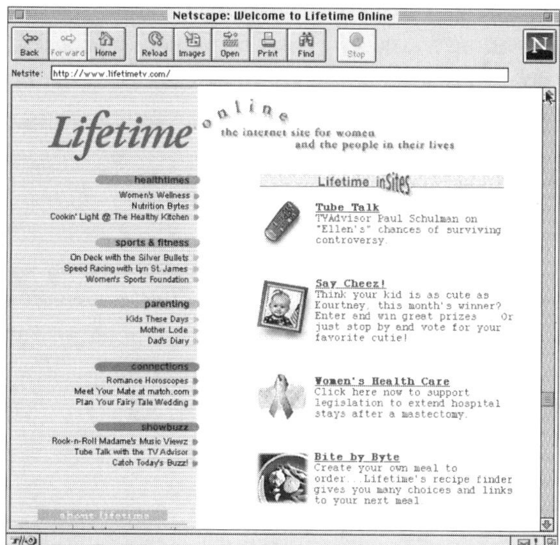

Figure 4.8

Lifetime Online, *http://www.lifetimetv.com*

MTV Online

http://www.mtv.com

The music television channel that revolutionized the music industry is online with a Web site. Naturally, it features the programs and personalities that make MTV popular, including *The Real World* and *120 Minutes,* and of course *Beavis and Butt-head.*

The Women of Star Trek

http://www.helsinki.fi/~mmtmakel/Women_of_ST.html

When Nichelle Nichols appeared on *Star Trek* in 1966, she became the first black woman regular on a television series. Since then, *Star Trek* has featured some outstanding female characters in high positions, including *Star Trek: Voyager's* Captain Kathryn Janeway. All of the show's regular female characters are listed at this site, complete with quotes, short bios, and links.

TV Tonight

http://www.tvtonight.com

This site for TV listings is less impersonal than many, with highlights and opinion delivered in a witty and sardonic manner that makes it much more fun to read than other guides of its kind. It's also easy to read and maneuver, without too much extra clutter.

TV Guide Online

http://www.iguide.com

Just like the popular print version, TV Guide Online provides television listings for every region in the U.S. This flashy Web site is a little bit cluttered and visitors may feel a little shell-shocked at first, but it does exactly what it's supposed to: tell the nation what's on the tube this week.

TRAVEL

Travlang

http://www.travlang.com

This site is fun even for those who aren't going anywhere. With the use of sound files, Travlang endeavors to teach potential tourists words in different languages. Travelers can come, pick the language of choice, then learn simple words and phrases that every international citizen should know. There are other resources, too, such as weather, train info, a currency converter, and European road rules.

Travelocity

http://www.travelocity.com

Vacationers planning a dream trip or a visit to a relative's house will be well served by Travelocity (see Figure 4.9). The site provides flight timetables, information on worldwide attractions, and a useful "Map It" feature to give you the fastest route from one place to another.

Pathfinder Travel

http://pathfinder.com/Travel

At yet another Pathfinder location (an umbrella site worth surfing for just about everything), users can access information for every step of the way: from deciding where to go, to booking flights, and planning vacation activities. Many tools exist for the traveler, including maps, advice, and a section on learning languages.

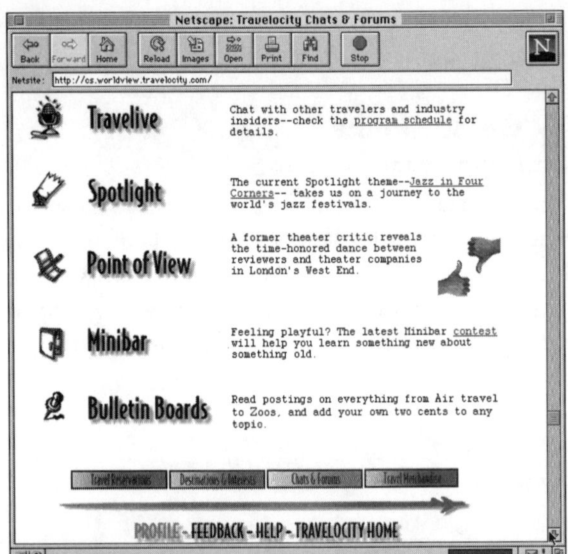

Figure 4.9
Travelocity, *http://www.travelocity.com*

Preview Travel
http://www.vacations.com

The overworked and underpaid in desperate need of a dream vacation should visit Preview Travel, a site that features details on many kinds of pleasure trips all over the world. It includes a Find-A-Trip feature and contests, including one in which travelers write their sob stories, users view them, and then vote on the one who most deserves a vacation.

The Internet Guide to Hostelling
http://www.hostels.com

This site is a cornucopia of information on these low-cost, communal accommodations for weary backpackers, with a worldwide hostel guide that is a great resource for money-challenged travelers. Not only can surfers find the guide here, they can also seek out tips on traveling for less and post to a virtual bulletin board.

MapQuest
http://www.mapquest.com

Web surfers who want a better idea of where to go, how to get there, and what to do once they arrive should use this Web site, which contains an interactive atlas. Using TripQuest, you can input starting points and destinations and receive clear instructions on how to get there—even including which routes are toll roads. MapQuest requires a quick, free registration.

The National Park Service
http://www.nps.gov

The country's national parks are wonderful places to experience nature. And thanks to this guide, travelers have a comprehensive source of information about them all at the click of a mouse. Information on sights, prices, climate, campgrounds, even recent press releases, are provided for intrepid explorers.

Rec.Travel Library
http://WWW.Solutions.Net/rec-travel

This extensive database is one of the best ways on the Net to get information on destinations around the world—from Taipei, Taiwan to Frankfurt, Germany. Other resources here include info on transportation, hobbies, and travel tips. Even those who just want to look up their home states will probably discover something new.

Time Out Net
http://www.timeout.co.uk

Full of weekly events and tourist guides for those traveling to Rome, Amsterdam, Barcelona, Paris, Berlin, and other exciting cities, Time Out Net offers worldwide travelers a way to plan their trips without too much hassle. For those who aren't going anywhere, it provides fodder for ultimate vacation daydreams (sigh).

Lonely Planet
http://www.lonelyplanet.com

Travelers who have more adventurous souls, who'd maybe like to avoid tourist traps and go somewhere more original should pay a visit to Lonely Planet. Users can find out all the pertinent facts about destinations like Arugam Bay, Sri Lanka, view slides and first-hand accounts, and get travel tips on such topics as border crossings between Western Australia and the Northern Territory.

SPOTLIGHT ON TRAVEL

On the Web, you can visit Denmark, Disneyland, and Mt. Denali all from your desk. And when you want to close down your laptop and hit the road for real, the Web can be a big help. Information online makes travel planning a much more immediate task. No more yellowing brochures and out-of-date schedules. The Internet houses a wealth of information for the traveller, from locales sojourners have enjoyed to places where caution is called for, as well as healthy travelling tips and best values around the world.

Five Sites Worth Traveling To

1 Now you can make airline reservations and other travel arrangements online. Also before you go, check the travel forecasts for reports on airport delays at this comprehensive, full-service travel site.
http://www.travelocity.com

2 Whether you're a stressed-out executive or stressed-out mother, you can find a vacation package suited to your needs.
http://www.wildwomanadv.com

3 Lonely Planet's clickable world map helps you learn all about off-beat travel destinations around the world. You'll find facts, information about the climate and local transportation, as well as lists of attractions and event—even a slide show.
http://www.lonelyplanet.com

4 Learn a few choice phrases, find out the meaning of symbols on foreign street signs, and pick up a few tips about healthy flying on Virtuocity's Travel Tips Page.
http://www.virtuocity.com/travel/tips

5 Link up to the lowest prices on airline tickets, hotels, cruises, and find budget travel agencies and companies on Discount Tickets.
http://www.etn.nl/dttickets

HOBBIES

Gardening Web Directory

http://www.btw.com/urls/toc.html

From Books That Work, this page includes many links to different gardening sites, with information on insects, landscaping, and other topics of interest. A link to Garden.com, also maintained by BTW, provides visitors not only with links to hundreds of different places, but short and useful starred reviews of gardening-related sites from all over cyberspace.

Astronomy and Space on the Internet

http://www.nuance.com/~cwbol/astro.html

This site is a great resource for people who are able to instantly understand proper nouns like these: Schmidt-Cassagrain, Palomar, Hubble, Shoemaker-Levy, and Messier. The sky's the limit with this page, which has links to some of the best star-struck sites on the Web. It's the perfect place for amateur stargazers to spend those cloudy evenings.

Inkspot
http://www.inkspot.com/~ohi/inkspot/home.html

Budding writers should use these pages, which contain lists of resources for writers in every genre, including children's literature and non-fiction. There's a list of classified ads for authors seeking publication, along with feature articles that focus on editing, writing, and getting published. A writer's forum allows people to network and solicit ideas and discussion.

The Elements of Style
http://www.columbia.edu/acis/bartleby/strunk

Strunk and White's book is a fountain of useful information on English grammar and usage—many journalists and writers would never be caught dead without it. Now it is available online, and there are no better resources of its kind on the Web. Those with Web access have no more good excuses for badly written stories and essays.

Harmony Central
http://www.harmony-central.com

This is a great list of resources for musicians, whether they want to learn guitar or find out what kind of synthesizer to buy. For those who have bands, there is information on how to copyright band names and get gigs. It's an all-around useful site, with links to sites of interest to music lovers of all kinds.

Wonderful Stitches
http://www.needlework.com

Decorative needlework enthusiasts with Web access should point their browsers to Wonderful Stitches, a well-organized site featuring cybersamplers of patterns and designs and decorative stitches to use (see Figure 4.10). The list of links to other resources on crafts is likely one of the best on its topic in cyberspace, including exhibitions of textiles from around the world.

The Dast Library of Photography
http://www.goodnet.com/~tibbits

This Macintosh-friendly site was created as a dedicated information service for photographers. This means it doesn't just include a large number of links to photographic resources, but also tries to add more general information that might be of interest to photographers. For those who are less impressed by the workings of the art, there are links to online exhibitions of photography.

Joseph Wu's Origami page
http://www.datt.co.jp/Origami

Those who haven't yet taken up the Japanese art of paper folding will certainly want to try it after viewing this page. It's truly astounding what one can do with just a few square pieces of paper, and Wu spotlights his own collection as well as providing resources for enterprising Origami enthusiasts.

Action Girl's Guide to Female Figures
http://users.aol.com/sarahdyer/index.htm

Part of a larger Web site called Action Girl Online, this guide is for collectors of action figures that happen to portray female characters. There's a definitive listing of figures from Xena: The Warrior Princess to Princess Leia and tips on collecting; but the best section is Missing in Action: female action figures that never made it to store shelves—it's a travesty.

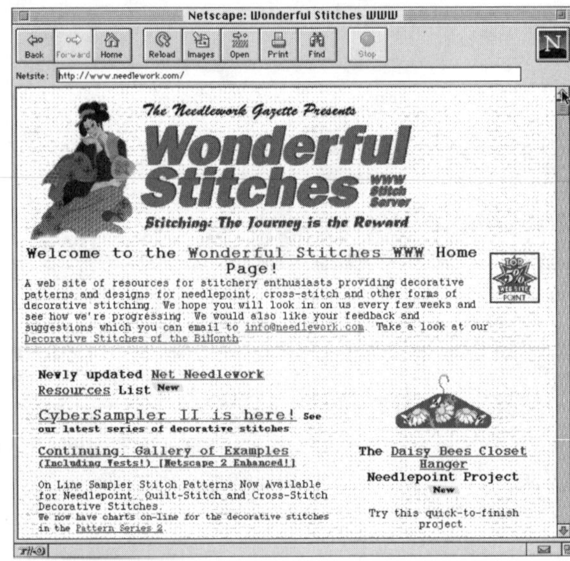

Figure 4.10
Wonderful Stitches, *http://www.needlework.com*

The Plastic Princess page

http://deepthought.armory.com/~zenugirl/barbie.html#Intro

Every little girl, it seems, played with Barbie, and over the years she turned from mere glamorous toy to serious collectible item. This page is for Barbie enthusiasts of every age, with photos of the original supermodel and friends, the latest happenings in the Barbie world and resources for Barbie lovers. Check the link to Nell's Doll List for a more comprehensive, less plastic, doll resource site.

MAGS AND 'ZINES

Hot Wired

http://www.hotwired.com

This site takes users into the geeky yet unbearably hip world of HotWired, run by the enterprising people who brought *Wired* magazine into the world. With departments on travel, dream jobs, drinks, features on the Internet, and just about everything else, it's required surfing for netizens everywhere.

Buzz Online

http://pathfinder.com/buzz

Another Pathfinder site worth visiting is Buzz Online, an entertainment rag based in Los Angeles. Its editors, however, view the City of Angels as a state of mind, not a geographic location. What this means is that Buzz gives visitors the scoop on pop culture from the center of the entertainment industry.

Yush Ponline

http://www.ftech.net/~yush

This magazine is the U.K.'s first publication to cover black culture, and the online version is an ultra-cool Webzine that covers a variety of topics, from style to politics to art and musical genres like reggae, rap, and hip-hop. Features cover everything from artists to conspiracy stories.

The Atlantic Monthly

http://www.theatlantic.com/atlantic

The cyber version of this politics and culture magazine holds much for Web users trying to find meaning on the Internet (see Figure 4.11). Atlantic Unbound, the magazine's online journal, has an excellent poetry section—and the literature and culture sections aren't bad either.

Vibe Online

http://www.vibe.com

The print version of *Vibe* covers jazz, R&B, rap, hip-hop, and all sorts of topics of interest to African Americans—politics, entertainment, personalities, and fashion. Vibe's attractive online companion includes much of the content of the monthly issues and updates the magazine with more reviews and news, sound, and video.

where they surf

Surfer: Marisa Bowe,
Editor-in-chief of *Word.*

Her favorite sites of the moment:

Cow Sounds

http://www.brandonu.ca/~ennsnr/Cows/Sounds/moo.au

"I like to visit cow sites on the Web. I find them calming. This one has a moo and a cowbell. I grew up next to a veal farm in Minnesota, and after 11 years in NYC, I crave that cow ambience."

Brazzil

http://204.140.220.54/index.htm

"This is one of several English-language, Third World Web publications I found while researching "Guyana," the multimedia Web documentary I recently produced for *Word.* One of the best things about the Web is that you're not limited to your own country—thank God."

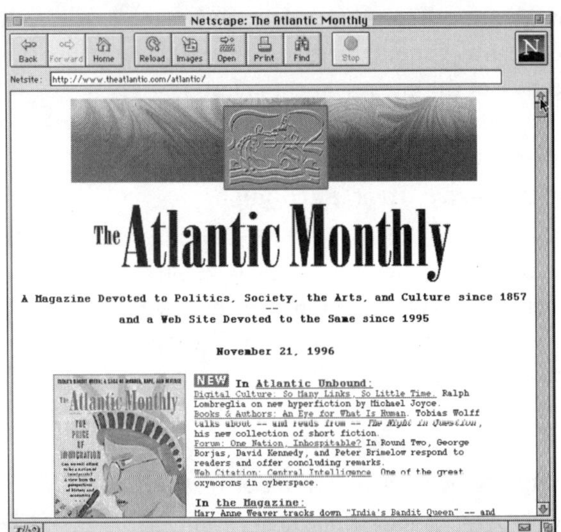

Figure 4.11
The Atlantic Monthly,
http://www.theatlantic.com/atlantic

Salon
http://www.salon1999.com

A well-written daily Webzine about books, arts, and ideas, Salon is a sophisticated and intelligent publication that will appeal to your literary side. You will find up-to-date and informed reviews of music, books, and movies as well as media circus which offers biting commentary on the press.

I·N·T·E·R·N·E·T M·I·N·U·T·E

WHAT'S A 'ZINE?

Originally 'zines were cheap magazine wannabes created by writers, artists, punks, fans, and others to get their work in print, their views aired, their stars worshipped. When the online world opened up, 'zines migrated to the Net, where they're sometimes called ezines or Webzines.

In the print world it was easy to distinguish the low budget, limited circulation, amateurish 'zines from larger circulation magazines. On the Web, that distinction blurs: everyone with genius or chutzpah and a few bucks is a publisher. 'Zines are usually produced by an individual or small group, often for fun or personal reasons rather than profit. They tend to be irreverent, bizarre, esoteric and FUN.

Some Women's Wire favorites include:

gURL
http://www.itp.tsoa.nyu.edu/~gURL

Foxy
http://www.tumyeto.com/tydu/foxy/foxy.html

Crisp
http://www.crispzine.com

Cupcake
http://www.cupcake.com

Take a look at a collection of links to women's 'zines at *http://www.zoom.com/personal/taci/ezines.htm* .

But to get a real appreciation of 'zine variety, scroll through Yahoo's Ezine Directory at *http://www.yahoo.com/Entertainment/Magazines.*

Internet Underground Online

http://www.underground-online.com

The magazine *Internet Underground* doesn't just cover cyberspace—it covers cyberspace with intelligence and a sense of humor. And the electronic version is more than just a good jumping-off point to find stuff online—it's a place to explore the entire culture of the Internet with all its darkness and light and weirdness, and find out what the future of the Web might look like.

Entertainment Weekly

http://pathfinder.com/ew

There are literally thousands of entertainment sites on the Web, but a few of the best ones fall under the umbrella of Pathfinder. For instance, for news of all things Hollywood, Websurfers should make it a point to visit Entertainment Weekly Online, which is the snazzy cyberspace version of the entertainment bible. Visitors won't be disappointed.

gURL

http://www.tsoa.nyu.edu/gURL

This peppy e-zine is an intelligent, playful site for girls (see Figure 4.12). With stories on body image, smoking, and interviews with people like teenage athletes and Judy Blume, it's not false advertising—this is like the early *Sassy* magazines. gURL also includes enjoyable sections, such as Paper Doll Psychology and Ha! The only beef: it should come out more often.

Word

http://www.word.com

This whimsical and wonderful magazine on the Web (see Figure 4.13) has articles on such topics as whether or not cows lie down before it rains and the life of a bike messenger in New York City. The layout is original and fresh and the stories are absolutely fascinating.

John Labovitz's e-zine list

http://www.meer.net/~johnl/e-zine-list/index.html#ezine

Subjects covered by e-zines tend to range from the bizarre to the esoteric—and there are thousands upon

Figure 4.12
gURL, *http://www.tsoa.nyu.edu/gURL*

Figure 4.13
Word, *http://www.word.com*

thousands of them on the Internet. Thankfully, John Labovitz provides a thorough, user-friendly way to find these fan-based publications on tophics from poetry and computers to the King James Bible...and beyond. Way beyond.

Bitch

http://www.bitchmag.com

This well-designed, well-maintained fanzine is a great read for feminists, Internet junkies, and all thinking people. The editors write features on a multitude of subjects, including Barbie dolls, changing views on marriage, and women's roles in the movies. They've also included rants on topics like girls who wear glasses and women and technology.

Suck

http://www.suck.com

This is a 'zine that doesn't live up to its name—and the entire Web community is grateful. Suck's articles cover culture, the Internet, and just about everything else that's vaguely interesting. It also sports clever cartoons, plus some of the most intriguing (and most disturbing) quotes from current popular media.

Nrv8

http://www.nrv8.com

From the pitfalls of the carpool lane to new poetry and tragic love stories, this 'zine is full of energy, humor, and all-around excellent content, updated on a daily basis. For a dose of culture on the Web that's both thoughtful and entertaining, Nrv8 is the place to go.

Urban Desires

http://desires.com

There are actually a large number of quality 'zines online, which is a good sign for the Internet—but many of them get lost in the sea of cybercontent. Urban Desires, with its unique hipness, will never be one of them. This hip culture 'zine covers dogs and Spam along, with more serious pursuits like literature, style, travel, and food—all with a healthy dose of urban insight.

DINING

INTERNATIONAL APPEAL

Fodor's

http://www.fodors.com

Netheads may already know the Fodor's name from restaurant and hotel guides, and this Web site is as good a resource as the printed books. Not only can visitors find places to eat and stay, they can also read reviews for fine restaurants and hotels in cities around the world.

McDonald's

http://www.mcdonalds.com

For those who actually want to explore the world of McDonald's more closely, this site gives the lowdown on the latest Happy Meal toys, the Ronald McDonald charities, commercial jingles, and nutrition information on its food.

INTERNATIONAL APPEAL

The Ultimate Restaurant Guide

http://www2.orbweavers.com/cgi-win/ULTIMAT.exe/GUID

The actual database for this search engine isn't very big, but it links to so many other restaurant guides that it really doesn't matter. The Guide allows visitors to find restaurants that will satisfy their craving of the moment, whether it's for Ethiopian cuisine in NYC or Chinese dumplings in Lawrence, Kansas.

INTERNATIONAL APPEAL

Richard's Restaurant Ranking

http://www.lagerling.se/rest.html

Whoever Richard is, he understands good food. He has compiled a list of the 21 finest restaurants in the world, complete with menus and descriptions that will make any epicure's taste buds water. Many Websurfers will never be able to travel to Stockholm to sample Paul and Norbert's fjord salmon with grilled scallops and lenient curry sauce...but they can dream.

INTERNATIONAL APPEAL

The Diner's Grapevine

http://www.dinersgrapevine.com

The creators of this site wanted to make sure Internet users could walk (virtually, of course) into any restaurant and view reviews and menus. So far the searchable database of 6,000 restaurants is only concentrated in a few major areas, and restaurant owners must pay $850.00 to have more than just a small listing on the site. Still, some interesting features like Today's Featured Restaurant make it worth surfing.

MUSIC

Internet Underground Music Archive

http://www.iuma.com

This is the place for music fans to discover the next big thing: IUMA prides itself on giving space to bands and artists from all different genres, from folk to rock and beyond. Listen to sound clips of The Bobs, Panel Donor, and Jack Tempchin—tomorrow's biggest stars—with any luck, that is. Fans will also find different musical publications here for the latest in music news.

The Ultimate Band List

http://www.ubl.com

Whether one's interests lie in classical melodies, hardcore punk, or reggae, one thing is certain: this site rocks. The Ultimate Band List is a resource that provides the lowdown on all major (and many obscure) performers and bands from the Amps to Ziggy Marley.

SonicNet

http://www.sonicnet.com

This music site based in New York City is one of the best of its kind. With cybercasts of hip hop, rock, and best of all, the spoken word, it's much more than just another magazine-style page. Certainly reviews, news, and features with audio clips are available, but there is always something new here, no matter when users come.

Addicted to Noise

http://www.addict.com

This site for rock fans is exactly what a Web magazine on music should be—chock full of reviews, features, interviews, columns, news, and special highlights such as Radio ATN and Sonic Lodge, where full albums are available online. Best of all, most articles and reviews hold sound files so users can actually hear what's being discussed.

Sub Pop Online

http://www.subpop.com

From one of the pioneers of grunge comes a Web site dedicated to all the bands that reside on the Sub Pop label. For the uninitiated, bands that have come from Sub Pop include Mudhoney, Soundgarden, Nirvana, L7, and the Reverend Horton Heat. Here visitors can find sound files, discographies, and biographies.

The Women of 1970s Punk

http://www.comnet.ca/~rina/index.html

Women interested in punk rock might take a detour to visit this site, which is a good place to find information on the women who were part of the classic punk scene. It does seem a bit sparse on content, but it includes a few good links to other sites that feature ska and the different schools of punk (including the Women of Ska page).

Music Boulevard

http://www.musicblvd.com

Not only can Websurfers buy over 150,000 CDs from all genres at this site, they can preview them with sound samples. The presence of such a useful way to shop is really the main attraction here, but Music Boulevard is also the online home to several movie magazines, including Spin and @Country. The site also features daily news and music charts.

Classical Net

http://www.classical.net

Classical music lovers will find much to enjoy on Classical Net, such as reviews and a searchable index with a plethora of information on the greatest composers of all time. There's a guide on how to build a great classical CD collection complete with information on the best operas, and a list of recommended CDs for keyboard music, chamber music, and concertos. The only things missing here are sound files.

INTERNATIONAL APPEAL

OperaWeb

http://www.opera.it

This site reminds surfers that opera is not always unapproachable and stuffy—and that it can be fun. Users can find reviews of both CDs and live performances here, along with a history of opera, an Opera Sing-Along, and Guinness world records about opera (anyone know that the highest note ever sung was a C5)?

INTERNATIONAL APPEAL

Operabase
http://operabase.com/do.cgi?index=&id=cust58_max4_chicago_il_ms_uu_net&lang=en

This is the site for opera fans to discover what's playing anywhere in the world in four languages. The database here includes 300 opera houses throughout the world, so Netheads can use Operabase to find out when Richard Wagner's *Gotterdammerung* is playing in Chicago or where to find Puccini in South Africa.

The Blue Highway
http://www.vivanet.com/~blues/intro.html

This page covers a style of music which has its roots in Africa and rhythms that still strongly influence today's sounds. With essays, tributes to around 20 blues greats like Muddy Waters and B.B. King, blues radio listings, and other information, it's a fine journey for blues lovers anywhere.

Jazz Central Station
http://www.jazzcentralstation.com

Jazz Central Online gets some of its content from *JazzTimes Magazine,* but it has much more than that. Surfers will find RealAudio interviews with jazz greats, information on jazz festivals, reviews complete with sound, a monthly featured artist, and much more. This is a site that really knows how to utilize its medium, and it does so with style and intelligence.

The Mudcat Cafe Presents Deltablues.com
http://www.deltablues.com

This site covers blues and folk, but it isn't merely a music site. It contains everything one might find at a cafe—philosophy talk, poetry, and music. Well, everything except coffee, maybe, although a link to a beer site is included for the thirsty. One of the best things here is the Digital Tradition Folksong Database, which contains lyrics to over 6,000 songs.

The Blue Note
http://interjazz.com/bluenote.html

Now people outside of New York City can get a taste of jazz at the Blue Note, by way of a Web site that features the sights and sounds of the club over the Internet. Since the menu has been posted and a giftshop is also included, the virtual experience is complete. The site is a bit small, but that doesn't seem to matter at all.

Cybergrass
http://www.banjo.com

This is the online source for bluegrass fans, with information and sound files for all kinds of bluegrass bands and performers along with features, reviews, and information on festivals, events, and publications. Anyone with a soft spot for the banjo or the mandolin will find something to like here—and others will be surprised at how many bluegrass fans are surfing the Web.

Primarily A Cappella
http://www.singers.com

A cappella music may not be the most popular form of music, but it definitely has a small and loyal following. This is the site for them. Actually, there's a lot of variety within this genre: these normally unaccompanied singers can be jazzy or folksy, singing Christian contemporary, doowop, or world music. All of it is found here.

COMICS AND CARTOONS

The Doonesbury Electronic Town Hall
http://www.doonesbury.com

The often controversial, always witty cartoon Doonesbury is online at a site which celebrates not only the comic strip, but the main topic of the strip—politics. As a result, it isn't just a site that has comics on it, it focuses on the pertinent news of the day. Still, users can buy merchandise here, such as a Mr. Butts ashtray or the Zonker Delta Kite, and view a few topical Doonesbury strips in the Flashback section.

Jonah Weiland's Comic Book Resources

http://envisionww.com/jonahw/comics

Comic books, despite what one might hear, were never just for kids. And they aren't all about superheroes, either. This page, which has reviews, a chat, TV themes, and other comic-related information, is a great site to start exploring the *X-Men,* the lives of twenty-something women in *Strangers in Paradise,* or the adventures of a little creature named Bone.

The Women of Marvel Comics

http://www.geocities.com/Hollywood/2855

Granted, many comic books are usually aimed at prepubescent males. And it's also true that many visitors to this site ask when a special "lingerie edition" is coming. Nevertheless, some of the strongest fictional women in the world are superheroines, and this site (maintained by a woman, in case you were wondering) is a tribute to all of them (see Figure 4.14).

Figure 4.14
The Women of Marvel Comics,
http://www.geocities.com/Hollywood/2855

[OVERHEARD ON WOMEN'S WIRE]

http://chat.women.com

"Sylvia has a certain attitude and that attitude doesn't have to do with gender."

ON WHAT SHE LIKES AND DOESN'T LIKE ABOUT SYLVIA:

"She has a lot more nerve than I do, and she's quicker on the draw. But she sits around too much. I'd like to draw her rollerskating but that's not her nature."

ON WHY SHE DRAWS ABOUT THE NET:

"The Web is like a new planet to me-I know so little about it. What I do know-is (it's) another world that people get obsessed with and I'm interested in obsession."

—Cartoonist Nicole Hollander discussing Sylvia and other topics in a live chat on Women's Wire.

The Dilbert Zone

http://www.unitedmedia.com/comics/dilbert

Anyone who's ever worked in an office environment can relate to Dilbert, America's favorite overworked, underappreciated employee. The Dilbert Zone is updated daily with new cartoons and includes information on Dilbert products as well as some shameless self-promotion (his own words) by creator Scott Adams himself.

The Non-Stick Looney Page

KID Appeal

http://www.nonstick.com

Bugs Bunny, Daffy Duck, Marvin the Martian...who could forget them? All the Looney Toons characters from Warner Bros. are featured at this attractive site, which has all kinds of information ranging from when they'll be on television to information on the animators. Fans won't want for anything, because their needs have already been anticipated by the Webmaster.

The Calvin and Hobbes Gallery

KID Appeal

http://eos.kub.nl:2080/calvin_hobbes

Although Bill Watterson's comic strip is gone, the irrepressible boy (some would say incorrigible) and his tiger are online at an unofficial but still amusing fan site. Calvin is so much more than just a six-year-old boy playing with an imaginary pal, and visitors to this page will have just as much fun as Calvin does.

ASTROLOGY AND MYSTICISM

The Hartford Courant Daily Horoscopes

http://www.tms.tribune.com/courant_horoscopes

This site is updated daily for the faithful horoscope reader. It features a message board and a way for people to assess their compatibility with their mates. Plus, there's an Instant Reading for those who'd like a silly, pre-programmed answer to their questions about life.

The Astrology Zone by Susan Miller

http://pathfinder.com/twep/astrology

Not only can users find monthly horoscopes at this attractive site, they can figure out the best ways to woo a Taurean lover or learn about the current planetary trends and the history of astrology. In the news section, Miller includes such interesting tidbits as the complete reading for Madonna's daughter.

The Peace Page

http://members.aol.com/elsajoy

Looking for meaning on the Internet can sometimes seem a daunting, if not downright impossible, task. The Peace Page, however, seeks to provide just that. This site isn't so much an astrology site as it is a calm, spiritual experience. Don't look for horoscopes here—look for life-affirming messages.

The Land of Oz

http://members.gnn.com/shickman/index.htm

Once visitors have come here, they'll truly believe they've entered a fantasy land. This site is much more than a tribute to L. Frank Baum and his series of children's books, although the full texts of these can be found here. It's also a tribute to spirituality, complete with poetry, stories, games, and Net resources.

The Matrix Space

http://205.186.189.2/ms/ms_root.html

The Matrix Space is more than just another horoscope site, although the curious can certainly find those here. The question is, through which medium do users want to discover their future? Runes? Numerology? The I-Ching? They're all here, along with extensive information about astrology.

HUMOR

Auntie Lois

http://www2.best.com/~tyrtle/aunt.html

Although the site advertises its content as, "Advice you did not ask for from a woman you will not like," this really isn't true. At least, the part about not liking Auntie

Lois. Yes, she has an attitude and sometimes she skips the tact. But she's funny and irreverent, and she actually gives some very good advice.

The Book of Bitterness

http://www.webfeats.com/sealander/Bitter_Book.html

Everyone's felt bitter at some time in their life, and many of the Internet junkies who find themselves feeling that way write about it and post messages to alt.bitterness—a newsgroup that's often funny, sometimes mean, and occasionally poignant. The Book of Bitterness takes the best writings from the newsgroup and makes them available for all Websurfers to read and relate to.

The Keepers of Lists

http://www.dtd.com/keepers

Everyone loves a top 10 list, and the Keepers of Lists go far beyond the top 10. They pick a daily topic, such as Top 96 Madonna's Baby's First Words or Top 248 Horror Movies Starring Cows, then let users submit their own entries and vote on them. They'll have visitors giggling hysterically, at the very least.

Joe's Amazing Relationship Problem Solver

http://studsys.mscs.mu.edu/~carpent1/probsolv/rltprob0.html

Anyone having a problem with her lovelife can come here and get some advice on what to do, although Joe, whoever he is, isn't a very sympathetic listener and makes no attempt to be tactful. Still, he's funny and sometimes, people just need to look back and laugh about their relationship problems.

Cruel Site of the Day

http://www.cruel.com

You've heard of the Cool Site of the Day—well, this is its evil twin. Here users will find links to sites maligning all the major celebrities and other Web sites that are just, well, cruel. Find, for instance, the Joey Lawrence Makes Me Physically Ill page, or learn why David Hasselhoff is the Anti-Christ. Many self-proclaimed bitter people and losers can be found here.

Dave's Web of Lies

http://www.cs.man.ac.uk/~hancockd/lies.html

Oh, what a tangled web we weave...So much of what is on the Web is speculation, rumor, or just an outright lie—which makes this page a breath of fresh air. Everything on the page is a lie, even its declaration that the page was last updated in 1998. Discover lies like this one: The Beatles' "I am the Walrus" was originally "I am the Wombat."

Addicted to Stuff

http://www.morestuff.com

Anyone who's ever been addicted to...well, stuff, should come here and hang out for a while. This is a site of first-hand accounts from obsessive people who collect dead batteries, eat pickle-salsa-peanutbutter-banana-wheat-germ sandwiches, lose their jobs because they're watching Montel Williams, and love their cars way too much. Funny, there seem to be a lot of them on the Net.

Centre for the Easily Amused

http://www.amused.com

Those in need of some amusement would do well to utilize the Centre for the Easily Amused, a site that has a trivia game and tips on how to avoid work at work as well as a whole slew of links to sites for those with short attention spans.

INTERNATIONAL APPEAL

HumorNet UK

http://www.netlink.co.uk/users/humornet

This page targets people who like to laugh, which is basically everyone. Not just a humor site, it's a tribute to anything funny—whether that means photos of Bill and Ted's Excellent Adventure or links to the U.K.'s adorable Mr. Bean, Rowan Atkinson. There are even sound clips of Instant Laughter and research on how women's stand-up differs from men's.

Yecch!

http://www.yeeeoww.com/yecch/yecchhome.html

Everyone on the Net has probably used Yahoo! at one time or another, so this parody of one of the Web's most popular sites is especially entertaining. What does Yecch!

search for? Well, the worst and weirdest in cyberspace. Here are some of the categories: What Were They Drinking?, See You in Hell, and Night of the Living Gilligan.

FUN AND GAMES

Riddler

http://www.riddler.com

Riddler is a multifaceted game system with cash prizes. Be sure to bring your thinking cap, though: you're competing against everyone else on the Net, and it's no cakewalk. The site does require that you register to play most of the games which range from trivia to crosswords to scavenger hunts. Advertisers supply the prize money (there's no fees for playing).

Web-A-Sketch

http://www.digitalstuff.com/web-a-sketch

The Etch-A-Sketch, available at stores everywhere, is a toy that continues to frustrate many because it can be a struggle to draw anything but up and down lines. Well, it is now online, with a cyber version called Web-A-Sketch (see Figure 4.15). Netheads can test their drawing abilities here and then have their pieces of art displayed at the gallery for all to see. It's truly amazing what some can do with a couple of lines.

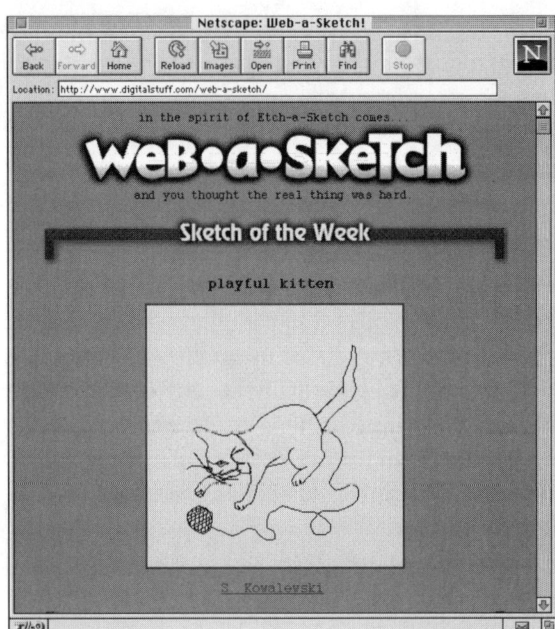

Figure 4.15
Web-A-Sketch,
http://www.digitalstuff.com/web-a-sketch

Games at Road to Nowhere

http://sp1.berkeley.edu/games.html

One of the great things about the Web is the amount of interactivity. Well, at this fun site users can play games called find-the-spam (the amount of bandwidth dedicated to Spam on the WWW is truly frightening) and guess-the-dictator, or add new lines to an interactive poem or piece of fiction.

The Web Poetry Kit

http://www2.best.com/~jnc/cd/poetrykit.html

This site is the online equivalent of Magnetic Poetry: using a list of words provided by the maintainer of the site, users can create their own free verse and have it posted online. Naturally, everyone else's poetry is also listed, so wanna be poets can view them all and decide firmly that their poetry is better than the rest of the world's.

The Keirsey Temperament Sorter

http://sunsite.unc.edu/personality/keirsey.html

It's not just a game, it's David Kiersey's famous personality test. Still, users should have fun determining what their psychological profiles are by answering 70 questions regarding sensation/intuition, extrovert/introvert, thinking/feeling and judging/perceiving. Then they can read about themselves and what their results mean.

duJour.com

http://www.dujour.com/riddle

Anyone who thinks she's smart enough to match wits with the Sphinx should visit duJour.com, where thousands of surfers will participate in games like Labyrinth, Jacque du Jour, MondoTrivia, or Riddle duJour. In Riddle duJour, users are invited to submit answers to questions and brain-teasers posed by an Online Sphinx, then win prizes for their trouble.

POP CULTURE

Women's Wire Buzz Channel

http://www.women.com/buzz

This is the place to catch the latest buzz about pop culture (see Figure 4.16). It has all that fun, dishy fluff from how much George Clooney got paid for his latest movie deal to whom Sharon Stone is dating these days, as well as cheeky reviews about the latest books, mags, TV shows, and cybersoaps. If your own life sometimes seems like a soap opera, talk to the resident guy-expert who gives humorous answers about relationship questions—the eMale. And check in everyday for your daily horoscope. If you're the kind of person who wants a taste of everything pop, but doesn't have a lot of time, check it out.

Cybermad

http://www.cybermad.com

One hundred years from now, this online magazine will be the best example for historians of what passes for pop culture in this era. Usually interesting, sometimes silly, and often bizarre, this site has taught users disco's four beat turn and shown pictures of the *A-Team* lunchbox. On a more contemporary note, the site includes an art gallery, a movies department full of irreverent reviews, and a whole lot more.

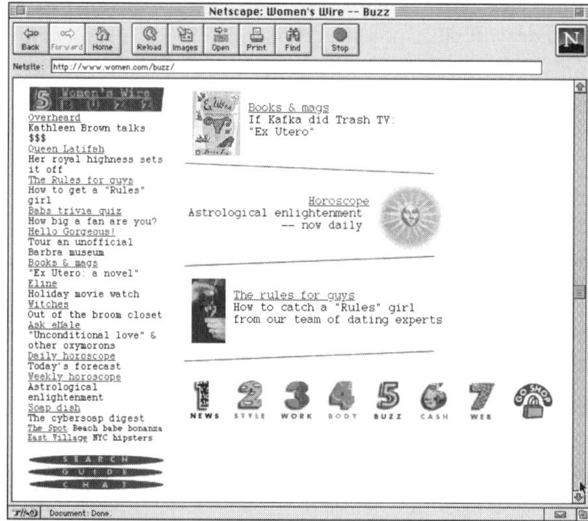

Figure 4.16

Women's Wire Buzz Channel, *http://www.women.com/buzz*

Dischord

http://www.gold.net/Dischord

Rather than celebrating pop culture, this electronic 'zine would rather deconstruct it. And it does so in biting, sometimes controversial, usually thoughtful essays. These are the stories behind the stories, and they cover raves, easy listening music, Quentin Tarentino, the new breed of male 30something authors, Malcolm X—all the trappings of society.

24 Hours in Cyberspace

http://www.Cyber24.com

This site is a digital time capsule of one day in 1996, documenting how online technology is changing the world. Stories about the way the Internet has entered real lives are paired with high-quality photographs all taken within one 24-hour period, by both amateur and professional photographers. The design is second to none and the written accounts are both informative and lively.

t@ponline.com

http://www.taponline.com

T@p Online targets the college-age members of the notoriously hard-to-categorize next generation and does a great job of it, incorporating high culture (poetry, fiction) with pop culture (movies, music, games) and adding sections on travel, politics, and of course, jobs. In the Virtual Dorm, users can vicariously live college life through seven students with a Spycam—hmm, sounds suspiciously like *The Real World.*

Los Negroes Café

http://www.losnegroes.com

This site holds content of interest to anyone into art, the spoken word, independent film, music, fashion, or poetry. There are movies and sound files for the ultimate multimedia creative experience, and it's pretty butta stuff (for the uninitiated, that means real phat).

Retro

http://www.retroactive.com/toc.html

This nostalgia mag celebrates 20th Century pop culture, anything that was ever cool. This ranges from music and hints for living a retro lifestyle to feature topics that change every two months and include Art Deco and Vintage Holiday celebrations. Also here is a City Guide to San Francisco, where the site is located, and a discussion section.

The 80s Server

http://www.80s.com

Remember Valley girls? One-hit wonders? Leg warmers? People who admit to remembering these distinctly 1980s terms should definitely visit The 80s Server. Users can play games and trivia, reminisce about fashion and fads, download RealAudio songs. Really, this site is worth visiting for one feature alone: ValleyURL, in which any URL on the Web can be translated into Valleyspeak.

The Super 70s

http://www.wwnet.com/~densmore

Shake your groove thang (yeah, yeah) at this site, which celebrates leisure suits and supergroups by linking users to other places on the Web where tributes to the 1970s can be found (see Figure 4.17). Everything from lava lamps to blaxploitation films like *Shaft* will bring visitors back to a decade that, well, some might consider better left dead. Others, however, will find this site to be dyn-o-mite.

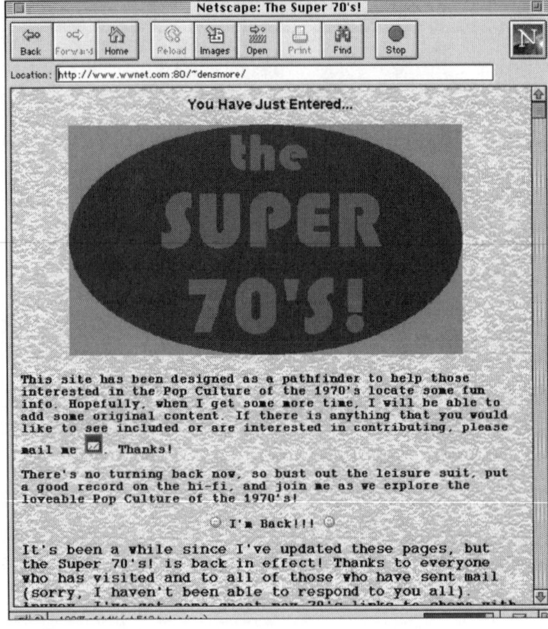

Figure 4.17

The Super 70s, *http://www.wwnet.com/~densmore*

CreatAbiliTOYS

http://www.toymuseum.com

Who can forget the Green Giant, Frankenberry, or Woodsy Owl ("Give a hoot, don't pollute!")? Relive memories of sometimes cute, often annoying characters from the past and the present at this museum for advertising icons that includes facts you never wanted to know on everyone from Snap! Crackle! and Pop! to the Green Giant.

50 Greatest Conspiracies of All Time—Online

http://www.conspire.com

Believers in UFOs and searchers of conspiracies will find a home here. In this increasingly paranoid era when a television show like The *X-Files* has become the most imitated show on television, anyone who wants to know about the murder of John Lennon, the story behind Roswell, or many other conspiracy stories can come here and discover for themselves whether or not the truth is out there.

Sony Online

http://www.sony.com

Everyone in the family will find something to like at Sony Online, which covers the company's many endeavors into film, television, video games, and music. Here, users will find all types of multimedia on shows like *Party of Five, Dark Skies,* and *Seinfeld*. Or they can find out what the tour dates are for the Presidents of the United States of America and what the latest PlayStation games are.

Twentieth Century Fox

http://www.fox.com

An all-encompassing site for Twentieth Century Fox's products, this site is perfect for fans of TV shows like *Melrose Place* and films like the recent William Shakespeare's *Romeo and Juliet* or the Star Wars Trilogy. It includes information on episodes, trailers, and a lot more, with separate sites for Fox TV, Home Entertainment, and Fox Interactive. Fox Online is definitely worth a visit.

Warner Bros.

http://www.warnerbros.com

TV favorites like *Friends, Pinky and the Brain,* and *Babylon 5* can be found at the Warner Bros. site, which also features a Virtual Lot, the history of rock 'n' roll, movies, music, and DC Comics. It's exactly what you expect from the site of huge entertainment corporation, so it doesn't disappoint.

Universal Studios

http://www.mca.com

More fun than a barrel of monkeys, the Universal Studios site is a virtual mecca for all of the company's entertainment products, including bands like Weezer and Sonic Youth plus movies like *The Lost World,* Steven Spielberg's *Jurassic Park* sequel. Universal TV shows like *Xena: Warrior Princess,* the Universal Studios amusement parks, and much more have official places here.

Paramount

http://www.paramount.com

Yet another entertainment monolith, Paramount is the home of *Star Trek, Entertainment Tonight,* and a plethora of popular films. This is a nicely interactive site with some cool features, including Other People's Problems, a daily online chat show where people can solicit advice and give it to others in need.

Disney.com

http://www.disney.com

Does this site really require any explanation? The online home of everyone's favorite cartoon mouse contains much more than the company's animated features, although all of those can be found here in abundance. This is a fine place to spend many long hours browsing through sound, video, and easy-to-read text to discover the magical world of Disney.

1. Ask the magic bra cups your future at this funky page called Net Chick Clubhouse. Includes hot-links to other fun sites, too.
   http://www.cyborganic.com/People/carla/Rumpus
2. Listen to a new house music track, then vote on whether you think it's a "smash" or just "trash" at Club iMusic.
   http://www.clubimusic.com
3. Check out what's going on in these (almost) real-time photos at the Web Voyeur page. They've got cameras set up all over the country taking current pictures of different indoor and outdoor locations.
4. Play a game at the Happy Puppy page. You'll find the most current online games and games reviews.
   http://www.happypuppy.com

☞ KEYWORDS

For more information on topics in this chapter, start your Web search with these keywords:

The Arts: humanities, museums, dance

Books: book publishers, book reviews, women in literature, popular authors

Movies: movie reviews, movie listings, movie tickets, movie festivals, and events

Celebrities: fan clubs, celebrity news

Television: TV shows, soap operas, talk shows, TV listings

Web serials: cybersoap operas

Travel: travel guides, tour and travel companies, national parks, travel guidebooks

Hobbies: crafts, sewing, cooking

Mags and 'zines: magazines, ezines, Webzines

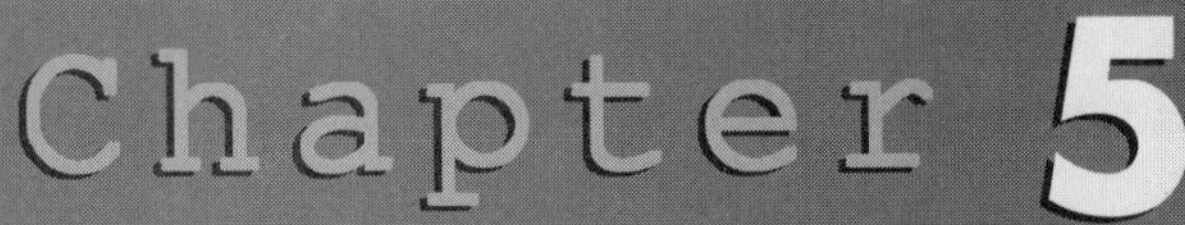

News, Politics, and the Law

- GENERAL NEWS
- NEWS MAGAZINES
- TELEVISION AND RADIO NEWS
- NEWSPAPERS AND NEWSWIRES
- WEATHER
- FACTS AND FIGURES
- THE LAW
- POLITICAL MEDIA
- PUBLIC POLICY AND ORGANIZATIONS

10 THINGS YOU CAN DO TO KEEP UP WITH THE NEWS *RIGHT NOW*

1. Read Women's Wire's Hot Off the Wire each day to learn about women making headlines around the world.

   http://www.women.com/how.html

2. Turn your desktop into a newsroom with a ticker showing the day's headline news.

   http://www.boston.com/globe/glohome.htm

3. Send a Netgram to your favorite (or not so favorite) politician.

   http://www.voxpop.org/netgrams

4. Vote in the Backtalk poll and read what other backtalkers have to say in Women's Wire's weekly news survey.

   http://www.women.com/news/backtalkForm.html

5. Before you hit the road, check out weather warnings from the National Weather Service for the continental USA.

   http://iwin.nws.noaa.gov/iwin/nationalwarnings.html

6. Locate any country or region using the CIA's World Fact Book.

   http://www.odci.gov/cia/publications/95fact

7. Use the court locator service provided by Villanova State University to search by state for the court and legal association in your area.

   http://ming.law.vill.edu/State-Ct

8. Read the *Christian Science Monitor's* 1996 Pulitzer Prize winning entries on Bosnia.

   http://www.csmonitor.com/bosnia/winning.html

9. Choose among a substantial list of foreign newspapers to brush up on the latest news from abroad.

   http://users.deltanet.com/users/taxicat/e_papers.html

10. Fight back! Learn how to resolve your consumer complaint through self-help or class action with legal info from a consumer law firm.

    http://seamless.com/alexanderlaw/txt/article/complain.shtml

By eliminating the traditional obstacles to news gathering—time, space, and cost—the Internet makes accessing general news, politics, and even narrow fields of interests efficient and virtually effortless. If you've ever read a news item and hankered for more depth, most Web sites now provide exhaustive links to related articles, reports, and sites that can make you a virtual expert on any subject.

Read the transcript of your favorite evening radio or TV broadcast; listen to the audio version; or simply view the broadcast from your desktop. And now reading the daily newspaper or your favorite magazine includes an interactive component, too: you can post to a discussion forum, send an e-mail to the editor, or view dynamic photos and graphics that illustrate the headlines.

News on the Internet accommodates your schedule. You'll never miss a program or wait for the morning edition of a paper again. Customized news options deliver the specific items that you want—including updated stock quotes (you choose the ticker symbols), hourly weather reports, news headlines from wire services, even local traffic conditions. For example, Pathfinder, the all-in-one news and entertainment magazine site (http://www.pathfinder.com) is free, but you can subscribe for an annual fee to receive the personal edition which customizes the news delivered according to your interests. Some personal news services are free of subscription charges like the MSNBC Personal Edition news-as-you-like-it feature (http://www.msnbc.com/choices.asp) where you register and choose your news each time you enter.

Keep up with the international scene by going directly to newspapers from countries all over the world. With hundreds upon hundreds of newspapers, magazines, journals, and specialty news services online at little or no cost, the only limitation is the extent of one's own curiosity.

GENERAL NEWS

100 BEST SITES

Pathfinder

http://www.pathfinder.com

From media giant Time Warner, Pathfinder houses some of the most well-known media brands in the world all under a single searchable Web site. Divided into the major categories of news, money and business, people and entertainment, sports, net culture and living, here you will find reliable news sources including CNN, Time, Life, The Weather Channel, Money magazine, Fortune, CNNfn, People, Entertainment Weekly and Sports Illustrated. And for a monthly fee, the site offers Pathfinder Personal Edition which delivers a personalized news service based on criteria that you select.

INTERNATIONAL APPEAL

The Canadian Press

http://www.xe.com/canpress

Stay abreast of general news and politics from Canada with this site. Find today's headlines gathered from press, broadcast, and photo services in Canada. If you're a French Canadian ex-patriot, you'll find some information in French, although the bulk of the news is in English.

Investigative Reporters & Editors

http://www.ire.org

Access the nation's hottest investigative reporters and editors resource. The IRE site has a wealth of information on the latest databases for research on subjects like government, health care, business, and more. Aspiring reporters and researchers may want to sign on to the current events discussion group, attend the conferences advertised here, order publications, or simply fish around for potential stories.

INTERNATIONAL APPEAL

The Online Intelligence Project

http://www.icg.org/intelweb/index.html

Journalists, scholars, business executives, or anyone with a keen interest in international affairs will agree with Web watchers that this is a great source for news. Peruse the regional watch section to check on general news or receive updates on world trouble spots. Information is culled from such sources as Knight Ridder and Voice of America as well as field reports from academics.

The Consortium

http://www.delve.com/consort.html

A bi-weekly online magazine and newsletter from Robert Parry (a former journalist with The Associated Press, *Newsweek,* and Public Broadcasting System), this is definitely an alternative investigative news site. The purpose of this site, visitors are told, is to compensate for the failure of mainstream journalists to provide fair and accurate reporting. Whatever your opinion of the media, there are some interesting stories online here.

Women's Wire News Channel

http://www.women.com/news

You'll find women on the front page here (see Figure 5.1). Hot Off the Wire covers the top news stories for and about women every day. Keep up with prominent women around the world, including Hillary Clinton, astronaut Shannon Lucid, and Mother Teresa. In Backtalk, the weekly poll, take an interactive look at the issues that affect women's lives—from Barbie to Bosnia, from the presidential elections to the latest health and entertainment news. Chuckle with Sylvia, Nicole Hollander's single gal in the '90s comic strip, or voice your viewpoint in Fast Take, the quick op/ed. It's the place for the busy woman who wants to know what's going on but doesn't have time to waste.

Newspapers/Media

http://netspace.net.au/~malcolm/media.htm

A site produced by Malcolm Farnsworth, a politics and English teacher from "down under," this is a fabulous source for newspaper and media links. One can find an index of newspapers, magazines, and broadcasters within the U.S. and abroad, as well as hotlinks with commentary to news sources on the Web. Updated regulary, text driven, and simple to use, a visit here will give a news weary traveller some direction.

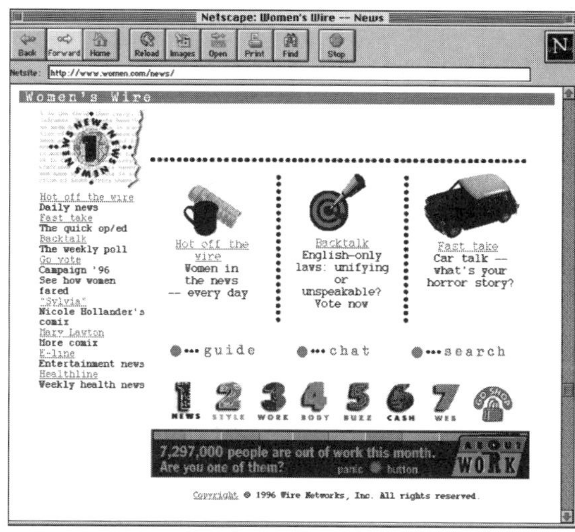

Figure 5.1

Women's Wire News Channel, *http://www.women.com/news*

Latino Web

www.latinoweb.com/favision/newspapers.html

This home page boasts a resource site with close to 100 links to Latino Web newspapers and magazines. This site will take you away to news from Brazil, Peru, and Honduras, as well as the *Chicago Tribune* and the *Los Angeles Times*. The site welcomes user comments and encourages all Latino news sources to be listed. If you are looking for a comprehensive listing of Lation sources, this is one to bookmark.

New Century Network

http://www.newcentury.net/about/index.htm

It's best to think of this site as a one-stop visit to 225 newspapers merged together. The product of nine major media conglomerates including Gannett Co., Knight-Ridder, Inc., the New York Times Company and Times-Mirror Inc., the New Century Network delivers news, politics, sports, business, travel and leisure, and more in one convenient location. Surprisingly, the information-packed site is easy to navigate via a clear graphical directory of components.

Journals and Newspapers

http://eng.hss.cmu.edu/journals

Journals and Newspapers delivers an alphabetical listing of some well-known, little-known and alternative newspapers, journals, and periodicals. So, if you're surfing the Web with a mind to read an varied mixture of news, check out this site. For example, you can locate and read up on *American Demographics, The New Yorker, The Hemmingway Review,* or *Electronic Antiquity* all from one source.

INTERNATIONAL APPEAL

Taxi's Newspaper List

http://users.deltanet.com/users/taxicat/e_papers.html

Not sure if your favorite newspaper is online? Taxi's Newspaper List is probably the most efficient way to find out. Arranged by country, simply click on the flag of the country where the newspaper originates and find yourself reading headlines from anywhere in the world. Visitors should note that Taxi's Newspaper List doesn't promise to be the most exhaustive source for newspapers but it's still a good starting point.

INTERNATIONAL APPEAL

WorldNews Online

http://worldnews.net

For those with a keen interest in Latin American news, WorldNews OnLine should be a regular stop. The site carries the full text of the leading daily newspapers as well as reports from the wires and other information networks. Although it's far from reaching its full potential, WorldNews Online promises that it will be adding European and Asian News.

INTERNATIONAL APPEAL

Asia One

http://www.asia1.com.sg

Online versions of news sites such as Asia One prove that surfing the Web for current events doesn't have to be dull or dry. This site is chock full of interesting and vibrant news, business, entertainment, sports, and travel from a variety of sources in Singapore and Thailand. Although still under construction, Asia One "hot stories" promises to organize the most popular stories from selected news services and arrange them in one place.

The Newsroom

http://www.auburn.edu/~vestmon/news.html

Just as walking into a department store for a bit of this and bit of that is often the most convenient stop for busy shoppers, sites like The Newsroom are the best bet for busy but hungry news junkies. Loaded with links to various newspapers, radio, and television Internet sites, the site is sufficiently thorough and simple to navigate when you're pressed for time.

NEWS MAGAZINES

The Atlantic Monthly

http://www.TheAtlantic.com

Those in pursuit of intelligent, witty commentary should stop by The Atlantic Monthly on the Web. Simply and elegantly designed, this site features in-depth analysis of the news of the day, editorials, politics, the arts, and culture. This site is an ideal example of traditional journalism (circa 1857) which adapts to modern times without compromising its regality.

A Magazine: Inside Asian America

http://www.amagazine.com

Asiaphiles interested in popular culture, entertainment, news, and social issues in this diverse community will enjoy this site. It includes a great reference tool in the site's "Asian American Nexus" which provides information and links to newsgroups and associations in the Asian American community. The Webmasters are correct in their claim that Asians comprise the largest ethnic group of users on the Internet, this site will experience rapid growth.

The Economist

http://www.economist.com

The online version of this weekly international journal is currently in an experimental phase and is constantly being revised. Currently, you will only find only bits and bytes of the Economist. The site is overly simplistic with little to catch the eye but it offers a free subscription to the "Politics this Week" and "Business this Week" summaries by e-mail.

Foreign Affairs

http://www.foreignaffairs.org

This high-brow, cerebral publication of the Council on Foreign Relations shuns the trendy practice of placing its entire contents online. Instead, the policy wonks and scholars at the prestigious journal tease readers with summaries and excerpts of the current issue, placing only the full text of their lead article online. However, the news summaries are valuable for people who want a concise synopsis of world events without having to purchase the costly journal each month. The site offers indexed access to leading journals, books, documents, and online resources on foreign policy and international relations.

Time Out

http://www.timeout.co.uk

What a cool place to find information on major world cities, weekly arts and entertainment, and generally what's hip and happening around you! Although you won't find hard news at this site, you'll find listings and reviews on theatre shows, concerts, restaurants, and much more. Celebrity profiles and Hollywood gossip are found here.

The Daily Muse

http://www.cais.com/aschnedr/muse.htm

Under its title banner, the statement "much ado about nothing at all" is displayed prominently giving visitors their first indication that business is not as usual at this site. You will find a satirical and wry look at the news of the day. Whether it's Michael Jackson, the President, or the Royal family, nothing is sacred. This is an amusing site for an irreverent look at the news.

Hispanic Magazine

http://www.hisp.com

Of the ethnic magazines around, *Hispanic* magazine is one of the best at serving a diverse readership of professionals, community activists, students, and entrepreneurs (its target audience). The monthly magazine covers business, politics, arts, music, culture, media, career and other issues relevant to Hispanics. This site has been awarded the Lycos top 5% distinction, as well as the Magellan 4 star and Zask awards for it's user-friendly features and content.

Life

http://pathfinder.com/Life

If you're tired of getting your news through traditional means, the Life photo home page is a great way to "read" the news through still photos, visual interpretations of the same stories we see in print. Though feature articles aren't available online, visitors will find online exclusives such as the Jack and Jackie Kennedy Virtual Photo Album and archival pictures of presidential candidates at the political conventions from 1948 to 1996.

New England Journal of Medicine

http://www.nejm.org

Read what your doctors and health practitioners read before they even get their hard copies in the mail. In fact, read as little or as much of the full text articles online even before the major news organizations report on the published findings. This weekly medical journal is on the cutting edge of medical research and science and now leads the cutting edge in Web sites. Search previous issues online or find out more about the activities of the Massachusetts Medical Society which owns the journal.

U.S. News & World Report

http://www.usnews.com

The online edition of U.S. News & World Report, like the paper edition, is a reliable, easy-to-read source for national and international news. It's a great place to visit to stay current with breaking news through Associated Press wire stories (as well as the current issue of the magazine). One should also stop by the "Soundbytes" section to hear Real Audio clips of major stories dating back several months. For political junkies, the Washington Infobank has useful links to historic documents, key speeches, and more.

Free Burma

http://freeburma.org

Monitor the turbulent, dynamic political situation in Burma through this source. The Free Burma site keeps visitors up to date on the rapid changes occuring in the political landscape. Find links here to archives, news, reports, and Burma press statements concerning Aung San Suu Kyi's release from house arrest.

Berskerkistan
http://www.linder.com/berserk/berserk.html

For an alternative perspective on the war in Bosnia, this online magazine is devoted to bringing news, photos, and commentary on one of the world's plaguing troublespots. A recent college graduate and photojournalist, Jim Bartlett, roves the streets of Bosnia in search of fresh news and unique angles to the war. Berserkistan also offers detailed maps and travel information for interested parties.

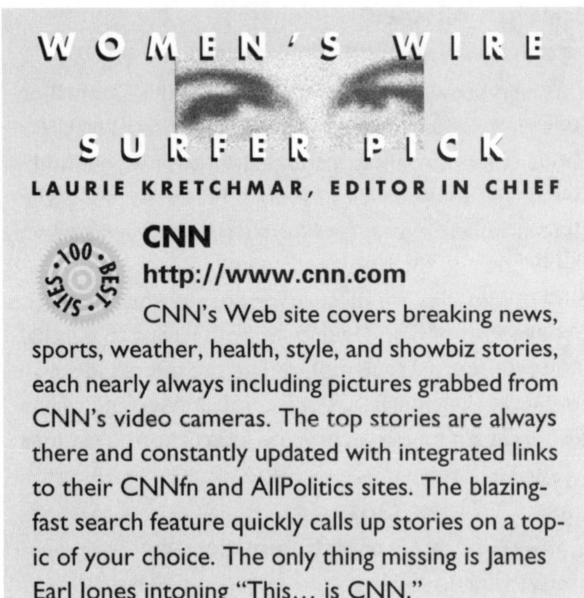

LAURIE KRETCHMAR, EDITOR IN CHIEF

CNN
http://www.cnn.com

CNN's Web site covers breaking news, sports, weather, health, style, and showbiz stories, each nearly always including pictures grabbed from CNN's video cameras. The top stories are always there and constantly updated with integrated links to their CNNfn and AllPolitics sites. The blazing-fast search feature quickly calls up stories on a topic of your choice. The only thing missing is James Earl Jones intoning "This… is CNN."

TELEVISION AND RADIO NEWS

CBS News
http://www.cbsnews.com

Stop by the CBS News home page for a glimpse of national and international news, as well as David Letterman's Top 10 list. The site is easy to navigate and provides some additional depth on the top stories. Feeling nostalgic? You'll find the CBS video archives containing highlights from years gone by. Notable among these are pictures of Mike Wallace wrestled to the convention floor by Chicago police during the 1968 Democratic National Convention.

Corporation for Public Broadcasting
http://www.cpb.org

The Corporation for Public Broadcasting is the private entity that oversees the federal government's interest in public broadcasting. Functioning as a nonprofit organization, the corporation funds Public Broadcasting Service and National Public Radio. Visit the site to find information on how to apply for funding, get in touch with your favorite programs, look for employment with the corporation or gather information on the public policy that drives this mighty media engine.

National Public Radio
http://www.npr.org

If you're one of National Public Radio's 17 million listeners, you'll never lament missing a program again. The online version brings programs such as Morning Edition and Talk of the Nation right to your desktop, at your convenience. Tune in to the hourly newscast or click on the stories you want to hear in the national and international sections.

ABC Radio Net
http://www.abcradionet.com

ABC Radio Net online is home to the ABC NEWS lineup of broadcast news as well as local newscasts in San Francisco, Los Angeles, Chicago, and New York. Listeners will also find commentary from Peter Jennings, Hugh Downs, the latest from Court TV, Business Week's radio broadcast, and a wrap up of political news from "Inside Washington."

News From Around the World
http://www.funet.fi/pub/sounds/news.html

Hear the latest news from abroad at the News From Around the World site in English, Russian, and Chinese from two reputable sources, the Canadian Broadcasting Corporation (CBC) and the U.S. government's Voice of America. You don't have to go far to stay in touch with transforming world events.

Microsoft NBC

http://www.msnbc.com

In coordination with the live 24-hour cable television news network, the MSNBC interactive site brings you breaking news, politics, money, sports, entertainment, weather, commentary, and lifestyle pieces. Although MSNBC Online has yet to achieve the caliber of CNN Interactive, respected journalists from NBC News and original contributors writing for the Web bring a new perspective to online news. MSNBC also offers a comprehensive Australian news service and a great personal page for free.

The BBC

http://www.bbcnc.org.uk

BBC, the distinguished English programming network has come into the cyber age. This is not a location for hard or soft news—the BBC site is a simple information site listing the BBC's programming schedules and summaries of its programs. There is little information on the long history of the BBC, but if you are in the market for employment with this organization, job opportunities are posted online.

Canadian Broadcasting Corporation (CBC)

http://www.radio.cbc.ca

A public broadcasting corporation funded by the government of Ottawa, CBC Radio has long been the mainstay of news for the majority of Canadians. This site delivers television and radio programming, listing, contacts, and interesting facts in both French and English. Visitors may wish to talk back to CBC with their editorial comments as well.

NBC News

http://www.nbc.com

The NBC News home page features updates from NBC's Sports, Entertainment, and News divisions. Visitors will find programming details/times, information on favorite news correspondents, TV personalities, as well as links to NBC's business channel, CNBC, and its other global holdings.

Unsolved Mysteries

http://www.unsolved.com/home.html

The long running television show that profiles missing persons, lost loves, and "wanted" bulletins brings the same information and more to their Web site. By visiting the site, TV fans will receive updates on pending cases and solved mysteries. There is even a "gallery of fugitives" for those wanting to view photos of dangerous individuals.

where they surf

Surfer: Charlayne Hunter-Gault

National correspondent on "The News Hour with Jim Lehrer" on PBS.

Her favorite sites of the moment:

Global Vision, Africa News

http://www.igc.apc.org/glencree

"I visit the Global Vision site because it helps me keep in touch with human rights issues. The Africa News site has the most comprehensive information available about Africa. There are not a lot of other sources out there for these particular areas."

NetNoir

http://www.netnoir.com

"The one other site I really use is NetNoir, a black cultural, social, and political site."

NEWSPAPERS AND NEWSWIRES

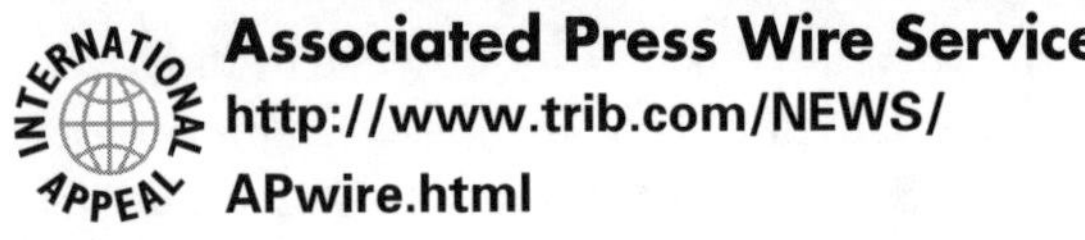

Associated Press Wire Service
http://www.trib.com/NEWS/APwire.html

This site offers Associated Press and other wire services through which news leads are updated every five minutes. Search for news by clicking on the relevant topics or by selecting the region you wish to search through. This news service, is akin to having a 24-hour newsroom in your own home or office.

PR Newswire
http://www.prnewswire.com

In the market for news with spin? The PR Newswire electronically distributes industry and company news to the media and financial sector. So if you can find a use for such material, you can read press releases pertaining to virtually any major industry, product, or company. Private investors can find quarterlies, corporate profiles, annual reports, stock quotes, and links to desired home pages. The site is also likely to be useful for researchers, industry analysts, journalists, or ambitious consumers looking for the release of a specific product.

Reuters
http://www.reuters.com/reutersnews/index.html

For around the clock news seven days a week, Reuters Wire Service online provides constant updates on national, international, political, business, and sports news. Visit this site for news summaries but don't expect flashy graphics or lots of photos. If you are looking for hard news without the trimmings, this site should definitely be bookmarked.

I·N·T·E·R·N·E·T M·I·N·U·T·E

AUDIO ON THE WEB

Browsing the Internet doesn't need to be a silent experience anymore—now you can listen to real-time audio while you are surfing the Web. To listen to live radio broadcasts and other live and taped audio on the Web, you first need to download the technology that makes it all possible. The RealAudio player is available for free at http://www.realaudio.com. Once you download the RealAudio player, follow the instructions and install it on your machine. It's easy to do.

When you're equipped with RealAudio, there are lots of live and taped programs to listen to. Here are three great sources:

Net Radio
http://www.netradio.net

Listen to the world's first 24-hour-a-day, live, Internet-only, radio network.

AudioNet
http://www.audionet.com

Live sports, including women's basketball, live talk radio, novels online, and a number of live radio stations, are available here.

Timecast
http://www.timecast.com

RealAudio program guide lists a schedule of the daily offerings of RealAudio programs including broadcasts from ABC, NPR, and the House of Blues.

The amazing thing about live or taped RealAudio is that you can tune in and then continue doing whatever you're doing on the Web. You can go from site to site and even download files. The audio continues to play.

One caveat: We're not talking audiophile quality here. Definitely check it out, however; you'll get a sense of how pioneer radio users felt.

The Washington Post

http://www.washingtonpost.com

The Washington Post home page carries today's top news as well as the full content of the current day's edition of the paper. Its version carries national, international news, sports, weather, style, entertainment, and a strong business section with links to useful directories and reference materials. If you're interested in the metropolitan D.C. area, check " Washington World" for local news and discussions about life in and around the nation's capitol. You can also search the site for Post stories dating two weeks back.

Christian Science Monitor

http://www.csmonitor.com

Always an excellent source for insightful international news, the Christian Science Monitor's Internet edition adds value to a consistently good newspaper. Online, the Christian Science Monitor brings the same great foreign and domestic reporting on diverse subjects from politics to entertainment reviews. Probably the best feature of the site is the Monitor Radio newscasts. Also check out the Mixed Media section with multimedia presentations of original art, audio, animation, and hot links.

ClariNet News

http://www.clari.net

Find news, politics, business, entertainment, sports, technology and special features, and columns at this news site. Plus there are special features and columns, press releases from major companies, and information about the U.S. government.

The Advocat

http://www.the dvocate.com/welcome.htm

From the heart of Baton Rouge, Louisiana's daily newspaper, The Advocate, delivers news, politics, sports, weather, traffic, and local events online. This fun site is extremely colorful and filled with great features such as an innovative food site loaded with recipes, a comprehensive restaurant guide, and even a "fun" page devoted to whimsical and seriously fun things to do in town.

Africa News Service

http://www.nando.net/ans

This site is marketed as a "one-stop source" for news on Africa, a claim which is fairly close to the mark. A service of the non-profit U.S. news agency and the Africa News Service, "Africa News Online, offers daily reports gathered from the major newspapers, magazines, journals, broadcast programs, and other significant news sources covering this vast continent.

Asahi Shimbun

http://www.asahi.com/information/AENsubscribe.html

Stay in touch with Japanese news via a direct source: Asahi Shimbun evening newspaper. This daily paper provides general news, financial reports, and sports updates online to anyone with a hankering for Japanese and Asian news.

USA Today

http://www.usatoday.com

Using all of the primary colors and more, USA Today's candy-colored home page is a useful quick-glance resource for breaking news, and interesting lifestyle stories. The best of this consumer site is the "what's hot" section that has everything from fun interactive crossword puzzles, to a "Web traveler" that notes hottest new Web pages, to a link to a money section that is updated every two minutes. The weather section is updated frequently and provides forecasts along major interstate highways.

Boston Globe

http://www.boston.com/globe/glohome.htm

Void of savvy graphics or flashing signs, the Boston Globe's Web page is content rich with news, editorials, business, and a strong metro/regional section. For those who need to be informed of breaking news minute-by-minute, the GlobeWire allows one to keep a mini-window open on your desktop that carries national, regional, sports, and business headlines. An archival system allows the users to search for newspaper articles in the Globe as far back as 15 years ago for a charge of between \$1.50 and \$2.95 per story.

The New York Times
http://www.nytimes.com

The New York Times online includes all of the news found in its daily edition with the option of customizing your electronic news delivery. Before rushing out the door in the morning, glance at the headlines found in the "quick read" section for short synopses of front page stories. The online issue is also updated at 1:00PM for midday readers. If you need an added incentive to visit, the "specials" section has full text of such memorable series' such as "The Downsizing of America" and the World Series.

The Jerusalem Post
http://www.jpost.co.il

If you are in the market for up-to-date information about Jerusalem and beyond, this is the site for you. Don't look to this site for extensive world news coverage, but if staying current with Jerusalem is the game, this site is a must see. Of note, the Tourism section gives adventurous travellers sites of interest, complete with information on costs, location, and hours of operation. The online Jerusalem Post Market Place sells the visitor multimedia, music, Hebrew lessons, and more with a four week airmail delivery.

The Chicago Tribune
http://www.chicago.tribune.com

This online version of the world famous *Chicago Tribune* not only boasts a complete print edition of the latest *Tribune*, it provides "between edition" news, weather, stock reports (on a 20-minute delay), sports, and features updated 24 hours a day. Value added areas are user friendly and geared towards today's fast paced lifestyles. The TV Guide is an interactive system which can search for your favorite shows and stars. For the visitor looking for an overall, comprehensive news site, this is it.

Miami Herald
http://www.herald.kri.com

Looking for an online news site that is geared towards cyberjunkies? The Miami Herald online is a fresh, savvy, news site with 24-hour updates. This site caters to the cyberspace community through its CyberHerald section featuring news, technology, and scientific updates of particular interest to online audiences. This is one of only a few news services to provide internet access as well. For a cost of $19.95 per month, the Herald will provide unlimited access to the Internet as well as to its news archives, and other Net offerings. A convenient package for those looking for both reliable news and a reliable service provider.

The Atlanta Journal-Constitution
http://www.ajc.com

A cooperative venture between the Journal-Constitution, AM750 WSB Radio, and Cox Interactive Media, this site is the place to start for news and information on Atlanta and the south. This page provides links to several areas of interest, from sports to attractions. The design is simple and links are easy to navigate. However, this site is more a collection of links to be used as a resource page for the south rather than as a news source.

The Sidney Herald Online
http://www.smh.com.au

For quick headlines on the daily news of Sidney, give The Sidney Herald Online a try. The site incorporates the daily news section of its print paper and adds special features specifically geared for the Internet. A bit cluttered, the site provides links, FAQ's, and specific selected topics with ongoing articles such as the Atlanta Olympics and the Budget 96. A good site for those interested only in a cursory glance at the day's events.

Charlotte.com
http://www.charlotte.com

Charlotte, North Carolina's daily paper delivers everything you'd want from a home town paper and more (see Figure 5.2). The online edition of the paper carries breaking news from Associated Press wires and prominently displays two to three top stories of the day with striking photos. In the mix of daily news, you'll find articles on business, local government, health, education, a regular food section, as well as featured entertainment in the city. Charlotte.com hosts a virtual "meeting places" for singles to post personal ads.

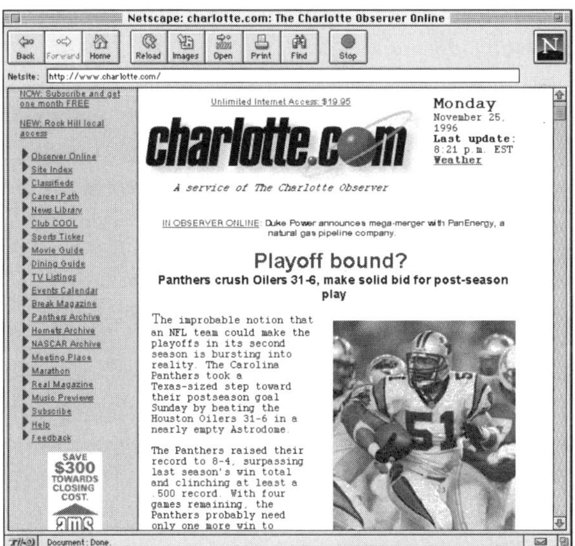

Figure 5.2

Charlotte.com, *http://www.charlotte.com*

Philadelphia Online

http://www.phillynews.com

Together, The Philadelphia Inquirer and the Philadelphia Daily News have created an authoritative source for news on their state. In addition to all of the local, national, and international news from the newspapers, there are fun components to visit, too. The "Philly Life" section is a terrific index of entertainment, restaurants, local events, and distinctly unique things to do if you live in the city or are planning to visit.

Rocky Mountain News

http://www.phillynews.com

One of Colorado's leading newspapers, *Rocky Mountain News* distinguishes its journalistic niche with a value added online version. Visitors can peruse the classifieds, sports, recreation, and local news. Or read the in-depth investigations that have been archived online.

United Media

http://www.unitedmedia.com

News just isn't the news without comics to illustrate the oddities and peculiarities of life. This will quickly become one of your favorite stops. United Media brings a vast collection of nationally syndicated feature and editorial comics to the Web in living color.

@The Post

http://www.cincypost.com

The *Cincinnati Post* delivers current regional and national news with a distinct hometown perspective. Their Web edition carries all of the highlights of its paper edition with additional features such as brief news summaries, updated weather, and wire stories from the Associated Press.

The Gate

http://www.sfgate.com

The San Francisco Chronicle and *The San Francisco Examiner* deliver daily regional and national news including sports and classifieds to your desktop with all the bells and whistles that make news gathering on the Internet so convenient. The "really useful gizmos" section allows the participant to custom design their news page, personalize their TV guide for the San Francisco Bay area, and participate in "bulletin board" discussions.

INTERNATIONAL APPEAL

The St. Petersburg Times

http://www.spb.su/times/index.html

If you're a news hound who's tired of purchasing expensive foreign newspapers at specialty shops, catch the news from the St. Petersburg Times for a timely update on Russian news. Visitors should note that the online edition is current for the week. News, politics, and general business news are readily available here.

Daily Record

http://www.record-mail.co.uk/rm/drsm/front1.html

Scotland's daily newspaper brings the traditional components of a newspaper (local and international news) with a twist. You can spend a considerable amount of time just browsing through fun stuff like the photo section that brings the news and newsmakers of the day to life and visiting the promotional contests and letters section.

San Jose Mercury News

http://www.sjmercury.com/main.htm

This innovative, technically savvy page is redefining newspaper journalism on the Internet. In fact, the investigative unit at the San Jose Mercury News broke a major story on the CIA's involvement with the Nicaraguan Contras that was specially designed for the Internet. Don't be fooled by the hip, fresh look of this page because it's truly the great reporting that distinguishes this site.

The Bergen Record

http://www.bergen.com

A leading paper from the Garden State, The Bergen Record online brings all of the news from New Jersey and its neighbors with great convenience. Drop by the section devoted to a "quick look at the news on the run" for headlines and briefs. Online readers should note the special section dedicated to health in the Garden State.

New York Post

http://www.nypostonline.com

Dishing for gossip on celebs? Stop by the New York Post at their online location for the latest. Fans of the tabloids can now access gossip, entertainment, sports and more by clicking on bright neon-colored buttons that fill the page.

Dallas Morning News

http://www.dallasnews.com

Although some may find the home page of the Dallas Morning News a tad cluttered, the advantage of having such a wealth of news at your fingertips tends to mitigate any irritation one might feel. Updated frequently, headlines of the day can be easily found here in addition to updates on local government, national politics, business, sports, weather, and more. The metropolitan section is a great resource for local news.

INTERNATIONAL APPEAL

The International Herald Tribune

http://www.iht.com

Published by *The New York Times* and *The Washington Post,* The International Herald Tribune online site is one of the most intelligent sources of foreign and domestic news, politics and business. Browse the front page for the top stories or drop by the "dispatches" section for special reports from the world's hot spots.

INTERNATIONAL APPEAL

The Star and SA Times

http://www.satimes.press.net

Despite widespread censorship under apartheid, South African journalism survived and is now disseminating news on the Internet as a joint venture between Independent Group Gauteng (part of one of South Africa's largest newspaper publishing groups) and the London-based *SA Times*. This publication delivers timely information from South Africa by bringing together leading newspapers such as *The Star, The Business Report, The Cape Argus, The Cape Times, The Pretoria News,* and *The Natal Mercury.*

INTERNATIONAL APPEAL

The Financial Times

http://www.ft.com

Based in London, this highbrow newspaper is an authoritative source on financial news and European politics. Its innovative and interesting Web site offers a good place to follow the markets and read wry commentary on American politics from English columnists.

Editor & Publisher

http://www.mediainfo.com

The trade magazine for print journalists, the Editor & Publisher site contains a thorough list of links to online newspapers. Search by keyword or country to find that obscure newspaper you've just got to read. The site also features outstanding work by print journalists and their papers.

WEATHER

Intellicast Weather

http://www.intellicast.com/weather/intl

Travelers and weather watchers will appreciate the weather serviceprovided by Intellicast and MSNBC. The site provides full earth and regional satellite forecasts which are updated every 12 hours.

100 BEST SITES

The Weather Channel

http://www.weather.com

This site has everything you would expect from the 24-hour weather cable channel: detailed weather conditions and forecasts for locations all over the world. It also has special timely areas like the skier's forecast and the fall folliage report. The "Drops of History" section is a fun look back at a weather event that happened on the same day of a previous year.

National Oceanic and Atmospheric Administration

http://ferret.wrc.noaa.gov/fbin/climate_server

For weather watchers everywhere, the National Oceanic and Atmospheric Administration (NOAA) delivers live access to climate data on their Web site. The winner of multiple awards for everything from its content to its layout, this site provides constant updates on climate from an extremely reliable source. Just select the region of interest and zoom in.

National Weather Service

http://www.nws.noaa.gov

A convenient way to discern the movements of the skies is to check out the National Weather Service Web site. You'll find U.S. continental weather bulletins, local weather updates, active warnings about hurricanes/tropical storms, and much more. There are also striking stills taken from weather videos that brings weathercasting to life.

Bermuda Weather Page

http://www.bbsr.edu/Weather

Brought to you by the Bermuda Biological Station for Research (BBSR), this cool site has tons of links to weather

I·N·T·E·R·N·E·T M·I·N·U·T·E

REGISTRATION

You've found the site you're looking for. But wait! You've been asked to register, choose a password, or provide information about yourself. What gives? Some Web sites ask you to register before entering: Many are free (Charles Schwab online financial site asks for free registration to browse certain "privileged access" areas.), though some require paid subscription (Wall Street Journal online, for example).

If you do come across a site requiring registration, there's no reason to be alarmed. Most content sites on the Web are free and entirely supported by advertising. These sites need demographic information about their typical visitors in order to sell advertising and continue to operate the site at no charge to the surfer. If a paid subscription is required, the site will specify this very clearly. You'll probably be asked for a credit card number (often, you can provide the information by phone if you prefer). You won't be charged or held responsible for any services unless you do provide payment and very clearly agree to the terms of the subscription.

Some free sites require registration as well (some ask for voluntary registration, others require it to enter the site). Companies that host Web sites want as much information about their visitors as possible to share with advertisers or help direct their marketing efforts. Or, they may just want to verify the number of registered users to determine the site's effectiveness. You may be asked for your name, address, or information preferences, but they will tell you if the information will be used for anything other than demographic information. Net users sometimes revolt, boycott and flame content providers who sell their e-mail addresses to spammers (online marketers), so most don't do it, and they're obligated to tell you if they're going to.

Some tips: If you've chosen a user name or password to register for a site, jot it down in a safe place in case you've forgotten it the next time. If you do choose a paid subscription, be sure to keep a record of it so you're not surprised when your credit card bill arrives.

resources on the Internet. If you're following weather patterns in the North Atlantic or Bermuda, this is a great place to start. Satellite images are also available here as are storm predictions for these regions.

Earth Watch Weather On Demand

http://www.earthwatch.com/SKYWATCH/skywatch.html

Simply one of the best weather sites in terms of content and sheer design, the Earth Watch Weather On Demand brings great 3-D satellite imagery, weather headlines, a storm watch center, and arresting visual graphics to make checking the weather hardly mundane (see Figure 5.3).

Environment Canada

http://www.dow.on.doe.ca

Environment Canada's Web site monitors weather forecasts for Canadian regions and delivers marine forecasts, charts, maps, and satellite images. There are additional links to the Canadian Meteorological Center, the National Weather Service, and independent weather centers. Mandated by the federal government, this service is available in both official languages.

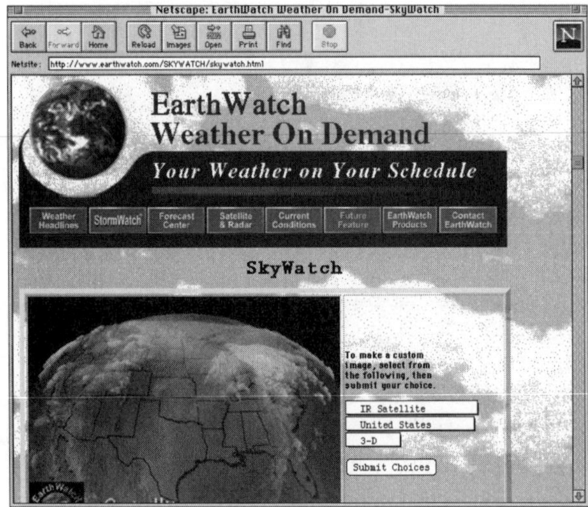

Figure 5.3
Earth Watch Weather On Demand,
http://www.earthwatch.com/SKYWATCH/skywatch.html

Hurricane Home Page

http://www.hurricane.com

Residents of Florida's Broward, Dade, Monroe, and Palm Beach Counties can be prepared for the next hurricane by monitoring tropical storms through this commercial Web site maintained by Coral Technologies Inc. Here, hurricane watchers can view radar and satellite images of storms.

National Earthquake Information Center

http://wwwneic.cr.usgs.gov

Want to feel the Earth move? Well, almost. Here at the National Earthquake Information Center of the U.S. Geological Survey (USGS), they provide near-real-time seismicity information for the concerned and the curious. Get bulletins of the last 21 earthquakes around the world, with maps, as well as information on how to get automatic earthquake alert, and links to related sites. Your new answer to "What's shakin'?"

FACTS AND FIGURES

Perry-Casta-eda Library Map Collection

http://www.lib.utexas.edu/Libs/PCL/Map_collection/Map_collection.html

Reference materials like electronic maps are outstanding resources when they are brought to life on the Internet. The University of Texas electronically maps the globe with cutting edge technology. Why invest in expensive atlases that take up a lot of room on your desk when you can access 275 maps of the U.S and much more on your computer?

Local Times Around the World—Asia & Australia

http://www.hilink.com.au/times/asia.html

Do you wake up your relatives and friends abroad with phone calls in the middle of the night because you've failed in your overseas time calculation? You no longer have an excuse! This cool site breaks down all of the perplexities of time zone calculations and leaves you with no guess work at all. Simply choose the city or region you're interested in and the correct time is displayed.

The CIA World Fact Book

http://www.odci.gov/cia/publications/95fact

Peruse this handy reference tool published by the Central Intelligence Agency for information on virtually all the countries of the world. From demographics like population and birth rate figures to the current governments, this fact book will answer your reference questions with a simple click on the country of choice. Tourists or frequent travelers will appreciate the handy facts. Users should be warned however, that only the 1995 edition is online.

The Quotations Page

http://www.starlingtech.com/quotes

News is what you make of it, right? The Quotations Page delivers news in bite-size chunks that range from the humorous to the thoughtful. Stop by this site to contribute or read a quote, or search for a quote that's on the tip of your tongue.

The Nando Times

http://www2.nando.net/nt/nando.cgi

The Nando Times, better known as the *North Carolina News and Observer* is one of the best sites for comprehensive American political coverage. The online version is updated continuously, easily navigated, and visually appealing. As well as the usual news areas, the Nando Times publishes news specifically written for the Net. Other things to note: the Toy Box for new and exciting games, and a low graphics option for quick downloading.

THE LAW

Indiana University School of Law

http://www.law.indiana.edu/law/v-lib/lawindex.html

The Indiana University School of Law offers the contents of its library online making this an invaluable site for research. It offers access to hundreds of law-related documents and research tools. Notably, there are listings for U.S. law schools, law firms, publishing firms, legal associations, and a catalog of legal research on the Internet.

Law Student Web

http://darkwing.uoregon.edu/~ddunn/l_schl.htm

The brain child of a second year law student at the University of Oregon, this site holds several items of interest to law students or those interested in pursuing a career in law. On one page, there are links to law journals, law schools in the U.S., and "offbeat" court opinions. The "fun" components to this page are the short biographies and quirky home pages of law students.

Arent Fox

http://www.webcom.com/~lewrose/home.html

A reputable advertising and marketing law firm based in Washington, D.C., Arent Fox Kitner Plotkin & Kahn, has created a site for beginners researching American advertising law. Visitors should peruse the Federal Trade Commission's laws and regulations governing the advertising industry as well as recent decisions issued by the Council of Better Business Bureaus.

Law Talk

http://www.law.indiana.edu/law/lawtalk.html

Indiana University's Law School has created a novel way to study law with its "law talk" lectures delivered by faculty members through real audio files on their Web site. You can find lectures on criminal law, civil law, amendments to the U.S. Constitution, and business and personal finance law.

Rutgers University Law School

http://info.rutgers.edu/lawschool.html

Anyone considering a career in law should visit the site created by Rutgers University Law School. It lists accreditation standards of U.S. law schools, guides on entrance to law school, information on the bar exam, a review page for the exam, professional organizations to join, and much more. Finally, the site hosts the law school's online catalogs and information on virtual reference desks.

Saint Louis University School of Law

http://lawlib.slu.edu/home.htm

Digging for information on employment, health, human rights, and international law? The Saint Louis University School of Law offers some alternatives to costly legal advice. Internet training guides have been specially prepared for lawyers, law students, and faculty members.

Richmond Journal of Law & Technology

http://www.urich.edu/~jolt

It's no surprise that the growth of the Internet is raising complex legal questions. Whether you're posing the questions or looking for answers, the Richmond Journal of Law & Technology online is a valuable resource. The site features the current issue of the journal with articles, book reviews, and interesting commentary on such topics as federal broadband law and issues of liability when accidents occur on the "information superhighway."

Patent Law

http://www.law.cornell.edu/topics/patent.html

Curious about patent and intellectual property law? Cornell University's Law School has created a site to answer basic questions and offer detailed information on how to find resources on the Internet. Visitors will also find recent Supreme Court decisions and international agreements outlining patent law.

U.S. Patent Office

http://www.uspto.gov

If you're an entrepreneur or inventor who's looking to protect your intellectual property, stop by the virtual U.S. Patent Office and apply for your own patent without having to leave home (see Figure 5.4). You can also search through the U.S. patents index and order copies of existing patents and trademarks.

American Bar Association

http://www.abanet.org

Attorneys, legal professionals, and members of the public may wish to browse through The American Bar Association's colorful home page for up-to-date information on the professional activities and publications of this organization. In addition to news for members, the public information section provides information on how to file a complaint about lawyer misconduct, get help on simple legal procedures, buy legal insurance, or find a lawyer.

Psychiatry & the Law

http://ua1vm.ua.edu/~jhooper/tableofc.html

The University of Alabama's Psychiatry & the Law Web page is a rich source for information on mental illness and the law. This forensic psychiatry resource page has data on landmark cases, U.S. Supreme Court rulings, links to psychiatry and law databases, and more. The layperson will appreciate the primer on mental illness: what it is, how it is legally defined, and how the illness is treated.

U.S. House of Representaties Internet Law Library

http://law.house.gov

The mission statement of the U.S. House of Representatives Internet Law Library Web site states its mandate to "provide free public access to basic documents of U.S. law." Indeed, visitors to the site will find U.S. state, federal, and territorial law information. In addition, the Library boasts 7,500 catalogued resources such as attorney directories and legal publishers.

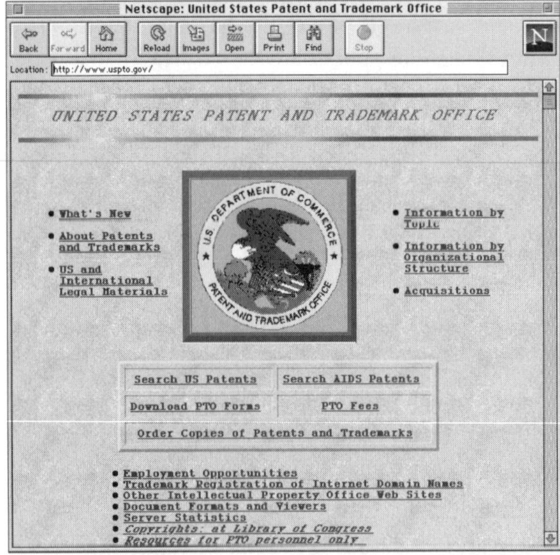

Figure 5.4

U.S. Patent Office, *http://www.uspto.gov*

University of Cincinnati College of Law

http://www.law.uc.edu/CCL

Learn the fundamentals of corporate law from the College of Law at the University of Cincinnati. Here, beginners to this specialty can read up on basic regulations and laws including the Securities Act of 1993 and 1934. Although it doesn't promise to be the most comprehensive source for business law, beginners will find it a handy resource.

Chicago-Kent College of Law

http://www.kentlaw.edu/lawnet/lawlinks.html

If you need to do research on computer, environmental, intellectual property, litigation alternative dispute resolution, and tax issues, drop by the Chicago-Kent College of Law. This site offers a searchable database of legal resources and the college's pick for law site of the week.

Women & Family Law

http://lawlib.wuacc.edu/washlaw/reflaw/reflistfam.html

This site focuses on women and the law with a particular emphasis on family law. You will find a tidy list of useful links on such subjects as family medical leaves, the glass ceiling, family law, and women's organizations. Although it's not comprehensive, the list highlights some of the larger, more prominent resources for women.

Court Locator Service

http://ming.law.vill.edu/State-Ct

The Court Locator Service provided by the Villanova Center for Information Law and Policy helps you find state courts. Simply click on the state of your choice and find the hours of operation, information on small claims court, traffic court, and much more, including recent opinions by the state's judiciary.

Court TV

http://www.courttv.com

If you're an avid fan of Court TV, their Web site has even more of the same juicy news on the hottest trials as well as consumer friendly legal information. Read case files and discover little known details, found in the full text of transcripts and depositions, on trials like the Oklahoma City bombing. Other perks: research legal terms in their glossary or find an attorney online.

The Copyright Web Site

http://www.benedict.com/index.html

Ignorance of the law is no excuse for breaking it, especially when it comes to copyright infringement. So, if you're trying to discern whether a lyric or phrase falls under public domain or fair use law, a quick glance at the Copyright Web site should suffice in answering the question. The site explains the basic rules governing copyright law. There's also a special section that deals with the thorny issue of copyright on the Internet.

'Lectric Law Library

http://www.lectlaw.com

The winner of numerous awards, the 'Lectric Law Library's site is probably the best site basic legal information. From current news on trials, pending legislation to information for the layperson like consumer rip-offs and taxes, this is a warehouse of information. Judges and attorneys will appreciate the special section dedicated to them, and consumers will enjoy heading over to the periodical reading or reference room.

The Consumer Law Page

http://seamless.com/alexanderlaw/txt/intro.html

The Consumer Law offers a wealth of useful and practical information to consumers. From feature articles on consumer rip-offs to tactics on how to protect yourself from fraud, consumers are likely to learn something new every time they visit the site. Of note, there is updated information on specific scams, industries, and products, as well as suggestions on "how to fight back."

The Electronic Privacy Information Center

http://www.epic.org

This site does a thorough job of informing people how to protect their civil liberties, constitutional rights, and right to privacy. The Electronic Privacy Information Center or EPIC is a public-interest research center established in 1994 to study issues of concern on the information su-

SPOTLIGHT ON WOMEN AND THE LAW

Women in the legal profession have a mixed record of advancement, despite the common perception that this is among the most promising profession for females.

Some Facts

1 According to the American Bar Association's 1995 Commission on Women, half of all students enrolled in American law schools are women.

2 The same commission found that female lawyers in the first to three years of their careers face an income disparity of $7,000 compared to their male counterparts.

3 A Colorado study cited in the commission's report concluded that women earn only 82% of men's annual salary while men stand at 300% percent greater chance than women do at rising to the ranks of partner.

4 More than half of the women responding to a 1993 National Law Journal study said they experienced some form of harassment.

Some Sites

1 Learn more about the professional associations and organizations that support legal practitioners at this section of the American Bar Association.

http://207.49.1.6/lawlink/associations.html

2 Access hundreds of law-related documents, listings for U.S. law schools, law firms, publishing firms and legal associations; and a catalog of legal research on the Internet at the Indiana University School of Law.

http://www.law.indiana.edu/law/v-lib/lawindex.html

3 Read the conclusions from the 1996 Fifteenth Session of Committee on Elimination of Discrimination against Women at the United Nations Division for the Advancement of Women, and find out what you can do to end workplace discrimination.

http://www.undp.org/fwcw/daw.htm

4 Peruse LawInfo for an international directory of attorneys, databases for expert witnesses, law firms, bar associations, and sources for legal research.

http://www.lawinfo.com

5 Read about women's experiences with the justice system and the ways in which the system has been unresponsive to women by visiting the online version of The Yale Journal of Law and Feminism's Web site. Submissions are encouraged.

http://www.yale.edu/lawnfem/law&fem.html

perhighway. Visitors should check out formerly secret documents now available to the public under the Freedom of Information Act.

INTERNATIONAL APPEAL

Global Law Net
http://www.lawnet.net

Global Law Net, the handiwork of lawyers is a fairly comprehensive resource for anyone searching for legal information. There are lists of state, federal, and international governments as well as links to numerous legal Internet resources. Visitors will also find handy reference tools like *Bartlett's Familiar Quotations* and *Webster's Dictionary*.

National Law Journal
http://www.ljx.com

Who said a law journal couldn't include humor, travel, and leisure? In addition to these non-traditional features, the Law Journal Extra provides legal news, the top stories of the day, and updates on the federal circuit every day. The site also holds a listing of online law firms and an employment center where aspiring professionals can post their "employment wanted" ads, or firms may post their "employee wanted" ads. This is a fun, uncluttered site for clear synopses of legal news.

LawInfo
http://www.lawinfo.com

Sponsored by Counsel Connect, an online service for lawyers, the LawInfo site provides an international directory of attorneys, databases for expert witnesses, law firms, bar associations, and sources for legal research. It delivers exactly what it promises. Legal scholars and lawyers might enjoy the opportunity to publish their legal research and articles online in the "forum" section of this site.

Supreme Court Decisions
http://www.law.cornell.edu/supct/supct.table.html

At the Legal Information Institute's Web site, search for the landmark decisions of our time by keyword, topic, or name of party for all Supreme Court Decisions dating back to 1990.

Trusts and Estate
http://www.rbvdnr.com/te/tepage.htm

A private law firm specializing in trusts and estates, this Web site provides a laypersons guide to handling one's assets. For interested parties, there are articles and links to the latest news in tax laws, estate planning, litigation, and planned charitable giving. Overall, a fairly thorough guide to managing all of the aspects of one's estate.

U.S. Department of Justice
http://www.usdoj.gov

It's hard to dispute the claim that the U.S. Department of Justice is indeed the nation's largest law firm. With major branches of enforcement including the F.B.I., the Federal Bureau of Prisons, the Drug Enforcement Agency, litigation, and executive offices, the infrastructure is somewhat complicated. This home page is a good place to learn about the divisions and or jurisdictions within the Department.

The National Journal of Sexual Orientation Law
http://sunsite.unc.edu/gaylaw

For recent updates, thoughtful commentary, reports, and studies on gay and lesbian legal issues, the National Journal of Sexual Orientation Law will meet your needs. Browsers should be warned that the site is not much to look at. However, there are original briefs filed by litigators, transcriptions of proceedings, and extremely relevant information for advocates of gay and lesbian issues.

Language in the Judicial Process
http://hamlet.la.utk.edu

This online newsletter devoted to language and law is for the legal scholar or anyone fascinated by the uses and structure of language. For interested parties, there are archives of abstracts, current citations in the field, and related links.

The Letter of the Law
http://rampages.onramp.net/~collier/newsltr.htm

A private law firm, Collier and Associates brings an electronic newsletter online to advise the business community. The newsletter concentrates on the most common legal landmines executives are likely to fall on. Even if you're not managing a staff of your own, the site is just as useful for describing employee rights and employer prerogatives. The site has substantive articles on sexual harassment, employee contracts, as well as interesting little known facts.

Lawyers Cooperative Publishing

http://www.lcp.com

For an idea of upcoming legal publications or an index of prominent publications, browse through the Lawyers Cooperative Publishing site. The most useful feature is likely to be the "legal list" which is actually "The Legal List, Fall 1995 Internet Desk Reference, Law-Related Resources on the Internet and Elsewhere." Now in its seventh edition, the legal list is a terrific guide to numerous law-related resources found on the Internet and elsewhere.

Attorney Net

http://www.attorneynet.com

Attorney Internet Marketing of Mountain View, CA delivers a useful and efficient means of finding an attorney without having to endlessly peruse your phone book. By entering in the specified location and the area of expertise desired, the site will provide matching hits. An added incentive is the list of additional legal resources provided.

The Freedom Forum First Amendment Center

http://www.fac.org

This site is created by the nonprofit media watch dog organization based at Vanderbilt University. The site provides current information through its First Amendment Legal Watch and monthly newsletter. In addition, the site advertises the numerous activities of the center such as the visiting scholars program, the "Freedom Speaks" television program, and its media panels. Of course, the site wouldn't be complete without full text and summaries of vital First Amendment decisions by the Supreme Court since 1990.

Center for Democracy and Technology

http://www.fac.org

The home page of the Washington, D.C. Center for Democracy and Technology is an informative site about issues of constitutional civil liberties and privacy. A solid resource for those interested in the direction of public policy, legislation, and government regulation of communications technology.

The Divorce Page

http://hughson.com

A resource page for those going through a divorce or ending a relationship, this site was established by a food consultant who was compelled to help others complete the process of untying the knot. From the practical need

[OVERHEARD ON WOMEN'S WIRE]

http://chat.women.com

"It's patronizing, I think, to presume that women who choose to make their livings in the sex industry are necessarily victimized, as opposed to women who choose to work as lawyers—a job that can also involve lots of unpleasantness!"

—Nadine Strossen, attorney, ACLU president and author of *Defending Pornography,* in a live chat on Women's Wire.

of finding an attorney to information on support groups, relevant books, parenting and children, and resources for women, this site fulfills its intended purpose.

Prison Legal News

http://www.synapse.net/~arrakis/pln/pln.html

Who better to inform other prisoners and families of convicted prisoners, about news from within the jails and courts than the individuals incarcerated within that same system? The brain child of Washington State prisoners Dan Pens and Paul Wright, the Prison Legal News is a monthly newsletter covering relevant news nationally and internationally with a particular focus on prisoner advocacy issues.

Citation Guide

http://www.law.cornell.edu/citation/citation.table.html

Another reference item from the Legal Information Institute at Cornell University Law School, this site is the laypersons citation guide. For all aspiring writers and researchers of legal briefs, this online guide provides all of the rules of legal citation.

National Political Index

http://www.politicalindex.com

Sponsored by AWWL or "Americans Who Work for a Living" this site is attempting to the become the one and only source for political news on the Web. It has thousands of links to political figures. The mandate as stated in their introduction is "locating, carefully indexing, and promoting the political work of others."

Law Journal EXTRA!

http://www.ljextra.com/nlj

The National Law Journal succeeds as a Web site by delivering legal news to a sophisticated target audience utilizing a bright, visually appealing page (see Figure 5.5). Updated weekly, the journal features the latest articles and news briefs on significant trials and issues relevant to the legal community.

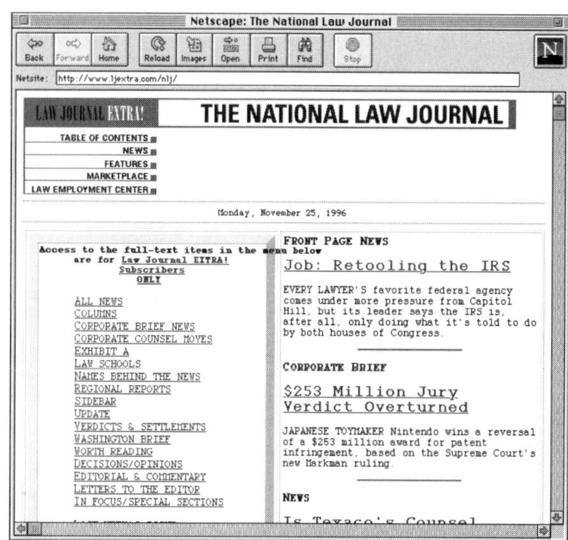

Figure 5.5

Law Journal EXTRA!, *http://www.ljextra.com/nlj*

POLITICAL MEDIA

Z Magazine

http://www.lbbs.org/ZMag.htm

Any magazine that contains the Noam Chomsky archives can easily be touted "alternative" and left wing. Although this site fails to be visually captivating, the content is the lure. Z magazine's monthly focus on political, cultural, social, and economic issues in the U.S. promises to provides a critical look at society.

WebActive

www.webactive com

Political activists are encouraged to get involved and share their political concerns and passions on Webactive. Well laid out with great design and graphics, this one fulfills its mandate to keep you informed of leading edge politics while providing opportunities and information about activism. A one-stop shop for all the hot issues of today.

Washington Weekly

http://www.federal.com/Political.html

A service of the alternative *Washington Weekly,* this site is appropriately titled "all things political." Offering speeches, discussion groups, scandals, and opinion polls.

Webmasters at Washington Weekly succeed in their mission to transmit political news.

PoliticsNow

http://www.politicsnow.com

A joint effort of ABC, *National Journal, Washington Post, the LA Times,* the Associated Press, and *Newsweek Magazine,* this virtual panoply of political information is invaluable. The site contains up-to-date information such as transcripts of speeches by the major players and extensive links to other sites. PoliticsNow offers all the features of ElectionLine and PoliticsUSA. One of the best features is Michael Barone's classic Almanac of Politics.

Mother Jones

http://www.mojones.com

Following the header of Mother Jones Interactive is the statement ,"More damned liberal media bias." This is indicative of the wry approach to news and politics that can be found here. For the interested, this site has some thoughtful features to peruse. Example: the MoJo Wire's list of America's biggest political donors and the politicians they donate to.

DeMOCKracy

http://www.clark.net/pub/theme/demockracy

Visit this site for a hillarious political comic strip. Distributed three times a week through the Internet, these political comics offer a lighter take on the often dry business of politics.

The Doonesbury Electronic Town Hall

http://www.doonesbury.com

Get your daily political updates with a smile. The familiar Doonesbury crew lights the way with daily briefings, ways to get involved in politics, flashbacks to past elections, and more. Be sure to vote in the daily Straw Poll, a humorous take on the news of the day.

Women in Politics

http:// www.westga.edu/~wandp/w+p.html

Women in Politics is an academic journal about women's place in the political spectrum. The site for this quarterly journal includes abstracts of articles from the journal, links to other political sites, and discussion lists...and, of course, subscription information for ordering the paper-based version of the journal.

[OVERHEARD ON WOMEN'S WIRE]

http://chat.women.com

ON HER ROLE AS A PIONEERING WOMAN IN CONGRESS:

"We didn't knock down these doors for our health. We want women to come through them."

ON THE ANTI-SINGLE-SEX MARRIAGE BILL:

"I think the Defense of Marriage Act is nothing but a wedge issue. The Republicans are simply trying to plant more seeds of hate by getting people to organize against gays and lesbians. A wedge issue is where you drive a wedge between different groups that make up your community. You can either drive a wedge or build a bridge. I want to be a bridge-builder."

—Former Congresswoman Pat Schroeder in a live chat on Women's Wire. Schroeder served 12 terms in Congress. That's longer than any other woman in U.S. history. She retired in 1996.

National Opinion Registry

http://www.opinion-reg.com

Concerned citizens are invited to exercise their civic rights and register their opinions on the questions that influence their lives through QUICK-POLL USA. This is an interesting site if you're trying to gauge the zeitgeist of the age or the pervasive mood of the public on significant issues. NOR compiles your opinions to form NORSTATS and promises to publicize them through timely newsletters sent to legislators on local, state, and national levels.

What's Newt: Keeping Track of Newt Gingrich

http://www.wolfe.net/~danfs/newt.html

The controversial House Speaker some call "revolutionary" has a Web site dedicated to his latest sound byte, quotable quote, and vision for America. Whether fan or foe, check out this site for news on Newt, past stories in the archives, funny quotes, or the full text of the "Contract with America."

Internet Conservative Network

http://world.std.com/~icrn

The Internet Conservative Resource Network is a political junkie's dream. Visit this site to read "great conservative" speeches, find links to other conservative sites, log onto a discussion group to debate right-wing agenda issues, or simply follow the news among compatriots for the conservative cause. Find phone numbers, e-mail, and other contact information for your elected representatives.

Foreign Report

http://www.thomson.com/janes/pay_view/default.html

Visit this weekly foreign-affairs newsletter published by Jane's Information Group for a serious, thoughtful look at international affairs. Scholars, journalists, and investors flock to this report for predictions on world events and insightful analysis. The annual subscription rate to access FOREIGN REPORT via the World Wide Web is £125 US$260.00. Interested parties should browse the sample issue on the Web with various articles on international monetary policy, foreign policy, and updates on world hot spots.

George Magazine

http://www.georgemag.com/hfm/index.html

Although not the most substantive site for political news, *George Magazine,* the brain child of John F. Kennedy Jr. is one of the more entertaining and light-hearted ones. Like its print counterpart, the on-line version is a wry, tongue-in-cheek approach to politics. In addition to current issues of interest, political junkies will find weekly polls, and an interactive "forum" on issues such as the media and society.

C-Span

http://www.c-span.org/schedexp.htm

Unfiltered and hardly processed political coverage is the name of the game for C-SPAN's television broadcast. The same goes for its Web site. Fans will find the current C-SPAN schedule, upcoming events, and archival news from the Public Affairs Video Archives at Purdue University in a simple layout. It's faster than flipping through your *TV Guide* and you can order tapes of missed programs.

All Politics

http://www.AllPolitics.com

A joint production of CNN and *Time,* you need not turn elsewhere for political news summaries, detailed analysis, commentary, and editorials (see Figure 5.6). Two very reliable sources have gathered their best in a user-friendly format. With constant updates on state and federal politics and politicians, this site is invaluable to Washington watchers.

100 BEST SITES

Salon Magazine

http://www.salon1999.com

The irreverent journalists responsible for this site provide a welcome break from identical news headlines and boring media reviews. Salon serves up news, book reviews, arts and ideas with a healthy dose of editorial opinion, including lively discussion from well-known media and political personalities. A highlight: Frisky Washington insider James Carville's Swamp Fever column. (http://www.salon1999.com/archives/carville.html), in which the columnist donates his hip, insightful view on everything from election politics to Hollywood. Your participation is encouraged.

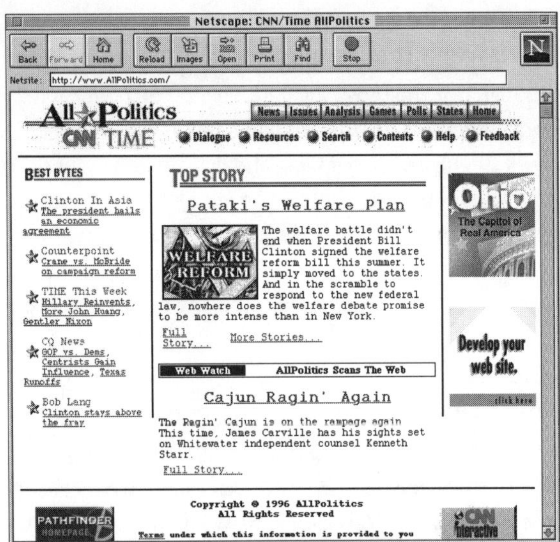

Figure 5.6

All Politics, *http://www.AllPolitics.com*

PUBLIC POLICY AND ORGANIZATIONS

Thomas

http://thomas.loc.gov

Thomas should be the first stop for Congressional legislative news. Established by the U.S. Library of Congress in 1995, the site contains among other things a Congressional record text, a bill summary and status, a list of floor activity for the current week, "hot legislation" categories, and committee reports from the 104th Congress. There is a wealth of information to be gleaned from this site. If participatory democracy requires an informed populace, this site should adequately equip inquiring minds.

ACLU

http://www.aclu.org

The ACLU "Freedom Network" breaks down topics of interest ranging from racial equality to reproductive rights to women's rights. "In the Courts" and "In Congress" give visitors current information on the battles being waged around the country.

Democratic Party

http://www.democrats.org

The party of Andrew Jackson, William Jennings Bryan, Harry Truman, and now Bill Clinton offers their partisan approach to politics with a lively, informative Web site. The content ranges from the important—the 1996 Democratic Platform, to the amusing—the history of the Democratic Donkey symbol.

Reform Party

http://www.reformparty.org

Ross Perot and the Reform Party may be unsuccessful in the national race for America's top CEO, but this site is clearly a winner in the online race. This Web site gets its political message across without forgetting the fun stuff. Namely, the interactive gallery hosts an online chat room, a photo album, and online audio/video of party landmarks.

Republican National Committee

http://www.rnc.org

"Welcome to Republican Main Street" is the greeting that visitors to the RNC site will receive. The Grand Old Party offers news releases, excerpts of the party platform, updates from the GOP news wire, and the latest on RNC radio and television spots. Compared to it's democratic counterpart, this Web site has superior content and design. The Web site also has fun stuff like the RNC crossword puzzle and the RNC gift shop where you can order hats, mugs, and gifts for your the conservatives in your life.

United Nations

http://www.undcp.org/unlinks.html

Although it's not the most efficiently designed Web page, there's a significant amount of useful information on the United Nations and its activities here. Of note to international watchers are the listings for U.N. country offices, Security Council resolutions, and keyword search functions for other important U.N. documents.

League of Women Voters

http://www.lwv.org/~lwvus

Using a hip Web site, the League of Women Voters, a nonpartisan organization, is spreading their message of political participation and community activism. Visitors to the site will find back issues of the league's publication, *The National Voter,* as well as ideas on how to get involved politically.

Feminist Majority Foundation

http://www.feminist.org

The driving force behind The Feminist Majority site is to provide timely updates on political issues that concern women and, when appropriate, point people to the e-mail addresses of their members of Congress. The site includes a summary of feminist issues in the news, a calendar of conferences and concerts, as well as some well-organized lists of links to other women's resources on the Internet.

Center for the American Woman and Politics

http://www.rci.rutgers.edu/~cawp

Created by the Eagleton Institute of Politics at Rutgers, The Center for the American Woman and Politics (CAWP) has built this modest Web site to showcase their research and their organization. The site provides fact sheets on women in politics including a detailed list by state of women candidates from recent U.S. congressional and statewide elections, statistics about the gender gap, and details about the number of women in elective office.

EMILY's List

http://www.emilyslist.org

EMILY's List, the organization established in 1985 to help elect pro-choice Democratic women, has a well-designed site featuring information about the organization and the candidates they support. You can learn about the people behind EMILY's List, become a member, and join an e-mail network to keep you informed about their activities. You can also check out their host of links to other political and women's sites.

Project Vote Smart

http://www.vote-smart.org

A nonprofit, nonpartisan organization, Project Vote Smart is a useful tool to verify facts or gather information on politicians and their parties in government (see Figure 5.7). At this site, citizens and journalists alike are encouraged to get involved in the political process by reading biographies, voting records, campaign finances and promises, and performance evaluations of elected officials and candidates. The site lists a toll free number for voters to call in with their questions.

National Organization of Women

http://www.now.org

This site is a great way to stay in touch with NOW and find out about the activities of your local chapter. Check out the "Key Issues" area for informative pieces on important issues including abortion rights, lesbian rights, affirmative action, and the "Take Action" section for informative legislative updates. You can also join NOW's action alert mailing list to keep up with the latest issues in e-mail.

Cato Institute

http://www.cato.org

The mandate of this public policy think tank is to "promote public policy based on individual liberty, limited government, free markets, and peace." Visit this site for the institute's calendar of events, list of special speakers, and updates on current legislation. The site also holds their policy report, their monthly journal, and interesting fea-

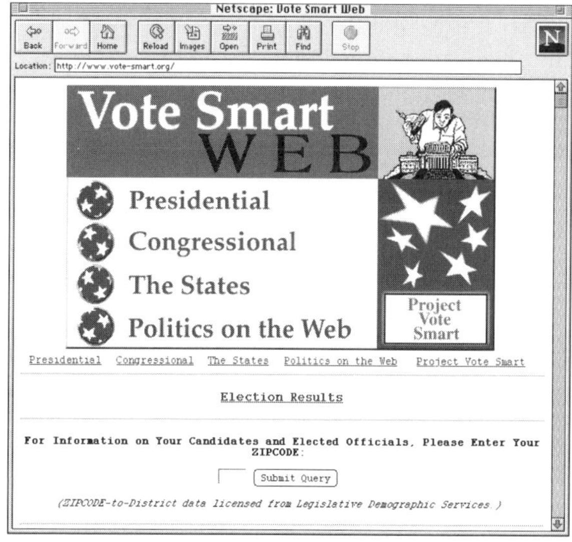

Figure 5.7

Project Vote Smart, *http://www.vote-smart.org*

ture articles on the economy, technology,and communications, political theory, and general public policy issues.

Baker Institute for Public Policy

http://riceinfo.rice.edu/projects/baker

Find updates on public policy and American politics by visiting the site maintained by the Baker Institute for Public Policy at Rice University. Although there is substantial information on events at the institute, profiles of in-house scholars, and general information on policy resources, the "publications" section of this Web site is probably the most useful feature. There, you'll find speeches, studies, working papers, and other findings of the institute.

Christian Coalition

http://cc.org

This vibrant site invites people to linger and look around, whatever their political inclinations may be. It features news on topics concerning religious liberties, national politics, and more. For example, you'll find information on membership, family resources, contacts for local chapters of the Coalition, special events, and policy statements.

Students for a Democratic Society

http://www.cpcug.org/user/kopp/bob/sds

The organization made famous in the 1960s for their contribution to the Civil Rights Movement lives on through the Internet. Students for a Democratic Society spreads its message on the Web with this site that holds key policy statements such as the 1962 Port Huron Statement, links to leftish youth organizations, and left-wing resources. To see how you can get involved, the site's "action alert" calls your attention toward events and news that demand a response.

Democratic Socialists of America Home Page

http://www.dsausa.org/index.html

Left-leaning political activists and curious citizens can learn more about the Chicago based Democratic Socialists of America. Part of the larger umbrella organization, Socialist International, this site holds relevant news items, commentary, and general information on the activities and mission of this political party.

Vox Pop

100 BEST SITES

http://www.voxpop.org

The slogan for this political site says it all: "Your Internet. Your Voice." Vox Pop makes great use of the Web with snazzy images, searchable databases, and feature categories such as The Left, Political Humor, Magazines and News, and general resources for news and politics. Give "The Zipper" a spin: Enter your ZIP code and get info on your senators and representatives. It's political news with a good dose of creativity.

National Rifle Association

http://www.nra.org

Americans who are determined to exercise their "right to bear arms" may wish to stop by the National Rifle Association's Institute for Legislative Action site to learn more about the activities of this organization and the benefits of membership. Download news, the latest press releases, research, and a firearms law review.

World Liberalism

http://www.ftech.net/~worldlib

Liberals will find a wellspring of like-minded folks at this page. Liberal news, links to political hotspots worldwide, and the world's smallest political quiz are found on this site, maintained by Liberal International, a union of liberal parties worldwide.

Peace Net

htttp://www.igc.org/igc/peacenet

PeaceNet is a resource dedicated to peace, social justice, human rights, and the struggle against racism. The organization's home page explains its goals and posts news items of topical interest. Also find listings of related organizations like Amnesty International and the Center for Third World Organizing.

The Concord Coalition

http://sunsite.unc.edu/concord

This site describes the Concord Coalition's hopes to "eliminate the deficit and bring entitlements down to a level that's fair to all generations." Peruse U.S. budget news and read the coalition's "Zero Deficit Plan." Founded by Senators Warren B. Rudman and Paul E. Tsongas, the site is a good source of information for budget watchers and those concerned about the growth of the economy. There are interesting facts and updates as well as links to other like-minded organizations.

Whitehouse.Net

http://www.whitehouse.net

This site contains information about the the White House and its functions. This site offers a briefing room for hot topics, a virtual library for speech and photo archives, and an interactive citizens handbook on government services and programs. Even a map of the offices of the key players and a way to contact your head of state via e-mail.

Heritage Foundation

http://www.heritage.org

This site has eye-catching graphics which favor the good old red, white, and blue. Easy to navigate and quick download times. Updated daily, this online site offers *Today@Heritage, Policy Reviews,* current and back issues of the *Journal of American Citizenship,* a publications library, and specifically geared cyber forums. Of note, the Internship Program for undergraduates with a downloadable application form.

Federal Election Commission

http://www.fec.gov

This site incorporates a citizen's guide to election contributions, help for candidates, parties, and PACs, as well as stats and financial info about all the key players. Employment opportunities at the FEC are also available online. Of note, the site offers a convenient way to download the national mail voter registration form.

Netizen

www.netizen.com

Netizen offers a humorous and irreverent view of politics in America. Created by Brock Meeks, journalist and cyberspace master, the site touches on the hot topic of the day.

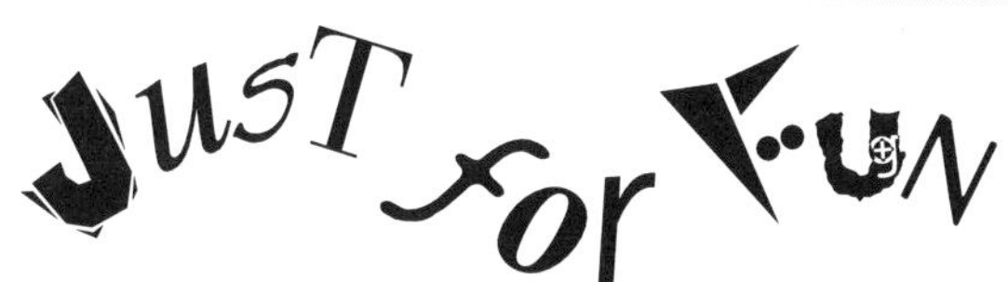

1. Listen to a bedtime story from James Finn Garner's best selling book, *Politically Correct Bedtime Stories.* Download real audio excerpts from this comical, satirical look at bedtime stories adapted for our modern age.
   http://www.mcp.com/380863822881789/general/news2/polit.html
2. If you're behind on your terminology for the '90s, browse a hilarious list of politically correct terms.
   http://pubweb.acns.nwu.edu/~bil874/comedy/misc/morepcte.htm
3. Review the ever-changing hairstyles of first lady Hillary Rodham Clinton.
   http://hillaryshair.com/index.shtml
4. Edit and view hysterical distortions of President Clinton, Dan Quayle, Newt Gingrich, and others at the aptly named "Political Distortions."
   http://www.ibsnet.com/ndl/distortion

☞ KEYWORDS

News: daily news, world news, national news, newspapers, radio, television, entertainment, weather

Politics: activism, associations, organizations, political action, public policy, politicians, political parties, U.S. Congress, White House, federal government

Law: legal advice, advocacy, civil rights, lawyers, law enforcement, law firms, gender issues, discrimination, harassment

Chapter 6 Family

PREGNANCY AND CHILDBIRTH

PARENTING

CHILDREN WITH DISABILITIES

FAMILY EDUCATION

GAMES

PLACES TO GO

FAMILY ENTERTAINMENT

HOLIDAY GOODIES

TEENS

FAMILY ISSUES

ADOPTION

DIVORCE

CARING FOR ELDER PARENTS

10 THINGS YOU CAN DO FOR YOUR FAMILY *RIGHT NOW*

1. Search a database of more than 2,000 summer camps organized by location and activities to find just the right one for your camper.

   http://www.intercamp.com

2. Check Family Planet's Parents' Daily for a daily report on news affecting families, including product recalls and health and safety news.

   http://family.starwave.com/news/index.html

3. Keep your children healthy and strong. Download an immunization guide to help keep track of your children's shots.

   http://rain.org/~medmall

4. Get advice from parenting experts. Visit the National Parenting Center, and read the A-to-Zs for raising happy and well-adjusted children.

   http://www.tnpc.com

5. Find entertaining and fun movies the whole family can enjoy. You can read how the latest movies and videos are rated by other parents.

   http://www.parentsoup.com/parentspicks/movie.html

6. Get rid of those pesky, hard-to-get-out stains! Let the Tide Stain Detector rid you of your laundry woes.

   http://www.clothesline.com/stainDet/index.html

7. Go on vacation. Find the perfect family destination, or a romantic getaway *a deux* with Epicurious' Destination Finder.

   http://travel.epicurious.com/traveler/concierge/concierge.html

8. Research the daycare options in your neighborhood by searching the more than 10,000 entries in the Daycare Page database.

   http://www.thegrapevine.com

9. Stumped on what to cook for dinner tonight? Try these terrific recipes for healthy and hearty family fare.

   http://www.cookinglight.com/recipebox.html

10. Help your kids start a garden. They will learn about different plants and also learn about the environment in the process.

    http://aggie-horticulture.tamu.edu/Kinder/index.html

Every generation has something that makes it unique. The youth of today are growing up in an information age that is unparalleled.

The Internet is helping parents to raise not just computer-savvy children, but responsible, better educated human beings. Kids are learning with amazing ease, not only how to use computers as a tool, but as a device that brings the world closer together.

The Internet is stocked with wisdom for parents, kids, even the family pet. There are Web sites that cover every stage of life from conception to death. Find out how to adopt a child, or trace your family's geneaology. Investigate the various methods of childbirth. Even plug in your conception date to find out what to expect when.

Learn how to protect your children from illness and disease. If it's support you're looking for, find organizations where you'll meet others in similar situations. Learn from others and share what it's like to be the parent of a child with a learning disability, a medical condition such as blindness or deafness, or a genetic disease.

Teach your kids to read or garden, or visit far-off lands and explore museums. Find out about movies the entire family can watch together. Check what the experts and other parents say are the A-to-Zs of parenting, for every age from tot to teen. Find ideas for daycare or eldercare wherever you live.

PREGNANCY AND CHILDBIRTH

Interactive Pregnancy Calendar
http://www.olen.com/baby

This is the ultimate in interactive medicine (see Figure 6.1). Plug in your conception date, or the last day of your period, and the site whips up an instant, printable calendar that takes you through every day of your baby's development. It also clues new moms into the changes happening to a woman's body. This also links to other pregnancy, childbirth, and infant care informational sites on the Web.

Childbirth.org
http://www.childbirth.org

With an extensive list on every method of birthing, this is a superb resource for women looking into their childbirth options. Information on caesarean births, episiotomies, the need for pregnancy classes, and the hiring of childbirth assistants (or doulas), is just some of the information that is here. Check it out before you go into labor.

Pillow Talk's Stork Site
http://www.storksite.com

New mothers and moms-to-be will find a strong sense of community at this site. At their bulletin boards and chat rooms, there's some major bonding going on as everyone shares this magical time with one another. Run by Tori Kropp, R.N. as an offspring of her childbirth education

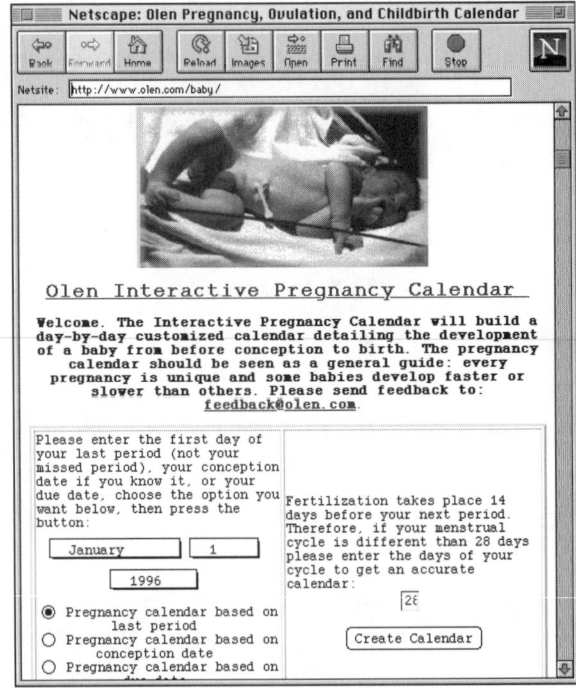

Figure 6.1
Interactive Pregnancy Calendar,
http://www.olen.com/baby

classes, there's a section to answer some of the most common pregnancy questions. A small, but growing, medical library is housed here, too.

INTERNATIONAL APPEAL

Online Birth Center

http://www.efn.org/~djz/birth/birthindex.html

If you're contemplating having your baby at home or using a midwife instead of a doctor, this site is full of information that can help you decide. A listing of midwives throughout the U.S., Canada, England, and Australia will make contacting a midwife easier. The site is searchable, and that helps navigate the plethora of information that is here.

INTERNATIONAL APPEAL

Babyonline

http://www.babyonline.com

This site, based in the U.K., is packed with articles for the mother-to-be anywhere. Advice on teething, how to lose post-pregnancy weight, talking to your baby during pregnancy, and even child safety tips are just some of the fare offered. There's even an interactive forum where you can post questions, share parenting tips with other new moms, and find support.

The Breastfeeding Page

http://www.islandnet.com/lbedford/brstfeed.html

The site does a good job of weaving the basics of breastfeeding with personal anecdotes by nursing mothers. The result: a well-designed site that gives insight into the close bonds developed by breastfeeding. Besides providing the answers to questions like how to prevent sore nipples, it also shows you how to choose the right breast pump.

Names!

http://members.aol.com/fishware/name.html

No bells and whistles here, but you'll find a thorough and concise dictionary on some of the most popular and common girls' and boys' names. Find the original meaning of the name of your choice, or just click over to see what names you should not name your baby. Sorry, but this year's most infamous ladies' names, Kathie Lee and Soon-Yi, are definitely out.

Jellinek's Baby Name Chooser

http://www.jellinek.com/baby

Tired of squabbling over whose side of the family to name the baby after? Let the computer do it for you. This site will randomly choose a name for the wee one. Just don't get upset when you can't find personalized attire for babies, Ciara and Bax.

American Association of Pediatrics

http://www.aap.org

An outstanding vaccination chart and information on how to prevent childhood diseases is the core of the parenting area. The country's largest association of pediatricians' home page also renders sound advice for parents on how to protect your children from violence. What is missing is online help in finding a pediatrician, but you can send in a request by snail mail.

Medical Mall

http://www.rain.org/~medmall

Allergies, bed wetting, attention deficit disorder, and asthma are just some of the conditions that can affect children. At this site, Dr. Chris Landon, Director of the Landon Pediatric Foundation in southern California, dispenses answers on those topics and a lot more. Links to other relevant health sites are available in Spanish and English, making this site a real asset.

Sudden Infant Death Syndrome Network

http://sids-network.org

Every hour a baby dies in the U.S. from sudden infant death syndrome. This site provides important information that every parent needs to know about this baffling and frightening disease. There is also a support group for grieving parents and a Real Audio interview with a leading medical expert from the Mayo Clinic.

PARENTING

Kid Safety

http://www.uoknor.edu/oupd/kidsafe/start.htm

This is a great site for parents and kids to look at together. The University of Oklahoma has put together a safety quiz for kids that can educate and enlighten everyone about safety practices. Safety on the Internet, what to do in an accident, and how to handle strange pets are just a few of the helpful areas here.

Safe Surf

http://www.safesurf.com

The movement for a safer Internet for kids is on, and Safe Surf is leading the charge. The company is one of the original Internet rating systems that help parents choose appropriate sites for their children. There is a detailed description of the current rating system that it uses and the opportunity to upgrade your browser to support the company's program. A helpful Kid's Wave section, lists kid-friendly and Safe Surf approved sites.

Parent Soup

http://www.parentsoup.com

This is the place for cyber-savvy parents to meet and exchange views on the joys and challenges of parenting (see Figure 6.2). Whether you're a single parent, a stepparent, a working parent, or a stay-at-home mom, there is lively discussion along with information and support for you. Take part in their daily poll on today's parenting issues or join one of their many chat sessions; it's all here.

The National Parenting Center

http://www.tnpc.com

With a library of answers to the most common, uncommon, and unusual parenting issues for children of all ages, this site is the virtual manual on parenting. Their experts run the gamut from medical doctors to child psychologists, to published authors on the topic of parenting. Guidance and help are available on all stages of child development: from newborn to adolescent. It's like having your own parenting consultant on call 24 hours a day.

Figure 6.2

Parent Soup, *http://www.parentsoup.com*

The American Academy of Child and Adolescent Psychiatry

http://www.psych.med.umich.edu/web/aacp

How to help children deal with divorce, stepfamily problems, depression, and teen suicide are just a few of the topics the academy advises parents on. These mental health professionals offer help on more than 50 tough parenting issues and give families solid advice on how to help their children. The award-winning, "Facts for Families" section is available in English, French, and Spanish.

National Parent Information Network

http://ericps.edu.uiuc.edu/npin/npinhome.html

You can find out if your child is gifted or learn how to develop a strong relationship with your child's school at this site. You will also find information on how to tackle many other concerns facing today's parents. Sponsored by Columbia University's Teacher's College and the University of Illinois, there are links to discussion groups and an area where you can ask the experts for more help.

Family Planet

http://family.starwave.com

The latest news affecting families and tons of fun things to do with your kids are just the beginning of some of the neat stuff here. At the site's "Sound Off" section, parents get their say on hot topics, such as: how to discipline your kids, the effects of working overtime on your children, and sexual harassment by kids at school. Updated daily, so if you have a spare half hour, you can always learn something here.

Parents Place

http://www.parentsplace.com

If you're a parent who wished directions came with your newborn, you're not alone. Started by a couple who quit the rat race to spend more time with their baby, and recently merged with Parent Soup, Parents Place offers practical help on birth, health, nutrition, and shopping. Don't know what to make for dinner? Check out their online menus for some family favorites. A searchable index makes navigation easy.

Parenthood Web

http://www.parenthoodweb.com

New moms and prospective parents will appreciate this site with information geared toward easing their anxieties. A panel of expert physicians answers questions, such as: how to know your child is getting enough breastmilk; the possibility of a vaginal birth after a caesarean; and even when to start children on solid foods. Their "I Wish I Knew" section passes on information every pregnant woman wishes she knew before the whole process.

All About Kids

http://www.aak.com

How do you raise strong, sensitive, responsible children? This site, an extension of *All About Kids* newspaper, based in Cincinnati, tries to answer that question (see Figure 6.3). An interactive forum on child rearing, from birth to those terrible twos, is available. You will also find a plethora of articles; including, how to choose the right preschool; and how to find out if your child has a learning disability.

Fathering Magazine

http://www.fathermag.com

You can take an illuminating look at the "other" person in the parenting equation at this site. The magazine has a mix of news, interviews and articles with a decidedly male skew. It's a good place to find out why there is a growing movement that considers circumcision "mutilation" or why some dads do NOT want to be called Mr. Mom.

where they surf

Surfer: Bonnie Scott

Director of Multimedia Mom Network

Favorite Web picks of the moment:

ParentsPlace.com

http://www.parentsplace.com

"This site is run by a couple in Berkeley, CA, who want to be home with their two-year-old and want to connect with other parents. They provide chat, bulletin boards, and a variety of useful articles all from other parents. No one claims to be an "expert; rather, we are all in this parent mode together."

SafeSurf

http://www.safesurf.com

"My kids are four and five so they are just getting old enough to start surfing, and I am concerned about content access. SafeSurf is committed to free speech on the Net. They, and I too, believe that parents are quite capable of making choices for their children."

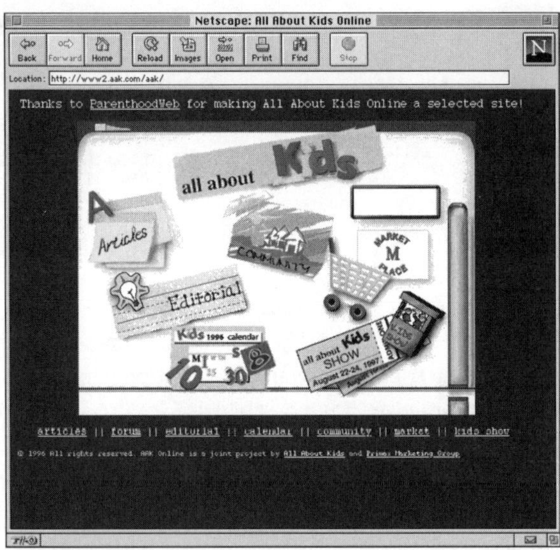

Figure 6.3
All About Kids, *http://www.aak.com*

FatherNet

http://www.cyfc.umn.edu/fathernet.html

This site explores the role fathers play in their children's lives. Brought to you by the University of Minnesota's Children, Youth and Family Consortium, FatherNet attempts to bring diverse voices together by providing an electronic discussion group, articles and essays, links to resources, and information on Father to Father, a program started in response to Vice President Gore's call to action. Plenty of adorable pictures of Dad and the kids.

National Center for Fathering

http://www.fathers.com

This is one of the best sites for fostering strong family ties. Great advice and guidelines for fathers on almost every parenting situation including, expectations when they come home from work, and the importance of having a strong, loving relationship with the mothers of their children. With articles from *Today's Father* magazine, this site provides helpful and reassuring guidance for men.

CyberMom

http://www.cybermom.com

CyberMom dishes out sassy advice that you would get from your Mom, without the virtual guilt. Check out her tips for the best way to keep your car clean; or, look for new adventurous ways of making macaroni dinners. There's even a top 10 list that could make Letterman run for cover.

Multimedia Mom

http://www.harbornet.com/mediamom

Anyone who has ever struggled to find fun, entertaining, and kid-friendly videos for their children will appreciate

[OVERHEARD ON WOMEN'S WIRE]

http://chat.women.com

"A woman commented to me she heard her little boy in the back of the car: A friend of his said: 'We went to Disneyland for four days.' Second boy: 'We stayed five days!' Her own darling child: 'We're moving there!' She felt she should tell her boy not to lie! But after seeing my clips and hearing me talk about it, she said, 'Now I realize that's just how boys talk.'"

—Deborah Tannen, author of best-selling book *You Just Don't Understand*, in a live chat on Women's Wire.

this site. Started by Bonnie Scott, a mom who was tired of shows that weren't healthy for kids, started this site that reports monthly on the latest video releases and computer software. There are also plenty of links to buy the materials online if you so choose.

Parent News

http://moss.fgreen.com/parent/parent/index.html

Started by a child psychologist, this site features an extensive set of articles, such as: raising children with social interest, nine things to do instead of spanking, and the harmful effect of criticism. All of the articles, in full, can be e-mailed to you. A special section for stepparents and families going through divorce offers support and sound advice.

The Daycare page

http://www.thegrapevine.com

This site houses a treasure-trove of daycare information with more than 10,000 entries to help you choose the right daycare provider for you. You can search by city and state, or by zip code. It's not limited to daycare, but also includes private schools, group homes, preschools, and even nannies, too. The section on daycare questions is a bit skimpy…a FAQ would be better.

American Childcare Solutions

http://www.parentsplace.com/readroom/ACS

No need for a repeat of Nanny Gate! This handy site explains the legalities of hiring a nanny or an au pair, and even of placing your children in daycare. With printable forms to fill out for tax and other government purposes.

Family.com

http://www.family.com

Fun-filled, family activities are the main focus of this site (see Figure 6.4). Its big, colorful menu points the way to their food, travel, and family-ties sections full of ideas on things to do. Kudos for the special sections that direct you to family stuff happening in your region of the country. It's a great place to surf when the kids say, "We're bored!"

Parenting Twins or Other Multiples

http://www.parentsplace.com/readroom/multiples.html

Located on the ParentsPlace site, this page holds a wealth of resources on twins, triplets, etc. You can scroll through interesting questions at The Misc.Kids Twins FAQ, check out the latest issue of *TWINS* magazine, or join a mailing list, and more. Get the kids involved (both of them!) with a list of childrens' books for and about twins. If parenting twins has you seeing double, bookmark this site for creative ideas.

INTERNATIONAL APPEAL

Twinless Twins

http://www.iserv.net/twinless

The Twinless Twins Support Group International is a non-profit organization founded to support twins who have suffered the loss of their twin through death or estrangement. What you'll find at the site: Information on the upcoming annual Twinless Twins Conference, plus links to publications (including *Twinless Times*), mailing lists, and more. Most importantly, though, TTSGI

Figure 6.4

Disney's Family.com, *http://www.family.com*

provides a comforting place to find people who understand one another as no one else can.

Twins Book Research

http://www.gbd.com/twins

If you're a twin, here's your chance to tell your story. Leila Brown-Swanson, mother of twin daughters, is writing a book about the relationships of twins, and she's got a series of questions she'd like you to tackle to help her with her research. Question topics include "Siblings of Twins," "Individual Identity," and "Living on Your Own," to name a few. You can also subscribe to Leila's free newsletter, *Di-Alogue.*

CHILDREN WITH DISABILITIES

The Arc

http://TheArc.org/welcome.html

The Association of Retarded Citizens sponsors this site where you can find valuable information on the disabled; including how to help children who are developmentally disabled, residential and employment options for the disabled, and respite care for parents. The site guides you through the lengthy landmark legislation, American Disabilities Act, and links to the group's local chapters.

The National Federation of the Blind

http://www.nfb.org

For parents searching for information for their visually impaired children, this is a good place to start. The Federation's *Future Reflections* magazine is available here online. The presentation is bare-bones, but it has essential information for both parents and teachers of blind children. The site does a good job of keeping track of current and pending legislation and it has links to government and community resources.

Deaf World Web

http://dww.deafworldweb.org/dww

Articles, pictures, and information for deaf people all over the world, is available here at this Web site. You can download and print the American Sign Language chart; or, find out how to protect your children from sexual predators. A wealth of knowledge for the deaf is here, but the confusing layout of the site means it will take a little while to find it.

National Tourette's Syndrome

http://neuro-www2mgh.harvard.edu.tsa/tsamain.nclk

Famous surgeons, baseball players, and even Mozart was afflicted with this disorder. Sponsored by the neurology department at Massachusetts General Hospital, you'll find the latest medical and scientific information that will help you better understand Tourette's Syndrome. Excerpts from publications helping both parents and children cope, and more important, thrive despite the disorder, are available at the site.

Children and Adults with Attention Deficit Disorder

http://www.chadd.org

More children and adults are diagnosed with Attention Deficit Disorder and Attention Deficit Hyperactivity Disorder than any other learning disability in the U.S. With the growing numbers comes a need for more information. The parents-based organization CHADD, (Children and Adults with Attention Deficit Disorder) renders the support and information given in their meetings at their home page. The site offers techniques for parents and teachers helping children, and advice for adults dealing with the disorder.

The Autism Society of America

http://www.autism-society.org

This is a very parent-friendly site and includes a "Getting Started" package for those families whose children have been diagnosed with Autism. The society has been working for the last 30 years to help educate and enlighten parents and professionals about the disorder. There is lots of solid information here including therapies, treatments, and support groups for both kids and parents. Also included are links to the many Autism resources available on the Web.

Rare Genetic Diseases in Children

http://mcrc4.med.nyu.edu/~murphp01/homenew.htm

What did Paul Murphy do when he could not find information on his child's rare genetic disease on the Web? He started his own home page to pool the resources he has uncovered and is giving parents, whose children are battling these diseases, their own voice. This is a clearinghouse of information with information on gene therapy, bone and organ transplants, and a guide to research institutes and hospitals actively working in genetic research.

Children with Diabetes

http://www.castleweb.com/diabetes

Concise, well-organized information for anyone living with, or affected by diabetes is available at this fantastic resource. Youngsters can vent their feelings about their condition or find a pen pal at the site's special kids' section. Parents will find all the basics about the disease, facts on insulin therapy, a guide to camps for kids with diabetes, and an area to discuss how diabetes is affecting their family.

FAMILY EDUCATION

Internet for Kids

http://www.internet-for-kids.com

Victoria Williams, a parent, a teacher, and a school's superintendent, started this site to encourage kids, ages seven and under, to become more familiar with the Internet. The result: an explosive and exciting site that's dynamic and interesting. Parents can find out the latest on how to get your babies interested in computing, while kids check out the tons of fun activities.

Midlink Magazine

http://longwood.cs.ucf.edu:80/~MidLink

Kids in the middle grades, ages 10-15, now have an online e-zine geared specifically for them. Published four times a year, each with a different theme, this site encourages kids all over the globe to interact and learn from each other. Some of the compelling content includes: haikus from a seventh grade class, forums on the importance of good character, and even multimedia profiles of authors.

KidsCom

http://www.kidscom.com

KidsCom blends savvy advice for parents and a great kid's site. Kids can learn about other cultures, tell humorous stories about their pets, or just vent on important issues to them. Parent have a place here, too, as Dr. Sylvia Rimm, child care expert, answers the question of the week and has a superb top 10 list for smart parenting. Kudos to KidsCom for making such a smart site available in English, French, German, and Spanish.

Big Busy House

http://www.harpercollins.com/kids

Brought to you by publishing giant, Harper Collins, this site serves up entertaining tidbits and background on many of their popular children's books, with a good dose of humor (see Figure 6.5). Kids can find out how to make their own pop-up book on noodles and then download the correct pronunciation for gnocchi and other great pastas. A spectacular area explaining "How a Book is Made" is one of the most delightful and entertaining areas on the Web.

Figure 6.5

Big Busy House, *http://www.harpercollins.com/kids*

LOURDES LIVINGSTON, DESIGNER

National Geographic

http://www.nationalgeographic.com

Take a digital trek through the Fantastic Forest with the folks from National Geographic. Explore habitats complete with animals and sound effects. The site has lots of graphics and will take a long time to load at slower speeds, but it's worth the wait to go on an expedition to the Brazilian frontier with this great expedition team. Also available are back issues of the magazine complete with the beautiful photographs that have become synonymous with the magazine.

The Page at Pooh Corner

http://www.public.iastate.edu/~jmilne/pooh.html

Most of the space at the Pooh Page is devoted to Winnie the Pooh creator, A. A. Milne and his tubby little cubby all stuffed with fluff. You can find out how toys from the author's son, Christopher Robin Milne, became the inspiration for the children's classic; learn the lyrics from this enduring classic; you'll find lots of informative tidbits here.

The Roald Dahl Index

http://www.tridel.com.ph/user/bula/rdahl.htm

Willie Wonka and the Chocolate Factory, James and the Giant Peach, and *Matilda* are just a few literary highlights of Roald Dahl's distinguished career as a children's author. Lia Bulaong, an ardent fan of Dahl's work, started this site and it's loaded with everything any Dahl fan would love: critiques of Dahl's most famous books, a filmography, biographical information, and even a recipe for Stink Bug's Eggs.

Grimm's Fairy Tales

http://ul.cs.cmu.edu/books/GrimmFairy

This no-frills site houses 209 tales from the Brothers Grimm. Transform bedtime into magical time with old classics like "Hansel and Gretel," "Rumpelstiltskin," and "Cinderella." Or, start a new tradition with stories of "Three Little Birds," "The Four Skillful Brothers," and "Six Servants." There is enough here to keep everyone in the family entertained.

Aesop's Fables

gopher://spinaltap.micro.umn.edu/11/Ebooks/By%20Title/aesop

The moral of this site is simple: spartan design with tons of content gets straight to the readers' hearts and minds. This gopher site contains the complete works of Aesop and has all the morals, or tales, that you may have forgotten. For instance, find out why the lion and the mouse became such good friends. This site isn't much to look at, but the information here has definitely passed the test of time.

The Children's Literature Web Guide

http://www.ucalgary.ca/~dkbrown/index.html

Long before the classic *Little Women* became a movie, it was a successful children's book. David K. Brown, librarian and founder of this terrific site, hopes to use the interest in popular movies to draw kids back to books. The site has a broad compilation of links to books available online: including classics like *Alice in Wonderland* and the popular Goosebumps series. You can also find listings of the latest award-winning children's books authors.

Van DerGrift's Children's' Literature Page

http://www.scils.rutgers.edu/special/kay/childlit.html

This site is a treasure for any parent who wished women and minorities were treated more equally in children's literature. Written by Kay Van DerGrift, an associate professor at Rutgers University, this clever site guides you to books that help promote self-esteem and cultural sensitivity in young children. Along with insightful critiques on how the books they read affect children's development, the site includes lists of books that have positive female, Asian, Hispanic, Native, and African-American role models.

Tales of Wonder

http://www.ece.ucdavis.edu/~darsie/tales.html

Here children's bedtime stories take on an international twist. You will find enchanting stories from all over the globe. You can travel to Africa where you can find out why "The Rabbit Steals the Elephant's Dinner," take a slow boat to China or, read about "The Jeweled Sea." You can even visit the ends of the Earth, and let the Siberians tell you "How the Sun was Rescued."

Children's Literature-Fairrosa Cyber-Library

http://www.users.interport.net/~fairrosa

When the school's library is closed you can still search through the virtual stacks at this Cyber-Library. *1001 Arabian Nights, The Jungle Book,* and *Anne of Avonlea* are waiting to be downloaded at the site's Book section. There are Booklists that will help you on your next visit to the "real" thing; and, a guide to finding books with a holiday, cultural, or religious theme.

Carol Hurst's Children Literature

http://www.crocker.com/~rebotis

Carol Otis Hurst has put together a wonderful site that parents who enjoy reading to their children will love. There are thorough reviews of current and classic children's books that include fun activities based on the book, that you and your child can do together. There are also questions that promote a deeper understanding of the themes discussed, and links to more information available online.

IPL Youth Division

http://ipl.sils.umich.edu/youth

This is the kind of library that kids will never want to leave (see Figure 6.6). At the Story Hour area, you can sample stories like "The Fisherman and his Wife" and "The Tortoise and the Hare." They are available in either picture book format or can be download as an animated video. A must stop is the Reading Room; where kids can file a book report of their own, or just peruse through what everyone else is reading.

A&E Classroom

http://www.aetv.com/classroom.index

"Time Well Spent" is cable channel A&E's motto and it applies to their Web site, too. Although, the original idea for the site is to help teachers use their programs to inspire learning, who says that has to end at school? Questions on the network's biographies, historical shows, and classics like Jane Austen's *Pride and Prejudice,* can be used by families who want to get more out of their TV viewing.

Safari Splash home page

http://oberon.educ.sfu.ca/splash.htm

Something fishy is going on at this site. Safari Splash gives a virtual tour of what's at the bottom of Barkley Sound, British Columbia. You can click on the 3-D fish tank and find out more about dogfish sharks or watch

Figure 6.6
IPL Youth Division, *http://ipl.sils.umich.edu/youth*

them move in a Quicktime video. You can even explore the expansive ocean floor and uncover the rich, undersea life. Links to other marine biology sites on the Web are here, too.

A.Word.A.Day

http://lrdc5.lrdc.pitt.edu

Anyone studying for the S.A.T. or who just wants a dazzling vocabulary should not miss this site. Learning a new word a day is the goal here. Did you know that "fustigate" means to criticize severely? You can also pick up daily inspirational quotations, such as Ralph Waldo Emerson's thoughts on the human condition. "Our greatest glory is not in never failing, but in rising up every time we fail."

The JASON Project

http://seawifs.gsfc.nasa.gov/scripts/JASON.HTML

The JASON Project is a huge, global field-trip that brings kids along on the journey. The project's mission: is to explore new scientific frontiers in environmental sciences. Sponsored by NASA, the group interacts with children, in grades 4–8, by assigning projects that kids can do on their own. So far, JASON has globetrotted to the Galapagos Islands, the Mediterranean, and even an exploding volcano in Iceland.

Beakman's Electric Motor

http://fly.hiwaay.net/~palmer/motor.html

You don't have to be MacGyver to help build this motor for your child's next science project. Originally featured on the kids show, *Beakman's World,* this site gives you step-by-step directions on how to build an electric motor. All you need is a D size battery, a magnet, a toilet paper tube, and some wiring; and you will have a working motor. The step-by-step diagrams make assembly a cinch.

KinderGarden

http://aggie-horticulture.tamu.edu/Kinder/index.html

This fun and informative site is jam-packed with hundreds of things that kids can do in a garden. They can plant flowers that attract butterflies; or, learn how to raise an ant farm. Behind the fun are lessons to teach kids how to be responsible about the environment. The seeds of information at this site will not only grow in your child's mind, but in your garden, too.

Star Child...Astronomy for Kids

http://heasarc.gsfc.nasa.gov/docs/StarChild

From the labs of NASA, comes the latest scientific information for young, budding astronomers. Data on the solar system, the universe, and lots of neat space stuff (like a lab on high-energy astrophysics) is furnished in rich detail with the help of some very cool graphics (see Figure 6.7). Some of the stuff went over my head, but it's ideal for kids ages 9–15 with an interest in science.

Volcano World

http://volcano.und.nodak.edu

Visit the world's volcanoes without getting lava on your feet. Kids ages 10–15 will enjoy this fascinating site dedicated to everything volcanic. Find out the latest updates on volcanic activity around the world, or learn how volcanos work. They can even find out how to become a volcanologist.

Figure 6.7
Star Child,
http://heasarc.gsfc.nasa.gov/docs/StarChild

GAMES

Games Domain

http://www.gamesdomain.com

One of the most helpful areas on this family-friendly site, is the kids' area which features downloadable commercial software for children's games, software reviews and ratings, and a handy parent's guide to the Web. The holiday section includes practical, fun things to do; and teens will appreciate the extensive links to FAQ's for almost every video game imaginable.

Games Kids Play

http://www.corpcomm.net/~gnieboer/gamehome.htm

This simple, yet charming, site is a monument to all those games we played as children. Classics, like, "Red Light/ Green Light," "Red Rover," and "Duck, Duck, Goose" are all recounted here. Geof Nieboer started this Web site so that these childhood games that are mostly passed on by word-of-mouth, would find a place in posterity. It's a great site for kids and a refreshing walk down a memory lane for adults.

MCA/Universal Home Video Kid's page

http://www.mca.com/home/playroom

Come meet Balto, Babe, Casper and other stars of MCA's children's movies. The coloring corner, the online arcade games and the downloadable sounds, from the studio's most popular kids' flicks, will mesmerize the younger folk (kids ages 4–8). You can even help Babe herd a flock of sheep into their pen. There are hours worth of fun at this site.

Mr. Edible Starchy Tuber Head home page

http://winnie.acsu.buffalo.edu/potatoe

He looks like him. He acts like him. Yes, this is Mr. Potato Head's alter ego. You can rearrange his face, electronically this time, and then have the joy of putting him back together again. While you're here, be sure to check Mr. E.S.T.H's fan mail and find out why he's becoming a Web phenom. They changed the name, due to copyright infringement, but the fun is still the same.

Hangman

http://www.cm.cf.ac.uk/htbin/RobH/hangman

Before *Wheel of Fortune* ever became TV's most popular game show, there was this simple word game with the menacing name. This time around you're up against the computer and the ornery computer-animated stick man. Choose your letters carefully, because each wrong guess leads to a step closer to the noose. This is such a simple and yet, challenging game, that is fun for the whole family.

Tic-Tac-Toe

http://lobster.bu.edu/TTT/play

This unpretentious game teaches the basics of game strategy and mental maneuvering that can keep you involved for hours. You choose who gets to go first (some say therein lays the secret in winning) and then the computer takes it from there. In an electronic world where the most sophisticated games are being designed every day, it's good to know that there is still a place for some great classics.

Fun Stuff

http://info.gte.com/gtel/fun

This neat-o site from the folks at GTE brings some of the most popular games of yesterday to today's electronic audience. Web Battleship, Minesweeper, Rubik's Magic Cube, and a Virtual Maze are all here and render hours of delight. The rules for each game are explained in detail. The only thing missing here is more games.

Happy Puppy

http://www.happypuppy.com

Happy Puppy packs in so many games, demos, news, reviews, and PC screen savers at this site; it's easy to see why this is one of THE most popular gaming sites on the Web. Started by game designer Jennifer Diane Reitz, there's enough here to keep kids busy for months. Parents may want to review some of the high-octane games that generally best suit kids over the age of 10.

Fake Out!

http://www.eduplace.com/dictionary

Fake Out! blends learning and laughing for kids. The words are arranged in separate categories for kids in Kindergarten to the sixth grade, and then they choose the right definition for a word, among many humorous clues. For instance, second graders can guess if "fogu" is related to tofu or a poisonous fish. Participants can also submit some "fake" clues for next week's set of words.

John's Word Search Puzzles

http://www.neosoft.com/~jrpotter/puzzles.html

Puzzles, puzzles, and more puzzles! This site houses those amazing word-search puzzles where you have to search forwards, backwards, and even diagonally for the words you're looking for. The puzzles here all have themes: kids area, city and states, sports, TV and movies, the Bible, space, and even the Old West. You can print them out when you want to give your kids hours of educational and fun stuff to do.

Mad Libs

http://he1.uns.tju.edu/madlib

Mad Libs, that wild, wacky game that makes up wild and funny stories, hits the Web. Put in the type of word the puzzle asks for, such as a noun, verb, or adjective, and the computer whips up a zany tale. You can choose from a theme, such as: a dream vacation, a cottage in the woods or, the great wizard. Or, let the computer choose for you. It's fun and inventive word play for kids of all ages.

PLACES TO GO

The Franklin Institute of Science Museum

http://sln.fi.edu

Explore science and wonder at the museum's online exhibits. The Franklin Institute offers science know-how and learning opportunities to kids through a variety of exhibits, such as: the workings of the heart; the inquirer's guide to the universe; and the experiments of a hometown boy made good, Benjamin Franklin. There's lots of multimedia stuff here, too, so you get a real flavor of the museum without going all the way to Philadelphia.

The Museum of Science and Industry of Chicago

http://www.msichicago.org

Fun, engaging, and practical exhibits are available here on almost every aspect of life. Some of the best fare include: the transportation zone, where you can download rare footage of a 1931 record-breaking flight from New York to Los Angeles, or watch a Quicktime video showing cities of the past in a salute to Yesterday's Main Street. The site is so terrific. You don't have to be a science buff to appreciate it.

The Exploratorium

http://www.exploratorium.edu

For the first time, you can learn from an online exhibit while giving it the Bronx Cheer. Don't worry it's all part of the experiment. That's just one of the many innovative ways to test perception at San Francisco's leading technical museum. Visit the digital library and they'll show you how the Mona Lisa is being used in a new and unconventional way.

The Field Museum of Natural History

http://www.bvis.uic.edu/museum/home.html

Natural history is here and it's big! Follow the online exhibits and see an Albertosaurus run in a full-motion movie, or listen to mammoth-bone music. There's fun prehistoric goodies for kids, paleontologists, and parents alike. You can follow the time line to the pre-dinosaur era and watch how dinosaurs took over the Earth. Challenge your wits and try to figure out what species survived evolution and which ones were left in the stone age.

The Children's Museum of Indianapolis

http://a1.com/children/home.html

This is one museum site that plays to the hearts of both kids and their parents. The home of the largest children's museum in the nation offers engaging exhibits for kids and fun activities for parents that will rekindle the kid in them. Youngsters can visit the planetarium; or, learn the mechanics of flight and pick up extensive directions on how to make the most sophisticated paper airplanes.

Hands on Children Museum
http://www.wln.com/~deltapac/hocm.html

Kids, ages 10 and under, will enjoy having a museum site just for them. They can travel along on an ocean odyssey or find out more about Casbah the camel. The Washington museum specializes in unusual delights for the younger set. You can even learn the nautical language of signal flags and learn how to spell your name out.

White House for Kids
http://www.whitehouse.gov/WH/kids/html/home.html

Socks, the Clinton family cat, hosts the White House tour for kids (see Figure 6.8), which introduces youngsters to America's greatest house and living museum. Follow along to find out how they built Washington, D.C.; meet other kids, like J.F.K. Jr. and Amy Carter, who have lived in the White House; or get up close and personal with Bill, Al, Hillary, and Tipper. This site has a fantastic e-zine, "Inside the White House" that explains how the government works.

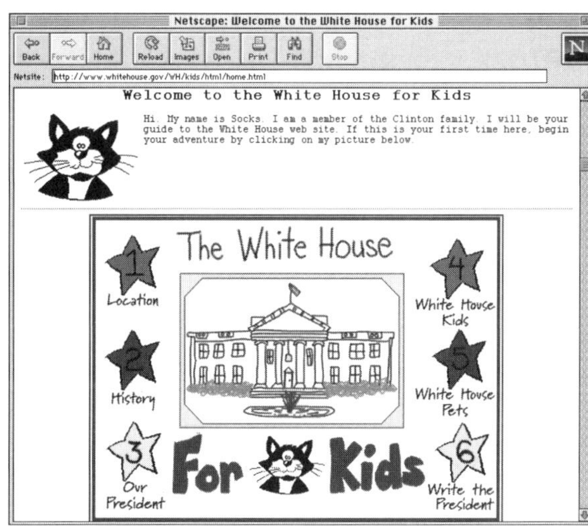

Figure 6.8
The White House for Kids, *http://www.whitehouse.gov/WH/kids/html/home.html*

Polynesian Cultural Center
http://www.polynesia.com

Take a virtual trip to Bali Hai and learn more about Polynesian cultures. Started by the Mormons to preserve the many distinct heritages of Polynesia, this site is a primer on more than 10 islands, including: Tahiti, Hawaii, New Zealand, and Samoa. Visit the Fiji Islands and download an authentic greeting from the tribe. After your junket, say "Aloha" to your friends with an electronic postcard from the Islands.

Minnesota Zoo
http://www.wcco.com/community/mnzoo

Learn about the more than 2,300 animals at the Minnesota Zoo, at this well-designed and clever Web site. Find out about the sleeping habits of the Amur Leopard or why the Burmese Brown Tortoise lays more eggs than any other reptile. While you're here, check out the range and habitat of the Minnesota Bats. There are so many interesting and intriguing animal facts here that can keep kids busy for hours.

The Wildlife Conservation Society
http://www.wcs.org

The society is host to five different locations throughout New York City: The Bronx Zoo, The New York Aquarium, and the three Wildlife Centers in Central Park, Queens, and Prospect Park. Here, you can visit them all. Download a clip of Casey, the Beluga Whale, giving birth; or find out what makes Chinstrap Penguins unique.

Busch Gardens/Sea World Animal Resource Information
http://www.bev.net/education/SeaWorld/homepage.html

This is a great site for kids who have always wanted to see what goes on behind the theme park's closed doors. Check in on a Bengal tiger or learn what makes the Killer Whale tick. Kids interested in an adventurous future can check out the guide for marine and zoological careers.

Monterey Bay Aquarium
http://www.mbayaq.org

Visitors to the largest marine sanctuary will be delighted with the "E-Quarium." Visit the towering Kelp forests or take a tour through deep ocean canyons and shale reefs. You can explore the rocky tidepools off this northern California paradise. This site is so well designed you can almost smell the sea spray off California's magnificent coast.

FishNet
http://www.huge.net.hk/~peterg/fishnet

Peter George, marine biologist and an environmental consultant in Hong Kong, hosts this site, that blends humor and a genuine love of everything aquatic. You will find underwater photographs taken during diving treks throughout the South Pacific, and a plethora of info on diving in the South Seas. The graphic-intense pages are slow to download, but they are worth the wait.

Disney World
http://www.disney.com/DisneyWorld

The family entertainment behemoth offers family fun like nobody else. Now you can plan your vacation to the world's happiest place, online: Make a reservation at any of Disney's hotels and resorts; buy your tickets in advance; or, just sample the nightlife. You can even take a live sneak peak at Disney's Main Street. This is Disney-rama at its peak.

Universal Studios
http://www.mca.com/unitemp/index.html

Back to the Future, Terminator 2, Jaws, all popular movies, now very popular rides. You can visit them all at Universal Studios. Find out the lay of the land and download maps of both Universal's parks in both Florida and California. You can get information on tickets, packages, and hotels at the site's speedy reservations area. These parks are jam-packed with fun, family frolics.

Intercamp: Internet Summer Camp Directory and Resource
http://www.intercamp.com

Parents can search through a database of more than 2,000 camps and find the right one for their child. Put in the general location, the amount you want to pay, special interests, and *Voila!* The site comes up with a report on the camps that meet your criteria. They can then compile your choices in a report that you can print. Great site for parents who want to get rid of those summertime blues.

Outdoor Action
http://www.princeton.edu/~rcurtis/oa.html

Run by the Outdoor Action program of Princeton University, this is the site to check out before you go on the family-favorite trip: camping. Find out what to pack in your First Aid kit, how to choose a camping sight, and what every backpacker should know. This site is a great resource for anyone considering a trip outdoors. With links to almost every outdoor activity, it's a sure bet.

National Park Service
http://www.nps.gov

The National Park Service has put its massive network of parks online. That's good news for everyone who wants to visit any of these marvelous national treasures. You can select a park by state or search for the parks that you know. The site also features an in-depth profile on one park each month and a section on how to prepare for your visit.

FAMILY ENTERTAINMENT

Disney
http://www.disney.com

When it comes to family entertainment, Disney does it all: movies, TV, home videos, music, books, shopping, and software. Mickey's reach seems limitless. At this first-class site, you can find out the latest on all of the Giant Mouse's ventures. There are video clips, sound bytes, and pictures a-plenty on almost every Disney production there is. This site will keep kids, of any age, busy for weeks.

The Family Channel: FamFun

http://www.familychannel.com

The FamFun site focuses more on family values than on family entertainment. Find out what books, movies, and even travel spots get their Family Seal of Approval. There are even forums for parents to share their views on favorite books and suggestions for things to do with the kids on a rainy day. The program listings for the channel are skimpy, but there are games for the kids in the member's only section.

Warner Bros. Animation

http://www.wbanimation.com

Welcome to the wonderful world of Warner Bros. animation. This lushly-produced site houses the genius of the legendary studio's animation department (see Figure 6.9). Kids will find games, pictures, sounds, and clips on favorites like *Animaniacs, Pinky and the Brain,* and *Freakazoid,* as well as cartoon classics. There's a spectacular section called, "Animation 101" that pulls the curtain back on the intricate process of putting a cartoon together.

TBS Kids Disaster Area

http://www.turner.com/tbs/disaste

Fans of Hannah-Barbara cartoons, like *Scooby Doo,* the *Flintstones,* and the *Jetsons,* will love the TBS Disaster Area. Kids can read bios on the Flintstones' Fred and Wilma, and Scooby Doo's Fred and Velma. You can even try to guess what family of dinosaurs Dino belongs to (hint: he's a snorkasaurus). Wacky and irreverent humor means this site is strictly for the younger set.

Cartoon Network

http://www.filmzone.com/SpaceGhost/cartoonnet.html

As part of the Turner cartoon legacy, the Cartoon Network broadcasts its impressive library of 8,500 cartoons, 24 hours a day, seven days a week. The site has a nifty program guide to the station's daunting toon selection, but the real focus here is on their very hip show, *Space Ghost, Coast to Coast.* Currently, Space Ghost claims to be the "only late-night host who was evaded the Council of Doom."

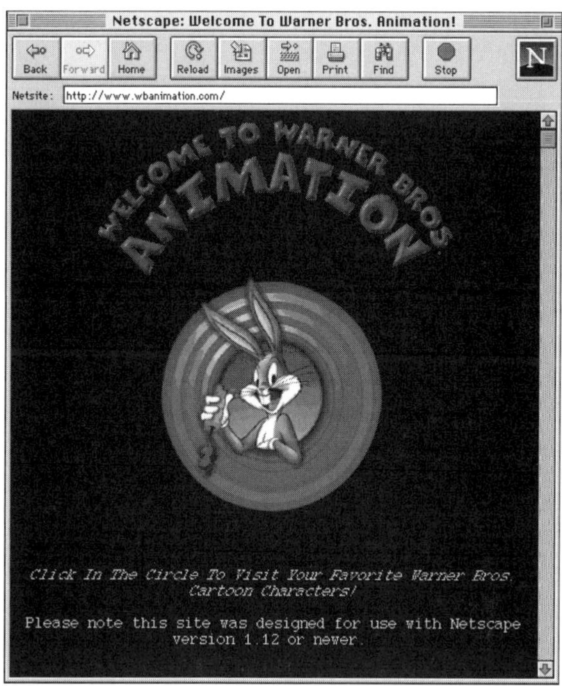

Figure 6.9
Warner Bros. Animation,
http://www.wbanimation.com

The School House Rock page

http://iquest.com/~bamafan/shr

If you're aching to remember the words from ditties like: "Lolly, lolly, lolly, get your adverbs here," or "Conjunction, junction, what's your function?" look no further. School House Rock's goal is teaching children, in a fun way, about words, numbers, and even civic duty. This is an amazing resource that lists the words and downloadable sounds from every one of *School House Rock's* segments: from America Rock, to Grammar Rock, to Science Rock.

Carlos' Coloring Book

http://www.ravenna.com/coloringboo

This simple, yet engaging, site will keep young children enraptured for hours with coloring fun. The site's low-tech appeal adds to its charm. Kids can even design their own coloring book, with the site's server, for a fee. But, there's enough here that will make you want to come back for more. The possibilities are only limited by your child's imagination.

Crayola

http://www.crayola.com/crayola

The official home site of the world's largest crayon giant, is loaded with crayon trivia, info on their new products, corporate history, and even a guide for parents on how to get stains out. Do you know what are the two most popular colors, or how many crayons would it take to go around the world? The answers to those questions, and so many others, are here.

Kristen's Unofficial Play-Doh Page

http://www.prism.gatech.edu/~gt6923b/play.html

Kristen has made Play Doh an art form. You can sneak a peek at her Play-Doh pizza or just look at some of her other creations. There are recipes galore for how to make your own Play Doh at home, including a salty-oily version and a sweet version. Play Doh was introduced in 1972 and you can even listen to the original commercial.

Lamb Chop's Play Along

http://www2.pbs.org/lambchop/intro.html

Preschoolers, who love Shari Lewis' creation, will appreciate this site. There are printable pictures for their coloring pleasure of all the gang: Lamb Chop, Charlie Horse, Hush Puppy, and Buster Bus. There's even a trove of delightful knock-knock jokes that will have the little ones guffawing with pleasure.

Virtual LEGO

http://www.lego.com

At the official corporate site, kids can play, surf, and learn about the wide world of LEGO. Young adventurers can play a treasure hunt game or find out more about those addicting building blocks. There's an online guide to washing and storing LEGOs here, too. The only thing it will not do is pick up the blocks for you.

Kids Crafts

http://ucunix.san.uc.edu/~edavis/kids-list/crafts.html

Ellen Davis gives parents some rudimentary ideas on how to take items from your household and turn them into

where they surf

Surfer: Toria Tolley

Creator of CNN Anchor and single parent of a 10-year-old son.

Toria's official Web page is:

http://cnn.com/CNN/anchors_reporters/tolley.html

Her favorite sites of the moment:

Yahooligans!

http://www.yahooligans.com

"I expected something only my son, Taylor, would enjoy, but I found 'I' spent more time exploring this site than he did! I appreciated the vast library with topics that are up to date and of great use to those of us who don't have vast research books on our shelves. My favorite thing about this site, though, is the fact it brings news to our children...on their level...that doesn't require my constant screening."

Virtual LEGO

http://www.lego.com

"My son LOVED this site...at age 10 he wasn't affected by the fact this was a bit commercialized. He played some games, made some things move, and actually learned a few things. And yes, when he finished, he DID want a LEGOS kit, but when I said no, it didn't deter his interest in the site."

beautiful and useful crafts. The ideas here, all stuff you can do with the kids, include how to turn leftover baby jars into an engaging Christmas tree. You can also learn to entertain kids with homemade versions of the ever-popular finger paints and gak. There's loads of holiday crafts, too.

Aunt Annie's Craft page

http://www.auntannie.com

With Aunt Annie's help, now, no one can say that they're all thumbs when it comes to making crafts. There are step-by-step instructions, and photos to help everyone make fabulous projects. There are more than 50 different crafts that range from the sublime to the sophisticated. Both parents and children will share hours of fun.

Joseph Wu's Origami page

INTERNATIONAL APPEAL

http://www.datt.co.jp/origami

The exquisite art of origami, or paper folding, is featured at this site in detail. There are diagrams that will teach you how to make many figures, including how to make the bird base that is the foundation for other more intricate designs. Learn the history of origami and where you can buy the special paper that is used by Origami Masters.

I·N·T·E·R·N·E·T M·I·N·U·T·E

CHILD-PROOFING THE WEB

There's no question that the Internet is a fabulous resource for kids. But you've probably also heard that there are Web sites that are inappropriate for children. If you are worried that your children will run into (or find) improper material on the Web, you can investigate several software companies that have created filtering applications parents use to child-proof the Web. These programs block out parts of the Internet, including discussion forums and graphically explicit material, that parents may find inappropriate for children. Here are several software packages available—each uses a slightly different method to block obscene or pornographic material, so explore the different programs to see which best matches your needs.

Cyber Patrol

http://www.microsys.com/cyber/default.htm

Cybersitter

http://www.solidoak.com/cysitter.htm

InterGo and KinderGuard

http://www.intergo.com/whoweare/protect.htm

NewView's Specs

http://www.newview.com

NetNanny

http://www.netnanny.com/home.html

SurfWatch

http://www.surfwatch.com

But remember, nothing is fool-proof and software is no substitute for parental guidance. How well your strategies and software work depends on how old, how curious, and how resourceful your children are. The best way to ensure that your children have positive online experiences is to stay in touch with what they are doing while they're online.

Interactive Creativity: Funny People Puppets

http://www.isisnet.com/stagehand/puppets/fpp-shp.html

Puppets and children go together. At this site, youngsters can make their own puppets online. After carefully selecting the eyes, nose, mouth and hair of a puppet: *Voila!* It is done. They can also pick up some tips on paper and scrap puppets and visit an online puppet theater.

Information Collection

http://www.xs4all.nl/~swanson/history/chapter0102.html

Kids, ages 10 and up, can enjoy a virtual field trip around the world, at this site. There are exciting and challenging things to do and see: including a multicultural calender for most of the world's holidays. You can read posts from students who have trekked through Oregon Trail, or learn about Russian history. There are tons of links to fun, entertaining, and informational sites on the Web.

Toys R'Us

http://www.toysrus.com

The super toy store dishes up fantastically fun games, puzzles and cool things to do for younger kids. It's a virtual color explosion at this site, where kids can play the classic game, Concentration, or just create a face. While you're here, you will want to get a glimpse of some hot toy picks for the kids.

Yahooligans!

http://www.yahooligans.com

The creators of Yahoo!, the Internet's most popular search engine, realized that when it comes to computers and kids, it's not just child's play. So, they created Yahooligans!, the largest directory for kid-approved sites on the Internet. The well-designed site has plenty of content to keep everyone from tykes to teens busy, with links to everything from sports and recreation sites, to museums and movies.

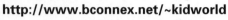

Kid World

http://www.bconnex.net/~kidworld

This is a great site for kids, and more important, by kids. Kids can post their most imaginative questions to "Dear Ashley," make pen-pals, read poems, or submit original story ideas. With lots of stories and jokes for the youngsters, aged 16 and under, the friendly and fresh attitude here will make you want to keep coming back.

Freezone

http://www.freezone.com/home

A vibrant start page beckons kids to come into the Freezone: a very cool place for kids online. They can learn how to build their own home page; join a kids-only chat room; find an e-mail pen pal; or, just surf the music and movie reviews. This is a safe and friendly haven that will interest kids, ages 7–12.

CyberKids

http://www.cyberkids.com/cyberkids

Kids are joining to form their own online community at this site. They can enter a writing contest; compose music and share it with their peers; or, download an original story and watch it come to life with Shockwave. They can even visit a virtual art gallery.

Sports Illustrated for Kids

http://www.sikids.com

Sports' most popular magazine comes online with a special kid's version, including a girl's zone area that puts the spotlight on women's sports. Find out what a day in the life of figure skater, Michelle Kwan, is like; or, read the Olympic diaries of Dominique Dawes. In the special "Created by Kids" section, the most pressing baseball, football, and hockey questions get answers.

HOLIDAY GOODIES

The World Book of Holiday Traditions

INTERNATIONAL APPEAL

http://mgfx.com/holiday

Does your family celebrate a holiday tradition that is special to you? If so, you can add it to the wonderful, and growing, World Book for Holiday Traditions. The goal is to share with other children, around the world, the many different ways traditions are passed on through cultures and generations.

Haunted Home Page

KID Appeal

http://www.hauntedhome.com

Spooky creatures that go bump in the night may only come out on Halloween, but on this page, you can enjoy the holiday year-round. Check out the downloadable spooky sounds, the history of Halloween, pumpkin-carving tips, and even some yummy treats to make, whenever you want a hauntingly good time.

Santa's Home Page

http://www.mofile.fi/rec/santa

At the oldest Christmas site on the Net, you can you can read an exclusive interview with the man in the red suit himself. Meet the reindeer, even find out how Santa Claus came to be. But probably the most important thing you can do here is send Santa your wish list. Yes, he's got e-mail, too! And he'll send you back an electronic card, just so you know he's close by.

Season's Greetings

http://www.christmas.com

Celebrate the holiday season the global way. Christmas, Hanukkah, and Kwanzaa are all represented here. Find out the words to all those carols, you mumble through. You can even find out how the holidays are celebrated throughout the world. There's a Santa Sighting section for the little ones, and a countdown to remind us when the big day is (as if we could forget).

Simply Easter

http://holiday.ritech.com/easter/easter.html

This is a superb holiday site. Find out the history and customs of Easter, and how different cultures celebrate the holiday. You can learn about Easter traditions all over the world and the wonderful, savory dishes made to celebrate the special day. But, one of the best sections, are the scrum-deli-icious desert recipes for year-round goodies, like Chocolate Cheesecake, Chocolate Egg-Nog, and Peanut Butter Cups.

TEENS

Cyberteens

http://www.cyberteens.com

Amazingly talented teens worked to put this site together, a spinoff from Cyberkids. Sensitive and insightful articles, art, and beautiful compositions are tailored here to a teen audience. Hear what it's like to live with HIV, read a Sci-fi series, or watch memorable designs in the site's Shockwave movie theater. Leave it to teens to develop a site that's both sassy and ingenious.

Reverse Link

http://www.io.org/~sward

Reverse Link is edgy, bitting, sarcastic, and full of teen angst. It's definitely not your parents e-zine. Music reviews, movie critiques, and open forums on teen topics make up the dark and trendy site. One of the positives is that any teen can submit their work to the site for consideration. It's definitely a place teenagers will find funky-fresh.

Virtually React

http://www.react.com

This site is the oh-so hip and colorful version of *React* magazine that they distribute with newspapers nationwide. There's plenty for teens here including news, games, jokes, sports, and advice columns (see Figure 6.10). Take part in the poll of the day or amaze your friends with a new joke each day. There's always fresh stuff here and the site is updated weekly.

Figure 6.10

Virtually React, *http://www.react.com*

Adolescence Directory Online

http://education.indiana.edu/cas/adol/adol.html

The Center for Adolescent Studies at Indiana University runs this solid resource for parents and teenagers. There is solid advice and guidance on how to help your child through many parenting minefields of raising a teenager in the '90s. Topics like eating disorders, depression, alcohol, conflict, and violence are discussed in-depth. There's also a teen only section with fun and informational stuff that addresses the concerns of today's youth.

KidLink

http://www.kidlink.org

Getting today's youth talking and communicating with each other is the goal of this site. The KidLink organization acts as a giant bulletin board, allowing kids from all over the globe to discuss, vent, question, and comment on the world. Its efforts (specifically aimed at youngsters, ages 10–15) have not gone unnoticed. Currently, more than 87 countries have participated in this global exchange.

Voices of Youth: World Summit

http:/www.unicef.org/voy

At this UNICEF site, it is the youth of the world that voices their opinions on world issues. Youngsters from around the globe share their thoughts on heavy topics like: the effect of urbanization on children and how war affects youth and children's rights. There's even a forum to discuss how they treat young women throughout the world.

The Safer Sex Page

http://www.safersex.org

Parents be advised: This is a frank and sometimes explicit site about how to have safer sex. Sponsored and written by John Troyer, head of pharmacology at the University of California at San Francisco, this site explains how to avoid sexually transmitted diseases, pregnancy, birth control, and how to use condoms.

Planned Parenthood Federation

http://www.igc.apc.org/ppfa

The world's oldest and largest voluntary family planning organization brings its considerable resources to the Net. There is extensive information on sexual health, sex education, contraception, and reproductive rights. Parents should note, there are guides here for how to talk to your children and your teens about sexuality. They stress the importance of family communication here, as well.

FAMILY ISSUES

Families-Priority 1

http://www.ag.ohio-state.edu/~ohioline/hyg-fact/5000/toc.html

Compiled by the Ohio State University Extension Family and Consumer Services department this site is dedicated to the intricate relationships between family members, providing info-packed articles and essays on a wide range of issues faced by the modern family. Topics include, Growing Up in Multicultural Families, You and Your Aging

Parents, even Growing Up with Exceptional Children. You'll also find extensive bibiliographies with each article.

Queer Resources Directory

http://www.qrd.org/QRD

There are helpful guides for gay or lesbian parents at the Directory's site. They discuss topics of interest to single parenting and same-sex parents here, as well. Adoption, custody, divorce, and dating are all topics that the "Families" site covers. There are also links to support groups for other parents facing the same situation.

Support for Stepfamilies

http://www.parentsplace.com/readroom/stepfamily

The Stepfamily Association reports that two out of three remarriages end in divorce. Unfortunately, for children and their parents, these traumas can have devastating effects. At this site, the Stepfamily Association offers help for parents to ease children's transition into a stepfamily, and, if necessary, reduce the effects of dissolving a family. There are downloadable articles, such as the one that dispels the 60 most common myths of stepfamily parenting and a guide to effective child discipline.

ACME Pet

http://www.acmepet.com

The family pet: one of the most revered members of the household has this site strictly devoted to them. There are guides for dogs, cats, birds, horses, fish and even more exotic silent members of the home. Check out the latest news in pet land with the Acme Pet Times, or get your most pressing questions answered at the Q&A area.

National Coalition for the Homeless

http://nch.ari.net

With more families living from paycheck to paycheck, the alarming chance of becoming homeless is growing. The National Coalition for the Homeless works to help families get back on their feet: by preventing them from becoming homeless, or help them get appropriate shelter once they are. You can also find out about how to become a volunteer in your community, or read about pending legislation in this ongoing battle.

American Red Cross

http://www.redcross.org

As one of the oldest and largest relief organizations in the world, the Red Cross continues to help families in need around the world. Whether it's a devastating storm, earthquake, famine, or war, the Red Cross is there. At their site, you can find out how you can help; download their official child safety calender; or, even take a virtual tour of the history of the Red Cross.

United Way

http://www.unitedway.org

The United Way reaches out to needy families in a variety of ways: they support many health and education programs, provide counseling and support, and they raise funds for charitable organizations. At their Web site, you can find out how the United Way is involved in your local community, or find out how you can become more involved with their program.

First Aid Online

http://www.prairinet.org/~cicely/firstaid

When the kids have a boo-boo, or when you want to know whether to apply ice or heat to an injury, this is the site to check out. There's lots of practical advice for parents, including how to treat burns, frostbite, sprains, bruising, puncture wounds, and shocks. Considering that most accidents happen in the home, this is a very handy resource for treating minor injuries.

Kids Health-Children's Health and Parenting Info

http://www.kidshealth.org

This is a super site on the Net on children's health issues. Sponsored by the Nemours Foundation, which owns the duPont Hospital in Delaware, and the Nemours Children's Clinic in Florida, this site offers parents an abundance of information, including facts on almost every childhood infection imaginable. Bravo to the foundation for a special kids area that answers sensitive questions about children's health in an entertaining and non-threatening manner.

Kid Source OnLine

http://www.kidsource.com

Kid Source offers timely and in-depth coverage of education and health care issues for children. Parents can read about how to nurture the development of their gifted children, how to help a child with Attention Deficit Disorder, the latest on car safety and air bags, or speak out at the "Kid Source Forum" on issues that are important to them. The site is searchable, which is definitely helpful, as there is a substantial amount of useful info here.

SPOTLIGHT ON DOMESTIC VIOLENCE

Deliberate physical abuse of women results in more injuries to women than rape, muggings, and car accidents combined. Here are some startling statistics and Web sites designed to help women in abusive situations.

Five Facts

1. On average, each year almost half a million women in the U.S. are violently attacked by an intimate partner.
2. The F.B.I reports that in 1995, 26% of all the murders committed in the U.S. were by husbands or boyfriends.
3. Almost six times as many women victimized by intimate partners did not report their violent victimization to police because they feared reprisal from the offender.
4. About 75% of the calls to law enforcement for intervention and assistance in domestic violence occur after separation from batterers.
5. Violence is the reason stated for divorce in 22% of middle-class marriages.

Five Sites

1. The Wounded Healer offers a comprehensive list of prevention and recovery resources, survivor's stories, and employment and disability information.
   http://www.idealist.com/wounded_healer
2. The DomesticViolence section of the Metro Nashville Police Department offers sound advice on warning signs, progression of violence, and common characteristics of abusers.
   http://www.telalink.net/~police/abuse
3. Safety Net provides hotline and referral numbers to domestic violence centers nationwide. You can also find out how abused women are helping each other, and develop a personalized safety plan.
   http://www.cybergrrl.com/dv.html
4. The Family Violence Prevention Fund is a national, nonprofit organization that stresses prevention and awareness.
   http://www.fvpf.org/fund
5. The Minnesota Higher Education Center Against Violence and Abuse has put together the definitive site to information and resources available on the Internet to help abused women world-wide.
   http://www.umn.edu/mincava/vaw.htm

Child Quest International

http://childquest.org

According to Child Quest International, a global non-profit organization, every 40 seconds a child is reported missing. The pain for parents is unimaginable. Child Quest has photos of both children who are missing and a comprehensive list of known abductors. The company has a hotline in case you recognize any of the children here. There's also a very helpful safety guide for children and parents, on how to avoid dangerous situations.

National Center for Missing and Exploited Children

http://www.missingkids.org

The National Center for Missing and Exploited Children works with the U.S. Department of Justice to find abducted children throughout the country. At their Web site, you can search through the database of cases that are still open and find an informative guide on child safety and the Internet. Since 1984, this organization that works with the U.S. Department of Justice, has found 29,000 children out of the 44,000 cases of abducted kids.

ADOPTION

The Adoption Network

http://www.adoption.org

Anyone even considering adoption should stop here first. This site, started by an adoptive parent, provides a wealth of information. It includes a listing of more than 2,500 adoption agencies in the U.S. and links to foreign agencies, as well. The well-designed site answers questions, such as: How do you get started? How much does it cost? What is the whole process like? Everyone from birth parents, to prospective parents to adoptees will find answers to their questions here.

Adoptees Mailing List

http://psy.ucsd.edu/~jhartung/adoptees.html

Jeff Hartung, an adoptee, founded this site which tackles the daunting and extensivelegislation that surrounds adoption. You'll find a guide that explains adoption laws from state to state plus the latest laws on open adoption, of which Hartung is a strong proponent. One of the most useful things here is the step-by-step guide on how to find birth parents.

Adoption: Assistance, Information, Support

http://www.adopting.org

This site blends useful information on the adoption process with helpful parenting advice. Features written mostly by child psychologists deal with a variety of hot topics like: how to explain adoption to your children, how to handle interracial adoptions, and how to manage an identity crisis. Great support system for anyone involved with any aspect of adoption!

DIVORCE

Divorce home page

http://hughson.com

Dean Hughson, food consultant and divorcee, has put together an impressive site that discusses the painful trauma of divorce. This a virtual A–Z divorce guide is a terrific resource for anyone who is going through a divorce, or is still recovering from one. There are insightful articles, such as "Steps toward Recovery," along with links to some very helpful and humorous sites on the Net.

Flying Solo

http://www.flyingsolo.com

This joint offering of a matrimonial and eldercare attorney and a writer, is an offshoot of the weekly life-after-divorce column of the same name that appears in newspapers throughout the U.S. Although paid subscription is necessary for regular updates, free registration gets you a look at their offerings, with good advice on legal and emotional issues that can arise when a marriage ends.

Divorce Helpline Webworks

http://www.divorcehelp.com

Divorce Helpline is a good site to check out when you're considering a divorce but don't want to entangle yourself in extensive legal red-tape. They propose that divorce in the U.S. is too messy. This is a virtual self-help guide and even teaches a course on short divorces. With a directory of self-help services in the U.S. and abroad, this is the ultimate do-it-yourself divorce center.

Family Law News

http://adams.patriot.net/~crouch/fln.html

Aimed largely at the layperson and as such, loaded with disclaimers, Family Law News covers not only divorce and child custody issues but such equally pleasant topics as child abuse and neglect, and domestic violence. Thankfully, there's also a section devoted to divorce prevention. Family Law News offers quite an education on a topic that no one wants to face, but, sadly, many of us will.

Dead Beat Victims Voice

http://home.navisoft.com/alphmega/deadbeat.htm

Here's a site where children and ex-spouses of parents who fail to pay child support can air their gripes...for a $99.00 annual fee. It's a place to hang virtual wanted posters so the slothful parents are exposed to the online universe. So what's to stop an angry ex-spouse from putting up a libelous "poster"? Worse things have happened in divorces.

Divorce Online

http://www.divorce-online.com/index.html

At a time when every little thing can help, here's a useful collection of resources; including articles and information on custody, single parenting, and more; and a list of professionals (lawyers, therapists), when you need some outside assistance (they're the ones who sponsor the site). Useful feature: A bulletin board where you can "talk" to others who have been there, too.

CARING FOR ELDER PARENTS

The Eldercare Locator

http://www.aoa.dhhs.gov/aoa/pages/loctrnew.html

The Eldercare Locator helps families find resources for older family members. The Locator, a public service from the U.S. Department of Health and Human Services, aids older people by finding the right service for their needs. Whether you live in the same city or across the country from a relative who may need food or health assistance, this group will help you find it.

Eldercare Web

http://www.elderweb.com

As more of the U.S. population ages, the need for services for older Americans is becoming more important. Karen Stevenson Brown, a C.P.A. and health care consultant, has provided an outstanding resource for families who are exploring health care options for older members of their families or for themselves (see Figure 6.11). There are articles on a variety of health, financial, legal and educational topics, including care giver resources, and a look at gerontology around the world.

Sandwich Generation

http://www.cris.com/~Rdkennen/sandwich%20generation.html

This page is part of Midlife Mommies, a site aimed at older moms. "Sandwich Generation" is a current media term used to describe the generation of people reaching middle age and dealing with the dual pressures of elderly parents and young children. If you're in this situation, and feeling squeezed, this is a good place to start looking for helpful resources on relating to and caring for aging parents.

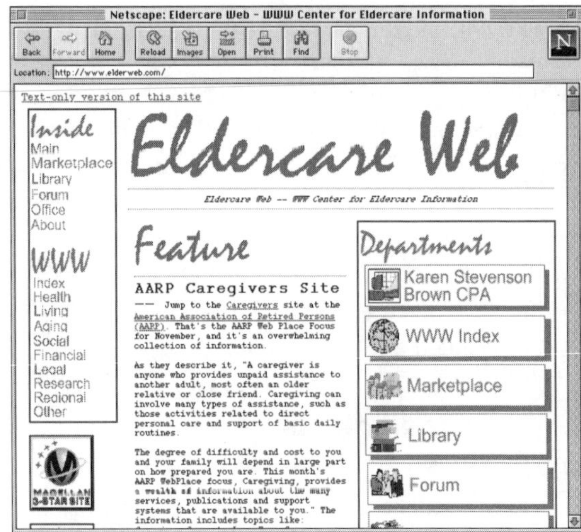

Figure 6.11

Eldercare Web, *http://www.elderweb.com*

Aging and Aging Parents Index

http://cybertowers.com/selfhelp/articles/aging

Psychology and *Self-Help Magazine* have compiled this index to provide helpful insight on the serious subject of parenting one's aging parents. Expert Emily Carton answers questions and features essays on topics like Depression in Older Adults, Alzheimer's, Before a Parent Moves In, and An Attorney's View (relating to *Powers of Attorney* issues)—not pretty subjects, but ones that often must be faced, and it's helpful to know the facts.

Fairview Health System

http://www.fairview.org/healthwise/summer/parent.html

Fairview Health System brings you this informative article on "The Sandwich Generation" —those with both young children and aging parents to care for. There are some insightful suggestions here, and if you live in Minnesota, you can get info on a United Way sponsored senior care program.

Eldercare and the Modem-Two Frontiers

http://kcmo.com/htm/owe03.htm

Part of an informative series on eldercare, by William R. Eubank, this site is an elegant compendium of stories, resources, links, and insights on the subject of caring for elderly parents and how the computer can help. Eubank describes the evolution of his own entry into cyberspace, as well the development of his interest in online eldercare resources. More evidence that your modem can truly be a lifeline.

Answers

http://www.service.com/answers/cover.html

This (paper) magazine for adult children of aging parents has come online with a sampling what's between the covers. You can read selected articles on topics like Health Insurance and No More Guilt. If you subscribe, they'll send you the first issue free.

ElderCare Help page

http://www.mindspring.com/~eldrcare/elderweb.htm

ElderCare is a financial management outfit helping Baby Boomers navigate the elder care maze. The ElderCare Lady, Laura Beller, offers more than just a pitch for her company here. You can participate in a forum for the elderly and their caregivers, or get advice on things like "Medical Self-Care for Healthy Aging." Although you don't get the entire *Caregiver Newsletter* online, there's enough good sense here to be helpful and comforting.

1 Enter your children's art into a virtual art show and showcase their work with other entries from around the world. Global Show and Tell—The Online Museum for Kids ages 0–17 Years Old.
http://www.telenaut.com/gst/parents.html

2 Play a game (or several games) of hangman.
http://www.cm.cf.ac.uk/htbin/RobH/hangman

3 Visit the bottom of Barkley Sound in British Columbia with a virtual 3-D Safari Splash tour.
http://oberon.educ.sfu.ca/splash.htm

☞ KEYWORDS

Parenting: infant care, adoption, teenagers, single parents, mothers, child care, family travel, children's health, birth order.

Kids' Stuff: games, children's books, children's' museums, zoos and aquariums, holidays, outdoor activities

Family Issues: domestic violence, family law, organizations and associations, widowhood, child safety, children with disabilities, gifted children, siblings, twins.

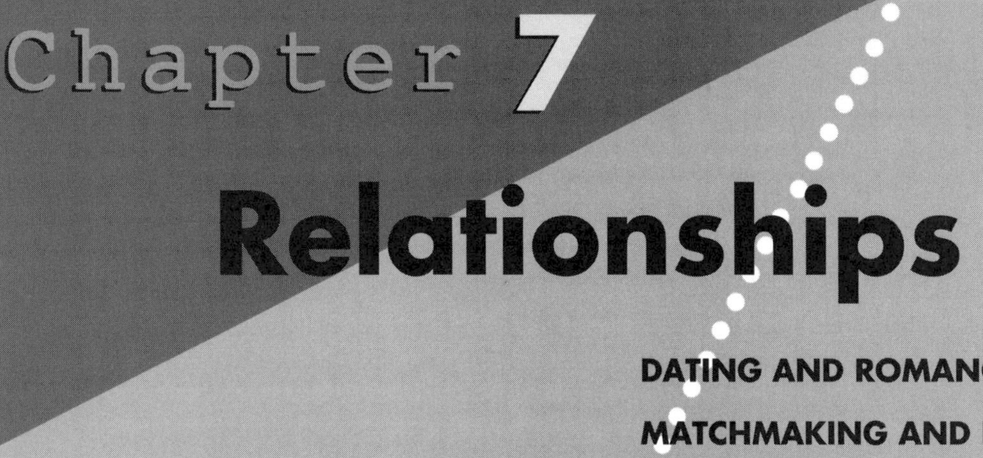

Chapter 7

Relationships

- DATING AND ROMANCE
- MATCHMAKING AND PERSONALS
- GAY AND LESBIAN
- SINGLE LIFE
- FRIENDSHIP
- WEDDING PLANNING AND MARRIAGE

10 WAYS YOU CAN RELATE *RIGHT NOW*

1 Create and send a personalized Valentine in seconds.

http://www.marlo.com/val.htm

2 Tell a loved one you're sorry with the help of Mark's Apology Note Generator.

http://net.indra.com/~karma/formletter.html

3 Learn how to say, "I love you," in almost any language from Albanian to Zuni.

http://www.hials.no/~ga/love/love.you.html

4 Solve your romantic dilemmas using Joe's Amazing Relationship Problem Solver.

http://studsys.mscs.mu.edu./~carpent1/probsolv/rltprob0.html

5 Wedding plans got you stressed? Check out the wedding jokes at BridalNet.

http://www.bridalnet.com/nethome.htm

6 Test your date-ability with the Vivarin Date-Ability Index.

http://www.vivarin.com/date

7 Send your sweetie an electronic Love Coupon using Cupid's Cove CityLink.

http://banzai.neosoft.com/citylink/cupid/doit.html

8 Send flowers to a loved one.

http://www.flowerstop.com

9 Write a funny love letter with some help from a pro at the Cyrano Server.

http://www.nando.net/toys/cyrano.html

10 When you get really serious: a digital proposal form!

http://hollywoodandvine.com/ltheeweb/proposal.html

So, you've heard that the Internet is the new hot spot for love and romance, and you'd like to join the party.

The Web is buzzing with places you can go to throw together a few words (and pictures, if you like) about yourself and cast them out for someone who has been looking for someone just like you. There are many dating services on the Web and, just like their offline counterparts, they have varying degrees of professional quality. But after you have checked the best ones out, give it a whirl—you can be someone's Prince Charming (or even meet your own). You can browse through hundreds of contenders and "check out the merchandise" in the privacy of your own home. Of course, just like in the real world, you should be very careful about giving out any personal information like your address or telephone number to people you do not know.

Frogs more your cup of tea? There are plenty of them out there, too. Countless stories of marriages-made-in-cyberspace couldn't be wrong. Find a special someone? Chat rooms and e-mail provide the perfect pressure-free getting-to-know-you atmosphere. Find pen (or mouse!) pals all around the world, with no phone bills or snail mail to get in the way. You can even get married online.

The Web is also a good place to turn if troubling questions start to pop up. Modern relationship issues like stepfamilies, AIDS, gender identity, and office etiquette make for at least a few good head-scratchers. Whether you want to break up or keep your romance alive, you can get advice from the love doctors and read heartfelt confessions from the lovelorn. Advice from a neutral outsider, or the discovery that others share your concerns, can shed some light on your dilemma.

DATING AND ROMANCE

Friends & Lovers

http://cyberspud.com/friends_lovers/index1.html

This magazine is for anyone dealing with mystifying and often painful relationship/dating issues. Read insightful articles, or try out the free personals page: you can specify whether you seek a romantic partner or just a friend, and there are separate sections for each. Get some advice, or have fun with the Astrology Page. Whatever you find here will help you feel less intimidated by the thorny world of relationships and dating.

Swoon

http://www.swoon.com

Beginning with "A Laypersons Guide to Sex Laws," this site is jam-packed with fun things to do and see in the area of dating and relationships (see Figure 7.1). It's all here, and more: Check out your daily horoscope by resident astrologer Celeste E. Smith; bizarre dating stories from various contributors; the Magazine Rack, which offers an archive of love-related stories from *Vogue*, *GQ*, and more; the latest celebrity-couple gossip; and, of course, the free personal ads.

Figure 7.1
Swoon, *http://www.swoon.com*

The Romance Web

http://www.public.com/romance

Cherubs adorn this site, brought to you by L&L Information Services. You'll find reflections on romance, a personal quiz (is naked Twister really appropriate on a first date?), and a dissertation titled, "Every Man Can Be A Romeo." And if you don't like the suggested titles on the list of romantic poetry, there's a link to the Random Love Poem Server. Also included: links to personal ads with 17,000 potential mates.

Vivarin Date-Ability Index

http://www.vivarin.com/date

The makers of Vivarin have a very funny quiz to test your "date-ability," followed by a brief guide to dating. The quiz features questions ranging from your "genetic disposition" to the "lamest thing to say on a date." Then, as a catalyst for a real-life dating adventure, they also provide commercial gift and entertainment guide links.

Cyber-Romance 101

http://web2.airmail.net/walraven/romance.htm

As the name implies, this collection of essays serves as an introduction to issues surrounding love found on the Internet. Many of these are from psychiatrists or therapists, and include some short, gossipy case studies. Relationships made through chat lines are still too new for anyone to be drawing conclusions, and these articles reflect that understanding. Instead, they serve to make people aware of the potentials as well as the pitfalls.

Jimbo's Big Book of Dating

http://www.pond.com/nelson/dating.htm

Jimbo's had some interesting dating experiences, and he wants to hear yours. After distinguishing between the different kinds of dating (Fun Dating, Undating, Looking-For-the-One Dating), he provides a deep trove of tongue-in-cheek dating and relating pages. Get some insights at the Institute of Relationshipology, then, for some laughs, read Saying I Love You, Erogenous Zones, and The Kiss. And pass along some stories of your own.

Gender Issues at Work: Office Romance

http://esther.som.umass.edu/som/resource/place/P0376.html

From the SOM graduate placement center at UMASS, here's a comprehensive article based on a panel discussion on the topic of office romance, beginning with a discussion of the reasons why romance springs up in the office to begin with. Several participants offer their opinions, and it's interesting to note the difference in the men's and the women's responses. Text only, but it's interesting reading.

MonasteryNET

http://www.calpoly.edu/~ttokuuke

It's tough to figure whether MonasteryNET is intended for amusement or edification, but it delivers both. Friar Wally offers an extensive "Monk's Guide to Dating," good for clinical analysis of relations between the sexes and insights on flirting. You can consult with the resident shrink, Dr. Psycho M.F.C.C., or take in serious discourse on questions like: "Can You Be a Modern-Day Job?" Go figure.

INTERNATIONAL APPEAL

The Definitive Guide to Relationships

http://www.odyssee.net/~jlevy

This raucous guide to relationships is brought to you by a pair of Canadians with an X-rated sense of humor and a bit of a chip on their shoulders. Complete with background music, you'll either love this site or hate it, but it's not for the faint of heart. A sample from their short discourse on Human Nature: "Relationships. Why? Because you need it, stupid."

Mark's Apology Note Generator

http://net.indra.com/~karma/formletter.html

If you can overlook the sexist overtones, Mark's Apology Note Generator (and its female counterpart, the Bitch Letter for Women), might come in handy when you just can't find the words to say, "I'm sorry," or "You're going to be sorry." Or gently direct a loved one to this witty form letter when you feel that you should be on the receiving end of that apology.

The Foolproof Guide to Making Any Woman Your Platonic Friend

http://www.phantom.com/~joelogon/platonic.html

Although it's clearly addressed to guys, this site is also for women who've had the experience of falling in love with someone who ends up saying, "I just want to be friends." Author Joe Logon offers bitterly funny tips, and visitors have posted their equally bitter stories of getting dumped. As Joe tells one contributor, "Why date when you can seethe?"

Gard's Laws on Love

http://www.hials.no/~ga/love/laws.html

At times witty and wise, Gard has a unique view of love. He devotes an entire section to pondering whether it's true that women are suckers for men with blue eyes.

[OVERHEARD ON WOMEN'S WIRE]

http://www.women.com/buzz/qa.ema.html

Women's Wire eMale, a.k.a. Andy Erdman, answers all questions about men and their (sometimes strange) behavior. If you've got a question for him, send it to *emale@women.com.*

"Despite being paid to explain why men are different, weird, or incomprehensible, the fact is we are not—even the morning after a bad date. Same holds true, I believe, in the other direction. Could it be that the sexes have more things in common than not? Let's take a look:

1 According to opinion polls, both men AND women think the biggest problem with TV dinners is the fact that the peas always spill over into the dessert.

2 As former British Prime Minister Margaret Thatcher demonstrated in the Falklands, both female AND male political leaders are equally capable of waging costly, meaningless wars over tiny land masses most people have never heard of. (See: Reagan and Grenada.)

3 Both men and women have to put up with a great deal of social and cultural baggage which forces them to think they should be one way, when in fact, they'd be happier being themselves. What did Simone de Beauvoir say? 'One is not born a woman, but, rather, becomes one.' The truth is, one 'becomes' a guy too, but this fact is often ignored.

So, yeah, we are all human—all laden with the same kinds of problems, though perhaps in slight, gendered variations. Wait! What's that sound? Could it be the sound of civilization itself lumbering slowly forward?!? Yup, I think it is."

(Gard, of course, has blue eyes.) The only drawback to his wildly funny reflections is that Sir Gard is Norwegian, so some of the English isn't perfect. Useful: hundreds of translations for "I love you," from Chicksaw to Esperanto.

101 Easy Ways to Say No

http://www.rain.org/~uring/jokes/101no.htm

No one should be without this handy list of sticky-situation-preventers. Topping the list: "I have to floss my cat." There are no fancy graphics here, just a text list with 101 useful excuses like, "My favorite commercial is on TV."

1-800-Dedicate

http://ahbqs.com/cat4.html

This ad describes 1-800-Dedicate, which for a fee will deliver "your specially selected song and personally recorded message...over the phone anywhere in the U.S.A." Make a blunder? You can send Brenda Lee's "Sorry" or "Please Forgive Me" by Bryan Adams along with your apology. Other stylistic options include "sexy," "get lost," and "birthday."

The Book of Bitterness

http://www.webfeats.com/sealander/Bitter_Book.html

This kooky anthology promises "unflinching accounts of a world that doesn't work." Relationships, whether with lovers or nations, are the main ingredient, with a pinch of "adult language." Actually, these stories are funny. Struggling artists, four-kilometer walks in the rain, yuppies toting worn-out copies of *The Celestine Prophecy*—they're all here, along with a survey that could help you discover a bitter side of yourself.

Literal Lies

http://www.he.net/~literal

This collection of fiction is at times disturbing and unsettling, but clearly there's a craft here to admire. Text-only, its gray tones match the themes and events described (see Figure 7.2): intensely personal and often cold musings on relationships between people and the fictions they create. Not stories in the traditional sense, but all very modern, featuring dissection of mind and body both literally and figuratively. A good example of some very crafty fiction.

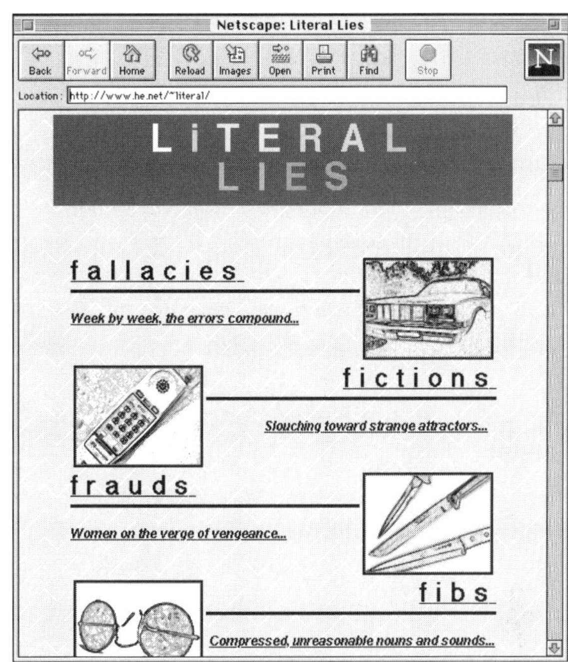

Figure 7.2
Literal Lies, *http://www.he.net/~literal*

The Couch

http://www.geocities.com/SunsetStrip/9458/advice.htm

This sex-and-relationship advice site, brought to you by Thomas and Courtney, a happy couple who "went through hell getting there," does not mince words, so it's not for the squeamish. Most of the questions they receive deal more with sex than relationships, though the answers do try to focus on more than just the physical aspects. From the But Were Afraid To Ask department: check out the Men's Underwear Survey.

Stan's Place

http://www.snj.com/telecouples/claire.htm

Stan is the founder of a New Jersey teen crisis center, and he's willing to handle your crisis, too. You can send him your relationship questions, and he'll try to help solve them for all the online world to see. You can browse through others' queries, with titles like "Real life 90210," and "Should I tell her?" You might well stumble across a topic that you've been struggling with as well.

BizCom '96 Love and Relationship Resources

http://www.bizcom.com/online/direct/love.htm

This site, hosted by BizCom Online, covers a wide range of relationship issues, from the cheerful Ms. Loquita's weekly Advice on Love column to links to Match.Com's well-stocked "date-a-base." You can meet the perfect match, work through the rough spots, and if it doesn't work out, there's a link to the Divorce Page, too.

Joe's Amazing Relationship Problem Solver

http://studsys.mscs.mu.edu./~carpent1/probsolv/rltprob0.html

Had enough of trying to figure out your romantic life on your own? Try Joe's Amazing Relationship Problem Solver. Just answer a series of simple questions until you reach The Truth about your relationships. A disclaimer warns that Joe's page is for entertainment purposes only. Joe may not be able to solve your problems, but you may laugh enough here to forget them.

Ask Dr. Tracy

http://www.loveadvice.com

Dr. Tracy Cabot is the author of *How to Make a Man Fall in Love With You* and other popular relationship books. Her online advice is usually pretty sensible. Even if you don't like her advice, eavesdropping on relationship tales is endlessly entertaining, and some of the best come from Dr. Tracy her own bad self.

The Official Hopeless Romantics page

http://www.primenet.com/~ejones/hrhome.html

Are you one? The features for those just along for the ride include a section of visitor-submitted love poems and tales of romantic encounters (positive ones), a nice set of annotated love links and more. The real service here, however, is all the advice. In fact, you can even apply to become an ad hoc love advisor! A list of resources for those who are in seriously bad relationships injects a serious note.

Lucy Lipps

http://www.lucylipps.com

Lucy Lipps is a radio "love doctor" and advice columnist who's not shy about self-promotion. Advice to the lovelorn, and suggestions for how to avoid becoming that way, are two of Lucy Lipps' specialties; her advice is serious, but given with a touch of humor. Lucy accepts e-mail queries, too.

Journey to Love

http://vegasnet.com/journey/radio.htm

Advice-show radio host Carol Reynolds offers a generous assortment of excerpts from her new book, *Journey to Love*. Carol isn't above mixing a little raunch in with her life-altering memoir. Okay, so her prose is about Fabio-quality, but her enthusiasm is high, and that alone makes this an entertaining book plug. She also offers playbacks of her show in VoxWare real-time format.

Philippa's Problem Page

http://www.agony.com

The emotionally supportive Philippa Perry invites all to please, e-mail her with any relationship problem, which she promises to answer. Often, submissions will end up on the home page (albeit with names and places changed to protect the innocent). Among the categories covered in her impressive archive of down-to-earth advice: Family Problems, For Transvestites and Their Partners, and Managing Your Parents.

INTERNATIONAL APPEAL

Doc Love

http://www.schwaben.de/home/pallmer/framedoc_e.htm

At this German-based site, choose the international version (unless you want the German version). There, you'll find a picture-index guiding you toward various symbols for that thing called Love. You can send anonymous letters to the Love Doc, and expect an answer to your burning love question within 48 hours. That's pretty much it here, but the pictures are cute and, hey, it's good to get an outside opinion sometimes.

One Day at a Time: Survival Guide for Relationships

http://nsonline.com/odat

Bernd and Lynda Hansen have stumbled on a few truths in their long (17 years) and (very) rocky marriage. Now they'd like to share them with you. Though entries from August onward are "under construction," the insights the Hansens share in previous months are timeless. With topics that include, Trust, Intuition, Priorities and Acceptance, you can probably find a few "me too's," and maybe a few new truths of your own.

World Hug Week

http://oac3.hsc.uth.tmc.edu/~bardoin/hugs

Site founder Denise Quick is promoting July 14–20, 1997 as World Hug Week. At the site, you can send an electronic hug to a special someone, read the reasoning behind the Hug Week observance (promoting unconditional acceptance), and find out how you can participate.

The Love Blender

http://www.alienbill.com/romance

With stories and tales, poetry and pictures, hopeless romantic Kirk Logan Israel offers up everything from the last lines of Woody Allen's *Annie Hall* to a real 1928 love letter from a 70-year romance. You'll find dozens of touching, funny, and thought-provoking snippets and stories about romance. The page also contains a shot of perhaps the ultimate 20th-Century romantic moment: the final scene from Casablanca.

Interactive Ego Booster

http://web.syr.edu/~ablampac/ego

Empty praise from our friends is expected, but why burden our loved ones with the job of having to tell us all those lies? That's where Syracuse University student Andrew Lampach's Ego Booster comes in. Just one click unleashes its tongue-in-cheek barrage of saccharine personal affirmations. "You are very very very special." Maybe so, but after two or three of these, you'll start to feel the tooth decay setting in.

From the Heart

http://www.wbm.ca/users/kgreggai/html/heart.html

Get ready for Valentine's Day. Complete with syrupy music as it loads, this site positively drips with love. What you'll find: poetry, stories, pictures, cupids, and more hearts and flowers than you can throw a box of chocolates at. Submit your own labour of love, or browse the works of others. As if there weren't enough love here, site overseers Kevin and Heather have added a list of links to other romantic sites.

The Love Test

http://www.topchoice.com/~psyche/lovetest

Betty Harris and Jim Glover bring you this interesting test as part of their research on how we love. Fill out a series of questions about yourself and your beliefs on the subject of love. Then, submit your answers and receive a score based on criteria such as "Passion," "Emotional Intimacy," and "Commitment." Score breakdown is well-explained, and you can see your answers in a different light. You might be surprised.

Loveplex

http://www.loveplex.com

Like a suburban movie theater, you can see it all here if it relates to love and romance (see Figure 7.3). Brought to you by multimedia firm AXA Virtual, you'll find all the love you need at this Valentine of a site: Racy 'zines, love stories, a collection of love and romance tests, information about love and relationships. There's so much fun stuff here, check out the page entitled, "A Woman's Brain."

Romance Novel Database

http://www.sils.umich.edu/~sooty/romance/romance.html

The site was created at the University of Michigan by Chris Powell, as part of her senior project. Categorized by title, author, and subgenre, the Romance Novel Database presents a thorough catalog of more than 50 titles, with publisher info, a one-to-four heart rating system and in some cases, a review of the book. You can even submit your own rating of the book if you found it to be lustier than the given review indicates.

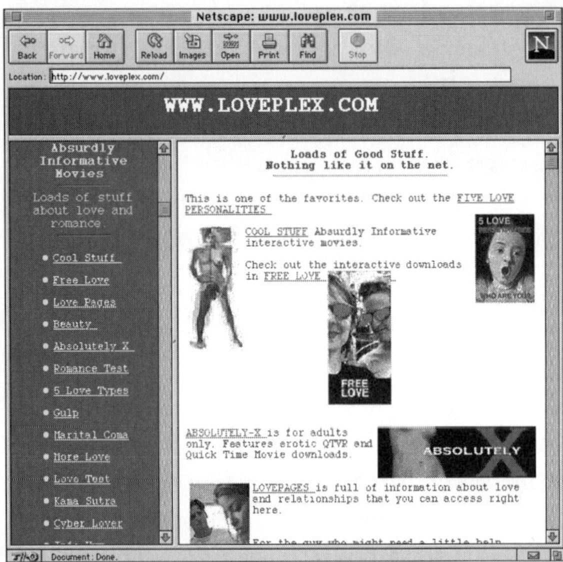

Figure 7.3

Loveplex, *http://www.loveplex.com*

Lovesongs

http://www.ravensoft.com

Hopeless romantics will love this Australian database of love song lyrics, and everyone else will love the site for its unusually high cheese level. Site maintainer Michael Buenaventura's database is impressively large (even Mr. Mister gets the nod), but that's okay: Sometimes "You've Lost That Loving Feeling" is more appropriate than "Tonight I Celebrate My Love."

Cupid's Cove CityLink

http://banzai.neosoft.com/citylink/cupid/default.html

Blake and Associates, an Internet marketing agency developed this modest little shop for lovers, with an emphasis on gifts for loved ones. Several cute (and free) ready-made "coupons" promise your sweetie a selection of Net-related promises ("I promise not to talk about the Internet"). The main attraction, however, is a list of commercial sites where more sure-fire gifts can be purchased. These guys are in marketing, after all.

The Virtual Kissing Booth

http://www.whitehawk.com/vkb

You load the page and get a picture of a female puckering up. You then get to kiss her. Against all reason, this site reports 50,000 accesses a week. It's becoming so popular, they now have monthly issues—each month they'll have a new female, and in the future, they'll have a group of females from which you can choose. And there's no maximum kissing limit.

The Soundbite Kiss

http://www.echonyc.com/~aeonflux

The Soundbite Kiss is full of poetry and art collected and created by the site's maintainer, Astrida Valigorsky. The subjects for the mini-galleries range from social commentary to silly (romance novel models imposed on Cheez Wiz labels). The poetry, however, conjures up melan-

where they surf

Surfer: Patrizia DiLucchio

The resident sex and relationship expert at Women's Wire.

Web picks of the moment:

The Cigar Journal

http://www.cigarjournal.com

"As much a noir diary of one guy's life as it is a rating system for cigars. This site proves once again that Freud was oh-so-misguided—because most times a cigar is more than just a cigar...."

Troma

http://www.troma.com

"Because how can you not love the people who took the True Tale of Alfred Packer—the only guy ever tried by the U.S. judicial system for cannablism—and turned it into a musical comedy?"

choly romance and love gone wrong. Just the thing to suit your mood on a rainy day.

Flower Stop

http://www.flowerstop.com

This online fresh-flower market offers next-day delivery (in the U.S.) of bouquets, vases, and that grand standby, the single long-stemmed rose. The "Romance and Roses CD Set" features two centuries of the world's greatest love themes to accompany your flower purchase. A nice example of online shopping. It's colorful, quick, and lets you see the product without provoking your allergies.

Kaplan's Muskrat Love

http://www.kaplan.com/holiday/muskrat.html

This fun site from test-prep gurus at Kaplan Educational Centers celebrates Valentine's Day, with a passing nod to Groundhog Day—you'll find the lyrics to "Muskrat Love" in the listing of the groundhog's "rodent friends." The links for lovers here are organized into categories like Bodice-Ripping Careers and Wooing Tools, and the downloadable Cupid Attack Game incorporates Presidents' Day into the February festivities.

Cyrano server

http://www.nando.net/toys/cyrano.html

Every romantic should visit the Cyrano server, courtesy of the Nando Net of Raleigh, North Carolina, which writes love letters on command (see Figure 7.4). Answer a few questions about your beloved, select a style from poetic to steamy, and let Cyrano do the romantic heavy lifting. On the flip side, Cyrano will also compose a Dear John letter, which runs more like, "It is time for you to remove your pathetic clogs from my closet and to detach your annoying pet ferret from my leg."

Love and Relationships

http://okcforum.osrhe.edu/~psyche/love

This is part of Betty and Jim's home page, which is subtitled "At Home in the Heartland," and their hobby is Love. Those with time to kill and love in their hearts can take The Love Test and compare their idea of love with their experience. And guess what: Love means never having to say you're sorry!

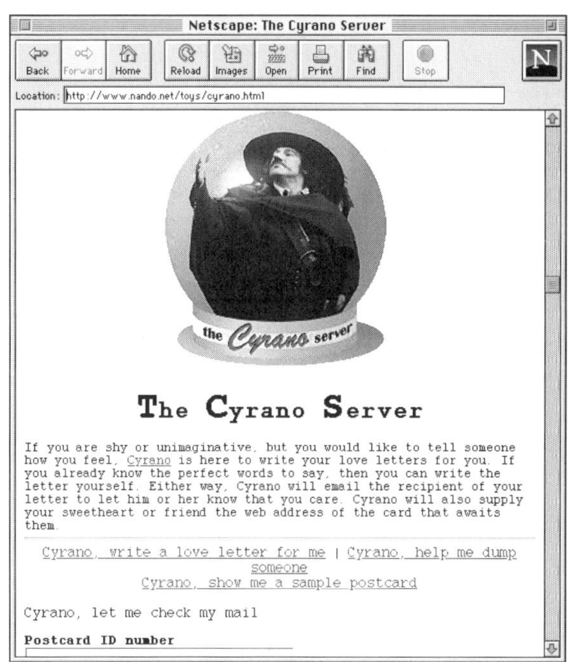

Figure 7.4
Cyrano Server,
http://www.nando.net/toys/cyrano.html

Natalie Engel's Chest of Lust, Longing and Obsession

http://hamp.hampshire.edu/~dbtF93/index.html

Natalie Engel is bubbling over with problems: obsession, bad relationships, a lot of anger. She's the creation of Hampshire College student Danielle Tropea who put together this fictional site as part of a multimedia project. Not really a soap, though—just an intense and funny character study. Check out stuff Natalie has stolen from boys she likes, tips on how to stalk, and her favorite pick-up lines. Interesting lady.

The Relationship Game

http://tiger.towson.edu/~bjohns1/relation/relamain.htm

Having trouble meeting that perfect someone? Can't get along with the one you've got? Maybe you just need a little practice. Enter the relationship of two young lovers, Jason and Cindy. You decide the outcome of this interactive romance, so be careful when you head down the path of love. A few rounds of this, with trial-and-error behind you, you'll be ready for the real thing.

Survey of Men: Sex, Virginity, Dating, Commitment, Marriage

http://www.frontiernet.net/~survey

Because a friend (presumably a woman) of the site's creator got burned by a cad, he set out to help women avoid similar letdowns by exposing the truth about the wild beast that is man. Chosen at random from the Rochester, NY phonebook, the participants answer detailed questions about love, sex, marriage, and waiting for any of the above. Take a look: Some of the answers may surprise you.

MATCHMAKING AND PERSONALS

Match.com

http://www.match.com

The fun personals site (see Figure 7.5). First you register (it's free). Then you can either browse categories by gender preference, or try your search by geographical region. Detailed information is available. Match.com Zine features modern dating dilemmas, like actually meeting your date. The site's coolest feature, measures the distance between you and each person whose ad you peruse. You'll know when you're just 313 miles from that mystery date in Pittsburgh.

Prodigy Web Personals

http://prodigy.telepub.com/Prodigy

Prodigy Web Personals brings you listings for what seems like every walk of human life. There's a membership system, so you can stop by and browse a few of the listings, but you have to join (it's free) to respond to the ads. Responses are e-mail and code word driven, so you only reveal as much as you intend to.

Figure 7.5

Match.com, *http://www.match.com*

WEB Personals

http://www.webpersonals.com

WEB Personals is a user-friendly site where date seekers and seekees are categorized in the appropriate straight or gay directory—you'll even find a guide to what the initials mean when DWM seeks DDFW. The site allows you to browse or submit your ad, and the Love Hound will notify you of any suitable matches in case you don't have the time to check for yourself.

One-and-Only Internet Personals

http://www.one-and-only.com

Access here is very easy, with only a few steps between you and that potential someone. The staff offers sensible tips on how to write your ad to grab more attention. However, this is of the type with arranged telephone connections—no pictures here—assisted by the staff. The catalog is just beginning, but there are still a fair number of ads, especially for "pen pals."

Amoreee!

http://www.kaiwan.com/~bayers/mates.html

The site allows you to post facts and (if you're really bold) photos of yourself with the goal of ferreting out a mate, but without the risk of cyberstalking—all e-mail addresses are confidential. Ad approaches vary; some men prefer half-clothed pictures of themselves, which make nifty screen savers. Amoreee! is run by a fellow named Jim, who says he's hoping to meet the woman of his dreams here.

Virtual MeetMarket

http://wwa.com:1111

A state-by-state listing of personal ads, MeetMarket allows you to scan a menu of bylines ranging from "Lonely in Texas" to "Meet the Man of Your Nightmares." You can then respond by e-mail if you like what you see. Visitors can place ads and pictures, depending on their desire to be mysterious or flagrantly available. The selection is relatively small, but management guarantees that available women will hear from interesting men!

Worldport Personals

http://www.worldport.com/cgi shl/dbml.exe?template=/webcat/personal.dbm

Offering quick and direct access to other lonely hearts via e-mail, this page has some promise. Brought to you as part of Worldport, a multiservice provider, the spirited postings here run the gamut from sincere to spicy. Ads for both men and women; light on ads for gays and lesbians. Postings are free, though you do need to open an account before you advertise. Don't feel like dinner and a movie? Try the pen-pal section.

Internet Personals

http://www.montagar.com/personals/index.html

No pictures, no audio. So far, most of these Internet personal ads look just about like the plain ol' newspaper type. As always, the alternative lifestyles category (here called variations) is both amusing and unsettling. On the plus side, it's all free!

Get Met on the Net

http://getmet1.etw.net

These folks seem to have it all covered at this well-organized personal ad site. They'll create a start page for you when you register ($7.00/month), complete with a batch of matches in your area. Then, anonymously submit a profile on yourself, along with a photo, if you wish, to be checked out by all who seek new companionship. You can also search the "alt.personal" newsgroups on the Net from here.

where they surf

Surfer: Fran Maier

General manager of Match.Com, the leading matchmaking service on the Web, http://www.match.com

Web picks of the moment:

Amazon.Com

http://www.amazon.com

"I love giving gifts and I love books. And I'm extremely busy. So I've found this site to be terrific when I want to send a present to a friend. And when I'm at their site it seems like I'm at a bookstore in reality. Great selection, fast delivery, convenient, and good prices. Hard to beat."

My Yahoo

http://edit.my.yahoo.com/config/login

"This is a personalized part of Yahoo where I have selected the information I'm interested in: Stock Quotes, Weather in San Francisco and Santa Fe, Sport Scores, Internet News, and links to my favorite sites. For me, this is 'one-stop shopping' for my news needs. I'm highly into everyday convenience!"

LDS Friends Worldwide

http://www.downtown-web.com/cfw/search.htm

There's something for everyone on the Web: this matchmaking resource for the Church of Jesus Christ of the Latter Day Saints (Mormons), maintained by an LDS brother, includes categories for Single, Divorced, Widowed, and Married (well, they *are* Mormons) Brothers and Sisters, divided further by age group. If you join, be sure to specify whether you're looking for a pen-pal, friend, dating partner, or the love of your life.

World Singles

http://www.infinityquest.com/world_singles

World Singles is based on a simple concept: you place an ad, you browse the ads of others, all free. The categories are unsurprising: Men seeking Women, etc., although the "Persons seeking Others" category is a bit baffling (turns out to be the slightly racier "alternative lifestyle" section). If you want to cast a wide Net, toss a line out here, too.

Romantic Rendezvous

http://www.start.com/romance

Aimed at 18-and-over date seekers, Romantic Rendezvous allows you to describe yourself or search the listings of those who have forged ahead with their own. You can search by age, gender, and state and get more specific, if necessary. You can also throw an animal icon in with your ad.

Date Net

http://Date.Net

DateNet offers a variety of membership packages which range from basic to complex. Some of the postings have pictures, some don't. The listings are categorized by heterosexuals and homosexuals seeking partners and then listed by state—you can also search by keyword—although a test search revealed that "good-looking" yielded many, many more responses than "smart."

LoveSearch

http://www.lovesearch.com

A new entry to the online dating scene, this personals site is souped up with lots of Java-based bells and whistles. You can Search or Browse the member profiles to find a potential match that is the right age, sex, religion, and one who has the right hobbies, musical preferences, and piercings. Take the ultimate love quiz and test your online dating personality. You can register for free, but there is a charge when you wish to contact a member whose profile interests you.

How to Date a Millionaire

http://amsquare.com/million/index.html

Columnist and author L.A. Johnson has received over 35 proposals of marriage, "most of them from the very wealthy." She works her experience here, pitching her book of the same name. She's put a sampling of her advice online, and it makes for interesting reading. Browse through topics like, "How Can I Dress to Get a Wealthy Man's Attention?" then go have breakfast at Tiffany's.

INTERNATIONAL APPEAL

International Hearts Club

http://www.netdata-intl.com/hearts

After registration at this site, (free, but to actually e-mail your chosen party, you must pay a small fee) you can anonymously submit your profile and peruse the profiles of others, then get in touch with them via e-mail. Members are categorized by ethnic group, and hail from around the world. A great way to find a pen- (or mouse-) pal!

Blind Date on the Net

http://carrcom.com/date

This is your basic online dating board, and it seems to be a popular one at that. "Expose Yourself" that is, submit your personal information, then browse the bios of your fellow seekers, all at no charge. For racier ads, check out the Alternative Lifestyles board. There's also a chat room for a more interactive experience. Why not try it out? Brad from Boston and Alex from Minnesota are waiting.

The Matchmaking Game

http://asylum.cid.com/matchmaking

Hosted by BrainTainment Center, this game is just like the TV version: with the help of the "Internet audience," you choose between four contestants (chosen by the hosts), who have been asked a series of questions. (To be a contestant, fill out and submit a form.) The winning couple gets an all-expenses (up to $75.00) reimbursed "date." Then you return to the site and tell all. How brave are you?

The Authoritative Matchmaker

http://www.awarenet.com/amm

This aptly named site could also be called the Thinking Person's Dating Service (see Figure 7.6): beautiful drawings, thought provoking forums (How to Recognize Your Soul Mate), and sound yet inspirational advice (including "flirtation behavior"), comprise the preparation phase. Head to the free personal ads when you're ready to use what you've learned.

Yenta—The Student.Net Matchmaker

http://www.student.net/yenta

Yenta makes her home at the slick 'zine Student.Net, and she wants to set you up with somebody's cute son (or daughter). Get yourself a Student.net user ID (it's free, and enables you to remain anonymous) then fill out a questionnaire with details of your real or imagined personality. Yenta puts her skills to work to find compatible Student.net users for you. Choose carefully: You can only do this once.

Figure 7.6
The Authoratative Matchmaker, *http://www.awarenet.com/amm*

GAY AND LESBIAN

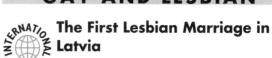

The First Lesbian Marriage in Latvia

http://dspace.dial.pipex.com/town/parade/gf96/wedding.htm

Complete with cute pictures of the happy couple, the page, and the site itself, shows just how much the Web is doing to promote international cultural unity. Do you think you'd ever know of the wedded bliss of Latvian lesbian Astra Indricane and her German girlfriend Birgit Böhvinger? Witness love in the time of Glasnost.

Out.com

http://www.out.com

America's best-selling gay and lesbian magazine brings its glossy style online in an impressive translation—you'll find all the printed articles here. The site also takes advantage of the electronic medium to present the News and Gossip of the Day: entertainment and political news updated regularly—though not quite daily. And, finally, you'll find the infamous Boy and Girl photos. Flippant and fun, but with plenty to say.

Youth Action Online

http://www.youth.org

Youth Action Online is a volunteer organization dedicated to providing a "safe space online" for gay, lesbian, and bisexual youth. Its content-rich monthly 'zine, Oasis, features advice from parents on coming out plus poetry and stories written by gay and lesbian teens and interviews with prominent activists. In the News and Reviews section : an item on censorship, and a rundown on "queercore" bands, for example. Newsy, informative, hip.

GaySource

http://www.gaysource.com

This monthly online general-interest magazine for the gay, lesbian, bisexual, and transgendered community features timely pieces such as an interesting update on the movement in Hawaii to legalize same-sex marriages. Also included were pieces on meeting Mr. or Ms. Right and where to see and be seen in cities like San Francisco,

Miami, and Houston. Lots of links to AIDS service organizations, political sites, and activist groups.

Igloo
http://www.actwin.com:80/chiltern/igloo.html

The International Gay and Lesbian Outdoor Organization's home page lists more than 112 outdoor organizations and events for its members. IGLOO is maintained by the Chiltern Mountain Club of New England. Members are into skiing and more traditional sports, and hail from everywhere from Japan to New Zealand. Interested parties may subscribe online to a newsletter, add a link to their home page, or post a blurb about their group.

Qworld
http://www.qworld.org

In addition to links to several little-known 'zines, you'll find message boards, regional resources, and a QMall. Especially interesting are the QFiles, which offer everything from health information to shareware. Click on Queer History here, and you'll find background on the rainbow flag, pink triangle, lambda symbol, and slogans. Lots of links to other gay-related pages, including entertainment, health, community, and youth sites.

Open Prairie Syndicate
http://www.visi.com/~oprairie

This syndicate features the work of well- and lesser-known cartoonists who have their strips in "queer friendly" publications. Included are, a Native American strip, "The Northern Mystique" by Richard MacPhie, and Chris Monroe's "Invisible Fence," among many others. The comics deal mostly with contemporary relationship issues, more wry and ironic than gut-bustingly funny.

Straight Spouse Support Network
http://www.qrd.org/qrd/www/orgs/sssn/home.htm

The Straight Spouse Support Network (SSSN) is an international support network of straight current or former spouses of gay, lesbian, bisexual, or transgendered individuals. The group also addresses the issues of children, parents, and other relatives who often feel shut out when Junior (or Mom) comes out. You can join mailing lists specific to your own relationship, or obtain info on how to contact various related organizations in your area.

A Dyke's World
http://www.qworld.org/DykesWorld

Site-creator Indina Beuche welcomes you to A Dyke's World. What you'll find at this beautifully-designed site is an eclectic collection of links, images, news, and rants. Stay abreast of what groups like the National Alliance are up to. In Same Sex Marriages, you'll get the scoop on the wedding of Eva Dahlgren and Efva Attling, united on January 25. Plus: Sisters Onstage, a list of pages devoted to female musicians.

Kakasarian: Queer Resources for Filipinos
http://www.tribo.org/bakla/bakla.html

Med student Kenneth Yerro Ilio offers far more than tips on finding a decent gay bar in Manila. Part of his much larger Trudong Pinoy Philippine site, this guide for gay, lesbian, and bisexual Filipinos features a cultural history of homosexuality and transvestitism (for religious purposes) on the island nation. An impressive collection of links follows, along with a sizable list of AIDS/HIV connections geared toward Filipinos.

gay.guide New York
http://www.gayguidenewyork.com

This monthly guide for the gay and lesbian community in New York City promises to provide community service listings as well as advertisements from businesses catering to the gay and lesbian community. The site's creator sums up *the raison d'être* for such a guide as follows: "I wanted to find a store where I could rent a gay-themed video, the name of a good therapist, and a bar where I could unwind."

D.Y.K.E.
http://dspace.dial.pipex.com/town/square/ad454/index.htm

This British lesbian page features fun stuff for dykes and others. What to do tonight? Check out the Cruise Me

Now! Cafe, an international venue guide. You can also read about famous and infamous queer hipsters, or peruse the News. Then talk about it in "D.Y.K.E.'s Talking," the girls-only chat room.

Visibilities

http://www.qworld.org/Visi/visib_home.html

The editors have put together a "place to learn about each other's cultures, lives, experiences, problems, joys, and to just have fun." This lesbian 'zine is an interesting mix of features, columns, book reviews, and cartoons. Especially intriguing is Elynor Vine's guide to interpreting dreams. Also fun is Pot Luck, an eclectic list of recipes, including coconut salad, curried chick peas, and chopped liver delight.

SINGLE LIFE

Conscious Singles Connection and The Single Life

http://www.cscsoulmate.com/life.htm

This simple, respectful resource board is host to a broad collection of singles- and dating-related resources, including Academic Companions "for intellectually accomplished individuals," sites featuring outdoor singles events, and a series of free reports by CSC director Joan Goldstein, covering topics like "Soulmates vs. 'Sole-Mates.'" Bookmarked by bookworms everywhere.

The Single Life Institute

http://www.abilene.com/tsli

The Single Life Institute is a non-profit ministry that deals with the issues of being single again after divorce. There's an emphasis on ties to the church, and they want you to order a pamphlet, but you will find informative articles such as, "Does Divorce Mean Disqualified?" and "When Your Ex Won't Pay."

National Gothic Singles Network

http://www.gothic-classifieds.com

A great way to meet the other undead in a new city, or just keep up on Siouxie's latest projects (see Figure 7.7). Whether you're a hard-core Goth, weekend warrior, or just like to wear black, this page is a must-see. Use the classifieds to find a coffin-mate, chat with other lost souls, and much more. Get on the e-mail list, and you'll receive regular updates, so you never have to see daylight.

Cupid's Network, Inc.

http://www.cupidnet.com

Beat Cupid and his arrows to the target. While browsing in Cupid's Bookstore, you can download "How to Find a Lasting Relationship," or get the low-down on titles like "A Good Man is Easy to Find in Southern California." The Cupid News link includes items like the one about a fraudulent dating service that had to refund millions. Also: links to singles services, magazines, travel organizations, and personal ad services.

American Singles

http://www.as.org/index.html

This singles ad site is rather straightforward. The form is standard: what you look like, what church you go to, what recreational toxins you eschew (or embrace). The service exists on voluntary donations; maybe that explains why there are so many entries. They provide a phone service, too, called "Cupid's Switchboard" (there's a joke in there somewhere).

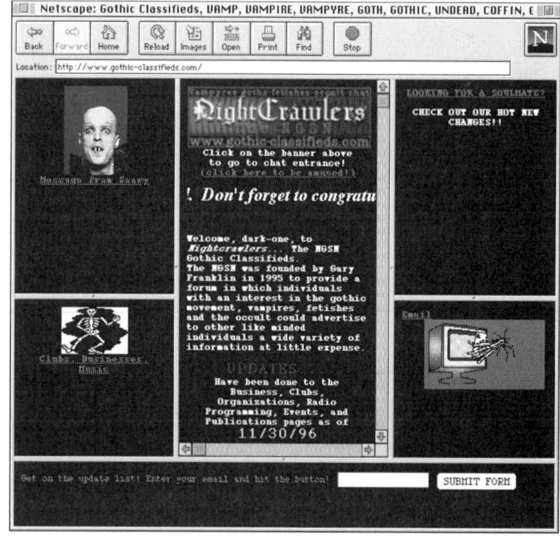

Figure 7.7

National Gothic Singles Network, *http://www.gothic-classifieds.com*

A Man's Life

http://www.manslife.com

This new Web 'zine is like a kind of mutant *Cosmo* for men. There are articles about relationships ("Rate Your Mate" against your ex-girlfriend, in an interactive quiz), clothing ("Dress for Sex!"), food, and health (about manly stuff like rashes). Also: Editor Stefan Kanfer critiques the current week's crop of news magazines.

The Singles Web

http://www.jjplaza.com/singles

Pickup lines? Massage techniques? Yup, sounds like singlesville. That's just what you'll get at this site courtesy of JJ Electronic Plaza. Brush up on Flower Types, and learn how to say "I love you" in several languages, and you'll be ready to try your luck with a free personal ad, which you can also submit here.

I·N·T·E·R·N·E·T M·I·N·U·T·E

ALL ABOUT BOOKMARKS

When you come across a site that you like, add it to your list of bookmarks or favorites. Bookmarks are like the speed dialer of the Internet—they save you the time and hassle of remembering specific Web addresses.

Some general tips about bookmarks:

1. Bookmark specific sections of a Web site (e.g. a page with daily news), so that you don't have to click down from the home page to your favorite section every time you visit the site.
2. Organize your bookmarks into topical categories for easy access.
3. Clean out your bookmarks at least once a month. Today's favorite site might be passé tomorrow.

Bookmarks work slightly differently on Netscape and Internet Explorer.

To add a bookmark on Netscape: When you reach a site that you want to bookmark, simply go to the Bookmark menu in your browser and select "Add Bookmark."

In order to organize and clean out your bookmarks, access your bookmark file by pulling down the Window menu on the top of your screen. Choose the "Bookmarks" option. Your bookmark file, which displays all your bookmarks, will open in a new window. You can change the order of your bookmarks or organize them into folders by selecting and dragging them.

To delete a bookmark, select it and choose "Delete Bookmark" from the Edit menu.

While this file is open, experiment with the bookmark options. Create new bookmarks or folders (they all can be deleted in exactly the same way).

To add a favorite on Internet Explorer: When you reach a site that you want to save, go to the Favorites menu in your browser and select "Add to Favorites."

In order to organize and clean out your favorites, you need to access your Favorites file: Pull down the Favorites menu, and then choose the "Organize Favorites" option. Your bookmark file, which displays all your favorites, will open in a new window. You can change the order of your favorites or organize them into folders by selecting and drgagging them.

To delete a favorite, select it and choose the "Delete" button.

While this window is open, experiment with the bookmark options. Create new favorites and folders (they all can be deleted in exactly the same way).

Roommates From Hell

http://orion.lab.csuchico.edu/Archives/Volume35/Issue10/Opinion/Roofrohell.html

Thinking of renting out that extra room in your place? Read through this hilarious story by columnist R. Eirik Ott. You may decide that your sanity is worth the few extra bucks you have to pay.

Roommate Bulletin Board

http://www.gromco.com/roommate

This online service is a useful way to find a place to hang your hat or someone to fill that emptiness in your apartment. Just select the state you're interested in, as well as a few details to narrow your search, and *voila,* you're on the road to cohabitation. There actually is some busy exchanging going on here, and it's completely free.

FRIENDSHIP

CU-SeeMe Event Guide

http://www-personal.umich.edu/~johnlaue/cuseeme

Okay, so you and your friends installed CU-SeeMe, played with it for a while...and now you're tired of connecting and doing nothing but make goofy faces at each other. What now? Hit the Event Guide, where you can catch a plethora of CUSM events. Or, if you want to make funny faces at new people, you can check the People Pages for people willing to stare back at you.

A Girl's World

http://www.agirlsworld.com

A Girl's World is an exceptional site where Amy, Rachel, Geri, and Tessa act as your guides to exploring their clubhouse, making new friends, meeting incredible women, and creating fun stuff (see Figure 7.8). You're treated to everything from an interview with Shari Lewis to an in-depth examination of gum. In addition, parents and teachers will find a page devoted to them.

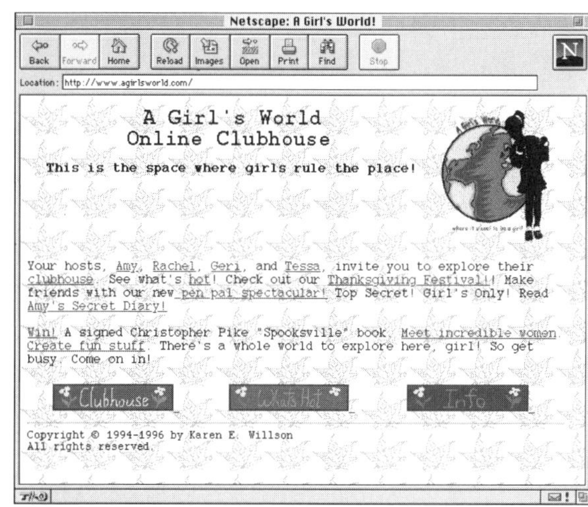

Figure 7.8
A Girl's World, *http://www.agirlsworld.com*

Friends and Partners

http://www.friends-partners.org/friends/opt-tables-mac-english

Like a post-Cold War "Brady Bunch"-style mix-up-the-family story, this joint project was developed by American Greg Cole and Russian Natasha Bulashova. Transatlantic surfers can learn about Russian and American culture through language, music, art, economics, and more than a dozen other topics. Then, check into a cool "hypertexted babblebox" for intra-continental conversations between Yanks and Russkies.

PeopleFind

http://www.yahoo.com/search/people

Find an old friend, high school classmate, or former flame. You can search for e-mail addresses, too. It's like having a very big "little black book." However, they won't be responsible for what happens after you reacquaint yourselves with one another...

WEDDING PLANNING AND MARRIAGE

David Slack's Automatic Wedding Speech Writer

http://speeches.com/auto.html

"Click Here to Miss the Nightmare" of having to give your Best Man's, Bride's or Groom's speech and being at a loss for words. Here's a stroke of genius from writer David Slack, who appears never to be at a loss for words (see Figure 7.9). Just fill in the blanks on the automatic form, and you'll actually have a pretty good wedding speech in minutes. Because you've got other things on your mind.

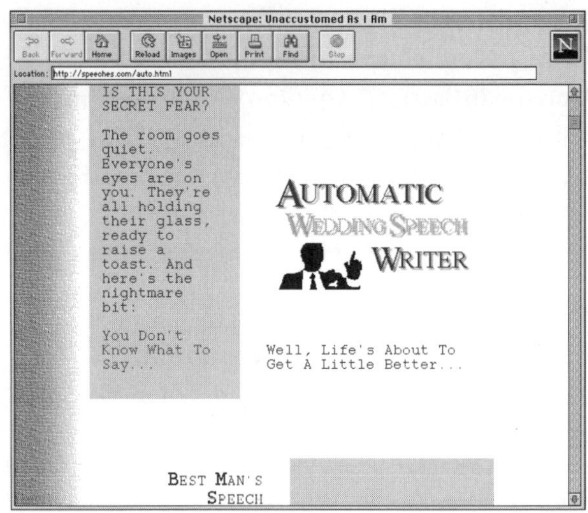

Figure 7.9
David Slack's Automatic Wedding Speech Writer, *http://speeches.com/auto.html*

Bridal Mag

http://www.BridalMag.com

Any bride-to-be will tell you: the most important purchase of them all is The Dress. Here's an online gallery of gowns to view, each with a short description and suggested price tag. You can also find out retail information specific to your area. Like having a front-row seat at your own bridal runway show.

Wedding Circle

http://www.weddingcircle.com

This all-encompassing wedding publication, from Continuum Internet Publishing Services, Inc., has its share of advertising, as do all things wedding-related. Yet it's also a surprisingly good resource for useful planning tips and interesting information on everything from ring shopping to learning about the wedding traditions of various cultures. They're all at this site, so only one bookmark is necessary. You can even post a wedding announcement online.

Rachel's Wedding Frugality Page

http://www.achiever.com/freehmpg/rachel/wedding.html

Rachel Shreckengast put this page of money-saving tips together for a friend, and she's gained a bit of recognition as well (a mention in the *LA Times'* Personal Finance column, for one). Her text-only guide outlines ways to save on everything from the ring (Cubic Zirconia? 10k gold?) to the gown (wear a relative's), plus budget-cutting tips for the ceremony. You may even have cash to spare for the honeymoon.

Wedding Web

http://www.weddingweb.com

Anyone who's been a bride-to-be knows: You can never get enough help in planning your wedding. And since the assistance offered at Wedding Web is online, it gives you the option of quietly perusing the tips rather than murdering your fiance or the florist. You'll find listings of regional services and downloadable planning guides full of advice on staying on schedule, getting a marriage license or changing your name (see Figure 7.10). Also interesting: the "bright ideas."

Agenda Online

http://www.agendaonline.com

Whether you're holding a reunion in Philadelphia or a wedding in Washington, D.C. Agenda Online is a solid resource for events planning. Register (free), then tap into descriptive directories of caterers, events planners, entertainers, photographers, and more for New York, DC, Philadelphia, Boston, and Dallas. The material comes from the company's collection of planning guides (order the hard-copy versions here). If you want the ease of an all-in-one resource, Agenda Online is a cool party zone.

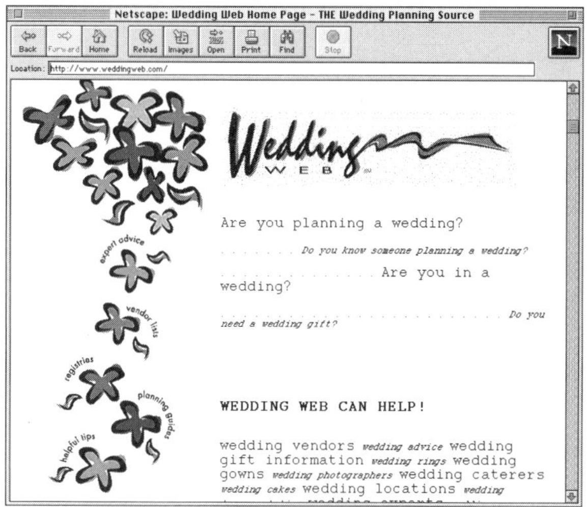

Figure 7.10
Wedding Web, *http://www.weddingweb.com*

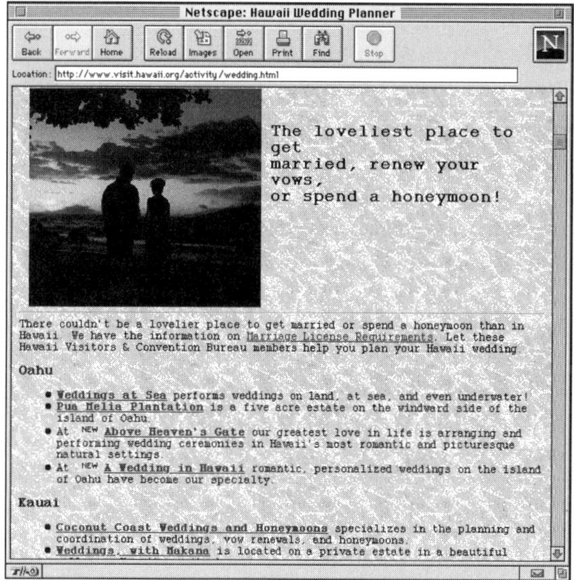

Figure 7.11
Hawaii Visitor Bureau,
http://www.visit.hawaii.org/activity/wedding.html

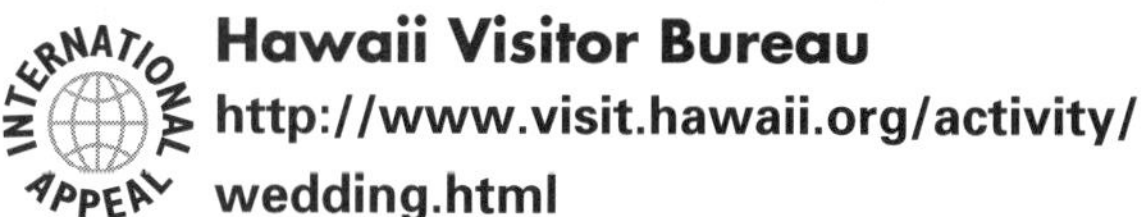

Hawaii Visitor Bureau
http://www.visit.hawaii.org/activity/wedding.html

This one's just for the Hawaiian traveler (see Figure 7.11). Browse through the listing of wedding services. One company offers an exchange of vows 30 feet below the surface of Hanauma Bay. Then have the honeymoon right nearby: an interactive map of the islands gives information on some of them. If you're really thinking ahead, visit the site that translates names into Hawaiian. This site also available in Japanese.

Wedding Bells
http://www.weddingbells.com

Along with the prerequisite advertising that seems to be present at everything related to nuptials, this site serves up a collection of wedding ideas and inspirations that would make even Martha Stewart envious, as well as the lowdown on wedding planning and the latest in trends and traditions, and fashions. By the time the Big Day comes, you may need to look to Romance Central for ideas on keeping romance alive.

BridalNet
http://www.bridalnet.com/nethome.htm

This site, one of the original wedding sites on the Web, is devoted to bringing the bride-to-be everything she needs to know for a picture-perfect wedding. What you'll find: beautiful soft-focus photos that will make you want to have a wedding even if you're not getting married, updates on bridal fashion, honeymoon ideas, and, just in case you're getting too serious about all this, an archive of wedding jokes.

WedNet
http://www.wednet.com

Here's another comprehensive resource site for those in (or anticipating) the agonizing throes of wedding planning. You can subscribe to the free newsletter, WedNews, with its monthly helping of unique wedding ideas and useful resources (it gets e-mailed to you, so there's minimal effort on your part). You'll also find budgeting tips, links to other wedding sites, and more. A valuable resource for planning that perfect wedding.

WeddingLine

http://www.weddingline.com

Everything you need to plan the perfect wedding is here at this site. From tips on the reception to ideas for the honeymoon, this free bi-monthly newsletter has you covered. Well organized and eye-catching, too. A great feature: generate a custom calendar for your own wedding planning needs.

I Thee Web

http://hollywoodandvine.com/Itheeweb

Part of Capitol Records' busybox of a site, I Thee Web is an online wedding chapel that promises to make even quickie Las Vegas ceremonies seem tired and traditional. Just follow their instructions on how to get married in "3 easy steps" (smarmy music included). If you can't find the words to pop the question, there's even a digital proposal form.

GlamOrama Wedding Chapel

http://www.glamorama.com/wed

Thanks to something called a "Weddimatic marriage and commitment system," you and your significant other can participate in a live, online wedding ceremony, and tie the knot in cyberspace (see Figure 7.12). The folks at GlamOrama are still researching state wedding laws and are currently only authorized to perform legal marriages in about half the country. Forego the legal hassles by participating in the chapel's commitment, re-commitment, or best friend ceremonies.

The Wedding Source

http://www.pep.com/pep/tws/tws.html

Prospective brides and grooms get numerous nuptial options on this page. The main attraction is an index of wedding related sites, including "Melanet" (for the African-American market), the French West Indies Page (for honeymooners), and Peachtree (featuring luggage tag

SPOTLIGHT ON PLANNING YOUR WEDDING

Your wedding: It's one of the most important events of your life. Yet preparing for a wedding can be stressful and confusing, especially if you're working with friends and family members who have conflicting ideas about the Big Day. It helps to be organized, and have a clear list of details that need to be addressed. Some basic questions to keep in mind:

The Place: Location, location, location.

Food and Drink: Brunch? Hors d'ouevres? Dinner? Bubbly?

Guests and Gifts: Who? How many? Where to put them? Where to register?

The Honeymoon: If you make it that far, you're doing okay…

Some sites that can help

1. Wedding Line is a great place to get your plans off the ground.
   http://www.weddingline.com
2. Look for fashion tips, honeymoon ideas, and more at BridalNet.
   http://www.bridalnet.com/nethome.htm
3. Find downloadable planning guides and bright ideas at the Wedding Web.
   http://www.weddingweb.com
4. Plan your wedding on a budget using Rachel's Wedding Frugality Page.
   http://www.achiever.com/freehmpg/rachel/wedding.html
5. Check out a wedding gown fashion show at Bridal Mag.
   http://www.BridalMag.com

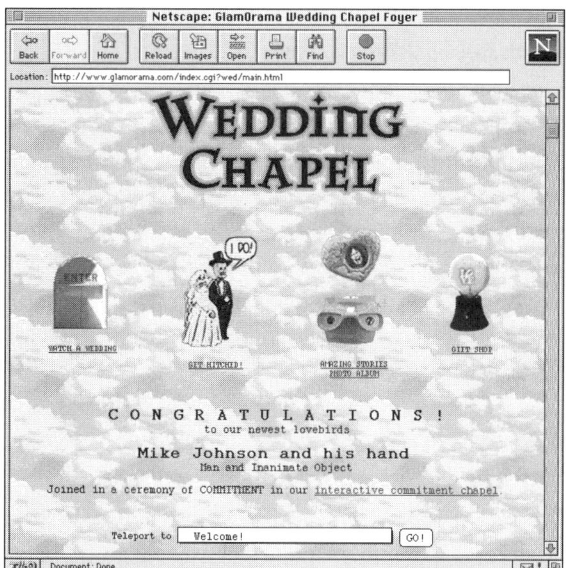

Figure 7.12
GlamOrama Wedding Chapel,
http://www.glamorama.com/wed

earrings, and other junky—er—distinctive attendant gifts). Check out Sonja's home page for questions of compatibility and the assurance that "not all marriages become devitalized over time."

The Bride Wore

http://www.visi.com/~dheaton/the_bride_wore.html

When Dave Heaton's friend was planning her wedding, she saved examples of the "strange, odd, and unflattering" wedding dresses that she saw depicted in the pages of bridal magazines. At this site, Dave has put up those photos, which feature such nuptial puffery as "sleeves bigger than my head" and "butt plumage." Anyone who's felt alarmed at the more-is-more philosophy of many bridal wear designers will especially appreciate the captions.

Oasis

http://www-leland.stanford.edu/~rmahony

This savvy online magazine is devoted to women's economic equality issues, and how they affect and relate to parenting concerns. Editor Rhona Mahoney looks at the number of househusbands in the U.S. and asks, "are women biologically programmed to seek a husband who is a good provider?" Provocative reading that will have you and your spouse debating for hours.

Vegas.COM presents Las Vegas

http://www.vegas.com/vegas/lasvegas.html

Vegas.COM collects everything you could ever want to know about Las Vegas under one domain name. The page on Vegas wedding chapels makes eloping easy. Long Fung Wedding Chapel, conveniently located in Las Vegas Chinatown, offers a bargain hitchin' for $168.00 including roses and music. Why wait?

The American Humanist Association-Wedding Section

http://www.infidels.org/org/aha/#weddings

For those who want to minimize the influence of other people's deities in their lives, here are several samples of secular, non-theistic wedding ceremonies, ranging from formal (with full orchestra) to more down-to-earth. These examples can serve as well-organized guidelines for those dealing with the touchy situation of a mixed faith marriage, or anyone who just doesn't want the usual dogmatic restraints.

Honeymoons.com

http://www.Honeymoons.com

A former producer of *Modern Bride* magazine, Susan Wagner puts her experience to work here, to help guide you to (and through) a successful honeymoon. Her Honeymoon Tips are practical ("Don't leave anything to chance"), and her destination section lists some real gems. You can almost feel your toes in that sand!

Honeymoon Magazine

http://www.honeymoonmagazine.com

There isn't too much here, simply because they want you to subscribe to the paper mag, but you can check out your sexual astrology, preview the soon-to-be-released *Destination Weddings* magazine, and check out some romantic hotels and resorts to put you in the mood.

Our Honeymoon: Two City Slickers in the Middle of Nowhere

http://www.tezcat.com/~jalfrank/honwel.html

Once upon a time, Dennis and Dana got married. And they shared the experience with everyone via the World Wide Web. Then they went on their honeymoon, and, guess what...? Follow D & D on their 7-day trek from Telluride to Moab, as they discover—sometimes painfully—that the great outdoors is "not like an L.L. Bean ad."

Famous Marriages

http://us.imdb.com/Couples

This mindblowing cross-reference of celebrity pairings is brought to you from the Internet Movie Database at Mississippi University. It's a seemingly endless string of couples (from David Bowie and Iman to Meat Loaf and Leslie Aday) with links to individual biographies. The people who gather all this data either have good common sense or a good sense of humor—they've left a field open for "Rosanne and ?"

Marriage

http://PersonalWebs.myriad.net/Roland/lect.htm

This offering by storyteller Roland H. Johnson III, gives some down-to-earth insight on some less than simple topics, such as love, marriage, and all the thorny issues in between. As the parent of a 13-year-old, Johnson is mystified by the attention his son receives from the little girls, who phone him and pass love notes. Johnson's brief study of love from those puppy-love days onward is a must-read.

Why? The Failed Marriages of Generation X

http://members.aol.com/WhyPage/index.html

This site is dedicated to exploring the failure of Gen-X marriages in language that Gen-Xers can relate to. The funky, eye-catching graphics don't detract from thought-provoking topics like "unconditional love," "marriage," "expectations," and "divorce." Nick Iacona, the man behind the site, draws on his personal experience to bite into questions like, "Why can't generation X seemingly hold marriages together?" and he manages to reveal some truly helpful answers.

LifeMatters

http://www.lifematters.com

A group of licensed marriage and family therapists in California pooled their backgrounds to create this forum for those who take responsibility for their own health and well-being. Articles and discussion areas are smartly presented on a variety of topics. Those include personal fitness, community relations, parenting and those OTHER kind of relationships. Another series of articles explores the "Mid-Life Transition." Empowering stuff here, for averting crises.

After the Affair

http://www.inforamp.net/~kmarlowe

This page, part of an article on extramarital affairs, provides answers for those in the unfortunate situation of having fallen out of one. Sufferers can track down the underlying reasons behind their emotions at this time of crisis, and gain some insight on intimacy. There are also discussion groups and links to other resources, and you can participate in the Affair Lady's doctoral study on the subject.

Marriage and Relationships

http://www.webcom.com/pleasant/sarah/marriage/marriage.html

This site, compiled by husband-and-wife team Sarah and Kyle Pleasant, provides a wealth of insight into the winding relationship roads that weave through dating, engagement, marriage, and anniversaries. Read their down-to-earth treatment of subjects like "Committed Relationships and School" and "How to Minimize In-Law Problems." And if you want the Cliff Notes, read about 14 tips to help your relationship now.

The Marriage Toolbox

http://www.marriagetools.com

At this well-crafted site, Publisher Paul Michael and Illustrator Kelly Kroll have created a magazine devoted to all aspects of marriage, from planning to maintenance. Topics are organized into, fittingly, a toolbox. Drawers are stuffed with articles, both fun ("Why Toothpaste and Deodorant are So Popular") and helpful, as well as tips ("Ask a Priest" for example) and resources. There are new additions every week. Idea: this toolbox makes a great wedding gift!!

1. Read a funny story about some Roommates From Hell.
   http://orion.lab.csuchico.edu/Archives/Volume35/Issue10/Opinion/Roofrohell.html
2. Check out 101 Easy Ways to Say No.
   http://www.rain.org/~uring/jokes/101no.htm/
3. Read up on the results of the Men's Underwear Survey at The Couch.
   http://www.geocities.com/SunsetStrip/9458/advice.htm
4. Take The Love Test—the results may surprise you!
   http://www.topchoice.com/~psyche/lovetest
5. Try your hand at The Relationship Game—just like the real thing!
   http://tiger.towson.edu/~bjohns1/relation/relamain.htm

☞ KEYWORDS

Dating: dating services, matchmaking, office romance, personals

Relating: love, relationship advice, friendship, roommates, gay, lesbian, single life, marriage

Weddings: bride, wedding planning, honeymoons

Divorce: separation, divorce counseling

Chapter 8

Fashion and Beauty

FASHION MEDIA

FASHION DESIGNERS

APPAREL AND ACCESSORIES

SHOES

MODELS AND MODELING AGENCIES

BEAUTY

COSMETICS

INFORMATIONAL

INSTITUTES AND ORGANIZATIONS

10
FASHIONABLE THINGS YOU CAN DO *RIGHT NOW*

1. Learn how to tie everything from an ascot to a waist sash at fashionmall.com's scarf-tying guide.

   http://www.fashionmall.com/media/acces/doc/scarftie.htm

2. Read the definitive guide to packing (including step-by-step illustrations for avoiding wrinkles), courtesy of Louis Vuitton.

   http://www.vuitton.com/spirit/packing/packing.htm

3. Don't let your burning questions about cosmetics and beauty go unanswered: e-mail them to makeup pro Bobbi Brown.

   http://www.bobbibrowncosmetics.com/askbobbi

4. Browse the breaking-into-modeling guide compiled by photographers at Hello beautiful!, which includes how to spot scams and a U.S. agency listing.

   http://www.hellobeautiful.Com/breaking/index.htm

5. Take this week's pop quiz for a shot at winning Armani Exchange merchandise or a gift certificate.

   http://www.armaniexchange.com/ax/quiz/qform.html

6. Find out the significant elements for each New York runway trend with Fashionwire on Women's Wire.

   http://www.women.com/style/fashion_wire.html

7. Locate the Vidal Sassoon salon nearest you, and make an appointment for a free consultation.

   http://www.vidalsassoon.com/html/somedays.html

8. Read Beauty Net's tip of the week.

   http://www.salonline.com/tip.html

9. Check out the image gallery, with selections from designer runway collections, on the Fashion TV site.

   http://www.citytv.com/ditytv/fashiontv

10. Stay on the pulse of the fashion universe—read British Vogue's Fashion Daily.

    http://www.vogue.co.uk/ms

Once upon a time, the world of fashion was for insiders only. Designers, editors, stylists, retailers, and their hangers-on were fashion's inner circle, and only those diehard fashionistas with P.R. connections could crack it. Thank goodness those days are over.

Now, design houses are experimenting with Internet simulcasts of their collections, so you don't have to be the editor of *Vogue Magazine* to get the best view of hot-ticket fashion shows. Names and clients of international fashion players are now at your fingertips, quite often with their e-mail addresses. Dates and locations of events on the glimmer circuit are listed and reported on—often with "backstage" photos and gossipy tidbits. Fashion fans who don't reside in the world's style capitals can live vicariously through the digital dispatches of reporters on the scene; look the part by locating specialty retailers; and even order wardrobe staples online. Everyone with a modem and a decent browser is welcome under the fashion tent.

Moreover, online fashion 'zines—covering classical to cutting edge style—entertain and inform using the latest technological toys. And Web versions of established fashion mags are holding their own—often with international editions in multiple languages. To top it off, the whole lot is basically free to Internet users.

It seems *"le Net"* (as the French say) has forever altered the realm of the fabulous.

FASHION MEDIA

Women's Wire Style Channel
http://www.women.com/style

The Style Channel is dedicated to both the fun of fashion and the reality of what women wear. Visit the fabulous circus of New York's runway shows in Fashion Notebook, and check out the season's themes (defined in photos and videos) with Fashionwire. E-mail a question to Fashion Plate—who rejects being a slave to style—and get Catwalk's amusing take on what's upcoming and what should be long gone. Cut through perfectionist hype and hoopla with Imagewire's discussion of body image issues. In Women's Wire's report on styles and trends the fashion police don't give tickets.

INTERNATIONAL APPEAL

Conde Nast Publications, Ltd.
http://www.condenast.co.uk/ms

A short registration form is the only hindrance to entering the Web home of Condé Nast's British publications—*GQ, Vogue, Tatler,* and *The World of Interiors.* Both British *Vogue* and *GQ* have daily Internet editions. This site has a graphics-heavy design, but the witty, scoop-filled content is worth the long download time.

INTERNATIONAL APPEAL

Cosmopolitan (Italian edition)
http://www.wonderpro.com/cosmopolitan

Italian Cosmo was the first edition of the international magazine to go online. This site is primarily in Italian; however, forums and certain features are written in English. The online version of the magazine highlights select articles and photo editorials from the newsstand edition.

Cosmo
http://www.cosmomag.com

Hey Cosmo girls, your mag is finally on the Web and it's got bedside astrologer updated weekly! (Say goodbye to those once-a-year, low-tech, pull-out bedside astrologers that never tear out quite right.) This glam site has all the wonderfully frivolous features of the monthly magazine we never admit to loving—bachelor of the month, agony advice, tips and quizzes, quizzes, quizzes! The legacy of Helen Gurley Brown lives on.

100 BEST SITES

Elle
http://www.ellemag.com

On this site, you'll find popular features from the printed version of *Elle Magazine* (numerology, photo editorials, shopping guide, *Elle*'s retail events), as well as a good selection of the monthly's articles. While the large glossy photos in the printed magazine usually aren't done justice with the site's colorful but small graphics, *Elle*'s written features translate to its online version just fine.

Elle International
http://www.elle.com

Fans of the numerous international editions of *Elle Magazine* (Elle USA, Japan, Germany, Spain, France, and Quebec) need one central site where they can link to all the magazine sites, and Elle International is it. While this site is relatively low-tech, and light on meaty content, it does serve as a good jumping off point to specific features in Elle's many country-specific editions.

French Elle
http://www.elle.fr

With all the different *Elle Magazine* sites on the Web (see Elle International, Elle Magazine, etc.), it's easy to get confused and a little overwhelmed. However, if you've ever wondered what it's like to cover the *prêt-à-porter* scene in Paris, this is the place to be—complete with news tidbits, guest commentators, and the low-down on the City of Light's hotspots. Read the pages in English or in French.

Esquire
http://www.designercity.com/esquire/index.htm

A small site composed of the British magazine's photo spreads, maintained on Designercity. Get the complete contents of the monthly, and click to pages with select fashion editorial. In addition to getting detailed information about the clothing pictured in the site's graphics, you can also search *Esquire's* database for your nearest retailer—that is, if you happen to live near London.

HomeArts, Network—Runway
http://homearts.com

If you're a fan of *Marie Claire, Redbook,* or *Good Housekeeping,* you'll love *HomeArts.* The Hearst Magazines site brings fashion coverage straight from the magazines' pages to our browsers in their unmistakable style. Features are well-designed, well-written and servicey—with price and retail information, if appropriate.

McCall's Patterns
http://www.mccall.com/homedec.html

Subscribe to McCall's Patterns directly from this site, or just browse the pages for the numbers and descriptions of patterns that catch your eye. McCall's Web pages will definitely not replace the printed magazine; however, they do serve as a good preview for the popular patterns of the season.

Papermag's Stylin Section
http://www.papermag.com/stylin

The New York-based manual of hipness brings street style online with a clean, colorful interface (see

[OVERHEARD ON WOMEN'S WIRE]
http://chat.women.com

"They were thinking about developing a women's basketball shoe. I was joking around with them. 'What are you going to name it? Air Swoopes?' They said, 'Air Something.' Five or six weeks later, they called. I was speechless. 'No way! Are you serious?!' A lot of female basketball players say, 'What took them so long?'"

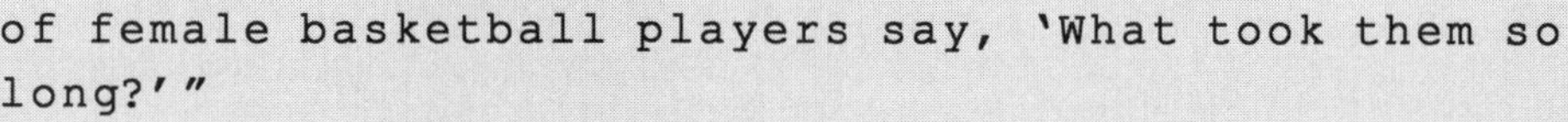

—Sheryl Swoopes, 24, Olympian-in-training to Women's Wire on how Nike's Air Swoopes, the first shoe named after a woman athlete, came about.

Figure 8.1
Papermag's Stylin Section, *http://www.papermag.com/stylin*

Figure 8.1). Papermag's "Fashion Schmashion" mavens take a wry look at the runways, and "Street" covers the latest in youthquake style. During the fashion collections, Papermag kicks into high gear, with daily coverage of the shows and reviews with downtown flava as only the magazine's own Lauren Ezersky, Kim Hastreiter, and Mister Mickey can deliver.

RAGS Magazine

http://204.189.12.10/R/RAGS

RAGS is a quarterly dealing with clothing, costume, ethnic textiles, jewelry, masks, et al. Its Web site is simple, straightforward promotion of the magazine. R.L. Shep Publications, the magazine's publishers, offers a bit of insight into the Mendocino, CA-based operation, and has an order form you can print out and snail mail. The *RAGS* costume and textile link page provides plenty of Web resources on the subject matter.

South Florida Magazine

http://sfl.com

Oh, to be part of the glamour set—jetting down to Palm Beach for a day of shopping or fashionably blading down the streets of South Beach. It's okay to dream, isn't it? *South Florida Magazine* invites you to the playgrounds of the sunshine state's elite on its pretty pages. Read their interviews, reviews, and the word on what's happening in the south's style capital.

ViaBazaar

http://viabazaar.com/index.html

Harper's Bazaar's site is devoted to promoting Italian fashion designers. Although graphics-intensive and not for the impatient (read: expect three or more clicks to reach your desired content), this site contains great biographical information, company profiles, news and international store information, not to mention highlights from designer collections. You can also get e-mail contact information for designers, and link to their Web sites.

@mode

http://www.ntt.fr/at-mode

This snazzy 'zine helps lead the charge of France-based fashion sites to the Web. Not quite ready to counter the resistance of French designers to displaying runway fashions on *le Net,* @mode presents a funky, opinionated tri-lingual (English, French, Japanese) take on street style, trends, and urban fashion phenomena.

Culture Zone

http://www.culturezone.com

A stylish yet low-on-substance bi-monthly 'zine. Culture Zone's fashion and beauty features are, for the most part, shockwave-enhanced photo essays. In addition to fashion, this 'zine covers film, art, music and culture. At press time, the latest issue of Culture Zone available on the Web was three months old, so proceed with caution.

Designercity

http://www.designercity.com

Designercity, the U.K.-based company responsible for the look and maintenance of various fashion sites (such as *Esquire Magazine)* hosts a fashion/lifestyle Webstravaganza. Not content to just report the trends or advertise for their paying customers, Designercity is an online monthly loaded (we're talking a heap of new content with each click) with witty columns, fashion editorials, and a guide to all that is hip in merry old England.

Dolce Vita

http://www.dolcevita.com

The fashion section of this Italian lifestyle magazine offers a bite-sized morsel of the Italian fashion scene. Clearly advertising-driven (judging from the constant mention of the same two or three Italian designers), *Dolce Vita* contains a few informational articles, a calendar of events in the Italian fashion industry, and a helpful "fashion finder," for locating retailers worldwide carrying Italian designer labels.

FAD Megazine

http://www.fadmag.com

The international quarterly "megazine" brings its art, design, and music content to the Internet. *FAD* includes a large number of brief "Web worthy" articles (often first-person) on its site, often with accompanying photos and specialized design. You can subscribe to *FAD*'s print version (at special Web-user prices) directly from the site.

fashionfirst

http://www.fashionfirst.com

The product of enterprising college students and recent grads with the fashion bug, this online 'zine attempts to create yet another place on the Web for articles on men's and women's trends, beauty, and popular culture. At press time, fashionfirst was in its third month of existence, so keep an eye on this site to see how it evolves.

Fashion Icon

http://www.fashion-icon.com

Once you get past the cute "I Dream of Jeannie" inspired clip art on Fashion Icon's opening page, you've done half the site. It's not clear exactly who the "fashion icon" is, though we're assured that she has good credentials and connections. Too bad the only content here are a few lengthy fashion show wrap-ups.

Fashion Internet

http://www.finy.com

FI set the industry standard for fashion Web sites with its attractive blend of insider scoop, fashion pictorials, intelligent articles, and witty reviews (see Figure 8.2). Especially great are its trailblazing features ("Ethnic Makeup: Beauty quirks of ethnic women"), and their hip, attitudinal advice column, "Ask Alex." Can Fashion Internet keep it up now that they have the attention of the fashion world (not to mention an entirely new masthead)?

Fashion Live

http://pclinux.worldmedia.fr/fashion

World Media Live's Paris-based publication delivers the Paris ready-to-wear collections and more. In addition to a schedule of fashion week shows, Fashion Live contains an extensive, informative database of designers presenting runway shows in Paris, trend reports and dispatches from wonderfully sarcastic roving reporters. Keep an eye out for exclusives like Yves Saint Laurent's Rive Gauche collection online.

Fashion Net

http://www.fashion.net

Links, links, and more links. If a site is remotely fashion-related, chances are you can link to it from here. Fashion Net hosts active message boards on beauty, modeling

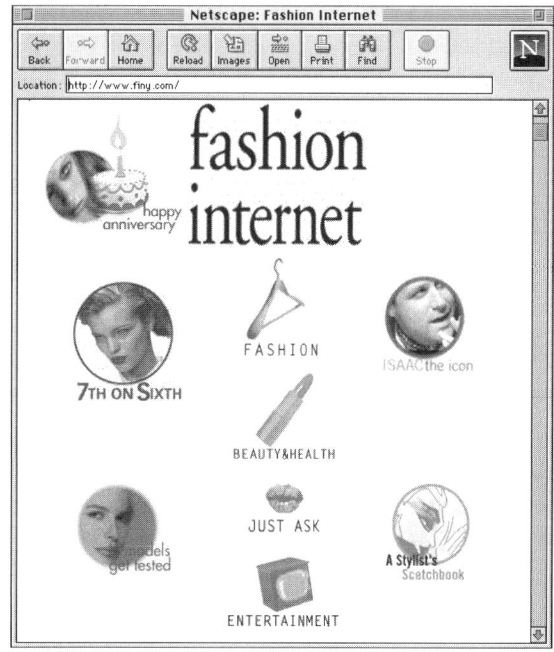

Figure 8.2

Fashion Internet, *http://www.finy.com*

and fitness, in addition to its employment boards for job seekers and employers (although there are many more seekers than employers on the "positions offered" list). The draw here is the international Fashion Yellow Pages, an extensive directory of industry contacts.

Fashion Online

http://fashion.com.sg

Fashion Online is an Asia-based trade publication primarily consisting of reprinted trend and market reports. The design of this site is a bit dense (three or more clicks to get to the features), and a good percentage of the content is for fashion industry folk on the marketing/financial side. Still, this site is worth joining and browsing for its employment listings (for jobs in Singapore), and business contacts.

Fashion UK

http://www.widemedia.com/fashionuk

The consummate British fashion site. Fashion UK is the place to find informative pieces laced with attitude and British wit on subjects as diverse as fashion prediction agencies and couture swap shops in Sydney, Australia. This site leaves no stone unturned with its coverage of the London fashion scene, detailed listings of industry contacts in the U.K., editorial spreads, and shopping guides.

FashionWeb UK

http://www.fashionweb.co.uk

A cluttered site for U.K. fashion industry links, advertising, and online versions of trade magazines distributed by London-based Streamline Fashion Publishing Ltd. The idea was to create an online gathering place for fashion industry professionals with contact listings, job postings, a message board, and links, links, links. It's all there, albeit on a somewhat clumsy, cumbersome site.

Hypermode

http://www.hypermode.com

Hypermode is all about fashion photography, visually arresting editorial spreads, high-tech toys, and bandwidth-sucking. As cool as it is to surf Hypermode, you probably want to stay away if you have less than a 28.8 modem and a Shockwave-enabled browser. If you are equipped the experience is worth the wait. The site's visuals are hype, but don't expect much in the area of written content... it ain't there.

The Look On-Line

http://www.lookonline.com

For fashion industry professionals or those who just wannabe. The Look Online, the labor of love of New York-based fashion photographer/Internet junkie Ernest Schmatolla, includes updates on trade events, New York fashion calendar highlights, and schmaltzy dish on the industry's players. Runway show photos, the occasionally funny "fashion fairy tales," and the priceless "Who's who in New York fashion public relations" warrant a bookmark for this site.

Lumiere

http://www.lumiere.com

Lumiere looks great, with its *de rigeur* black background, frames-enhanced design, and stylized, animated photos. But once you get past all that it is a glorified advertising site. At Lumiere, three out of four links lead to "a word from our sponsors." Looks like the initial fascination of maintaining the site is waning—updates are done once monthly.

MBA Style Magazine

http://members.aol.com/mbastyle/web

A fashion magazine for the business school set. MBA Style includes write-ups of designer collections (as they relate to businesspersons, of course), relevant guides (e.g., how to buy an interview suit), and practical non-fashion information (resume, salary info, links to business school sites). The online publication's articles are distributed for free at graduate business schools in the U.S., and supplemented with monthly chat sessions on America Online.

NYStyle

http://www.nystyle.com

NYStyle is a magazine/shopping site where you can read print pieces by established professionals in the field of fashion (Bernadine Morris), design (Evelyn Jablow), and artificial beauty (Dr. Sobel, Cosmetic Surgeon). But journalism is clearly not the point here. The interesting yet brief insider articles serve as a good segue to the goods and services (from "carefully selected, high quality companies") sold in NYStyle's shopping area.

N-touch Magazine

http://www.dircon.co.uk/lcf/ntouch.html

A conscientious online fashion magazine written and produced by students in the B.A. Fashion Promotion program at the London College of Fashion. Using the latest technological toys available at production time, the N-touch staff devotes as much reportage and Web space to the hot shots of the fashion establishment as to the oddities of the underground fashion scene.

Parade Fashion Consulate

http://www.theparade.com

Animation! Applets! Parade Fashion Consulate's site assaults the senses (and your browser) with its bandwidth requirements. Click through pages with brief trend reports, sample the random rants on the bulletin board, and check out photos from Parade's online fashion show. But there's more. Parade Fashion Consulate, should you wish to apply for membership, is an online buying service.

7Avenue

http://bytesizemag.com/7AVENUE/7AVENUE.HTM

A well-designed style sheet, which features a brief, interesting fashion report. Get an overview of the latest trends in "Details," and an in-depth analysis of each trend in its corresponding feature article. Not much material to work with here, but looking good never hurts.

StreetStyle

http://streetsound.clever.net/style/fashion.html

File this under Something Different. It's not for the faint of heart, but it does dish some real insider tips on hip hop and club style—straight from the keyboards of "correspondents" on the front line. In other words, leave any notions of self-censorship at the door, and get ready to rant, rave, and mix it up with club and hip-hop kids on the subject of phat gear.

Style Front

http://teleparc.com/stylefront/en/index.html

If it's Paris fashion week, it must be Style Front for runway reports, gossip, trends, and the after-hour parties. Plus there are interviews and hot features with the cool plug-ins. Don't even think of visiting without the proper gear... sneakers, jeans, and out-of-date Web browsers not permitted. For multi-lingual fashionphiles, the site has Japanese and French versions, in addition to English.

t@p Style

http://www.taponline.com/tap/culture/style

The 'zine devoted to the university set has a fashion/style section worthy of its audience. Here you'll find fashion commentary ("uh-oh, fur is in again"), service pieces ("new wardrobe for next to nothing!"), and those ubiquitous editorial rants. Although some features are more *Seventeen Magazine* than *Swing,* features are entertaining and useful. Now if only t@p would start sprucing up their design.

Urban Desires

http://www.desires.com

This envelope-pushing 'zine sets the technological, design, and content standards for all other 'zines to follow (see Figure 8.3). Lyrical, substantive prose, high-quality graphics, and an element of unpredictability are the hallmarks of Urban Desires, a production of Agency.com. Urban Desires' Style section is never short on action, adventure, and information with its hip, interactive features.

CNN Style

http://www.cnn.com/STYLE

Don't cancel your basic cable just yet. Style with Elsa Klensch, the CNN showcase of fashion, interior design, and the high life, features a select few story segments on its small, wordy site. Klensch files dispatches from style capitals around the world, often using video, sound clips, and animated photos. Although news items are informative, style just isn't the same without the omnipresence of Elsa Klensch.

Figure 8.3
Urban Desires, *http://www.desires.com*

The Detroit News

http://www.detnews.com

Okay, so this is an online newspaper in the truest sense—a reprint of the day's news shoveled on a Web page. But the Detroit News always has cutting-edge (or at least interesting and well-done) fashion features in its Accent section. Don't expect to find fancy toys and graphics here—you'll get the printed word and perhaps a photo or two. The fashion coverage is worth reading, really.

Fashion TV

http://www.citytv.com/citytv/fashiontv

The perfect complement to the weekly television program devoted to fashion, style, models, and art. This site features detailed episode guides with photo highlights of segments from each show, an image gallery with selections from designer runway collections, a list of international markets where the program is broadcast, but nary a trace of FT's charismatic host Jeanne Beker. Jeanne, where are you?

Style by Suzy Menkes

http://www.iht.com/IHT/FASH

The International Herald Tribune's pompadored fashion editor brings her award-winning dispatches to the Web. Visit this site for an index of available fashion articles. Most stories are text-only, however, on occasion photos do accompany Menkes' prose. A must-see for *International Herald Tribune* and Suzy Menkes fans—without the necessity of a trip to the international newsstand.

WWD (Womens Wear Daily)

http://www.wwd.com

The Holy Grail of fashion trade pubs presents a daily dose of headlines and happenings in its caustic signature style. This page is updated daily and features the full front page photo and caption from the day's paper in addition to news tidbits. For those who need more than just a distilled version of WWD (the entire paper, in other words), you can submit a request for an e-mail subscription.

FASHION DESIGNERS

jhanebarnes.com

http://www.jhanebarnes.com

How did a girl from rural Maryland become one of America's foremost designers? Click through and read about Jhane Barnes's ascent from designing band outfits in high school to winning prestigious awards from the Seventh Avenue fashion establishment. You can browse Barnes's men's wear, furniture, textile and bedding designs, a searchable store database, and press clippings on this smart, substantive site.

INTERNATIONAL APPEAL

BERNSHAW

http://www.fashion.net/bernshaw

BERNSHAW, a U.K.-based design and manufacturing company, previews their high-fashion women's wear on this small and simple site. Having trouble finding a retailer that stocks BERNSHAW label designs? E-mail your request for a catalog or the location of the retailer in your area, or as the Brits say, your "nearest stockist."

Chanel

http://www.elle.fr/chanel

INTERNATIONAL APPEAL Primarily an advertising site on *Elle France,* Chanel's pages offer something a little extra: makeup trends for the season, an introduction to its latest fragrance, and a brief history of the company's legendary namesake, Coco Chanel. The pages are written in both English and French.

Dollhouse

http://www.dollhouse.com

INTERNATIONAL APPEAL The funky clothing line for juniors has an animated, psychedelic site (see Figure 8.4). Not just content to toot their own horn, this site includes media clippings, an international store finder, photos of seasonal fashions, a quirky company backgrounder, a feedback page, and trade show dates. If you're moved to buy any Dollhouse fashions, you can link to the AirShop page on fashionmall.com, where the clothes are sold online.

Figure 8.4
Dollhouse, *http://www.dollhouse.com*

Romeo Gigli

http://www.energymedia.com/gigli

Romeo Gigli counts INXS's Michael Hutchence and the actor John Turturro among the many celebrity fans of his fashions...but do we really need 15 minutes of download time to learn this? Gigli's downtown-inspired site is frame-enhanced and consists of oversized fashion and publicity photos of personalities wearing Gigli designs. To scroll or not to scroll? You decide.

Norma Kamali

http://www.omo-norma-kamali.com

The design veteran who made headlines by banning black clothing in her showroom took the plunge online by simulcasting her Fall 1996 collection over the Internet. Kamali's site contains photos of her press clippings, highlights of her collections, and an extensive biographical timeline. Proving the infamous "ban on black" could actually play in monochrome New York City, the site includes a large picture of Kamali and her staff clad in technicolor fashions.

Donna Karan

http://www.donnakaran.com

A slick site done in basic black where you can get a front-row view of DK's latest men's wear and women's wear collections, not to mention her line of beauty products. You'll also find a bio, store locator, and info on Donna Karan's involvement with the Newman/Haas (that's Newman, as in Paul) Indy Car Racing Team.

Walter Moszel

http://wmoszel.com

INTERNATIONAL APPEAL Buenos Aires-based Walter Moszel invites Internet users to view designs from his women's and men's casual, formal, and resort collections. This high-bandwidth site also features various beautiful and sexy advertising campaign photos to view or download. Moszel's home page is available in both English and Spanish.

Nicole Miller

http://www.nicolemiller.com

One of the first designers on the Net, Nicole Miller's site delivers video clips, close-up views of Miller's collections, ordering information for her signature line of funky printed scarves, ties and accessories, and a listing of stores in the U.S. and abroad.

Thierry Mugler

http://www.energymedia.com/mugler

Thierry Mugler's Universe offers a glance at the man behind the arresting runway fashions. Although this infrequently updated site doesn't deliver many of the much-touted celebrity models Mugler woos to his runways, it does showcase some of the Parisian designer/shutterbug's extraordinary fashion photos. Don't be fooled by the French titles, the site is in English.

Aldo Negri Fashion

http://www.doit.it/NegriFashion

INTERNATIONAL APPEAL The Italian manufacturer/distributor of women's wear offers a look at four of their lines: Fascino (daywear), Ellison (knitwear), Benedetta (junior), and MariaLuisa Negri (large sizes). Although the lines are sold at boutiques throughout the globe, you must e-mail the company for specific locations or further information. Since no online sales, store databases, or extensive looks at each line are available at this somewhat sparse site, the goal seems to be securing more worldwide distributors of their fashions.

Massimo Osti Production

http://www.production.it

INTERNATIONAL APPEAL This Italian design/manufacturing house has a sleekly designed Web site, with their collections for men and women beautifully displayed online. The pages list retailers where the sporty collections are available, which is throughout Italy and other European countries, but unfortunately not the U.S. Pages are in English and Italian.

Yves Saint Laurent

http://pclinux.worldmedia.fr/YSL

INTERNATIONAL APPEAL This treat from World Media Live's Fashion Live site details the so-called "Yves-olution" from the French designer's days working for the house of Dior in the early 1960's to Saint Laurent's exclusive Internet broadcasts of his '96/'97 couture and ready-to-wear collections. The site contains interviews, a photo slide show, diaries from the days leading up to the couture collection, and an area where users can "interact with YSL."

2B!

http://weborama.com/2b

At press time, 2B!, the sassy, downtown design house whose fashions are sold at (among other places) Saks, is a Web site in progress (see Figure 8.5). Ever-so-slightly reminiscent of a virtual ride on New York's subways (get on the desired line and pray it gets you where you want to go), the 2B! pages present a brief introduction to the

Designer Rozy Lewis and partner, Max Gross

where they surf

Surfer: Rozy Lewis

Designer 2B! http://weborama.com/2b

Favorite sites of the moment:

firstVIEW

http://www.firstview.com

"This site is incredible! I can see the collections of over 200 designers from Paris, Milan, London, and New York from my computer. As a designer, I find it an educational and inspirational resource."

Paper Magazine

http://www.papermag.com

"The definitive New York City guide that lists monthly descriptions of the hippest bars, restaurants, clubs and lounges so even jaded New Yorkers can act like tourists."

names, faces, and funky philosophies behind this street-inspired line. Be patient… this site is graphics-heavy.

Geoffrey B. Small
http://www.tiac.net/users/gbs/index.html

Geoffrey B. Small is a Boston-based designer who wows the fashion community each year with his vintage-inspired creations, often of spruced-up "recycled" clothes. He has the distinction of being the only U.S.-based designer to officially show during the Paris collections. Small's site, a labor of love (he often updates it himself) is loaded with runway highlights, designer notes, press clippings, and international tour dates.

Paul Smith
http://www.paulsmith.co.uk

This "true Brit's" site is full of biographical information, highlights of his chic collections from 1987 to the present, and the 411 on his traveling exhibition. Video clips, witty backgrounders, and worldwide store locations make Paul Smith's home on the Web worth dropping in. He promises that more interactive features are coming soon.

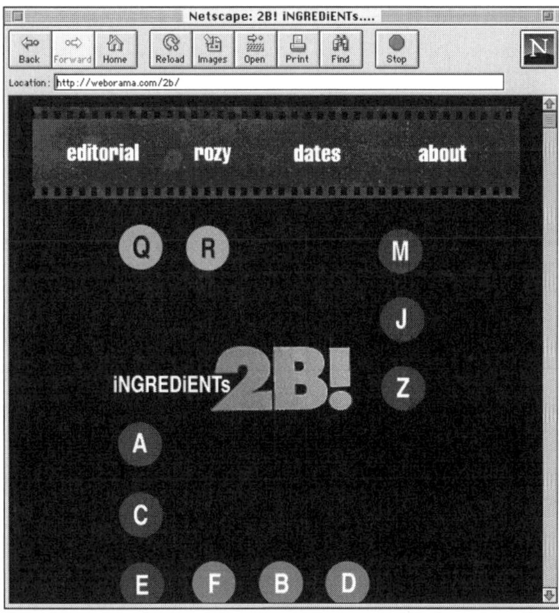

Figure 8.5
2B!, *http://weborama.com/2b*

W.&L.T.
http://www.walt.de

While you can view avant-garde designer Walt Van Beerendonck's futuristic collections and get purchasing info at Wild and Lethal Trash, the experience goes way beyond fashion (see Figure 8.6). You can take a virtual trip to the W.&L.T. Paris runway show, and if you're game for a bit of whimsy, sample some of the plug-in enhanced fun spots on the site. This is the future of fashion.

Gianni Versace
http://www.energymedia.com/versace

A frames-enhanced manual slide show of all things Versace. This site allows addicts of the Italian designer's fashions, fragrances, and ad campaign photos (by Bruce Weber) to get a nice fix. Versace's home page transcends any language barriers his international fans may face—there's no text on this site, just photos.

Madeleine Vionnet
http://www.vionnet.com

Madeleine Vionnet, one of the pioneers of French haute couture, is beautifully remembered and honored at this well-done site. Read about Madeleine Vionnet's history,

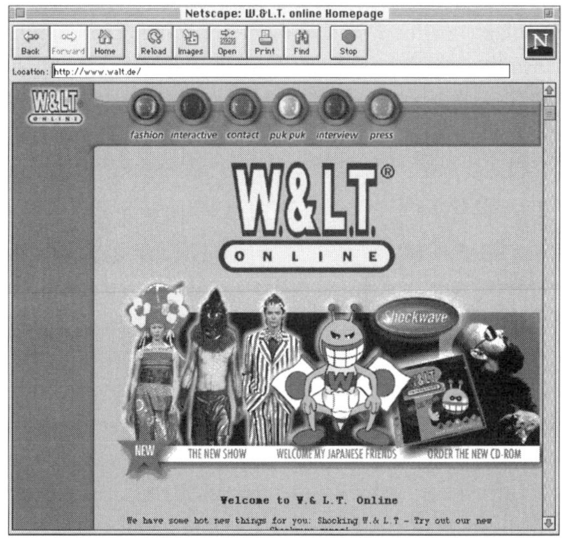

Figure 8.6
W.&L.T., *http://www.walt.de*

her historical contributions in the fashion timeline ("In 1932, the first breast ever revealed in the pages of Vogue was wearing Madeleine Vionnet."), and the revival of the Vionnet label. The site also hosts a boutique where you can purchase silk Vionnet scarves woven in Lyon, France priced at $495.00 and up.

APPAREL AND ACCESSORIES

Levi's

http://www.levi.com

A slick, hip, and happening shrine to the American blue jean. Read the history (jean-eology) of Levi's, download commercials, send animated cards, or participate in the latest in interactive advertising. That is, send your suggestion for the "501 reasons" campaign, and, if you're up for it, play the game based on the wildly popular "pool boy" commercial.

INTERNATIONAL APPEAL

United Colors of Benetton

http://www.benetton.com

The Benetton Group—the label behind those striking, shocking advertising campaigns—has a searchable site with corporate background information, their manufacturing and marketing philosophies (to keep those pesky MBA students from bombarding their switchboards, no doubt), as well as a peek at their avant-garde magazine, *Colors*. This site isn't all corporate, there are Quick Time movies, and eyebrow-raising postcards you can send via e-mail.

Guess?

http://www.guess.com

The world of Guess? is a stylish place where you can download videos and pictures from their famous commercial campaigns, take a virtual getaway to Florida, Hawaii, or a new hotspot, learn company history (or "how the Guess? was won"), and play high tech games for prizes. Oh, and if you have the inclination, there's always the "Prop and Wardrobe" area for what's in stores, and the worldwide Guess? store locator.

Diesel Jeans

http://www.diesel.co.uk

Diesel Jeans superstores are shrines to decadence, the avant garde, design, and, of course, fashion. The bright, dynamic Diesel Jeans Web site is no different. Here's where you can send funky e-mail postcards, advertise for a mate, take a virtual tour of the company's hotel properties, and, last but not least, visit the Diesel Jeans boutique.

INTERNATIONAL APPEAL

Esprit

http://www.esprit.com

The Esprit site offers glimpses via stylized (if not substantive) photos of Esprit clothing, eyewear, timepiece, and bedding collections. The pages also boast an international store locator. The real draw, however, is the serialized story of the birth and growth of this company from a home-based business in San Francisco to one of the most recognized brands in the world.

INTERNATIONAL APPEAL

Giesswein

http://www.giesswein.com

The Austrian Knitwear manufacturer maintains a promotional/informational site, where you can order a snail mail catalog, win a Giesswein original, or learn the history of the company. Giesswein manufactures clothing for men, women, and children, and offers glimpses of its different product lines. Web pages are in English, French, Italian, and German.

KID APPEAL

Joe Boxer

http://www.joeboxer.com

The underwear company with the smiley face logo also sells outerwear, kids apparel, accessories, and housewares; but the merchandise is not the focus of this slightly gaudy, graphics-intensive site...the real goal here is creating a sideshow atmosphere, complete with games, freaks, a wacky message board, and a kooky poodle story.

INTERNATIONAL APPEAL

KOOKAI

http://www.gci.fr/kookai

KOOKAI, the French label popular in Europe, Asia, northern and southern Africa, South America, and Australia has a dynamic, informative site. It is written in

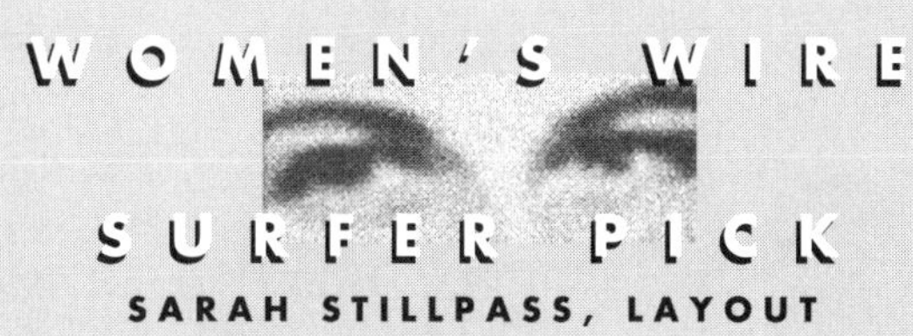

SARAH STILLPASS, LAYOUT

Armani Exchange

http://www.armaniexchange.com

At A/X's sleek but overly industrial site, you can browse the latest collections (fabric descriptions and prices are included), go behind the scenes of a campaign photo shoot, get store locations, and the lowdown on the Armani Exchange party scene. Just in case there's no A/X in your area, the store is selling T-shirts hipsters can buy exclusively on the Net.

French as KOOKAI doesn't have any stores stateside. Francophiles just might enjoy practicing *la langue,* reading KOOKAI's style and trend reports for the season, or scrolling through the exhaustive list of KOOKAI stores worldwide.

Lee Jeans

http://www.leejeans.com

Lee's home on the Web is a showcase for the various jean styles the company sells, and an FAQ on caring for your denim. While the site refers all specific questions to the company's 1-800 number, Lee Jeans devotes much of its pages to info on its community involvement (breast cancer awareness, for example), and commercial sponsorships.

Poot!

http://www.tumyeto.com/tydu/poot!/poot.html

If hipster chords, snap-on minis, and spaghetti tanks are your thang, then Poot! is the site for you. Order items from the online catalog, get store info, and click over to Foxy, the 'zine where Poot! grrls mingle. Poot! is self-described as "anti-fashion," designed for "girls on the go."

INTERNATIONAL APPEAL

Sisley

http://www.sisley.com

This sharp site wasn't fashioned primarily to sell clothes, or even to locate stores where merchandise from this Benetton offshoot is sold...if that were the case, perhaps then the Web pages would allow a lot more space than a tiny frame for that information. Instead, the attractive pages focus on the "Sisley Diary"—a wide-eyed, romantic-yet-informative jaunt around the globe.

Wool Home

http://www.woolmark.com

Woolmark has a bright, informative spot on the Web that not only furthers the purpose of the IWS (a promotion and marketing organization for wool), but aims to expand the horizons of visitors surfing the site (see Figure 8.7). In simple and interesting fashion, the Woolmark folks explain (in great detail) the wool manufacturing process, present a specialized glossary of wool-related terms, and provide an in-depth seasonal style report.

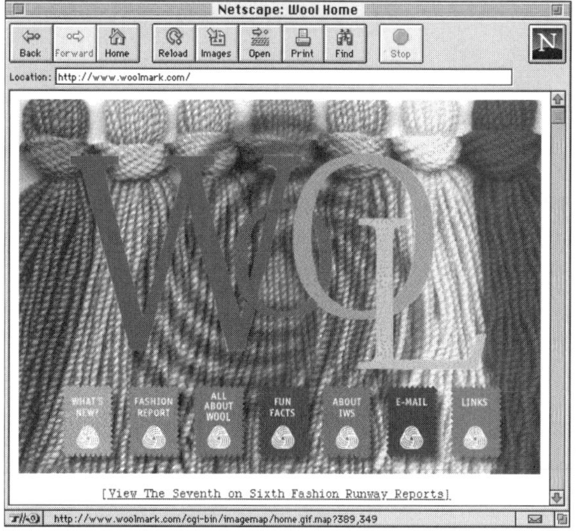

Figure 8.7

Wool Home, *http://www.woolmark.com*

SHOES

Adidas Webzine

http://www.adidas.com

A sport shoe junkie's dream. Adidas' stylin', animated, high-tech Webzine has loads of sports news, a multimedia sports hall of fame, photos of just about every Adidas sneaker on the market today, as well as a good amount of self-hype. In English and German, with links to Adidas Canada and Adidas Deutschland.

Airwalk Online

http://www.airwalk.com

The manufacturer of footwear for the snow/skate/street/bike set has a site overflowing with photos, event listings (like snowboarding competitions and skateboard league events), profiles of extreme athletes, and a database of Airwalk shoe retailers (so we'll forgive the outdated sponsorship info on Lollapalooza '96). As if that's not enough, the folks at Airwalk online promise to keep you updated on additions/changes to their site in "The Spot."

Buffalo Boots

http://www.buffalo-boots.com

Enter Buffalo Boots' dayglo pages to discover the hip spots to party, shop, and hang in London (see Figure 8.8). Take to the streets to check out the phattest fashions, and, if you dare, browse the Buffalo Boots online catalog of the British store's newest styles of platform footgear. Merchandise can be ordered online or by telephone or fax.

Figure 8.8
Buffalo Boots, *http://www.buffalo-boots.com*

Margapita

http://www.margapita.com

Shoe lovers beware—this site may cause serious drooling. Margapita's shoes, advertised as "the most beautiful shoes in the world," are gorgeous, if pricey. The Ft. Lauderdale-based retailer brings its hottest designer styles to its Web pages—the better to entice us to visit the store or order their catalog online, no doubt. The "Ann's top 10 shoe secrets" page is a must-read.

Minnetonka Moccasins

http://www.minnetonkamocc.com

A low-tech online catalog site, through and through. Exactly how many different styles of moccasins are there? You'd be surprised. Browse through selections of Minnetonka's shoes, coats, and hats, with detailed info on pricing and sizing. To order a selection, you must call in or fax in a printout of your order page.

Reebok

http://www.reebok.com

If you're expecting nothing more than an over-hyped repository of online sneaker ads, you're in for a treat. Reebok's mammoth site combines the requisite shoe and retailer information along with loads of content on exercise; sports news, scores, and rankings; and features from their content partners (including *Swing Magazine,* PE-TV and Fit-TV). You can also post to Reebok's bulletin boards, participate in chats, and register to receive site updates and product discounts.

ShoeInfoNet

http://www.shoeinfonet.com

A repository of worldwide information on shoe manufacturers, retailers, importers, agencies, and more. ShoeInfoNet aspires to provide the maximum amount of objective information about footwear. Judging from the many specialized categories of information on shoes provided at this site (not to mention the 14 languages besides English in which the info is presented), we'd say they're succeeding.

Shoes on the Net

http://www.shoesonthenet.com

Shoes on the Net presents up-to-date information on the footwear industry in Milan, Paris, and New York. In addition, these pages also contain great links to footwear sites (from the Al Bundy Page to the Vans Web site), a free newsletter, and a guest area where shoe fetishists can rendezvous.

Shoeworld

http://www.shoeworld.com

Advertised as Europe's premier shoe site, Shoeworld is the place on the Web where you can link to the home pages of the designers and manufacturers of shoes for men, women, and children throughout the EU. Shoe World also has an extensive page of links to other worldwide shoe and footwear-related sites.

Oilily

http://www.oilily.com

The Netherlands-based company which designs clothes for women and children (in addition to shoes, accessories, cosmetics, and stationery), has a bright, simple site. Users can order merchandise catalogs, find locations of Oilily stores throughout the world, submit ideas for new products, and join the international fan club.

Fashionmall.com

http://www.fashionmall.com

Ben Narasin's site is a stylish, one-stop-shop for the beautiful people (see Figure 8.9). Not only can you see photo highlights from designer runway shows in the U.S. and abroad, you can also sample fashion magazines such as the *Fashion Reporter,* and learn useful tips (e.g., how to tie an ascot, buy lingerie, and judge a Cuban cigar). RayBans, designer fashions, and specialized gifts can be purchased here. Watch for live online broadcasts of ready-to-wear runway shows.

Figure 8.9

Fashionmall.com, *http://www.fashionmall.com*

Swatch

http://www.swatch-art.com

Primarily an advertising site, Swatch offers visitors the opportunity to join a fan club, chat with other Swatch watch fanatics, and download screensavers, videos, and artsy photos from its "artist" area. The site is visually arresting, yet dated—you can still play Swatch's net.hunt game here although the competition is officially over.

Louis Vuitton

http://www.vuitton.com

Learn about Louis Vuitton's contributions to the art of travel. This site contains Louis Vuitton "news" items, store/repair information, and pictures/descriptions of the French luggage manufacturing house's best sellers; but the highlight is the "Musee du Voyage," an historical showcase printed in English and French. Users are encouraged to respond to the customer service feedback form with the promise of a gift—no, not a key chain, but a special edition Louis Vuitton GIF (digital photo).

MODELS AND MODELING AGENCIES

BangkokNet-Thai Models and Celebrities

http://www.bangkoknet.com/tim.html

Take a gander at the hottest models, celebrities, and beauty pageant contestants in Thailand, or further your own modeling career in Asia with the contacts you'll make via BangkokNet. Thai-Inter Models, whose clients decorate this site's pages, welcomes wannabe European, Asian, and Eurasian supermodels to e-mail vital stats and professional digitized photos.

Barbizon International Schools of Modeling

http://www.modelingschools.com

Barbizon Schools promise training to "be a model or just look like one." Their site offers a peek into their network of schools and annual modeling competitions. Visit the site for a curriculum description, search the international model database, tour the Barbizon boutique, or discover which "Baywatch babe" is a former Barbizon School grad.

INTERNATIONAL APPEAL

Boss Models

http://www.bossmodels.com

The agency that invented the male supermodel (or so they claim) has a Web site overflowing with stunning fashion photos of their buff and beautiful mannequins. Here's where you can order their glossy pictorial book, *Male Supermodels: The Men of Boss Models,* write fan e-mail to their stars, or get instructions on how to enter the Boss Online Model Search.

John Casablancas Modeling and Career Centers

http://www.jc-centers.com

In addition to being the founder and CEO of the mammoth Elite Modeling Agency, John Casablancas serves as the namesake to over 40 modeling and career centers in the U.S. and overseas. At the John Casablancas Modeling and Career Centers site, you can get the FAQ on this modeling school franchise, submit an electronic request for more info and request a free copy of their *Model News Magazine*.

INTERNATIONAL APPEAL

Elite Models

http://www.elitemodels.com

Elite, home to supermodels Linda, Christy, et al., has an informational yet stylish site, complete with contact information for their offices worldwide, a brief history of the agency, a monthly spotlight feature on an Elite model, and everything you ever wanted to know about the annual "Elite Model Look" competition.

Headbooks Online

http://www.headbooks.com

Headbooks Online attempts to simplify the casting process by letting professionals in casting surf the Web to find their desired talent. Registered members in the fashion print, commercial print, and TV/film industries have the ability to view headsheets on the Web and search the Headbooks Online database to locate talent by specific qualifications and physical attributes.

IMAGE

http://www.imagewrld.com/index.html

The Independent Models and Actors Guild is yet another full-service Web site—a place for photographers, casting agents, and models to meet under one virtual roof. Judging from the model portfolios and advertising for the Glamour Illustrated newsletter, the only difference between this and other sites of this kind is that IMAGE represents the up-and-coming faces on the boudoir photography scene.

LA Models

http://www.lamodels.com

The largest modeling agency on the west coast has a funky little site where you can take a look at their cache of male, female, runway, and television/commercial talent...we're talking pictures galore! And for those surfers who want to do a bit of paid promotion for the company (meaning you pay, you promote), you can order LA Models-emblazoned merchandise online.

SPOTLIGHT ON THE RUNWAYS

Runway fashion is a year-round, cross-Atlantic scene both on and off the Web. In 1996, fashion icon Yves Saint Laurent previewed his entire fall/winter collection on the World Media Live Web site, and Italian designers Dolce and Gabbana had their D & G spring/summer 1997 show broadcast live on the fashionmall.com site. The trend is slowly catching on...runway shows are no longer just for the fashion elite.

Five Facts

1. Ready-to-wear shows are held biannually in New York, London, Paris, and Milan.
2. Haute couture collections are held twice a year in Paris.
3. New York's 7th on Sixth was established in 1993 by the Council of Fashion Designers of America (CFDA) to organize and centralize the U.S.'s most well-known runway shows.
4. According to the Elite Model Management agency, runway models make anywhere from $500.00 to $2,000.00 an hour.
5. In early 1996, the French guild for haute couture and deluxe ready-to-wear designers *(Le Chambre Syndicale du Prêt-à-Porter des Couturiers et des Créateurs de Mode)* threatened to sue an Internet fashion photo company for posting couture on the Web. Their fear is that designs seen on the Web will be pirated by lower-end knock-off manufacturers.

Five Sites

1. The Council of Fashion Designers of America documents the fashion mania of the New York 7th on Sixth women's collections and men's shows.
   http://www.7thonSixth.com
2. The up-to-the-minute online photo service, firstVIEW, offers members the first look at international collections from the hottest designers worldwide. Non-members can take close-up looks at highlights from previous seasons.
   http://www.firstview.com
3. PaperMag's Fashion Shmashion mavens give you their downtown fashion 411, straight from the runways and streets of New York and Paris.
   http://www.papermag.com/stylin
4. World Media's Fashion Live presents extensive runway/backstage coverage of the Paris *prêt-à-porter* (ready-to-wear) shows.
   http://pclinux.worldmedia.fr/fashion
5. The stylemeisters at Fashion U.K. leave no details or gossip unmentioned in their recap of London Fashion Week.
   http://www.widemedia.com/fashionuk

Model's Lynk

http://www.modelslynk.com

A "members only" meeting place for up-and-coming models and actors and those ever-elusive casting directors. For a fee, models can display their pictures/vital statistics online, and have access to casting calls. Casting professionals who are members can search the Talent Quest Interactive database. Model's Lynk also offers Web site hosting and development.

Models Online

http://www.models-online.com/Gateway/mo.acgi$home

This Toronto-based home page aims to be the Web site where aspiring models can gain exposure (as much as possible, judging from the cheesecake photos). The entire searchable model database is available free of charge to industry professionals and curious Web surfers. On the other hand, aspiring models are charged a fee to be listed.

NEXT Online

http://www.nextmodels.com/index.html

NEXT Model Management, the international agency that counts Angie Everheart among the pretty faces it represents, offers you the opportunity to get in touch with its clients. Visit the Model Lounge for the vital stats on your favorite NEXT model, and to complete a form to e-mail her a question. If that's not enough excitement for ya, perhaps you'll enjoy The Loft, the NEXT site's cheesy online *Models Inc.*-like soap.

SUPERMODEL.COM

http://www.supermodel.com

An online shrine to "supermodeldom"—complete with fashion and paparazzi photos, interviews, a news wire (where tasty gossip items from newspapers and magazines is compiled), and chat sessions with an international talent scout (see Figure 8.10). The site features a calendar with a fashion event/news tidbit for every day of the month—usually reported after the fact, but interesting all the same.

Figure 8.10
SUPERMODEL.COM, *http://www.supermodel.com*

Arlene Wilson Models

http://www.mindspring.com/~arlene

Arlene Wilson Models isn't just another agency with downloadable headshots of its talent. The Atlanta-based agency also has a voiceover talent listening room with over 75 Real Audio audition clips. AW Models has an area on its site for portfolio shots from its resident hair/makeup artist, and a page devoted to modeling-related merchandise (portfolio, modeling directory) that clients or those who wannabe can order by telephone.

BEAUTY

BeautyLink

http://www.beautylink.com

100 BEST SITES

Don't let the graphics-intensive nature of this site get you down—the content is worth the wait if you have the time and patience (see Figure 8.11). Step into the member's parlor (after transmitting membership

Figure 8.11
BeautyLink, *http://www.beautylink.com*

information, natch), and read up on beauty tips and remedies. BeautyLink is where you can find natural cures to what ails you (acne, insomnia, wrinkles, etc.), and humorous dispatches on nail care, mind and body tips, and fashion magazine gossip.

BeautyNet
http://www.salonline.com

Toronto-based Salon Communications Inc., the publishers responsible for providing salon patrons hours of dryer-time reading material, brings its advertising-laden content to a simple, well-designed Web site. The features on hair, makeup, and nail trends frequently mention specific products (usually sold at salons), and plenty of salon pros are lurking in the BeautyNet chat room, ready to push their services. The weekly 'zine's "ask the pros" and "tip of the week" features are worth a glance.

Beautyspot
http://www.beautyspot.com

A somewhat busy advertising/sales site for drugstore beauty products such as fragrances, deodorants, after-shave, and nail care paraphernalia. Locate a store near you that sells Beautyspot products (Tabu, Musk, Canoe), or do a little online shopping. If you have the inclination (and the patience to click through this frames-enhanced site's endless pages), e-mail questions to Beautyspot's Nail Doctor.

BeautyTech
http://www.beautytech.com

This certainly isn't the prettiest or the most orderly site, but there's a lot here. BeautyTech is a virtual beauty community where you can link to salons across the U.S. that participate in their worldwide salon referral program, chat with cosmetologists and nail care professionals, and join mailing lists to connect with people in the beauty business.

BeautyWorks
http://www.salonpro.com

This quarterly online publication presents photos of the latest short, long, and specialty hair styles for men and women, as well as a small database of salons in the U.S. with Web pages. There's not much else to this site, although users can order a handful of hair trade publications online or by telephone, and register to receive notification via e-mail when BeautyWorks is updated.

KID Appeal

BodyFX
http://www.bodyfx.com

The company responsible for products such as Brain Stain (temporary hair color) and Dread Head (dreadlock-forming gel) have a site tailored especially for the *Seventeen Magazine* set. Browse the list of hair and body products—with descriptions and the occasional video clip; locate your nearest store location; visit the rasta/patois dictionary; or send e-mail to join the exclusive On the Edge club.

Women's Link by Bristol Myers
http://www.womenslink.com

Enter this cozy spa-like "cyberclub" for women, loaded with information on everything from hair care to fitness, health care to momness. Even though Women's Link's primary goal is advertising (notice the strategic plugs for products like Excedrin and Clairol hair color), the site's contests, interactive-ness, and interesting features make it worth visiting.

Main Floor

http://www.mainfloor.com

This syndicated beauty and fashion television show continues its practice of blurring the line between editorial content and advertising on its Web site. Main Floor, which appears to be loaded with features departments such as good advice, health and fitness, and who's hot, simply clutters its pages with columns of fluffy prose, the occasional photo, and plugs for the show's various fashion and beauty sponsors.

StudioNet

http://studionet.com/index.html

The "world virtual studio production network" site has enough animation, scrolling text, and photos to make surfing it a major time commitment. Still, this members-only site (registration required) succeeds in its goal to bring photographers, modeling agencies, agents, stylists, and other fashion professionals under one virtual roof.

HairNet

http://www.hairnet.com

A gathering place for hair and beauty professionals. HairNet boasts nationwide databases of hair salons and beauty schools, in addition to an advertiser-free telephone hotline. This site is the place to read industry press releases in Beauty On-line (described as a "beauty cyberzine"), and the home of the online version of American Salon magazine.

Your Personal Salon

http://www.yoursalon.com/salon/default.html

This site is entirely devoted to promoting the use of the Salon Selectives line of hair care products. If you're game to participate in some mindless fun, get your monthly hair horoscope, play a game to learn some amusing facts about the history of hair, or be the star of the site's monthly serial stories. Of course, you can also click through to find out the Salon Selectives products best suited for your hair type.

Salons USA

http://www.gosalon.com

Salons USA wants you to treat yourself or someone you care about to salon/spa services. They have established a network of salons nationwide that accept its gift certificates for services such as waxing, manicures, and massage. Neither the names and addresses of participating salons, nor the charges for using the service are listed, although you can order the gift certificates online.

Vidal Sassoon Academy

http://www.vidalsassoon.com

Advice, trends, and product suggestions courtesy of Vidal Sassoon professionals. No matter how you style it, this site is about Vidal Sassoon products, schools, and salons. Enjoy the humorous hair timeline, and the "hairoglyphics" quiz.

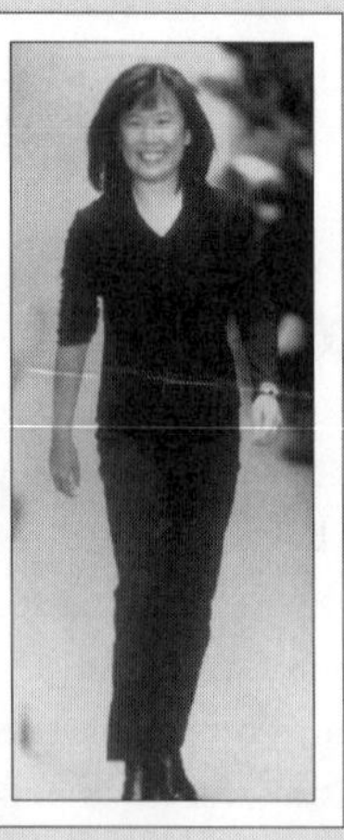

where they surf

Surfer: Yeohlee

Fashion Designer

Favorite sites of the moment:

MTV

http://www.mtv.com

"It's a great overview of the network and allows you to be tuned in to current trends."

Ticketmaster

http://www.ticketmaster.com

"It has all the information you need about different concerts and events occurring throughout the U.S."

COSMETICS

Aveda

http://www.aveda.com

Aveda isn't just a product, salon, or clothing line, it's a way of life. In addition to providing a searchable database of Aveda salons/retailers, courses offered at Aveda Institutes, and articles from their magazine, this site provides detailed information on ayervedic medicine and aromaology (see Figure 8.12). You can also sample organic recipes, Aveda's natural clothing line, new additions/trends in cosmetics, and learn the history of this environmentally conscious company.

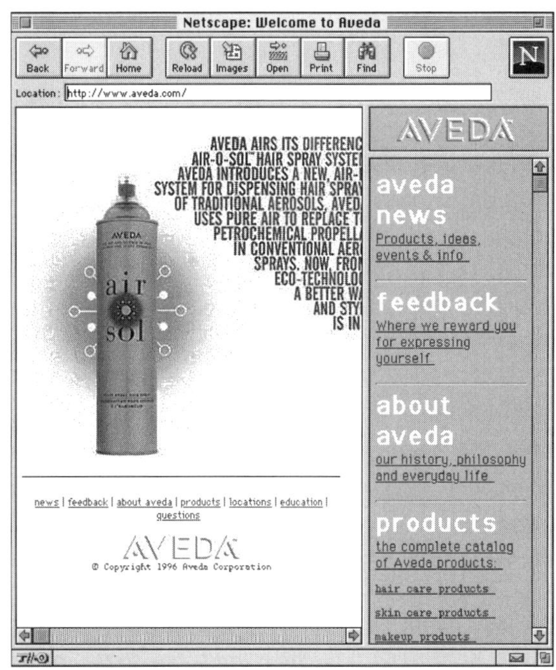

Figure 8.12
Aveda, *http://www.aveda.com*

Avon

http://www.avon.com

Visit this site's purple pages to request info on becoming a sales representative or ordering a catalog. You can also use the "Talk to Avon" feature for comments, questions, or advice via e-mail forms.

[OVERHEARD ON WOMEN'S WIRE]

http://chat.women.com

"Women today have vast interests and are expected to do everything. They're no longer categorized as ladies who lunch. They want to know about everything. And, by the way, they also want to be amused."

ON WHAT'S FASHIONABLE:

"I think that probably it's getting harder and harder to define specifically what is fashionable, possibly because there is so much out there in such varied guises that there are no specific fashion trends."

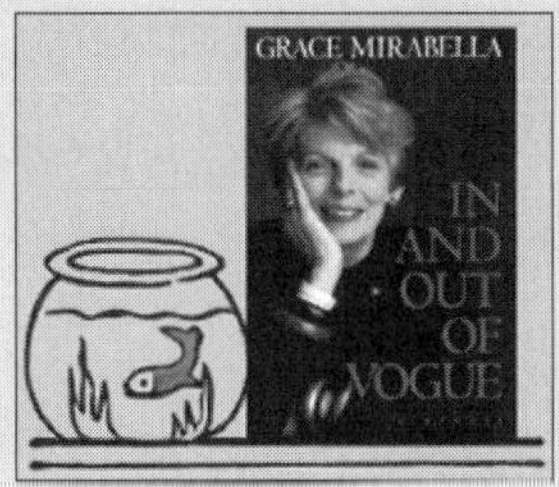

—Grace Mirabella, author of memoir *In and Out of Vogue*, and former editor-in-chief of *Vogue* in a live chat on Women's Wire.

The Body Shop

http://www.the-body-shop.com

The eco-friendly and socially conscious cosmetics retailer has a site where you can get advice on skin care regimens, background on The Body Shop's anti-animal testing policy, as well as directions on where to direct correspondence to support international prisoners of conscience. No store locator or specific product pitches here...but who needs 'em online when there's a Body Shop in just about every local mall?

Bobbi Brown Cosmetics Online

http://www.bobbibrowncosmetics.com

The makeup artist to the stars, and namesake of the well-known international cosmetics line has brought her makeup tips and down-home approach to beauty to the Web. This site contains the requisite store finder, product descriptions, advice column, and media clips. Thankfully, it also contains a price list for Bobbi Brown makeup and brushes.

Clinique

http://www.clinique.com

Just like a visit to your local Clinique counter, this site is all about clean design, and providing lots of information. The site's many features on men's products, expert tips, and personalized information offer beauty and skin care tips involving only their products, natch. The bonuses here are the guide to the Net, and the Men's Health pages, offering advice and useful information.

Ask CoverGirl

http://www.covergirl.com

Each page contains nothing more than a large graphic with either advertising information or makeup tips. There is an area devoted to answering user questions, via e-mail or using CoverGirl's toll-free hotline.

The Lipstick Page

http://www.users.wineasy.se/bjornt/lip.html

A makeup junkie's dream. The amazing Lipstick Library organizes thousands of lipsticks of all brands into basic color categories, complete with color swatches. Join the Cosmetics Exchange Network to link up with fellow lipstick-lovers, read the witty, comprehensive guides to lipstick shopping in New York, London, and Stockholm, or download the latest edition of FashionStance magazine.

Lancôme

http://www.lancome-usa.com

The elegantly designed Lancôme site focuses on products and gift ideas. It's reminiscent of an advertisement—using delicious words to describe everyday beauty items—but better: You can see lists of colors for different makeup, and they do cool graphic tricks with the text. The site includes a do-it-yourself, simplistic skin analysis (dry, oily, or combo?), a product-endorsing feature called "What's French, What's not?" and an extensive national store locator.

L'Oreal

http://www.lorealcosmetics.com

L'Oreal's site is a product-minded spot with personalized cosmetics advice. Find information about L'Oreal's newest products, fashion tips, product recommendations, in addition to a makeup quiz.

Mary Kay, Inc.

http://www.marykay.com

No pink Cadillacs here, just hype for the cosmetics company whose merchandise is sold exclusively through individual sales representatives. Take a look at Mary Kay's newest products, and read through kudos from various fashion magazines; but if you're looking to purchase products you'll still have to call the company's 1-800 number to locate your nearest rep.

Revlon

http://www.revlon.com

Revlon's busy site combines different ads for its various makeup lines. Each page contains graphics with lipstick, nail color, and foundation spectrums, in addition to instructions for achieving those flawless daytime and evening looks Revlon says we all can achieve. Look for the site's contest entry page.

Shiseido
http://www.toppan.co.jp/shiseido/e/index.html

The Japanese cosmetics corporation has a detailed site with clean, fluid design. Information—which ranges from company backgrounders to annual reports to the makeup line—is served as a well-planned corporate presentation, complete with QuickTime movies and interactive pages. Every bit of info, whether an introduction to Shiseido's fragrance line or a short bio of the company's founder, is written in lyrical, enticing prose. In English and Japanese.

Urban Decay
http://www.urbandecay.com

Browse Urban Decay's Web pages to find products with names like "smog," "acid rain," and "asphyxia" (in blacks, dark purples, and mustardy yellows). The most decadent this site gets is with its first-person accounts of fun and revelry. Otherwise, it's your average store-finding, product-introducing, link-filled cosmetics site—except it's advertising makeup with oddly named, eclectic colors.

INFORMATIONAL

Angel of Fashion
http://www.fashionangel.com/angel.html

The "angels" monitor the Web for fashion and beauty-related sites, then bestow their coveted seal of approval on those deemed worthy. How do they pick winner sites? "If on the first page we see a price, we move on. Blatant selling is rejected," says creator Rodney Dunetz. The result, despite cumbersome design, is a pretty well-stocked clearinghouse for fashion and style information.

ApparelNet
http://www.apparel.net

An organized, if somewhat outdated, repository of fashion and apparel-related links. The searchable ApparelNet site consists of pages devoted to retailers, fashion media, trade show events, and other subjects relevant to the business. Each page is loaded with Internet links and brief descriptions of the services/information available at the sites listed.

The Fashion Biz
http://www.fashionbiz.com

A surprisingly un-fashionable site devoted to linking online fashion resources. A limited number of international designers, manufacturers, and retailers are available on the Fashion Biz database, and news/industry information is often provided via direct links to content on other fashion-related Web sites. Well-intentioned, but confusing. In English and French.

FashionLink Hong Kong
http://www.fashionlink.com.hk/~cerfab

A link-laden fashion site with Hong Kong flava. Visit FashionLink to participate in forum discussions, link to the requisite beauty, fashion, and designer home pages, and get info about Hong Kong. This site includes links to government Web pages, a who's who directory for the Hong Kong fashion industry, and an area for posting/responding to job opportunity listings.

Fur Online
http://www.furs.com

Advertised as the largest resource on the Web for fur fashion, Fur Online is more of a promotional than informational site. These pages contain fur highlights from the runways, a fur FAQ, a page devoted to unflattering soundbytes from animal rights organizations, and an online version of Fur Age, the newsmagazine of the industry. This site is heavy on graphics, so patience is required.

INSTITUTES AND ORGANIZATIONS

Fashion Careers of California College
http://www.fashioncollege.com

San Diego-based Fashion Careers of California College is a private postsecondary business school offering students certificate and degree programs in fashion design and fashion merchandising. Although some of this site's pages might present a challenge to some (with its teeny-tiny type), all relevant tuition, course, academic calendar, and credit information is available here. You can also e-mail questions, or request for a course catalog.

The Fashion Institute of Design & Merchandising

http://www.fidm.com

FIDM, an accredited college based in Los Angeles, offers degree and specialized programs in fashion and interior design. Their site is an award-winning, thorough, and dynamic introduction to the institution. Rather than serving as an online repository of course and program information, FIDM's site contains among other things, a calendar, spotlights on alumni and student work, a resource center, and a gallery of exhibits.

Fashion Institute of Technology

http://www.apparel.net/fit

The renowned fashion college located in the heart of New York's garment district has a simple, seldom-updated page on the ApparelNet server. This small site is where you can find snippets from the Fashion Institute of Technology (FIT) student handbook or catalog—with its

I·N·T·E·R·N·E·T M·I·N·U·T·E

VIDEO ON THE WEB

Attention MTV fans and film buffs: Live action videos, film clips, and animation are available now on a monitor near you. You can view video clips on the Web—with a little help from some viewing software—most of which can be downloaded free. The only limitation is lack of bandwidth: A rough download time estimate is: 1MB = 5 minutes (at 28.8kbps). An average film clip is 1MB. So—before you download—check the size of the file and the speed of your modem.

Most video viewing software is also available as a "plug-in" for your Web browser (primarily Netscape or Internet Explorer). Plug-ins let you obtain the software—via your browser—and view the movie directly on the Web page. The movie will open automatically upon being downloaded.

Common Formats for Viewing Video Files

- QuickTime—A majority of video files can be viewed with Windows or Mac software called QuickTime, which may already be included in your system software if you have purchased or upgraded your system recently. If not, you can download it:

  http://quicktime.apple.com

  Or get the Netscape plug-in:

  http://www.quickTime.apple.com/sw

- MPEG—Another standard for viewing video clips. MPEG viewing software for Mac:

  ftp://mirror.apple.com/mirrors/info-mac/gst/mov/sparkle-245.hqx

  For Windows:

  http://www.mpeg.org/MSSG

  As a Netscape plug-in for Mac and Windows:

  http://www.intervu.com/player/player.html

- AVI—Yet another video format, primarily for Microsoft Windows. AVI viewing software for Windows:

  ftp://ftp.microsoft.com/softlib/mslfiles/WV1160.EXE

  For Mac, AVI to Windows converter:

  ftp://mirror.apple.com/mirrors/infomac/gst/mov/video-for-windows-11p.hqx

  Netscape plug-in for Windows:

  http://support.intel.com/tools/help/t-vidply.htm

sanitized prose and nary a mention of the fashion institution's esteemed alumni.

Ida Ferri (Italy)

http://www.pagemaster.it/idaferri

INTERNATIONAL APPEAL This Roman fashion design school, which offers degree and certificate programs in fashion, dress, and pattern design, has little more than a symbolic presence on the Internet. Their site, available in English or Italian, offers short descriptions of their programs, and the ability to e-mail the school for more information.

London College of Fashion

http://www.dircon.co.uk/lcf/lcf/lcf.html

At this site, you can read a short backgrounder on the London College of Fashion, a part of the prestigious London Institute. Also, get brief descriptions of course and study programs available at the LCF, along with some examples of student work. The main draw of this site, however, is its link to N-touch, an online fashion magazine produced by the college's students.

I·N·T·E·R·N·E·T M·I·N·U·T·E

VIDEO ON THE WEB

Something New

The newest formats for video compression allow you to view real time video. You can play audio and video "streams" (signal transfers in digital form, which are then downloaded on your computer and played back using various tools) directly from the network. A tool you can use to access this format is StreamWorks. It works as a plug-in with Netscape or Internet Explorer, and can be configured to your modem speed, avoiding unnecessarily long download time.

You can ownload StreamWorks for Mac or Windows at:

www.streamworks.com

Now that you've got the tools, on with the show! Some sites where you can check out video and movies on the Web:

http://www.cnn.com/video_vault

CNN daily news site, often with video clips. Also includes an archive of past coverage.

http://www.mediacast.com

Live media events.

http://www.virtuallot.com/bin/mm_lib.cgi?video+WBVaults:_Video+va.htm+WB_Vaults

Video clips from *Friends, Lois & Clark,* and other Warner Brothers TV programs.

http://film.softcenter.se/flics

Quicktime's archive, with Quicktime clips and trailers from new and old movies.

http://www.webmovie.com

Sci-fi drama, considered the first made-on-a-PC movie. With live actors, digital sets, special effects. (Requires a Java-enabled browser—another Netscape plug-in.)

If you find a movie clip or music video you like, you can save it, e-mail it to a friend, and include it in your Web site. Or, think about creating your own. Your only limitations are your imagination—and, of course, the viewer's bandwidth.

Parsons School of Design

http://www.newschool.edu/academic/parsons.htm

Designers Isaac Mizrahi, Donna Karan, and Anna Sui are all graduates of the world-renowned Parsons School of Design. The school, a division of The New School for Social Research, has a comprehensive introduction to its history and course offerings online, as well as extraordinary portfolio items from students in various programs of study (see Figure 8.13). You can also read about programs offered at Parsons' various international locations (Paris, Malaysia, Dominican Republic), and can e-mail a request for admission materials.

Pratt Institute

http://www.pratt.edu/schools/artdes/fashion/index.html

In the 1940s, Brooklyn, NY-based Pratt Institute was the first school in the U.S. to grant a degree in fashion design. Pratt's visually pleasing information-laden Web site is where you can read about the school's fashion design program, required courses, course descriptions, and faculty bios. If you're still interested in surfing the site after reading all about the fashion program, then take a tour of the campus, and play voyeur with the site's three PrattCams.

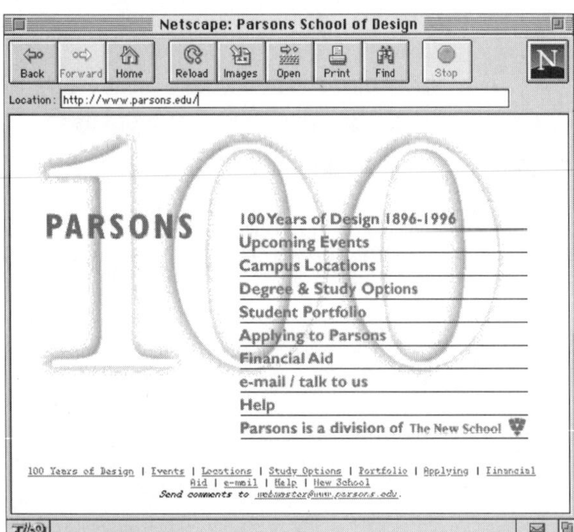

Figure 8.13

Parsons School of Design, *http://www.newschool.edu/academic/parsons.htm*

Shenkar College (Israel)

http://www.shenkar.ac.il

Shenkar College of Textile Technology and Fashion has a site as small as its student body (approx. 560). This institute offers five programs of study, including fashion design, textile design, textile chemistry, textile marketing, industrial management, and textile/plastics engineering. Besides brief descriptions of each department, Shenkar's site includes a listing of alumni/friends groups worldwide, and the opportunity to e-mail a request for more information.

The Apparel and Textile Network

http://www.at-net.com

ATnet, as it is called, is a members-only meeting place for apparel/textile buyers and manufacturers. Membership is free, and members can access product and ordering information from retailers with "showroom" areas (which they pay a fee to maintain). In addition, ATnet members can get international trade show information, link to trade association sites, and get the latest business stories in Fashion Bytes, ATnet's weekly publication.

Bobbin Blenheim Online

http://www.bobbin.com

Bobbin Blenheim, the company that publishes a magazine and produces apparel industry conventions and expos world-wide, maintains this promotional site. Navigating this site is confusing, however; non-insiders with no prior knowledge of Bobbin Blenheim, its printed version, or its productions have little reason to surf this site. Link to sponsors' sites, relevant news items, and a schedule of Bobbin's international trade shows.

CaliforniaMart

http://www.californiamart.com

Diehard fashionistas refuse to acknowledge that the fashion industry exists and thrives in the U.S. anywhere outside of New York City. It does, and CaliforniaMart is the west coast's answer to Seventh Avenue. Though thin in the content area, the site presents schedules for the California Collections—a database of designers, showrooms, and representatives affiliated with CaliforniaMart, as well as membership information/forms for the buyer's club VIP program.

Camera Nazionale della Moda Italiana

http://www.italycollections.it/index.html

The National Chamber of Italian Fashion, a nonprofit promotional organization, maintains this site. This is the page to visit for the scheduled dates for men's and women's fashion shows in Milan and Rome, contact information, and public relations snippets about Italian fashion designers. Not much more content or even meaty information available here. In English and Italian.

Fashion Beauty Internet Association—FBIA

http://www.fbia.com

A new association of fashion industry professionals and businesses who have taken the leap online. Get membership profiles and information here, but not much else. FBIA sets its sights high, with short- and long-term plans for an advertising network, seminars, and fashion industry benefits for the wired set.

Fashion Group International

http://www.fgi.org

Fashion Group International, the first nonprofit organization established by and for women, maintains an informational site to help boost its membership of 6,000+ fashion professionals. These Web pages offer a detailed profile of the organization with a few extras, such as industry and market reports filed by members. However, in order to reap the benefits of FGI's bulletin boards (job opportunities, conferences, databases), you must pay a fee ($18.00/month for non-members).

firstVIEW

http://www.firstview.com

For a large fee ($999.00/year), members of firstVIEW, the professional photography service, have instant access to photos from the hottest designers' haute couture and ready-to-wear shows. For yet another fee, members can purchase the publishing rights to these photos. This site is well done and gets the recognition it deserves…from editors, publishers, designers (and designer knock off artists, no doubt). Non-members have access to selections from the previous season's shows, and NY Style, firstVIEW's magazine supplement.

ICA Gem Site

http://www.gemstone.org

A mine of information about gemstones, courtesy of the International Colored Gemstone Association. The nonprofit organization, which represents the international gemstone industry, has a fun, fact-filled site, complete with news (market trends, mining reports), helpful hints (how to judge gem quality), and a guide to gems. In English, German, and French.

In-StyleWorks Online

http://www.styleworks.com

A snazzy, toy-filled (Shockwave, VRML) online trade and accessory show featuring hundreds of fashion retailers and manufacturers. Scan the directory for companies on display, then visit their virtual booths for glimpses at their exhibits. Download VRML to take a tour of the Intercontinental Hotel. Contact information is available for all companies on display.

The Mart

http://www.themart.com

The Mart caters to store retailers by allowing them to view and purchase clothing and goods from manufacturers online. This is a members-only service, although curious retailers, manufacturers, and surfers are welcome to try out The Mart's sample session. Created by Carlsbad, CA-based JDS Solutions Corporation, The Mart aspires to be a full-service showroom using the latest electronic technologies.

7th on Sixth

http://www.7thonSixth.com

So, you're not in New York City for the 7th on Sixth collections. Or, if you are in New York City, there's no way you're getting anywhere near the fashion show venues. Worry not, you'll feel like you're a part of the glamour set when you surf this site. In addition to show schedules, designer bios, and runway photos, the 7th on Sixth Webmeisters up the ante every season, adding interesting interviews or features to their highly visible pages.

1 Got a message for the citizens of Gotham? Post it to the Joe Boxer Interactive billboard, located in the heart of Times Square, New York City.
http://www.joeboxer.com/new/talktalk/times/zip_message.html

2 High fashion meets high technology at designer Walt Van Beerendonck's Wild and Lethal Trash site. Create a future face using your Shockwave-enhanced browser.
http://www.walt.de/new/new.html

3 Send a love letter to Marcus Schenkenberg, Joel West, or another Boss Models mannequin.
http://www.bossmodels.com/fanemail.html

4 Thinking of getting a Jamaican-style dreadlocked coif? First learn the lingo in the Rasta/Patois dictionary.
http://www.bodyfx.com/glossary.html

Virtual Garment Center

http://www.garment.com

Membership in the Virtual Garment Center is free, and open to retailers, manufacturers, suppliers, textile companies, and all other business types relevant to the rag trade. From what we can see, the idea is slowly taking hold of international fashionphiles. Although the site's many bulletin boards aren't very active, they do receive posts from people doing business in the U.S., as well as importers/exporters from remote parts of the Middle East and Asia.

☞ KEYWORDS

Fashion Designers: apparel, shoes, kids clothes, maternity, large sizes, accessories

Beauty: hair, makeup, cosmetics, skin care

Fashion: news, history, institutes, magazines

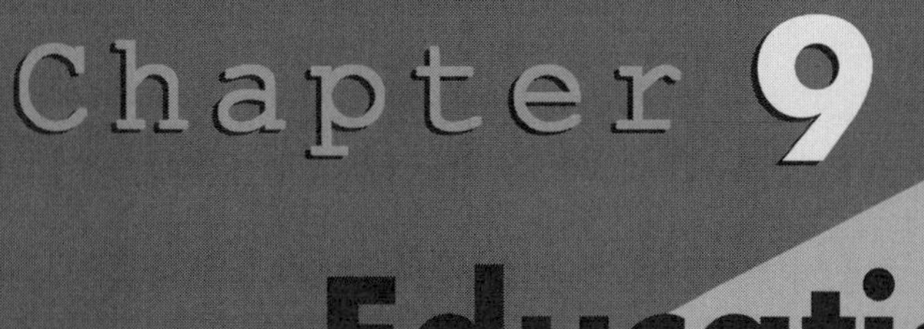

Chapter 9

Education

EARLY CHILDHOOD RESOURCES

K THROUGH 12 RESOURCES

COLLEGE AND POST GRADUATE

WOMEN'S STUDIES

FINANCIAL AID, SCHOLARSHIPS, AND LOANS

LIBRARIES

TEACHERS AND SCHOLARS

EDUCATIONAL SERVICES AND RESOURCES

10
EDUCATIONAL THINGS YOU CAN DO *RIGHT NOW*

1 Use the fastWEB search engine for immediate results on what financial aid resources might be available to you.

http://web.studentservices.com/fastweb

2 Learn how to cite bibliographic information obtained from the Internet in your academic papers.

http://www.uvm.edu/~xli/reference/estyles.html

3 Visit College Net and conduct a detailed search to find the right college for you.

http://www.collegenet.com/cgibin/Webdriver?MIval=search_choices

4 Entertain your child by introducing him or her to Cyberschool Magazine.

http://www.infoshare.ca/csm/index.htm

5 Submit your own commentary on the biggest or most obscure issues on education to the Educational Policy Analysis Archives.

http://seamonkey.ed.asu.edu/epaa/commentary.html

6 If you are, or know, a senior citizen interested in continuing education, search the Elderhostel Home Page catalog index to find their short-term continuing education location nearest you.

http://www.elderhostel.org/catindex.html

7 Read about George Eliot's life at the "Celebration of Women Writers" site.

http://www.cs.cmu.edu/afs/cs.cmu.edu/user/mmbt/www/women/writers.html

8 Conduct a virtual frog dissection.

http://curry.edschool.Virginia.EDU/go/frog/home.html

9 Search for government documents at Yale University's Government Documents Home Page.

http://www.library.yale.edu/govdocs/govdoc2.html

10 Get some art project ideas for your students or your own children.

http://www.ceismc.gatech.edu/BusyT

When the popularity of the World Wide Web really hit the public eye, the emphasis was on the dissemination of information (hence the term "Information Highway"). It makes sense that the world of education, whose currency is information, would be one of the biggest players in the field. The Internet has changed the face of education drastically.

Stay-at-home parents, professionals in transition, or anyone who wants to take courses and can't get to a campus, can take continuing education classes without having to leave the house. Teachers across the globe can share ideas faster and cheaper than ever before. Prospective college students can search for the right college, find out what financial aid opportunities are available, and apply to college—all from their computer.

Best of all, there are loads of sites out there that are targeted to—and can be used as a learning tool for—a younger crowd. Parents who are sick of watching their children vegetate in front of the television have an alternative that kids think is fun, and that is educational at the same time.

For those already in—or done with—college, the vast collection of information available in online libraries and other educational sites will keep you learning forever.

And this is just the tip of the iceberg. The available technology is constantly improving. Before you know it, playing hooky might mean not turning on the computer in the morning.

EARLY CHILDHOOD RESOURCES

Building Blocks to Reading
http://www.NeoSoft.com/~jrpotter/karen.html

Karen Potter, a mother of two in Dallas, shares her copyrighted "Building Blocks to Reading" program in this helpful page for parents struggling to enliven early literacy lessons. Pages cover Potter's reading tips, monthly activity suggestions, and A–Z ideas associating words with letters as in "Activity L: Children make great lazy lumps on logs." Potter doesn't seem to be selling anything here (you can't order her program online), just sharing her ideas—she also offers links to related early childhood learning sites.

ReadyWeb
http://ericps.ed.uiuc.edu/readyweb/readyweb.html

Making sure your child is ready for school goes beyond first-day outfits and cool lunch boxes—it's about educational readiness. And ReadyWeb, sponsored by the U.S. Department of Education's ERIC Clearinghouse on Elementary and Early Childhood Education, is loaded with resources for parents and educators of kids new to, or preparing for, school. The site features links to Department of Education publications for parents, including "Helping Your Child Get Ready for School," and, on the flip side, "Getting Schools Ready for Children."

Lamb Chop's Play-Along
http://www.pbs.org/lambchop/welcome.html

"Knock Knock…Who's there?…Freddie O.…Freddie O. who?…(sing) Who's a Freddie O. Big, Bad Wolf…" Who indeed but a little lamb chop? Shari Lewis' Lamb Chop, actually, whose PBS series, *Lamb Chop's Play-Along,* has spawned this site of activities and yes, knock-knock jokes for preschoolers. Among the highlights is a page of drawings of the hand-puppet and its cohorts Charlie Horse, Hush Puppy, and Buster the Bus, for printing out and coloring. A thrill for any kid who watches the show.

Mister Rogers' Neighborhood
http://www.pbs.org/rogers

PBS legend Fred McFeely Rogers offers a RealAudio greeting to his cyberspace neighbors here (see Figure 9.1). In his Sing Along section, Mr. Rogers displays lyrics to the songs that have been staples of his show for more than three decades, including the smash hit, "Won't You Be My Neighbor." The site's other sections include Parents' Pages, Plan and Play Activities, Neighborhood

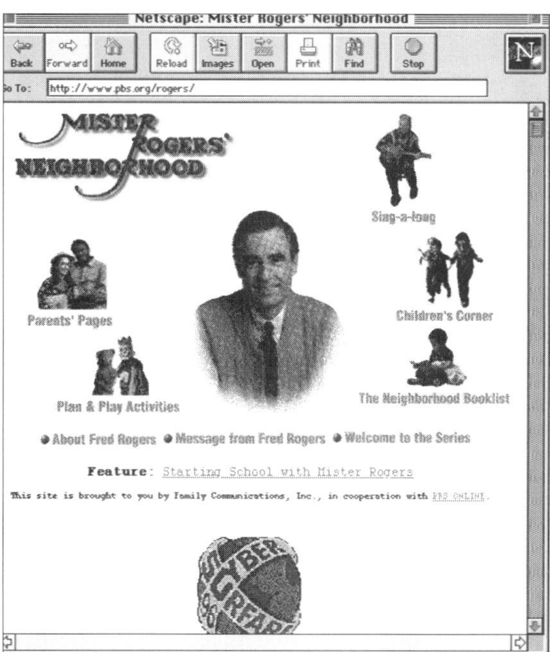

Figure 9.1

Mister Rogers' Neighborhood, *http://www.pbs.org/rogers*

Book list, a Children's Corner for kids to explore, and even features like, "Starting School with Mr. Rogers."

The Preschool Page

http://www.ames.net/preschool_page/index.html

"Hi! I'm Michael, and I'm a CyberKid!" is the greeting you will get at the Preschool Page. Michael's mommy created the site because she "thought that there should be a place on the World Wide Web that kids can visit with their Mommies and Daddies." Well CyberKids and their mommies and daddies will find pages on the zoo, the circus, worms and bugs, and other kid-tested topics. Each page has photos, illustrations, and text written for a preschool audience.

Montessori for Moms

http://www.primenet.com/~gojess/mfm/mfmhome.htm

This attractive, active site offers parents and teachers ideas for using the Montessori method for early school preparation (see Figure 9.2). You can download "Montessori for Moms," a free book about the sensory-based developmental program. Or sample the Example Lesson, which features a project called Sandpaper Letters, designed for children "to gain kinesthetic (shape) memory of the letters." Then pay a visit to the Montessori Equipment Room, with its images and brief descriptions of their teaching tools.

The Parents of Preschoolers Resource Page

http://lonestar.texas.net/~maverixx/parents.html

This resource site offers loads of useful links for coping, living, and learning with preschoolers. Organized into categories such as General Parenting and Activities and Crafts, the site is a good bookmark for newbie parents. Along with the links, the page creator offers some sage advice about raising kids today: "I have come to the conclusion that I will never stop learning, because just as we are here to teach our children, our children are also here to teach us…"

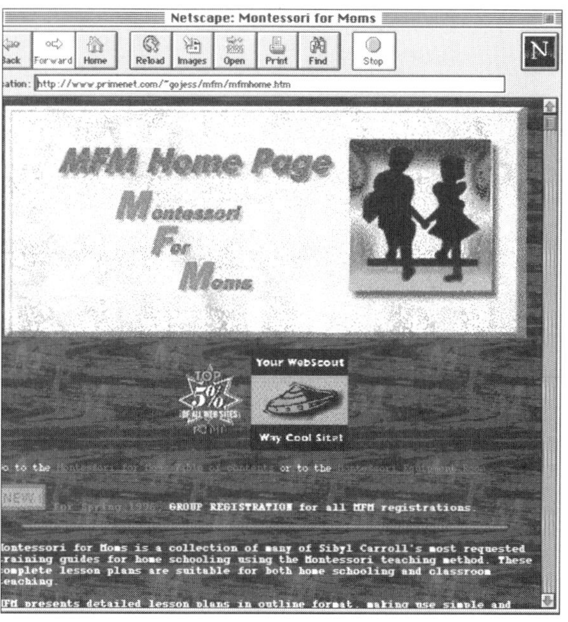

Figure 9.2

Montessori for Moms, *http://www.primenet.com/~gojess/mfm/mfmhome.htm*

Hedgehog's Classroom Resources

http://www.hedgehog-review.com/index.html

A snappy, Java-created hedgehog mascots this review and index site that spotlights the latest early childhood education (K through 1) resources, both online and off. The selection is small, though updated frequently, and Internet sites are arranged according to how much "beef" (meaningful content) they feature. Hedgehog also reviews educational CD-ROMs and software, such as the "Dr. Seuss ABC CD-ROM."

National Association for the Education of Young Children (NAEYC)

http://www.naeyc.org/naeyc

The Web site for the Washington, DC-based organization spells out the organization's work and provides online access to its resources (see Figure 9.3). Though the design and much of the content is about as tasty as school cafeteria tuna casserole, the site does offer useful material for early childhood educators. The Public Affairs pages are particularly rich, with online consumer information brochures such as, "Toys: Tools for Learning," and articles from the NAEYC's journal, *Young Children* (full issues also are online).

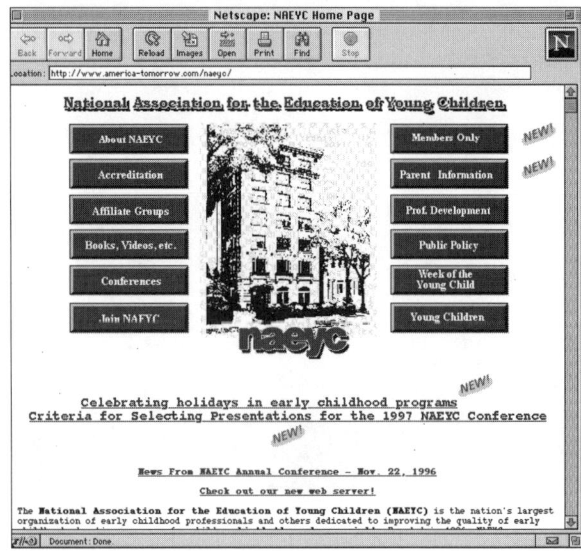

Figure 9.3
National Association for the Education of Young Children (NAEYC), *http://www.naeyc.org/naeyc*

[OVERHEARD ON WOMEN'S WIRE]

http://chat.women.com

"Parents seem to think that software is all about making up for deficiencies in schools by providing drill and practice type learning. For forty bucks they want their kids to become geniuses. There's a great opportunity to give kids great entertainment that also opens up new worlds to them, develops reasoning, problem-solving and creativity skills without being didactic.

"I think some of the namebrand stuff is the worst because people have been rushing repurposed content to market and this usually suffers in the translation. The best software is packed with rich, open-ended varied activities that accommodate different learning styles. I think the best software is coming out of the newer companies like Headbone, Humongous, Theatrix."

—Susan Lammers, president of Headbone Interactive, a Seattle-based publisher of children's CD-ROM titles.

The Hanen Early Language Program

http://www.hanen.org

The Toronto-based Hanen Early Language Program's Web site offers information and background on this program aimed at young children with special needs and language skill deficits. The site includes information on the latest research, as well as pages about the program's training and educational materials. A site highlight is, "The Caring Connections that Help Children Communicate," excerpted from the Hanen guidebook, *It Takes Two to Talk.*

K THROUGH 12 RESOURCES

Frank Potter's Science Gems

http://www-sci.lib.uci.edu/SEP/SEP.html

Physicist Frank Potter and colleague Jim Martindale here feature links to over 2,000 Web resources that are appropriate for math and science classrooms. It's selective and extremely well organized. Main categories such as Physical Science, Life Science, and Engineering are sub-divided into the likes of Biology of Viruses, Introduction to Quantum Mechanics, and Algebraic Geometry. Resources are also sorted by grade level. This is an excellent K through 16 math and science index.

Ask Dr. Math

http://forum.swarthmore.edu/dr.math/dr-math.html

The ultimate problem-solver, Dr. Math, helps kids of all ages with their toughest math questions. For brain teasers turned tormentors, Dr. Math's answers add up—not that kids should get this numerical guru to do all their homework. Dr. Math is actually a pseudonym for a batch of college students in the Math Forum, based at Swarthmore College. Their answers are archived by grade level (Elementary, Middle, High School, and College Level). Educators will also find Ask Dr. Math a treasure trove of fun math puzzlers.

Beakman's Electric Motor

http://fly.hiwaay.net/~palmer/motor.html

This is a great amateur-science page. It includes just one project—the construction of a homemade electric motor out of a toilet-paper tube and some paper clips. Although the number of parts is amazingly small and it looks easy, it would make a serious contender for first prize in any science fair. The instructions are actually taken from Paul Zaloom's *Beakman's World TV* show, but they're presented by a friendly engineer-type with nice clear diagrams.

Blind Children's Center

http://www.blindcntr.org/bcc

Parents and educators of blind children will appreciate this site, from the Los Angeles-based Center, which has been aiding sight impaired youngsters for over 55 years. Visitors can expect overviews of BCC's Infant Stimulation Program. In addition to publications such as "Dancing Cheek to Cheek: Beginning social, play, and language interactions." Pointers are offered to National Library Services for the Blind, and other pertinent sites. Also a good starting point for would-be supporters and volunteers.

K-5 Cybertrail

http://www.wmht.org/trail/trail.htm

Teachers have long been leading their students down the pathways of knowledge; with today's technologies, even educators need some guidance. The K–5 Cybertrail, a colorful selection of pre-tested surfing safaris, is a new kind of tour guide (see Figure 9.4). Designed by WMHT, a public broadcast station, the site offers the Tenderfoot Trail (a collection of elementary school sites) and the Explorer's Trail (K-5 resources online); a recent addition is the Syd's Kid Picks, with child-friendly links for surfing students.

Exploring Your Future in Math & Science

http://www.cs.wisc.edu/~karavan/afl/home.html

"Girls say they enjoy math in earlier grades, but tend to shy away in adolescence," point out these University of Wisconsin students, who created this page to help

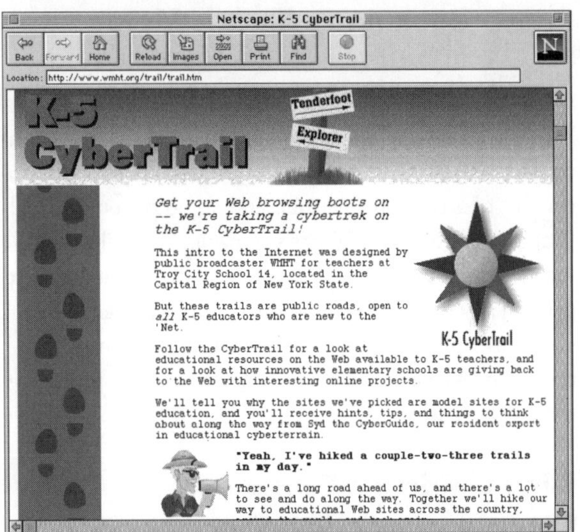

Figure 9.4

K-5 Cybertrail, *http://www.wmht.org/trail/trail.htm*

reverse the trend. Here's some encouragement: chief engineers earn an average of $79,998.00, and retail brokers break in at $90,000.00. Critical thinking for classroom projects and links to Cal Tech's "Women's Center" add to this resource for pre-college females who'd put pi into an equation before the oven.

Busy Teachers' Web Site K-12

http://www.ceismc.gatech.edu/BusyT

On a winter break from Georgia Institute of Technology, Carolyn Cole was frustrated by "a gazillion hours" spent surfing the Net for K through 12 resources, so she created this beginner-friendly site, giving teachers fast access to lesson plans, virtual exhibits, and more. The reptiles link under Biology leads to a "Complete Guide To Keeping Green Iguanas in Captivity," while Recess features a chance to assemble "Mr. Edible Starchy Tuber Head" electronically. Dozens of photos, online books, and the like will interest students as well as their mentors.

AskERIC Virtual Library

http://ericir.syr.edu

AskERIC is a massive online question-and-answer service primarily for teachers, but parents will be amazed at the depth and breadth of resources here. Language arts teachers will find great guides to directing a "whole language experience," and science teachers can browse mini-lessons on topics from soil erosion to elementary astronomy. A super bonus: learning materials which can be used with children's programming on The Discovery Channel or PBS's *Newton's Apple* series. Hats off to Syracuse University, the U.S. Department of Education, and Sun Microsystems for sponsoring this terrific page.

Cool School Tools

http://www.bham.lib.al.us/cooltools

Where in the world can you find the Bible in Swahili, JFK Resources, and French Paleolithic Cave Paintings? At the Birmingham (AL) Public Library's Cool School Tools site, naturally. This great site offers links on subjects ranging from Customs, Etiquette, and Folklore to Space and Aviation (see Figure 9.5). Its Quick Reference page has simple, kid-friendly forms for searching for online versions of such resources as *Roget's Thesaurus* and *Bartlett's Book of Familiar Quotations*. Adults will find the links and information just as rewarding.

Figure 9.5

Cool School Tools, *http://www.bham.lib.al.us/cooltools*

Cornell Theory Math and Science Gateway

http://www.tc.cornell.edu/Edu/MathSciGateway

Useful for high school educators and students, this site offers smooth sailing through the Net's best math and science resources. Briefly annotated links are organized in 10 categories from astronomy to physics. For example: "C++—Introduction to Object Oriented Programming Using...won two awards in the 'Best of the Web 94' contest." Teachers will find help with methods and curriculum, as well as an extensive journal and research article archive. An excellent educational index.

Challenger Center for Space Science Education

http://www.challenger.org

This site promotes the work of the Alexandria, VA-based Challenger Center, founded by the families of the lost Challenger astronauts to develop and inspire space science education. Visitors can explore pages offering links to other space science sites, a teacher training page—"Explore simulation as an instructional tool and find out how to integrate the theme of space"—and information on learning center and classroom programs. There is a tribute page that includes biographies of the crew who died in the disaster and also describes the organization's founding.

Cyberschool Magazine

http://www.infoshare.ca/csm/index.htm

Ring the bells and clap the erasers: Cyberschool Magazine is in session, and kids are likely to learn a lot from this fun educational 'zine. Each issue includes departments with articles covering science (Nuclear Newton), the arts (Bionic Bard), history (The Time Machine) and other curricular standards. And if you're ready to link out on your own, the Surfin' Librarian features hundreds of great sites worth exploring. It's one worth bookmarking for return visits.

The Cyberspace Middle School

http://www.scri.fsu.edu/~dennisl/CMS.html

The Cyberspace Middle School (CMS), a project that evolved from a Florida State University summer program, is a resource site created to help illuminate the Web's educational potential. Designed for sixth through ninth graders, CMS has stuff for both kids and teachers: Students can hit Surf City for fun links to sites such as YO SHARK!, or visit Topics of Interest for subject-oriented resources, covering everything from astronomy to wildlife. Educational Resources for Teachers suggests sites for K through 12 educators. A nice mix of student-friendly and teacher-savvy links, CMS delivers on its promise of proving the Web's educational appeal.

EdLinks

http://webpages.marshall.edu/~jmullens/edlinks.html

John L. Mullens, a West Virginia high school principal, weaves some of the Net's best education sites into his Web. Biggies like Educom, AskEric, and the Library of Congress are all here, elegantly categorized and succinctly described. There are also dozens of links to not-so-big but still-impressive sites, like "Kathy Schrock's Guide for Educators," which features a classified index of resource materials from arts and literature to world news. Or try "Teacher Talk," an online conferencing system for K through 12 instructors to share advice and anecdotes about the latest classroom snafu...or miracle!

KID Appeal

Education Place

http://www.hmco.com/school

Publisher Houghton Mifflin's Education Place is a vivid learning site that helps promote its educational products (see Figure 9.6). Teachers and parents can check into centers devoted to mathematics, reading/language arts, and social studies for curriculum planning tools and activities (plus a pitch for Houghton Mifflin offerings). In the Math Center, for instance, you'll find Brain Teasers puzzles and a searchable activities index. Students can visit the Just For Kids area, while the more grown-up Parent's Place offers the site's resource guides.

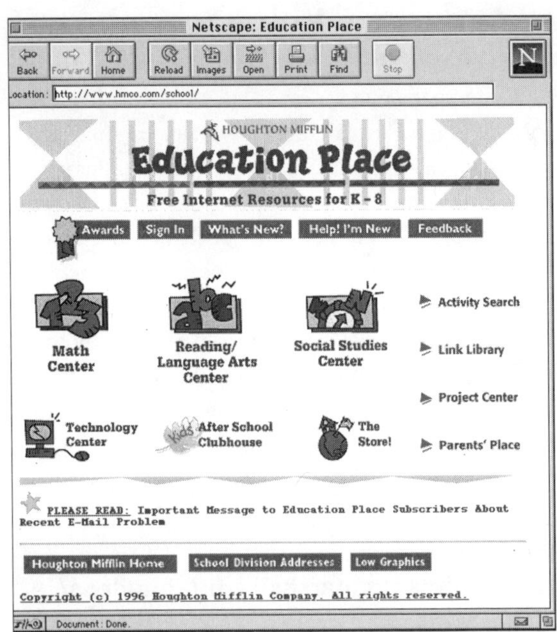

Figure 9.6

Education Place, *http://www.hmco.com/school*

The History Channel Classroom

http://www.historychannel.com/classroom/classroom.html

The Classroom, part of the History Channel's Web site, offers resource guides designed to help teachers turn the boob tube into an educational tool. The site features discussion and activities guides relating to particular programs—most of which are documentaries on historic figures or events—such as *Pompeii: Buried Alive* and *Modern Marvels: The Empire State Building*. From this site, you also can link back over to the Arts & Entertainment Classroom site, which features similar teaching guides to that network's programming.

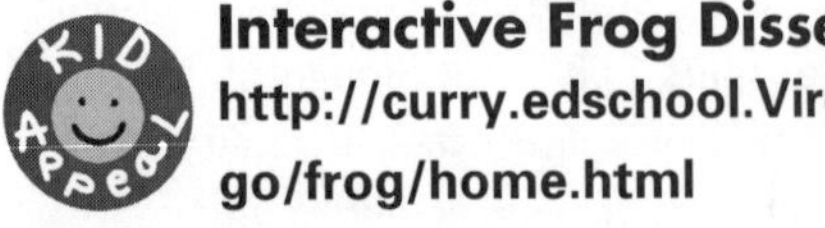

Interactive Frog Dissection

http://curry.edschool.Virginia.EDU/go/frog/home.html

Thanks to the University of Virginia's Instructional Technology department, there's an alternative to the now famous Whole Frog Project. This virtual frog dissection is billed as good preparation and even a "useful substitute" for doing the real thing in a laboratory. Commentary, photos, and QuickTime video guide you step-by-step from beginning to end. Those without fast modems will have time to run down to the river and catch a live specimen while many of these features are loading. Otherwise, this is a practical and interesting guide for K through 12 students.

The Franklin Institute Science Museum

http://sln.fi.edu

This virtual museum dedicated to scientific inquiry has plenty to keep you busy (see Figure 9.7). Start at the "heart of the matter," and find out why red blood cells are so important to us. Then move on to electricity (a Franklin favorite) or to shipbuilding on the Delaware. Ben even has his own video, but beware of its long download time. the site could stand some more serious interactive stuff, but the experiments for kids will give parents some great rainy-day ideas.

Invention Dimension

http://web.mit.edu/invent

This MIT inventor's site profiles a different creative innovator every week, in breezy, picture-filled

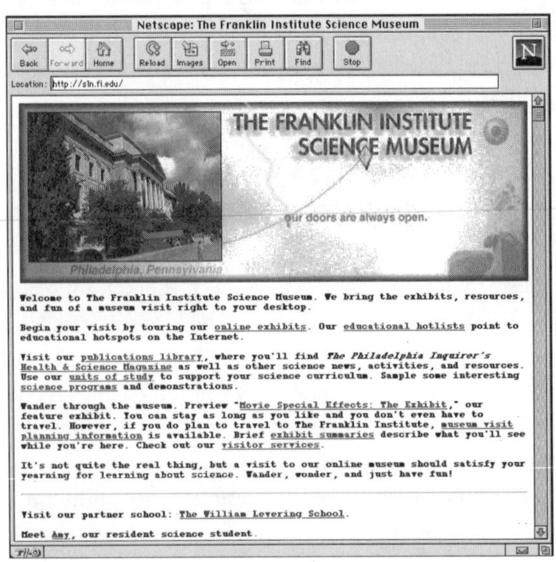

Figure 9.7

The Franklin Institute Science Museum, *http://sln.fi.edu*

bios. The Invention Dimension series introduces the world of inventors to students—or anyone else interested—and helps paint a portrait of how their inventions have affected our lives. The great names are here, including Benjamin Franklin and Eli Whitney. But so are the lesser-known inventors—geniuses such as Norbert Rillieux, the son of a black slave and a white plantation owner who invented the sugar processing evaporator.

Keypals International
http://www.collegebound.com/keypals

Keypals International is sort of an online phone book for finding high schools on the Net. It's a simple site, no fancy bells and whistles, but it does its job well. Just click on a continent or country and Keypals guides you to the URLs and e-mail addresses for, it claims, every high school online. It's a great tool for schools seeking sister sites with which to share their experiences.

Odyssey of the Mind
http://www.odyssey.org/odyssey

This home page for the Odyssey of the Mind (OM) School Program, a creative group-learning competition for K through college students, spells out the program's philosophy and background, as well as its rules and regulations. Visitors will find synopses of recent OM projects, such as the 1995-96 "Amusin' Cruisin" assignment: "This problem requires teams to design, build and drive a vehicle on two journeys that will take a driver(s) to see 'attractions' that are part of a team-created theme." Those interested in getting involved can read an FAQ about how to enroll their schools in the program, which is run by the nonprofit OM Association of Glassboro, NJ.

Star Child
http://heasarc.gsfc.nasa.gov/docs/StarChild

Stylized into an electronic storybook, the Star Child, a NASA project, introduces basic concepts such as astronomy, the earth, the moon, stars, and space in individual pages dotted with hypertext links to material like tours of the solar system provided by NASA's Jet Propulsion Laboratory, University of Arizona, and the Los Alamos National Laboratory. Pages feature colorful photos and MPEG movies of the planets in motion, turning the mysteries of the universe into a teaching tool for down-to-earth education.

The Incredible Art Department
http://www.in.net/~kenroar

Like taking a trip back to the art room in elementary school, this is an invitation for educators, parents, and kids to get hip deep in fun art projects (see Figure 9.8). Favorite Lessons is the place to go for all kinds of ideas for creative lessons. In the Art Room are some samples of student art from guest departments around the country, and the fun section on Pet Peeves is a cheerleading call to overcome the "I Can't Draw" syndrome.

Quest: NASA K-12 Internet Initiative
http://quest.arc.nasa.gov

This is another NASA-sponsored Web site. It includes a dynamic assortment of past, present, and future projects such as "TOPEX/Poseidon" (kids collaborate with scientists on ocean topography experiments) and "Online From Jupiter" (tracking the Galileo spacecraft's progress).

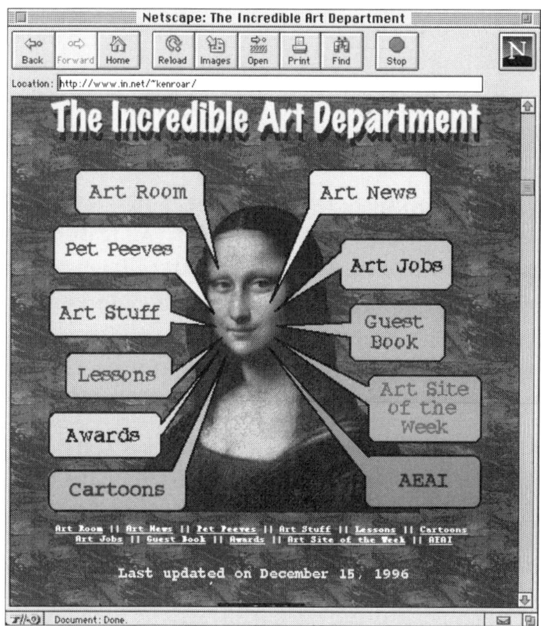

Figure 9.8
The Incredible Art Department, *http://www.in.net/~kenroar*

Teachers may want to check out the action here, too; say, for information on available grant money. Meanwhile, a "Using the Net in School" section is great for those who don't know FTP from PTA.

Sea World/Busch Gardens Animal Information Database
http://www.bev.net/education/SeaWorld/homepage.html

Sea World and Busch Gardens present this site as an animal information database. Rather than covering every animal, they've chosen a few particularly cool ones, like vampire bats and Bengal tigers, and loaded the site up with fun facts on them. Did you know that vampire bat saliva contains an anticoagulant that is 20 times stronger than any other known anti-clotting agent? Bat spit could someday be used in hospitals. If you've got questions about ocean-dwelling animals, you can "Ask Shamu"—or get some marine life of your own following the advice in Aquariums as a Hobby.

Montessori Network
http://www.montessori.org

"Ours was a house for children, rather than a real school. We had prepared a place for children where a diffused culture could be assimilated, without any need for direct instruction." So wrote Maria Montessori, whose experiential educational philosophy spawned the Montessori schools. This official Web site of the Montessori Foundation offers a lengthy selection of Maria Montessori's writings, along with electronic issues of the organization's *Tomorrow's Child Magazine*. If you're inspired to give your child the Montessori experience, the site includes a searchable Montessori School Directory.

CEA Science Education Home Page
http://www.cea.berkeley.edu/Education

From Berkeley's Center for Extreme Ultraviolet Astrophysics comes this home page, a gateway to a variety of K through 12 science sections within the server, including the Internet-based Classroom Resources for K–12 pages, with teacher-developed lesson plans that incorporate the Web. The site also serves the Science Information Infrastructure, which links earth and space science data to American science museums; and the NASA-funded Science Online project, which offers tool kits for K through 12 teachers and students with classroom activities on topics such as weather, the solar system, and space science.

USGS Learning Web
http://www.usgs.gov/education

The U.S. Geological Survey is famous for its maps, geological information guides, and other educational goodies. Now those resources are coming online at the USGS Learning Web, an earth science education clearinghouse. The site's Teaching area offers in-depth coverage of applied earth science issues. Its first major offering, about global change, has pages on the Brazilian rain forest, tree rings, and suggested activities.

Environmental Education Network
http://envirolink.org/enviroed

Students can explore the solar system, learn about deforestation in the world's rain forests, or poke around some old dinosaur bones in Honolulu. "Earth Viewer" generates instant real-time images of the Earth as seen from the vantage point of the Sun, the Moon, or a satellite in Earth orbit. Teachers will find a wealth of K–12 resources, including air quality lesson plans designed to teach kids about acid rain, carbon monoxide, and the ozone layer. EnviroLink, which sponsors the site, also offers links to a "Green" market which promotes and sells eco-friendly products, and a huge library containing shelf after virtual shelf of "EnviroEvents," activist information, and government resources.

Gallery of Interactive Geometry
http://www.geom.umn.edu/apps/gallery.html

Even if you haven't lost any sleep wondering what the projection of a surface in n-dimensional space would look like, the Gallery of Interactive Online Geometry makes a game out of stuff that used to put you to sleep in high school (see Figure 9.9). Thrill to the effects of negatively-curved space in Orbifold Pinball; gaze upon Escher-like tilings and infinite knots in 17 planar groups with Kali (a Silicon Graphics program). The Geometry Center Home Page at the University of Minnesota requires an HTML 2.0 compatible Web Browser.

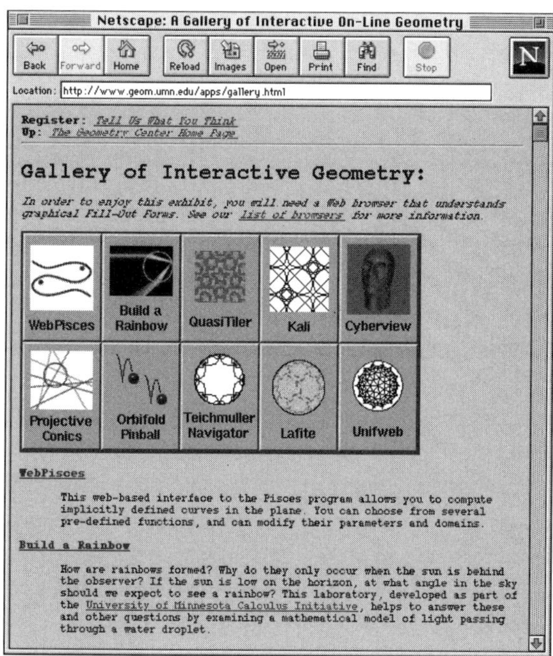

Figure 9.9
Gallery of Interactive Geometry,
http://www.geom.umn.edu/apps/gallery.html

COLLEGE AND POST GRADUATE

College and University Home Pages
http://www.mit.edu:8001/people/cdemello/univ.html

At this site, MIT's Christina DeMello provides an extremely useful service: a directory of university home pages. Visitors can download the entire list in compressed formats or search by letter. A glimpse at the "L" listings, for instance, yields everything from La Salle University in Philadelphia, to Lycee de Garcons Esch in Luxembourg. The site has geographical listings, as well.

Internet Headquarters for Student Governments
http://www.umr.edu/~stuco/national.html

The University of Missouri at Rolla student council forged this electronic meeting-house, making international student government easier than ever. Over 100 student governments have already signed on, including American University in Bulgaria, University of Toronto, Universitaet Gesamthochschule, and many schools in the U.S. Links to those student government sites are categorized by location, school size, type, and other criteria. Another promising feature here is the issues page—a forum for discussing student interests and strategies.

The Main Quad
http://www.mainquad.com

Like its campus counterpart, this virtual quad is a meeting place for college students, created by enrollees and recent graduates of Stanford University, Duke, and The Art Center. So, as you might expect, The Main Quad is efficient and pleasing to the eye, while also featuring stimulation for the mind. Essays such as "Working Your Way Through Europe" and "Getting a Ph.D." are offered in answer to The Big Question: "So...what are you doing after college?" The Dean's List is an index of cool college sites, and the Student Services Center is filled with all sorts of help.

Loci
http://www.loci.com

Loci aims to be a center of activity for college students seeking online entertainment, news, or simply a place to hang out and chat (see Figure 9.10). Its slick layout and content are created and maintained by college students who are in tune with the proclivities of youth in the higher education process. Changing features have included a chance to chat with hip-hoppers "TLC," message boards dedicated to great pickup lines, for instance, and Loci's 8-step "Breaking Into the Real World Guide."

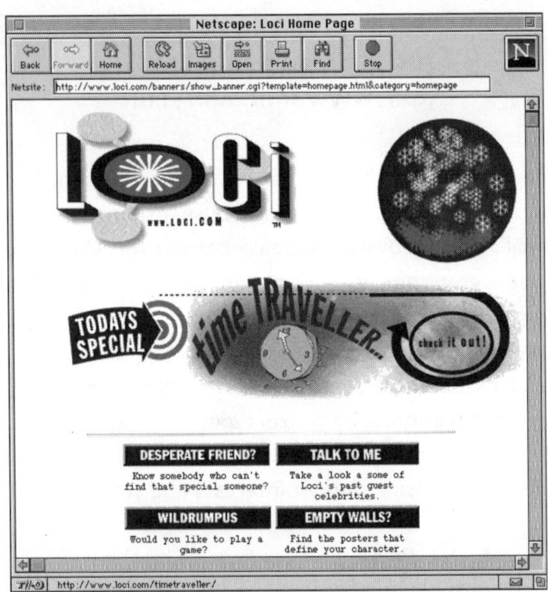

Figure 9.10
Loci, *http://www.loci.com*

Once Upon a Time in the Eighties

http://www.engl.virginia.edu/~enwr1016/index.html

The students of Matthew Kirschenbaum's 1995 Introductory Composition seminar at the University of Virginia liked their final, collaborative project so much, they turned it into a Web page. The students' essays are serious, nostalgic and humorous—from Jarett Epstein's "The Challenger: Our Disaster;" to Keya Veney's "The Vanessa Williams Story;" to Will Thompson's "My Adidas," which states, "In the eighties, the [athletic] shoe transformed from a clothing necessity into an intricate accessory of an outfit, inner city identification, or a symbol of social status." Yes, it's that deep.

U.S. Two-Year Colleges

http://www.sp.utoledo.edu/twoyrcol.html

This is billed as "the most complete" two- year college list available on the Net, with links to over 590 such institutions categorized by state. One special delight of these junior colleges is the unusual names: consider Capital Community-Technical College-Flatbush (Connecticut), or Fond du Lac Tribal & Community College (Cloquet, Minnesota). A similar list of Canadian schools is accessible here as well.

Erick's Guide to Medical School Admissions

http://lonestar.texas.net/~santos/MedGuide.html

"Apply as early as possible!" rings out loud and clear on this page of wisdom for getting into med-school. University of Pennsylvania admissions committee member Erick Santos encourages prospects to consider why they want to get an M.D. or D.O., and proceeds to offer MCAT and application essay pointers, along with other shrewd advice. According to Santos, "all told, you will probably spend in excess of $1,000.00 in application fees, not including interview and travel expenses." The site has a special section for minority and foreign students—great stuff for pre-docs.

BioTech

http://biotech.chem.indiana.edu

BioTech is a "hybrid biology/chemistry educational resource and research tool." They've collected a huge number of links to other biotechnology Web sites, and organized them into searchable databases. Intending to be of use to high school students, they provide a hypertext dictionary of science terms. To please grad students, there's Professional Resources collection of links to jobs and funding. The writing is a little dry, but the collection is a goldmine for anybody at any level studying biochemistry.

Law School Dot Com

http://www.lawschool.com

West Publishing has created a site targeting current and prospective law students. It helps you prepare for exams (visitors can download sections of "Sum & Substance," a quick review guide) and offers some job-hunting resources as well. Other features include a Legal Challenge question of the day and a Law Library. The site is in progress and looks promising. Coming soon: "Moot Courtroom," live online.

The MBA Page

http://www.cob.ohio-state.edu/dept/fin/mba.htm

Courtesy of Ohio State University's Max M. Fisher School of Business, here's a huge hyper-index of resources from all over the Web, designed to help MBA students "survive and thrive." School directories and rankings are included, with publications like the Wharton Journal Online, and course materials in, say, "Management, Logistics, and Operations." Soothsaying and whimsy also have a place here. For instance, there's "Deep Thoughts," where MBA students reflect on how the Net will impact business education's future.

College Board Online

http://www.collegeboard.org

Founded in 1900, the venerable College Board is a U.S. educational association, "whose aim is to facilitate the student transition to higher education." Information here is specifically categorized for parents, students, guidance counselors, teachers, and just about anyone else involved in helping kids and adults gain a college education. The ExPan College Search hunts down schools to suit students' own specified criteria. Other features include a sample SAT question of the day, a student art gallery (nice painting JPEGs), and financial aid calculator.

World Lecture Hall

http://www.utexas.edu/world/lecture

University of Texas' World Lecture Hall offers the most comprehensive list of distance learning courses available online. Searchable by topic, it lists the school, instructor, and even links to lessons you can follow on the Web and related resources you can check out before signing up for the course. From accounting to zoology—it's all there.

Adventures in Education

http://www.tgslc.org

Take a guided tour through this galaxy of financial aid, college selection, and career advice. The sci-fi theme is presumably aimed at young people embarking on the adventure of higher education in order to prepare for a

[OVERHEARD ON WOMEN'S WIRE]

http://chat.women.com

ON AFFIRMATIVE ACTION

"There are still kids who have such limited possibilities that they can use education to improve their lives. It continues to be one of the best stories told in this country, children who come along and are transformed by their educational experience… (Affirmative action) has been one of the best public policies in my time. It's clear that not a lot of advancement would have occurred had certain guidelines not been in place."

ON WOMEN'S COLLEGES

"If anything, the role of women's colleges will be even more important in the future because of the tremendous range of things that women are now expected to do."

—Ruth Simmons, president of Smith College in Northampton, MA, in an interview with Women's Wire.

fierce job market, but these provisions are also suited for parents and school professionals. The tour will lead you through Federal Pell Grant and other aid application procedures, while urging the likes of skills and interest assessments as part of a career plan.

CollegeNet
http://www.collegenet.com

CollegeNet offers an efficient and practical way to access and browse U.S. and Canadian higher education institutions. Their database is searchable by criteria, including geography (state or province), price, and enrollment (see Figure 9.11). Click Massachusetts on the sensitive map, for example, and up comes an alphabetical list of schools such as Amherst College, with contact information, annual tuition, and a pointer to their official home page. Financial aid and graduate program directories, links to standardized test discussion groups, as well as the Complete Works of William Shakespeare, and other academic resources are featured.

Association for Support of Graduate Students
http://www.asgs.org

Here's help for students earning a Ph.D. or masters degree, and looking to "improve their lives during the thesis process." To get full support, you'll have to pony up some cash for an ASGS membership. Yet, to help you decide if that's a good deal, there are free samples of member services, such as tips on how to "maximize the return on your investment in graduate school…either in professional advancement or cold, hard cash—or, better yet, in both!"

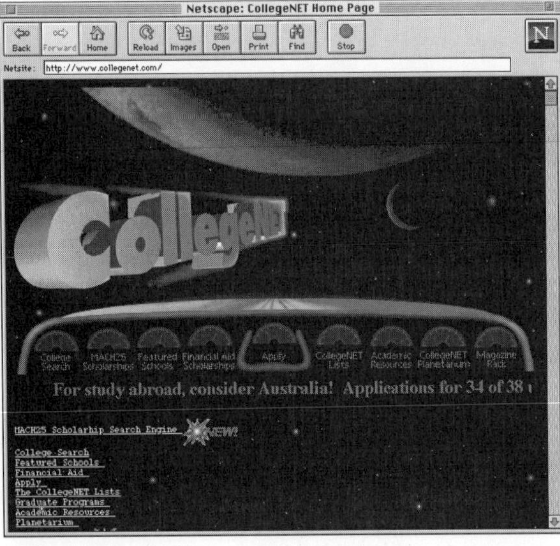

Figure 9.11
CollegeNet, *http://www.collegenet.com*

Internet College Exchange
http://www.usmall.com/college

The main event here is a chance for college prospects to discover their ideal higher educational institution via the ICX search engine. Simply enter criteria such as 4-year private, small–medium size, up to $8,000.00 cost per year, and you get back a list of possible U.S. schools running from Abilene Christian U. to York College Pennsylvania. ICX's "irreverent" newsletter, The Dunce's Cap, is "dedicated to the absurd thought that getting in…should not be the hard part of going to college." Registration is free.

Campus Voice: The College Site
http://www.campusvoice.com

College kids who want to be hip to world news, pop culture, and "what's throwing down on campuses" across the U.S. will want to stop in here. "The College Site" addresses issues ranging from money to eating to studying to sex. Don't miss the chance to "Ask Spike" Gillespie for advice, or peruse "Top of the Tabs: Shelly Ridenour's Tilt-a-Whirl of Tattle Titillation." Then again, profiles of "Cool Profs" like Lisa Bowleg, an AIDS researcher at Georgetown, prove seriousness also has a place here. Student contributions are welcome.

Greek Pages
http://www.greekpages.com

Evidently nostalgic for pledge weeks and Friday night "functions," Rutgers law student Glenn Kurtzrock maintains this site, formerly known as Fraternities and Sororities on the Web. It offers pointers to over 300 chapters, in order from Alpha to Omega. The is good stuff if you're searching for information on your sorority or co-ed society, but of little interest to others.

WOMEN'S STUDIES

The American Association of University Women

http://www.aauw.org

The American Association of University Women is a national organization that "promotes education and equity for all women and girls." At this site you'll find links to AAUW issues, a list of fellowships, grants, and awards and information on how to become involved in the organization. Also includes an in-depth look at the association (a 160,000-member organization; the AAUW Educational Foundation funds research on girls and education, community action projects, and grants for outstanding women around the globe); and the AAUW Legal Advocacy Fund.

Wellesley College

http://www.wellesley.edu

Founded in 1870 to educate "the calico girl as well as the velvet girl," Wellesley College is now the undergraduate home to some 2,300 women. After a rather drab front page, their Web site sneaks up on you. Academic requirements, cross-registration with M.I.T., study abroad program information, and the like are provided in detail, but there's lots more to Wellesley than curriculum. Other features here include their preeminent Center for Research on Women, virtual tours of Davis Museum exhibits, and more. Alumni will appreciate the worldwide club directory.

Barnard College

http://www.barnard.columbia.edu

New York-based Barnard College—the women's college affiliated to Columbia University—features general admissions and program information along with a school history and details about information technology on campus through this home page. Check out the link to the Paperless Guide to New York City for those thinking of applying to or visiting Barnard.

Encyclopedia of Women's History

http://www.teleport.com/~megaines/women.html

This is a great page that began as a classroom assignment by the Portland Jewish Academy to write research papers on figures in Women's History in March of 1995. They liked it so much, they decided to distribute the assignment over the Internet and invite all K through 12 students to submit entries to a Web encyclopedia, or "K12opedia," that the Academy would then maintain for all to use. Entries are not edited for content, so you get what you'd expect from this intellectually diverse, but very young, age group.

A Celebration of Women Writers

http://www.cs.cmu.edu/afs/cs.cmu.edu/user/mmbt/www/women/writers.html

It's nothing flashy, but this is an incredibly helpful site. Simply search the extensive alphabetical list of women writers to find out whether your favorite women writers have Web sites dedicated to them. Looking for Dorothy Parker? Just click on "P," and you'll find a link to a home page dedicated to her. Another bonus: The list is so large, you'll probably end up discovering a lot of writers you've never heard of just by clicking on their links.

InforM Women's Studies Database

http://www.inform.umd.edu/EdRes/Topic/WomensStudies

More than a database, this page provides loads of information for anyone interested in women's studies. Link to "Computing" for a discussion of gender issues in the computer industry, or use pointers to a host of electronic women's forums. An index of electronic and real-time conference announcements is impressive and eclectic. An unusual collection of feminist film reviews puts a new spin on Hollywood (ever want to get the feminist perspective on Home Alone?). Then there's the job bank, calls for paper submissions, and dozens more gender-related links. Solid photos and design do wonders for this academic material.

Diotima: Materials for the Study of Women and Gender in the Ancient World

http://www.uky.edu/ArtsSciences/Classics/gender.html

This historical resource focuses on women in antiquity, and provides a wealth of university materials for study. The site is named "Diotima," for the woman who supposedly taught Socrates about love. Featured are college courses from around the U.S., including biographical essays on Hypatia and women of the ancient world, and discussions of gender issues in antiquity, from politics to architecture. From Palestinian Bronze Age figurines to Roman portraits, plenty of images can be found, as well as reviews of historical texts and links to ancient history materials.

Women's International Center

http://www.wic.org

WIC is a nonprofit foundation that honors women who make positive contributions to humanity. This page outlines their mission and projects, including the annual Living Legacy Awards. Among the projects detailed here: scholarship assistance to older women reentering the work force; medical studies scholarships; and "Operation Greentrees," an ongoing donation of tree seedlings to organizations and schools. Biographies, a "global town hall," and a terrific history of women in America make this one of the better resources for women on the Net.

Multimedia Exhibits in Women's History

http://frank.mtsu.edu/~kmiddlet/history/women/wom-mm.html

Here's a decent, but limited, resource for women's history, courtesy of Kenneth Middleton at Middle Tennessee State University. The links represented are well-ordered sites ranging from the Suffrage Movement (celebrating 75 years of women's rights to vote) to Florence Nightingale (including facsimiles of her famous letters), to "The Women's Land Army" (a WWII group which harvested crops as part of the Emergency Farm Labor Service).

The Womanist

http://www.uga.edu/~womanist/home.html

From the Institute for African-American Studies at the University of Georgia, this scholarly journal looks at issues in feminist theory from an African-American perspective. The Womanist began as a newsletter but after just two issues, the editors say that the response was so positive they started another publication, *Womanist Theory & Research,* which is also posted on the Web. The term "womanist," by the way, was coined by Alice Walker, author of the Color Purple in her 1983 book *In Search of Our Mothers' Gardens.*

Women's Campaign School

http://www.yale.edu/wcsyale/index.html

Politics—long the domain of cigar-smoking old men making deals in back rooms. Many agree it's time for more fresh faces and new ideas, so this Yale program organizes seminars for women in politics—from fundraising to running a campaign. Most of the speakers are women; people like Julie Belaga, the director of the U.S. Ex-Im Bank and Jodi Rell, Connecticut's Lieutenant Governor. This site is basically an introduction to the program and a schedule of upcoming events, but it's likely to become a storehouse of information for prospective female candidates.

Women's Studies Research Guide

http://www.nypl.org/research/chss/grd/resguides/women.html

Presented by the New York Public Library, this site provides indexes of materials available from the library. The indexes are sorted by categories such as Feminist Theory, Biography, History, Social, Legal and Health Resources, Literature and Periodicals, among others. Their Women's Studies Resources on the Internet also provides annotated links to a broad range of women's studies topic, from activism to health to feminist science fiction.

Women's Studies

http://www.lib.berkeley.edu/Collections/Womstu

This site, part of the larger University of California at Berkeley library page (see library section), is a huge storehouse of women's studies information. It includes sections on conferences, electronic books and journals, listservs, organizations and research institutes, references sources, and more. Standout features include an online exhibition of Emma Goldman, which includes samples of her writings, a guide to her life and documentary sources, document highlights and pictorial highlights of the late radical feminist.

Biographies of Women Mathematicians

http://www.scottlan.edu/lriddle/women/women.htm

Exactly as advertised, the offerings here are brief biographies of women mathematicians. From Hypatia on up to Florence Nightingale ("invented the pie chart"), and now filling out with contemporary mathematicians, this wonderful site offers something you won't find anywhere else, and that's the beauty of it. The bios of the dead mathematicians read like history books, but the contemporary bios read a little like magazine articles.

Roe v. Wade, 410 U.S. 113 (1973)

http://www.law.cornell.edu/supct/classics/410us113.ovr.html

The case that started generations of hubbub is covered from Amniocentesis to Zygote on this page from Cornell University Law School. If you've ever wondered exactly what the U.S. Supreme Court had to say about the case of Ms. Roe, Justice Harry Blackmun's full opinion is reprinted here. You'll also find Justice Potter Stewart's consenting opinion, as well as the controversial dissent filed by Justice (now Chief Justice) William Rehnquist. Excellent legal detail on this subject.

The Kassandra Project

http://www.reed.edu/~ccampbel/tkp

This project's goal is to introduce and encourage the study of "German women writers, artists, and thinkers" of the 18th and 19th centuries. The foundation of the project is the Karoline von Günderrode Pages, supported by the short biographies of other German women writers such as Bettina von Arnim, Sophie von La Roche, and Sophie Mereau. Some of the poetry of von Günderrode, who committed suicide at age 26, is here, in German and English.

Collaborative Bibliography of Women in Philosophy

http://billyboy.ius.indiana.edu/WomeninPhilosophy/WomeninPhilo.html

This site is devoted exclusively to the writings of women philosophers. It's a collaborative, scholarly bibliography, which welcomes additions to its over 7,200 entries representing more than 3,200 women philosophers. The database is searchable by author, title, and other standard criteria. For instance, key *in Rand, Ayn,* and up comes a bibliographic record of *For the New Intellectual,* among other of her works, plus pointers to related Web resources where available.

Internet Resources for Women's Legal and Public Policy Information

http://asa.ugl.lib.umich.edu/chdocs/womenpolicy/womenlawpolicy.html

This meta-index of resources is a gold mine for anyone interested in hot public policy issues like women's reproductive rights, sexual harassment, and women in the military. It offers a link to the "Glass Ceiling Newsletter," a publication edited by a former placement professional which reports on sex discrimination in the workplace. The Women of Color Resource Center explores minority issues, while the Women's Environment and Development Organization (linked in five languages) examines women's roles in achieving world ecological and economic sustainability.

FINANCIAL AID, SCHOLARSHIPS, AND LOANS

Fulbright Scholar Program

http://www.cies.org

University students, teachers, and scholars interested in taking their act abroad will want to consider this resource for Fulbright grant opportunities. It includes an overview of the Fulbright program, established in 1946 under Congressional legislation "to increase mutual understanding between the people of the United States and the people of other countries." Descriptions of 5,000 annual grants may be accessed in a searchable index. Application requests and alumni information are here as well.

Student Services

http://www.studentservices.com

For higher education prospects in the U.S., Student Services maintains a database of more than 180,000 private financial aid resources. Simply type in an academic major (e.g. humanities), and the search engine will return contact information and deadlines for, say, Rockefeller Foundation arts fellowships, $11,000.00 Charlotte W. Newcombe doctoral dissertation awards, and on. You can also e-order the Money For College Directory at no charge.

College Guides and Aid Home Page

http://www.collegeguides.com

The benevolent aim here is to save prospective students and their parents time and money in their search for a college and financial aid. The "independent" Resource Pathways College Information Community serves up reviews and ratings of admissions and financial aid guides and services, which are available in print and on the Web. Resources are described (e.g. "This company…compiles videos of colleges you select onto a single videotape…"), rated from 1–4 stars, and listed with price and availability information.

Signet Bank College Money Matters

http://www.signet.com/collegemoney

Signet Bank wants to lend you money for college. Ulterior motives aside, this is a helpful site. Parents and guidance counselors too may appreciate the "College Planning & Budgeting" section, information on government programs, and what they call "alternative funding options"—e.g., home equity loans, savings, and investing schemes from (you guessed it) Signet Bank. An online dictionary defining terms like "amortization" and "garnishing" is a good resource.

Don't Miss Out: A Student's Guide to Financial Aid

http://www.signet.com/collegemoney/toc1.html

These pages are part of the larger Signet Bank College Money Matters site (above), but are worth special consideration in themselves. Each year, Signet produces this guide to help a variety of ambitious college students find financial aid, and the entire text is placed online.

fastWEB

http://web.studentservices.com/fastweb

And you thought "f.a.s.t." stood for financial aid search through the Web, eh? Actually, it does. And after your first visit here you may find yourself registering for a mailbox and keying in your biography in order for this search engine to return all the Web's financial aid resources appropriate to your personal criteria. The service is free, thanks to Student Services, Inc.

GrantsWeb

http://infoserv.rttonet.psu.edu/gweb.htm

Higher education professionals, non-profit developers, and other reputable types who need money will find GrantsWeb a good place to start an Internet search. Though just emerging, it's already loaded with pointers to a number of U.S. public and private funding sources like the National Science Foundation, National Institute for Humanities, and the Foundation Center, to name a few. Though text heavy, the primers on legal considerations affecting grants, proposal development aids, and other resources make this a commendable research tool.

National Research Council Fellowship Office

http://fellowships.nas.edu/index.html

This site has information on pre- and postdoctoral fellowships administered by the U.S. National Research Council. Those include grants from the Howard Hughes Medical Institute (in biological sciences), the U.S. Department of Energy (for integrated manufacturing), and Ford Foundation Dissertation Fellowships For Minorities. In

I·N·T·E·R·N·E·T M·I·N·U·T·E

ALL ABOUT NETIQUETTE

The technology behind the internet may be advanced, but the rules for navigating through it are simple. Proper netiquette (that's net etiquette) is based on concepts you probably learned in grade school.

Be Polite. A good rule of thumb is not to say something via e-mail that you wouldn't be comfortable saying in person. Avoid using ALL CAPS unless you are really really angry because this is equivalent to screaming.

Don't Tell Secrets. Don't give out personal information such as your home address or phone number in public areas of the Web. Also, don't forward or post a private message that someone sent to you.

Don't Steal. Copyright violations for graphics and text fall under that category of netiquette where it's not just rude, it may be illegal. Check out Brad Templeton's Copyright Myths for more information:

http://www.clarinet.com/brad/copymyths.html

Read the Directions before Beginning. Newsgroups generally have an FAQ (frequently asked questions) section.

Don't Ask People for Lunch Money. Although sending junk e-mail, a.k.a. spamming, isn't illegal, it is certainly annoying.

Learn the Alphabet. The world of chat rooms and newsgroups is full of acronyms. IMHO (in my humble opinion) you should familiarize yourself with some of these and, BTW (by the way), then you won't come off looking like a newbie (net neophyte).

Learn the Local Language. Punctuation marks are used to form emoticons, a form of expressing emotions in a text environment. When viewed from the side, these symbols form faces. For example, if you think something is funny, you can add a :) (smiley face); or if you are sad or displeased, you might try a : ((sad face). It's a good idea to put a wink ;) after a sarcastic comment so the reader will know that you are joking.

Keep in mind that copyright infringement, obscenity and harassment can be subject to punishment—in the simplest situations, you could be thrown out of a chat room or newsgroup. You should get to know your limits and your rights.

Here are some good sites to check out for more netiquette tips:

http://bookfair.com/Services/Albion/nqhome.html
The Albion Publishing's Netiquette home page is linked to Virginia Shea's book, *Netiqutte,* and offers a netiquette quiz.

http://www.screen.com/UNDERSTAND/Netiquette.html
Cochran Interactives Guide to Life on the Internet features tongue-in-cheek advice from Emily Postnews.

http://www.primenet.com/~vez/neti.html
This is Vince Zima's "Netiquette Primer."

most cases you can apply, or at least request application materials online. Definitely worth a visit by science-oriented grad students in search of further funding.

The Student Guide: Financial Aid from the U.S. Department of Education

http://www.ed.gov/prog_info/SFA/StudentGuide

According to the U.S. Department of Education, more than 80 percent of all student financial aid comes from government sources. Another 19 percent comes from school-sponsored sources. (One percent is stolen, apparently.) You can find out about the first 99% right here. So-so advice ("contact the financial aid administrator") is supplemented by hard details on eligibility for Pell Grants, state grant programs, and student eligibility status.

Scholarship Foundation of America

http://cen.cenet.com/sfa/sfahome.html

Calling all high school whiz kids, gifted young artists, 3.7 GPA college students, and technological wunderkind. The Scholarship Foundation of America has something green for you! We're talkin' from $1,000.00–$5,000.00 in cash, if you're a U.S. citizen and plan to further your education at a U.S. institution. SFA also offers Project C.O.R.P., a student/business match-making service for internships and jobs. Application available online.

Financial Aid Information

http://www.finaid.org

College grant and loan information doesn't come any straighter than this index, maintained by Mark Kantrowitz of Carnegie Mellon University (the author of *The Prentice Hall Guide to Scholarships and Fellowships for Math and Science Students*). Students of all ages will appreciate links to bank student loan programs of all types, plus extras. Direct links to fellowship databases will be of particular interest to grad students, and the grants and scholarship pages go on for days.

LIBRARIES

Library of Congress

100 BEST SITES

http://www.loc.gov

The mother of all libaries, the Libary of Congress offers the ability to search its extensive catalog by book title, author, or keyword. The site also offers special features about its collections like the recent exhibit on the architecture of Frank Lloyd Wright and the extensive handbook of Latin American Studies. Each month the server is updated with new exhibits, new prints, and incredible photographs.

The American War Library

http://members.aol.com/veterans/index.html

Click on War Library Offerings to discover an immense list of topics, including America's involvement in World Wars I and II, Vietnam, Korea, Somalia, and the Persian Gulf, as well as information about anti-Mao operations, the Civil War, and the Iran-Contra Affair. If you're interested in a particular administration, you can read the text of battle-related speeches given by Presidents during war time. In addition the library has several Quick-Search wings, where you can get the scoop on personnel, international organizations and groups.

Berkeley Earth Sciences & Map Libraries

INTERNATIONAL APPEAL

http://library.berkeley.edu/EART

One of the Web's best sources of digitized maps. From its colorful global graphics to its growing collection of online maps, the site is as visually appealing as it is informative (see Figure 9.12). The digital maps are organized into areas such as nautical charts, topographic maps, transportation and communications maps, facsimile maps and reproductions, and aerial photography. You'll also find research round-ups of fire insurance maps—invaluable historical, building-by-building cartographic community portraits.

National Library of Education

http://www.ed.gov/NLE/index.html

The National Library of Education's Web site serves as a user's guide to the U.S. Department of Education resource center. Unless you're headed for DC, pages on

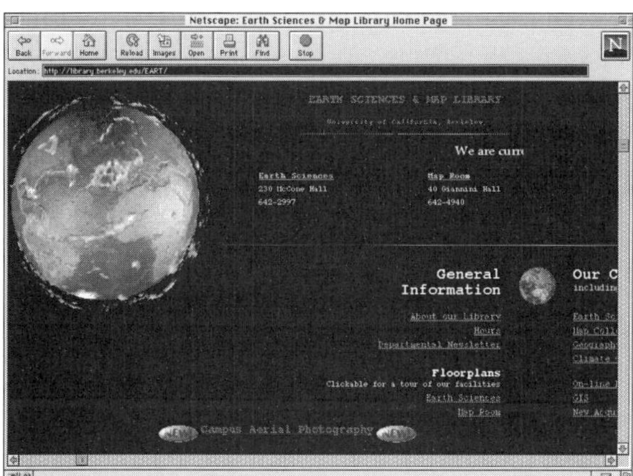

Figure 9.12
Berkeley Earth Sciences & Map Libraries,
http://library.berkeley.edu/EART

hours, location, and upcoming lecture series are relatively meaningless; but the site does include terrific bibliographies on a range of topics, from Collective Bargaining for Teachers to Family Literacy. It also provides a list of publications available for free.

Government Documents

http://www.library.yale.edu/govdocs/gdchome.html

This Web page provides links to many government documents in a friendly way: Visitors can simply look through a list of "I am looking for..." statements and click on the ones they want, with topics such as census statistics, court decisions, directories, and declassified documents. And since this is a library, you'll find more than links—Yale provides brief descriptions of document collections and publishers on and off the Net. Not flashy, but a solid resource.

National Agricultural Library

http://www.nalusda.gov

As the world's largest agricultural library, the National Agricultural Library's vast resources range from research on food-borne illnesses to references on crop rotation. Its Web site offers an assortment of publications and reference packages such as the Global Change Information Packet, Global Climate Change, as well as selected bibliographies and research guides. A link to Agricultural Images from Special Collections has an eclectic sampling of images on topics that include Natural Phenomenon, Rare Botanical Prints, Plants, Pests, and Diseases.

INTERNATIONAL APPEAL

Smithsonian Institutions Libraries

http://www.sil.si.edu/mschp.htm

For those who thought the Smithsonian was just an attic filled with Archie Bunker's chair and the Hope Diamond, the SIL home page is an eye-opening discovery. SIL branch libraries cover everything from archeology to zoology, and they're coming online fast, offering access to the institution's collective resources. For instance, the Political History Resources page will direct you to George Washington's boyhood home in Falmouth, Virginia, as well as to other presidential libraries and archives; the History of Computers Resources section includes a link to the Chronology of Events in the History of Microcomputers.

The History Buff's Reference Library

http://www.serve.com/ephemera/library/refmain.html

A product of the Newspaper Collectors Society of America (NSCA), it's more of a history of journalism library than anything else, but worthwhile for the job it does in that area (see Figure 9.13). The library has articles by editor R. J. Brown and other NSCA members, who culled through old newspapers for fascinating stories. Most of them are related to the journalism history, and the site also features early article reprints and loads of photos. You can search for specific names or events, or just browse the 17 categories, arranged visually as file drawers.

LibraryWeb: Columbia University Libraries WWW Information System

http://www.columbia.edu/cu/libraries

Columbia seems to have a library for every field of study, and its LibraryWeb lets online users tap into some of these extraordinary resources. The site lets you search by subject or by library, and features background pages on institutional history and collection highlights. Search the Selected Subject Guides & Resources section for topical overviews of library and Internet resources in areas

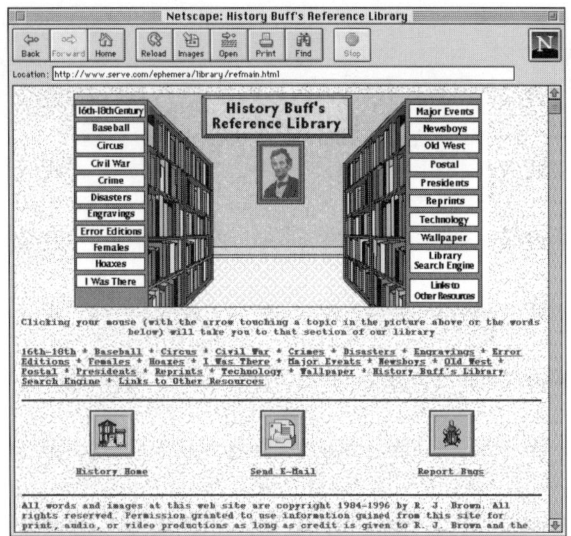

Figure 9.13

The History Buff's Reference Library, *http://www.serve.com/ephemera/library/refmain.html*

such as Business and Economics, Latin American Studies, and Mathematics. It also includes electronic texts of references and literature such as the complete *Oxford English Dictionary* and the *Federalist Papers.*

The U.C. Berkeley Libraries

http://www.lib.berkeley.edu

You suspect up front that the University of California at Berkeley's library Web site will be a winner, and it certainly lives up to the university's cutting-edge reputation. You can find general information on the library system, but it's more fun to browse the home pages for Berkeley's 20-plus libraries, which range from the Anthropology Library to the Teaching Library. You can also search the famous Digital Library SunSITE for a world of knowledge sources.

American Library Association

http://www.ala.org

The American Library Association (ALA) is the nation's symbolic head librarian, a 57,000 member organization that addresses issues ranging from technology policy to children's literature. Its Web page serves mainly as an attractive gateway to the ALA's no-nonsense gopher site; pages offer brief descriptions of ALA functions such Library Outreach and Awards, then link to the appropriate gopher pages. Tap into the gopher to grab goodies such as a history of the Caldecott and Newbery medals, and the prestigious children's book awards given annually by the ALA.

Presidential Libraries IDEA Network

http://sunsite.unc.edu/lia/president

If you just gotta know Harry Truman's hat size or how many of the Watergate tapes are available for your listening pleasure, PRESIDENT has the scoop. The site serves as a storehouse of information and materials from the nation's official Presidential Libraries. The nine libraries (along with two Presidential Materials Projects) are run by the National Archives and Records Administration; the non-federal PRESIDENT hails the chiefs with content culled from their collections, from trivia about presidential pets to the texts of campaign speeches.

Professional Organizations in the Information Sciences

http://witloof.sjsu.edu/peo/organizations.html

Somewhere out there, a librarian knows how to get a book, magazine, or paper you need. But how to find the right library? This index is a very good place to start. It has links to site after site, and it doesn't stop with libraries, but includes archivists, linguistic resources (like, say, dictionaries) and artificial intelligence. This should be an instant bookmark for grad students, professors, and research librarians.

TEACHERS AND SCHOLARS

Counterpoint

http://www.mit.edu:8001/activities/cpt/home.html

Published 10 times a year by students and alumni of M.I.T. and Wellesley College, *Counterpoint* is a journal of "rational discourse," intended to offset an alleged "ideological balkanization" taking place on many campuses. Visitors to their Web site get generously reprinted articles and features from current and back issues of the print edition. Some issues are humorous, but this is mostly a read on serious issues affecting higher education and society.

HEPROC

http://rrpubs.com/heproc/index.shtml

Internet and higher education enthusiast Carl Reimann created this virtual community for "educators, students, and all who labor in their support." Online discussion is a HEPROC priority. For example, you're invited to share thoughts on what "teaching excellence" means, as well as resources on, say, getting students more involved, or institutional development. HEPROC maintains an archive of the great ideas that have come out of such discussions, and, hey, they'll even help you with research questions.

Global SchoolNet Foundation

http://www.gsn.org

Since one of the missions of Global SchoolNet is to bring the latest communications technology to classrooms, it figures they'd have a rich Web site like this one. With so much information being disseminated, however, the page could stand to be a bit more focused. It is a resource for "linking kids around the world" via newsgroups and even videoconferencing. Educators are also offered training and consultation on "Designing On-line Courses," among other options. Its a good site for education pros looking to incorporate the Web into their curricula.

INTERNATIONAL APPEAL

H-Net: Humanities Online

http://h-net2.msu.edu

Based at Michigan State University, the H-Net initiative supports scholars and teachers of the humanities and social sciences with a host of electronic discussion lists, plus other helpful features. Those include the latest professional book, software, film and video reviews, as well as descriptions and syllabi appropriate for K–12 and collegiate courses. The H-Net Job Guide, humanities advocacy reports, and a selective related link index round out this generous resource, already boasting 40,000 list subscribers and over 200 editors worldwide.

Information on Academic Careers and Academic Life

http://bunny.cs.uiuc.edu/sigmod/funding/academicCareers.html

Courtesy of ACM SIGMOD, here's a database filled with counsel and networking info for professionals who want to succeed, or at least survive, in academia. It's especially geared toward women, because discussions of tenure, making connections, teaching, and other issues were transcribed from a women's academic careers workshop. There's a section on where to obtain grants and other funding, along with stuff to interest grad students, experimental computer scientists, and engineers.

Scholarly Journals Distributed Via the World-Wide Web

http://info.lib.uh.edu/wj/webjour.html

Robert Spragg at the University of Houston maintains this neat index of free Web-based scholarly journals. Journals are listed by searchable alphabetical order. Click on "C," for instance, and you'll find links to Classics Ireland, Contributions to Algebra & Geometry, and Cornell Law Review. Information may be had on forthcoming e-journals, while a more comprehensive periodicals listing is also available, sometimes for a price. A fine index for professors, as well as scholars at large.

UniSci

http://unisci.com

In the never-ending quest for the answers to sticky questions, UniSci is a messenger. When a significant scientific breakthrough occurs at one of America's universities, this page usually has the story. As Editor Don Radler explains, "People need to know what is going on in their own field and in related fields." So from top awards for molecular nanotechnology to the busy Arctic research season, UniSci has brief reports on the big news in science.

Educational Policy Analysis Archives

http://seamonkey.ed.asu.edu/epaa

Arizona State University's College of Education publishes this peer-reviewed e-journal, dedicated to "education policy at all levels and in all nations." Visitors can browse issue-by-issue abstracts; and, should something strike their fancy, proceed to the article archives to read full text selections like "Choosing Higher Education: Educationally Ambitious Chicanos and the Path to Social Mobility." Free subscriptions and submission and discussion opportunities make this a fine site for educational policy buffs.

Pathways to School Improvement

http://www.ncrel.org/sdrs/pathwayg.htm

Consider this site an online road map for enhancing America's educational system (see Figure 9.14). The North Central Regional Educational Laboratory's Pathways project has developed a schemata of critical educational issues, organized into areas such as Professional Development, School to Work, Math, Science, and Learning. Each area is broken down into "Critical Issues" and combined with links to other useful online resources. Though somewhat lacking in dealing with the arts and humanities, this site lights the crossroads at which American education now stands, and offers suggested routes for the future.

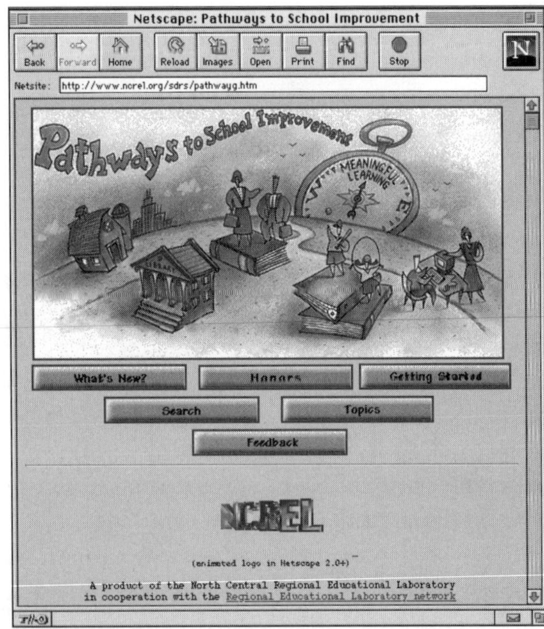

Figure 9.14
Pathways to School Improvement,
http://www.ncrel.org/sdrs/pathwayg.htm

Mission Critical

http://arachne.SJSU.EDU/depts/itl

San Jose State University created this virtual lab, utilizing the Web's interactive capacities to help teach basic critical thinking skills (e.g. deduction, induction), which are part of the transfer core curriculum in California's higher education system. Visitors are encouraged to work through detailed tutorials and multiple choice exercises on, for instance, "Vagueness & Ambiguity" and "Universal Syllogisms." Along the way, you'll learn about "Ad Hominem Attacks" and "Non Sequiturs." The only drawback is its text-only presentation of literate logic lessons.

CEARCH: Cisco Educational Archive

http://sunsite.unc.edu/cisco

This site is good for educators and schools hoping to "internetwork" via the Web. CEARCH is an acronym for the Cisco Educational Archive and Resources Catalog (it's a joint project between Cisco Systems and the University of North Carolina). You can "CEARCH" topics using the keywords and a list of links will appear. The site also invites you to the Virtual Schoolhouse, a "meta-library of K–12 links" to nearly every online education resource imaginable, from Doctor Fun to Mega Math to Declassified Spy Photos.

Educom

http://www.educom.edu

Educom is a nonprofit consortium of colleges and corporations seeking to integrate information technology into classrooms, curricula, and research. This site is excellent for those with a vested interest in "the changing ways we will work, learn, and communicate in the digital world of the 21st century." Articles such as "The Role of Publishers in the Digital Age" may be found online in current and back issues of Educom Review, and the "Edupage," updated three times per week, offers digested educational technology news.

EdWeb

http://k12.cnidr.org:90

Sponsored in part by the Corporation for Public Broadcasting, author Andy Carvin maintains this hyperbook as a means to explore school reform in light of new information technologies. After considering issues such as whether the World Wide Web really will revolutionize education, you can take an HTML crash course, or follow the progress of U.S. school projects utilizing Internet curricula. The graphic interface will take you through a history of the Web, education reforms currently being implemented, and on to scores of other pertinent Web sites and discussion groups.

From Now On

http://www.pacificrim.net/~mckenzie

Teacher/administrator/consultant/info specialist Jamie McKenzie authors this lively educational technology issues page. Updated monthly, and free, it offers more than McKenzie's expertise—delivering, for instance, full text of a book he published in 1991, which begins: "The Odysseus who served as hero to the Greeks would rate poorly as a leader for this Age of Information." Educational innovators will find support and encouragement here.

TeachNet: The Teachers Network

http://www.teachnet.org

From the moment the yellow, ruled paper background appears, you know TeachNet is a quick study in capturing the essence of creative education. The site is sponsored by Impact II/The Teachers Network, a nationwide, educational, nonprofit organization. TeachNet lets educators share their techniques and ideas through the Let's Talk bulletin board and the Sharing Curriculum database of classroom projects. Search by subject area, grade level and region for terrific projects posted by contributing teachers.

Electronic Archives for Teaching the American Literatures

http://www.georgetown.edu/tamlit/tamlit-home.html

This Web offshoot of Georgetown University's American Studies Program features full-text resources for teachers of various U.S. literatures and culture studies. Those include the likes of an essay on "Teaching Chicano Literature: An Historical Approach" by Raymund Paredes, a Dialect and Vernacular bibliography, and the syllabus for a course on "Century's End: Race and Gender at the Turn of the Century." T-AMLIT discussion lists on "High School Canons," among other issues, are also available, with The Heath Anthology of American Literature Newsletter online edition.

New Tools for Teaching

http://ccat.sas.upenn.edu/teachdemo

University of Pennsylvania classics professor James J. O'Donnell created this interactive guide to using the Net in higher education teaching. With friendly hypertext commentary that leads in any number of directions, it should prove an especially good resource for college instructors who want to become more Web-active, but aren't exactly sure where to start. Visitors also get primers on enhancing communication with students via e-mail, Web applications in the library, a look "over the horizon," plus lots more pertinent stuff.

Scholarly Societies Project

http://www.lib.uwaterloo.ca/society/overview.html

This University of Waterloo (Canada) site is a gateway to worldwide scholarly societies. For higher education professionals under the publish or perish gun, this might just be the ticket. Indeed, one of the aims here is addressing what has been called a "Crisis in Scholarly Publishing." It's an academic extravaganza, featuring links to more than 500 scholarly Web pages, submission resources, and an archive of full-text serial publications.

EE-Link

http://nceet.snre.umich.edu

This site is for K–12 professionals looking to lead students on an environmental issues expedition. The no-frills interface belies a database rich in consiousness raising resources. Those include air quality lesson plans, access to the Kunosoura (population and resource management) Project, *Electronic Green Journal,* and other publications. Regional information is also provided for a number of U.S. states. This is a good index for anyone who wants to be environmentally educated.

The University Financing Foundation
http://www.tuff.gatech.edu/HOME2.html

For research equipment and facilities, this Atlanta-based nonprofit foundation offers "less than tax-exempt rate" loans and leases to college and universities. Read all about how "overhead recovery financing" helped Georgia Tech construct a building which shot research performance up to a level not enjoyed since the "heyday" of the mid-'70s. Budget pros at U.S. institutions needing to grow beyond their apparent means will want to consider the services offered here.

EDUCATIONAL SERVICES AND RESOURCES

Star-Brite Learning Program
http://www.primenet.com/~starbrit

Designed for do-it-yourself parents planning to unplug Barney and home-educate their preschoolers, the Star-Brite Learning Program is marketed at this resource-rich Web site. The program is sold in monthly packages of lessons and materials; the site offers a sample day's plan, with highly structured activities ranging from an apple puzzle project to jumping exercises. For browsers, the most useful element is the Child Care Resources page, with descriptions of and links to everything from the National Parent Information Network to the USDA's Administration for Children and Families.

Kaplan Educational Centers
http://www.kaplan.com

The standardized-test gurus at Kaplan Educational Centers provide info on just about every fill-in-the-bubble test that prospective American students might want to take, along with plugs for Kaplan's books, software, and classes. Some downloadable test-prep games are available for a trial run, and you'll also find a library of links to "higher-education Web resources."

Princeton Review
http://www.review.com/index.html-ssi

The Princeton Review claims to be "the nation's leader in test preparation," and they make a case for themselves here. They offer bone-up courses for standardized college and grad school entrance exams, such as the SAT, LSAT, and MCAT. This sales pitch is dressed up in a cool graphic interface, giving access to "best schools" lists, financial aid info, and more.

UnCover
http://www.carl.org/uncover/unchome.html

Approximately six million pieces from 17,000 magazines and journals are available through this "online table of contents index and article delivery service." UnCover remains in compliance with all copyright laws, because you pay individually for the articles ordered, but searching their database is free. This looks to be an especially fine service for those needing information quickly, as UnCover will fax the goods to your computer "within 24 hours—often in less than 1 hour." They also offer special library and institutional rates.

Apple Education
http://education.apple.com

Apple Education markets its products only to public, private, and parochial schools in the U.S., but if you're eligible, there are some special deals. At press time, those included a Power Macintosh 6100/66 DOS Compatible Computer (described in full detail), multimedia tools such as the Apple QuickTake 100 digital camera, and Early Childhood Connections, a literacy program for tykes. In addition to a fine array of curriculum software offered here, educators may be interested in Apple's purported efforts to help schools meet the Goals 2000: Education America Act.

Cliff's Notes
http://www.cliffs.com/cliffs/cliffs.html

The official Cliff's Notes Web site is sort of a Cliff's Notes for Cliff's Notes—it boils down the company's lines of literature outlines, study aids, test prep guides, and software, and tells you where to buy them. There's even a collection of Cliff's FAQs, including bread-and-butter questions such as, "Will teachers get mad if I use Cliffs Notes?" But like the best commercial sites, this one does more than sell: It has a giveaway page with an order form for a free Hot Tips disk to help students study more effectively.

Dragonfly Toy Company

http://www.magic.mb.ca/~dragon

For children with special play needs, The Dragonfly Toy Company sells (and ships) toys worldwide. In categories such as Fine Motor Skills, Cognitive, and Sensory Stimulation, you can browse an inventory that includes Texture Dominos, a Sound Puzzle Box, and Curved Martian Canal—a semicircular sandbox on legs designed to fit around a wheelchair. Here as well is a selection of books, and a toy search service, in case you didn't find exactly what you had in mind.

Educational Software Institute

http://www.edsoft.com:80/q/@006847yrxljg/index.html

For parents, educators, and students, this "one-stop educational software center" features a catalog of over 7,000 titles for sale from more than 300 publishers, available for both PC and Macintosh. Middle-schoolers can learn critical thinking skills using programs like "Granny Applebee's Cookie Factory." Selections for older students include "The Secret Island of Dr. Quandary," and "Museum Madness," a problem-solving application using a "mixed-up" virtual museum as its setting. This enormous, well-organized resource promises many items not available in the average retail market, some of which are offered in both Spanish and English.

Gryphon House Books, Inc.

http://www.ghbooks.com

Gryphon House Books, Inc. is a seller of children's books, both for them and for the teachers and parents who care for them. The site is geared more towards the adults, though—the children's books aren't listed (but you can order a free catalog of them online). All their teaching books are sold here, with full descriptions. But what makes this site stand out is its free list of activities, sampled from their book collection.

Knowledge Adventure

http://www.adventure.com

The Knowledge Adventure Web site features samplers of its products, but it's more than just a bunch of sales pitches—you'll also find engaging stand-alone learning pages. For parents confused by the jungle of children's computer programs, the KA Info area includes a Children's Software Revue article about "How to Buy Educational Software." The site also features an online edition of the Random House Kids Encyclopedia, an A–Z collection of articles culled from the CD-ROM version.

Home Education Resource Center

http://www.cts.com/~netsales/herc

This page of home schooling resources for browsers and buyers will also be of interest to conventional school teachers. HERC's catalog includes "American History Simulations," "Beginning Map Skills," math study kits, and much more. Valuable state-by-state home schooling regulations are outlined in detail. An index of support groups across the nation provides added value for parents who are thinking of "opting out" of the system. Great links to other Internet education resources, and a special bonus: guidance for keeping kids out of the seamier "adult" side of the Web.

Microsoft Kids

http://www.microsoft.com./kids

Here's a detailed catalog of Microsoft's K–12 educational products and services. Software includes "The Magic School Bus Explores the Human Body," another package promising to bring kids "face-to-face with more than 250 of the deadliest creatures on Earth," plus lots of arts and music options. Teachers get curriculum integration tips. Some discounts are also offered through this well-organized page.

Pitsco Technology Education

http://www.pitsco.com/wel.html

Hands-on (rather than computer-oriented) educational technology products are offered here. Pitco's most popular products include Epicenter, a model construction package challenging students "to design and build a tower (simulating an office building) that will resist high magnitude earthquakes," and The Seeker, an "exciting and unique device for teaching the principles of robotics!" Teachers will also be attracted by an index of links to the hypertext edition of books like "Rip Van Winkle." Mostly of interest to K through 12 folk.

Schoolhouse Videos and CDs

http://www.nando.net/ads/gift/school.htm

This site sells educational videos and CD-ROMs geared in particular toward students who are being schooled at home. Software titles like "Portraits of American Presidents" and "Undersea Adventure," and videos are available in a wide range of subjects like languages, medicine, and martial arts. Not all of the titles are for kids, but the business owners are on a mission to provide "wholesome" instructional and Christian inspirational materials, and to try to ensure that the 4,000+ products they offer are appropriate for the entire family.

Big Top Productions

http://www.bigtop.com

This fun site is a good example of how a company can represent itself on the Web without sounding like a promotional leaflet all the time. Big Top makes educational and entertainment software like Keroppi Day Hopper, an ingenious program that encourages kids to keep a journal. More than just ads, though, the site serves up resources for parents of young children and activities for kids.

Women's Studies on Disc: The Women's Studies Index on CD-ROM

http://www.mcp.com/12516545986406/mlr/books/821395/821395a.html

Part of a promotional page presented by MacMillan publishing, the site claims that "G.K. Hall & Co.'s Women's Studies Index has gathered and organized this wealth of popular and scholarly journals on women's issues to provide the scholar, student, and researcher with easy access these essential sources." Now, Women's Studies on Disc makes accessing the material even easier by cumulating the last five years of the printed index on a single CD-ROM. It includes scholarly articles, book reviews, film reviews, and popular material, searchable by keyword, author, title, and journal.

Bibliographic Formats for Citing Electronic Information

http://www.uvm.edu/~xli/reference/estyles.html

Attention students: here's the answer to the nagging question, "But how do I cite an Internet resource?" Online sources and bibliographies are now part and parcel of academic work, so it's good to have this resource, which tells you how to cite home pages, online newspapers, journals, and encyclopedias. All in American Psychological Association or Modern Language Association style. It saves you the trouble of buying the latest APA or MLA update, too.

The Language and Culture Center

http://bentley.uh.edu/English/LCC/home.htm

The University of Houston-based Language and Culture Center offers intensive English language/English as a Second Language programs to international college or graduate students and professionals. That includes GRE and TOEFL preparation, as well as pronunciation courses. Interested browsers may consider housing options, financial aid opportunities, or airport pickups. Photos and testimonials from the likes of Makoto Kato break up what is mostly an information onslaught here.

The Piano Education Page

http://www.unm.edu/~loritaf/pnoedmn.html

Here the West Mesa Music Teachers Association of New Mexico has compiled a grand array of keyboard resources. Both the Alfred and Suzuki teaching methods are explored. Studio etiquette requires that the parent who arrives early to pick up a child from lessons "remain quiet and do not interrupt." The buying tips advise that, "It's worth the extra time and effort to seek a grand piano made prior to World War II," while adult students are counseled that they shouldn't "expect to learn as fast as a seven-year-old child." Good software reviews, too.

Educational Marketing International

http://www.christusrex.org/www1/EMI/EMI-index.html

Andreea M. Bensaia, author of the annual *Guide to International Schools,* maintains this gateway to foreign program / internship enrollment information, appropriate to students of all ages and interests. Options for high schoolers include a summer "in the heart of Oxfordshire" preparing for the SAT at Abacus College, or a year in the Swiss Alps at Gstaad International School.

National Defense University

http://www.ndu.edu

The classes at the National War College (like "Strategic Decisionmaking" and "Joint Military Logistics" probably

SPOTLIGHT ON DISTANCE LEARNING

The advent of the Internet was like a revolution for those who learn or teach in their homes, referred to as distance learning.

Five Facts

1 It can take as little as 15 minutes to send an assignment to a teacher and have it graded and returned.

2 Online conferencing and discussion forums have made school hour requirements unnecessary.

3 International and cross-coastal personal communication between students is now immediate and free of costs.

4 Some Professors' office hours are occasionally held in chat rooms.

5 Procedures that used to be hands-on only—like biology class dissections—can be done "virtually" on the computer.

Five Sites

The Adult Distance Education Internet Surf Shack

http://www.helix.net/~jmtaylor/edsurf.html

This page explains distance learning opportunities on the Net.

CASO

http://www.caso.com/iuhome.html

The CASO home page has a centralized listing of over 700 courses you can take via the Internet.

LOLU

http://www.lbbs.org/lolu/index.htm

LOLU: The Left On Line University offers alternative distance learning opportunities for political, social, economic, and historical activists.

Global Campus

http://www.csulb.edu/gc

The Global Campus site is a free collection of Web resources for learning and teaching.

Virtual Online University

http://www.athena.edu

An upstart organization named Virtual Online University offers college-level and K through 12 classes and is presently applying for accreditation.

weren't on your college transcripts), but other stuff is here, too—like a nice big list of defense-related links and publications. The famous McNair papers—studies by some of the leading military academicians—can be found here, although most aren't available yet. Still, papers like "NATO from Berlin to Bosnia: Trans-Atlantic Security in Transition" offer good insights into the military mind. And the INSS's annual Strategic Assessment is one of the benchmarks of American defense policy.

Gender-Free Pronoun FAQ

http://www.eecis.udel.edu/~chao/gfp

Tired of dodging the gender issue when writing papers? This lengthy document is the total guide to gender-free pronouns (GFPs). This site provides lots of information, background, and resources, ranging from technical, to clever, to vaguely surreal.

National Center to Improve Practice

http://www.edc.org/FSC/NCIP

NCIP promotes technology to enhance education of students with sensory, cognitive, physical and social/emotional disabilities. Their home page features facilitated discussion forums on issues like Augmentative & Alternative Communication, Inclusion, or Early Childhood Technology. They also have an online library, offering articles and resources on everything from "Motivating the Reluctant Writer" to "The Journal of Visual Impairment & Blindness." Among the educational technology products for sale, visitors can order videos, for which preview clips are offered.

ICLnet: Institute for Christian Leadership

http://www.iclnet.org

Since 1983, the Institute for Christian Leadership has provided publications, seminars, and other services to those concerned with critical issues in Christian higher education. Now, their home page furthers that tradition. Articles such as "The Pedagogical Impulse in The Pilgrim's Progress" can be found in the electronic archive of ICL's tri-yearly Faculty Dialogue journal. Extensive Christian Web resources are indexed, with a software library, a prolific "Reading Room," and so on. This vast database is searchable, and hosts electronic discussion groups, too.

The MU Online Writery

http://www.missouri.edu/~wleric/writery.html

The MU Online Writery is a school hang-out for writers seeking cyber companionship (see Figure 9.15). Designed as an electronic accompaniment to University of Missouri's writing program, "This place is about writers talking with other writers." Chat areas and news groups let authors share their innermost works, while "Cybertutors" are available for those needing a little extra help. Much of what's here is geared toward MU students, but anyone can join in, and outside scribes will appreciate the links to other useful writer's resources.

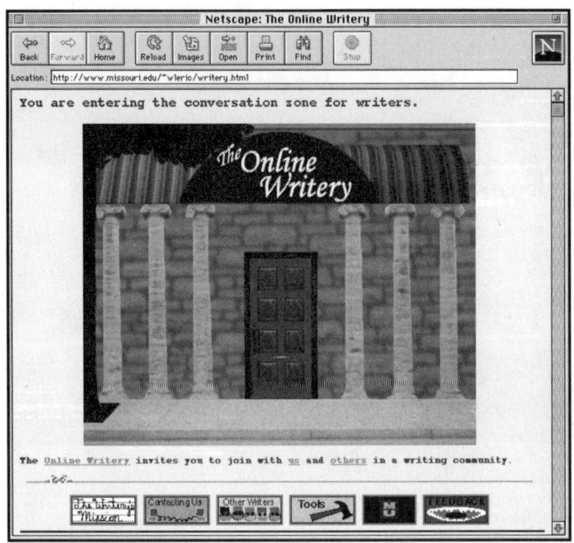

Figure 9.15
The MU Online Writery,
http://www.missouri.edu/~wleric/writery.html

KEYWORDS

Education: colleges, universities, libraries, K–12 resources, women's studies, early childhood, higher education, education issues, law schools, MBA, distance learning

Financial aid: grants, fellowships, scholarships, school loans

1. Take a virtual tour of the human heart at the Franklin Institute Science Museums' online exhibit.
   http://sln.fi.edu/tfi/virtual/vir-summ.html
2. Visit Once Upon A Time in The Eighties, a page put together by a class at the University of Virginia for a humorous and smart wrap-up of the last decade.
   http://www.engl.virginia.edu/~enwr1016/index.html
3. Take the "Nine Planets: Solar System Tour," at the Students for the Exploration and Development of Space home page.
   http://www.seds.org/nineplanets/nineplanets/nineplanets.html
4. Hang out and communicate with college students across the country and around the world at The Main Quad or at Loci.
   http://www.mainquad.com and **http://www.Loci.com**

Chapter 10 Personal Finance and Business

- INVESTING
- FINANCIAL MARKETS
- TAX PREPARATION
- PERSONAL FINANCE
- SAVING
- REAL ESTATE
- BUSINESS AND SMALL BUSINESS
- BUSINESS NEWS

10 THINGS YOU CAN DO FOR YOUR FINANCES *RIGHT NOW*

1. Create a personal portfolio of 15 stocks and mutual funds and monitor their performance at InvestorsEdge.

   http://www.irnet.com/pages/login.stm

2. Crunch the numbers: everything from how much house you can afford, to how much it'll cost to send Junior to college.

   http://alfredo.wustl.edu/mort_links.html

3. Use Smith Barney's interactive IRA calculator to add up your retirement savings.

   http://nestegg.iddis.com/smithbarney/interact.html

4. See how your stocks are doing with the Security APL Stock Quote Server.

   http://www.secapl.com/cgi-bin/qs

5. Calculate your taxes with a little help from The Tax Prophet.

   http://www.taxprophet.com/apps/apps.html

6. Find out the current best rates nationwide on credit cards, savings, and loans, at Money Online.

   http://pathfinder.com/money/rates/index.html

7. Rate the value of the latest models and calculate the cost of owning a new car at FinanCenter.

   http://www.financenter.com/newautos.htm

8. Ask Cash Flo, resident finance expert at Women's Wire, about anything from how to start a nest egg to what are the intricacies of zero coupon bonds.

   http://www.women.com/cash/qa.cas.html

9. Get today's latest-breaking financial news from the business front.

   http://www.cnnfn.com

10. Enter in your data and determine if your mutual fund has holdings in the tobacco industry.

    http://www.calvertgroup.com

Is managing your personal finances forever on your list of things to do? The Web can help you get matters in hand and money in the bank (or wherever you'd like it to be). Use the Net's wealth of commercial and non-commercial resources to save, plan your retirement, shop for a home, or beef up your portfolio. When you're ready, you can shop online for the right professionals to help you.

If you're at all intimidated by the complex world of saving and investing, you can find answers and advice online, without pushy salespeople or embarrassment about your lack of financial savvy (or cash).

If you're a small business entrepreneur, you can add a whole stack of new names and contacts to your Rolodex by networking on the Net. It's also a great way to find resources like funding, advice, and regulations pertaining to small businesses. The Web is enjoying star status as an advertising tool: reach customers you never would have encountered, at little cost.

Already a pro? Make life easier by plugging into the Web for delivered-to-your-desktop business news and up-to-the-minute stock and fund quotes. You can even buy and sell online.

In this chapter you'll find out how you can use the Web to take steps toward putting your financial house in order—or shopping for a new one. You've got a hotline to money management, whenever you need it.

INVESTING

Money Talks Magazine

http://www.talks.com

Sponsored by the P.R. Newswire news service, this free online investment magazine is a great daily news-and-information fix for investors (see Figure 10.1). Features include articles by top names in finance (like author and *New York Times* columnist Robert Metz), Money Saving Daily Travel Tips from a personal finance expert, as well as archives of articles past. Questions? You can "Ask the Authors" here, too.

Investor's Network

INTERNATIONAL APPEAL

http://www.worldnt.com/invest

Pinnacle Financial Advisors Inc. serves up sumptuous Web design and bite-sized investment tips. The company tends to focus on a single international pick in the "Fund Forum" and "Growth Stock" entries of its World Class Investor department. But if you return often, you may eventually amass some global-trading savvy. Also: the Investment Resources section, has a nicely organized collection of links to other trading-related destinations on the Web.

PR Newswire

httt://www.prnewswire.com

PR Newswire provides an excellent resource for the active investor. You can get the latest full-text news about a wealth of public and private companies as well as an archive of these news articles from the past year in News On Call. This service is free, although all of the news releases come from PR Newswire members. Also worth a look: The weekly articles in Money Talks.

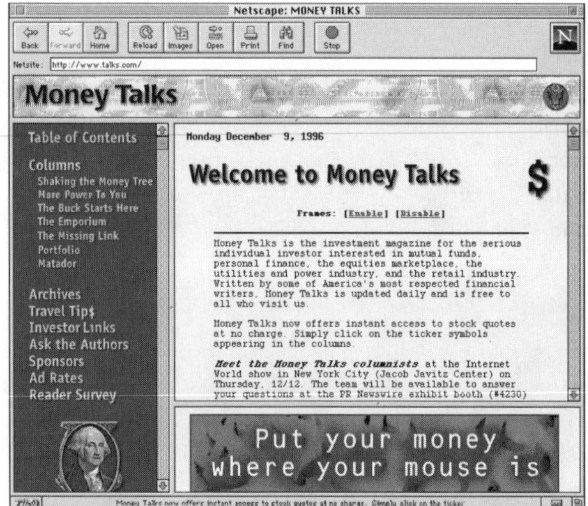

Figure 10.1

Money Talks Magazine, *http://www.talks.com*

The GreenMoney Online Guide

http://www.greenmoney.com

This online arm of the GreenMoney Journal is dedicated to promoting socially and environmentally responsible investing. You'll find up-to-date excerpts from the newsletter (a recent article: "Simplicity and Commerce: Don't Shop, Be Happy"), an events calendar, and a gallery of "green" links and businesses, featuring everything from organic foods to "PC" mutual funds, plus links to other publications. Do your part and still come out ahead.

TD Bank

http://www.tdbank.ca

The home page of the Toronto-Dominion Bank carries a hefty load of information about personal and business investing and finances—and it's available in English, French, and Japanese. Of note: The Business Forum, where experts field financial questions, and tips on managing the family money in Your Home, Your Future and Your Finances. If investment advice could make you a millionaire, you'd hit the jackpot here.

Creative Investment Research

http://www2.ari.net/cirm

Creative Investment Research is an investment advisory firm dedicated to providing information on investments, brokerage firms, and banks owned by women and minorities. Download the Minority Bank Study, or scan the partial transcript from the White House Conference on Corporate Responsibility. Then browse the listings of minority-owned banks. For a deeper search, order the Minority Bank Web Monitor, which includes "summary data on every Asian, Black, Hispanic, Native-American and Woman-owned Bank in the U.S."

Finance Wat.ch

http://finance.wat.ch

This is a superbly designed site that brings into reach everything from derivatives to a financial glossary (see Figure 10.2). You'll find exchange rates, stock market data, and even an online training course in futures and options, and the regularly updated hotlist brings you the newest global financial sites. If you can't put your money in a Swiss bank, you can at least put some time into this treasure trove of world financial information from Switzerland.

Figure 10.2

Finance Watch, *http://finance.wat.ch*

Investment Wizard from Online Intelligence

http://www.ozsoft.com/iwhome.html

The folks at Oz Software are keen on providing investors with the proverbial Second Opinion. You'll find investment advice and articles from the *Wall Street Journal*'s top wizards as well as market news. Check out the regularly updated analyses of IPOs and other big money moves in the Hot Hands section. You must subscribe ($5.00 monthly), but you can try it free for two weeks. A wise alternative to the blindfold-and-dartboard method.

NumaWeb

http://www.numa.com

Numa Financial Systems shows off its technological prowess here with some online utilities that should impress investors. The UK company has created forms-based "webulators" to help visitors analyze such arcane investment vehicles as warrants, convertible bonds, and options. If you need a break, you can visit the Neural Broker. There you'll find an artificial intelligence system that, happily, always seems to agree with your own market analyses.

Investors Edge

http://www.irnet.com

The Investors Edge is cutting through the financial services bureaucracy by providing free investment information—from stock and fund quotes to corporate profiles to the latest news from the business world. A cool interactive feature lets users create a virtual portfolio of six stocks and monitor their performance. The Edge also includes a huge directory of companies sorted by industry groupings. So much for so little.

SEC EDGAR Database

http://www.sec.gov/edgarhp.htm

If you don't mind poring through fine print, you'll appreciate this vast database of U.S. corporate filings to the SEC. It's a way of getting information you probably won't find in annual reports, and you don't have to fiddle with stacks of paper. It searches only for keywords in the title of the document; you'll need to download the document to do further searching from your Web browser or word processor.

The Chicago Board Options Exchange

http://www.cboe.com

This site answers the question "What is an Option?" for investment newbies, and offers an options FAQ. Pros can get the latest market stats or the CBOE new option listings. Of course, before buying or selling options, you must receive a copy of the Characteristics and Risks of Standardized Options. It's here online!

The Municipal Resource Center

http://www.municipal.com

Investors in the municipal bond market will love this site. Financial publisher R.R. Donnelley currently runs the place as a no-cost experiment. Donnelley says there's a $1.2-trillion market for those who'd rather invest in, say, the village of Fairmont, Nebraska, than blue-chip stocks. All the dope on bond offerings across the country is online, indexed alphabetically and by state. Also: A growing list of links useful to those researching local governments.

The Syndicate

http://www.moneypages.com/syndicate

Ever wonder just what exactly the Dow Jones Industrial Average is? You'll find the answer here in William Rini's Syndicate. You'll also find links to more than 1000 finance pages. Take a look at the scorecard showing the change in seven key investment indexes during the last calendar year, or compare your portfolio with a professional's. The misc.invest FAQs make this an informative investment page.

The Motley Fool

100 BEST SITES

http://www.fool.com

These Fools have taken their place as the online keepers of Wall Street tomfoolery. For individual investors looking for daily news, predictions and advice on how to stay on top, this site is a familiar stop. 13 Steps to Investing Foolishly outlines a fool-proof investment approach and the Fool Portfolio tracks investments daily, plus you'll find daily news updates, links to real-time stock quotes, a daily Pitch (market dilemma), and more. You won't have to feel foolish for seeking some good investment advice.

Insider Watch

http://www.cda.com/investnet

This online investment magazine is brought to you by CDA/Investnet. It's a good dose of mainstream advertising, but the slick pages also bring you useful investment information, and you can download an Acrobat version of the latest copy of Insiders' Chronicle, CDA's investment newsletter. Don't miss top dog Bob Gabele showing off his investment picks on the Hall of Fame page.

Douglas Gerlach's Invest-o-rama

http://www.investorama.com

If you had a dime for every Web link on Douglas Gerlach's Invest-o-rama, you wouldn't have to worry about money. The page is divided into useful subheadings like "Quotes," "Brokers," and '"Funds". Choose "Funds," for instance, and you'll find links to mutual fund big dogs like Fidelity, and Dreyfus (see Figure 10.3). Throw tasty morsels of economic wisdom, and you have a comfortable (and pretty) little investment neighborhood.

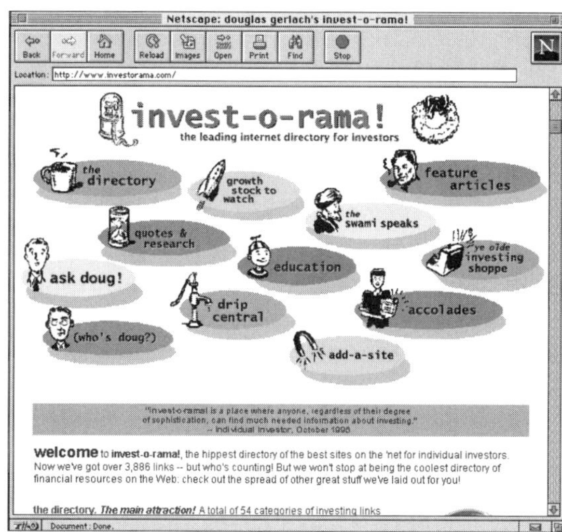

Figure 10.3
Douglas Gerlach's Invest-o-rama,
http://www.investorama.com

Barra

http://www.barra.com

Here's a slick Web page from some slick salesmen. Barra specializes in computer-assisted investing. Believers in such programs can get Equity Money Managers, Fixed Income Money Managers, Equity Traders, Plan Sponsors, Consultants, and Master Trust Banks...all from Barra's computer wonderland. They also provide access to the BARRA research publications (such as Miscellaneous Quantitative Analysis), so you can get somethin' for nothin'.

Kiplinger Online

http://www.kiplinger.com

The well-known publisher of the Kiplinger letters for investors is showing off its stuff on the Web. You'll find selections from recent newsletter issues and Kiplinger's Magazine. Recent offerings included the magazine reprint "21 Ways to Cut Your Own Taxes," offering detailed advice for the April 15 tax deadline. Also available here: Stock quotations and a stock ticker search, with data provided by PAWWS.

FINdex

http://www.findex.com

FINdex is an index and search engine that helps visitors find related Web sites. It's a low-bandwidth site created by a company called FinSource Ltd. that gets straight to the point: select a business type (such as brokerage house or stock exchange) from a pop-up list, choose a country and add an optional keyword to narrow your search.

The Securities Law Home Page

http://www.seclaw.com

Investing used to be a hands-off business. Now, brokers and investors need to know the laws and what the Internet will mean to securities trading. Here, Mark J. Astarita looks at corporate finance, Direct Public Offerings, and the uncertainties posed by stock rumors on the Web. You can also get stock quotes or read about the latest securities law decisions. This site holds promise for even the newest investors.

J.P. Morgan

http://www.jpmorgan.com

The firm that practically invented global financial services takes to the Web with this collection of corporate information and financial research. You'll learn a little about the 150-year-old company: They're still making daring loans to governments, for example. They also aim to help corporations and wealthy investors manage their money wisely. Free information on commodities and governments bonds, updated often. Most valuable if your bank balance hits seven figures.

Zack's Investor's Window

http://iw.zacks.com

Zack's Investment Research Inc. offers this list as the perfect tool for investors tired of wading through hip graphics and Netscape-enhanced HTML just to find the financial dope on corporations. Looking for the latest investor info on Rockwell International's site? Zacks says, "Click on the second image from the bottom for the Corporate Overview, and click on the second image from the top for Press Releases." Fast and easy.

Ethical Business
http://www.bath.ac.uk/Centres/Ethical

Brokers of the world take note! Ethical Business is a directory of businesses and investments that are environmentally and socially responsible. The site also includes an explanation of ethical investing. If you don't like investing in companies that test their products on animals, check out the NPI Global Care Fund. An excellent resource for folks who want to keep the Earth green and make a little green on the side.

FILL: Financial Information Link Library
http://www.mbnet.mb.ca/~russell

Serious investors need financial information from around the globe, and the Financial Information Link Library has most of the bases covered. Check out the Banco del Pacifico in Equador or the Zagreb Stock Exchange in Croatia. The U.S. section, the most complete, is a veritable who's who of the financial sector in this country. Local color: Webmaster John Russell throws in flags from all the countries represented.

I·N·T·E·R·N·E·T M·I·N·U·T·E

CUSTOMIZING YOUR BROWSER

It's a good idea to change your default home page, although most people don't know it can be done or don't get around to doing it. Your default home page is the page your browser automatically opens to each time you connect to the Web so changing it to a site you visit often saves time. Usually it is set to open to either Netscape's or Microsoft's home page. If you'd like to change it to another home page, follow these instructions for your browser type.

Using Netscape:

1. Fire up your Netscape browser, and take a look at the Menu Bar that runs across the top of the window.
2. Under the Options Menu, find "General Preferences" and select it. A dialog box with several options will come up: "Browser starts with" is the one you're after.
3. Replace the URL currently in the "Home Page Location" box—*http://home.netscape.com.*
4. Enter the URL of your favorite Web site, e.g., *http://www.women.com/guide.* Once that's done, click the OK button to save your change and exit Preferences. That's all there is to it.

Using Microsoft Internet Explorer:

1. To replace the default home page (in this case, the Microsoft Network Homepage), open Internet Explorer and access the Web page that you want to use for your new home page e.g., Women's Wire at *http://www.women.com/guide.*
2. Once there, go to the Internet Explorer Edit menu at the top of the window, and choose "Options."
3. In the Options dialog box, click on the "Home/Search Page."
4. Locate the "Change Address" option.
5. Click on the "Use Current" button in the "Change Address" box to change your default home page to the page you're currently on. The URL, will appear just above the Change Address Box.
6. Click OK, and you're done.

If you're looking for a more serious browser makeover, check out font options, font sizes and link colors. Experiment. Browsers don't break, and you can undo anything. Just have fun with it.

Charles Schwab Online

http://www.Schwab.com

Helping investors help themselves is the name of the game at Charles Schwab. Get information here on any of the multitude of Schwab investment services, like reinvesting your stock dividends for free with the Schwab No-Fee StockBuilder Plan. You can also register (it's currently free) for a "privileged access account" which lets you into privileged pages on the Schwab site.

National Association of Investors Corporation

http://www.better-investing.org

The National Association of Investors Corporation (NAIC) provides training and support for fledgling investors, with a special focus on investment clubs. NAIC's club network is one way to find out what's going on in your region. There's an emphasis on using personal computers to track finances, and the volunteers who operate the NAIC Web site do a pretty good job of monitoring the latest software tools for investors.

INTERNATIONAL APPEAL

Eco-Rating International

http://www.eco-rating.com

Determining whether your company is investing in "green" stocks or mutual funds, or if your commercial winery qualifies as organic, is the aim of this Pasadena, California company. Rather than simply labeling a company environmentally friendly, they assign degrees of "environmental soundness" on a ten-point scale. They promise objectivity and neutrality using up-to-date research on sustainability and evaluating a company's use of available "green" technology.

INTERNATIONAL APPEAL

Mark Twain Bank

http://www.marktwain.com

What makes the site stand out: Efforts to enlighten customers of the joys—and risks—of international investing. Visitors will find WorldWide Wizdom, a forum on international investing that includes daily commentary from an MTB bond trader, market strategies from other traders, and a Global Colloquium for posting questions or ideas. If you're considering a plunge into the pool of foreign stocks and bonds, you can test the waters here.

Wall Street Direct

http://www.cts.com/~wallst

This "discount financial superstore" gathers brochures from scores of financial service companies all in one place. Browsing the catalog, you'll find listings for software like "MetaStock for Windows" and books like "Fatten Your Wallet". A little clumsy to navigate at times, and don't expect much information without a price tag attached, but the typical investor is likely to find something of interest buried here.

Investment Brokerages Guide

http://www.cs.cmu.edu/~jdg/invest_brokers

Compiled at Carnegie Mellon University, this simple listing of brokerage companies offers a valuable service for the potential online stock trader. You get an alphabetical listing, estimated commission prices, and links to Web sites. Most listings are for discount brokerages like National Discount Brokers and Charles Schwab & Co., but you'll also find some "upscale" entries. A good starting point for the do-it-yourself investor wanting to shop for commission prices.

TIPnet

http://www.tipnet.com

TIPnet is an online information service with lots to offer investors—those who'll invest in a subscription, that is. It looks promising: quote services for the whole gamut of investments (stocks, bonds, mutual funds, options, futures, commodities), company reports and a searchable database that lets you find stocks that meet your specific investment objectives. The good news: Subscriptions seem fairly reasonably priced.

Hoover's Online

http://www.hoovers.com

Hoover's (no relation to Herbert) is an independent investment firm offering popular blue-ribbon profiles on some 1,500 of America's best-known companies. Updated as needed, they include specifics like key personnel, competitors, and financial performance—and they're written in a surprisingly punchy style. Recommended: The searchable database with 8,000+ records. It's simple, concise, and fun to read for potential investors.

Berkshire Online
http://www.growth.com

A (currently) free service of Berkshire International Finance, Inc., this little gem of a site provides timely information (company profiles, research reports, financials, etc.) on small, growth-oriented companies. Companies are organized by industry, so potential investors can navigate easily. The What's New section, along with Daily Market Watch and Commentaries provide up-to-date cutting edge market news. Definitely a find for the savvy investor.

International Finance Encyclopaedia
http://www.euro.net/innovation/Finance_Base/Fin_encyc.html

If you stocked up on ear candy when your Dad suggested you invest in CDs perhaps a trip to the International Finance Encyclopaedia, from Information Innovation, is in order. It's an exhaustive glossary of banking and investment terms, from the familiar to the foreign. The site's greatest strength is the international scope—it covers the stock exchanges, currency, and other money matters relevant to nations large and small.

Chicago Board of Trade
http://www.cbot.com

The world's leading futures exchange has a fattened pork belly of a site here, packed with information. Speculators will find closing prices for commodities exchanges worldwide, and agricultural market commentaries at both midday and closing. The Visitors Center contains histories of the market; a guide to futures market jargon; even a QuickTime movie of the trading floor. Nice graphics to boot, though a bit slow to load.

Net Profit Private Investor Service
http://www.bozeman.com

Portfolio Alert, from Zacks Investment Research, Inc., allows subscribers to receive stock and mutual fund price quotes daily by e-mail for your portfolio. More good news: subscriptions are free (up to 10 symbols). You can also do the work yourself by entering the ticker symbol of the stock you're looking for and getting graphs and prices for your trouble. Another way the Net makes it easier to manage your investments.

The Internet Securities
http://www.securities.com

Eastern Europe has become a promising international market. This fee-based service offers financial news and info to those who want to enter that market. Subscribers can access company profiles throughout Russia and the Baltic States, plus stock quotes. News briefs from Polish and Russian news agencies can tell you about industry growth. Priced by the country, and not cheap, but you can try out some features before deciding on the whole package.

Holt Report Index
http://metro.turnpike.net/holt/index.html

Wheeler-dealers can get a daily dose of financial market activity from this excellent investment resource. From the basics like the Dow Jones averages, to currency and metals trading news, to info on stock options, this could be the individual investor's best friend. Plus: The excellent archive of reports dates back to March of 1995; not long in real-world terms, but not bad for the Web.

Chicago Mercantile Exchange
http://www.cme.com

If you're ready to learn about the volatile futures market, this is the place to start on the Web. The "Merc" (as it's known) stakes its claim as the first of the world's exchanges on the Web. You'll find hot trading of Eurodollar futures, information about new offerings, and the latest quotes and exchange news. Most useful for experienced investors.

RINACO Plus
http://www.fe.msk.ru/infomarket/rinacoplus

For a change of pace (and currency), visitors can discover one of the world's newest and largest investment markets from this Russian securities broker. This is a great

RAMONA AMBROZIC, MARKETING

QuoteCom

http://www.quote.com

Whether it's pork bellies or mutual funds, QuoteCom is among the broadest financial Web services we've found yet (although it needs a better interface). Investors can check PR Newswire or BusinessWire Report for company press releases by industry, finding out if financial results are better or worse than expected. Many services are free but require registration; others are available by subscription.

place to learn about Russia's new brand of capitalism. Documents are in English and well-written; graphics are limited to a few well-placed charts and graphs.

Futures Magazine

http://www.futuresmag.com

The online version of Futures magazine attempts to help investors navigate the murky waters of futures, options, and derivatives trading. It offers articles like "Mining London's Metals Market," lists of upcoming industry events and lots of things for sale (including videotapes like "How to Capture Big Profits from Explosive Markets") to help befuddled buyers pick through the pork bellies.

Stocks

Stock Research Group

http://www.stockgroup.com/index.html

The goal of the Canada-based Stock Research Group is to provide an environment where investors can receive up-to-date stock and investment information. Visitors can read thorough profiles of companies like International Tasty Fries, Inc. By focusing on "small fry" like these, SRG offers an extremely valuable service to smaller investors.

E-TRADE

http://www.etrade.com

This site brings the complexity of stock trading together with the simplicity of the Web. You must pay for an account to do any real business— E-TRADE claims to have the lowest and simplest commissions of any broker, but you can get free stock quotes on a 20-minute delay. Nonmembers can also play the Stock Game: See what you would have made if you were a Virtual Marc Andreesen.

Smith Barney Wall Street Watch

http://nestegg.iddis.com/smithbarney

At Smith Barney's Wall Street Watch Web pages, you'll be surrounded by late-breaking stock market summaries and tantalizing glimpses of the kind of research usually reserved for paying clients, like an overview of the year ahead for small-cap stocks. Each day, a Stock Hit List ranks the ten most-requested stocks, complete with charts. There's even an online IRA Calculator to help you plan your tax-deferred retirement account.

Alert-IPO

http://www.ostman.com/alert-ipo/index.html

Brought to you by Ostman Information and Engineering Service, this online service provides analysis of the Securities and Exchange Commission's database for companies filing for initial public offering. Subscribers get detailed summary reports on the companies that have filed via automated e-mail, so they can research the companies and decide whether or not to participate in the IPO (membership is only $34.95 yearly) Non-members can browse previous months' reports.

WealthWEB

http://www.aufhauser.com

This brokerage site from K. Aufhauser & Company is designed for clients who manage their own accounts. (If you can't balance your checkbook, you're not ready for this.) Once you register for an account, you can get delayed quotes on equity, option, mutual fund, and bond investments; you must be a customer to access most services. The free demo account is worth trying to see if it's for you.

Stock Club

www.stockclub.com

This site is an easy-to-dig treasure trove of all things stock-related (see Figure 10.4). Register first (free), and you have access to, well, everything. Choose from diverse, bustling forums, and a "real-time 3-D virtual trading floor." If you have the voice/avatar software, you can be virtually present at chats between investors, "trading" information on individual stocks. Also: News and forums on broader investment topics. There's even a Young Investors forum: "Kids Only."

Stock Master at MIT

http://www.ai.mit.edu/stocks

The experimental StockMaster at Massachusetts Institute of Technology spits out historical price/volume charts for stocks trading on U.S. markets, with the most recent closing prices and graphs with historical data for some 500 companies—all part of a project masterminded by MIT Artificial Intelligence Lab's Mark Torrance. Also available is the raw data behind each chart, so visitors can download the numbers and do their own analyses.

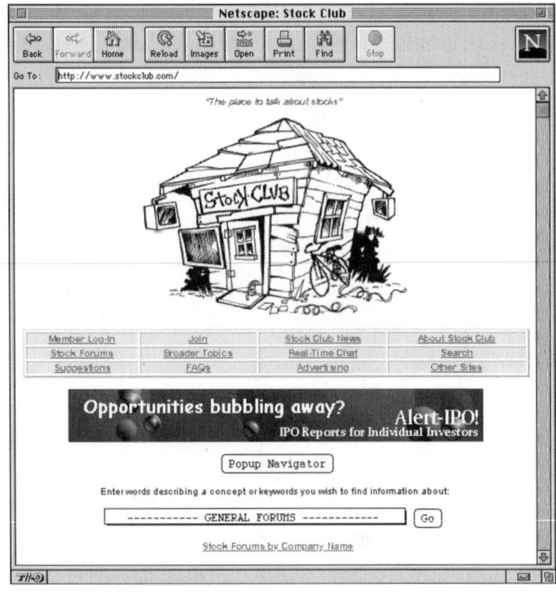

Figure 10.4

Stock Club, *www.stockclub.com*

StockDeck

http://www.stockdeck.com

Corporate information on more than 600 of the largest publicly traded companies can be found on StockDeck. The Corporate Gallery allows surfers to select an industry group and then retrieve an alphabetical list of companies registered with StockDeck. You can also get recent quotes from a select group of stocks. As a bonus, StockDeck throws in a nice hotlist of publications on the Web.

American Stock Exchange

http://www.amex.com

This blue chip site from the American Stock Exchange offers wonderful returns on your investment, featuring top-notch graphics and impressive information. It includes a list of all exchange companies; a news database of AMEX events; and the Information Exchange, a forum on topics like shareholder litigation reform. You'll also find market summaries and a photo gallery of trading in action. At least for now, AMEX has the Internet edge over its competitors.

Home of the H$H Investment Club

http://hh-club.com

The H$H Investment Club is into the high-risk world of making big volume trades on low dollar value companies. This Web site is basically a gateway to the Club's "free" e-mail newsletter. Want in on the action? Read the investment prospectus. Otherwise, a ton of links—to stock quotes, FAQs, and market predictions for the U.S. and Canada—await to entertain those who choose to take a plunge.

The Silicon Investor

http://www.techstocks.com

Look here before investing wads of cash in high-tech stocks (It's free!). Though in its early stages, Silicon Investor helps you track stocks from Adobe Systems to Zycad (charts help the numerically impaired). Follow an industry, a product line, or trends. You can even customize groups worth tracking. Silicon Investor's profiles give the necessary background on companies you're curious about—or, query one of its discussion forums. Expect growth here.

Inter-Quote

http://www.interquote.com

This online stock quote service sells a gateway to its subscription-based services here. Choose from five different packages, from up-to-the-second quotes, to a simple end-of-day service. The real-time service is unique on the Net: Special (free) software lets you watch stocks rising and falling on your screen (a hypnotic experience). You can register for a 15-day trial. For the hard-core investor, this is an innovate use of the Net.

Lombard Institutional Brokerage

http://www.lombard.com

Welcome to the Brave New World of online stock trading. At the Lombard Institutional Brokerage-sponsored real-time trading and information center, traders must register (no cost), and can then buy and sell stocks, options, and mutual funds as well as retrieve 15 minute delayed quotes. The firm is a member of the NASD and MSRB, and it's running a Netscape SSL server (your transactions are secure). All in all, a bold venture.

The Investor Channel

http://vanbc.wimsey.com/~jchow/Magnet/mc/index105.html

The Investor Channel, from Vancouver, Canada, will turn you on to their Hot Stocks—companies they think will be on the move over the next few months. These reviews of firms like California Amplifier, Inc. include a corporate "snapshot," a detailed report, company news releases, and more. Since this is all free of charge, expect to find a bit of advertising here. A small price to pay.

Wall Street Online

http://www.wso.com/wso

Bold claims made by this subscription-based investment advisory service may interest U.S. stock market players. Their electronic newsletter is offered here, with other daily market slants. Samples are provided, and free trial subscriptions are currently offered. Other features include an index of online brokers, financially pertinent Web pointers, and real-time stock quotes.

Corporate Financials Online

http://www.cfonews.com

Investors may find this free service useful because it allows them to peruse the electronic filings and news releases from more than 25 companies (even though not all of them provide the same data). Some biggies like Motorola and IBM are here, but the companies listed are mostly smaller technology-related companies. Often, you can get the latest stock quote and earnings releases—if not, link to the company's home page.

where they surf

Surfer: David Gardner

Co-author of "The Motley Fool Investment Guide" (Simon & Schuster, 1996) and co-founder of The Motley Fool, the popular investment service geared toward individual investors at *http://www.fool.com.*

Favorite Web sites of the moment:

PointCast Network

http://www.pointcast.com

"Really more an application than a web site, but it's a darn useful application. It creates a new screensaver for your machine that is actually an updated news page with the news that you request."

c|net

http://www.cnet.com

"A good catch-all hub for computer users, whether prospective buyers of new computers, peripherals, or software. It's a fine site, and worth clicking in when you want to see reviews of the latest stuff available from computer manufacturers."

Investment Research

http://www.thegroup.net/invest

The folks at the Data Transfer Group have put their investments in order. The best items here for investors are the series of articles about investing, including the excellent Warren Buffett quote, "You won't know who's naked until the tide goes out." You will also find a running series about the MIDAS Method of Technical Analysis, a new way of charting stocks.

PAWWS: Wall Street on the Internet

http://pawws.secapl.com/top.html

This virtual one-stop brokerage and portfolio management server offers you everything from online trading to the latest dish on takeover rumors. (PAWWS is a fee-based subscription service, but you can check the service with an online demo.) The page offers enough details to make your head spin; it also links directly to the APL Quote Server and the National Discount Brokers page.

StreetNet

http://www.streetnet.com

The "street" here is Wall Street, and it will take some street smarts to use this online financial guide to make a killing on the market. Directories of financial resources get you started, but the rest is up to you. Highlights include Selected Stock Information (links to stock markets around the world) and Corporate Portfolios (financial data from StreetNet's business subscribers). Just enough to point you in the right direction.

Security APL Stock Quote Server

http://www.secapl.com/cgi-bin/qs

This slick service provides stock quotes on a 15-minute delay. Enter a stock symbol, call up the latest price, and get links to other spots on the Net where you could order the stock, thanks to Security APL. Avoid loading the graphics here—too slow. Still, the quotes are free, and watching the rise and fall of investors' fortunes can bring entertainment in the best Web tradition.

Mutual Funds

NETworth

100 BEST SITES

http://networth.galt.com

This slick site offers sophisticated mutual fund information and a delayed stock quote server (you must fill out the free registration form). The Mutual Fund Market Manager lets users search a database of more than 5,000 mutual fund profiles, and you can look at a prospectus for a selected fund. You'll like "The Insider," an excellent searchable guide to the Net's financial resources.

Tradeline Investor Center

http://nestegg.iddis.com/mutfund

The Tradeline Investor Center is a hot tip for investors looking for statistical highlights of the mutual funds business. IDD Information Services offers tempting tidbits from its Tradeline electronic stock guides, including lists of the best-performing mutual funds, updated daily. Online information includes full-screen charts detailing performance of each fund, as well as a section for the market's most capitalized funds.

Fidelity Investments

http://www.fid-inv.com

The nation's largest mutual fund company (and second largest discount brokerage) offers useful guides to its services here. You'll find detailed reports on mutual funds, and articles on topics like "What is Your Savings Personality?" You may even find "giveaways" like CD-ROM drives for correctly guessing the rise and fall of the stock market (and filling out a survey). A worthy browse if you're considering doing business with Fidelity.

Strong Funds

http://www.strong-funds.com

The Strong Funds are an assortment of mutual funds managed by Milwaukee-based Strong Capital Management. If you're searching for mutual funds, Strong uses these Web pages to provide a comprehensive rundown on its offerings, including fund profile, you can download. You'll also find a cache of investment tips, including the Eight Basic Principles of managing your portfolio.

Mutual Funds Magazine Online

http://www.mfmag.com

Free registration is required for full access to the online edition of Mutual Funds Magazine (from the non-fund-affiliated Institute for Econometric Research), and it's worth it! In addition to various departments and reader services, feature articles are printed in hypertext with downloadable graphs and charts. Investors can also follow the performance of specific funds via a searchable database with over 7000 entries. If you're into mutual funds, you'll love this site!

The Fund Library

http://fundlib.com/home.cfm

Canadian mutual funds are the main focus, but there's plenty here for non-Canadians. Eye-pleasing graphics and clever organization make it easy to find your way to daily market updates, news flashes, fund prices, a busy online discussion forum, and a well-stocked newsletter list (see Figure 10.5). In the works: Fun with Funds, a chance to test your portfolio management skills. Anyone with an interest in mutual funds would do well to visit this library.

[OVERHEARD ON WOMEN'S WIRE]

http://chat.women.com

"My financial struggles began when I was bedridden for five years in my 20's after the birth of my second child. We had to survive not just on one income but on huge medical and personal caretaker expenses as well.

Although I have worked hard since then, I will always be in a worse financial position than someone who started saving in their 20's and was able to commit a lot of money every month into investments."

WHAT EVERYONE SHOULD DO:

"Spend less than you make. Do your best to get out of debt. Have an investment strategy no matter how much or how little you have. Make sure you are protected from catastrophe."

ON CHOOSING A MUTUAL FUND:

"Check Morningstar. This service rates mutual funds according to how well they have done in the past and how much risk they had to take to do so—You can also ask a financial planner, stock broker, etc.—stay away from your hair dresser or brother-in-law or anyone else who does not do this for a living."

—Personal finance planner Ginger Applegarth, author of "The Money Diet," in a live conference on Women's Wire.

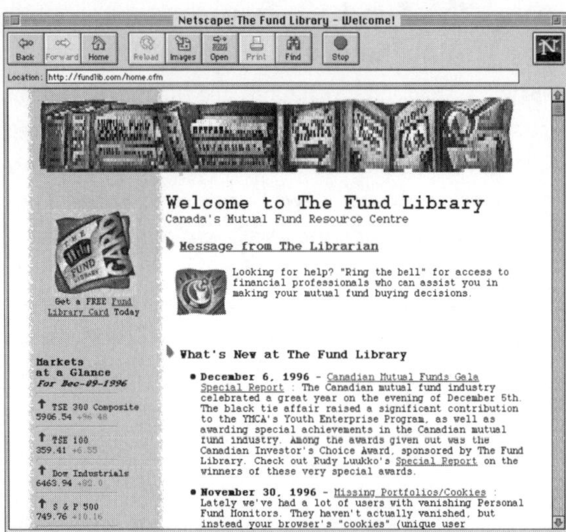

Figure 10.5
The Fund Library, *http://fundlib.com/home.cfm*

The Money Manager Review Page
http://www.slip.net/~mmreview/index.html

This site is the online incarnation of the printed guide to the nation's top money managers. The online version includes short reviews of the top fund managers, as well as rankings according to various criteria. You can also check out a handful of featured managers. For more, you'll have to subscribe to the printed newsletter, but there's enough here for you to see if you're interested.

Mutual Funds Interactive
http://www.fundsinteractive.com/#con

Brill Editorial Services brings you this definitive bookmark-able mutual fund page where you'll find price charts and quotes, links to top financial newswire services and other resources, FAQs, and mutual fund 800 numbers. Collect pearls of wisdom from guest experts in the Expert's Corner, check out fund manager profiles, and much more. It's the all-in-one stop for the mutual fund investor.

TAX PREPARATION

Browse the Federal Tax Code
http://www.tns.lcs.mit.edu/uscode

Here it is, kids: Title 26—the Internal Revenue Code—the rules the IRS plays by. This is complete in a big way: The Table of Contents alone takes minutes to download. (A nifty search interface helps you get around that.) Pick your favorite section, like Subtitle A, Chapter 5—Tax on Transfers to Avoid Income Tax. Volumes (and volumes) of information—your tax dollars at work!

Taxing Times
http://www..com/tax

If you're a little paranoid about getting tax forms directly from the IRS Web site, Taxing Times gives you a lighthearted alternative. It's a public service by Maxwell Labs, a military research company. No rocket science here, just the forms, some links to other tax sites, and a picture of a miniature taxpayer getting the squeeze. Why tax forms from military scientists? Sorry, that's classified info.

NetTax '96
http://www.vni.net/~nettax

You like the idea of electronic tax help, but you're still too scared to visit the IRS site. Here's your compromise solution. NetTax allows visitors to download tax forms and calculates their taxes online. For folks filing a single return, it's a good place to get a second opinion (or check your math). All of the data you enter in the forms is encrypted, so you aren't sharing your financial secrets.

The Internal Revenue Service Digital Daily
http://www.irs.ustreas.gov/prod

Dealing with the IRS just got less complicated. At this fresh, funny site, the folks who make sure you've paid your taxes dispense helpful information—and they're good sports about it. An example: Concise, logical (!) explanations of the tax code. Lots of cool graphics, and navigation is nearly effortless. It may even change the way you view the IRS. If not, it'll give you another way to complain.

1040.com

http://www.1040.com

All the tax information you can eat, from Drake Software. You'll find State and Federal tax forms (save yourself a trip to the post office), late breaking news, and other general information and data. You'll also find links to other sources of tax information. Maybe you'll even file on time this year.

1-800-TAX-LAWS

http://www.5010geary.com

This telephone referral network for tax professionals adds the additional feature of letting you file your taxes electronically over the Web. San Francisco CPA Jerry Newman is behind the innovative service, charging you $75 to $200 for most returns. A good start at what's likely to become the tax filing method of the future.

The Tax Prophet

http://www.taxprophet.com

Robert Sommers, a San Francisco practitioner, created this site to help with the tax law blues (see Figure 10.6). You'll find Hot Tax Topics, like the possibility of a new flat tax on income. Peruse the Tax Prophet's professional record and download any of his newspaper columns published semi-regularly in the *San Francisco Examiner*. Enjoy cool graphics and complete a test to see whether you owe Social Security taxes on your babysitter.

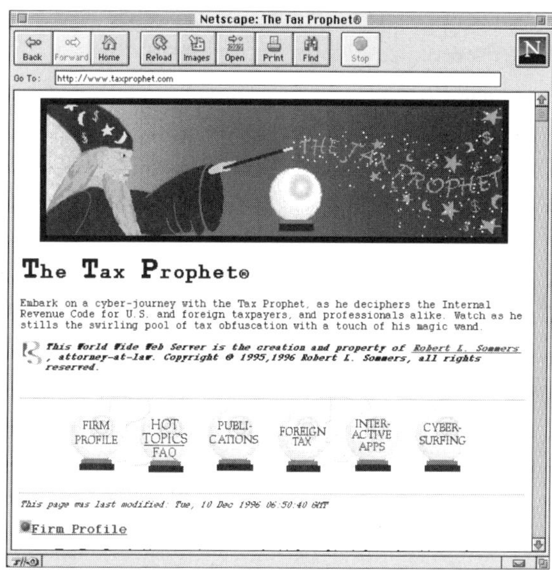

Figure 10.6

The Tax Prophet, *http://www.taxprophet.com*

PERSONAL FINANCE

Financial Players Center

http://fpc.net66.com

The Financial Players Center is an Illinois company bent on spreading the word of financial empowerment to individuals everywhere. At their online spot, you'll find interesting interactive evaluations: Test your financial knowledge, see how much you know about the Time Value of Money, try your hand at the Trivia Questions, and more. There's also a discussion forum and resource list. Impressed? You can register for their curriculum, currently free for first-timers.

American Association of Individual Investors (AAII)

http://www.aaii.org

AAII are providers of educational materials to help individuals better manage their personal finances. Their online presence is helpful, well-organized and can provide a healthy amount of information on financial topics like retirement planning, stocks, portfolio mangagement, and many others. The retirement planning section, for example, covers the topic thoroughly, from "The Myths of Retirement Planning" to "Retirement Investing: A Look at the Tax Considerations." All of this, and no book pitch, either.

Personal Finance Network

http://wwbroadcast.com/pfin

Brought to you by World Wide Broadcasting Network (WWBN), a real-audio news service provider, this true multimedia financial news and advice service gives you a choice. With Real Audio, you can kick back and listen to Daily Briefings on timely personal finance topics. If you're more lo-tech, you get the text version. Check out useful articles in categories like Save & Invest, Women & Pensions, Mutual Funds, and more.

Consumer Information Catalog: Money

http://www.pueblo.gsa.gov/money.htm

It's compiled by the U.S. Government. And it's free. You can send away for the brochures (free or $.50), but most of the information is here at the (text-only) Web site. You'll find basic info on consumer finance topics from bankruptcy to taxes, debt to annuities, fair collection laws to buying a new water heater. If you're doing research on any of these topics, this thumbnail-library will provide some answers.

WomenBiz

http://www.frsa.com/womenbiz

With a home page that crackles with three-deck headlines proclaiming victory for womankind, who wouldn't be inspired by this resource exchange site for the female business owner? Technology, money, networking, advice—they've got it covered. The Money Matters section is especially useful, offering timely articles on investment and taxes, with plenty of room for you to add your two cents.

Hugh's Mortgage and Financial Calculators

http://alfredo.wustl.edu/mort_links.html

Who's Hugh? He's a guy at the Biomedical Computing Institute at Washington University who wants to help people learn how to use their computers to gain control of their finances. His handy empowerment tools include the Simple Savings Calculator, Tuition Savings Calculator, Retirement Calculator, Prepayment Calculator, as well as calculators for more complicated financial transactions. He's also included his own "financial common sense page." Be the master of your financial destiny.

USA Recovery from debt home page

http://www.voicenet.com/~blowry/debt.html

This text-only page features tools and advice for getting and staying out of debt by changing debt-prone behavior. Included are a 12-step plan for getting out of debt, information on credit regulations and laws, plus links to debt FAQs, credit counselors, and related sites. You'll even be asked to consider the possibility that your debt problems are merely a symptom of deeper troubles: See "12 step recovery information for other problems."

Altamira Investment Services

http://www.altamira.com

Altamira is a large Canadian mutual funds company whose Web site offers daily updates on key market indicators in Canada and the U.S. Almost anyone can take advantage of the personal finance information provided by experts (not all from Altamira). Also, an online glossary explains finance and investment terms.

The Screaming Capitalist

http://www.cadvision.com/screaming

The Screaming Capitalist doesn't offer the complete sensory experience its name implies, but you will find some strongly worded investment advice from Canadian financial planner Kevin Cork (see Figure 10.7). In his disclaimer, Cork warns you that he's in the business of flogging investments and insurance, but that his Web pages reflect his personal views on his first love, personal finance. The first big secret of personal finance: "Spend less than you make."

LifeNet

http://www.lifenet.com

LifeNet has a decent amount of information to go along with the sales pitches by some companies that sell investment products, and the site provides lots of tips on home

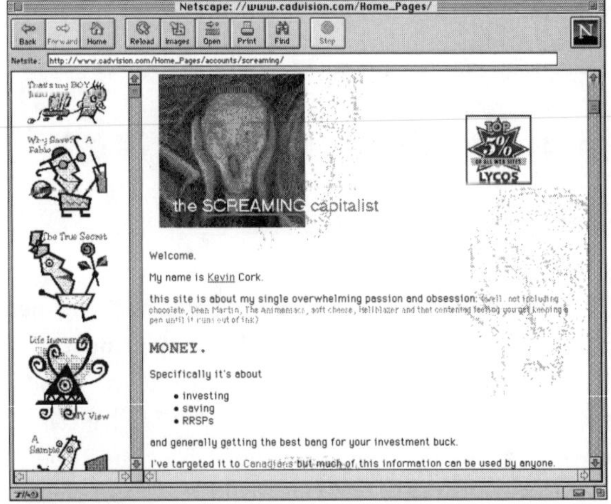

Figure 10.7
The Screaming Capitalist, *http://www.cadvision.com/screaming*

buying, estate planning, and other aspects of personal finance. A nifty feature here: interactive "calculators"—you plug in details about your situation, and they determine how many months it will take to make up the cost of refinancing a loan, for example.

YPN Net News and Money

http://www.ypn.com/mm-bin/genobject/news_money

Your Personal Net, from Wolff New Media, has put together a great-looking magazine-style personal finance site that really lives up to its name. You'll find articles like, "Beyond the Piggy Bank: Learn the Basics of Finance," aimed at newcomers to the money game, as well as a brimming plate of advice, investing and business info, and real-time news and stock quotes. A painless way to boost your financial IQ.

Quicken Financial Networks

http://www.qfn.com

Intuit's official site here focuses on its software for managing personal and business finances. The magazine-style interface features articles designed to convince readers how Quicken and related products will improve their lives. The company has joined forces with GALT Technologies' excellent investors' information site, NETworth. Even non-Quicken users may find financial info they can use here, but Quicken converts will get the most out of this site.

Money Online

http://pathfinder.com/money

This online version of the popular finance magazine is sponsored by Time Warner's Pathfinder site (see Figure 10.8). The good selection of articles here changes weekly, with offerings like "How to Cut Your College Costs in Half" and "What's Hot in the Market." Useful feature: A version of *Money*'s "Best Places to Live in America" which lets you search for your ideal city based on the attributes you think are important.

Consumer World

http://www. consumerworld.org

Consumer Advocate Edgar Dworsky has collected over 1000 useful consumer resource links for your browsing pleasure—and business. From discount travel to mortgage rates, car deals to credit cards, you'll find links that can help you get the most for your dollar. You also get Consumer News (has your computer been recalled?), stock and fund prices in Money & Credit, and much more to add to your smart-money Web arsenal.

Microquest

http://www.microquest.com

This is the home page of the Microquest computer company, as well as the home of InsideTrack investment tracking and analysis software. InsideTrack automatically retrieves your stocks and mutual funds every 15 minutes, notifies you if pre-determined objectives have been reached, records buys, sells, splits and dividends, and more. You can download a free copy of a "lite" version of it here, and you can order it if you're impressed.

FinanCenter

http://www.financenter.com

This super site has all you need to nail down your personal borrowing and investment options. Before you buy that new car or home, for instance, you can calculate the annual cost of ownership including depreciation and insurance. For hints on managing those vexing credit cards,

Figure 10.8
Money Online, http://pathfinder.com/money

you'll have to wait a bit: FinanCenter's still under construction, but the foundation is impressive.

Crestar Student Lending
http://www.student-loans.com

Okay, so applying for a loan can be dehumanizing. This commercial page promises financial aid lending with a personal touch. Featured are virtual guides like Celeste, a fine arts major/gymnast, who will walk you through the entire Crestar lending process, while introducing other options. Students, parents, and guidance counselors will find detailed and worthwhile information here.

NetShare
INTERNATIONAL APPEAL

http://www.netshare.co.uk/home.htm

For those struggling to plan a sound financial future, NetShare stands ready to assist. NetShare was created by Saunderson House Ltd, a financial planning company. The site lays out some excellent investment resources. You can fill out an online questionnaire to get direct insurance quotes along with an e-mail outlining the quotations. Some interesting Britain-only items are included as well.

Nest Egg Magazine
http://iddmz4.iddis.com

This slick stop is the plugged-in version of *Nest Egg Magazine,* your information source for financial survival. The target audience is the upper income bracket—how many other publications can tell you that their marketing plan reflects the coming of age of America's suburbs? Back issues, mutual fund news, and other market info give this site plenty of meat.

Credit Card Network
http://www.creditnet.com

If you've still got space in your wallet, the Credit Card Network offers what are surely the Web's most comprehensive links to online applications for plastic. From VISA and MasterCard to credit cards offered by department stores, oil companies, or airlines, this site helps you apply for them all. You'll also find an extensive database of news reports related to the industry.

Internet Bankruptcy Library
INTERNATIONAL APPEAL

http://bankrupt.com

Bankruptcy attorneys take note! The Bankruptcy Creditors' Service has created a huge index of bankruptcy resources. You'll find plenty here, from Chapter 13 consumer bankruptcy to the latest conferences, organizations, and publications. Also included: a directory of bankruptcy and insolvency professionals from around the world. This is a great guide to going broke.

The Better Business Bureau Web Server
http://www.bbb.org/bbb

The BBB is the place for information on everything from "work-at-home" schemes to complaint reports on local businesses. Plans are in the works for individual bureaus to offer "reliability reports" on area businesses. For now, you can find money-saving tips and advice on refinancing

where they surf
Surfer: Karen Southwick

Executive editor of *Upside* magazine, *http://www.upside.com.*

Favorite Web sites of the moment:

Atlanta Reproductive Health Centre
http://www.ivf.com

"Offers information on women's health issues—everything from fertility to PMS to Pap smears—and a lot of good links to other sites."

Dog-Play: Dog Links to Dog Links
http://www.dog-play.com/links.html

"As the loving owner of a basset hound named Eeyore, I enjoy surfing sites that feature dogs. This site is especially useful because it lists all the major breeds of dogs and links to web sites that feature them.

a mortgage loan. It's also a great place to find the nearest bureau. It's nice to have somebody looking out for you.

Persfin Digest/Personal Finance Web Sites

http://www.tiac.net/users/ikrakow/pagerefs.htmlf

Persfin Digest, a (free) interactive personal finance e-newsletter published by Ira Krakow, attempts to answer subscribers' personal finance questions. If you want to do the legwork yourself, Krakow's monster link collection is a good first stop for anyone searching on the Web for information on financial planning, investing, or saving. As with all great resource directories, if it's not here, it probably doesn't exist.

Deloitte & Touche Online

http://www.dtonline.com

Financial consultants Deloitte & Touche bring you this top-notch guide to personal finance, taxes, and business. In addition to weekly updates of the latest business news, small business owners can find valuable advice from the Small Business Advisor, and everyone else can check out the Personal Finance Advisor. There's a spot devoted to tax news, a well-stocked Library of resources, and don't miss the Tip of the Week.

Financial Advice

Women's Wire Cash Channel

100 BEST SITES

http://www.women.com/cash

Women's Wire puts together a useful package of advice and wisdom on saving, spending, investing, and understanding the green stuff (see Figure 10.9). Dedicated to helping women maintain financial freedom, the site offers regularly updated columns like Ask Cash Flo, Cover Your Assets, and Savvy Spender to help everyone from a starving artist to an heiress manage personal finances. A wealth of plainspoken information.

The Center For Financial Well-Being

http://www.ns.net/cash

Grady Cash (!), "Values Based Money Management" consultant, brings you this ever-expanding site dedicated to improving personal finance skills by re-examining actions and attitudes. Features like Financial Secret of the Week and Deadly Money Mistakes include nuggets of good advice. Cash even explores the relationship between money and happiness. There's enough good stuff here to point you (and your spending habits) in the right direction.

Automobile Leasing

http://www.mindspring.com/~ahearn/lease/lease.html

Al Hearn, kind creator of this no-strings page explains and promotes the benefits of auto leasing based on his own positive experiences. "Who Should Lease?" is addressed, alongside definitions of "Cap cost," "residual value," and other terms. And, should you favor this option, Hearn offers advice on lease negotiation, in theory and real life ("most dealer salespeople don't really understand leases themselves..."). Thanks, Al!

Peter Schmidt, CTA

INTERNATIONAL APPEAL

http://206.29.188.10/pschmidt.cta

This home page of futures investment advisor Peter Schmidt is an addendum to the pages of the Commodities llc brokerage. The aim here is to sell Schmidt's expertise in the commodities markets. Once you get past background graphics the size of feeder cattle, you'll dis-

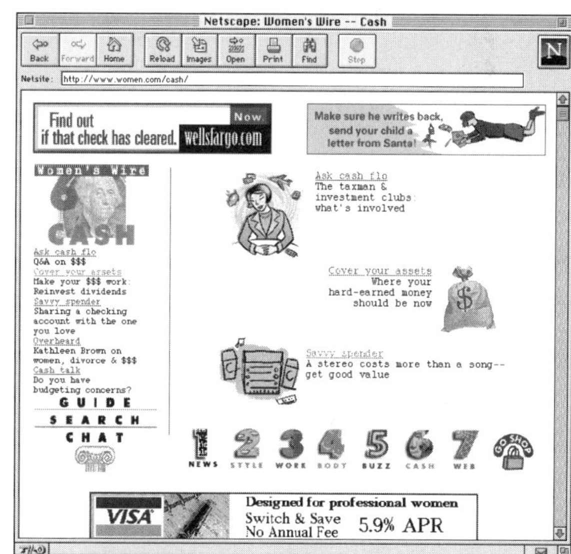

Figure 10.9
Women's Wire Cash Channel, *http://www.women.com/cash*

cover a promo for an investment analysis system Schmidt has dubbed Pathfinder, and a cache of investment wisdom. It's quirky: The Web at its personal best.

Signet Bank College Money Matters

http://www.signet.com/collegemoney

Signet Bank wants to lend you money for college. Ulterior motives aside, give them credit here for the e-edition of their acclaimed "Don't Miss Out: An Ambitious Student's Guide to Financial Aid." Parents and guidance counselors may appreciate the "College Planning & Budgeting" section, info on government programs, and what they call "alternative funding options"—e.g., home equity loans, savings, and investing schemes from (you guessed it) Signet Bank!

Jackpot! What to Do Before and After You Win the Lottery

http://www.note.com/note/pp/jackpot.html

Americans spend over $25.1 billion yearly on lottery tickets. Someone's gotta win, right? Brought to you by Prosperity Partners, Inc., a company that helps people deal with "unusual cash flow," this site offers useful, interesting, no-promises tips for beating the odds, claiming your rightful winnings, and holding on to as much dough as possible after you win. Of course, it's more likely that you'll be struck by lightning. Is that thunder I hear?

Home Banking

Wells Fargo

http://www.wellsfargo.conm/index.html

That stage coach that tore across 19th-Century America is now a California bank cruising the infobahn, offering its customers access to their credit-card histories, checking-account balances, finance news, and more. Stay ahead with Weekly Economic Commentary and News Update. History buffs: Read from the diary of Charles Blake, a Gold Rush era Wells Fargo driver.

Financial Services Technology Consortium

http://www.fstc.org

A research group, co-sponsored by U.S. banks, universities, and the federal government, uses this site to foster support for the new generation of electronic banking. They're looking for ways to improve standards and security so the masses can soon be using the Net to pay bills and manage investments. Big players like Citibank and Chase Manhattan are sponsors. This project is an interesting peek at what's to come.

INTERNATIONAL APPEAL

Banca della Svizzera Italiana

http://www.tinet.ch/bsi/bsien00.htm

Ever wonder what it's like to have a Swiss bank account? Why not contact a Swiss bank? Here BSI—since 1873, the oldest bank in southern Switzerland (and the first Swiss bank on the Internet!)—provides basic info on its branches from St. Moritz to Lugano, and preaches bank philosophy and services including "securities brokerage in Switzerland and abroad." Dream on!

First Union Corp.

http://www.firstunion.com

This forward-thinking bank holding company is serious about "cyberbanking," and they've reserved it as a service mark for future online banking services. This site outlines what you may see, allowing you to "leave your slippers on" while transferring funds, making investments, or applying for a home loan. First Union is asking for input, so now's the time to express your opinion. Don't miss: The Consumer's Guide to Credit.

SAVING

The Dollar Stretcher

http://www.stretcher.com/dollar/index.htm

A weekly offering from family finance columnist Gary Foreman, this entertaining site is a penny-pinching resource (see Figure 10.10). Weekly columns on topics like "Where do we spend our money?" are aimed at saving dollars without losing quality of life. You can check out past columns, or link to other saving sites. Save time, too, by subscribing (free) and having this useful newsletter e-mailed to you every week.

Consumer Prices and Price Indexes

http://stats.bls.gov/cpandpi.html

The answer to the popular question "What is a consumer price index?" can be found here. This site is chock-full of statistics on the prices of food, clothing, and pretty much anything. The Bureau of Labor, which compiles the data,

SPOTLIGHT ON RETIREMENT PLANNING

Time is one of the most powerful tools in the accumulation of wealth. The sooner you start to accumulate assets and plan for your retirement years, the better, and the less you will need to set aside each year in order to achieve the same objective.

Five Facts

1 Among female baby boomers, 20% to 25% are expected to see age 85—twice the number of males who will live that long. The American Association of Individual Investors stresses that with increasing life expectancy, your retirement savings may have to last much longer.

2 Inflation is still the biggest threat to the financial security of retirees. Over a period of 20 years, at 4% inflation, the purchasing power of one dollar falls to 44 cents! From 1980 through 1991 inflation averaged 4.66% per year.

3 Social Security accounted for approximately 38% of average retirees' income in 1990.

4 This year, the average Social Security benefit for all retired persons was approximately $602.00 per month. Although increases in benefits have occurred and may continue to occur, it is likely they may become less generous than they have in the past.

5 Typically, Medicare pays less than half of a retiree's medical bills, and you usually cannot start collecting until age 65.

Five Sites

1 First Union Retirement Information Page offers basic info on investing for the long run.
http://cmg.firstunion.com

2 Retirement and Savings Directory—Retirement Zone is a great resource for all things retirement-related.
http://www.savingsnet.com/retindex.htm

3 American Association of Individual Investors—Retirement Planning offers information on saving, investing, and planning for your whole life.
http://www.aaii.org/finplann/finplanindex.html

4 RetireWeb (Canadian) provides information and resources on financial planning for retirement.
http://www.retireweb.com

5 Maturity USA is a Monthly Web magazine with articles like, "Can You Afford to Retire?"
http://www.maturityusa.com

Figure 10.10
The Dollar Stretcher,
http://www.stretcher.com/dollar/index.htm

gets most of the info through personal interviews. Yet another labor-saving device for comparison shoppers.

The Sensible Saver

http://www.sensiblesaver.com

Mark W. Miller wants you to invest in his newsletter on how to save and invest your hard-earned cash. Though this site plugs the publication, Miller provides some useful goodies right here, like his weekly $aving Tips (one great tip: check your credit report for errors), and free special reports on request. Selected articles and back issues from the newsletter are here, too, and might even convince you to subscribe.

Retirement Planning

International Association for Financial Planning (IAFP)

http://www.iafp.org

This international membership association is aimed at both industry professionals and individuals working toward their financial goals. The site is straightforward, amounting to a collection of informational brochures online. It's a thorough collection, though, and a useful one. You'll find Financial Tips for everyone from young professionals to retirees, pointers on looking for a financial adviser, important facts about retirement accounts, as well as resources to turn to for further information.

American Savings Education Center (ASEC)

http://www.asec.org

The American Savings Education Center is a partnership of private and public sector institutions dedicated to educating Americans on savings issues and providing help in achieving savings goals. The site features useful Savings Tools, articles covering topics like the importance (and widespread ignorance) of 401(k) plans, an up-to-date calendar of savings/planning related events (like the AARP's retirement planning series), and links to other useful Web sites. Control your retirement destiny.

REAL ESTATE

Homeowner's Finance Center

http://www.homeowners.com

If you're clueless about covenants, appurtenances, and ARMs, this page can help you unravel the mysteries of the mortgage. First-time buyers will get a kick out the mortgage calculator, which instantly computes monthly outlay using the interest rate of your (or more likely, your lender's) choice. You even get daily updates on economic factors affecting home loan rates. Even pros will appreciate the useful tips on buying and refinancing.

International Real Estate Directory and News

http://www.ired.com

The International Real Estate Directory and News (IRED) is not just a terrific jumpstation to some 5,000 real estate sites on the Web. It's also an online magazine jam-packed with articles that both buyers and sellers will find useful. As an independent source for real estate information on the Web, IRED also keeps tabs on the industry's use of the Internet. IRED looks like a good source for good research.

Cyberhomes

http://www.cyberhomes.com

Cyberhomes introduces a nifty approach to house-shopping across the U.S., backed by data from regional multiple-listing services. Shop for a home by clicking on a map of your chosen state, then zoom in on a community until you can see its streets. Select price range and features to come up with your dream home. Links to other Web sites to provide information on weather, population stats, and attractions in each region.

Homes and Land Electronic Magazine

http://www.homes.com/Welcome.html

This site from Homes & Land Electronic Magazines offers true nationwide (U.S.) home shopping, and what it lacks in depth it makes up in quantity. Click on the state and city you want, then browse the brief home descriptions and agent names and phone numbers. Most useful for those moving across the country, or wanting to compare notes on home values.

The Appraisal Institute

http://www.realworks.com:80/ai/index.htm

If you're looking for an appraisal on your property, this site can get you started. The Appraisal Institute is a training institute, so course descriptions and enrollment information are provided here. Additionally, you can find an online index of publications, audiovisual resources, software, and textbooks for sale. The handy search engine will locate a registered appraiser by name, company, or location—a nice online treatment of the topic.

Consumer Mortgage Information Network

http://www.pacificrim.net/~proactiv/cmin

This site, brought to you by consumer information and product provider ProActive, is dedicated to using technology to help demystify the home-buying process. Here you'll find software (and some freeware) that you can download to calculate mortgage eligibility, financing estimates, and more. You'll also have (free) access to information, articles, and resources pertaining to mortgage and home buying, as well as links to real estate listings. Be an informed consumer.

Real Estate Listings

HomeScout

http://homescout.com

The Cobalt Group brings you a service that lets you search the more than 300,000 homes listed on the Web through one central database (see Figure 10.11). Narrow your search by choosing location, price range, and other relevant info, and then view (pictures, too!) your future dream home. There's also a library of helpful tips and articles to help you in your search. If you surfed here would you be home by now?

Rent Net

http://www.rent.net

RentNet is just what you think it is: a service that lets you search the 1,095,000 rental listings in the U.S. and Canada. Search by location, number of bedrooms, price, and other keywords. Something new: View 360, which lets you "step in and walk around" many of the apartments in major cities. There are links for moving van services here, too. Everything you need for a smooth move.

Figure 10.11
HomeScout, *http://homescout.com*

BUSINESS AND SMALL BUSINESS

Inc. Online

http://www.inc.com

This familiar handbook for entrepreneurs has made good use of the online medium by providing services beyond its monthly magazine articles. Some examples: The Virtual Consultant, featuring interactive worksheets, searchable databases, bulletin boards, and resources; and Beyond the Magazine, offering the rare feature of material written expressly for the Web site. If Inc. Online readers are as forward-thinking as its creators, they'll undoubtedly achieve the level of success outlined in these pages.

Bank of Montreal

http://www.bmo.com

The home page of the Bank of Montreal is a doorway to some great resources for small businesses—even those that don't bank in Canada. The Virtual Head Office section offers strategic planning tips and info on entrepreneurial success. The "office water cooler" leads to discussion groups on business topics. The bank has reserved other space for students, including a personal budget calculator: Compare your spending habits with those of the "average" student.

CAPEX Capital Exchange, Inc.

http://www.broker.cube.net/capex.html

CAPEX, based in Munich, Germany, introduces those who think they've invented that better mousetrap to people who have the kind of money it takes to turn an idea into a business. Would-be entrepreneurs can fill out form-based business plans describing their ventures. Financiers can then monitor the CAPEX databases for promising investments. It's a nifty idea that's still fun reading for those of us who are simply nosy.

The International Small Business Consortium

http://www.isbc.com

This site provides a listing of the 1,000 or so members of the International Business Consortium, an association of small businesses around the world. Potential investors or customers are invited to browse through a database that includes cashmere exporters in China, furniture manufacturers in England, and incense manufacturers in Thailand. From here you can jump to over 30 international trade organizations, as well as general business and finance sites.

FinanceHub

http://www.FinanceHub.com

If you're an entrepreneur looking for dough, you'll find not only a listing of venture capital firms here, but links to pages on banking, law, investing, consultants, and advice. If you've got money to invest, check the searchable listing of ventures in fields from software to microbrewing. Currently, entrepreneurs can list for free, but a small maintenance fee looms on the horizon. Well-researched links make this a useful stop.

The Business Page

http://www.sgn.com/4sale.html#TOP

International opportunities abound here, from distributorship of revolutionary concrete products to partnership in a Hanoi supermarket. Offbeat investors will enjoy pondering prospects like a Swedish robotic device to assist in brain surgery, and a line of Spanish undergarments "designed to create a sense of calm in office workers." You can place your own classified ad, too.

Trade Point USA

http://www.tpusa.com

One stop on a global network of "Trade Points" designed to foster international trade through the dissemination of information and coordination of effort, Trade Points like this site offer support to smaller businesses aiming to compete in the big leagues. Free services include an Export Guide, a tutorial for fledgling international traders. Other goodies—like analysis from experts like Dun & Bradstreet—require subscription to the I-TRADE information service.

All Business Network

http://www.all-biz.com

The MarkeTech Group Inc. has compiled lists of resources on the Web in an effort to help surfers with a business bent save valuable time. You'll find useful articles, such as a piece on overcoming public-speaking anxiety. You'll find the usual links to business news services and job banks, plus a collection of online business databases. Worth a visit if you're serious about mixing the Web with work.

Entrepreneurial Edge Online

http://www.edgeonline.com

"Finding Affordable Health Care for Employees" is an example of articles you'll find at this e-zine for entrepreneurs. A few of the features are sneakily disguised ads, but there are so many articles per issue that they don't intrude much. The resource list includes links to help you develop ideas, resolve legal questions, and find venture capital. That combination laundromat and bowling alley of your dreams may be within reach.

Small- and Home-Based Business Links

http://www.ro.com/small_business/homebased.html

As the title suggests, this site is a list of connections to places that can help you with your small or home-based business. The Reference section contains helpful links to places like the Small Business Administration and the Home Business Review Magazine. If you don't have such a business and you're looking to get started, check the Opportunities and Franchises sections.

INTERNATIONAL APPEAL

Canada/British Columbia Business Service Centre

http://www.sb.gov.bc.ca/smallbus

The Canada/British Columbia Business Service Centre was designed to help beginning entrepreneurs set off on the right foot. The "Online Small Business Workshop," will be useful to fledgling tycoons everywhere. These comprehensive, tutorial-style pages cover techniques for starting a new venture or improving an existing one, with tips on researching your market, managing a payroll, and more. Can't find anything of use here? Your business probably isn't that small anymore.

Business Resource Center

http://www.kciLink.com/brc

If you're trying to start or expand a business, it's well worth spending a little time at what was formerly the Small Business Help Center. You'll find tips on marketing and setting up management plans; and if you want to do business with the government, the useful Government Contract Glossary can help you. Articles are top-notch and the Quote of the Week is a fun feature.

[OVERHEARD ON WOMEN'S WIRE]

http://chat.women.com

"What you were kidded about as a kid often contains clues as to what is different and special about you. For example, my mother was always teased about talking on the telephone and she used that to start a successful business. Find out what is special about you and then use it to differentiate yourself."

—Rebecca Maddox, author of *Inc. Your Dreams,* in a live conference on Women's Wire.

Black Enterprise

http://www.blackenterprise.com

Though largely a subscription pitch, this online supplement to a magazine aimed at African-American businessfolk contains some useful articles. It's more entrepreneurial than corporate, with articles about the pitfalls of running a home business and "The ABCs of Online Banking." Though rarely taking an overtly political tone, Black Enterprise is about empowerment.

The Small Business Journal

http://www.tsbj.com

The Small Business Journal is a magazine for entrepreneurs and small business owners. Its Web site features complete back issues to browse while you decide if you should subscribe. Recently, tax expert Roy Mitchell explained how the IRS determines who's next in line for an audit. Other pieces covered topics like selecting software to manage a small business, and maintaining a professional image as a home-based captain of industry.

Entrepreneurs on the Web

http://www.eotw.com

This eclectic list of links includes sites that promise to edify you on concepts like "Chutzpahology," and how to "Protect Your Idea Before Someone Steals It." The advantage of this listing is that it's very long; entrepreneurs looking for resources are likely to find something useful here—perhaps the Global Trade Center or the Internet Business Center. And why not explore business opportunities in Hawaii if you have the time?

Empowerment Zones and Enterprise Communities

http://www.ezec.gov

What do the Rio Grande Valley, Chicago, and Jackson County, Florida have in common? They're all empowerment zones or empowerment communities, where the federal government is trying to stimulate economic growth. This site is the official page of the program. Discover resources for businesses in EZ/EC areas, including tax credits and tax-exempt bond financing. It's a slick setup with lots of details on whom to contact to participate in the program.

MoneyHunter

100 BEST SITES

http://www.moneyhunter.com

MoneyHunter is a great resource for entrepreneurs seeking funding. Get the scoop on who's on top in the investor/entrepreneurial world, advice from leading business experts, and even download "the internet's most popular business plan template." The Web site will be joined by *The MoneyHunt Show* on PBS beginning in January 1997.

Cyberspace Field of Dreams

http://www.gridley.org/~imaging/links1.html

Gives the term "leveling the playing field" new meaning! This site is dedicated to helping women in business get past first base with resources, articles, advice, news, and freebies. Read "How to Network," then join the e-mail discussion group for support in achieving your dreams.

American Individual Magazine and Coffeehouse

http://aimc.com/aimc/foyer.html

Here's a publication for serious bootstrappers, with its emphasis on "following your own path." This Libertarian publication provides well-organized, useful tools, tips, and resources for all stages of the entrepreneurial/small business venture. Try out the (free) Virtual Business Cards, or stop in at the Roundtable to share ideas with others. Unique feature: You can download an Adobe Acrobat version of the magazine to read in the bathroom.

Franchise Source

http://www.axxs.com

There are hundreds of franchises listed here, each with general statistics such as how many stores are in the franchise and what the start-up cost is. Listings are organized by title, subject, and start-up cost, and if any of them awaken your entrepreneurial spirit, you can have info sent via postal mail for free. Also on the site is the rapidly growing Entrepreneur's Law Center.

Home Business Solutions

http://netmar.com/mall/shops/bopps.html

This "virtual shop" offers resources for people who have started, or who want to start, a business at home. Learn of "businesses that you can start on a shoestring," get "dirt cheap printing" on promotional postcards, and more—all at this location. A business library contains articles like "What To Do When Your Partner Lets You Down," and free tips are scattered among the items for sale.

SOHO central

http://www.hoaa.com

The name stands for Small Office/Home Office and the site is the online headquarters of the Home Office Association of America, the national organization for full-time, home-based professionals. They'll show you lots of reasons why home-based businesses are such a fast-growing trend. Includes updates on news, new products, links to home-office related sites and benefits of membership in the Association (including useful perks like airline discounts and free tax/accounting checkups).

BUSINESS NEWS

Bloomberg News

http://www.bloomberg.com

Need to monitor changes in the Dow Jones, the Nikkei, and the Hang Seng Index at a glance? Business news service provider Bloomberg's Web site allows you to do just that. Bright green "GO" buttons bring you to news on world markets, detailed analysis on industry trends, growth rates, or info on the Personal Business Magazine. In terms of financial news and analysis, they don't miss a trick.

Municipal Bond Scandals—The Web Site

http://lissack.com

Michael Lissack used to toil as a senior banker for Smith Barney. Now, Lissack throws the spotlight on alleged fraudulent practices in the municipal bond field. You'll find an extensive inventory of articles from familiar news sources detailing one bond market-related scandal after another, including reports of federal regulators scrutinizing Lissack's former employer, Smith Barney, in relation to a 1991 New Jersey municipal-bond issue.

Financial News Center

http://www.finnews.com

The Financial News Center is home to the News-A-Tron Financial and Commodity Reports. Hosted by Newswire Syndication Inc., the News-A-Tron offers up-to-date information on commodities markets. Daily data for prices on futures is available for paying subscribers. For another $89.00 a year, subscribers gain access to the site's Future Focus data, which attempts to forecast next week's trends. Non-subscribers can access old reports and forecasts.

INTERNATIONAL APPEAL

Weekend City Press

http://www.news-review.co.uk

If you're pressed for time but want to read business and financial news summaries from the British weekend press, this is the site for you. The Weekend City Press Review gathers news articles from 12 British newspapers and synthesizes them into short paragraphs. The summaries include leading Buy, Sell, and Hold recommendations of the London weekend papers and key weekly share tips from Friday's authoritative *London Investors Chronicle*.

Briefing

http://www.briefing.com

Can't afford the pricey information services the Wall Street traders use? Try Briefing, a scaled-down version of Reuters, Bloomberg, and their ilk. The stock and bond tickers, briefs, and market news here are free and frequently updated. You'll also find long-term outlooks and forecasts. Political winds blow here, too. If you don't mind a bit of stridently Republican editorializing, this is a quick and easy way to pick up financial facts.

100 BEST SITES

CNNfn

http://www.cnnfn.com

Cable News Network's all-business channel has loads of fast-breaking business scoops in the site's News In A Hurry section, plus continuously updated indicators from stocks and commodities markets. And if you can't get enough of "Moneyline" host Lou Dobbs, this is the place to hang out. Most fun: The Grapevine, where Webmasters cover the lighter side of business news, like Hoover's Dirt Finder vacuum with its built-in microphone to help detect carpet crud.

Fortune

http://pathfinder.com/fortune

This goldmine includes some excellent articles from *Fortune* magazine, but the mainstay items are its Fortune 500 and Global 500 profiles of the largest corporations in the U.S. and world. These lists are far more useful here than in print, allowing you to search the database and view rankings by different criteria. Lives up to its name as a "one-stop corporate scorebook."

Financial Times Group

http://www.ft.com

An abbreviated version of the *Financial Times* is better than no version at all. The *Times* is a London and world institution in economic journalism. Published Monday through Saturday, the Web version has each day's top story, news briefs, and a technology article ("Journey to the heart of cyberspace" was one recent story). The paper prints a U.S. edition and has its own American Web address.

Barron's Online

http://www.barrons.com

Barron's print edition content, fully duplicated here—including market perspectives, investment ideas, and expert insights for individuals—was free of charge until recently. Now, you'll have to subscribe to get "piping hot," fully framed e-issues by 8:00 AM each Saturday morning. Newbies can take a guided tour through the regular columns, to other features like mutual fund dossiers, stock performance snapshots, and Barron's New York Stock Exchange Report.

Business Wire

http://www.hnt.com/bizwire

The Business Wire home page is popular with journalists: The corporate news is about as fresh as it comes without an inside source. Business Wire is a leader in the delivery of unadulterated corporate press releases to investors, online databases, and the news media. See what the big stories looked like before the *Wall Street Journal* reporters added verbs.

GINA GURRUBBO, SALES AND MARKETING

Wall Street Journal

http://www.wsj.com

Faithful *WSJ* readers have flocked to the savvy online version for good reason. For $49.00 vs. $29.00 a year for print subscribers, the *Wall Street Journal* online delivers 24-hour updates of business and news. Personal investors and those with a keen interest in the movement of national and international markets will want to take advantage of the personalized portfolio updates which allow you to track current stock prices and mutual fund growths.

BusinessWeek

http://www.businessweek.com

If you want the latest word on the best business schools, mutual funds, or hot business books, try *BusinessWeek Magazine*'s online site which is updated every Thursday evening. Business-savvy women will appreciate the "Women and Business" feature, wherein women can search through the past year's archives to read such articles as "Shatterproof Glass Ceilings." An additional incentive for reading the magazine online: readers will find both the U.S. and international versions of this financial publication at their fingertips.

Bloomberg News Radio

http://www.bloomberg.com/wbbr/index.html

Bloomberg's 24-hour news radio station now comes to the Internet through the Streamworks rea-time audio player (non-Mac versions play rudimentary video, too). These are live broadcasts, the same ones you'd hear if you switched on the radio. If you're out of range of a Bloomberg affiliate and you absolutely must have your business news—here it is! In any case, this is one of the best business news services available, with Bloomberg's general news and sports material online via Streamworks as well.

Financial Scandals

http://www.ex.ac.uk/~RDavies/arian/scandals.html

From the collapse of Barings Bank in the U.K. to Whitewater in the U.S., this site is a jumpstation to information on financial scandals available elsewhere on the Net. Webmaster Roy Davies has compiled a fascinating index to high-profile financial intrigues as well as to background information like the role of forensic accountants. You'll find an international mix of impropriety—and then you'll go bury your money in the garden.

Asia, Inc.

http://www.asia-inc.com

Asia, Inc. Online corresponds to the print magazine *Asia, Inc.,* which covers the doings of businesses in the Far East. These slickly presented pages include a joint venture with news service Knight-Ridder to provide daily updates on international finance (see Figure 10.12). Feature articles cover topics like India's underground bankers and Japan's economic future. Lively writing makes these pages fun for dilettantes as well as for execs with an interest in Asia.

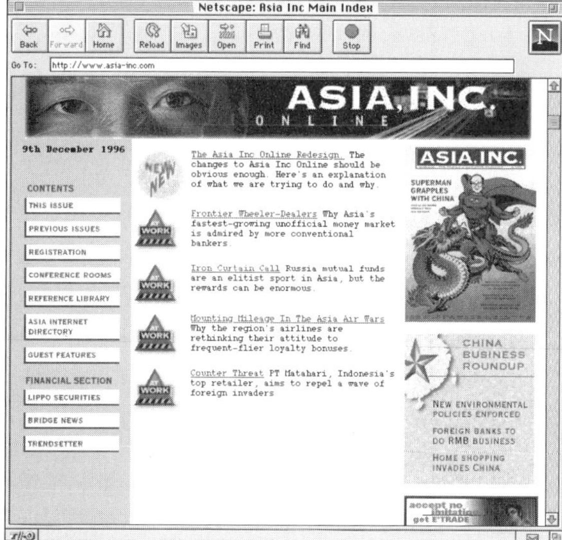

Figure 10.12

Asia, Inc., *http://www.asia-inc.com*

NAFTAnet

http://www.nafta.net

NAFTANet is a privately operated meeting place for small businesses hoping to cash in on opportunities resulting from the North American Free Trade Agreement (NAFTA). The site's comprehensive list of links to other sites containing news and regulatory information on NAFTA and the General Agreement on Tariffs and Trade (GATT), as well as a searchable online company database, makes it a useful international trade resource.

NewsPage

http://www.newspage.com

This impressive business news service lets you scan 25,000 pages of newspaper and trade magazine articles, and they're updated daily. Access to story headlines and news briefs is free, but to get full stories, you'll need to pay a monthly fee. Non-subscribers may find it useful to have a gander at the briefs. In addition to gaining access to the whole enchilada, members get to run searches of all NewsPages articles.

BizWomen

http://www.bizwomen.com

BizWomen, founder Marianne Babiera-Krammel's remedy for what she felt was a shortage of Web sites for women, mixes links to business news and information sources with opportunities for women to have an online presence. A good idea, but it could use some more depth in the coverage of business issues specific to women. The liveliest additions may be the business notices some members are already posting.

Worldclass

http://www.goldtiger.com

The people behind the Web pages of Worldclass have put serious effort into their guide to hundreds of business-related sites on the Net (see Figure 10.13). Most of the links you'll find here are accompanied by descriptions to help you determine if the trips will be worth the effort. The Worldclass Webmasters hand out Golden Tiger awards each month to the "best of the best" on the business side of the Web.

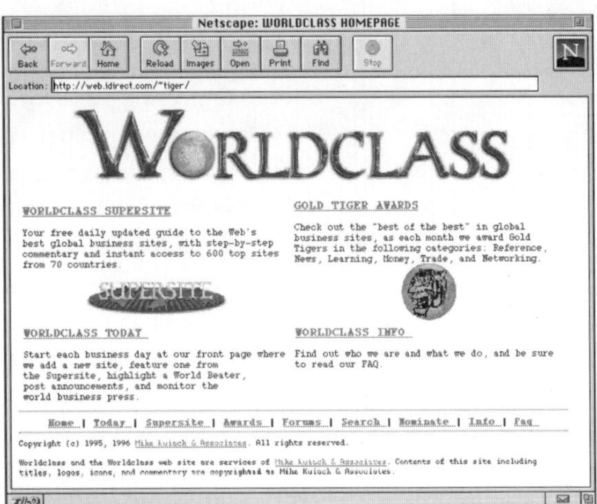

Figure 10.13

Worldclass, *http://www.goldtiger.com*

News Alert

http://www.newsalert.com

When you absolutely have to keep track of the business world—and don't mind paying to do so. This service of newspaper giant Knight-Ridder gives full-text access to financial news, including Hoover profiles and Moody's Reports. Investors wanting to stay abreast of world markets will find the latest news plus stock quotes and more, and you can take a demo spin before deciding if News Alert is for you.

Reuters Business Alert

INTERNATIONAL APPEAL

http://206.4.74.17

If British media giant Reuters is trying to hide this site, it shouldn't. Business Alert provides some great news updates from selected countries, and specific industry news for the financial world. They're trying to sell the product, which is up-to-date reporting, but you can take advantage of the freebies that are here. Reports from other countries (like the American automobile industry) are on the way, too. A hidden gem.

Dow Jones Business Information Services

http://dowvision.wais.net

The electronic publishing arm of Dow Jones provides news and information services to business people, students, and private investors. These services send you business news updates for a monthly fee. DowVision, for example, will update you, or your company, about news in your field or market. Not much in the way of sample demonstrations, but there are links to other sites, like the *WSJ* and *Smart Money* magazine.

Forbes Magazine

100 BEST SITES

http://www.forbes.com

The original "Capitalist Tool" hits cyberspace. Nearly all, if not all, articles in current paper issues are available here (including special editions like ASAP and FYI), arranged in an interesting format: Features are spread out over the month corresponding with each issue (you couldn't read it all at once anyway, right?). And just like the old faithful mag, articles cover current movers and shakers in corporate America, and what makes them tick (or fizzle).

Upside

http://upside.master.com

Tired of hearing about computer/new media moguls raking in millions at the age of 15? No? Good. Upside has just what you want: A fly-on-the-wall view of the high tech corporate world, with its tales of rollercoaster growth and obsolesence. Read about today's layoffs, mergers, and IPOs in Daily News, find out who's behind them in People, link to stock quotes, and more. Be an insider, or just feel like one.

1. Hunt for your dream house.
   http://www.cyberhomes.com

2. Do some caviar dreaming at Jackpot! What To Do Before and After You Win the Lottery.
   http://www.note.com/note/pp/jackpot.html

3. "Play the Stock Market Game" with real market prices and $100,000.00 worth of "game money" at E-trade.
   http://www.etrade.com/html/visitor_center/game.htm

4. Check out the Grapevine at CNNfn: the lighter side of business news.
   http://cnnfn.com/hotstories/bizbuzz

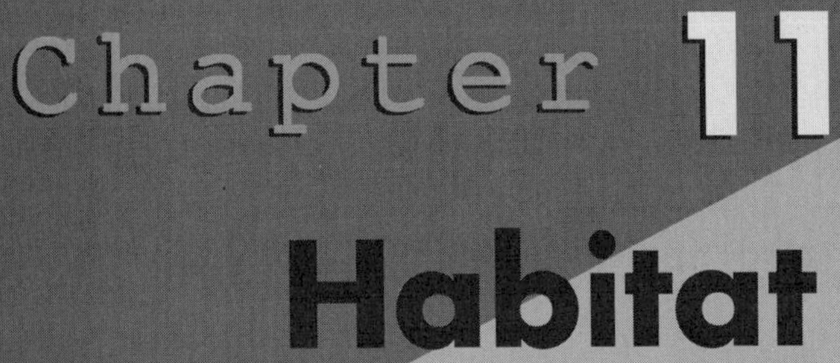

Chapter 11
Habitat

HOME IMPROVEMENT

DECOR

AUCTIONS, CLASSIFIEDS, AND REAL ESTATE LISTINGS

ENTERTAINING

COOKING

GARDENING AND HORTICULTURE

HOBBIES AND COLLECTING

PET CARE

10
HOME-BOUND THINGS YOU CAN DO *RIGHT NOW*

1. Turn your basement into a winery or a microbrewery.
   http://www.mono.org/~ritchie/wine/begin.html
2. Get your closet organized with products from the Container Store.
   http://containerstore.com
3. Adopt a whale.
   http://www.webcom.com/~iwcwww/whale_adoption/waphome.html
4. Grow orchids in your house.
   http://sciserv2.uwaterlooo.ca/orchids.html
5. Learn techniques to marbleize a wall.
   http://www.serv.net/faux
6. Make a birthday present last all year with monthly deliveries.
   http://www.800.flowers.com/reference/feature-flower/index.com
7. Plan a cigar party.
   http://www.cigarworld.com/library/la-2a.htm
8. Find out what it takes to add decorative ceramic tiles to brighten your kitchen or bathroom.
   http://hometimes.com/pc1.htm
9. Toilet train your cat.
   http://www.sff.net/people/karawynn/cat/catfaq.htp
10. Find a recipe that you saw on the Cable Food Network.
    http://www.foodtv.com/index.htm

As we near the millennium, the concept of "home" is changing—the need to have a comfortable refuge has become essential. Some Americans are choosing to work at home, and those that work in an office want to spend an increasing amount of their free time at home.

People are spending more time and money than ever before to improve and beautify their living spaces. For nesters, the Web contains information on design techniques, furniture, and hardware; it saves trips to the library or bookstore and can connect you to local designers and suppliers—all from your computer.

Even shopping for a new home can now be done on the Web, with virtual tours of houses. Live antique auctions are held online, offering items from all over the country.

Recipes abound on the Web and so, too, do celebrity chefs. Getting your hands on Julia's famed Peach Strudel no longer requires writing to her television program—you can now access it immediately.

Gardeners, botanical garden-snoopers, doll collectors, model-train enthusiasts—even snake lovers—can find sites devoted to their passion, and chat rooms to meet others that share their interests.

The transformation of "home" in this increasingly technological era is two-fold: The Web can help you turn your home into an office or fitness or entertainment center; the Web can also allow you to spend more time just enjoying your house and your family, by saving time and energy outside of it.

HOME IMPROVEMENT

Books That Work

http://www.btw.com

Offering home and garden CD-ROMs, this site covers a lot of ground: gardening, landscaping, home improvement, automobiles, and real estate (see Figure 11.1). The software is a great planning tool, including everything it takes to build a garage and map out a garden. Playing around with the CD-ROMs is actually much more fun than the project itself—wood and cement blocks move effortlessly and money is no object!

Paint It Yourself: Faux Finish Instructions

http://www.serv.net/faux

Marbleize a wall, sponge-paint a door, distress a piece of furniture. Techniques on how to create these popular effects are detailed in step-by-step instructions. If the instructions are not enough, work-in-progress photos are posted and, as a last resort, you can call their technical support hotline. The finishes you need can be bought here, too.

Hometimes

http://hometimes.com/pc1.htm

Brighten your kitchen or bathroom by adding decorative ceramic tiles. Visit the popular PBS home improvement show's online site, Hometimes, and access directions for this and other projects. Everything is outlined, from choosing the tile and carefully planning the layout to installing and long-term maintenance. Tons of other do-it-yourself home improvements are painstakingly detailed.

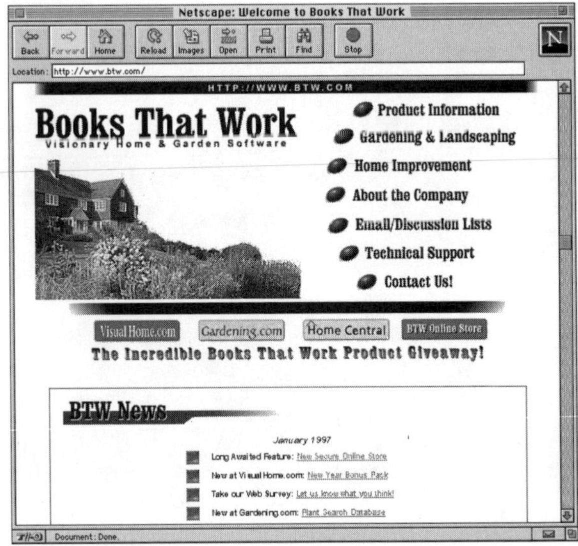

Figure 11.1
Books That Work, *http://www.btw.com*

Handyman Hints

http://ic.net/~epn/handyman.htm

Subscribe to Handyman Hints journal and get quick uncomplicated answers to nagging questions. Search the archives for loads of information including America's master handyman Glenn Haege's articles, which include everything from Get Rid Of Condensation to Ten Projects That Could Save You Money (And Your Life).

The Healthy Office

http://www.generalbusiness.com/cgi-bin/gb.cgi/healthy_office/healthyoffice.html

It's too bad that not every workplace designer visits this site before wedging people into their spots at the office. When you are designing your own area, you can address the things that, if unchecked, could lead to physical problems. Visit the useful Infobriefs for data detailing how to avoid repetitive strain injuries, back problems, and vision damage.

The Container Store

http://containerstore.com

The Container Store offers all the products you will need to transform a chaotic closet into a peaceful refuge for you clothes. This company has been shaping up closets for close to 20 years, so, although yours may seen unsalvageable, this online store can help. Pictures of their products at work are posted, but your best bet is to order a catalog online so that you can flip through a hard copy.

The Sharper Image

http://fir.enet.net:80/cgibin/WebObjects/SharperImageCatalogue/SIHome.wo

A great place to buy gadgets for home. Could you use a digitized tie rack that rotates like the racks at dry cleaners? Or do you want the longest range cordless phone? This Web site will let you peruse 100 of their unique goods which make living more techie and often easier.

INTERNATIONAL APPEAL

Metropolis Online

http://www.metropolismag.com

An entertaining, beautiful site dedicated to design—from bike racks and public housing to furniture. But this site is a teaser—you must subscribe to read it ($19.95 for 10 issues in the U.S.). A recent issue was dedicated to the design of health care facilities. Design lovers will really appreciate the content.

Net Tips

http://www.nettips.com/homepage.html

Are you about to venture into a home improvement project? Net Tips offers supply guides for do-it-yourselfers. Although the site was still evolving when visited,

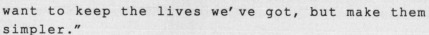

[OVERHEARD ON WOMEN'S WIRE]

http://chat.women.com

"Barbra Streisand simplified by getting rid of five of her seven houses. The person next door may simplify by getting a Honda instead of a BMW.

"It's not about dropping out and going to the woods. It's not about leaving the community. We want to simplify where we are. We want to keep the lives we've got, but make them simpler."

—Elaine St. James, author on the trend toward down-shifting (or "voluntary simplicity").

among the information offered was ways to tackle tacky walls, hints on how to keep your home safe, and the best tool choices.

Black & Decker

http://www.blackanddecker.com

You need tools to be a Ms. Fix-It. Black and Decker has always been a faithful place to turn for long-lasting ones. Loads of helpful product information are here. And step-by-step directions on how to build your own furniture, including a computer desk. You will also find tips for the bride-to-be. Definitely women-targeted.

The Rubbermaid Site

http://home.rubbermaid.com

Rubbermaid keeps rolling out helpful products to make our living easier. Come here to find the latest innovations. Yes, this site was designed to sell Rubbermaids goods, but we can all use some help when it comes to organizing, entertaining little ones, and, well, just keeping clean. You can't order online, but locating a store near you is available and you can order catalogs online.

Owens Corning

http://www.owenscorning.com/owens/around

Selling products to improve and maintain your home, such as insulation, housewrap, roofing, and vinyl siding, the Owens Corning site is great for home improvements. The site's The Front Porch section offers advice, a place to exchange stories, or just listen in. And the Literature Rack archives how-to principles, products, and advice. Just about any home building material you can think of is here—as well as a bunch you didn't know you needed.

Laughingbirds Mega Tips: Cleaning Tips

http://www.laughingbirds.com/tip.html

Laugh away your worries of spoiled, soiled goods. This web site offers creative and quirky solutions to cleaning just about anything. The tips are listed in a simple and rather dull 1-2-3 manner that you scroll through until you find one that applies to you. Unfortunately these creative solutions offer no mercy to mildew, grease, and lime deposits. Also check out Laughingbirds cooking, pet and organizing tips.

HearthNet

http://hearth.com

In the interest of "Fire and Comfort," this retailer-manufacturer consortium, HearthNet, has created an information stockpile on fireplaces, pellet stoves, BBQ grills, and other wood burning appliances. Visitors can expect features such as a generic "How to Install a Wood Stove" guide. Earth friendly home owners will also appreciate articles like "The Real Cost of Oil—Think it through."

DECOR

The Frank Lloyd Wright Page

http://www.mcs.com/~tgiesler/flw_home.htm

Are you are a fan of the modern style of Frank Lloyd Wright? Learn about his minimalist decor and furniture here. Not all the Wright linking sites work, but the ones that do will give you a good overview as well as offer reproduction mail-order goods.

HomeArts

http://www.homearts.com

This family-oriented Web site from the Hearst Corporation is dedicated to beautifying homes (see Figure 11.2). HomeArts offers access to the resources and columnists of Hearst magazines such as Good Housekeeping and Country Living. How-to articles for home repair, decorating, and techie-friendly living spaces are accessible. You can also post questions to Hearst's appointed experts on a range of subjects including, of all things, love. Especially good for homebodies and married folk.

Home Office Design

http://www.ccsi.canon.com/creative/homeoffice/index.html

Need to design a space for a home office? Canon's Web site offers the complete how-to. Here the planning process evolves as it should, allowing your work to define your work space. And just so you know you can trust Canon's ideas, a six-step design process is demonstrated as a case study. You be the judge.

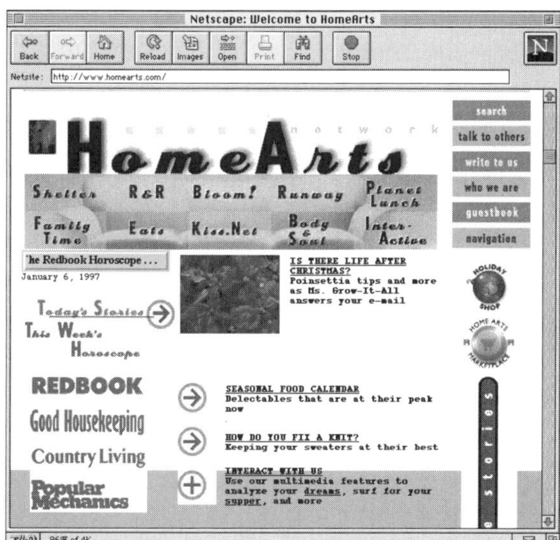

Figure 11.2
HomeArts, *http://www.homearts.com*

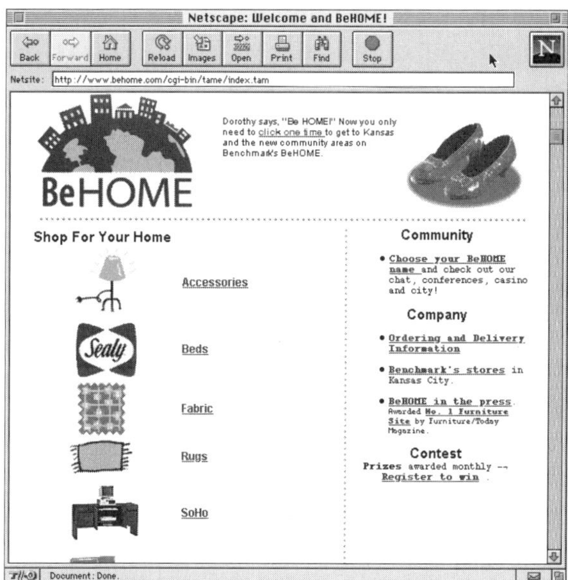

Figure 11.3
BeHome, *http://www.behome.com*

Skaff's Oriental Rugs

http://www.channel1.com/skaffrugs/index.html

A family business promoted online thanks to the grandson of the founder. Catalogued by index, a visitor can view over 70 small-to-intermediate sized Turkish, Persian, Caucasian, and Turkoman carpets for purchase from home. If you have any questions regarding the rugs on view, you can contact the company via e-mail Lots of information about the fine art of carpet making is here so its worth visiting if only for an introduction.

BeHome

http://www.behome.com

Not many magazines admit they are magazines and catalogs wrapped into one, but this site has no qualms stating its purpose (see Figure 11.3). BeHome offers furniture shopping online and a slew of decorating tips. It was created by Benchmark Home Furnishing, a retailer that would also do well as a Web site designer. Rather than posting static photos of their goods like most furniture retailers, BeHomes content is frequently changing. The products and content are presented in a lively, beautifully illustrated way.

INTERNATIONAL APPEAL

ArtNet

http://www.artnet.com

Go gallery shopping online, and fill up your home with your favorite artists work. If you haven't visited ArtNet and are a fan of fine art, you are missing out on the way the art world is evolving online. Thanks to the services provided here (which were propriety until last year), galleries can post their shows and asking prices over the Internet. You no longer need to travel the world round to attend gallery shows.

George Smith

http://www.georgesmith.com

If you read decorating magazines, you have definitely run across the venerable English furniture maker George Smith's advertisements. Even in the clutter of magazine advertisements, George Smith's lush fabrics jump off the page. Unfortunately, the site's graphics do not do justice to the fine textiles, but it is still a good place to visit to get an idea of what is offered. A special attraction: old Turkish kilims used as upholstery, transforming any sofa into a work of art.

Furniture Direct

http://www.furnitured.com/dens

Furniture Direct may need to jazz up its Web site and most definitely the photos of products, but, if you want to purchase hand-crafted furniture from the Furniture Capital of High Point, NC, check out this site. Here the middleman has been done away with, so the furniture is offered at a lower price. Delivery is nationwide and the furniture will be set up by the time the delivery people exit your home.

Ansel Adams: Fait Lux

http://bookweb.cwis.uci.edu:8042/AdamsHome.html

A site dedicated to the black and white photography of Ansel Adams—bring the majesty he captured home to adorn your walls. As you view his famed photographs, a recording plays with Adams describing each one. This site is a great place to visit to better understand his viewpoint, develop your own for his art, and, if one or two catch your eye, there are linking sites that allow you to buy prints.

Prints Plus

http://www.printsplus.com

A great place to shop for prints to jazz up a room that doesn't require fine oils. Over 1200 prints are offered at Prints Plus 150+ stores across the country, but here you can view and purchase effortlessly from home. An index lists prints by specific artists such as Klimt and Matisse and in more general categories such as African American art and celestial. Many linked sites give historical data about artists and movements.

Book Stacks Unlimited

http://www.books.com

Creating a library? Stack it from the convenience of your own home. Close to half a million books are offered, including a nice selection of home decorating titles. A search engine is provided to hunt for books, and order online through Unlimited's secure server. Noteworthy features are the daily newsletter Book of Days, which features the brief history of a famous author, and the Worthy Reading section that suggests a book and provides critics' reviews.

Collegian Fashionable Decor

http://www.spub.ksu.edu/ISSUES/v099B/SU/Preview/OFF.CAMPUS/pre-decorating-janney.html

Going off to college or packing up your teenager to do so? This site will help with decorating tight spaces on a minimal budget. Created by a trustworthy source—college student from Kansas State University—Collegian Fashionable Decor is basically a list of decorating tips (such as that lighter colors like beige or light gray make a room look larger) and other information about all aspects of creating a homey, familiar atmosphere away from the homestead—right down to buying used furniture.

Home Furnishing Netquarters

http://www.homefurnish.com/NHFA

This is a retail furniture trade association that offers links to a variety of retailers such as Pier 1, The Bombay Company, Domain Home Fashions, and Hudson Discount Furniture. The Netquarters also doles out very useful furniture first-aid advice, design ideas and details of trends in furniture. And, if you are in the trade, you can join the National Home Furnishing Association.

American Society of Interior Designers

http://www.interiors.org/one.HTM

Member Interior decorators for both residential and commercial spaces can be reached via this Web site. The Society's 1-800 contact numbers are posted, or you can fill out a form, listing your specifications, send it online, and the association will suggest a decorator or two to you.

INTERNATIONAL APPEAL

National Decorating Products Association

http://www.pdra.org

The National Decorating Products Association is a nonprofit trade affiliation of locally owned paint and decorating stores all over the U.S. and internationally. NDPA's 3,500 professional members can offer you advice, personal service and quality products for every paint, wall covering, window treatment and floor covering project (see Figure 11.4). Don't miss the decorating articles, updated weekly. For professionals, become a member and be privy to industry happenings.

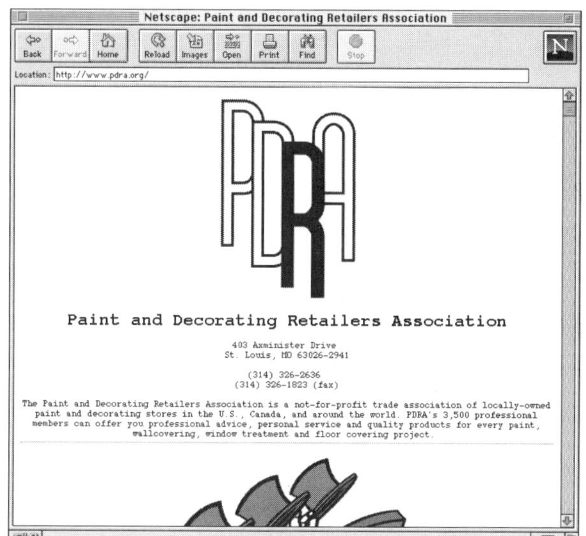

Figure 11.4
National Decorating Products Association, *http://www.pdra.org*

i3

http://www.i3.se

i3 is a forum for those interested in furniture and interior design. At i3's designers' site, visitors can search for information by design pictures, designers or manufacturers. Publications and essays are available under Skrift and commercial pages are ergonomically located, but a click away.

Architecture and Building Net Resources

http://www.nscee.edu/unlv/Libraries/arch/archhome.html

When in doubt, always refer to a professional—if you need advice for architecture and building, you'll find it here. Web resources for alternative design, real estate information, and interior ideas are provided at this site, courtesy of the libraries at the University of Nevada, Las Vegas.

Internet for the Fine Arts

http://www.fine-art.com

This site specializes in online sales of fine art reproductions by a variety of artists worldwide. Prices will seem steep to those accustomed to buying their posters in shopping malls, but many prints represented are limited editions from famous artists like Pablo Picasso. And even those who can't afford the more expensive prints will want to register for periodic online giveaways.

Indesign

http://www.intergate.bc.ca/business/indesign

Plain curtain rods hidden beneath layers of fabric just don't cut it anymore—drapery hardware and accessories have become increasingly stylized. Indesign manufactures fancy accoutrements for curtains, in a variety of finishes and styles. These solid wood accessories have been antiqued to give the impression of elegant aged wood. Choose from Indesign's line of French or Classical hardware, to add a delicate European flair to your home.

ArtSource

http://www.uky.edu/Artsource/artsourcehome.html

Anyone with an interest in art on the Web is liable to be sucked into this site for hours. Mary Molinaro, library director at the University of Kentucky, has produced a "selective, rather than comprehensive" catalogue of art and architecture-related pages. Visit to find valuable home decor tips and the latest in architectural design.

World Wide Arts Resources

http://www.wwar.com

Aside from offering links to more than 250 museums worldwide, 560 galleries and exhibitions, 50 publications and 40 arts-related institutions, visitors here can locate fine furniture dealers. You can shop for antiques or—if you think grandma's armchair in your attic is really a Chippendale—contact a dealer.

The Antique Gallery

http://membrane.com/chestnuthill/antique_gallery/index.html

The Antique Gallery was established in 1982 and has evolved from Philadelphian dealer Gerald D. Schultz's private collection to a place where many can post what they are selling. Offering ceramics, glass, paintings, bronzes, and antiques from the English arts and crafts movement, this is a great site to browse if you are a collector of antiques or want to unload a few. All you need do in order to post a product online is send a photo and pertinent information to Schultz.

Antique Alley's Dealers

http://www.bmark.com/aa/index.html

Explore Antique Alley's exquisite shops. If you just want to browse, each shop has a link to a color catalog of merchandise. There is a wide range of goods with prices and styles to suit all tastes. If you know what you're looking for, Antique Alley's search engine generates custom picture catalogs based on the criteria you provide. And if you want to venture outside, the antique shop guide lists the names, phone numbers and addresses of over 35 thousand antiques shops and dealers nationwide.

AUCTIONS, CLASSIFIEDS, AND REAL ESTATE LISTINGS

WorldWide Classifieds

http://wwclassads.com/home/a04010.htm

You can find a little of just about anything at this evolving site. WorldWide Classifieds offers a way to sell unwanted goods or promote your services. Two categories, Home Furnishings and Home Care Products currently have sparse offers. Ads such as Pro Leather Restoration and books on how to become a decorator are listed. Online classifieds are new, so be patient.

eBay Auction Web

http://www.ebay.com/aw

A modern-day tag sale and a 19th century trader wrapped up into one. Auction Web is a do-it-yourself auction house that brings together buyers and sellers. Charging only 10 cents per trade, this site monitors the activities as you sell and bargain for goods. It is a brilliant (and easy) way to get rid of old stuff cluttering your home and fill it with new. (Just think, you don't even have to make a tag sale sign!)

Phoebus Action Gallery Online Auction

http://phoebusauction.com

An upscale auction house based in Virginia. Phoebus is the middle person here; everything has to be delivered to them before it is hocked. If your item is acceptable by Phoebus and sold at auction, the Internet version of bidding is as exciting as traditional auctions. The downside may be the shipping cost to get your pieces to Phoebus.

Homebuyers Fair

http://www.homefair.com/home

Whether you are planning to rent or buy a home or apartment, this site is a great place to visit. The Fair's mission is to help you save as much money as possible when buying, selling, or relocating. Therefore, salary and moving calculators are offered to keep you on track, along with first-time buyer and mortgage information. If you are a real estate agent, the Broker section will be of interest to you.

INTERNATIONAL APPEAL

HomeSell

http://homesell.com/index2.htm

Want to avoid a brokers fee when selling your home? The Internet now offers you an outlet in addition to the traditional listing of your home in a newspaper. For a small fee, you can post pictures of every room in your home, the exterior, yard, and all pertinent info at HomeSell. Currently, HomeSell posts houses for sale in the U.S. and Canada, with plans to expand to other continents in the near future.

HomeNet

http://www.intertel.com

This real estate shopping page lets you sit in your $89,000 3-bedroom rancher in Manhattan, Kansas, and shop for a $649,000 3-bedroom loft in Manhattan, New York. HomeNet will make any New York/New Jersey home shopper happy with its uptown design and downtown ease of use. Thumbs up for the reports on school districts and neighborhood home values, but the grainy black-and-white pictures need work. Still, one of the best real estate sites around.

Cyberhomes

http://www.cyberhomes.com

Cyberhomes has unveiled a nifty approach to house-shopping in communities across the U.S., backed by data supplied by regional multiple-listing services. On a recent visit, the virtual doors had just opened and Cyberhomes was still adding information for many states. Aside from the listings, linking sites provide information on weather, population, services, and attractions in each region. This site will improve as more listings are added from other areas of the country.

ENTERTAINING

The Unofficial Martha Stewart Home Page

http://www.du.edu/~szerobni

This site is devoted to Martha Stewart, the often intimidating competent arbitress of good housekeeping, and it will appeal most to confirmed fans: It contains a mixed bag of Martha links, including book reviews, articles, and recipes. You can also find such engagingly trivial items as a People magazine interview with Stewart's Connecticut neighbors (they don't like the film crews that camp out at her estate). Lots of fun.

Beertown

http://www.aob.org/aob

Start and run a home brew club. Thanks to American Homebrewers Association, beer clubs are popping up all over the country. Starting one is a great way to meet new friends, learn more about the drink and enjoy interesting flavors of brew. Recipes for versions such as Bohemian Pilsner, Basic Dreher Vienna, and Raspberry Cider are posted here to help get you started. Once you have concocted your own flavors, you can trade recipes online with members of brew clubs nationwide.

The World of Macanudo and Partagas

http://www.cigarworld.com/library/la-2a.htm

No longer the province of males, today women are also enjoying a good smoke. Cigar-makers Macanudo and Partaga's Web site offers general entertainment tips. The specifics of a cigar party's menu and bar are not spelled out, so you will have to go to another source for help.

Southern Living

http://pathfinder.com/vg/Magazine-Rack/SoLiving

Visit the online home of the entertaining articles from Southern Living. Each issue of Southern Living also contains stories on gardening, home improvement, and decorating projects, and food, as well as other subjects that reflect the way Southerners enjoy life. The design of a traditional Southern gala offers wonderful tips that can

where they surf

Surfer: Tricia Nelson

Net personality and avid surfer, as well as a writer at Disney Online.

Her favorite sites of the moment:

Cafe Los Negroes

http://www.losnegroes.com

"The online hub for news, columns, gossip and fashion with a 'cybernegroidal' flair."

Crayon

http://www.crayola.com

"A great way to keep up with newspapers and noteworthy publications on the Web. Also satisfies my need to surf news, gossip, entertainment and 'cool' sites in some sort of orderly fashion every day."

be molded to fit your get together, wherever you are whooping it up.

Planning a Cocktail Party

http://www.angostura.com/barmans.htm

Angostura aromatic bitters has created a Web site full of party-giving tips (see Figure 11.5). The information is quite entertaining and very useful, especially for those not well versed in cocktail party etiquette. A well-stocked bar is detailed at great length, from the booze to the tools and accessories. The Six Basic Rules about mixing drinks are very handy, and suggestions and recipes for hors d'oeuvre a treat.

Rolling Your Own Sushi

http://www.rain.org/~hutch/suchi.html

Throw a sushi party complete with green tea. And make the rolls yourself. Mark Hutchenreuther leads you through the world of fishy delicacies, from California Rolls to Stuffed Fried Bean Curd Bags. Dishes are carefully described and Hutchenreuther provides helpful diagrams, but the lack of photos is a handicap.

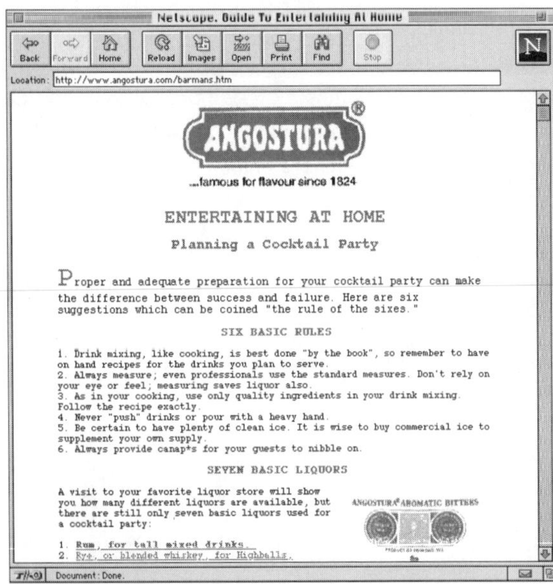

Figure 11.5

Planning a Cocktail Party,

http://www.angostura.com/barmans.htm

Clambake Celebrations

http://www.netplaza.com/plaza/strfrnts/1004/storepg1.html

Clambake Celebrations will whisk a fresh lobster to your office party or home doorstep overnight—complete with claw-crackers, bibs, and wetnaps. Choices range from a pot of soft-shell steamer clams, to a seaweed-lined crustacean extravaganza. The company has been in business for 10 years and guarantees that every lobster, clam, or mussel that hops on Federal Express has been hand-picked and quality checked. If you are landlocked and long for seafood, get online.

The Wine Making Pages

http://www.mono.org/~ritchie/wine/begin.html

This Web site offers all you need to start producing vino at home. There are no kits to order here, but all the equipment you will need is listed along with the ingredients and instructions. Even if you turn out to be a failure at the wine making game, a bottle of wine is always a nicer holiday gift than a fruit cake.

Virtual Vineyards

100 BEST SITES

http://www.virtualvin.com

If God is in the details, He (or She) probably spends time at Virtual Vineyards. Founder Peter Granoff, an experienced enologist, gives great advice on wines produced by small, well-respected wineries and makes it easy to order a case of Chardonnay to match your taste buds. If you choose, you can become a wine snob by visiting the interactive "tasting chart" of a wine's seven perceptions (oak, complexity, etc.), so that you can discuss and choose perfect vintages every time.

Michael Jackson's Beer Hunter Online

http://www.beerhunter.com

Although basically a plug for brew connoisseur Michael Jackson's CD-ROM, there are many recipes and reviews of home-brews from North America and Europe. Many of his home-brews come with nicely illustrated, well-written histories of the ancient recipes. It is a great site to visit to trade recipes with others.

Great American Beer Club

http://www.greatclubs.com/recipes.html

Woman certainly can't live on beer alone. Yes, this is a brew club, but also a super site to visit for recipes of food to indulge in with a brewski or two (either mixed into the stew or not). Italian sausages, chili, and casseroles all with the magical ingredient of beer will give you a buzz based on aroma alone.

The Captain Morgan CyberShip

http://sportsworld.line.com/demo/captain_morgan/index.html

The charm of these advertising pages for Captain Morgan Original Spiced Rum is that they often seem as if they were designed by a teeny bopper reared on MTV alone—lots of entertainment references and general silliness. Get past the inevitable shiver-our-timbers pirate speak and there's some fun stuff here. The site tells you, of course, how to mix up drinks with the Captain, and it's also got some recipes for foods with rum in them, like Grilled Calypso Shrimp.

Cocktail

http://www.hotwired.com/cocktail/96/45/index4a.html

This dynamic, highly graphic site offers drink recipes for unique or classic spirits (no Jello shots here), a bit of the history and folk lore behind each drink, and how-to suggestions concerning serving them. Cocktail is a part of Hot Wired and the text can slant towards the too clever by half approach but, if prepared, it is entertaining.

The World of Tea

http://www.stashtea.com

This Web site offers everything a tea lover could hope for online. The latest breaking tea news, history dating back to 2737 BC, recipes for tea of all seasons, exotica teas, tea-friendly bed and breakfast inns, and even site visitors' confessions of flamboyant uses of teas and the bags. (Don't ask. Go see for yourself.)

Japanese Green Tea

http://www.daisan.co.jp/cha2e.htm

The Japanese custom of drinking green tea came from China about 800 AD when Buddhist monks, who had gone to China for study, returned to Japan bringing tea with them as a medicinal beverage. Green tea was touted as the "elixir that creates the mountain-dwelling immortal," from that point on. Buying the long life-giving claim or not, it is still a flavorful and soothing drink for anytime of the day. Visit this site for the entire history.

The Tea Man

http://www.teatalk.com

The tea man has done some traveling. He can tell you about Chinese, Indian, and Japanese tea. Yes, this is a commercial tea site, but the creator's excessive adoration of the brew is clear. An entire encyclopedia and worldwide history is given. The many health benefits listed just may force you to test his medicinal tea theories. Aside from caffeine, it couldn't hurt.

Coffee a GoGo

http://www.illuminatus.com/fun/agogo/coffee_a_gogo.html

Presented in a 1950s version of the typical diner, here is all a good, old fashion diner could offer. Unpretentious chat about beans and brewing, history, the pluses and minuses of caffeine, shopping, and free samples.

Over the Coffee

http://www.cappuccino.com

Over the Coffee is for brewed bean enthusiasts and professionals. There is a reference desk, a search engine for 700 venders and a variety of discussion groups. A good deal of the information here are personal comments posted by site visitors.

Classique Image

http://www.partysupplies.com/ideas

Throwing a successful party is all about lists. Despite the cheesy name, Classique Image offers useful, straightforward tips for event planning and invitation mailing. You can print out a thorough check list that will whip even the most disorganized into shape and even learn what you need to throw a piñata party.

Tuppertime

http://www.tupperware.com

No, Tupperware parties didn't go out with the Cleaver's. Believe it or not, they still exist, offering a social way to make extra dough. Tupperware selling has moved out of the living room, and into gymnasiums where the pliable goods are used to fundraise. There is no chipping, cracking, breaking, or peeling at this site, but the noisy burp-and-seal demonstrations are sure to make any 1950s female prototype blush.

COOKING

Epicurious Food

http://www.epicurious.com

Magazine mammoth Condé Nast's Web site is, as the tagline reads, "for people who eat." It offers vast culinary information gleaned from its print magazines: Gourmet and Bon Appetit (see Figure 11.6). Tips from restaurants, diet fare, and scrumptious recipes (ranging from day long preparation events to completed under an hour) are easily accessible on this well-designed site. Also invaluable are the resources that cater to wine connoisseurs and beer snobs. If you possess a fondness for consumption, you will be satiated here.

Cornucopia!

http://www.mnsinc.com/cornucopia

They want to be your "Horn of Plenty," prodding you along the way to becoming an artist in the garden and the kitchen. This "basket full of gardening and culinary tips" hasn't quite left the shaping hands of the weavers yet, so it's still a little bit light on hints. One little fun feature is Cornucopia's tireless pithy-quote generator, called the "Fortune Cookie." Showing promise, it's worth a look even at this early stage.

The Gourmet Connection E-Zine

http://www.norwich.net/~gourmet/link1.htm

Despite the "gourmet" title, what distinguishes this cooking site from its fellows is an emphasis on health: its articles cover such subjects as food-borne illnesses and the medicinal uses of cayenne pepper. It also includes useful items like a recipe conversion chart (so that Americans can cook up British recipes without puzzling over what a "gas mark" is) and a calorie counter for supermarket and restaurant foods.

Grouchy Cafe

http://www.echonyc.com/~cafehrk/cafe.html

The name couldn't be more misleading. Your hostess/waitress, "Cafepark," is a completely pleasant woman, who runs this pretend Internet New York diner like it was a cable-access TV show. She bemoans New York's lack of a breakfast mentality and the apparent nonavailability of "spiritual breakfast" dishes, like Tofu Scramble, the recipe for which is included here, direct from Portland, Oregon's fabulous Bijou Cafe. Grouchy offers many other unique recipes for those who are experimental.

Figure 11.6
Epicurious Food, *http://www.epicurious.com*

The Dinner Co-Op

http://dinnercoop.cs.cmu.edu/dinnercoop/homo-page.html

More than 1,500 links to gastronomic delights await at the Dinner Co-Op, hosted by 15 funny folks in the Pittsburgh area who simply love food. Start with the group's mind-boggling assembly of favorite recipes, like "Sweet Noodle Kugel" and "Mango Rum Cake." The site features an excellent search engine. Links go to places like a culinary 'zine called Electronic Gourmet Guide, which features, among other things, a hopping good piece on homebrewing.

The Internet Chef

http://ichef.cycor.ca

When you're told the Internet Chef is "an electronic archive dedicated to the worship of food," you know you're not going to be getting a simple recipe list. This site of recipes, etc. is maintained by people who love food—and not just eating it, either. Possibly most interesting is the searchable "How to repair food" section of Tips and Tricks, which describes what to do when your food goes horribly, horribly wrong.

FoodWine.Com

http://www.2way.com/food/egg

The fare here ranges from classical country club menus (pheasants, turkey) to more exotic cuisines. For more exotic recipes go to the Global Gourmet cookbook section. American Wine is considered one of the most knowledgeable spots to choose wines. An all too short collection of toasts is posted to help you wow the crowd at your next formal get together.

The FOODplex!

http://www.gigaplex.com/food/index.htm

The highly amusing and artfully written site is part of the gargantuan Gigaplex entertainment complex. Shindler starts off slowly, pondering the imponderables (there are apparently 14 "H's" in a typical bowl of alphabet soup), then moves through Noshes & Nuggets to Mouthwatering Morsels. Don't discredit the serious food info, although the site is a tad goofy.

Yum Yum

http://www.yumyum.com

Looking for a recipe? Yum Yum has over 10,000 creative and delicious recipes categorized by types of cuisine. It is

[OVERHEARD ON WOMEN'S WIRE]

http://chat.women.com

ON TRACKING DOWN GOOD RESTAURANTS:

"I like browsing the amateur restaurant reviews. I tend to browse the reviews on America Online (AOL). I browse what people are saying about restaurants in New York and wherever else I'm traveling. I don't always believe professional reviews—not everyone is as picky as reviewers are. Lots of people leave a restaurant happy, which is nice to read about. And they're more honest about their basic feelings. They write candidly about what turned them on and what turned them off. So you can find out a lot about a restaurant."

—Tom Douglas, the self-described chubby, tall, middle-aged executive chef of Dahlia Lounge, Palace Kitchen, and Etta's Seafood in Seattle, WA. Check out his Web site at http://tomdouglas.com.

easy to find what you are looking for thanks to a search engine that allows you to hunt by ingredient in each category. Also worth viewing is Yum Yum's entertaining and gardening advice.

Copycat Recipes

http://www.netins.net/showcase/medca/copy.html

If you've ever been overcome after hours with a craving for a bucket of KFC fried chicken, help has arrived in the form of this page. In addition to some of the Colonel's best-kept secrets (buttermilk biscuits, anyone?), Copycat Recipes offers up a how-to for Long John Silver's fish batter. A must try is the guide to creating our own, at-home version of the Olive Garden's 5-Cheese lasagna.

Recipe Archive Index

http://www.cs.cmu.edu/~mjwl/recipes

The title says it all: Recipes range from appetizers to pasta to vegetarian dishes. Most come from the rec.food.recipes, newsgroup. Don't expect Julia Childs-type frills or virtual aromas here—it's just ingredients and instructions in plain text. But the recipe for jambalaya will make your mouth water nonetheless.

Cheesenet

http://www.wgx.com/cheesenet

Cheesenet offers a database of over 60 cheeses accompanied by cheezy verbiage and photos of the yellow stuff. If you are gaga about cheese, visit its Fun with Cheese section that offers games, puzzles, and trivia contests, or the Cheese Literature section to submit or read poems, short stories, and plays. Ode to the Big Cheese?

Caviar & Caviar, Ltd.

http://virtumall.com/Caviar

Pearls of the sea, regal roe, oviparous jewels...fish eggs? That's right, and the finest in the world, according to this page from Virtumall's online shopping service. Beluga still reigns as top sturgeon, having little salt ("malossol" in Russian) and a delicate skin. Get plenty of serving tips. Prices for the delicate ovum range from $4 to $61 for a 2 oz. jar.

Herbed Cheese Pretzels

http://miso.wwa.com/~dougp/pretzel.html

Cookin and Computing web site offers lots of great recipes including one that adds a twist to the old pretzel recipe. This recipe adds several cheeses and some of the dried green stuff to jazz up the original recipe circa 610 AD. As most recipes do, this one bring you thorough the steps but also offers photo illustrations.

Snax.com

http://www.snax.com

The Snack Food Association—the self-proclaimed voice of the American snack food industry—has set up this web site in the apparent interest of finding out what kinds of snacks surfers like best. The site lures potential survey respondents with prize offers and with some fun, frivolous fare. It's probably not endorsed by the American Heart Association, but given the eating habits of many of the Web's mouse potatoes, it's certainly appropriate.

Sally's Place

http://www.bpe.com

The Sally who oversees this food, drink, and travel guide is Sally Bernstein, lifestyle mentor for "the finer things in life." This little village is a dense news source for food-related articles and discussions, with something for everybody. Sally interviews some leading names in cooking and food writing, and other contributors offer all kinds of food, drink, and dining out guides.

The Gumbo Pages

http://www.webcom.com/gumbo

Bringing the vivacious spirit of New Orleans to your monitor, the Gumbo Pages is a great place to find Creole and Cajun recipes and, surprisingly, a host of other regional and world cuisines. You may not be able to travel to the festive cities listed here, but you can always create their alluring delicacies at home.

KID Appeal

Oscar-Mayer Cyber Cinema

http://www.oscar-mayer.com

Go to Oscar-Mayer's Cyber Cinema and avoid its sister site, which is a straight-forward unappetizing sales pitch of nakedly illustrated weenies. This site is a great one for kids to visit (see Figure 11.7). Oscar-Mayer's World Wide Weener leaps incredible bounds on the World Wide Web. He offers a Web tutorial that is perfect for beginners, a Oscar-Mayer sing-a-long and, for big kids, recipes.

Ragu Presents: Mama's Cucina

http://www.eat.com/index.html

Ragu is an enlightened Web advertiser—long on fun and short on sales pitch. And if you happen to get hungry for a certain brand of Old World Style Spaghetti Sauce, so much the better. Mama, the Ragu hostess, offers stories of the Old Country (even if the Old Country happens to be Hoboken), plus Ragu-drenched recipes like Spicy Apricot Chicken and Veal Cutlet Parmesan.

The Burrito Page

http://www.infobahn.com/pages/rito.html

"You can send flowers over the Internet!" is an oft-touted example of the miracles of the Net: Why doesn't anyone ever mention sending burritos? Now, the "Home of the Famous Flying Burrito" is online, and you can send your friends a gift box of burritos. The company has been airmailing their products since 1985, with the hefty prices around $37 for a six-pack.

Figure 11.7
Oscar-Mayer Cyber Cinema,
http://www.oscar-mayer.com

Chilegod

http://www.chilegod.com

Here's a site that could literally be termed a hot list—it's a database of hot sauces of nearly every description, from curry to chili to habanero. Several dozen varieties of hot sauce have been researched and reviewed by Andrew Gaines (the chilegod). If you're looking for something specific—say, to use at a Cajun crab boil or a Mexican fiesta—you can narrow things down with a search by brand, place of origin or ingredient.

Virtual Health

http://www.vhs.com

Virtual Health, an "interactive health store" based in Santa Monica, CA, offers an appetizing online collection of low-fat recipes designed to tempt Netizens into waistless fare. The site includes glossy photos, preparation, and nutritional info for dishes such as Melon-Berry Turkey Salad and Pumpkin-Filled Lasagna Rolls. The site also promotes the store's good-for-you gift sets, such as the Aromatherapy Basket filled with products exuding the sweet smell of well-being.

Fatfree: The Low Fat Vegetarian Archive

http://www.fatfree.com

The only thing fat here is the list of recipes: more than 2,000 of them at your disposal. These vegetarian entrees are collected from submissions to an e-mail list, and it's all done just for the love of fat-free cooking. The site also lets you search the USDA Nutrient Database which helps to answer burning questions like "Does broccoli have fat?" and "Is quinoa a good source of iron and zinc?" Naturally, you'll find no bloated graphics here.

Veggies Unite!

http://www.vegweb.com

Your online guide to every cows favorite utterance: I am a vegetarian. Become a member of Veggies Unite, and access recipes (equipped with users comments), a newsletter, menus, chat groups, recipe book reviews, and grocery lists.

World Guide to Vegetarianism

http://www.veg.org/veg./guide

This is the site to find veggie-friendly restaurant chains, national organizations, magazines, travel agencies, and

I·N·T·E·R·N·E·T M·I·N·U·T·E

LIVE CHAT ON THE WEB

A good way to think of a live chat is like a party. People gather in rooms and have real-time conversations via their keyboards. Just like at a party, you can opt to be a wall flower (in chat room lingo, "a lurker"), which means you aren't actually talking to anyone but just hanging out and taking things in, or you can choose to participate in the discussion.

Online chats offer a feature that many a party could use—if someone's comments bother or offend you, you can block their words from appearing on your screen (commonly referred to as a "bozo filter"). If that person bothers or offends a lot of people, he or she may be asked, or made, to leave the party by the administrators of the chat room.

The ability to be anyone you want is what draws some people to chat rooms. It's always interesting to see how people react when you say you're a female bodybuilder or a kindergarten teacher—or both. Keep in mind, that hunky fireman from Florida may really be a pimply pipsqueak from Peoria. So be aware and have fun.

While chats cover everything from gardening to bungee jumping, they can also be sexually oriented. Your sex and age are of keen interest to people, and some women have complained of being harassed in chats. Others have logged on and fallen in love, so you never know. Just choose your parties carefully. It's a good idea to stick with rooms that have a designated topic so you know what you're getting in to.

Where to go and how to get there

Then there are chats that you need a software plug-in to access. There are several different versions out there. They come with instructions on how to download the software (which is usually provided for free). Check out Parent Soup's Chat at *http://www.parentsoup.com/chat/indexnew.html.*

The latest in chats are 3-D rooms where you wander through virtual worlds as a character, or avatar, of your choosing. For 3-D worlds, try Worlds Chat at *http://www.worlds.net/wc.*

Another type of chat you may come across is Internet Rely Chat, better known as IRC. This text-only interface requires that you learn some simple commands and was the original way to chat on the Web. It is quickly being superseded by newer, easier-to-use chat programs.

For a calendar of chats taking place around the Web, go to Yahoo!'s NetEvents at *http://events.yahoo.com/events.html*.

And, in case you missed that celebrity chat you wanted to attend, go to Chat Soup at *http://www.chatsoup.com* to hear what the celebs had to say in their latest chats on the Web.

cooking schools. In the U.S., you can search by state, which is especially helpful for finding new restaurants in your area or when planning a trip.

Healthy Choice Home Page

http://www.HealthyChoice.com

You can't go to the supermarket anymore without seeing those green packages on the shelves. Now the diet dishes from Healthy Choice have a tasty, low-fat Web site rich in information, with a dollop of product information mixed in. Visit the Healthy Choice kitchens at Table One for menu planning guides and recipes, then go for the burn at the Personal Trainer's gym, where exercise tips motivate you to lift more than your fork.

M&M's Chocolate Mini Baking Bits

http://www.m-ms.com/bakery/index.html

If you didn't already know, M&M's Chocolate Mini Baking Bits are tiny versions of the famous M&M's Chocolate Candies, "designed from the start," the M&M/Mars company tells visitors, "to meet the strict demands of your baking needs." Okay, anyway, visit this site for recipes and tips like cookies cook faster on dark baking sheets. And take the online tour of the M&M's plant.

Godiva

http://www.godiva.com

Just be happy you can't grab the chocolates off your monitor screen, because the temptation is overwhelming. Check out the dessert recipes made with Godiva chocolate (or you favorite substitute). And if you want to send someone (maybe yourself) chocolates, you can design your own box and fill it with whatever combination of gooey pralines and crunchy nuts, smooth caramels, rich truffles, and exotic creams you prefer.

I Need My Chocolate

http://www.qrc.com/~sholubek/choco/start.htm

A woman from Hershey, PN, started this Web site several years ago and has, in the meantime, become quite an expert of the eatable temptress, chocolate. Don't get dissuaded from the banal opening comments—overall it is a fun site to visit. Chocolate trivia, chocolate talk from other countries, FAQs, and a loads of chocolate recipes to joyfully fatten you up are here.

Gingerbread House

http://dinnercoop.cs.cmu.edu/cgi-bin/mfs/01recipes/Karen/Gingerbreadhouse.html

Did you ever make a gingerbread house as a child? If not, it is never too late to start and a great thing to do to entertain the next generation for an afternoon. There is no need to construct a Martha Stewart-esque three-story Victorian with shingle roof and blooming garden—a simple one-story will do. This Web site gives all the instructions (see Figure 11.8); all you need supply is the patience.

Weight Watchers

http://www.weight-watchers.com

A Web site dedicated to promulgated good health and nutrition as well as Weight Watchers products. Aside from constant WWs refiguring of diet plans, who could pass up clicking on the link titled Eating Your Way to a New You? A variety of WWs programs, nutrition facts, secrets for success, and a sample 3-day diet to inspire you to join the ranks are here.

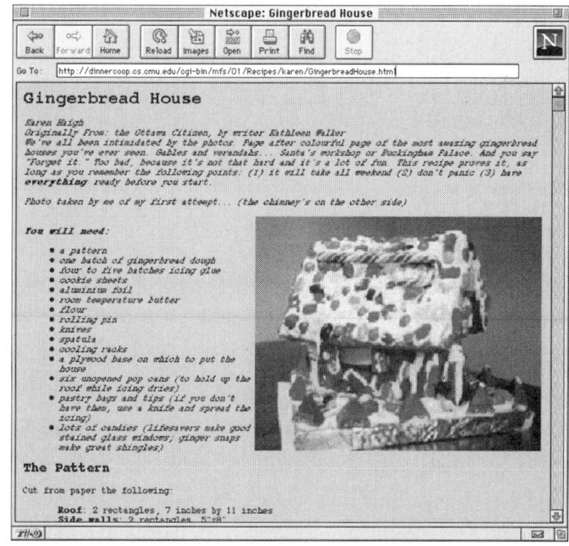

Figure 11.8

Gingerbread House, *http://dinnercoop.cs.cmu.edu/cgi bin/mfs/01recipes/Karen/Gingerbreadhouse.html*

National Food Safety Database (NFSD)

http://www.agen.ufl.edu/~foodsaf/foodsaf.html

A serious site for an important subject. There is nothing breezy about the information offered here. The purpose is to educate you about the dangers of things like salmonella and poor nutrition. Helpful documents such as USDA Complete guide to Home Canning and Handling Wild Game Meat Safety can be accessed and downloaded. And, if you don't find what you need, check their related links or contact the NFSD and ask for the information to be added.

Food TV

http://www.foodtv.com/index.htm

Are you a fan of the Food Network's on-air chefs? Then you will enjoy their Web site. Offered here are a slew of recipes from such foodie celebs as Julia and Mario Batali, and the concoctions of the networks guests. Also pushing food print magazines, discounts on subscriptions are offered. A cyberchef is on call to answer your questions, and program information for the channel can be accessed. You no longer have to write into a show to obtain a recipe; all you have to do is go online and immediately download it.

California Culinary Academy's Online SPICE

http://www.baychef.com

By the year 2000, demand for professional chefs is expected to grow by 38 percent, according to the California Culinary Academy. And if that's not reason enough to attend, this attractive site has a few more: information about its programs, its instructors, and its restaurants. A culinary education isn't the only thing for sale, here, though: Visitors will also find food products, videotapes, and cookbooks.

Cookin With Frito-Lay

http://www.fritolay.com/home/html

Odd as it may sound, people do actually concoct meals with the all-American corn chip, the Frito. Posted here

[OVERHEARD ON WOMEN'S WIRE]

http://chat.women.com

ON EDUCATION:

"Most of my education has been life. It taught me a lot of things. We were taught to cook in the house. I think most women weren't aware of careers back then."

WHY EVERYONE CALLS HER "MAMA":

"I would say it's the charisma we create in our restaurants. We're cooking with love. As we adopted more and more employees that became an extension of my family, everybody began to call me 'Mama.' Now the whole city does."

KEY TO SUCCESS:

"Quality and family. Everybody is involved."

—Mama Ninfa, founder and chair of the Board of Ninfa's Mexican Restaurants. With 23 restaurants and licensees around the South, her biz has become a $75 million "institution in Houston."

are recipes for Fritos Chicken Fried Steak and East Stuffed Peppers. If you are having trouble getting your 5-year-old to digest broccoli, then whip up Crunchy Broccoli and Cheese Lasagna and the little one is sure to gobble it down.

Cape Breton Pictorial Cookbook

http://www.taisbean.com/cbcookbook/hom.html

Anglophiles will love this pictorial cookbook, which offers selections from the paper version by Chef Yvonne LeVerte and Warren Gordon. (You can order the full version here, of course.) The hearty traditional recipes from the eastern tip of Nova Scotia are mixed with Cape Breton Island lore and a virtual landscape of photographs. The pictures are as sumptuous as the dishes.

The Wimmer Companies

http://ttx.com/wimmer

The Wimmer Companies are creators of something they call Community Cookbooks—books that feature American regional cooking, with part of the proceeds from the sale of each going to local nonprofit projects. At this site, you'll find a sampling of their wares: books like "Cajun Revelation" and "Cafe Oklahoma," which has down-home recipes like Rush Springs Watermelon Rind Preserves and Stratford Peach Fried Pies. As they say in Oklahoma, "Bon appetit, y'all."

GARDENING AND HORTICULTURE

Living Home

http://livinghome.com

Someday you're finally going to organize that closet. Get help in the Daily Dirt section of Living Home (and you can ask your own questions). You'll find daily tips on gardening, remodeling, decorating, and design, with plenty of handyman project wisdom as well as the latest loot for your home in "objects of desire." Perfect for those who aren't quite Martha Stewart, but want to spiff up their environs a bit.

Lowe's Home Improvement Page

http://www.lowes.com

This site could become the handyman's best friend. The Lowe's home improvement mega-chain brings you a useful resource for just about any home improvement project you can imagine, from how to fix broken pipes and install vinyl flooring to remodeling the entire kitchen. There's even a Pro's Corner for those in the contracting biz. Print a copy and slip it under your landlord's door.

The Internet Antique Shop

http://www.tias.com

If you're an antiques buff, you'll want to bookmark this online jackpot of sales, classifieds, news, store locations, and other info about antiques and collectibles. Find out about auctions, local shows, store openings and closings, online resources, and other ways to keep up with the lucrative and interesting antiques trade. You can also join discussion groups on topics like watches, fine china, and art glass. Buy, sell, or just keep up on what's (not) new.

This Old House

http://pathfinder.com/TOH

From the same folks that bring you the TV Show and magazine. The MO: They find a "fixer-upper" (it could be yours!) and go through the step-by-step process of turning it into a dream home. The Web site gives you selected articles from the magazine, but you have to subscribe to the paper version to get the whole enchilada. Still, it's enough to make you see that dilapidated wreck you pass on the way to work every day in a whole new light.

The Housepainting FAQ

http://www.osf.org/~macrakis/paint.html

Stavros Macrakis recently had his 120-year-old house repainted, with terriffic results. He found it to be quite a learning experience, and now he wants to share his knowledge with you. FAQ items include Choosing a Color for an Old House, Should I use Vinyl or Aluminum Siding Instead, and more. It's straight text, no bells and whistles, but if you're thinking of repainting, you'll be glad you found this.

United Homeowners Association

http://policy.net/uha

The UHA is a nonprofit organization dedicated to preserving and promoting home ownership. At their site, you'll find valuable information about mortgage rates and insurance, plus real estate services, home improvement resources, and more. Included are up-to-the minute news items like flood damage, and how they relate to home ownership (insurance resources, for example.). Useful feature: The Mortgage Rate Shopper, which supplies your loan information to lenders via the Net.

The Virtual Garden

http://www.pathfinder.com/vg

This Time Publishing Ventures gardening guide is likely to bring out the "green thumb" in anyone. You can look up a plant from among nearly 3,000 North American species, get a local weather forecast, or talk to a Garden Guru if things get sticky out there. Also featured are selected articles from home improvement/lifestyle mags like This Old House and Southern Living, and if you run out of tools, you can always shop The Marketplace.

GardenNet

http://trine.com/GardenNet/home.htm

This gardening resource hotspot has everything you need to make your garden grow. Don't have one? Check out Flora's Best for access to the best of garden stores. After a while you'll be ready to enjoy The Ardent Gardener, which features stories, tips, books, forums and more for the rabid garden fan. You'll also find info on magazines, local shows and events and catalogs. You'll be workin' that trowel by springtime.

The Garden Gate

http://www.prairienet.org/garden-gate/homepage.htm

Site publisher Karen Fletcher offers a virtual bouquet of links to floral and garden-related sites for recreational trowel users everywhere. She's also included her column, which can be found on the GardenWeb site, as well as helpful hints for finding information elsewhare on the Net. Links are well described, and she'll only list commercial sites if they contain valuable info beyond a sales pitch. A handy bookmark for your gardening research.

Cyndi's Catalog of Gardening Catalogs

http://www.cog.brown.edu/gardening

In site publisher Cyndi Johnson's words, "This is a large list of 1628 catalogs..." and so it is. The list includes items from listserv mailing lists, copyrighted articles, Web gardening catalogs like W. Atlee Burpee & Co. and Gourmet Gardener, as well as, well, nearly everything. Cyndi's Catalog also includes digital updates on what's growing in *her* garden.

Garden Escapes

http://www.garden.com

Online garden shopping at its best (see Figure 11.9)! Bulbs, seeds, plants, and gardening products from all over the world are available for mail-order. A full, lively description and photo is provided with most plants and goods sold. The Garden by Design feature allows you to plot and plan your ideal garden without lifting more than your fingers to the keyboard. Once you have submitted answers to questions about your property (real not virtual) and gardening preferences, Garden Escape suggests the necessary planting materials complete with full color images. If you are a gardener, you will go gaga over this site.

Figure 11.9
Garden Escapes, *http://www.garden.com*

The Cook's Garden

http://www.sover.net/~justso/index.html

The Ogdens of Cook's Garden are professional seed peddlers as well as cooks. Here you can order organically raised seeds for a variety of flowers, greens, and herbs to use in the kitchen. If you're still working your garden vegetables over with pesticides, fertilizers, and soil supplements, you may want to check out author Shepherd Ogden's books on organic growing.

Floriculture and Ornamental Horticulture

http://www.cals.cornell.edu/cals/dept/flori

Starting with floriculture and ornamental horticultural class offerings, and ending with a journey to the campus's A.D. Whitehouse Gardens, this Cornell University site offers plants aplenty. You can read about the school's research and tutorials, visit the Nutrient Analysis Lab, or browse admissions requirements. The information here is accessible and non-technical enough to be enjoyed by the armchair horticulturist.

Electronic Orchid Greenhouse

http://yakko.cs.wmich.edu/~charles/orchids

This page will shatter your preconceived notions about orchids (except about their price, of course). Charles Marsh, whose personal home page is devoted to the gorgeous buds, insists that orchids are not grown exclusively by geezers and eccentrics, and can be successfully cultivated on a household windowsill. Luscious photos are about as sensual as it gets in the virtual garden (see Figure 11.10). This page will work best for those with some previous orchid experience.

Bonsai

http://www.pass.wayne.edu/~dan/bonsai.html

This site (tended by a host of individual gardeners) is a bonsai bonanza. Literally translated, bonsai means "a plant grown in a dish," and this page has all the dish you need to plant your own little trees. Get inspired by a closer look at a knee-high wisteria or an elegant dwarf powder puff. You could call the page "short and sweet."

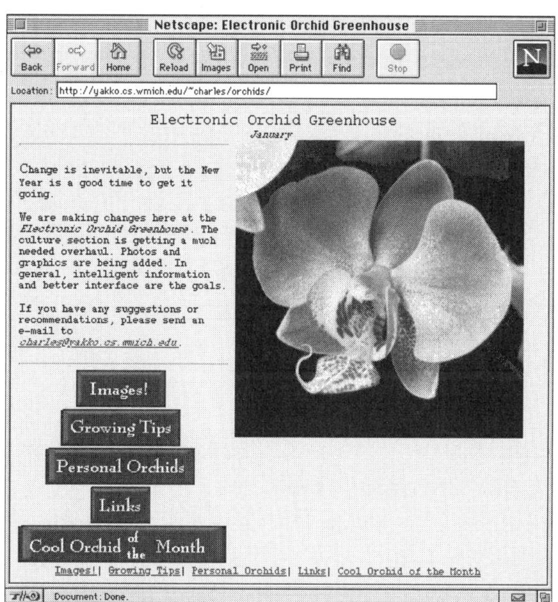

Figure 11.10

Electronic Orchid Greenhouse, *http://yakko.cs.wmich.edu/~charles/orchids*

American Horticultural Society

http://eMall.com/ahs/ahs.html

Presented by the American Horticulturist Magazine and News Edition, the site presents articles from the magazines and membership information and its privileges (free flower show and arboretum admittance nationwide). The site slants toward the enthusiast who will be intrigued by articles like one on the medicinal purposes and history of the Hoya.

American Association of Botanical Gardens and Arboreta

http://192.104.39.4/AABGA/aabga1.html

A national organization committed to the study, display, and conservation of plants, the AABGA site offers a list of member gardens and arboreta and links to them, and an index of publications and information on a proposed national Consortium. Also here are updates on the group's Web activities and a mini-directory of nonmember organizations and their links. Great for the garden crowd.

Florida Wildflower Page

http://www-wane.scri.fsu.edu/~mikems

This collection of beautiful photographs should appeal to all flower lovers, and most especially to nature and flower photographers. The dozens of large pictures of Florida wildflowers are certainly breathtaking. Wild Portulaca and Spider Lily, a good selection of orchids, or the spiky-leaf background of the Mexican Poppy—so many to choose from it's best to make more than one visit. One minor complaint: Thumbnails would be nice to spice up the laundry list of specimens.

National Wildflower Research Center

http://www.wildflower.org

The National Wildflower Research Center is the brainchild of former first Lady Bird Johnson. (Lady Bird welcomes you here herself.) The facility, in Texas, is both a botanical garden and a center to encourage public and private use of wildflowers. On this site you can take a virtual tour of the center's gardens, tower, library, and lush meadows. The staff will also answer wildflower questions.

The Orchid House

http://sciserv2.uwaterloo.ca/orchids.html

"In the world of flowers," boasts this lovely site, "orchids are the undisputed champions." Here's a mammoth guide to the much-loved blossom, complete with species-by-species breakdowns of color, size, ideal temperature, humidity...even appropriate fertilizers. Orchid myths are exploded right and left: They don't need a greenhouse to get started, not all blooms come from the jungle, and they're no longer just "a rich man's hobby."

INTERNATIONAL APPEAL

Australian National Botanic Gardens

http://155.187.10.12/anbg.html

These fine gardens are devoted to preserving Australia's botanic biodiversity by growing some 90,000 plants representing more than 5,000 species unique to Australia. As this home page exists to promote the Gardens, it would be far more effective if the beautiful gardens and aboriginal microcosms were actually pictured. Much more delightful is the thorough index of indigenous birds, complete with dozens of calls from birds like the infamous Kookabura (merry king of the Bush is he).

The New York Botanical Garden

http://www.nybg.org

Hoping to entice you to its 250 acres of gardens, this site was constructed in an attractive and helpful way. But the virtual tour of some garden highlights including the Victorian conservatory is mediocre. There is also a search engine, gardening tips, and the opportunity to e-mail questions to its staff.

The Brooklyn Botanical Garden

http://bbg.org

Also trying to entice you to its acreage, the Brooklyn Botanical Garden Web site is lovely (see Figure 11.11). You can take a picturesque tour of the gardens and plant collections. Aside from the allure of the Brooklyn gardens lush greenery, this site is considered one of the best botanical sites on the web given its extensive reference and education resources. Ask your gardening questions here.

INTERNATIONAL APPEAL

Missouri Botanical Garden

http://www.mobot.org

Originally designed for scientists of botanical research, this orderly site is now offering useful information for people like you and me under its education heading. Although based in Missouri, this site offers

Figure 11.11

The Brooklyn Botanical Garden, *http://bbg.org*

horticultural information for all the continents. There is a search engine, books available, and course and lectures to register online.

Buckingham Greenery, Inc.

http://home.erols.com/greenery/index.html

Although to purchase their plants and services you are going to have to live in Georgia, North Carolina or Virginia, Buckingham Greenery's Web site offers interior landscaping guidance we all can benefit from. There are no exciting graphics to entertain you, but horticultural services, holiday decorating tips, and suggestions of plants for clean air are here for the taking.

1-800-Flowers

http://www.800.flowers.com/reference/feature-flower/index.com

Send yourself (or a friend) a years worth of flowers. The worldwide flower deliver, 1-800-Flowers, will deliver one flowering plant a month to whomever you choose. Flowers always brighten a room, and in this arrangement, planted bulbs are sent so that the flowers should stay bright until the next package is received.

1st in Flowers!

http://www.1stinflowers.com

A cheerful, breezy design makes this flower selling site a fun place to visit. Photos for the potted plants, blooming buds, and gifts are provided for almost all the goods, helping you make a selection that is perfect for the recipient. Buy online or call the 1-800 number listed. Also offered are fruit baskets and gourmet foods.

The Telegarden

http://www.usc.edu/dept/garden

If you are a city dweller dying for just a small patch of soil, check out Telegarden. You won't dirty your hands here but you will be the controller of a robots arm that will do the grunt work for you as you plant a virtual garden. Since its inception in June of 1995, close to 10,000 people have cultivated their own gardens using this technology from the University of Southern California. You can also watch your garden prosper in techno color and review an online log that registers its growth.

INTERNATIONAL APPEAL

Flora of Europe

http://www.knoware.nl/flora

Although an amateur photo-herbarium with over 600 pictures of flowers, mostly of southern Europe, one would never guess that a professional wasn't at work recording the various flowers. Basically, this site is a photographic encyclopedia of European plant types. All flowers, alphabetized by their Latin names, are disappointedly accompanied by dry, scientific descriptions. Without the fantastic photos, this site would put all but a botanist to sleep.

INTERNATIONAL APPEAL

Pukeiti Rhododendron Trust

http://pluto.taranaki.ac.nz/pukeiti/welcome.html

Are you are rhododendron fan? Do you have trouble makes these colorful plants flourish in your gardens? This site offers research from a New Zealand garden with over 2,000 species of the plant. Given that this is an important research area for these plants, there is lots of helpful information and a vast photo collection.

INTERNATIONAL APPEAL

Conservation International

http://www.conservation.org

Conservation International believes that the "earth's natural heritage must be maintained if future generations are to thrive." Its mission is to conserve the "earth's living natural heritage, our global biodiversity, and to demonstrate that human societies are able to live harmoniously with nature." Among the world's biodiversity hot spots is the Atlantic forest region of eastern Brazil, as seen here. This site also includes information on joining CI and ways you can help save the planet.

The Amazing Story of Kudzu

http://www.sa.ua.edu/brent/kudzu.htm

Kudzu, that beautiful green vine that covers over 7 million acres in the southeastern U.S. is the subject of a video documentary made at the University of Alabama. This page offers a fascinating history via the video of the green monster since it hit the U.S. in 1876. Why a monster? It grows a foot a day and takes over everything, and is impervious to almost all herbicides. But it has some uses, including jelly, goat food, and a possible medicinal treatment for alcoholism (well, in rats anyway).

AGropolis

http://agcomwww.tamu.edu/agcom/agrotext/agcommap.html

This friendly site from Texas A & M University offers family farmers and gardeners science-based agriculture info. Most of the information is for Texans, featuring "Exotic Deer Farming in East Texas" which tells about new legislation that concerns raising deer for venison and the Pest Control Center's tips on dealing with the Africanized "killer" Honey Bee. But even those who work the land on a modest scale in other parts of the country will find useful material here.

University of Washington Medicinal Herb Garden

http://point.lycos.com/reviews/database/5_16_028.html

Wander the health-giving paths of the Seattle Campus of the University of Washington's Medicinal Herb Garden at this hypertour site. For a closer look at these leafy healers, the site features gorgeous individual plant GIFs. You won't find anything about the plants' medicinal uses here (a disclaimer advises to seek professional medical advice on using herbs)—but at least the next time you see a Arctium minus (a.k.a. Beggar's Buttons) you'll know it.

Aboriculture Trees & Timber

http://www.kernvalley.com/arbor/harbor.htm

Doug Mellor is an Arborist (or "tree surgeon") with nearly thirty years of experience in arboriculture. Sounds stuffy, eh? Not so—he learned from his father and grandfather, and after searching the Web on pages about his chosen craft and finding none, he decided to make his own. If you're willing to let some spelling and formatting errors slide, there's plenty of practical information on this esoteric topic.

The Tree Doctor

http://www.1stresource.com/t/treedoc

Although close to being a strict advertisement for various and sundry tree products, The Tree Doctor saves itself by providing useful information about pruning your trees (tree topping = bad) and the liability of your arborist (see Figure 11.12). There's also a handy list of "approved" arborists to prevent poor cropping of a beloved oak. Tree enthusiasts have likely seen all this before. For the novice, a good quick read.

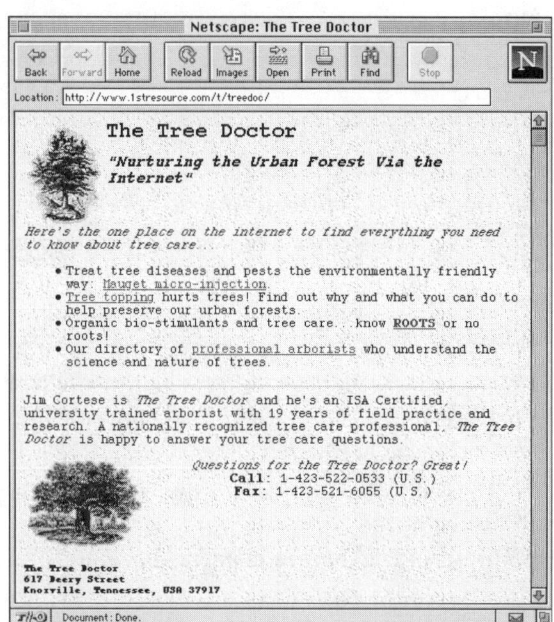

Figure 11.12

The Tree Doctor,
http://www.1stresource.com/t/treedoc

Pete's Pond Page

http://reality.sgi.com/employees/prto/index.htm

Pete Orelup built a 2400 gallon pond in his central California backyard, then stocked it with koi and goldfish. Along the way he documented the project, and this home page is a neighborly primer on building a pond; this one comes complete with a bridge, a waterfall, and a tricked out "biofilter." Pete's straightforward narrative is both charming and helpful, and gardeners and weekend builders will have fun touring this project.

Andrew and Jackie's Koi and Pond Page

http://www.byteline.com.au/koi/koi.html

Here's a homemade guide to better ponds and koi (the colored carp you see in Japanese gardens) from a couple in Australia who know what they're talking about. Even though it's clear that Andrew and Jackie are hobbyists, their page is very well done. Beyond the pond is a good section on koi, from feeding and breeding to those gnarly fish ailments, anchor worms and dropsy.

Snakebite Emergency Web Page

http://www.xmission.com/~gastown/herpmed/snbite.htm

Although it may be your garden, the snake thinks it is his home. Finding out what not to do about snakebites may be the thing that saves your life. For instance, your first instinct might be to reach for the nearest painkiller (or shot of Jack Daniels), but the experts here say "no way," on both counts. Antivenom resource numbers and a snakebite hotline are listed here too.

HOBBIES AND COLLECTING

The Plastic Princess Collector's Page

http://deepthought.armory.com/~zenugirl/barbie.html

You can't help but love this monument to Barbie, Ken, and a rainbow of other plastic fashion dolls (see Figure 11.17). If your Barbie feels like being politically incorrect, you can contact a woman who makes miniature mink stoles. And, meet "Billy, The World's First Out and Proud Gay Doll," manufactured by a company in England. Site-mistress Zoli Nazaari-Uebele, an engineer in real life, even reveals her dream item: a DKNY Barbie (brunette, please).

Action Girl's Guide to Female Figures

http://members.aol.com/sarahdyer/index.htm

This friendly collector's guide to female action figures is courtesy of Sarah Dyer, who produces Action Girl Comics. It's a huge list of cartoon and TV heroines and the action figures they inspired over the last thirty years. Sarah advocates trading, not dealing ("an evil practice"), and the emphasis is clearly on fun, fun, fun. It's refreshing to see someone collect toys because they like to play with them.

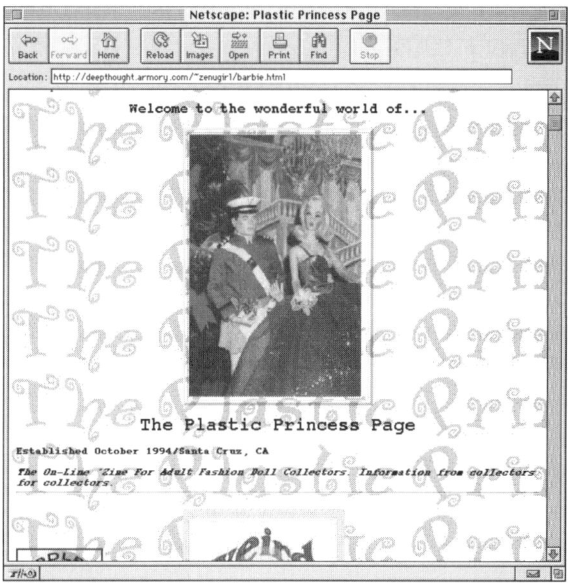

Figure 11.13
The Plastic Princess Collector's Page,
http://deepthought.armory.com/~zenugirl/barbie.html

AquaLink

http://www.aqualink.com

AquaLink is a searchable trove of info and resources pertinent to tropical fish tanks, and virtually all other aspects of hobby aquarium-dom. It was created primarily by University of Washington oceanography student David Kreg, who has since enlisted a staff of "help service" volunteers. Visitors get access to a free commercial product locator, nutrition FAQs, and aqua-columnists verbiage. And don't forget to check the stunning results of the last live rock survey!

Collector's Coin Universe

http://www.coin-universe.com

Numismatists of every denomination will want to put a bookmark in this excellent home page for coin and currency collecting. Among the offerings at this on-line collector's 'zine are news of upcoming coin shows, dealer ads, a U.S. Coin Directory, and a "Coin Dealer Newsletter." Links and searchable indexes will put you in touch with the "Israeli Government Coins and Medals Corp.," "Frank Chlebana's Coins Page," and lots more. There's even (inevitably) coin software to buy.

Where to Buy Model Railroad Supplies in the 1990s

http://www.tuscon.com/concor/buy.html

In addition to being a "Where to" buyer's guide for the latest model railroading equipment, Con-Cor Models company offers helpful how-to information here, for anyone just venturing into this popular hobby. Veterans will want to scroll down (through so much home page text) to the link—embedded graphic train, a gateway to all manner of other model train sites. Also found here is excellent shopping for the choo-choo enthusiast.

Virtual Flyshop

http://www.flyshop.com

The Virtual Flyshop is home to what it calls "The First Internet Journal of Flyfishing," featuring articles such as "If I Only Had One Fly," offering tactics for fishing the Woolly Bugger. Another onsite feature, "Riverkeeper," tracks fishing conditions across the U.S. A Forum combines, say, expert backcasting advice with a chance to brag about your Deschutes River catch, share photos and solicit suggestions for fishing in Switzerland, etc. It can certainly carry those big fish stories to new heights (or rather, lengths).

GI Joe—Action Soldier

http://www.netaxis.com/~petebuilt/gijoe

The irony of GI Joe is that Hasbro's soldier doll hit America's shores in 1964, at the brink of the Vietnam era when the military took a heroic hit in public opinion. This site, from a longtime GI Joe buff and collector named Pete, celebrates all that is Joe—from its olive drab background to its thorough history of the doll's evolution. Pete also arms his site with loads of GI Joes, accessories, and packaging. The page's funniest offering is a reprint of Previews Magazine's brutal GI Joe vs. Ken comparison.

CraftNet Village

http://www.craftnet.org

Two distinct images—the computer whiz, and the home craft maker—are brought together here in one site. Not only can you find a fair amount of crafty stuff to buy in the marketplace (and not to buy: the Prime Publishing database is full of contact info for free or postage-only items), but you can do some reading in the Magazine Rack, and trade project ideas with other crafters in the Project Exchange.

Collector Link

http://www.collector-link.com

For memorabilia-collecting hobbyists, this efficient search engine delivers hundreds of links to dealers, news groups, price guides, and other pertinent Web sites (see Figure 11.14). It's especially strong in the realm of cards—sports cards, phone cards, postcards, business cards. Then again, there are Coins & Currency links, too, with Dolls & Action Figures coming soon. A powerful networking and shopping index.

Internet Cigar Group

http://www.cigargroup.com

If you are new to cigar smoking or an old hand, this site is a joy to visit. Those who smoke cigars take it very seriously, and this site's founders are no acceptation. A smoky chat room, interactive cigar database, resource library, discounted cigars, and collectibles are all offered here.

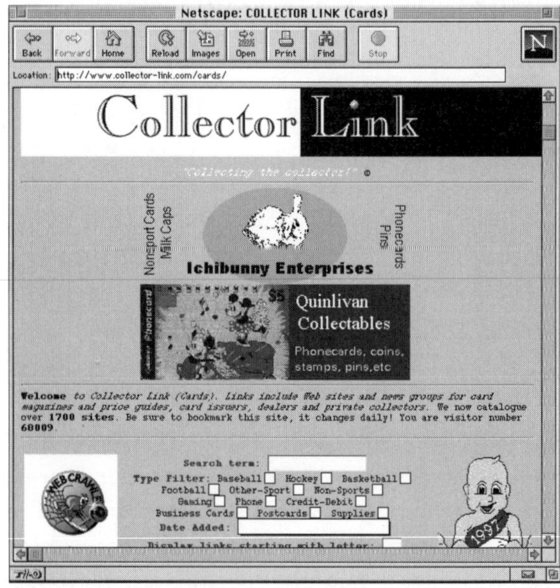

Figure 11.14
Collector Link, *http://www.collector-link.com*

Amateur Radio
http://www.acs.ncsu.edu/HamRadio

Newcomers and old pros of amateur radio will want to tune in to this site. There is an Amateur Radio NewsLine (weekly newspage), the FCC rules and regulations to follow, Amateur Radio software, newsgroups to join in and other ham radio and club web servers.

Ham Radio Outlet
http://www.hamradio.com

Best shopping online for ham buffs. Available online: product information, searching, pricing database (updated six days a week), and mail order shopping. Either hunt via WWW or request a free ham radio outlet catalog to satisfy all your enthusiast's needs.

Lighthouse Depot
http://www.sierra.com/games/lighthouse/sites.html

Are you a fan of the days of old, when lighthouses guided Mariners to port and were manned by daring, seafaring families? This site offers a taste of the old and newly modernized, electronically controlled lighthouses. There are many mementos to order: posters, calendars, books, cards and, even, videos detailing collections of lighthouses.

Dreamers Hobbies
KID Appeal

http://www.execpc.com/~dreamers

Just about all you need, from mini trains and scenery components to the tracks can be ordered and viewed at Dreamer Hobbies. An authorized dealer for Overland Models, Challenger Imports, Hallmark Models, Shoreham Shops, and Precision Scale brass models (only an enthusiast would realize the importance of this), Dreamers specializes in presenting a large collection of train consignment brass, books, and specialty items.

PET CARE

How to Toilet Train Your Cat FAQs
http://www.sff.net/people/Karawynn/cat/catfaq.htp

As long as you can remember to leave the lid up but seat down, the Web site will convince the greatest of skeptics that they too can potty train their cat. Step-by-step instructions and illustrations help in this most unusual process for all kinds of kitties: old, young, frisky, silly, and just plain dumb. Just imagine what you will save on kitty litter.

Purina Pet Care
KID Appeal

http://www.purina.com

Purina wants to help you create a positive owner and animal relationship. This Web site offers lots of pet care advise for cats and dogs. If you are still puzzled by a question, you can post it online to be answered by Purina employees. And, of course, get the skinny on all of Purinas pet food products.

Happy Household Pet Club
http://www.best.com/~slewis/HHPCC

For almost 30 years, the HHPCC club has been aiding the owners of show cats, but this site is a good place for any cat owner to visit. If you do show your cat, access to The Happenings (their bi-monthy newsletter), show results, and membership information are posted. And other cat owners, you can access humane society reports and cat care information.

Cat Fanciers
http://www.fanciers.com

Given that this Web site was developed by a group of cat breeders, this is a good place to visit if you are looking for a specific kitty. There are hundreds of links to almost every house cat breed imaginable. Cat Fanciers also posts a list of FAQs and veterinary medicine documents and resources for cat care.

Dog Fanciers
http://www.fancier.com

Dogs too have fan clubs, too. This site offers the latest information for show dogs. You can order their book,

Fancier Bible, a complete source for showing your canine. And peruse their list of rescue dogs, and access the breeders network.

Cats, Cats, & More Cats

http://catscats.index.htm/5.htm

Interesting gifts for ailurophiles (feline lovers). You can shop online or, if you live in the U.S., order a print catalog. Computer gifts, books, clothes for you and kitty, and many more items are available. Also: Many items can be personalized.

Horse Country

http://www.horse-country.com

A virtual equestrian experience for anyone interested in horses, especially geared towards teenagers and kids. Horse history, fiction, health advise, clubs, and associations. A special feature is the Jr. Riding Mailing digest where children can discuss with one another horses and other equestrian interests.

The Italian Greyhound Club of America

http://clever.net/ignca/info.html

Founded close to 50 years ago, the IG is a national breed club is for friends and aficionados in the U.S. The site is meant to further the interest of the breed and educate owners, breeders, and fanciers. If you are interested in another type of purebred dog, follow the links.

The Pet Bird Page

http://aloha.net/~granty

A fantastic site for pet bird information, especially if you are a parrot fan. A wide range of birds from the Gray Cheek Parakeet to the Senegal Parrot are covered here. Tips on how to raise your birdie, a host of insightful FAQ, newsgroup connections and, medical care referrals to keep your feathered friend swaking.

Acme Pet

http://www.acmepet.com

A local and international forum for pet enthusiasts, provider of pet products and services and non-profit organizations. Essential pet resources are here. You can also conduct pet research, join in on chat groups, and read the latest pet news. And, if you have a show dog, this site offers a listing of all canine shows in North America. And join in their chats.

Bird Dog News

http://www.bird-dog-news.com

Just because they like to go out and shoot animals doesn't mean they don't love their hunting dogs. This Web site offers important breeding and training information for anyone who like to target pheasants or ducks or other game. Bird Dog magazine posts many of its articles here so check out the archives.

Flea News

http://www.ent.iastate.edu/FleaNews/AboutFleaNews.html

Posted here is a bimonthly newsletter about those itchy little critters called fleas. The newsletter is really a compilation of news published about the flea to keep you abreast of important Siphonaptera (flea) news. How better to protect your pets?

Kneenbec River Company

http://www.acmepet.com/kennebec

Treat your cat to the ultimate in catnip toys—one that surrounds your fuzzy friend in irresistible catnip—by online mail-ordering a Cat-A-Tonic Catnip bed. The potency of this bed's herbs will lead your kitty to believe the stuff is illegal. Or buy your pooch a colorful sweater for those long winter months. This site doesn't offer many goods but the prices of the ones they do sell are low, especially for those of you who are use to paying city prices.

Ferret Central

http://www.optics..rochester.edu:8080/users/pgreene/central.html

Do you want a smelly little ferret as a house pet? (They can be deodorized, ya know.) Ferret Central answers all kinds of questions ranging from historic to medical about the little rodents. It also provides numerous links and lots of ferret photos. The most fun here can be had by clicking on the variety of sound bites from ferrets like hissing and chittering/chuckling.

SPOTLIGHT ON PETS

While the Web is a great place to go to chat with like-minded pet lovers, it is also being used to systematically help animals. The Web is a good resource for medical care, animal rights activism, and placement by shelters.

Five Facts

1 As many as 25 percent of dogs entering shelters each year are purebreds; approximately 61 percent of all dogs entering shelters are killed (and 75 percent of cats).

2 The organization Greyhounds Friends has saved and placed over 6,000 former racetrack greyhounds since 1983, partially through the use of its online placement service.

3 ASPCA/NAPCC Web site veterinarians advise on more animal toxicology (poison) cases in a day then most vets handle in a year.

4 The Web offers medical and behavioral tips for pet owners, including emergency care, homeopathic remedies, and psychology advice.

5 In particular, owners of exotic pets—ferrets, for example—have found like-minded souls via chat rooms and Web sites.

Five Sites

Save-A-Pet

http://pasture.ecn.purdue.edu/~laird/Dogs/Rescue

If you want to get a dog, go online to Save-A-Pet and find a shelter near you. This referral service offers a list of online breed rescue organizations and shelters both within the United States and internationally. This site also lists rescue organizations by state and links you to their sites.

Greyhound Friends

http://www.greyhound.org.

In recent history, greyhounds are used at racetracks for gambling and generally destroyed as soon as their money-making capabilities are finished. Greyhounds Friends is a nonprofit organization dedicated to saving racetrack greyhounds and placing them in new homes. Check out this site if you are interested in helping the cause or adopting a greyhound.

ASPCA/NAPCC

http://napcc-hp.cvm.uiuc.edu/difference.html

The American Society for the Prevention of Cruelty to Animals/National Animal Poison Control Center is the first animal-oriented poison control center in the United States. The organization has created a Web site to offer round-the-clock online advice and treatment for potentially poisoned animals.

Largest Pet Related Link Spots

http://www.exoticpets.com/exoticpets/links.html

This site delivers what it touts. And if your idea of the perfect pet is less than ordinary, you will feel right at home.

Pet Phocus

http://www.radix.net./~eallen/pet

Pet Phocus offers case studies of difficult and unusual pet problems, and the solutions doctors of animal behavior and veterinarians have used. Diagnosis is matched to treatment, and both behavioral and new age, holistic treatments are offered as remedies.

Virtual Pet Cemetery

http://www.lavamind.com/pet.html

Your pet (like it or not) can live on forever in what is the first online virtual pet burial ground. Pictures and written accounts of your beloved deceased fuzzy friends are posted here. It is questionable if anyone other than you will visit the virtual grave (aside for a hearty laugh.

Basic Rules for Cats Who Have a House to Run

http://geog.utoronto.ca/reynolds/pethumor/catrules.html

To get your cat's point of view, come hither. Topics covered include the vacuum cleaner, otherwise known as appalling beast or cat eater, and the secrets cats share about waking owners (one effective method of rejuvenating a dormant human is the direct approach, namely jumping on the bed and doing one or more of the following: trampling, licking and/or nibbling any exposed parts, pulling hair). It's a conspiracy!

Whale Adoption Project

http://www.webcom.com/~iwcwww/whale_adoption/waphome.html

So you aren't allowed any pets in your apartment building, don't let that stop you from adopting a 2-ton whale. By taking one in (not literally), you can help in the International Whaling Commission with their cause to protect whales. And, it doesn't cost much to adopt an entire humpback whale. Why not give one to your little girl the next time she cries, "I want a puppy!"?

Cockroach World

http://www.nj.com/yucky/roaches/index.html

This page, part of The Yuckiest Site on the Internet (where else?), gives you everything you ever wanted to know about cockroaches. And well, okay, maybe you were never really interested. But this site, geared mostly towards elementary school students, almost makes cockroaches look cute. Play "Around the World" to learn which bugs come from where (the hissing variety comes with a sound file), and ask Betty the Bug Lady your burning cockroach questions.

Why Cats Paint

http://www.netlink.co.nz/~monpa/index.html

You have to be a giant feline fan to visit this site (and perhaps a bit screwy). It is an outgrowth of writer Burton Silver and photograph Heather Busch's book *Why Cats Paint*. These two perceive the territorial marks cats make while walking with wet paint paws as art, and claim it demonstrates cat's creativity. There are books, calendars, and postcards that detail cats masterpieces to buy online. Is it art? You be the judge.

Hound Dog Fashions

http://www.gatewest.net/~hounddog

Designer doggie goods for people. This site offers an exclusive collection of 70 cat and dog drawings transposed onto T-shirts and sweatshirts. All drawings are of mommy with pup or kitten and the drawings render the breed perfectly.

The American Kennel Club

http://www.akc.org

The American Kennel Club has been dedicated to purebred dogs and responsible ownership since 1884. It has created a website that is especially helpful for first-time dog buyers. The responsibility of owning a canine is made clear, and tips are given on how to care for a new pup. If you already are a dog owner, you can register your pet with the AKC, mail-order shop for goodies for your dog, and keep abreast of AKC events and news.

The Breeders Guide

http://www.burgoyne.com/pages/breeders/breeders.htm

You have passed the AKCs test of responsible ownership. Now you want to find a breeder, but the phone book shows no listing for, say, Rhodesian Ridgeback pups. You can go online and access the Breeders Guide, a referral service to get in touch with the one nearest you. And, if you are a breeder, you can register your pups with the service.

Breed Specifics FAQ

http://www.bulldog.org/dogs/breedfqa.html

Have some questions about a certain breed of dog? Breed Specifics FQA offers a host of information of over 75 breeds ranging from the ubiquitous Labrador retrievers to infrequently sighted Nova Scotia Duck Tolling retriever. Access to linking sites offering history, breeders, and kennel clubs for each breed are available.

Pet Loss & Grieving Resource Pages

http:www.cowpoke.com/~twscan/Pet.html.

Offers 25 interlinking pages to help people deal with and prevent the loss of their fuzzy pals. Support hotlines, ways to cope with your grief, and tips on how to find lost pets are accessible.

Pet Hotline

http://www.deltanet.com/allstar/petline.htm

Have a basic pet question but don't want to have to pay for a visit to the vet? Go online and check out Pet Hotline. This Web site works the following way: You scroll through the questions, until you find yours. Once you make a match, you call their 1-900 number to access a recorded answer. This Web site offers help for cats, dogs, reptiles, hamsters, gerbils, and fish.

Home: home decorating, entertaining

Food: cooking, cookbooks, chefs, gourmet

Gardening: gardening associations, horticulture, gardening clubs

Hobbies: crafts, sewing, art

Pets: pet care, pets and kids

Look into the real estate market in the Canary Islands at Homenet's international directory.
http://www.intertel.com

Check out the weather and time of sunset at Pathfinder's virtual garden site.
http://www.homearts.com

Browse Antique Alley, with screensize photos of individual pieces, separated by categories ranging from "tribal art" to "weathervanes."
http://www.bmark.com/aa/index.html

Find a recipe for dinner tonight by entering the ingredients you have in your fridge into Epicurious' recipe search. Also search by type of cuisine and course.
http://www.epicurious.com/e_eating/e02_recipes/recipes.html

Punch in your gardens' parameters and see what perennials will be appropriate for a spring bloom.
http://www.garden.com

Send an animated, personalized "postcard from the web" to the e-mail address of your special someone or today's birthday girl.
http://homearts.com/postcard

Chapter 12

Technology and the Internet

- COMPUTER HARDWARE AND SOFTWARE
- INTERNET ACCESS AND HELP
- NETIQUETTE
- COOL SITE PAGES
- WEB PUBLISHING AND HTML
- SECURITY
- INDUSTRY NEWS

10
TECHNOLOGICAL THINGS YOU CAN DO *RIGHT NOW*

1. Download some new software.

   http://www.shareware.com

2. Sell the old stuff.

   http://www.hyperion.com/usox

3. Grab some new wallpaper for your desktop.

   http://www.sirius.com/~ratloaf

4. Compare Internet Access Providers, and see how they stack up.

   http://thelist.com

5. Get e-mail, free.

   http://www.juno.com

6. Ask Bit-Witch where to chat online—or any other Internet-related question—and expect an answer.

   http://www.cybertown.com/bitwitch.html

7. Download and print the beginner's guide to HTML.

   http://www.ncsa.uiuc.edu/General/Internet/WWW/HTMLPrimer.html

8. Download free graphical goodies.

   http://www.pixelsight.com

9. Check your Web page code at the HTML Validation Service.

   http://www.webtechs.com/html-val-svc

10. Choose the right font for any occasion.

    http://www.will-harris.com/esp1.htm

You've watched as computers have revolutionized the way people live, learn, and work. From spreadsheets to desktop publishing and databases, the technological age has improved efficiency and competence in all aspects of our lives.

Computers are advancing so rapidly that it seems nearly impossible to keep up with the latest information about them. What kind should you get? What can you do with it? What if you need help? What are the latest developments in the field? The Web can help you answer all of these questions and more.

You can read entire computer magazines and keep up with the latest technology news—all for free. You can comparison shop for computers and other electronics and even sample software before you buy it. From grabbing shareware and fonts off the Web to deciding on a new computer for your business, the Internet is a ready resource.

Once you have the right equipment, you are ready to join the millions who are using the Web for personal and business communication and maybe even create your own home page. With your own Web site, you can spread a message to thousands at very little cost. Whether it's a business, a 'zine, or a home page dedicated to your family, use this new freedom to express your creativity and connect with others.

Anyone can create a site and put it on the Web for all to see, and fortunately, the tools you'll need to create your own site are relatively simple and available online. You can find all the basic guidance you need: from HTML primers to software to jazz up your pages with multimedia, to the cool sites of others to inspire you.

COMPUTER HARDWARE AND SOFTWARE

PCs

INTERNATIONAL APPEAL

PC/Computing Online

http://www.zdnet.com/pccomp

PC/Computing is a great resource for Internet beginners, avoiding nerdy computer talk and aiming squarely at home computer users. Updated monthly, features include the perennial "101 Tips" and one-minute guides. The uncluttered interface clears your mind to concentrate on useful tips like "hold down the ALT key and click on the right mouse button to view an item's properties." Worth a look if you're dead-set on becoming a computer whiz.

Intel Corporation

http://www.intel.com

Intel's Web presence is conservative and full of technical documents, but some gems shine through, like a thorough article on 3D virtual communities. Best of all, the Pentium fiasco (insert your own math error joke here) turned into a great sideline for Intel marketing types.

Build Your Own PC

http://www.verinet.com/pc

Considering building your own PC from parts? You're not alone. While the terminology of PC guts can be daunting, veteran PC tinkerer Jeff Moe spells it out as simply as humanly possible. The interface is spare, but the tips are the kind of straight talk you'd expect if you pulled a friend aside and asked for advice. Gives a good idea what to expect when you do it yourself.

Jim Brain's Commodore Home Page

http://garnet.msen.com/~brain/cbmhome.html

Long before the 32-bit computers of today, clunky boxes like the Commodore Pet talked in abrupt 8-bit sentences. Host Jim Brain is committed to keeping these relics alive, explaining how they can still do stuff like e-mail and simple word processing. Documentation, instructions on useless trivia questions will reassure you that, someday, when your Pentium system is worth $20.00, somebody will be saying, "Don't give up!"

Zenith Data Systems

http://www.zds.com

Zenith Data Systems serves up product support and info for its computer line, but instead of the typical cold-looking company site, you'll find a refreshing "cyber-journal" with frequently updated feature stories. They don't just do PC clones, either. Check out the wireless handheld computer that gets its processing power straight from an existing server without a full PC. The site's design is a nice contrast to most corporate pages.

Compaq Computer Corp.

http://www.compaq.com

Computer shoppers and support pros will appreciate this no-nonsense archive from one of the world's top PC makers. Compaq promotes its latest, while also delivering a great online support service (for a fee). Thanks to a cuddly relationship with Microsoft, you'll find plenty of information on Windows95 and its "Plug and Play" technology. If it plugs but doesn't play, download diagnostic software or check a list of common questions to ease your headache.

Windows95.com

http://www.windows95.com

This huge, well-organized archive of Windows95 tips, trivia, and software looks just like the Windows95 desktop. Funny thing is, the site isn't from Microsoft; Brigham Young University grad student Steve Jenkins has put together this beautifully designed site with everything from reviews of Microsoft's Internet Explorer to a custom live chat system for users to share Windows war stories. And, yes, Jenkins registered the windows95.com domain first.

NetEx Unofficial Windows95 Software Archive

http://WWW.NetEx.NET/w95/index.html

Internet consulting company NetEx provides a free online forum for downloading the latest Windows95 shareware and discussing Windows95 problems (like configuring TCP/IP to connect to their Internet providers). Strong content, including Usenet-like discussion groups and frequently updated software archives with a wealth of good downloads, makes the site worth repeated visits.

Screen Savers for Windows From A-Z and WindowsWallpaper

http://www.sirius.com/~ratloaf

While it's in need of a new name, this collection features nearly 300 screen savers with subject matter ranging from the Grateful Dead's dancing bear to clocks that look like cheese (see Figure 12.1).

PC Lube and Tune

http://pclt.cis.yale.edu/pclt

Finally, a palatable use of the "Information Highway" metaphor: a virtual service station offering repairs, maps, and gas from a computer scientist at Yale. Howard Gilbert gives wise advice in articles like "The Storm before the COM," explaining how to avoid the pitfalls of COM ports on PCs. No glitzy graphics at this pit stop, but clarity and charm make it a recommended stop for PC users seeking friendly advice.

System Optimization

http://www.dfw.net/~sdw/index.html

Those who wage a constant war against disk fragmentation, poorly performing software, and incompatible

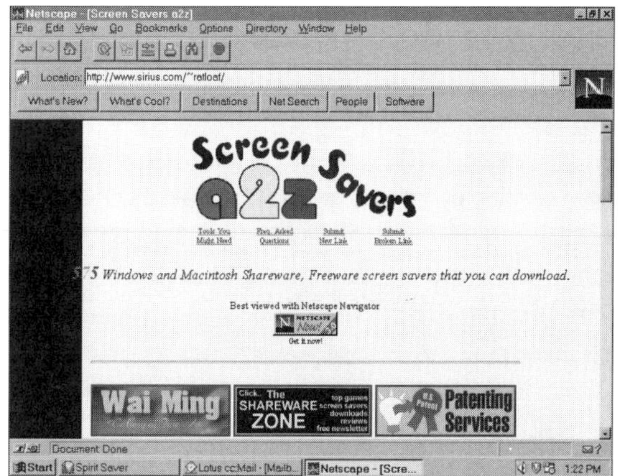

Figure 12.1

Screen Savers for Windows From A-Z and WindowsWallpaper, *http://www.sirius.com/~ratloaf*

hardware will find the tweaks listed here invaluable. Topics include proper BIOS settings for a PC, detailed information on motherboard chipsets, and an archive focusing on the controversial technique of "overclocking." Sounds scary, but PC geeks will eat it up.

Purchase Agenda: The Computer Buyer's URL

http://faraday.clas.virginia.edu/~jeg5s/buyers/buyers.html

University of Virginia grad student Ellis Godard knows the frustrations of trying to find a good PC at a decent price. His answer is this in-depth technical hand-holding that anyone from technophobe to techie should appreciate. DRAM or EDORAM? It's all explained here. The site is updated to keep current with the wildly changing market. If you're shopping for a PC, be glad someone is doing all this work for you.

PC LapTop Magazine

http://www.pclaptop.com

Laptop owners and prospective buyers will want to peruse this truncated, yet worthwhile, online version of *PC LapTop's* print edition. You'll find features like the abstracted cover story about the role of laptops in the O.J. Simpson trial, tips for extending battery life, and other guideposts for living life on the edge of technology.

Internet Shortcuts by CRE8

http://www.ratol.fi/~msiikani

Finnish PC guru Mikko Siikaniemi has turned his list of links to software, PC tips, and music sites into a work of art (see Figure 12.2). A stylish design helps you forget that you came by for shareware; also, there's tips on how to make your PC sing plus the inside scoop on the European rave and techno music scene. Intelligently organized and easy to navigate, this site holds some genuinely useful information.

PC Week Online

http://www.pcweek.com

This site has everything you've come to expect from Ziff-Davis's popular weekly and more. PC Week Online offers breaking computer news and product reviews as well as insightful commentary and editorials. Visit the download library, updated each week, where you can test drive the latest software. If you can't find what you are looking for here, link right to parent site ZDNet and it's bound to be there.

Figure 12.2
Internet Shortcuts by CRE8,
http://www.ratol.fi/~msiikani

PC Magazine Online

http://www.pcmagazine.com

Another useful site from computer publishing giant Ziff-Davis, PC Magazine Online offers up the contents of its print magazine plus much more. The site includes hundreds of reviews from PCLabs including ratings of the latest Internet tools, digital cameras, and the best home PCs. And check out their weekly tally of the 25 most popular Web sites.

Macintosh

Corey's MacOS Page

http://www.imc.sfu.ca/mac/default.html

MacOS page is clearly the work of a Mac devotee. With a fervor bordering on fanaticism, your host serves up a well-organized collection of software and other information about operating system updates (rated according to their usefulness), Apple's plans for the hardware line, and even System 8. There's also much more at this site, and it deserves some exploring.

Power Computing Corporation

http://www.powercc.com

The Mac clones are here. Apple has begun licensing Macintosh technology, and Power Computing offers some very fast machines, at prices that supposedly undercut the originals. The specs are interesting, but check out the interactive Build Your Own Box page, where you can get a price quote on the configuration you want. And for quirky fun, visit the Sam Cam page to see one of their programmers at work.

Cult of Macintosh

http://cult-of-mac.utu.fi

In terms of intelligence of design and useful pointers, Cult of Macintosh delivers, pushing nearly 1,500 links to Macintosh-related resources all over the Net. Frames and eye-catching icons put every one of the site's links within one or two clicks—a design that must be seen to be appreciated. Designed by Juhani Sirkia and Chris Stone, the Finland-based site should make Mac fans right at home.

Clock Chipping

http://bambam.cchem.berkeley.edu/~schrier/mhz.html

"Clock Chipping" refers to inexpensive speed upgrades you can make to many Macintosh models. The parts used in Macs are rated for certain speeds, but may often be capable of processing faster. This page lists which Macs can take advantage of such upgrades, and where to get the parts to do it. Most upgrades will require some soldering, so you'd better know what you're doing. Proceed at your own risk.

BMUG Online

http://www.bmug.org

The nonprofit Berkeley Macintosh Users Group is the largest Mac consumer advocacy user group in the world, and their site is a great resource for Mac aficionados worldwide. You'll find products and special interest groups here, as well as helpful tech support information and more. There's a great glossary of Mac and Internet terms and Mac error codes. Finally, you can find out what "type—129" error means.

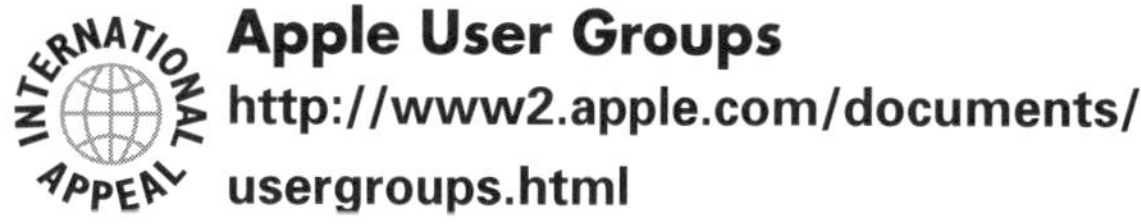

Apple User Groups

http://www2.apple.com/documents/usergroups.html

This page comes straight from the source (Apple Computer) and points you toward a Mac/Apple user group near you, wherever that may be. From MOUSE (Macintosh Owners and Users Society of Edmonton) to HUGE (Hartford User Group Exchange), you'll find links to user groups around the globe. Go local or global: Members get benefits like free clip-art and software, tech support, new product news, and answers to FAQs.

Mac Central

http://www.maccentral.com

MacCentral is a comprehensive monthly electronic magazine— independent of Apple—which promotes the World of Macintosh. In addition to feature reports, they offer hard news stories, like the brouhaha over the departure of Apple's CFO, plus news about the newest operating system. Lookout Larry provides updates on product releases and software updates (and site links for downloading them) and Central Sights showcases interesting new Mac-related Web sites.

Mac Today Online

http://www.avaloncity.com/MacToday/JuneIssu/default.html

Independent of Apple Computer, this e-edition of the monthly print "alternative Macintosh magazine" is quite generous, as readers get free access to "News From Apple," feature stories, and product reviews. Columns such as "Life in the Mac Lane" are also good. Efficient to browse, fun and informative. Lots of cool Mac links, too.

QuickTime Continuum

http://quicktime.apple.com

Both Mac and PC users will find plenty to do at Apple's site promoting its QuickTime digital video software. Apple updates you on the latest version of the software and points you to sites across the Web which offer free downloads of digital music videos. You'll need a fast Net connection to download most of these action-packed clips, but it's good fun.

MacWeek Online

http://www.macweek.com

This Ziff-Davis site brings you all the news from the world of Macintosh. Breaking stories, reviews, and opinion columns from the popular weekly are all available here. Plus the site offers a well-organized index of reviews and top-sellers as well as links to other useful Web pages for Mac enthusiasts. Link directly to parent site ZDNet for even more computer news and information.

Cross Platform

IEEE Computer Society

http://www.computer.org

Probably the largest computer society in the world, the IEEE Computer Society provides technical information and services to the world's computing professionals. You'll find the gamut of IEEE info here, including excerpts from the latest issues of magazines they publish, and a listing of all local and student chapters worldwide. And, boy, they must have gotten in early on the domain-name registration game.

The Used Software Exchange

http://www.hyperion.com/usox

The Used Software Exchange is a service for people to sell their used software to people who want to buy it. Looking for a copy of Novell 4.1 for less than $4,000.00? Want to sell your Sega Genesis carts, cheap? Buyers can browse the database; sellers must register (it's free); then add items, descriptions, and prices. Invaluable for anyone who's gone through the hassle of selling software via Usenet.

O'Reilly and Associates

http://www.ora.com

The creators of the Global Network Navigator offer this site for beginning Web publishers. You'll get support for their popular WebSite software and helpful ideas for Web publishing. You can even get WebSite for a 60-day free evaluation. For other technical tips, "Ora.com" magazine offers excerpts from books they've published. If you're interested in creating a new site or setting up your own server, this is a useful place to start.

Peachpit Press

http://www.peachpit.com

Unlike most computer book publishers, Peachpit focuses on largely non-technical guides. Sample chapters from hits like *The Macintosh Bible* are offered online. You'll find the interview-style author profiles, and the site's atmosphere in general, perky and refreshing.

InterFace

http://vvv.com/interface

There are plenty of magazines dedicated to the technical side of computers, but InterFace promises, "We no speak technobabble!" Segments include light interviews with significant people in modern industry. The "New Gadgets" section profiles recently released hi-tech toys. In essence, it's more a computer magazine for people who have "Gosh, that's neat!" reactions to computers and our technological age, but who don't need specs to build mainframes out of paper clips.

The Moan and Groan Page

http://eightof.tsixroads.com/Moan

Just about everyone's been burned by bad hardware or software at some time, but "The Moan and Groan Page" aims to change all that. This archive of war stories—"I spent three days on hold waiting for SlimeTech's customer support"—allows the Net's citizens to warn each other. The database is large, but mostly PC-related (stop laughing, Mac users), it might save you some hair yanking.

PowerPC

http://www.mot.com/powerpc

PowerPC is a speedy family of central-processor chips for personal computers from Motorola. Their Web site is eager to show off what this baby'll do in Macintoshes, NT machines, and probably toasters someday soon. Programmers and computer buyers will find much to ingest here. Regular folks may want to check in just to find out if their computer is already obsolete (it is), or to look at the funny TV commercials.

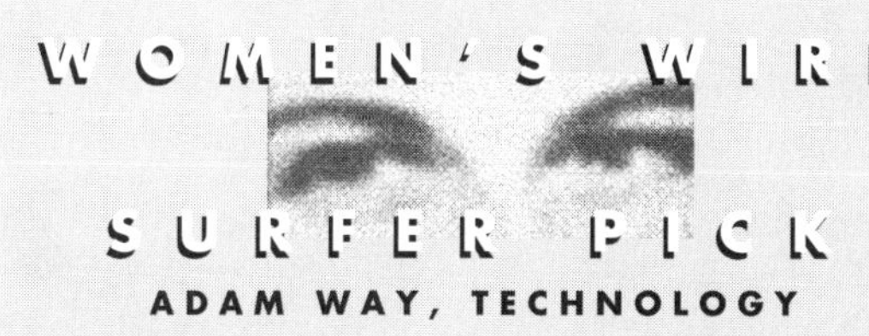

ADAM WAY, TECHNOLOGY

Tucows

http://www.tucows.com

If you're looking for your choice of free/shareware and demo software all in one place, you need look no further than TUCOWS (the name originally stood for "The Ultimate Collection of Winsock Software"). You'll find a well-organized collection of downloadable software for Windows 95, Windows 3.1, and Macintosh in an impressive array of categories including Sound, Movie Viewers, Internet, and much more. It's even performance rated and checked for viruses.

Abacab

http://abacab.mac.trincoll.edu

Hardware tinkerers shouldn't miss "Abacab," a computer made from garbage and spare parts. The brainchild of Trinity College student Frank Sikernitsky, Abacab is part Macintosh, part PC, and part Velcro. Hacked together from spare and junk parts, the machine runs Web, mail, and FTP servers. Read the whole story. Nicely annotated photos give you a close-up of the machine's inner workings. Check out the tongue-in-cheek sledgehammer upgrade system for old Macs.

Electronics Manufacturers on the Net

http://www.webscope.com/elx/homepage.html

This directory of switched-on Web sites will please nearly any technophile. You can peruse about 100 listings—mostly from computer manufacturers—or search by company name or product type, then link to Web pages. Most useful for gadget shoppers, although it's tough to make side-by-side product comparisons. Look for the number of listings here to increase with the growth of Web commerce.

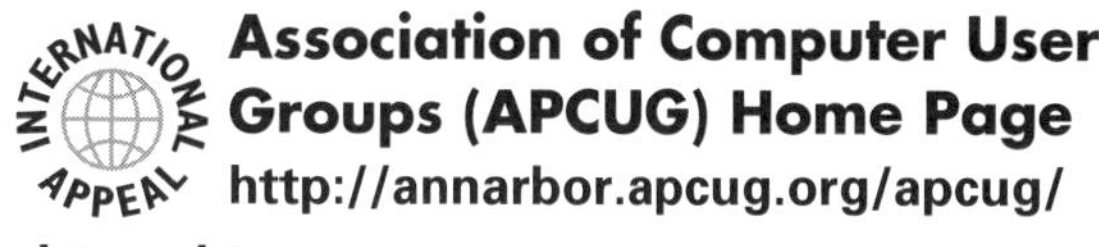

Association of Computer User Groups (APCUG) Home Page

http://annarbor.apcug.org/apcug/abtugs.htm

Computer users can get more value out of their experience if they join a user group or two, and this non-profit organization can help you find the group you're looking for, or the resources to start and manage one. Nearly every platform is represented here, as are more than a few countries and every U.S. state. And if your group isn't listed, there's a place for you to add it.

Jumbo!

http://www.jumbo.com

Jumbo! is a large, easily navigable index of quality shareware for PCs, Macs, and other platforms. Look for categories like Business, Games, and Utilities to find the software you're seeking, and a few clicks later you'll be reading a summary of the programs with the option to download them right away. All in all, this is an intelligently designed interface with good results.

Easter Egg Archive

http://weber.u.washington.edu/~davidnf/egg.html

David Nagy-Farkas collects Easter eggs, those little tricks and hidden features that programmers like to toss into their software. Some are well-known (like cheat codes for Doom), others aren't (an arduous series of keystrokes just to see a tiny picture of the programmer's dog). At the site, you can browse the large sorted-by-application collection of eggs. Need a quick Easter egg fix? Netscape users can press Control-Alt-F for a relaxing respite.

Maui Island Computing-Customer Support

http://www.maui.net/mic/tech1.html

Maui Island has put together this list of tech support contacts for hundreds of computer companies like Adobe Systems and Compaq. Next time you have a program blow up, and you lost the documentation six months ago—you can check here for the phone number, BBS, or Web page for tech support. It's nice to see a company providing a service like this to the Internet community.

Obsolete Computer Museum

http://www.ncsc.dni.us/fun/user/tcc/cmuseum/cmuseum.htm

Avocational curator Tom Carlson forged this virtual museum for those wanting to reminisce about outmoded personal computers of the "near past." Obsolescence enthusiasts may be interested in dinosaurs such as the Altaire 8800 (prototype PC), Osborn I, and Texas Instruments TI-99/4A. Includes personal history and opinions of machines such as the Commodore 64: "The nicest thing you could say about it was that it was faster than typing."

Notebooks.com

http://www.notebooks.com

More than just a price list, this notebook computers-only site serves up most everything you'd need to know to make an informed buying decision. Of course there's the sales motivation, but you'll be given accurate definitions of key terms and pros and cons of configuration options. Just a few clicks sends off a request for a price quote on the model you're looking for.

Children's Software Company

http://www.childsoft.com/childsoft

This Maryland software distributor offers dozens of titles here, indexed alphabetically and by categories like creativity, early learning, music, and foreign language. They offer an online newsletter for new products and interesting sites elsewhere on the Web. True fanatics can register their vote for the year's best children's software, too.

Techno Weenie

http://www.rubyslippers.com/spaceweenie

Gamers and graphics fanatics find a home at this graphically rich 'zine (see Figure 12.3). Look for solid reviews of new PC and Mac multimedia software, news of upcoming releases, and a chance to talk back to the site's creators, Ruby Slippers. Recent contents included reviews of the game F/A 18 Hornet 2.0 and Photoshop plug-in Black Box. And, they take the weenie motif as far as it can go.

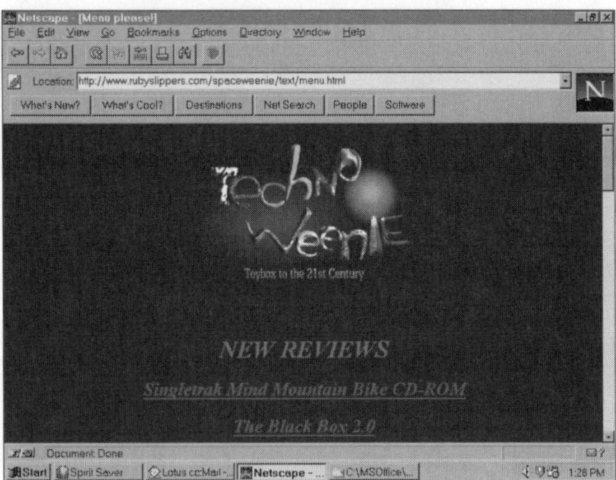

Figure 12.3
Techno Weenie,
http://www.rubyslippers.com/spaceweenie

WorldVillage

http://worldvillage.com

This site gives an impressive performance as an entertainment and educational software reviewer. Well-written columns focus on new or established software aimed at home users. Alongside announcements of upcoming preschool educational software, you'll find tips for the flashier games that are the real reasons so many parents are urged by their kids to buy a PC. A respectable online magazine, and worth a look.

Virtual Software Library

http://www.shareware.com

The mother of all software archives on the Net. This mind-blowing shareware server uses shase, a brilliant indexing system created by Dr. Ziga Turk of the University of Ljubljana, Slovenia. Click on an icon for your computer type, enter some search words, and a list of relevant shareware from servers around the world pops up nearly instantly. Or, you can get a list of the top 30 requested files. Staggeringly simple.

ZD Net Software Library

http://www.zdnet.com/zdi/software

Ziff-Davis's ZD Net is a strong Web resource for PC and Mac users. This sub-site should appeal to those looking for recommendations on which shareware applications are worth the time to download. In addition to categorized recommendations (games, utilities, Internet, etc.), the site offers a monthly shareware feature. The intent is to cut through copycat programs and ferret out the genuinely creative and useful ones.

Versions

http://www.versions.com

This site promises to send you announcements via e-mail whenever the software you select gets updated. Yes, it's a good idea, though there's no guarantee that the company is playing the game and willing to pay Versions to distribute its press releases. "You're still running WidgetScape 4.3?" you'll say with a scoff. "4.4 has been released for nearly an hour."

INTERNET ACCESS AND HELP

PSI Interramp

http://www.interramp.com

This launch pad for PSI's nationwide Internet service offers links to "hot spots" on the Web, or the ability to download from a useful library of utility software. Internet access shoppers shouldn't pass up the free Instant Interramp software, which lets you test the service for a week. Not the easiest site to navigate, but rich in technical support info. Links to weather, news, and sports, too.

SPRYNET

http://www.spry.com

The makers of Internet in a Box are quite energetic and eager as they describe their new Net products and offer enthusiastic online support. (Note: CompuServe purchased Spry in early 1995.) Expect frequent updates and cool new tools. Also, this Seattle-based site has added a handy search engine, the Spry Internet Wizard.

Telecom Information Resources

http://www.spp.umich.edu/telecom/telecom-info.html

This index lists more than 600 Internet access providers, telecom companies from the U.S. to Germany, and a list of Internet business directories. Pretty much anything that has to do with cable, wireless technology, and any other form of telecommunication is grouped into neat categories. These are the best of the best, and the list is updated regularly to keep it that way.

The Galactic User Group

http://www.galactic.london.on.ca

This Canada-based site is brought to you by a group of individuals dedicated to sharing their ever-

where they surf

Surfer: Stacy Horn

Founder of Echo, the "virtual salon of New York City," an online community and fun Web site with great links and a regular "Stacy's Obsessed!" column about Stacy's passion for, among other things, drumming (http://www.echonyc.com).

Her favorite sites of the moment:

Word

http://www.word.com

"An evolving collection of contemporary cultural artifacts and commentary."

Girls on Film

http://www.girlsonfilm.com

"Whenever I see a film, I go here to see what the rest of the girls think."

growing knowledge of the Internet. At their site, you'll find answers to questions on hardware, software and Web page authoring, as well as technical support. Membership is encouraged, but it's free (simply subscribe or attend one of their monthly "virtual meetings"). This is one group that may make your online life a little easier.

Internet Resource Center

http://www.software.net/internet.htm/SK:Inehfekmkgljidge

From online vendor Software.net comes this collection of links to an impressive collection of tools for browsing, building, or otherwise using the Internet. Most of the Software featured here isn't free, but it's often inexpensive, and free demo versions may be available (click the "more information" button). The site is well-organized, and offerings cover a huge range of needs, from Web Authoring tools to Plug-ins and Utilities. The name says it all.

INTERNATIONAL APPEAL

The List

http://thelist.com

The List is a database of 1,000+ Internet access providers around the globe, as well as tons of information: connection fees, customer service numbers, e-mail addresses, and more. You can pull listings by area code or by country, or search by the provider's business name. If your provider is listed, you can rate its service and provide notes—user support is one reason why these listings are so extensive and reliable.

How To Select An Internet Service Provider

http://www.cnam.fr/Network/Internet-access/how_to_select.html

This guide to finding the right Internet service provider (ISP) gives you tips on "looking under the hood" of prospective providers. Written by Rick Adams, president of UUNet, this site holds a lot of good information often overlooked, like network topologies, customer base, and the provider's internal network link speeds. Almost required reading if you're connecting your company to the Internet for the first time.

Juno—Free Internet E-mail

http://www.juno.com

Yes, free—the software, access time, data transmission—everything will be free to anyone who has access to a computer and modem. Software company Juno tells

[OVERHEARD ON WOMEN'S WIRE]

http://chat.women.com

ON THE INTERNET:

"I think it is a wonderful, wonderful invention and everyone should get into it."

ON HER FAVORITE SITES:

"Now I go into my own, because we have a site on AOL. But I go into all the programs. Oprah has one, there is one on parenting, the mothers forum, and I do a lot of it."

ON GETTING OTHER PEOPLE ONLINE:

"I know a lot of people my age, 35, they are sort of past the age where they think they can learn. But it's not that hard–get a Macintosh, point, and click. That's my advice."

—Comedian Rosie O'Donnell, *http://www.rosieo.com*

you how: Just download their free software, and you're ready to go. How is it free? Through advertising. (Which the company promises will be unobtrusive.) And using demographic information you supply, you'll only get ads in which you'd actually be interested. A site to watch.

The National Public Telecomputing Network

http://nptn.org

How can you have a superhighway without connecting back roads? The NPTN is attempting to connect people

I·N·T·E·R·N·E·T M·I·N·U·T·E

CREATING A WEB PAGE

Learning HTML programming is a piece of cake, because it only involves putting formatting tags around text. For example, the title of a document you want to publish would be tagged like this:

<TITLE>My Catchy Title</TITLE>

Get it? It's not hard.

One of the best ways to learn how to create your own Web site is simply to copy someone else's coding as a test.

Find a site that you like. Go to the "View" menu and click on "source" if you use Explorer, or "document source" if you use Netscape. You'll get a copy of the source code for the page. Next, you can download it, leave the HTML tags alone, change the text to suit your needs, save it, and name it something that ends in .html. Another option is to use free/shareware or a commercial HTML editor. When you have created a page, drag the icon for this new document across your Netscape or Explorer icon and there you have it: You've created a fantastic home page. This page is only located on your local hard drive, it is not yet on the Web.

To broadcast your site to the rest of the world, you'll need to find an Internet Service Provider (ISP) and get a SLIP or PPP account. Make sure that your monthly fee includes not just your Internet access, but also some disk space on the service provider's Web server.

Most ISPs give between 5MB and 50MB; 5MB to 10MB is sufficient, unless you use lots of multimedia in your site. Your ISP will tell you how to get your Web page onto their server.

You can find a local ISP by looking at The List, a comprehensive list of all ISPs:

http://thelist.iworld.com

There are lots of sites out there to help you create your home page. You can start with these sites, which link to other useful sites as well:

http://www.links.net/webpub/html.overview.html

http://oneworld.wa.com/htmldev/devpage/dev-page1.html#doc-a

http://info.med.yale.edu/caim/StyleManual_Top.HTML

In addition, there are informational books to help you out:

Teach Yourself Web Publishing with HTML, Laura Lemay, SAMS Publishing, (800) 858-7674.

http://slack.lne.com/Web/HTML3.2

HTML Sourcebook, Ian Graham, 1995 John Wiley & Sons, (800) CALL-WILEY.

HTML for Fun & Profit, Mary E.S. Morris, Prentice Hall, (800) 947-7700.

Every day, some new technology is being developed that allows Web page developers to do more than they could before. Keep abreast of what's new, and be prepared to update your site as needed. Most importantly, experiment and have fun.

in local communities by way of "Free-Nets"—central computers located in each area. Users can dial in at relatively little expense. It's inexpensive due to the volunteered expertise of local residents who want to get their community connected. They see it as a public service—providing medical, political, and educational information.

Mac Internet Helpers

http://www.tiac.net/users/mdw/machelp.html

This site's helpful pointers to Mac Internet software tools are made even better by a well-designed interface (see Figure 12.4). The pointers are organized into categories like Web browsers, e-mailers, and News Readers, so it's easy enough to get in and out with what you need. One great feature: For each item there's a short review on the application's own site.

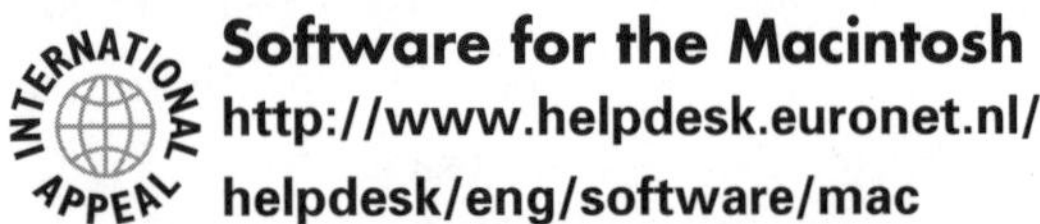

Software for the Macintosh

http://www.helpdesk.euronet.nl/helpdesk/eng/software/mac

Internet cowboys need to have the latest branding irons, and this site aims to please. You can download the Internet software you need to make your surfing/creating more satisfying. From Netscape to JPEG View, from GIF Converter to Fetch, the folks at EuroNet have created an excellent archive. As a bonus, the right brain is treated to nice icons rather than a boring FTP directory.

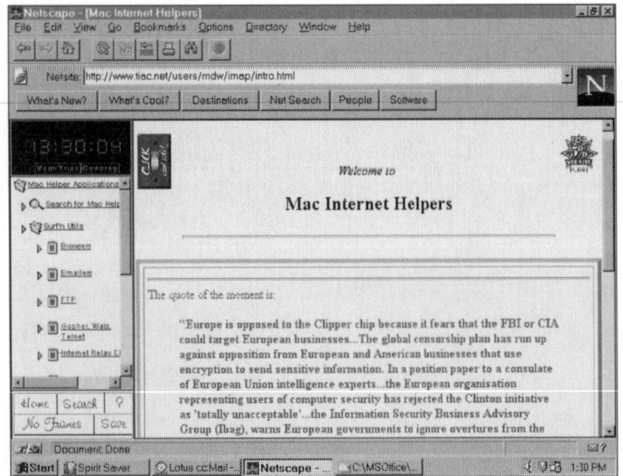

Figure 12.4
Mac Internet Helpers,
http://www.tiac.net/users/mdw/machelp.html

The Internet Help Desk

http://w3.one.net/~alward

Brimming with troubleshooting checklists for popular applications, networking, and even Microsoft Windows, this site makes for a great (free) technical reference. Mail bouncing back to you? There's a dictionary to explain why a message from MAILER-DAEMON is nothing to fear. Can't telnet to a site? You'll find a checklist of things to test. Site author Amy Ward even promises to answer e-mailed questions about things not covered on her site.

Net as a Telephone FAQ

http://www.northcoast.com/~savetz/voice-faq.html

Don't tell your phone company, but this FAQ explains how to use your Net connection to make unlimited phone calls across the world. You need special software and a fast Net connection, and the person you're calling has to have the same software, but this page is worth exploring for the curious. The text-only FAQ mainly covers the software available, and links you to sites where you can discover more.

Butterfly Glossary

http://www.rirr.cnuce.cnr.it/Glossario/glhpage.html

The graphics in this Net term glossary appear positively poetic against the reality of this useful site (see Figure 12.5), published by CNUCE Institute of the Italian National Research Council (CNR). Search by letter or keyword for thorough definitions of almost any acronym and code term imaginable, though new users may find that many definitions themselves require definition. Hypertext links make the jargon jungle more surfable.

Usenet Info Center Launch Pad

http://sunsite.unc.edu/usenet-b/home.html

A great resource for people who read Internet news. The Usenet Info Center Launch Pad can tell you what Usenet is, how to use newsgroups, how to create newsgroups, and more. This service was previously known as The Bible of Usenet, and it's still growing. A purely textual interface, so don't expect flashy graphics. If you want current and complete information about newsgroups, this may be just what you need.

Figure 12.5
Butterfly Glossary,
http://www.rirr.cnuce.cnr.it/Glossario/glhpage.html

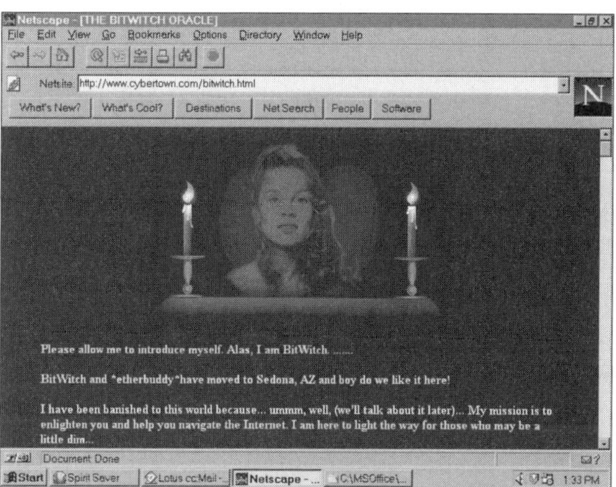

Figure 12.6
The BitWitch Oracle,
www.cybertown.com/bitwitch.html

Infinite Ink's Directory

http://www.jazzie.com/ii/toc.html

This mega-FAQ site, maintained by Nancy McGough, features a good foundation of links and FAQs on the basics of the Internet. Some examples: The Internet In a Nutshell provides pages of info on topics like Connecting to the Net, Marketing, Jargon, and MetaWeb. Electronic Conversation points to a stack of how-to's on news and e-mail. There's enough here to take you from novice to expert in no time.

The BitWitch Oracle

http://www.cybertown.com/bitwitch.html

Clever BitWitch (Susan Bush, owner of Inex online connectivity provider) offers to answer any and all Internet questions—from a "fuzzy perspective." Send her a question on anything from Net-phone software to hard drives, or you can browse through the questions of others to see if yours has already been addressed. Just the thing to help would-be Web-divas feel a bit more comfortable (see Figure 12.6).

Alt.Spam FAQ

http://ddi.digital.net/~gandalf/spamfaq.html

Here's a page that explains in detail how to deal with that pesky unsolicited e-mail known as spam. Although author Kris Coppieters obviously knows what he's talking about, the instructions he provides are written for the non-techie as well. For example, in instructing readers to check the origin of the mail, he translates: "the part after the (@) sign." These simple skills will make you feel very clever.

NETIQUETTE

The Net: User Guidelines and Netiquette

http://www.fau.edu/rinaldi/netiquette.html

Arlene Rinaldi wants to make it clear that she is "not the Miss Manners of the Internet." Yet she fills a definite need, providing a clearly articulated online etiquette guide. Dedicated to the idea that everyone is responsible for his or her own actions on the Net, this site covers topics like e-mail, Telnet Protocol, FTP, discussion groups, and the World Wide Web, plus NOT-iquette items like chain letters and offensive language.

The Netiquette Comic Strip

http://carbon.concom.com/~dmenter/Netiquette/netiquette_hmpge.html

Author David Menter gently pokes fun at clueless newcomers at this creative, funky site, while he provides information to help you learn the ropes and feel like an insider. Features include tongue-in-cheek Netisodes (which occasionally feature a bumbling character called Newbie), the Netiquette Archive page, and the Newbie for President pages, plus lots of great links. A fine example of Internet life that doesn't take itself too seriously.

Netiquette

http://www.primenet.com/~vez/neti.html

This text guide to Internet Newsgroup manners covers everything from the simple ("DO read the (To:) and (Cc:) lines in your message before you send it") to the more subtle ("Don't rely on the ability of your readers to tell the difference between serious statements and satire..."). Site host Vince Zema provides enough helpful pointers here to allow users to sound like they've been doing it for years.

Copyright and Netiquette Primer

http://www.abitec.com/home/page1.htm

This site "primer" from intellectual property consultants Abitech, Inc. is as helpful as it is adorable. The trial version (the company sells the real thing) includes an eye-catching story on what can happen if you don't bone up on the latest in copyright laws before publishing your Web page. Other easy-to-follow, picturesque guides include Netiquette (including e-mail), an Internet dictionary, and a spot where the truly overwhelmed can go for "HELP!"

COOL SITE PAGES

Lycos Top 5%

http://point.lycos.com/categories/index.html

Feeling overwhelmed by a seemingly uncharted sea of Web sites? Popular search engine Lycos does the research for you with this collection of top picks. Chosen sites are organized into logical categories and sub-categories, with each site being thoroughly reviewed and rated according to content, presentation, and overall experience. Also, you can search by topic to view the top picks in the subject area of your choice. Know where you're going before you get there.

Whoopie!

http://www.whoopie.com

The folks at Whoopie! have found their niche in audio/video: They index and rate audio and video clips on sites throughout the Web. One great feature: the Program Guide, a *TV Guide*-style listing of audio and video events and programs being broadcast on the Net each day; so when Pearl Jam does a live Net simulcast of a concert, you'll know in advance.

where they surf

Surfer: Drue Miller

Web mistress at Vivid Studios, a San Francisco-based Web site developer.

Her favorite sites of the moment:

Safer Sex Pages

http://www.safersex.org

"Information about HIV and AIDS, sexually transmitted diseases, reproduction and contraception, and more, presented in a very understandable, non-judgmental format. Resources like this are especially important at a time when our government is cracking down on available material about sex and sexuality."

Tweak

http://www.safersex.org

"Tweak is a 'zine filled with personal stories and no-nonsense journalism. I submitted a piece for it, but that's not the reason I like it so much :-). The design is simply exquisite. They're among the most beautiful and Web-friendly works I've ever seen."

Netsurfer Digest

http://www.netsurf.com/nsd/index.html

Subscribe to this free weekly service, and Netsurfer Communications will find new and interesting Web sites, classify them in topics like Thread Watch and Surfing Science, and ship them in a short hypertext document right to you. (Compliments of Netsurfer's advertisers, of course.) This site is for surfers who'd rather watch from the beach.

BitStreet Internet

http://www.bitstreet.com/cool.html

This "cool site" site has some special features that separate it from the pack. "If you've got pipes, we've got sites" points high-bandwidth surfers to sites that take full advantage of the Web's multimedia capabilities, and Toybox features games and entertainment links. It's updated frequently, with links to "Rubber Chicken.com" and the Ben & Jerry's Flavor Graveyard.

Cool Central

http://www.coolcentral.com

This JavaScript enhanced, animated cache of featured sites of the moment, hour, day, week, and…you get the picture (see Figure 12.7). These slick clickers have "presurfed" the Web for you, and unearthed some truly interesting destinations. New sites daily, so you'll stay busy. And you'll love the penguin.

Figure 12.7

Cool Central, *http://www.coolcentral.com*

Mirsky's Worst of the Web

http://mirsky.com/wow

For you cynical types, the snarly Mirsky has created this site to warn you of the Web's groaners, and point you toward sites that are so bad, they're good. By now a Web institution—it's considered a kind of compliment to be among the chosen—WOW offers carefully categorized current selections and past archives for your browsing dis-pleasure. When you've stopped giggling, check out more mouse-in-cheek stuff, like Mirsky's Drunk Browsing Test.

THE ANGLE

http://www.theangle.com

This very cool site points you to other cool sites—with an angle (see Figure 12.8). With information you provide, the links and news you receive (once you've registered, bookmark the site, then go straight to "regulars") are personalized to fit your taste in online fare. You'll have fun choosing from several stylin' interfaces, picking an "editor," and choosing an overall tone (*60 Minutes* meets *Life? Seinfeld* meets *People?*) for your info. Best of all, it's free.

CoolSchool

http://vassar.coolschool.edu

This cool blue site, maintained by Vassar College, is aimed at high school students and their teachers.

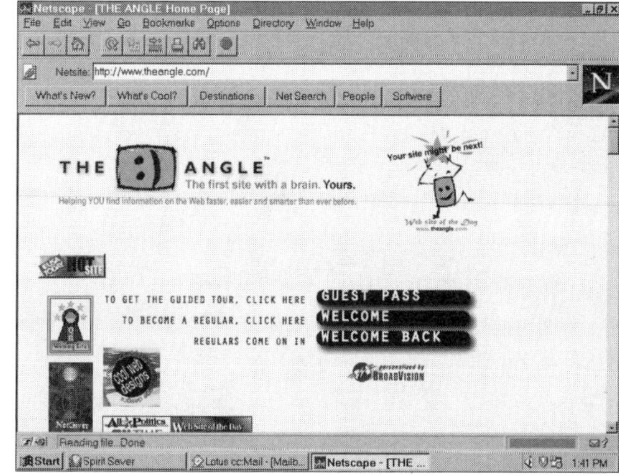

Figure 12.8

The Angle, *http://www.theangle.com*

It features links to educational (Go to School), Fun (Hang Out), and informative (SAT, etc.) sites, plus the Teacher's Lounge (see Figure 12.9). Featured links are interesting and useful (the Art section yielded links to the Metropolitan Museum of Modern Art and the Louvre, among others.) And it's hip enough to pass muster with teenagers.

Web Wise

http://webwise.walcoff.com

This corporate-sponsored guide to getting started on the Web is designed with new surfers in mind. Clean design and carefully selected links point out what's good, bad, and useful on the Web. Example: The Surf Shop, where you can stock up on the software tools you'll need to get every last Javafied, multimedia, animated ounce out of the Web.

Project Cool

http://www.projectcool.com

Glenn Davis, creator of the popular, often-imitated Cool Site of the Day, has moved on to bigger things. Project Cool is the result. This newer incarnation still points out cool sites, but with a fancier interface and added original content like Future Focus, a forum for essays on where technology and the Net are headed. Also look for the Developer Zone, a list of resources for programmers and Web developers.

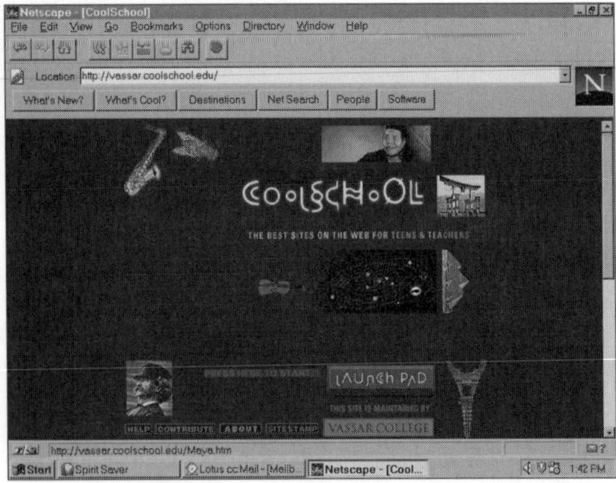

Figure 12.9

CoolSchool, *http://vassar.coolschool.edu*

Xplore

http://www.xplore.com

Xplore's creators have put together a site with links to what they've ranked as the top 500 sites on the Web. It's bigger than most people's bookmark lists, but much smaller than any of the well-known Web review sites. To someone who just signed up for their 10 free hours on AOL, one-stop shopping at Xplore may be a godsend. The well-Web-traveled won't find many surprises.

Daily Buzz

http://www.dailybuzz.com

Web fanatic Eric Bjorndahl hasn't really broken new ground with his Daily Buzz site, but it's enough that everything here is done unusually well. Look for organized, frequently updated links to the Web's best sites, daily news, comic strips, and more. Aesthetically, this hodgepodge of information is a treat. It's a strong site with clean, readable text and no obtrusive interface tricks. Enjoy the experience.

The Cool Site of the Day

http://cool.infi.net

The simple concept of picking an entertaining new site each day has built Glenn Davis's creation into one of the most compelling on the Web. The idea has built thousands of followers—creating a guaranteed flood of visitors to any site that makes the list—and many imitators. It will no doubt be one of the Web's kingmakers for a long time to come.

The Super 70s

http://www.wwnet.com/~densmore

Pop in an 8-track, slip on a mood ring, and slide into your beanbag chair: It's time to journey back to The Super '70s. This hilarious Web index is crammed full of links to sites celebrating the culture, entertainment, and artifacts of the decade. The perpetrator, Jamie Densmore, slices and dices the Disco era into sections covering TV shows, movies, music, fads, sports, and collectibles from Pet Rocks to Shaft.

WEB PUBLISHING AND HTML

Beginner's Guide to HTML

http://www.ncsa.uiuc.edu/General/Internet/WWW/HTMLPrimer.html

The National Center for Supercomputing Applications (NCSA)—one of the original Internet builders—brings you this all-you-need guide to HTML for beginners. This site is home to a very large document (download it and print it; we're talking 50+ pages here) that you'll find to be a complete reference manual to HTML coding, including tips on making your pages professional and pleasant to read. A must for first-time Web weavers.

The Web Multimedia Tour

http://ftp.digital.com/webmm/fbegin.html

John Faherty has conquered the snarled mess of competing multimedia tools on the Web. Before you dive in, load up on software at his well-stocked Supply Shop, since the rest of the site is filled to the gills with examples of real-time sounds, streaming video, MIDI clips, and every other multimedia bell and whistle. Scores of media formats are discussed at length, too. Impressive feature: daily updates and new commentary.

INTERNATIONAL APPEAL

Macromedia, Inc.

http://www.macromedia.com

At this site from the multimedia software giant, you'll find some of the finest graphics on the Web, plus a healthy library of articles and multimedia clips for both hobbyists and seasoned professionals. Beyond the usual support and product info, Macromedia creates a "virtual community" for the multimedia industry by offering news, a file library, and even a chat area. Highlights: Industry Pulse (daily industry news) and Free Toys.

Hyperstand

http://www.hyperstand.com

Some magazines consider their online counterparts a teaser for the paper version, but this site is chock full of solid articles, intelligently written columns, and product reviews of hardware. Then there's April One, a "multimedia development soap opera." The video editing junkie and Macromedia fans of the world will find plenty to chew on here.

Interactive Media Association

http://www.ima.org

Get insider information on the multimedia trade from one of the industry's most influential groups. You'll find the latest on standards for CD-ROM quality and discover how to attend a "Multimedia Boot Camp." ("Hit the ground and give me 20 hyperlinks.") If you're embarking on a multimedia profession, check your luggage here. If not, the Glossary of Multimedia Terms may be of interest.

Web Toolz Magazine

http://www.webtoolz.com

Accomplished and would-be Webmeisters will love its excellent assortment of Net-related news, articles, and reviews—not to mention tools and pertinent links. It's good for, say, the scoop on Netscape's newest browser version. Get access to VRML editors and browsers, hot plug-ins, and all sorts of other good stuff. A comprehensive, elegantly designed, and most generous resource.

Netscape's Creating Net Sites

http://home.netscape.com/assist/net_sites/index.html

Want to build your own Web site or home page? If you're starting at square one, this is it. This index is housed at the launch site for most Web surfers: Netscape. You'll find a well-chosen compendium of sites to help you on your way. Sections include Adding Functionality, Authoring Documents, and Developer tools. This index is aimed at the average human, so don't expect a collection of high-end tech toys.

Webreference.com

http://www.webreference.com

This catch-all site covers enough ground to appeal to new Web users and masters alike. Casual users will appreciate the beginners' guides. More experienced ones will want to check out articles like "A Day In the Life of a Webmeister." For anyone who fears falling behind trying to keep up with the Joneses (or at least Jones.com), this is a handy tool.

Mesh Mart

http://cedar.cic.net/~rtilmann/mm/index.htm

Mesh Mart is trying to fill the need for reusable 3D objects. Web designers and graphics gurus may find just what they're looking for among the site's free and commercial 3D objects. Need an eyeball for an anatomy lesson? Just download it, or post your request to the bulletin board. The site's inventory is extensive, and most items are currently free.

Web Master Magazine

http://www.cio.com/WebMaster/wmhome.html

This is the online half of *WebMaster* magazine, intended to enable IT professionals to use the Web more effectively. It's well-organized, with points of interest right at the top of each page. If you're new to the Web, check the Overview of the Web seminar notes, presented like overhead slides. There's a calendar, surveys, and interviews, and when you're done, relax with "What we learned today on the Web."

Photodisc, Inc.

http://www.photodisc.com

This home page, from stock photography supplier Photodisc, Inc., allows you to purchase images right over the Web. The graphically interfaced Web is a natural for this—you'll be amazed no one thought of it sooner. You'll have to register by phone to buy anything, but then you can browse their entire collection and buy one picture at a time. Also: Visit Design Mind for advice on design, Web creation, and other tidbits.

HTML Validation Service

http://www.webtechs.com/html-val-svc

Make sure your Web pages are up to HTML specifications: Give your URL, hit a button, and the Validation Service retrieves the source of your document and tells you what's wrong, at a "strict" level that catches a lot of niceties often ignored. There's also a place where you can type in a few lines and check them quickly. Find out if you really know your HTML.

The Web Developer's Virtual Library

http://www.stars.com

This site is a vast, organized array of links for the Web creator. The images and icons section gives you links (with detailed descriptions) to everything from where to grab pictures to software that creates pictures on the fly. There's also a whole "how-to" on 3D graphics on the Web, plus sample CGI scripts. As you'd imagine, the interface is packed with gratuitous graphics, but it's still a great resource.

Virtual Society on the Web

http://vs.spiw.com/vs

Sony's programmers have big plans to usher in the next wave of human communication via virtual reality. To that end, they offer CyberPassage, a Web-based VRML (Virtual Reality Markup Language) package that adds some non-standard extensions to VRML like sounds and interactive objects. They're also offering CyberPassage Conductor, which lets you build your own VRML worlds (both are free). There's also a VRML gallery that works with most VR browsers.

Pixelsight

http://www.pixelsight.com

Design firm Pixelsight's online graphics tools make it easy to create 3D logos and text for anyone who needs some spiffy images. Most impressive: all the tools are free. The real meat of the site is a tool that lets anyone create slick-looking 3D custom images with just a standard Web browser. There's also a huge clip art library of professional-looking images for personal use.

100 BEST SITES

Real Audio

http://www.RealAudio.com

The revolutionary Real Audio software lets you play sounds in real time, almost like playing a radio. You can download the player for free from this site and tune into live broadcasts from ABC News or NPR radio, among others. Or link to the many sites that have Real Audio files. You'll love the software's flexibility: Jump from the start of an audio file to any point in the file with a click, with only a slight delay.

JavaWorld

http://www.javaworld.com

JavaWorld is a full-fledged online magazine for the growing ranks of Java programmers. Produced by technical publisher IDG, the site's professionally written articles and reviews set it apart from the many "here's a link to a Java manual" sites. Contributors include one of Java's lead developers at Sun—you can be sure of good advice. And, you can get this great information at no cost.

Esperfonto

http://www.will-harris.com/esp1.htm

Esperfonto, maintained by self-professed type lover Daniel Will-Harris, is an online help system for choosing the right typeface for your project. Do you want formal or casual? Display type? Body type? Need to narrow it down? Friendly or serious? Modern or traditional? After you decide, you're given a list of suggested typefaces. Selected listings also include a sample of the font, and even a short history.

Netamorphix

http://www.netamorphix.com

Atlanta-based Web design firm Netamorphix brings you this useful site for aspiring Web publishers. You'll find concise tutorials on most popular Web design topics like Java, frames, VRML (Virtual Reality Modeling Language), and CGI scripting at one of the better generalized Web tutorials. Need to do HTML work offline while the tutorial is online? You're given the option of downloading the entire site. Have your cake and eat it, too.

Centripedus Center

http://www.centripedus.com

Centripedus is a graphics and Web design company, but it's almost difficult to tell. In addition to graphics and layout and terrific design advice, you get the added bonus of their opinions on life, with items like their Wiccan religion page and the Jeff Fahey fan page. This is passive advertisement at its most passive.

Dimension X, Inc.

http://www.dnx.com

Dimension X is a slick Web creation company, and their site shows off their talents. Although their X logo bears a resemblance to the *X-Files* logo you can't deny the originality present. They include their clients (including Imagination Network and the Who Shot Mr. Burns? pages) as examples. More original content: the chat rooms in The Cafe, movie reviews, and more.

Terra IncogNeta

http://www.netzone.com/~tti/whatsnew.html

This is the home of "The Stick," a monthly newsletter with news and tips about the Internet. Most of this online guide is devoted to "Surf Sites"—reviews each month of useful or fascinating sites—but recent issues have included a regular feature, "HTML Tips and Tricks," and a few other treats.

Lucidcafe

http://www.lucidcafe.com

The Web consultants at Lucid Interactive have put together this cyber-cafe—an eclectic mix of entertainment and services with a coffeehouse theme (see Figure 12.10). Learn about the lives of Thomas Edison, Mother Theresa, and Lorenzo de Medici, among others, or browse the directory of coffee-related sites. To round out the virtual decor, the Gallery features artworks from Lucid Interactive's Art Forum, a directory of artists, galleries, and art supply shops.

Java: Programming for the Internet

http://java.sun.com

Sun has a hit with Java, the platform-independent language that lets you embed applications (called "applets") in your Web pages. Java is built into Netscape and has been licensed for inclusion in Microsoft's Internet Explorer, too. A tour of this site shows just how much fun Java can be—and how easy it is to get started programming your own applets thanks to the many good resources provided here.

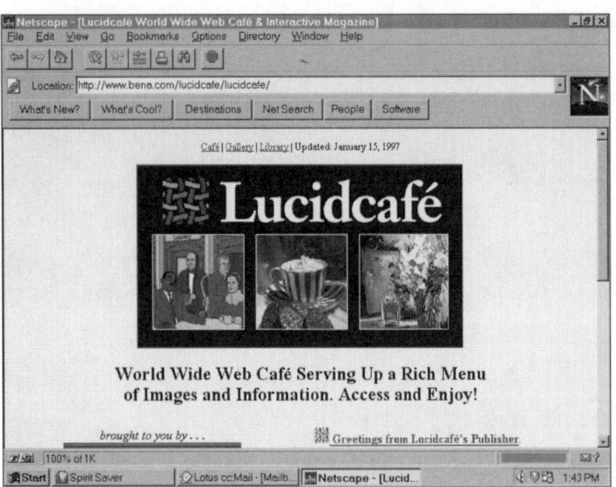

Figure 12.10
Lucidcafe,
http://www.lucidcafe.com/lucidcafe/lucidcafe

HTMLscript

http://htmlscript.volant.com

If you're running a Web service with subscribers who publish Web pages, they're probably clamoring for CGI ability, right? Not only is HTML script a powerful programming tool that users can enter into their HTML documents, it's fully configurable for security and activity logging, and it's completely independent of which browser is viewing the page. This should quell the cries of, "Gimme! Gimme!" from your users.

Yale C/AIM WWW Style Manual

http://info.med.yale.edu/caim/StyleManual_Top.HTML

Most "how-to's" for HTML composing will tell you how to create HTML so browsers will understand it; Yale's Center for Advanced Instructional Media (C/AIM) tells you how to create HTML so people will understand it. Each of their design principles is footnoted with sources, like the snippet that repetitive tasks that have more than a 20-second waiting time become intolerable. Good news: Their whole site is based on these principles.

InContext Systems

http://www.incontext.com

InContext's smooth site combines a little marketing with a lot of good information. The company's software tools, which include an HTML editor and a Web site link-checker, appeal to even inexperienced users. Notable features at this site include The Spider's Web, a high-quality electronic magazine geared toward businesses using the Web. This is a nice change of pace from most corporate sites.

The Internet Audit Bureau

http://www.internet-audit.com

The Internet Audit Bureau (iAudit) has made it easy to calculate usage statistics on your Web page: open a free account with them, and insert a line they give you into the HTML of your home page. That's all you need to have iAudit keep track of your Web traffic. The site now features The Top 25 Hit list, the most popular sites they track, plus weekly and monthly statistics.

BrowserCaps

http://www.pragmaticainc.com/bc

This form-based tool asks users of different browsers to go through HTML tests and "vote" on whether their browsers render it as described. Programmers and Webmasters know the difficulties of creating robust pages, because so many different browsers render HTML differently. This page can give you an idea of which browsers support which attributes. Takes a while to get through the tests, but it's for the good of the Web.

INTERNATIONAL APPEAL

How Do They Do That With HTML?

http://www.nashville.net/~carl/htmlguide

Green with envy at the neato stuff on other people's pages? Stop in here to get some tips on using those cool toys. Seasoned HTML writers might scoff at this page, but it's a good, conversational help document for first-timers. Most bits are Netscape-dependent (that's the most popular browser anyway), but other useful sniglets are provided, like how to get access counters and help on making transparent GIFs. Also in German.

HTML Bad Style Pages

http://www.earth.com/bad-style

This is a serious look at what to avoid when you're writing HTML. The site makes a strong case against using Netscape extensions: some estimates say 70 percent of the Web-faring public are using Netscape; but what if you move your site to another system, and try to use HTML tools that don't know about proprietary information? The site's not about Netscape-bashing, though, as there are plenty of solid tips here.

The Virtual Background Museum

http://www.teleport.com/~mtjans/VBM

Here's the Virtual Background Museum, a weighty collection of images you can add to your own home page for the benefit of Netscape users. Not only are there plenty of backgrounds to pilfer, but maintainer Lucas Jans updates frequently with new backgrounds. There are several feature sections, and a Top 25 section for the top backgrounds, chosen by users. Can't decide? Choose the new Random Background.

The Web Designer

http://web.canlink.com/webdesign/nl.htm

This is a page of links to resources for the beginning-to-intermediate Webmaster, including links to details on writing HTML. You'll even find an explanatory page, with a template you can copy and use for your own. Extras include Netiquette links (yes, that matters, too), and locations (with short descriptions) of programs for creating HTML documents on several platforms. If you concentrate on the content, this is a good starting resource.

[OVERHEARD ON WOMEN'S WIRE]

http://chat.women.com

ON CREATING A POPULAR SITE:

"Don't be afraid, just start browsing and exploring. It won't take long before you develop a good sense of what looks good, why it looks good, and what interests you. There is no substitute for experience. It is important to see what's out there and see how things are being done. Not that they are being done 'right,' but there are lots of ways of doing things."

ON WHAT WILL BRING A LARGER AMOUNT OF PEOPLE TO THE WEB:

"The most important factor is ease of use. We have to make it easy for people to get online."

ON THE COST:

"The ongoing expenses are what people don't expect. The sites have to be updated continuously. So, even if you have a simple site, you need to work on it all the time."

—Donna Hoffman, professor of management at Vanderbilt University and co-creator of Project 2000, a study of the commercialization of the Internet, in a live chat on Women's Wire.

Cold Fusion

http://www.allaire.com/cfusion

Cold Fusion is Windows software that puts databases on the Web by automatically fusing them into HTML code. If done correctly, it could save hours of work for companies wishing to market their valuable databases and enrich more Web sites with online conferences and searchable databases. The documentation here explains how it's done; you can even download a free 30-day evaluation version. A must-visit for Web developers.

Sausage Software

INTERNATIONAL APPEAL

http://www.sausage.com

Australian company Sausage Software makes the popular HTML editor HotDog Pro, and more recently they've developed Egor, a Java-based animation tool for Web sites. Egor, demonstrated via wild anthropomorphic sausages throughout the site, lets non-programmers develop Java animations with embedded sounds. While you're waiting for the large animations to load, you can read up on HotDog Pro to decide if you want to download the free trial version.

StarNine: WebStar

http://www.starnine.com

Software that turns a Macintosh computer into a Web server takes center-stage here. You'll get a chance to judge the software for yourself, since their own site is using WebStar running on a PowerMac with 8MB of RAM. If you're not ready to reach for the wallet, there's a useful resource guide to get an idea of how other people are building Web sites. An alternative for the Webmaster-to-be.

DeltaPoint

http://www.deltapoint.com

DeltaPoint is looking for a niche in the "I'd like a Web site but you can't make me learn HTML" market. Members of this group will want to check out the free evaluation version of QuickSite, a product that promises HTML-free Web authoring. Borland was impressed enough to license part of the program for inclusion in an upcoming product. Of course, DeltaPoint's own Web presence is created with QuickSite.

Interleaf, Inc.

http://www.ileaf.com

This electronic publishing site caters to users who've never written an HTML document and never hope to see one. Interleaf says its "Cyberleaf" software allows you to publish documents on the Web using your favorite word processing program. (The United Nations uses this software to publish online documents on nuclear disarmament.) Good reading for aspiring Net publishers.

Web Servers Comparison Chart

http://www.proper.com/www/servers-chart.html

This is an impartial guide and comparison chart to Web server software. Future Web publishers especially may want to visit this hypertext document, which lays out the facts and links you to sites where you can get the server software of your choice. Plenty technical and nothing glamorous; you'll need to know what you're looking for. Even so it's a great time-saver.

HTML: Working and Background Materials

http://www.w3.org/pub/WWW/MarkUp/MarkUp.html

Call this the Strunk and White style guide to HTML. You get all the whys and wherefores of HyperText Markup Language—the Swahili that makes the WorldWide Web possible—including its syntax and semantics, history, status of the standard, and development issues. Edited by Web vet Daniel Connolly, this site is complete, informative, and dense—a must for anyone who is designing their own home page.

The Common Gateway Interface

http://hoohoo.ncsa.uiuc.edu/cgi

You may not know what a CGI script is, but you've probably used one: They allow Web users to fill out online forms and click on pictures to get Web links. Here, they're explained by the gurus at NCSA. Those who intend to develop their own site will be glad they visited. Most valuable resource: a library of sample scripts to give you a head start.

SECURITY

EFFWeb

http://www.eff.org

The Electronic Frontier Foundation (EFF) is a nonprofit organization dedicated to promoting freedom of expression and responsibility in new media. EFFWeb backs that aim by bringing you news and information on the latest developments in privacy, intellectual property, and free speech. The site provides news about the battle against the Communications Decency Act of 1996, and the reasoning behind the organization's opposition to government regulation of content on the Internet. Now the Internet anti-censorship movement has the blue ribbon campaign which you will see on sites across the Web, courtesy of the EFF. You'll also find ways to get involved (letter writing, etc.), action alerts, and links to related sites. Contests, awards, and even cool T-shirts make it easy to leave apathy behind.

The WWW Virtual Library: Cryptography, PGP, and Your Privacy

http://world.std.com/~franl/crypto.html

This oft-linked site, part of the World-Wide Web Virtual Library, centers on cryptography and privacy issues on the Internet, providing sources and links to many privacy-related documents, such as the CRYPTONOMICON, possibly the largest FAQ in existence. The sources may

SPOTLIGHT ON SECURITY ON THE INTERNET

The Internet's global communications capabilities have led to the creation of many diverse online communities. Instead of basing communities on geographic proximity, virtual communities are formed around common interests—often by people who have never met f2f (face to face). Not surprisingly, Net communities sometimes contain online versions of some unpleasant real-life problems that can potentially impact your security. While these are rare and will probably not happen to you, it can't hurt to take the following common sense precautions:

1 Don't post your name, address, and telephone number in a public forum online. Many sites may ask that you give this information in a private form when you register with them—you might want to check if they plan to share this information with others.

2 Be careful when arranging to meet anyone face-to-face that you have only met on the computer. Plan to meet in a public place and consider taking along a friend.

3 Consider using a gende-neutral name in large live chat rooms.

4 If someone sends you unwanted messages in a live chat room or on a public bulletin board, ignore them. Chances are they will get bored and go away.

5 If you continue to be bothered by someone, keep copies of all e-mail and bulletin board messages, including your own.

Some sites that provide additional information and resources:

http://www.cyberangels.org
Neighborhood watch from cyberland's guardian angels.

http://www.anonymizer.com
A site devoted to surfing the Web anonymously.

http://www.io.com/~barton/harassment.html
Online Harassment Resources from the Webgrrls.

seem overly political at times, but they make plenty of good points. Great reference if you're looking for it; thought-provoking reading if you're not.

DigiCrime

http://www.digicrime.com

First, you're shown where you've just been surfing: "So much for privacy." This site is the home den of an organization of self-professed outlaw hackers, albeit a full-service one. Some services offered: Political Dirty Tricks, Internet Shoplifting Network, wealth redistribution service, and much more. You'll also find lots of disclaimers about incidents they claim not to be responsible for. Laugh hysterically, then be afraid. It'll make their day.

The National Computer Security Association (NCSA)

http://www.ncsa.org

Dedicated to providing information on security, ethics, and reliability issues, the NCSA maintains this mostly text site as a reference point for those issues. The site provides a clear picture of what the potential security risks of the Internet are, and what can be done to eliminate and protect against those risks. You'll also find intelligent discussion on the reasons these risks have arisen in the first place. Be an informed Netizen.

INDUSTRY NEWS

ZDNet

http://www.zdnet.com

Computer mag mega-publisher Ziff-Davis (*PCWeek*, *MacWeek*, etc.) brings their vast store of computer-life knowledge to the Web. The site provides a dizzying array of info on software, hardware, industry news, and insight on just about every platform you can think of. Test out software, get buying advice, and add your feedback on timely topics. Plus, you can check out the latest online editions of their seemingly endless array of magazines. A must-bookmark for the computer whiz wanna-be.

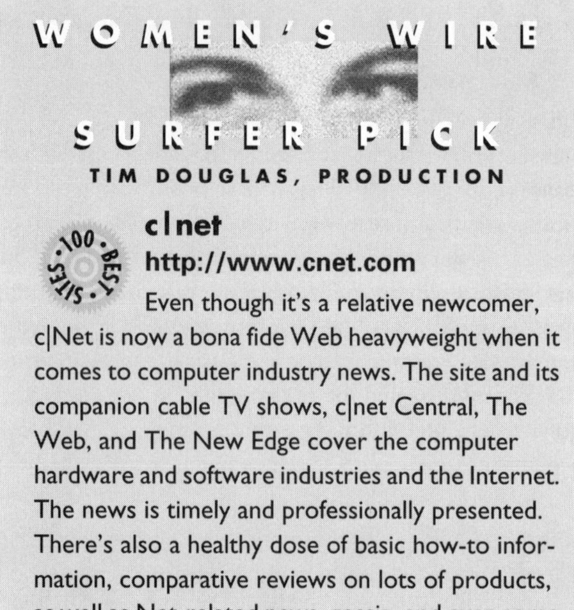

c|net

http://www.cnet.com

Even though it's a relative newcomer, c|Net is now a bona fide Web heavyweight when it comes to computer industry news. The site and its companion cable TV shows, c|net Central, The Web, and The New Edge cover the computer hardware and software industries and the Internet. The news is timely and professionally presented. There's also a healthy dose of basic how-to information, comparative reviews on lots of products, as well as Net-related news, gossip, and even some interactivity.

Andersen Consulting

http://www.ac.com

Take a look into this business technology consultant's crystal ball here. For a taste of their technology forecasting, Andersen Consulting publishes research reports here on issues like "The Possible Futures of Multimedia," where you'll find a series of scenarios businesses must face as consumers get more interactive power. Experiments like SmartStore Virtual show how "intelligent agent" software might affect Net commerce. Well worth a few thoughtful minutes of your time.

Off the Net

http://home.netscape.com/assist/net_sites/off_the_net.html

Housed on uber-browser Netscape's home pages, this monthly update keeps you current on the latest and greatest in developments and controversies on the Internet/Web Frontier. Publisher Chris Tacy, director of Web development at IDG Publications reports on industry conferences and other events, as well as shiny new software, protocols, and services for Net-izens.

HotWired Network

http://www.hotwired.com

By now you've probably heard of this online offering from digerati bible *Wired* magazine, but if you've never stopped by, you're missing out. HotWired features daily news and views on cutting-edge Internet and technology topics like spam-tagging, telecommuting, and Net-finance. You'll find interviews with major and minor luminaries from the pop-culture and online world, plus drink recipes, travel guides, a link to *Wired* magazine's site, and much more.

MMWire Weekly

http://www.mmwire.com

MMWire (Multimedia Wire) is a daily report on the industry, faxed to subscribers. Here, the newsletter is boiled down to a weekly online form. Emphasis is on commerce and corporations, with reports on major players along with smaller fish. The classifieds section has "help wanted" postings—there are some good jobs. Also included: back issues, events, trade associations, and much more. Essential reading for multimedia pros.

Howard Rheingold's Brainstorms

http://www.well.com/user/hlr

Brainstorms is an extended philosophical dissertation on how the Net will affect the future. Headed by Howard Rheingold, a speaker and writer on Net issues, it features an international roundtable of futurists, including Wavey Davey from London, and Digital Reiko (ex-teen idol from Japan). Also available are his Tomorrow columns, covering topics ranging from the use of MUDs to digital telephony opening the door for legalized phone tapping.

Steve Jackson Games vs. The Secret Service

http://www.io.com/SS

Steve Jackson was writing a book about credit card fraud in the future. The Secret Service injected themselves into the picture, touching off a lengthy legal battle over privacy and the Internet. This site meticulously retells the tale, from the March 1990 raid to the ruling against the Secret Service by a Texas judge three years later. A fascinating lesson on why policing the Internet could be the biggest problem in the Information Age.

TechWeb

http://www.techweb.com

From tech pub giant CMP comes this tech-news site to bring you the inside scoop from the front while remaining easy on the eyes. There's enough late-breaking news from Silicon Valley and points north to satisfy IPO groupies, plus thought-provoking features, summaries of stories past, and info on hi-tech careers, consumer pricing, and more. Added bonus: It's easy to navigate, and low on annoying ads, too.

Welcome to @WWWiz

http://www.wwwiz.com

This online version of the print magazine aims to help everybody understand the World Wide Web. Monthly feature articles are targeted to a general audience, while several columns address issues of concern to Web masters and authors. Great feature: An impressive list of HTML books, with reviews. This 'zine informs and entertains on all aspects of the Internet, from business news to the socio-political implications of a wired society.

Online PC Review

http://www.mg.co.za/mg/pc/pcrevie1.htm

An online mag from South Africa, Online PC Review is devoted to all things online, including Macs, other computers, and general Internet issues. Some items are South Africa-specific, but most are of general interest, like tests of chat room software, and the announcement that the Webmasters are mirroring the Cult of Macintosh Website. Arthur Goldstuck's column, "The Next Big Thing," is dependably entertaining.

WEBster

http://www.tgc.com/webster.html

WEBster is a twice-monthly index to news about the Web, with articles like "Pipeline Releases Web Browser for Macintosh" and "Telescan Investors Platform Redefines Financial Services." WEBster is geared to business clients, with some stories more promo than news. Hidden gems include the conference guide to help you plan your next junket. Fun master list of links.

Net Law News

http://www.mindspring.com/~moceyuna

Georgia lawyer Ann Moceyunas specializes in technology law so the developments on the Internet of the past couple of years fascinate her greatly. In clear, layman's language, Moceyunas covers the various legal problems of the online revolution—intellectual property, in particular. She summarizes specific cases as well as lots of background on the issues. An enlightening site for anyone confused by the legal niceties of the Net.

Surf News

http://www.newspage.com/NEWSPAGE/cgi-bin/walk.cgi/NEWSPAGE/info/d5/d1/d1

Up-and-coming Net businesses may want to follow this daily feature from NewsPage, a subscription clipping service. You'll find the latest business news about high-tech companies. The daily summary of news is free, but—aha!—only subscribers can get the full stories. Still useful as a daily update, and a must if you're trying to see if the name "Virtual CyberGlobal WebNet" is taken.

[OVERHEARD ON WOMEN'S WIRE]

http://chat.women.com

ON THE FIVE BEST TECHNOLOGY INVESTMENTS:

"Net, Internet, Web, Intranet, Online… Get the picture? Actually I think investors don't focus enough on the quality of the people. Technology and even business models change so rapidly that you can't count on anything other than quality people. Personally, I think service-intensive businesses, ones that know how to leverage content, are the most interesting."

ON THE ELECTRONIC FRONTIER FOUNDATION'S FIGHT AGAINST THE U.S. TELECOM ACT:

"We're hoping to have the whole thing overturned simply by taking it into court. Most sensible people (including many of the legislators who voted for it) and Al Gore (whose president signed it) openly acknowledge that it's unconstitutional. Beyond that, we're trying to get the general public to understand the importance of free speech and that the Net is not simply a gallery of dirty pictures and wicked perverts waiting to grab their children."

—Esther Dyson, technology industry insider and chairman of the Electronic Frontier Foundation, *http://www.eff.org*, a nonprofit advocate of civil liberties online.

Sunergy

http://www.sun.com/sunergy

This audio-visual education program from Sun Microsystems asks you to think about the future of technology in society. Executives and scientists from Sun join prominent users every two months for a forum broadcast worldwide on satellite TV. Audio clips and transcripts are here for those who miss it; topics cover issues like "Cyberjockeying in the 21st Century." It's useful for finding the "right" buzzwords and bibliographies. For the high-tech jet set.

Global Internet News Agency (GINA)

http://www.gina.com

GINA is one of the Web's most convenient sources for high-tech product news and announcements, offering a daily summary via e-mail. You can also visit the site for daily postings. News releases are mostly from the computer and entertainment industries, with titles like "L3 Interactive Ships Sports Title On New Platform."

Interactive Age

http://techweb.cmp.com/techweb/ia/current

Interactive Age is a digital magazine featuring daily trade stories like "Bug Hits AOL Chat Rooms." Its strength: coverage of trends in the hot new Web business. You'll find commercial links, a column titled "Tabloid Webism: A Penny a Peek," a terrific library of Web sites of top companies, as well as their choices for the top 25 commercial sites on the Net, and more. An authoritative, useful daily source.

Sam's Interactive Cable Guide

INTERNATIONAL APPEAL

http://www.teleport.com/~samc/cable1.html

The wave of the future: TV. And the Internet. Somehow. Sam Churchill's page provides some help sorting it out. Primarily a comprehensive set of links, it covers most ways that the Net is broadening its horizons. Cable modems? Real-time video on the Net? Two-way TV? Churchill test drives, or links to sources, every significant permutation of multimedia out there. Friendly, but bring your pocket protector; it's also available in French.

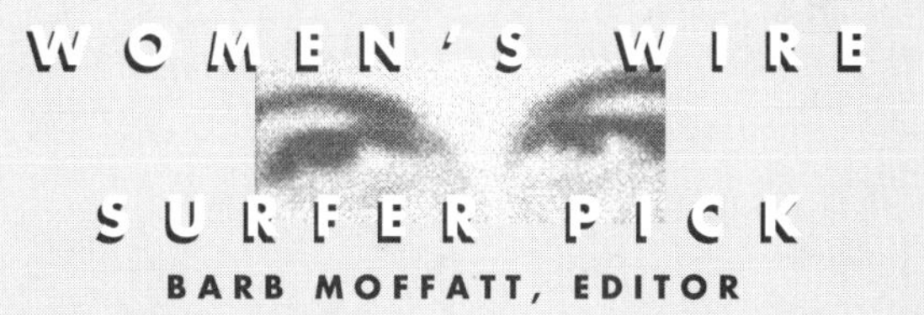

BARB MOFFATT, EDITOR

The Netly News

http://www.netlynews.com

Making its home on Time-Warner's Pathfinder, this site aims squarely for the same hip audience courted by the *Wired* offshoot, *Suck*. Best described as a sort of "News of the Weird" of the Web, with a bit of a political forum thrown in, Netly offers you bizarro news stories, as well as updates on controversial issues, plus fiction, fun and games, and FAQ. It's irreverent, it's interesting, but, as the small warning on the home page reads, "Netly is not for Kids."

Internet Magazine

INTERNATIONAL APPEAL

http://www.emap.com/internet/home.htm

Selected features of this online edition of the monthly print mag make for a worthwhile U.K. slant on the Web world (see Figure 12.11). Those include a Free Software Finder, numerous site reviews, British What's New on the Web, and listings of conferences and events throughout Europe, as well as the excellent Marketing Hot List. Of course, if you like what's offered free, a subscription form stands ready.

Where It's @

INTERNATIONAL APPEAL

http://www.whereitsat.com

This "fourtnightly" e-zine from Britain offers a concise update on Net business news and a useful guide to new sites (see Figure 12.12). You can learn, for example, the latest about a libel suit against Prodigy, and a brief update on Rupert Murdoch's plans for electronic newspapers. Great feature: "Best of British" collection of sites, including the intriguing Ecosystem entry. Useful if you want Web news in a hurry.

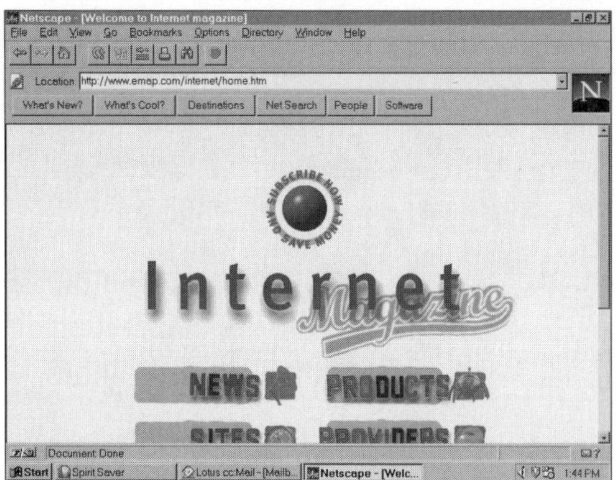

Figure 12.11
Internet Magazine,
http://www.emap.com/internet/home.htm

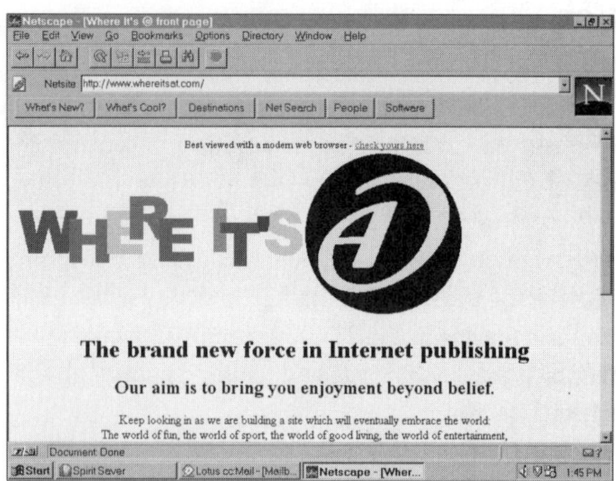

Figure 12.12
Where It's @, *http://www.whereitsat.com*

DaveNet: 24 Hours of Democracy

http://www.hotwired.com/davenet/96/07/index4a.html

Site creator Dave Winer was looking for brief, strong statements about the Internet that were positive. He received more than 1,000 responses. Devoted to the celebration of free speech on the Internet, 24 Hours of Democracy (hosted by Hotwired) contains the aforementioned essays plus images, news reports, and features. In addition to essays from regular folks, you'll find opinions from the likes of Bill Gates and Caleb John Clark.

NeWWW

http://grafton.dartmouth.edu:8023

NeWWW is a useful bi-weekly Web guide offering reviews of about 30 selected sites, plus feature articles on topics like the perils of e-mail and Web pornography, all from the perspective of Dartmouth students. Published during the school year, articles and descriptions of sites are student-written. It's a fresh view and a useful resource.

Survey.net

http://www.survey.net

Metairie, Louisiana-based Survey.net brings you this collection of online polls, invites you to participate, and offers the latest results on a variety of topics surveyed. You can turn your most cherished preferences and beliefs (on the O.J. Verdict, cyber-sex, who should be president) into anonymous statistics. Survey.Net offers plenty of discussion opportunities as well.

WorldWideWeb Consortium

http://www.w3.org/pub/WWW

Browsing this site is like walking in late on a heated debate. You'll find insider talk on hot topics like privacy and censorship on the Web and the latest Java technology (which allows browsers to run programs over the Web), for example. This site is a good place for programmers and Web designers to insert their two cents.

In, Around and Online

http://www.clark.net/pub/robert

Web users who travel via commercial online services like Prodigy or America Online can get the scoop on price wars from this weekly newsletter, brought to you by Robert Seidman of Westchester County, NY. He digs up comparisons and stock reports for the major consumer online services. Good, highly opinionated homespun reading—and a subscription is free.

Web Week

http://www.webweek.com

This online newspaper helps you fight a nearly impossible battle—keeping up to date on developments of the Web. Upstart Webmasters and avid cruisers will get the latest on browsing software and news from Web trade shows. The Web Watch page is a highlight, offering useful guides for Web publishers, and the News can be quite helpful.

Innovation Network

http://innovate.si.edu

This online awards ceremony for innovators in information technology isn't quite the Oscars, but it's worth a quick stop if you want to read about the latest crop of movers and shakers to get laurels from the computer and communications industries. If you must, shout out, "And the winner is" before clicking on each award.

Internet Herald—The Generation X Webzine

http://www.iherald.com

This University of California at Berkeley-based news-and-commentary monthly is written by and for 20-somethings. Themes include the political (a call to join a protest against Serbian oppression, for example) as well as Music, Humor, Game Reviews, and more random offerings like the Stud and Putz of the Month. It's news of the world with an irreverent twist. Outside submissions accepted, too.

Computer Currents Interactive

http://www.ccurrents.com/cc

Computer Currents is one of those free computer newspapers you'll find on street corners in big cities. Now you don't even have to go *that* far to get articles on computers and the Net. This complete online version offers local and regional advertising from computer stores, plus the clever Net Quote—a form that gets you customized price quotations from local dealers. Useful for local advertising.

Check out the Netiquette Comic Strip page:
http://carbon.concom.com/~dmenter/Netiquette/netiquette_hmpge.html

Find out what you're not missing, and take the Drunk Browsing Test at Mirsky's Worst of the Web:
http://mirsky.com/wow

If you have Netscape, press Control, Alt and F at the same time. Also find other hidden "Easter Eggs" in your software:
http://weber.u.washington.edu/~davidnf/egg.html

Hunt down some cool sites, like Ben & Jerry's Flavor Graveyard:
http://www.bitstreet.com/cool.html

 KEYWORDS

Technology: Internet news, business news, multimedia

Personal computers: PCs, Macintosh, user groups, software, customer support, shareware

Internet: Internet access, browsers, Internet FAQs, modems, Internet Service Provider (ISP), cool sites, Web publishing, HTML, Java, netiquette, cyberspace

Chapter 13

Shopping

DESIGNERS AND RETAILERS

APPAREL

VIRTUAL MALLS

AUTOMOTIVE

BOOKS

FOOD AND DRINK

MUSIC AND VIDEO

FLOWERS AND GIFTS

SALES AND BARGAINS

HOBBIES

TRAVEL

10
SMART SHOPPING THINGS YOU CAN DO *RIGHT NOW*

1 Register to become a member of the Express site, then print out a coupon for ten percent off your next in-store purchase.

http://express.style.com

2 Listen to sound samples from radio station WFMU's Catalog of Curiosities before ordering your musical selections.

http://www.wfmu.org/Catalog/Items/allsnd.html

3 Read Notes for the Beginning Collector at auction house Sotheby's Collector's Corner.

http://www.sothebys.com/Collector/emerge2.html

4 Register with Grapes, the online wine selection service, and get a free "wine enjoyment" kit.

http://www.grapes-wineline.com/joinin.html

5 Print out coupons that can be used at JCPenney for merchandise, photography, and salon services.

http://www.jcpenney.com/newhome/content/coupons.htm

6 Take a break from online buying, and let Derek's Free Stuff Page point you toward sites where you can get something for nothing.

http://www.ft-wayne.com/freestuff.html

7 Visit CraftNet Village's free project library for instructions on new crafts projects.

http://www.craftnet.org/projects

8 Comparison shop for the new or used car you want using DealerNet's car/dealer database.

http://www.dealernet.com

9 Link to dealers, trade shows, chats, classifieds, auctions, and price guides on everything from comic books to Star Trek memorabilia at the World-Wide Collectors Digest.

http://www.wwcd.com

10 Find the outlet centers and stores nearest you in Outlet Bound's database.

http://www.outletbound.com/omg/obfind.html

While many people are perfectly comfortable picking up a Victoria's Secret or Spiegel catalog and calling a 1-800 number to order clothes or merchandise, they hesitate to click through an online catalog and submit an electronic order form. Is it that viewing information on a screen is less satisfying than perusing a glossy catalog? Can it be that people just don't buy the concept of secure online transactions, or are we just too set in our ways?

There are many incentives on the Web to keep people shopping in the traditional ways: You can download coupons, preview merchandise, locate stores, get advance sales notices, and even print out order forms for faxing. More and more businesses are learning to utilize the medium, with Web sites that offer customers bona-fide virtual reality experiences complete with avatars and interactivity. They are realizing that it isn't enough to cut-and-paste traditional catalogs onto Web pages and expect customers to usher in a new era in shopping. Web sites with extensive databases and intelligent agents have taken comparison shopping to a new level, and some retailers have put their bridal/gift registry information on line.

Most importantly, software development companies are rushing to introduce new forms of payment to the Web to address the daunting concerns of submitting credit card numbers over the Internet. Move over, QVC. Analysts predict that if developers and retailers build secure, convenient virtual malls, customers will come. Cyberspace is poised to dominate the home shopping market.

DESIGNERS AND RETAILERS

INTERNATIONAL APPEAL

A.P.C.

http://www.apc.fr

The Paris-based design house, Atelier de Production et de Creation, creates and distributes clothing for men and women. If you're not familiar with A.P.C.'s designs, you are out of luck—no online fashion shows here. However, you can e-mail a request for a catalog, get a listing of store locations in Paris, Tokyo, London, Kobe, and New York City, as well as listen to snippets from CDs on A.P.C.'s record label.

Janell Beals Design

http://www.janellbeals.com

The story begins with a vest and ends with Alaskan Janell Beals making a splash on the Chicago fashion scene with her designs. Read about the designer's rise from "the Bering Sea to Barneys," take a look at items from her latest collection, or print out an order form. Her site preserves the store's Francophone flair with seasonal guides to French style, food, and culture.

INTERNATIONAL APPEAL

Product

http://www.productnet.com

Elaine Kim's Product is a full-service fashion and shopping site for the wired set and fashion mavens (see Figure 13.1). The site provides loads of information on the designer's background, international store locations (with particular focus on New York and LA), and editorial spreads. Not content to be just another promotional site, Product is also an online catalog.

J.C. Penney

http://www.jcpenney.com

America's national department store has an aesthetic yet functional site where you can shop for regular and sale merchandise on line, including gift items from their bridal and baby registry database. Coupons, a store locator, and contests will keep Penney devotees on line for hours.

Figure 13.1

Product, *http://www.productnet.com*

L. L. Bean

http://www.llbean.com

Learn about the company behind the outdoorsy catalog, browse popular L. L. Bean products, e-mail an order for a seasonal catalog, but don't try to order merchandise electronically from here, because that can only be done through L.L. Bean's 1-800 number. The site's nationwide parks database is a huge draw for the nature set, and the company's history and fantastic return/replacement policy guidelines are worth a read-through.

Macy's

http://www.macys.com

Macy's makes gift and holiday shopping just a bit easier with their Web site. Use the retailer's personal shopping service, Macy's By Appointment, for pre-picked present suggestions, then order your selections on line or by telephone for delivery. Browse listings of regional store locations and events, or peruse Weddingline, Macy's monthly newsletter for bridal planning.

INTERNATIONAL APPEAL

Spiegel Directions

http://spiegel.com/spiegel

This large, well-designed site offers cybershopping as well as an online magazine with its columns on work, play, home, and learning (see Figure 13.2). You can browse the entire Spiegel catalog, or simply peruse select items in each of the magazine's specific sections. The online inventory includes, among other things, household goods, electronics, fashionwear, childrenswear, and toys. There are also links to Spiegel's clearance center site and their European affiliate.

Neiman Marcus

http://www.neimanmarcus.com

The legendary Dallas-based emporium has a site which doesn't aim to replace, but rather to enhance the in-store shopping experience. Here's where you can locate a Neiman Marcus in your area, request guidance via e-mail from a personal shopper, get a heads-up on store events nationwide, and learn the real story behind the legend of the $250 Neiman Marcus cookie recipe.

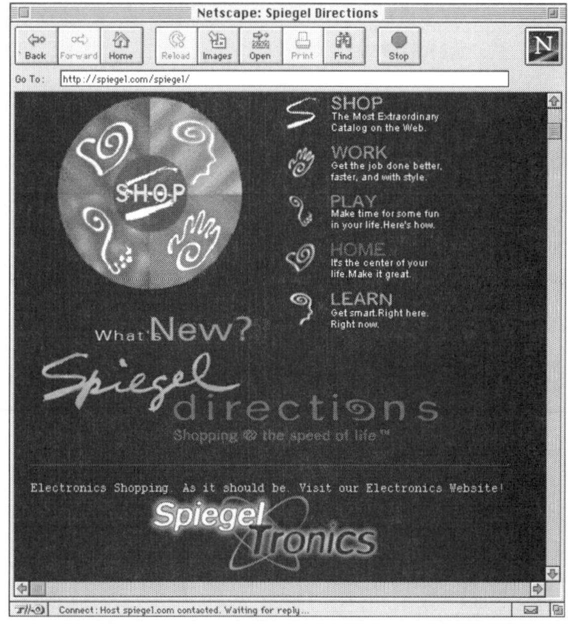

Figure 13.2

Spiegel Directions, *http://spiegel.com/spiegel*

Utilities Design Match

http://www.designsys.com/udm/index.html

Utilities Design Match is a women's clothing mail-order company whose catalog works like a flip book, showing multiple combinations of ready-to-wear designs—a "choose your own garment" adventure, if you will. At this site, you can flip through the online catalog then submit an electronic order form, or just e-mail your request for a catalog hardcopy.

Barneys New York

http://www.netcity.com/barneysny.html

Barneys New York, that haven for haughty couture buffs and the home of the SWA (salesperson with attitude), has a simple Web page on the Net City mall site. The site is devoted to Barneys locations worldwide, and has a brief merchandise spotlight (i.e., what's hot in men's/ women's shoes this month).

APPAREL

Women's Wire Shopping Channel

http://www.women.com/shop

For those with a passion for purchasing and an eye for a deal, Women's Wire's shopping channel is the place. Packed with trends, advice, and good stuff, this shopper's Eden provides the lowdown on brand-name bargain hunting, lists of hard-to-find outlets, and info on fab shops and gorgeous objects. For dreamers, it offers a look at great style, and for realists, there are hard-headed ways to stretch household dollars.

Clothestime

http://www.ctme.com/main.htm

Clothestime's site on the Internet allows you to pinpoint store locations, download commercial video clips, and explore job opportunities at the company's headquarters. As an extra-added perk, visitors to the site are given a heads-up on current sales, promotions, and featured separates.

Express

http://express.style.com

The ultimate mall store has a chic, informative, and fun home on the Web (see Figure 13.3). In addition to a database of stores and a shopping guide, those who register for free membership on the site can participate in chat sessions, shop for Express fashions online, and print out a personal coupon for ten percent off.

Chase Tavern Farm Alpacas

http://www.maine.com/ctalpacas

Chase Tavern Farm, an alpaca breeding ranch in Maine, invites you to read about its history, operations, and

where they surf

Surfer: Nicole Miller

Renowned fashion designer and business owner, noted for the colorful prints she uses in her collections, sportsware, and accessories. Her site is available at http://www.nicolemiller.com.

Her favorite sites of the moment:

Hotwired

http://www.hotwired.com

"The graphics are great, and it keeps you current."

Epicurious

http://www.epicurious.com

"I like Epicurious for its functionality. If you need a recipe, you just go there. I cook a lot, and I find the site very functional."

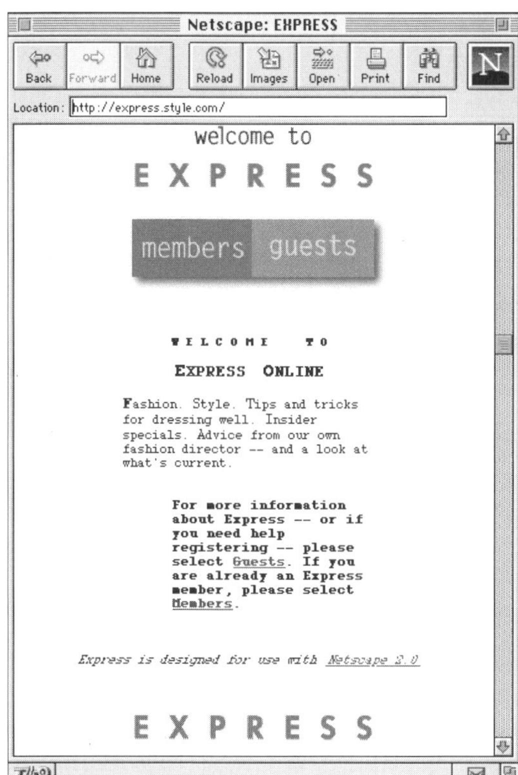

Figure 13.3

Express, *http://express.style.com*

everything you ever wondered about their South American animals. You can also shop for alpaca items such as shawls, blankets, mittens, and dolls at Chase Tavern Farm's online country store. Orders can be made by snailmail, phone, or fax.

Eddie Bauer

http://www.ebauer.com

Not content to be a run-of-the-mill retail Web page, Eddie Bauer's large and tasteful site embellishes Web page staples (store locators, product descriptions, online buying options, corporate background) with recruiting information, registration perks, and adventure travel packages. Now if we could only order Eddie Bauer limited edition four-wheel-drive vehicles here, we'd be totally set.

Edwin Jeans

http://www.edwinjeans.com

Men and women can order over ten different styles of Edwin Jeans (priced from $72 to $86) over the Net, in basic or made-to-order colors. Choose a desired fit and color, and make a secure transaction from the no-frills Edwin Jeans Web site. Associated with the Marianne shop based in San Rafael, CA.

Nine Lives Clothing Consignment Store

http://chezhal.slip.netcom.com

Nine Lives, the quality consignment clothing shop based in Los Gatos, California, has a simple yet functional site where you can browse their inventory of menswear and womenswear, or hire a personal shopping assistant. Register for shopping assistance by specifying your size and desired items, and you'll receive e-mail notices when clothing fitting your specifications is in stock.

Royal Cashmere

http://www.royalcashmere.com

Royal Cashmere, a North American importer/wholesaler of Royalle Himalayan Cashmere, has a no-frills site dedicated to the sale of their bargain-priced merchandise. Browse Royal Cashmere's accessories, home furnishings, jacquards, and prints, then visit the Bargain Trunk for samples at rock-bottom prices. You can e-mail, fax, snail mail, or phone in your order.

Suzi Saint Tropez

http://www.wp.com/SST

Suzi Saint Tropez has fashions from the French Riviera in her boutiques located in Boca Raton, Palm Beach, and North Miami. For those who don't live in the Sunshine State, users have the option of shopping for pricey custom-order evening gowns, Parasuco jeans, and the Basic Bodywear collection on line. Suzi offers discounts on some of the clothes ordered directly from her site.

Zac Attac

http://www.zacattac.com

The largest alternative clothing and bodywear retailer in Southern California brings its extreme scene on line. Browse through Zac's catalog of women's and men's hip hop, street, punk, alternative, and ska gear, shoes, boots, and body jewelry. Orders can be made via e-mail or by calling Zac Attac's 1-800 numbers—we're promised online transactions are coming soon.

VIRTUAL MALLS

Abbington Village

http://www.abbington.com

Shopping in New England is a tourist attraction in itself, one that this site attempts to recreate on the Web. Quaint little knick-knacks, folk art, homespun cotton blankets, and, of course—since all that strolling helps work up an appetite—those New England culinary staples maple sugar and Vermont cheddar cheese are all available for purchase in this virtual strip mall.

Above & Beyond—The Tall and All Mall

http://www.abmall.com

This mall offers a high, wide, and somewhat quirky range of goods and services. Above refers to tall folks' fashion outlets, links to social clubs like the Boston Beanstalks, and world's-tallest-woman Sandy Allen's home page, among other attractions for the vertically gifted. Beyond is for online advertising and marketing opportunities, "Gender Issue" shopping, "Web Sites With a Twist," and more.

Access Market Square

http://www.icw.com/ams.html

This virtual mall offers a wide and somewhat far-fetched array of goods and services. Online shoppers can browse an inventory that includes smoked sockeye salmon, "nuditude" T-shirts, left-handed products for the office, and children's clothes among other offerings. Cyber-vendors will find Internet advertising and marketing opportunities here. Lots of photos and graphics make things look great, but can also make for tedious site navigation on slower computers.

All-Internet Shopping Directory

http://www.webcom.com/~tbrown

This site is more like the yellow pages than a shopping mall itself, in that it charges companies for listings without participating in the transactions themselves. Actually, most vendors are listed for free, but in tightly-packed, difficult-to-read paragraphs. Companies that want visibility must pay to be moved into the virtual high-rent areas. Overall, the results are spotty, but useful when you have something specific in mind you want to buy.

America's Best!

http://www.sni.net/abest

This information mall is "designed and maintained by America's Best!" and is also reminiscent of those obnoxious "U-S-A!" chants at the Olympics because they keep beating you over the head with that America's Best! thing. Yet, America's Best! does offer a ready, state-by-state index of interesting U.S. Web sites, salable goods, and tourist resources.

Avant Garde: A Virtual Marketplace

http://www.infoanalytic.com

"Nebraska" and "avant garde" don't often appear together, but this contemporary market has a strong Cornhusker flavor. The page is keyed toward industrial and electronics shoppers, with links to the Laser Products and Services Group, Oasis Software International, US Robotics, and others. You'll find other products, too, like gift food baskets with honey, red popcorn, and beef chub.

BizWeb

http://www.bizweb.com

Bizweb is a link-filled, if not aesthetic, source for over 10,000 online businesses selling everything from antiques to videos. This is the place to find links to small, local businesses that have discovered the wonders of Internet commerce, as well as large, commercial Web sites. BizWeb is a great starting point if you know exactly what you want to buy on line and want to shop around.

Branch Mall

http://www.branchmall.com

One of the first malls on the Net, Branch has accumulated dozens of retailers and organized them into eight categories on this simple, frame-enhanced site. Twelve florists will sell you everything from orchids to miniature grapevines, while one hobby-department store offers personalized children's books. E-mail your encrypted order, or sign up for the Branch Mall mailing list, which announces special sales.

CyberShop

http://cybershop.com

This digital shopping mall injects an element that online shopping tends to lack: fun! The site promises "the ultimate shopping experience" and we won't spend much time arguing with that. Here, you can spend hours browsing and buying merchandise like bed and bath items, jewelry, gourmet food, electronics, toys, and office and travel items. Cybershop is a well-organized, dazzlingly displayed, fully searchable shopping site that's obviously easy on the feet (see Figure 13.4).

CyberTown

http://www.cybertown.com

CyberTown is a space-age themed shopping and services center that sprawls over the entire galaxy and across several centuries. Or maybe it just seems like it. The creators hope that CyberTown will become a central point for Web access and a sort of self-contained virtual village, with links to just about everything you can think of to enhance your virtual existence. By the look of things, they're well on their way.

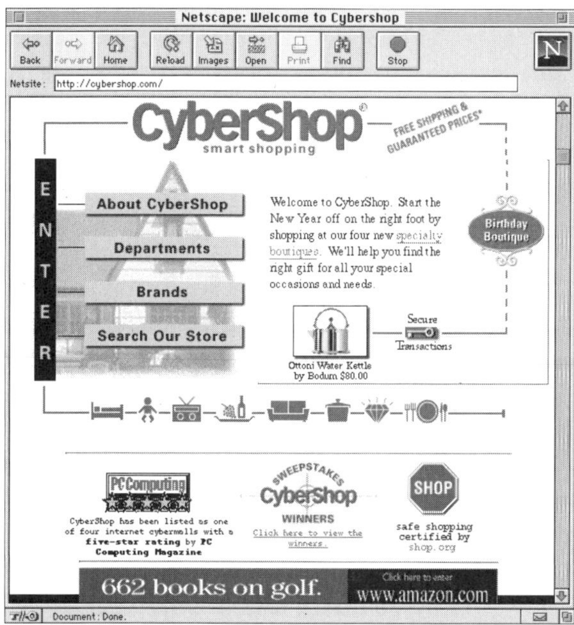

Figure 13.4

CyberShop, *http://cybershop.com*

eMall

http://www.emall.com/Home.html

eMall's cheery pastel graphics are a draw, yet its selection of links to food, spice, flower, and music vendor pages is rather sparse (although it does include much-coveted Rokerware of Al "Today Show" Roker fame). eMall's "Explore New York" pages are a nice treat for surfers in the mood for some virtual sightseeing.

Empire Mall

http://empiremall.com

This virtual mall offers a refreshingly diverse menu which includes CDs, futons, gourmet coffee, jet-aircraft consultants, and a detective referral service. OK—you may not need it to make tonight's macaroni, but the diversity is there, and the inventory links make for easy perusing. Order products by credit card on line, or by telephone.

eShop Plaza

http://www.eshop.com

eShop, MSN's brand new shopping pavilion, is snazzy if a tad sparse (at least it is for the moment). Expect major vendors like Tower Records, Avon, and 1-800-FLOWERS to lure you in with online specials and first-time shopper discounts. Toss desired items in your shopping cart, and keep track of your purchases with dated electronic receipts and tracking numbers.

The Gigaplex!

http://www.gigaplex.com/wow/homepage.htm

This "whopping 600-plus page Webmagazine devoted to arts and entertainment" definitely delivers the gigagoods: excellent coverage of film, music, food, theater, and photography, among other fields (see Figure 13.5). There's the TVPlex, TheaterPlex, BookPlex—you get the idea—even a YogaPlex. However subtle, these pages try to sell you something, whether it's a Hawaiian retreat or a photojournalism book. The Gigaplex is part shopping mall and part magazine, but wholly entertaining.

Figure 13.5
The Gigaplex!,
http://www.gigaplex.com/wow/homepage.htm

Good Stuff Cheap
http://206.251.122.9/index.html

The purveyors of Good Stuff Cheap boast that their site has offered "the best bargains on the Web since '94." Peruse GSC's shopping index of auto accessories, computer/office equipment, power tools, and "potpourri" (plenty of "Hey, they sell this for $100, but you can get it from us for $29.95"), and fill your virtual shopping basket.

Green Market
http://www.igc.apc.org/GreenMarket

Made from "100% recycled electrons," this environmentally friendly market hosts listings of "green" companies. It's a partnership with EcoNet and the Institute for Global Communications, and claims to feature "some of the hippest companies around." A super-efficient search function allows shoppers to locate specific products quickly. Much of the rest of the site is devoted to listing environmental education and discussion groups on the Net.

The Hall of Malls
http://nsns.com/MouseTracks/HallofMalls.html

The Hall of Malls features general, regional, and specialty online malls, with direct links to The Bizarre Bazaar, Web Warehouse, and dozens more Web shopping venues. Site creator New South Network Services has been "tracking mice" for quite some time; they don't take themselves too seriously, and that's part of the appeal here.

Health Trek
http://www.healthtrek.com/helthtrk.htm

Health Trek is a clearinghouse of info and products for homeopathic and other non-traditional health and wellness treatments. The site includes an online mall of ad pages for natural products and services; a Doctor's Office, where you can consult (for a fee) with a naturopathic practitioner; plus a library of informative pages on topics ranging from food allergies to premenstrual syndrome.

iMall
http://www.imall.com

Any single site that can offer computer hardware, a "100K Genuine Amethyst Jewelry Set," and TV's Amazing Discoveries is all right in our book. No, the vendors aren't all retail heavyweights, but the Web site makes a dandy storefront for smaller companies. The selection is both eclectic and extensive, so if you've longed to try out your browser's secure transaction abilities, it's likely you can find something worth buying here.

infoPost
http://www.infopost.com

This is headquarters for a California company specializing in putting small businesses on the Web. Here you'll find Bigelow Teas selling commemorative tins for $6.95, links to the sites for the Sheraton Grande in La Jolla, and just a flick of the wrist away from those links, the Private Label Cosmetics page, where you can order products to start your own personal cosmetics line.

INTERNATIONAL APPEAL

Innovations Gift Point
http://www.innovations.co.uk

The blokes at Innovative Gift Point present a selection of over 2000 products from seven leading

SPOTLIGHT ON ONLINE SALES AND BARGAINS

Retailers sold $254 million worth of goods and services on line in 1995, double the $105 million worth of sales in 1994. According to Melissa Bane, a senior analyst at the Yankee Group—a technology consulting firm in Boston—the online sales figure will grow to $10 billion by the year 2000.

Five Facts

1. In 1996, only about 25 percent of people on the Web had shopped on line.
2. The number of businesses on line with 20 or more employees was 150,000 in 1995—analysts expect that number to grow to approximately 2 million by the year 2000.
3. Books and magazines make up the largest percentage of products sold over the Net. Apparel, gifts, and food are among the least-sold products.
4. Web shopping can be cheaper than ordering by telephone. A bouquet ordered on the FTD Web site costs $5 less than the identical bouquet ordered on FTD's toll-free hotline.
5. Companies are developing new payment concepts to address the hesitancy of shoppers and retailers to transmit and receive credit card information. One example is CyberCash. Via your checking account or credit card company, you can put CyberCoins in your wallet, to be used for secure online purchases.

Five Sites

Onsale Steals and Deals

http://www.onsale.com

Get the lowest prices on hardware, software, and electronics at the Onsale Steals and Deals auction site. Sign up for a free e-mail newsletter, so you can bid on products from authorized resellers.

Nine Lives

http://www.los-gatos.scruznet.com

Let your online personal shopper notify you of bargains on designer thrift/consignment fashions from the Los Gatos, California-based Nine Lives consignment store.

World Wide Wanderer Cyberian Bucket Shop Guide

http://www.tmn.com/wwwanderer/flight_search_page.html

If you're looking for airfares at rock-bottom prices, search the World Wide Wanderer Cyberian Bucket Shop Guide for those outlets selling plane tickets at low, break-even costs.

Cybercash

http://www.cybercash.com

Pay for low-priced, online items—like software and services—with virtual currency at the Cybercash site.

Andersen Consulting

http://bf.cstar.ac.com/bf

Before you purchase a compact disc on one of the Web's many music sites, let Andersen Consulting's intelligent agent do your comparison shopping.

catalogs. Their inventory includes Stocking Fillas ("such an important part of Christmas," and many items under one pound sterling), The British Heart Foundation's gift catalog, and decorative art options from the Victoria & Albert Museum. Register for a PIN, or place your order on line. The site isn't really revolutionary: it's British.

The Internet Mall

http://www.internet-mall.com

Boasting more than 7,500 "stores," The Internet Mall is certainly an impressive array of shops. You'll find over thirty listings under "The Online Winerack" category alone, and each listing comes with a short description, so you don't have to run a tiresome point-and-click leapfrog just to see what's what. Be warned that some descriptions simply link to e-mail addresses for information requests, hence this can be a loose interpretation of the online stores concept.

Internet Shopping Network

http://www.internet.net

Run by TV's Home Shopping Network, this computer-oriented shopping page gives you everything but the frumpy TV hosts. The graphics and logos are nifty and the interface is easy to follow. High-brow techies can gobble up modems or hard drives, and the site is deemed secure, so you can one-stop shop without leaving your computer.

Internet Shopping Outlet

http://www.shoplet.com

In spite of its generic name, the main thrust at this simple online mall is computer hardware and software. Each of the three separate stores (CD-ROMs, software, and hardware) offers periodic specials and keyword searches for specific products, though category-based listings for the hardware and software areas would help. If you know what you're looking for, the selection is good, prices are moderate, and transactions are secure if your browser talks the talk.

London Mall

http://www.londonmall.co.uk

It's a shopping mall, a tourist info center, and online magazine, too, but, wait, there's an agency... oh, let's just come out and say it: Here's a virtual key to London! Commission a silver tea set from Langfords, order a suit from Savile Row, or read Grey Fox's editorials on, say, the differences in cuisine in the various classes of airplanes. We can't figure out whether this will encourage actual tourism or render it unnecessary.

MCI

http://www2.pcy.mci.net/marketplace/index.html

MCI's clout on the Net is drawing some well-know catalog stores to this online shopping site, more a mail order outlet than a "cybermall." So instead of getting stacks of catalogs from PC Zone, Day-Timer, and Damark, you can shop for air ionizers, planners, and rubberized keyboard covers right here on line.

Megabyte Mall

http://www.megabytemall.com

At Megabyte Mall, you can purchase computers, software, and hardware, if you know exactly what you want to buy. Don't expect to do any window shopping here, because they're no graphics or even descriptions of the computer products and peripherals being sold. What you *can* do is search this site for the name and make of your desired product, then call or fax in your order (no online transactions).

MegaMall

http://infotique.lm.com/megamall.html

Designed more like a mall directory than an actual mall, this site puts you in touch with more than 140 different vendors selling everything from CD-ROMs to lingerie. Vendors are divided into 49 categories, each corresponding to a floor on MegaMall's virtual 50-story skyscraper. The vendors themselves are reputable enough, but don't expect to do any real commerce at this site. The selection at this mall is broad enough to satisfy even esoteric tastes.

MexPlaza

http://mexplaza.udg.mx/Ingles

Though world-wide advertising and Latin America's first virtual shopping center are MexPlaza's main offerings, they've also spiced up this commercial site with an eye toward the arts (see Figure 13.6). Commercial offers range from clothing and investment firms to franchises and the Japanese Samurai Doll World. The Galeria MexPlaza features fine painting, sculpture, and photography by Mexican artists. In English and Spanish—expect to see many more of these in the future.

Modenet

http://www.mainstream.net/modenet

Modenet bills itself as "the global market-place." This site is the central point where you can purchase exotic goods from Italy ranging from leather accessories and handblown crystal housewares to jewelry and designer eveningwear. All purchasing can be done right from Modenet's Web pages, with free shipping and handling and a money-back guarantee.

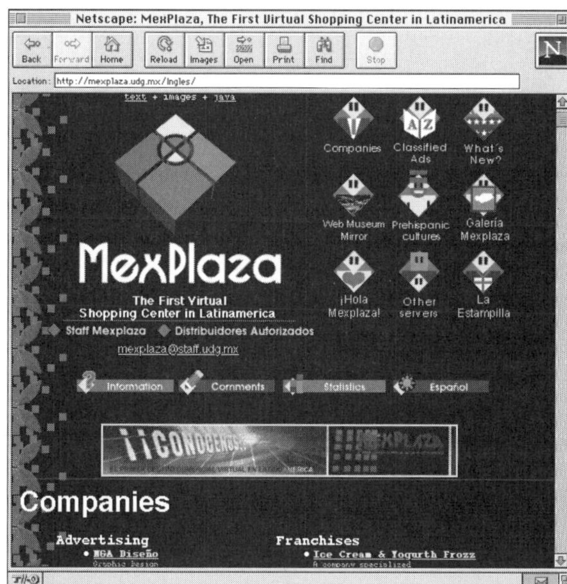

Figure 13.6

MexPlaza, *http://mexplaza.udg.mx/Ingles*

NetMall

http://www.netmall.com

Maybe they should have named this HyperMall, as the on-site shop selection is limited to a couple-dozen names, but the main attraction is a searchable index of links to more than 3000 other online merchandisers. Link to the United Airlines site, or do a little shopping at the Sara Lee Corporation's L'eggs Pantyhose site. NetMall promises a directory page with interest categories once their site construction is completed.

1World Plaza

http://www2.clever.net/1world/plaza/shop.htm

Classically decorated and well designed, 1 World Plaza is a virtual mall that clearly hopes to capture the feel of an upscale store. For the most part it succeeds, with a long list of vendors hawking everything from home electronics to movie posters. Some of the vendors and deals are too good to be missed, and the site is generally a smooth browsing experience without undue hype.

Pathfinder's DreamShop

http://www.dreamshop.com

Catalog and home shopping meet mall-crawling at Pathfinder's DreamShop. Toss items from Saks Fifth Avenue, The Bombay Company, Williams-Sonoma, and other upscale retailers in your virtual shopping bag, then go wild. The sales, values, and gift ideas areas are worth visiting, plus there's a free gift with purchase offer—always a nice touch. Security and customer service are guaranteed.

The Pennsylvania Dutch Marketplace

http://www.padutch.com

What? Amish on the Internet? Not quite. But this mall from "the Pennsylvania Dutch heartland" does offer "legendary hex signs," a one-pound chocolate computer from Hershey's, and meats from Kutztown's: certified makers of the world's largest salami! Order by phone; deliveries arrive in a few months by horse and buggy (just kidding).

Prodigy Shopping Net

http://www.shopnet.prodigy.com

You don't have to be a Prodigy subscriber to use the Prodigy Shopping Net, although registration on the Web site is necessary before you can shop. Browse through items from JC Penney, PC Flowers and Gifts, The CheeseBoard, and other stores from the handful of retailers represented in this virtual mini-mall.

Rocky Mountain Cyber Mall

http://www.hardiman.com/malls/rmcm/index.html

With information on everything from natural beauty products (goatmilk soaps!) to network search engines (Lycos, Yahoo, Open Text, and WebCrawler), the Rocky Mountain Cyber Mall doesn't offer up the usual shopping experience. Rather, it's a place for tips on everything from fine gifts, to gourmet food, to investment opportunities. Also includes info on environment-friendly cleaning products, the Denver area, and transportation.

The ShopSite Marketplace

http://www.shopsite.com

The ShopSite Marketplace (Figure 13.7) is an uncluttered, well-designed site where you can link to small businesses who've made the leap on line using the ShopSite Manager online storefront management system. Link to businesses as diverse as health food stores and gourmet food outlets, then do your shopping on line. Or, read ShopSite's FAQ and submit a form to purchase their software and open your own online store.

Speak to Me

http://clickshop.com/speak

Lonely? Need somebody to talk to? How about something to talk to you? With diligent seriousness and online sound demos, this theme-shop sells only stuff that talks: talking picture frames, talking note recorders, talking clocks, and talking kitchen helpers. Also available: "Marriage Savers," his-and-hers keyrings that spout (downloadable!) sayings such as "Just charge it, honey" and "Yes dear."

The Tarheel Mall

http://netmar.com/mall

Beneath a Carolina blue sky (graphic), past the helpful information-desk man, beyond a library of over 200 neophyte-friendly Web links, after the classified ad pages, and more, the Tarheel Mall features scores of online shopping venues, like Contact Lenses Online, and Uncle Henry's Pretzel Bakery. And, in a measure of their own security, the purveyors of this full-service shopping site offer links to other e-malls.

INTERNATIONAL APPEAL

TravelShop

http://www.travelshop.com

TravelShop is more about traveling to shop than travel-related shopping. This virtual mall is simultaneously a listing of posh boutiques in major cities around the world, and an online ordering system for those that choose to utilize a virtual storefront here. Shop for pricey sunglasses or stroll over to the London page where you can read up on the company billed as "a favorite of the queen for whips and gloves."

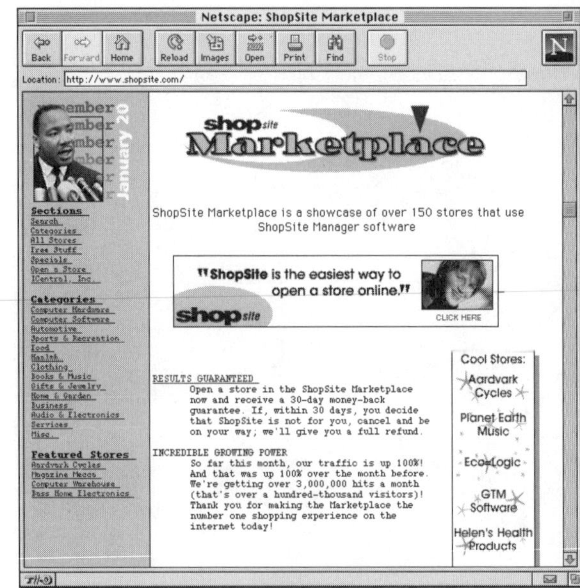

Figure 13.7

The ShopSite Marketplace, *http://www.shopsite.com*

Viamall

http://www.ishops.com

This isn't an online version of a sprawling suburban mega-mall. Instead, Viamall focuses on giving smaller companies a strong Web presence with minimal fuss. The teasers on the home page tell the whole story. While the product choices on each page aren't extensive, the stores within all offer secure encryption of orders, so you won't have to worry about your credit card number.

VirtuaLynx

http://www.virtualynx.com

VirtuaLynx is really two sites in one. The first half of the site, Commerce Place, is a free directory of vendors on the Web selling everything from snack foods to cars. Listings are free, but the company also creates full-blown corporate sites for a fee. The second half of the site, CooLynx, follows the lead of the time-worn Cool Site of the Day idea, adding the ability to vote for the best sites.

Web Warehouse

http://webwarehouse.com

Web Warehouse isn't the biggest collection of stores on the Net, but they just might have what you need. Everything here can be ordered via a secure transaction server, so whether you crave a diamond tennis bracelet, the "Evita" soundtrack, Corel software, or a blessed occasion bouquet, you're in business.

INTERNATIONAL APPEAL

Weekend a Firenze

http://www.nettuno.it/mall

Italian merchants vie for your mail-order dollars (and lire, and yen) at this online collection of vendors based in Florence. The site's creators have done everything they can to convince you that their site is just like traipsing through Florence's most prestigious shopping districts, though the experience is decidedly virtual. Everything from costume to expensive jewelry is available via the Web storefronts.

INTERNATIONAL APPEAL

Worldshop

http://www.worldshop.com

Products at this straightforward online mall cover the gamut from compact discs to aromatherapy oils. Credit card orders are taken on line, though there's no encryption mechanism available. Even those who aren't shopping may want to drop by. The site sponsors both a real-time chat system via the Web and an unusual armed forces online welcome center to put soldiers overseas in touch with their relatives.

where they surf

Surfer: Ben Narasin

Creator and fashion director of http://fashionmall.com

His favorite sites of the moment:

Perry Ellis

http://www.fashionmall.com/perryellis/htdocs/index/html

"I like Perry Ellis's site because it changes each month, and I like the use of frames and animation to create a relatively low bandwidth version of an animated cover."

Bay's Auction Web

http://www.ebay.com/aw

"I think that online auctions are one of the few truely compelling uses of this new medium which are unique and not re-purposing."

World Wide Magic

http://www.wwmagic.com

Here's a mall which is intended to house the more eclectic shop owner. For the most part, the shops here have a notably "New Age" feel, like The Cape, where you can buy "classical capes and other magical garments," Echo-Art ("Our hope is to convey... a remembrance of divinity within the human being"), and I Am the Love of God, a phone line for psychic readings.

World Wide Mall

http://www.olworld.com/olworld/mall/mall_us/index.html

This quirky New Mexico-based cybermall offers Native American jewelry alongside kidnap/detention insurance and Health Blend coffee with chromium. Yes, it's long on Southwestern themes, up to and including the question "Will I see Fido in Heaven?" (addressed in Mary Buddemeyer-Porter's book). This is a fun browse, but brides-to-be should probably register elsewhere.

WWWMall

http://www.clever.net/wwwmall

Right next to the run-of-the-mill golf equipment and travel agents you'd expect to find at this virtual strip mall are some genuinely weird offers. Where else could you order alligator or kangaroo jerky next door to a computer hardware dealer? It's all here, waiting for the 24-hour wave of Web shoppers to burst in, credit card in hand, shouting "I know it's 3 a.m., but I need kangaroo jerky!" It could happen.

X Avenue

http://www.avenue.com/x.html

This online mall cries out shamelessly to Generation X. Amongst ads for an SAT prep course and the National In-Line Hockey Association, Xers are invited to "design a soda" with a chance to win a free case of Skeleteens. Way down at the far end of the mall we spotted some interesting links (Islam, Central Intelligence Agency, Loads of Mammals), but opted to click "for those who prefer to be bored" (Interactive Hangman, The Vain Game).

AUTOMOTIVE

All Things Automotive Directory

http://www.webcom.com/~autodir

As if its title hasn't said it all, we're told that this mega-index "attempts to cover the waterfront for automotive information on the Internet." Access to a wide array of dealers and manufacturers is provided, with enthusiast pages, the likes of Vettes on the Net, AutoWeek Online, and tons more. If you're interested in alternatively fueled vehicles, you won't be disappointed here.

Auto-By-Tel

http://www.autobytel.com

Submit an electronic request form (on the seriously intended "honor system") for your desired car make and model, and Auto-By-Tel will have a subscribing dealer respond within 48 hours. They claim their sales volume accounts for the significant savings promised. It bodes well that potential buyers are encouraged to familiarize themselves with prices, via Consumer Reports and the like, before using this service. The site includes a "Weekly Auto Market Report" as well.

AutoMall

http://www.iclc.net/aol

AutoMall says its service is "like buying factory-direct." Visitors are invited to click through a series of vehicle selection options (make, model, color), type in extras (air conditioning, ejector seats), and calculate your purchase price. Then, contact a customer service representative to purchase the vehicle. The service claims to offer lower prices on everything from Buicks and Geos, to Jaguars and Infinitis.

AutoNetwork

http://www.autonetwork.com

Visit this slick site and take some of the mystery out of buying a car. AutoNetwork's Interactive Purchasing Agent site (Figure 13.8) is the place for preferred service and updated price listings that will get you the best deal possible on a new or used automobile. Use the dealer locator to find specific car dealerships by location, and use the virtual showroom to link to the car manufacturer of your choice.

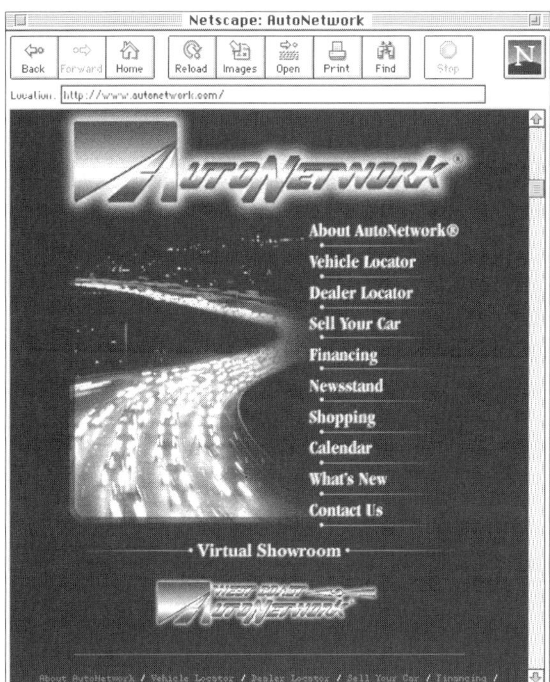

Figure 13.8
AutoNetwork, *http://www.autonetwork.com*

Autorow
http://www.autorow.com

Touche', Inc. offers here what may well be one of the Web's most complete automobile information centers. With more than 25,000 dealerships listed through a clickable U.S. map, you'll find links to the likes of auto racing info, a mega-showroom for browsing new models in every make from American Motors to Volvo, and other features like downloadable lease calculator shareware.

AutoSite
http://www.autosite.com

AutoSite is your Web key to "everything automotive," and that includes access to more than 30,000 pages of car-related info. Sounds too good to be free? You're right, as nominal subscriber's fees are required for, say, new car dealer invoice prices, model specs, reviews, and on. But wait! It won't cost you a thing to browse the troubleshooting diagnosis and repair tips, auto club links, consumer advisory articles, used car resources, and tons more worthwhile features.

AutoWeb Interactive
http://www.autoweb.com

AutoWeb Interactive, a Cupertino, California-based online guide for car buyers, offers detailed information and listings from dealers around the United States. Use AutoWeb's AutofinderGC to locate your desired used car, link to the Web sites of hundreds of member dealers nation-wide, and search the interactive specials for the best deals on new and used cars.

Brian's Harley-Davidson/Buell
http://www.netaxs.com/~brianshd

Harley-Davidson and Buell sport motorcycle enthusiasts may now virtually visit the Langhorne, Pennsylvania dealership that has earned owner Brian Bentley three Bar and Shield awards since 1985. This photographic inventory includes a full line of new and used vehicles, such as the "journeyman" H-D Sportster and the Ultra Classic Electra Glide. Brian's H.O.G. page is a calendar of Harley events. Motor clothes, accessories, and collectibles are also available for international shipping.

Cars @ Cost
http://www.webcom.com/~carscost/welcome.html

Cars @ Cost webmasters are using the Net to assemble virtually thousands of auto shoppers at a time, to help each one purchase new vehicles at the factory invoice (dealer's) prices. This strategy doesn't hold for exotic models, but would-be drivers of Detroit's best-sellers (as well as Japanese makes, and Saab) can get a Cars @ Cost quote for $29, while a $299 fee is charged if you actually buy the car.

Classic Car Source
http://www.classicar.com

Classic Car Source does a smashing job of backing up the claim that its classified ads and features are "the premier online source for Classic Vehicles, Automobilia, & Rare Parts"—it's great whether you want to buy or sell. Those looking for a good browse will find that here, too, including worldwide club and museum links as well as an archive full of articles.

Classic Automobiles, Inc.

http://www.starweb.net/classic.htm

"New York's Exotic Superstore" offers world-wide sales of previously owned exotic Bugatti, Audi, Lamborghini, Lotus, and Porsche vehicles. Classic Automobiles is located just "minutes from New York City." Sadly, we found no word on how you would get, say, that 1995 Hummer Hardtop delivered for safari use on the Serengeti. Still, this is a good virtual lot for high-end car shoppers.

DealerNet

http://www.dealernet.com

DealerNet is a useful tool for Internet car-shopping. Beyond info on new car dealers, the glossy interface also offers reviews, used cars, and financing help. One especially interesting gadget is Credit Check, in which DealerNet offers to send you the full details of your established credit rating for about 30 bucks. All the information stuffed in here can make pages slow to load, but the results are generally worth it.

Edelbrock Performance Products

http://www.edelbrock.com

California-based Edelbrock Corporation designs, makes, and markets their own line of performance vehicle parts and components, mainly for American-made automobiles, but also for Harley Davidson motorcycles. Read a company overview, order free print catalogs, search for the U.S. Edelbrock dealer nearest you, and post or consider "shop talk" in the chat room. Lots of good stuff here for vehicle sooper-uppers.

Exotic Automobile Showroom

http://vmarketing.com/autohp.html

Fort Lauderdale, FL dealer Tino Rossini teamed up with Virtual Marketing Corporation to create this dreamy classified ads page for exotic sports car enthusiasts. For sale are 12 cylinder 1973 Jaguar XKEs, assorted Rolls Royce Corniches, and lots of other roadsters suited for leisurely cruises around Monte Carlo. Prices aren't normally listed with the splendid photos and descriptions, but serious shoppers can contact Tino directly via e-mail.

Highway One Classic Autos

http://www.highway-one.com

This San Francisco Bay Area based virtual showroom provides auto enthusiasts with a salable inventory of vintage European and American sport and luxury cars. You can browse the Classic Classifieds (complete with photos and asking prices), a Photo Library, and related links. No-nonsense presentation and discussion complement this stately shopping site.

Hot Rods Worldwide

INTERNATIONAL APPEAL

http://www.hotrodsworldwide.com

Hot rod builders, buyers, sellers, and plain old enthusiasts will enjoy loads of information and resources via this custom car clearinghouse. Included are commercial

[OVERHEARD ON WOMEN'S WIRE]

http://chat.women.com

"Unless you have some innate, personal love of big houses and helicopters, don't let yourself buy into someone else's idea of the good life. If you do, you're in for a big letdown."

—Barbara Sher in her book, "Live the Life You Love in Ten Easy Step-by-Step Lessons".

and classified ads, show and events listings, articles, plus links to the likes of "Microsoft CarPoint" and "Fans of the Fish Carburetors." Hot rods for sale are categorized by make, while sellers' e-mail addresses are included for ready contact. A developing community for hot rodders worldwide, especially in the U.S.

Kanter Auto Products
http://www.kanter.com

Restorers of collector automobiles and trucks (years 1930-1986) will want to consult this online catalog of parts, listed alphabetically with page numbers corresponding to a hardcopy edition. Kanter has wheel bearings and pinion seals for your Desoto, Studebaker carburetor kits, Chevrolet piston pin bushings, and lots more. Restoration tips are also provided.

Motorcycle Shopper Online
http://www.mshopper.eurografix.com

This e-version of Motorcycle Shopper magazine is a virtual bikers' rally (minus most of the beards and tattoos). Offerings include vendor links, archived articles, and a rather fascinating U.S. salvage yard directory. A subscribers fee is required for access to the extensive vehicle/accessory classified ads section. Vintage and modern motorcycle enthusiasts will find interesting stuff here.

Sea Ray Boats
http://www.searay.com/boats

The longtime purveyor of pleasure boats makes waves on the Web with this splashy info-site and boat catalog. Click on "product families" to access photographs, descriptions, and mile-long specification lists for the company's 1997 lineup. You can also get practical tips on maintaining your bilge/engine compartment and removing scratches from your boat's shiny gel coating.

Special Car Journal
http://www.SpecialCar.com

This is an extensive and effective classic, exotic, and sports car site, with inventory lists of dealerships from Memory Lane Motors in Lake Bluff, IL to Old Cars Import/Export in Buenos Aires, Argentina—not to mention larger dealerships (see Figure 13.9). The site highlights specific cars and includes a Web yellow page

Figure 13.9
Special Car Journal, *http://www.SpecialCar.com*

directory (with car clubs and news groups) and a "Cruisin' the Net" review of motoring Websites, making it more than just an advertising vehicle.

BOOKS

Amazon.com Books
http://www.amazon.com

Amazon.com Books's site (Figure 13.10) features a database of one million titles. Ordering is quick and easy, and more than 20 categories can help ease the burden of browsing. The real achievement here is the free personal notification service—subscribe and the folks at Amazon.com will notify you of new titles in your category or tell you when a new book comes out by your favorite author.

Andromeda Books and Gifts
http://www.luckydog.com/andromeda/index.htm

Andromeda is an online bookstore that specializes in books off the beaten path. The books they carry are "alternative" in that they cover other cultures (Native

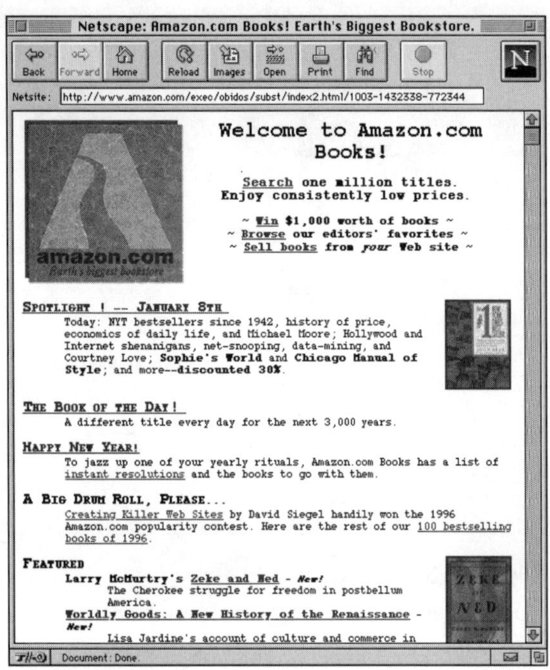

Figure 13.10

Amazon.com Books, *http://www.amazon.com*

American and Asian religion and history, for example) and "fringe" subjects like UFOs, astral projection, Atlantis, and alchemy. Books (and gifts such as tarot cards, oils, and incense), can be delivered within 48 hours of your order.

Audiobooks.com

http://www.audiobooks.com

Audio editions of books are all the rage now in publishing, and Audiobooks.com carries 15,000 titles in fiction and non-fiction, for sale here for worldwide shipping. Using the search and browse options, we found everything from children's books, to erotic readings, to bestsellers galore. Several titles, especially in non-fiction, are read by the authors. Others titles feature dramatic readings that include sound effects. Unfortunately, few details of the titles are provided beyond cost, author, and reader.

Book Stacks

http://www.books.com/scripts/news.exe

Book Stacks Unlimited, Inc. bills this page as, "Your local bookstore. No matter where you live." They boast of more than 425,000 titles; searches by author, title, or keyword; and major browsing capabilities—all without the Dewey Decimal System. You'll need to open an account to order titles from Book Stacks.

BookWire

100 BEST SITES

http://www.bookwire.com

The amount of options for BookWire visitors is daunting, so we recommend using the site's Navigator page. From there, link to the "Reading Room," an amazing online library of books for download. Or, skip to the BBR's page of essays and interviews with people like Camille Paglia and Allen Ginsberg. Looking at books always seems to lead to spending money, and that's easy enough to do here, too.

Borders on the Web

http://www.borders.com

Next time you're looking for those multicultural Cinderella books, you might check the Borders Books and Music page. The Michigan-based retailer offers limited online shopping for books, music, and videos, as recommended by staff members. Links are provided to Borders store locations in America, and Salon, the e-zine for people who read.

HarperCollins Publishers

http://www.harpercollins.com

HarperCollins, one of the heavy hitters in publishing, has been around since 1817. This is their book page, with press releases, schedules for author tour events, and, of course, the online bookstore. Read blurbs from hot new releases, listen to audio excerpts, or jump on over to HarperCollins Interactive to find out what's new on CD-ROM for kids or adults.

The Internet Book Shop

INTERNATIONAL APPEAL

http://www.bookshop.co.uk

With 912,000 titles, the IBS is one of the biggest bookshops on the Internet, although searching for titles and authors here may be a bit difficult. Features beyond the catalog include pleasant promotions of new titles and profiles of authors. A list of the top 50 bestsellers shows their strength is in U.K. titles, with names like Ian Banks and Neil Gaiman.

Intertain.com Internet Bookstore
http://intertain.com/store/welcome.html

Similar to other bookstores on the Net, Intertain.com boasts a huge catalog, only a little of which you can really effectively browse. A wide range of titles for adults and children is offered in English, Spanish, and French, which helps to set this store apart from a neighborhood shop. Prices are lower than the suggested retail, but you'll need to order a bunch to save some money on shipping.

Macmillan Publishing USA Information SuperLibrary
http://www.mcp.com

Here the world's largest computer book publisher implores you to shop electronically, then read bibliographically. A monthly newsletter alerts you to the latest books on software and hardware, then links you into online searching and ordering from a library of more than 1000. Even if you don't read computer books, this is a useful shopping site.

Penguin Books
http://www.penguin.com/usa

Penguin Books's site displays how diverse their catalog is. Besides all the paperbacks, there are hardcovers, academic resources, and multimedia products. Latest releases include Stephen King's "Rose Madder," "The Winnie-The-Pooh Collection," and the "The Pearl and The Red Pony CD-ROM." Get sneak peeks of new printed and electronic releases or link to book-related sites.

Sierra Club Books
http://www.sierraclub.org/books

Sierra Club Books' commercial site gives you a full account (with prices, too) of its nature and travel titles—including mountaineering, gardening, natural history, and National Park guides. Technoid nature lovers can buy environmental screen savers, or choose among a series of CD-ROMs ranging from "Blue Whale" to "Wildebeest Migration." A useful site, especially for holiday window shopping. Lengthier descriptions and online sales would be helpful.

Ventana Online
http://www.vmedia.com

Ventana Online serves as an electronic catalog for computer-book publisher Ventana Press. You can make purchases online after setting up a shopping account, and those who already own Ventana books can get follow-up support. You can download files here (just in case you misplaced the diskettes that came with your book), or read author bios and then link to their personal home pages.

The Word Mill
http://www.wordpr.com/book

The Word Mill site's (see Figure 13.11) nice, trim layout makes it easy to browse titles of their used books, categorized by subject matter. Although there aren't any snazzy snapshots of book covers or authors, these folks at least provide a short summary of EACH book. ALL books here are $2.50, whether hard or soft cover (and many are hard cover).

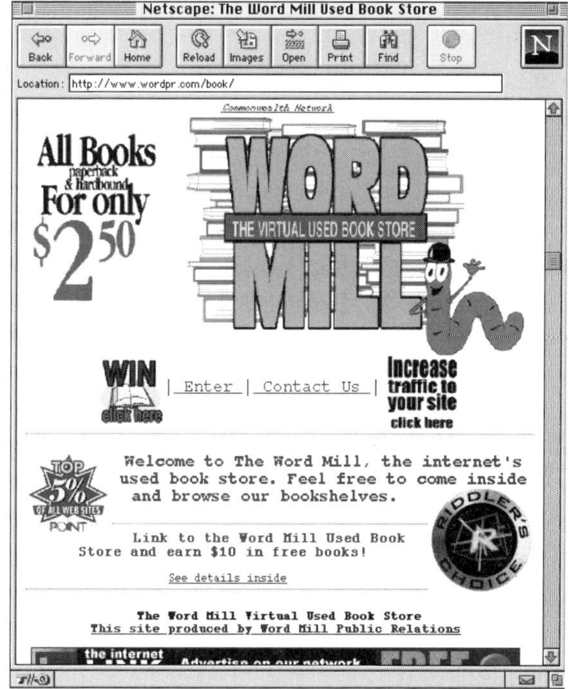

Figure 13.11

The Word Mill, *http://www.wordpr.com/book*

FOOD AND DRINK

A World of Tea

http://www.stashtea.com

Brought to you by the Stash Tea Company, an Oregon-based mail-order firm, this surprisingly entertaining sales site spins in some tea history ("Three great Zen priests restored tea to its original place in Japanese society.") and news ("Animal studies suggest tea is a cancer-preventing agent."). Stash's online catalog makes it easy to order teas, gift packs, kettles, and mugs. You'll find everything here but the tea party. In English and Japanese.

Balducci's

http://www.balducci.com

The gourmet goodies advertised at the Balducci's site look mighty fine, if a little pricey: the Balducci Beef Wellington goes for $135. This attractive, high-calorie, graphics-intensive site is heavy on elaborate descriptions like, "so dense and creamy that it coats the entire roof of your mouth and palate with an intensely rich, chocolate flavor."

Celestial Seasonings

http://www.usa.net/celestial/seasonings.html

Do you have a sudden craving for Ceylon Apricot Ginger tea? Who wouldn't, after visiting the Celestial Seasonings page. This company makes many different types of tea, including the standard black teas, herbal teas, and iced teas. Here, you can order up a gift set and have it mailed directly to a friend. Or, if you've become a big fan of their teas, you can pick up a few T-shirts and caps.

Clambake Celebrations

http://www.netplaza.com/plaza/strfrnts/1004/storepg1.html

Clambake Celebrations will whisk a fresh Lobster-Clambake to your office party or home doorstep overnight—complete with claw-crackers, bibs, and wetnaps. The company has been in business for 10 years and guarantees that every lobster, clam, or mussel that hops on Federal Express has been hand-picked and quality checked. If you're a landlocked lover of seafood, you'll be happy as a clam with this site.

@Farm Direct Marketplace

http://www.farmdirect.com

Just like an actual farmers' market, this site brings together an assortment of vendors who sell produce, specialty foods, and trendy-sounding produce like arrugula, Belgian shallots, lemon grass, and lobster mushrooms. Plenty of unusual food items here, as well as a search engine in case you can't find what you're looking for.

Gourmet Today

http://www.gourmettoday.com

Gourmet Today, "your online gourmet gift store," offers food and wine packages for all occasions. If you really want to splurge, you can arrange to send someone a Basket of the Month for as long as two to 12 months. Along the same lines, the International Stiff Upper Lip Wine Society, a wine-of-the-month club, is also on line at this site. Classy—or at least more so than a six-pack with a ribbon tied around it.

Grapes

http://www.grapes-wineline.com

Grapes, which bills itself as "America's Top Rated Wine Selection Specialists," has a straightforward site with one goal in mind: to make you a wine-lover, or at least convince you to shop like one. Take a peek into the wine cellar, join the wine program, chat, or contact the good folks at Grapes if you're inspired by their fun wine activity suggestions like starting your own cellar, or organizing a wine tasting.

Harvard Espresso Company

http://www.coffee.com

This Seattle-based coffee company offers a specialty line of coffee for sale over the Net, as well as information on brewing and drinking the perfect cup.

Indian River Gift Fruit Company

http://www.giftfruit.com

Indian River, "Where lush soil, rich Florida sunshine, and warm tropical rains combine perfectly," offers mangos, genuine Vidalia onions, Ruby Red grapefruit, and other online delectables. The Honeybell Tangelos are available only in January; the oranges all year around. Gift packages

I·N·T·E·R·N·E·T M·I·N·U·T·E

ONLINE ORDERING

Born to shop? With over 100,000 commercial sites up these days, the Web offers unlimited spending opportunities. The question for most of us is: Is it safe? A better question might be: Is shopping on line any less safe than giving your credit card number over the phone, fax, or even to a food server or sales clerk? The answer is no. Many companies use encryption technology to scramble your credit card number as it travels through cyberspace. As long as you shop smart, your biggest concern about cyber-shopping should probably be exceeding your credit limit.

There are a few things you might want to do when ordering on line. Make sure the Web site you order from has a geographic address as well as one for e-mail. You might want to call the business to confirm that their site is legitimate. Don't use your credit card at a sight you are not familiar with, and don't send a check either.

Organizations eager to promote online commerce are beginning to filter and screen Web sites for consumers. In 1997, the Better Business Bureau will be placing a seal of approval on sites that meet their business standards. Also on the horizon is CommerceNet's E-Trust, which will display "trustmarks" on sites participating in their security standards. Visa, Mastercard, and others are coming out with a single standard called SET (secure electronic transactions), which they say will safeguard all online transactions.

Some Sites with More Information

Better Business Bureau
http://www.bbb.org

E-Trust
http://www.etrust.org

Visa
http://www.visa.com

Mastercard
http://mastercard.com

If you still don't feel comfortable typing in your credit card number, most companies have work-arounds like 1-800 numbers or allowing you to set up a special online credit account. The following sites are examples of the later:

Cybercash
http://www.cybercash.com

First Virtual
http://www.fv.com

Netcash
http://nii.isi.edu/info/netcash

ecash
http://www.digicash.com/ecash/ecash-home.html

may be arranged for Easter or Hanukkah, among other occasions, and shipped all over creation.

The Interactive Gourmet

http://www.cuisine.com

The Interactive Gourmet offers over 900 wines for sale via retail powerhouse Sherry-Lehmann, as well as the food consulting services of celebrated restaurateur Drew Nieporent. The wine database is searchable by criteria that include region, varietals, body, and aroma. The interactive "Grapevine" allows you to put questions to the wine experts themselves, and a "Restaurant Specials/Events" feature lists going-ons at four New York hot spots.

The Matzah Market

http://www.marketnet.com/mktnet/kosher/index.html

The Matzah Market is an online catalog of more than 50 kosher products (mostly Manischewitz brand) offered by the suppliers at Kosher Express. As you might guess from the name, there's lots of matzo, including Honey and Spice, Egg and Onion, and Matzo Thins (diet!)—plus jars of gefilte fish, boxes of potato pancake mix, and other such items to help stock the Kosher kitchen.

Mother Nature's General Store

http://www.mothernature.com

This natural shopping mall-cum-hippie health clearinghouse is a cornucopia of info and products relating to alternative medicine, herbal supplements, and other earthy delights. When you shop the site, you'll find everything from Bricker Labs' diet products to pet supplies such as Mr. Barky's dog biscuits. The site also incorporates a fine selection of enhanced links to sites such as the farm fresh Veggies Unite! vegetarian recipe pages.

The Sumac Ridge Estate Winery

INTERNATIONAL APPEAL

http://www.sumacridge.com

The entire selection from the British Columbia winery is for sale on line at this site, and its shopping cart interface is designed to make it easy to buy in both U.S. and Canadian dollars. The '93 Cabernet Sauvignon looks appealing, but now that we can actually say "kab-er-nay so-vee-nyonh" (thanks to Sumac Ridge's online wine pronunciation guide), we're considering using the company's telephone-order option.

Sweet Seductions

INTERNATIONAL APPEAL

http://connexion.parallax.co.uk/seduct

Drop by this Leamington, England sweet shop next time you're feeling a little peckish to load up on Belgian truffles, chocolate-coated coffee beans, or Uncle Joe's Mint Balls. Delivery may take a while, but family-owned Sweet Seductions will ship anywhere in the world if you order on line with a major credit card.

Virtual Vineyards

100 BEST SITES

http://www.virtualvin.com

Virtual Vineyards (Figure 13.12) gives advice on how to buy the gourmet foods and fine wines recommended by renowned wine expert, Peter Granoff. Visit this site to use Peter's trademarked tasting chart; order food, wine, and gift selections on line; or browse Louise Fiszer's food column. Orders can be delivered to domestic and international locations.

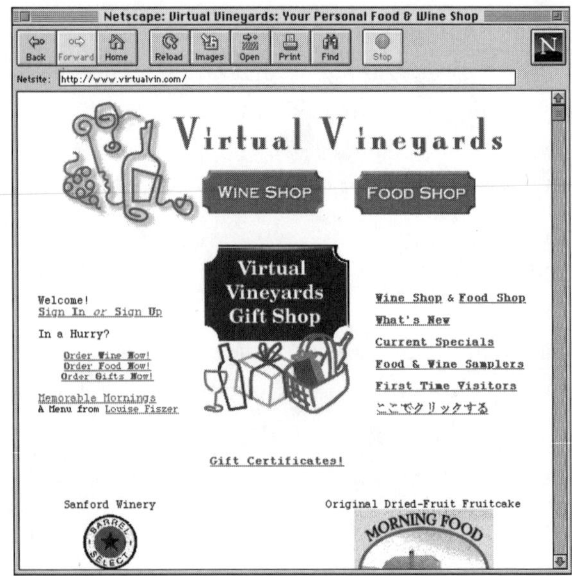

Figure 13.12

Virtual Vineyards, *http://www.virtualvin.com*

Wine.com

http://www.wine.com

"Connecting the World Wine Web together," Wines On-Line points to what's new, rare, "hot" and available through their monthly auction (where you can bid on rare bottles of wine). You'll find forums, online search resources shopping opportunities, and links to Napa Valley real estate sites. Of course, you can also purchase wine and gifts from featured companies.

Wines on the Internet

http://www.wines.com

This Internet clearinghouse for wineries does a fine job of mixing useful info with the ads for specific wines and wine-tasting events. Learn terminology at the Wine Lover's searchable database, read the WineWizard's introduction to popular wines, or submit questions to the Winemakers' Forum and have one of the pros fill you in. Various wineries offer their wares here by mail order.

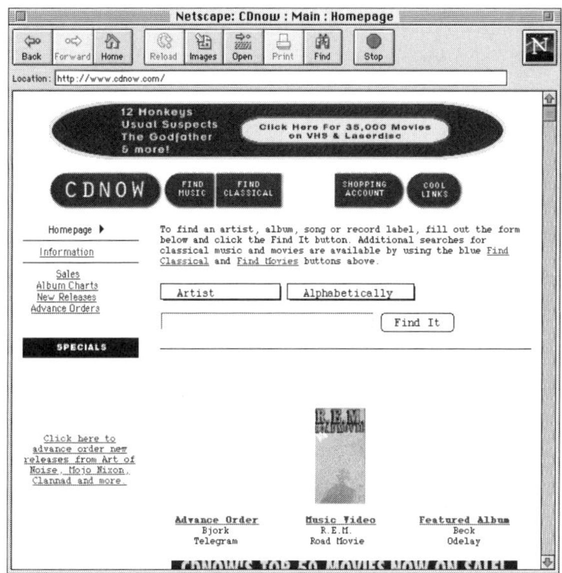

Figure 13.13

CD Now, *http://www.cdnow.com*

MUSIC AND VIDEO

Best Video

http://www.bestvideo.com

Order film-related merchandise and videos, including rare prints and cult films, right here at the Connecticut-based video retailer's site. Read monthly reviews, search for titles from more than 230 video categories, and link to the staff's favorite Web sites. Submit electronic requests to rent rare videos from Best Video's collection, or use their secure purchase option to buy.

CD Now

http://www.cdnow.com

The CD Now online music and video store (Figure 13.13) allows you to search for titles by artist, title, and record label, as well as toss your choices in a shopping cart for electronic purchase. Take advantage of CD Now's discounts, early releases, and hard-to-find import titles, or link to reviews and other music-related Web sites.

CDworld

http://cdworld.com

CD World carries more than 100,000 CDs on line, and their site offers a simple-enough search button, secure transactions, and fairly decent prices. Read from the feature-artist profiles and download samples of artists' work—New Age composer Steve Halpern was among five when we last dropped by. Our search on Bootsy Collins dug up three CDs, including his "Keepin' Dah Funk Alive." Elsewhere, Brian Wilson gets lavished with copy, thanks perhaps to his Don Was-produced "I Just Wasn't Made For These Times." Overall this is a solid site, worthy of a top 5 percent rating, but still not quite as high-powered as CDNow.

Emusic

http://www.emusic.com

This shopping site, with more than 100,000 CD titles available, stakes a claim as the "fastest, easiest, and most enjoyable way to browse the world of music today!" This fun way to shop for CDs allows surfers to search for discs by song, year, album, or artist. A search of 1976 turned up ten of that year's top-selling albums, including Marvin Gaye's "Greatest Hits" and the Eagles' "Hotel

California." Then we searched for Led Zeppelin under "artist" and found 16 Zep albums, with color graphics of album covers. Visitors can also enter their own reviews for albums, or read the reviews of others. Rock on.

Ticketmaster Online

http://www.ticketmaster.com

You won't hear Pearl Jam singing the praises of this ticket-selling giant, but those who don't mind attending events in its shadow may find this promotional site helpful. (It's another slick production from Starwave Corporation, partly owned by Paul Allen.) Rock groupies and theater people can peruse "onsale" tickets across the country here (Thrill Kill Kult in Pheonix!, Fiddler on the Roof in Buffalo!). The weekly "Tipsheet" dishes up gossip and celebrity news (Liz Taylor on Michael Jackson: "I think he's like litmus paper"), and fills visitors in on the previous week's top-grossing concert acts. As of our last visit you still couldn't order tickets on line here.

FLOWERS AND GIFTS

Brookstone

http://www.netplaza.com/plaza/strfrnts/1015/storepg1.html

Here's an online sampler from the store that thinks it has something for the person who's got everything. This is a fine gift shopping site, and they certainly "put the f-u-n into functional!" Some very handsome photos of the products are included. This is just one of the venues at netplaza, a mall to visit if unique is what you seek.

Eagle Express Flowers

http://www.eaglex.com

Eagle Express Flowers of Half Moon Bay, California—the name flows, and their bouquets aren't bad either. They'll ship fresh-cut roses, carnations, and other arrangements overnight to U.S. destinations (including territories). Emergency shoppers won't find a trove of options and images here, as the emphasis is on express. Check out the online catalog if one of the creations tickles your fancy.

Flower Stop

http://www.flowerstop.com

This online fresh-flower market (Figure 13.14) offers next-day delivery (in the U.S.) of bouquets, vases, and that grand standby, the single long-stemmed rose. Shoppers can frolic among "Gold 'N' Glow" and "Autumn Harvest" bouquets, delivered through FTD. The prices are probably higher than your local florist, but this site is colorful, graphic, and doesn't provoke allergies.

FTD Online

http://www.internet.net/FTD/index.html?source=DYHO

The original long-distance floral service with the prancing Mercury logo offers elegant online shopping at this site. For your perusal, the "Colors of Love," "Spring in a Basket," and "Stately Beauty," among other bouquets, are photo-linked and categorized under headings like "Holiday & Special Days." Once you've joined the Internet Shopping Network, you can order on line. Some bouquets are available for same day delivery if ordered by 11:00 A.M. EST.

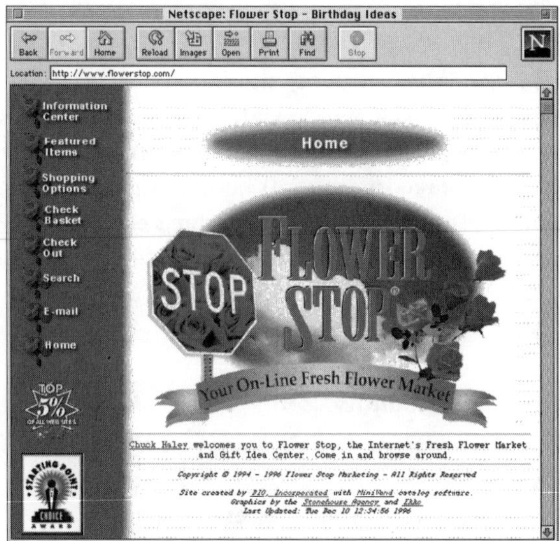

Figure 13.14
Flower Stop, *http://www.flowerstop.com*

1-800-USA-GIFT

http://www.800-usa-gift.com

Through a 23,000-member floral services network, 1-800-USA-GIFT "guarantees instant...worldwide delivery" of fresh-cut bouquets, fresh fruit and chocolate baskets, and other such gifts. Of their balloon bundle called "Avant-garde Celebration," they say: "The trendy set loves this oversized arrangement!" Hmm... does the avant-garde really send floral arrangements by phone? Either way, these gift items are suited to just about any occasion from births to funerals.

The Orchid Mall

http://www.netins.net/showcase/novacon/cyphaven/chorcmal.htm

This orchid lover's resource site has dozens of informational and commercial contacts for orchids and orchid supplies. Check here for sellers, traders, commercial dealers, and want-ads specially tailored for orchid fans. Hobbyists can investigate the international scope of the many orchid societies listed here, and casual browsers are bound to find some delightful blooms to view.

PC Flowers and Gifts

http://www.pcflowers.com

There's no excuse not to have a gift on the fly now that it's this easy to order flowers and select a personalized greeting card. PC Flowers, which has been handling electronic orders since 1989, serves up an attractive Web site in its incarnation as PC Flowers and Gifts. When you place flower orders, they're delivered by the FTD florist nearest your much-impressed recipient.

Perfect Present Picker

http://perfect.presentpicker.com

Click on assorted criteria—Occasion ("retirement"), Profession ("animal science"), Interest ("gambling"), Lifestyle ("world beat"), Personality ("controlling")—sit back, and let the Perfect Present Picker do its thing. When we tried, it returned race-horse analysis software called "Winning at the Rack," a Director King or Queen Chair, and other items, with ordering info from participating merchants. It's a nice idea that's worth a try, and kind of fun, too.

Spencer Gifts

http://www.mca.com/spencer

The mall store known for items such as lava lamps and naughty party games has an online site that's even more entertaining than visiting the store in person. The sales clerks put an inimitable spin on the merchandise. Looking for a novelty gift for a relative, but you're on a tight budget? How about a battery-operated back scratcher?

where they surf

Surfer: Kate Spade

Fashion accessory designer

Her favorite sites of the moment:

Salon

http://www.salon1999.com

"Because it is intelligent, but doesn't take itself too seriously, and covers an interesting array of topics."

Papermag

http://www.papermag.com

"Because it's the perfect resource when I want a dose of 'downtown'—a great guide to all that's hip in New York and the hysterical, immediate coverage of the fashion collections in Bryant Park."

Trade Mission, Inc.

http://www.neosoft.com/~tm/souk/index.htm

Houston's Trade Mission, an international crafts store, markets its collections in a beautifully wrapped package of cultural and experiential content. Inside, you'll find Trade Mission's art, crafts, and accessories, including items such as stone sculptures from Zimbabwe and costumed dolls from the hill tribes of Northern Thailand. Trade Mission also hosts the Travelers Club, a refined online gathering place for travelers to share their stories and resources.

WFMU's Catalog of Curiosities

http://www.wfmu.org/Catalog

WFMU, the independent freeform radio station based in the New York City area, brings its coveted catalog on line. Here's where you can indulge your love of Esquivel, books about conspiracy theories, outsider art, and theremin music all in one place. We won't give any more info away, because this site is a must-visit—if only for a priceless audio clip from William Shatner's out-of-print album, "The Transformed Man."

SALES AND BARGAINS

Derek's Free Stuff Page

http://www.ft-wayne.com/freestuff.html

We're really not sure exactly who Derek is or why he has assembled his Web page, but we do know that this site is pretty darn cool. If there's free stuff to be got, chances are you can find out about it here—or on one of the other eleven "free stuff" sites you can link to from Derek's page.

Onsale

http://www.onsale.com

Here's a fresh twist in Net commerce: Onsale has created a vibrant, photo-filled online auction in which you outbid other Web users for products ranging from digital cameras, to fine wine, to automobile radar jammers. The items remain on auction for a few days, and bidders even get e-mail updates on the proceedings.

Outlet Bound

http://www.outletbound.com

Outlet shoppers rejoice! Outlet Bound's site presents information about 12,000 factory outlet stores and 390 outlet centers in the United States and Canada. Search the store database by product category, store name, location, or brands sold, then get in-depth information about the desired outlets. An extra-added bonus: If you complete a survey, you receive VIP vouchers redeemable at select outlet centers.

SampleSale

http://www.samplesale.com

No longer are the hottest sample sales in New York limited to the well-connected. SampleSale's site (Figure 13.15) presents monthly calendars of sales in New York City featuring women's and men's apparel, jewelry, accessories, and housewares. Get the lowdown on the sales and the stores, and perhaps even get additional discounts on the merchandise—a perk of being a SampleSale surfer. Now if SampleSale would go regional.

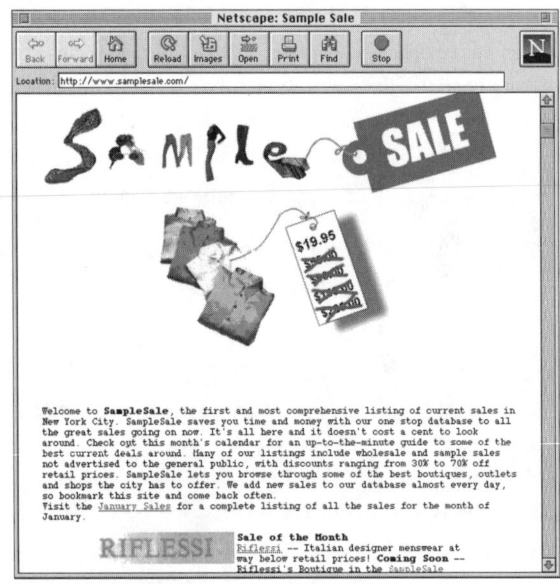

Figure 13.15

SampleSale, *http://www.samplesale.com*

HOBBIES

CraftNet Village

http://www.craftnet.org

Crafters can gather at CraftNet Village to get new ideas and trade tips. Post craft ideas at the project exchange, shop for supplies in the market square, or spend hours crafting at the free project library. The magazine rack is the place to go for craft reading pleasure from magazines like Home Express, Cross Country Stitching, and Craft & Needlework Age.

Fuji Publishing Group Cigar Page

http://www.netins.net/showcase/fujicig

At this jam-packed humidor of information from Fuji Publishing you can download the Windows Online Cigar Guide (all 4MB of it), flip through pages of the Web magazine The Double Corona, browse smoking-related newsgroups, and—take a breath here—jump to a host of other smoky pages (you'll be surprised at how many are out there).

Hobby Stores on the Net

http://www.hobbystores.com

One might expect that the stores indexed here are Hobbytyme dealers, since this site is run by toy wholesaler Hobbytyme Distributors. This is actually a good resource for hobby shoppers. U.S. stores like Classic Hobbies, Rocket Science, and Regiments Games are listed alphabetically (in HTML) alongside graphics signifying their products, which include model airplanes, trains, radio controls, and so on.

Hobby World of Montreal

http://www.odyssee.net/~hobbywld

Hobby World of Montreal is now marketing their international selection of models and collectibles via the Web. An extensive inventory is the main attraction here. Presented in a mostly text-only format is a long list of plastic model kits. There are some pictures of furniture and wooden dollhouse kits from the Tudor Period, American Colonial and Greek Revival, and other architectural eras. A very good shop for serious scale modelers.

The Magical World of Fisher-Price

http://www2.best.com/~elusive/fisher_price/index.html

Fisher-Price enthusiast Lanajean Vecchione of San Mateo, California offers this unofficial cache of information on the toy company and its products (see Figure 13.16). Collectors will find helpful features including an online marketplace, a dealer locator, and a guide to various Fisher-Price logos which can help you determine a toy's age going back to 1931. Fisher-Price's Two Tune TV and Music Box Record Player will at least bring back memories.

Movie Poster Page

http://www.musicman.com/mp/posters.html

Chock full of poster images, the Movie Poster Page entertains nearly as much as it makes a sales pitch. That's because these posters have skyrocketed in value in the last decade. Dig though its archives and you'll find a French version of Paris, Texas; or The Magic Carpet, from 1951 starring Lucille Ball. The image supply dries up all too soon, but collector Mahtab Moayeri says she's got many more.

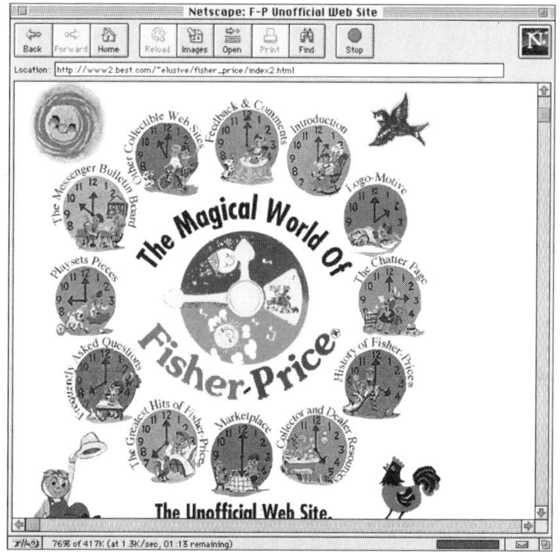

Figure 13.16

The Magical World of Fisher-Price, *http://www2.best.com/~elusive/fisher_price/index.html*

Online Sports

http://www.onlinesports.com

Those who "love sports, but hate shopping" can buy all sorts of equipment, instructional videos, and memorabilia through this online catalog. Products are organized by supplier, sport, and item (orange lacrosse balls, "The Original Pawleys Island Rope Hammock Pillow," and much more). Complementing the shopping are a sports newsletter and career center.

Philatelists Online

http://www.philatelists.com:8000/q/index.html

Yeah, we know that you know philately is a fancy word for stamp collecting. San Francisco-based Philatelists Online offers rare stamp buyers a chance to participate in auctions and Net price sales by American dealers like Midwest Stamp Exchange and The Estate Company Beverly Hills, California.

Stitcher's Source

http://www.crafterssource.com

Needleworkers can order fibers, fabrics, scissors, charts, and more via the Stitcher's Source. One gallery here offers the "finest Geometric Counted Thread designs in the World." Another features a photo profile of company owner Lesa Steele's work, which won her a Los Angeles County Fair blue ribbon. Electronic catalogs and stitch leaflets are available for downloading, if not for simple browsing. Pointers to other stitching-related companies and Web sites are offered as well.

Tennis Warehouse

http://web.xplain.com/tennis-warehouse.com

A sponsor of the WWW Tennis Server, Tennis Warehouse offers an equipment and apparel inventory for worldwide shipping, "with a guarantee of the absolute lowest prices." It includes Wilson, Prince, Head, and Dunlop racquets and accessories; K-Swiss and Adidas shoes; bags; grommets; and more. Links to other tennis-related sites are included as well.

Virtual Toystore

http://www.halcyon.com/uncomyn/home.html#Directory

The word eclectic leaps to mind. Japanimation collectibles, holographic earrings, lots of Star Trek stuff... oh, and a gallery of works by Pacific Northwest artists. They're all here in this Olympia, Washington toy store catalog. Check out photos of the Awesome Arm and Skeleton Arm, or listen to the sound made by the "Martian Popping Thing" before you decide if it's just the gift for you. Scattered, but fun.

World-Wide Collectors Digest

http://www.wwcd.com

This site may seem a tad busy, but that's because it is chock full of stuff. The World-Wide Collectors Digest is an online haven for collectors of everything from cards, comic books, and memorabilia, to figurines, toy trains, and planes. Browse a free classifieds section, a business section with ads, live auctions, chats, and trade show listings.

TRAVEL

Campus Travel

http://www.campustravel.co.uk

This U.K. site offers cheap deals for British students on the go. Campus Travel, the "retail wing of the global student travel organization, USIT International," includes contact info for the Telesales (trip booking) offices, and pages about student travel ID cards. Though U.K. students will get the most out of Campus Travel, there's something for everyone here. The Information pages, for instance, include a country-by-country disease and immunization checklist.

easySABRE

http://www.easysabre.com

AOL, Prodigy, and other online service users have been booking trips with the American Airlines-owned easySABRE system for years. Now its simple ASCII interface flies onto the Web. Register for an ID number and book air travel, hotel rooms, and rental cars by following a menu-based, fill in the blanks format.

European Travel Network

http://www.etn.nl

INTERNATIONAL APPEAL

ETN connects with ticket "consolidators," companies that buy tickets in bulk from airlines looking to make sure they fill all of their seats (most airlines dump tickets this way). As one would expect, buying cheap means selling cheap. Buying from a consolidator often means waiting until the last minute, but once you learn the ropes of discount travel, this is a way to potentially save a lot of money.

Internet Travel Network

http://www.itn.net

Connect to this site and research real-time availability of airline seats or hotel rooms, and then book your own reservation. Documentation and payment are routed through a member travel agency in your area. Minimal on-site registration is required, there's no need for credit card numbers, and easy user directions are provided with hints on finding the lowest rates and fares. If nothing else, now you can confirm flight times and prices for yourself.

LeisureWeb

http://www.leisureweb.com

LeisureWeb is a growing vacation package marketer with some big name product lines, including getaways from American Express, Delta Airlines, and AAA. The site features a RealAudio tour of its offerings and downloadable videos of destinations so you can get a leisurely taste of vacations to come. The presence here of name-brand players makes this a worthwhile site, though online vacation buyers will still want to shop around for the best deals.

PCTravel

http://www.pctravel.com

PCTravel lets you buy your airline tickets on line through a simplified interface with the same Apollo Reservation System used by many agents. Some cheap-seat airlines such as SouthWest don't participate in Apollo, so you may still need to shop around for those rock-bottom fares. You have to provide a credit card number to use the service, so those ill at ease with sending credit card info over the Internet can register by fax.

Preview Vacations

http://www.vacations.com

Preview Vacations created this site to help you plan worldwide pleasure trips from start to runway-touchdown finish. Presentation here is state-of-the-art, with a postcard-themed interface featuring postage stamp links to online airline ticketing, free trip contests, multimedia, and on. Features like the Hot Deals and Find-A-Trip (for those who want to go, but know not where) make this one delightful travel shop.

Travel Discounts

http://www.traveldiscounts.com

Travel Discount wants to be your all-in-one travel discount outlet, and it has set up an impressive site to attract your attention. With pages of info and offerings organized geographically or thematically (e.g., resorts, cruises, and railroads), you can find almost any kind of getaway, then ask the service for a price quote. Register for the free Travel Discount airfare war alert mailing list, and you'll always be up on the bargains.

TravelNow

http://www.travelnow.com

TravelNow offers cruise and package tour booking, but the site's strength is its whopping hotel database—with 20,000 properties worldwide, you can plan that 'round the world trip in one sitting. It lives up to its name with real-time availability, as well as pricing and reservations features, so what you book is what you get. Listings include distances to major attractions, check-out times, and other facility and policy information.

The World Wide Wanderer Cyberian Bucket Shop Guide

http://www.tmn.com/wwwanderer/WWWanderer_home_page.html

INTERNATIONAL APPEAL

What the heck IS a bucket shop anyway? According to the World Wide Wanderer site, it's a place where you can save up to 70 percent on flights from the U.S., U.K., and Canada to anywhere in the world. Search for budget flights, locate your nearest bucket shop, read the WWW's travel tips, and never pay full price for air travel again.

Ever heard the urban legend of the $250 Neiman Marcus cookie recipe? Get the lowdown.
http://www.neimanmarcus.com/cookie.htm

Put your sport gear to use—search L.L. Bean's national parks database for seasonal activities in the great outdoors.
http://www.llbean.com/parksearch

If you are tired of your car, build your own BMW 5 series on the computer screen.
http://www.bmwusa.com/ultimate/5series/byo5series/byo5series.html

Learn everything you ever wanted to know about coffee brewing at Harvard Espresso Company's site.
http://www.coffees.com/tips.html

Use the Find-A-Trip service on the Preview Vacations site to dream up your next vacation spot. Also, enter free trip contests, and check out airline fares.
http://www.vacations.com

☞ KEYWORDS

Shopping: autos, apparel, flowers, kids' stuff, gifts, home, online malls, food and drink.

Chapter 14

Community and Social Service

CHARITIES

ACTIVISM, ADVOCACY, AND SUPPORT

GENERAL NONPROFITS

MINORITIES

GAY AND LESBIAN RIGHTS

SENIORS

ENVIRONMENTAL AND ANIMAL RIGHTS

GOVERNMENT RELATED

CRIME AND FRAUD PREVENTION

10 WAYS YOU CAN CHANGE THE WORLD *RIGHT NOW*

1. Donate your frequent flyer miles to someone with a life threatening illness.
   http://www.unitedway.org/skywish.html
2. Become an organ donor and print out a donor card directly from the Web page.
   http://www.asf.org/doncard.html
3. Contribute an editorial on a poignant topic for all to see.
   http://www.women.com/news/fasttake.html
4. Make a donation toward books and scholarships for illiterate Indian girls.
   http://www.cs.duke.edu/~surendar/safe
5. Adopt an endangered mountain gorilla for $30.
   http://voyager.paramount.com/CAdopt.html
6. Join Amnesty's letter-writing campaigns to help free prisoners of conscience and victims of human rights violations.
   http://www.io.org/amnesty/campaign/index.html
7. Follow these re-use and recycling tips for household items from appliances to toys.
   http://www.knosso.com/Shoes/index.html
8. Find out where your talents and interests can be put to the best use for charity work: This database will consider your criteria and location and search for a volunteer position for you.
   http://www.impactonline.org
9. Are you or a loved one a smoker? Get help to stop smoking.
   http://www.chriscor.com/linkstoa.htm
10. Check the Edison Homelink for energy-saving ideas for your house and yard.
    http://www.edisonx.com/homelink/houseyard/index.html

Amidst the dazzle of entertainment and marketing homepages on the Web, there are thousands of community resource sites from nonprofit organizations, educational institutions, and individuals. Filled with information, these sites add a strong sense of compassion to the Internet, and offer ways for you to get involved in your community right from your computer.

It's now easier than ever for people with a common cause to come together on the Web to form, join, and support charities and nonprofit organizations. Even government agencies are reaching more of the public through the Web, offering services to make it easier to access government information and learn about citizens' rights.

You'll find more local and international groups than you ever knew existed, from political organizations to environmental groups. And you'll be amazed by the number of ways that you, personally, can take action. Learn how to "adopt" endangered species, or support women's groups that are making changes in all corners of the world. Send your political opinions directly to elected officials or world leaders.

From sites for minority and child advocacy, to those that fight crime, the Web is a resource tool that can assist you in supporting that for which you are most passionate. Your involvement is only a few keystrokes away.

CHARITIES

The American Red Cross
http://www.crossnet.org

Updated monthly, the Red Cross's site beckons you to get involved in the world around you. If you're unable to donate cash or blood to disaster victims, find out how to donate some of your time to volunteer for this charity. The site will also keep you up to date on the latest disaster news.

Habitat for Humanity
http://www.habitat.org

If you prefer not to give the homeless a handout, you can help build them a home. This site can help you locate the nearest home-development project of Habitat for Humanity, a non-profit, international group that works side-by-side with needy families to build and renovate houses. You can volunteer by swinging a hammer or by joining a committee.

Unicef
http://www.unicef.org

All of those donation cans and holiday cards comprise only a fraction of the action that Unicef takes to help children around the world. This site (see Figure 14.1) allows you to make a donation, volunteer, and learn about all their activities. As the primary branch of the United Nations that works for children, this group is working to universally ratify the first children's human rights treaty in history, explained on their Web page.

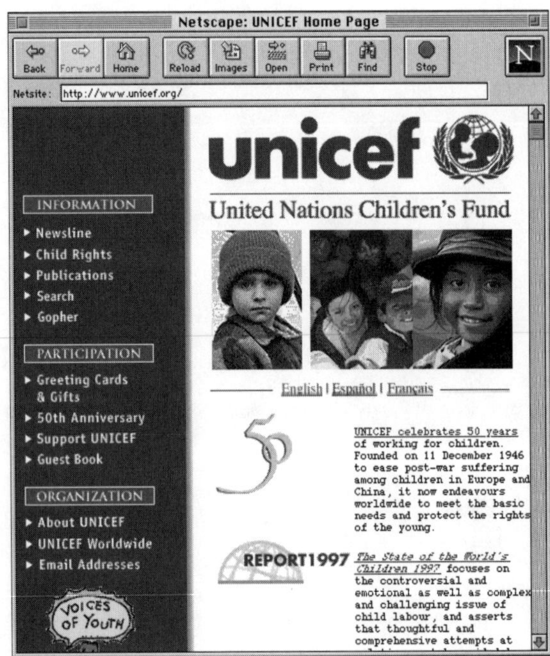

Figure 14.1
Unicef, *http://www.unicef.org*

Big Brothers and Sisters of America

http://www.bbbsa.org

Children involved in the Big Brother and Big Sister programs have a lesser occurrence of substance abuse and greater school attendance. Are you willing to offer your friendship and guidance to a child in need? Here you'll find a list of agencies in your area.

United Way Online

http://www.unitedway.org

This site (see Figure 14.2) is worth visiting for the beautiful stained-glass style graphics alone. If you look closer, you'll see that the United Way is an organization that helps anyone in need. Learn how you can contribute, or find out how you or someone you know can get help.

Nicole Brown Simpson Charitable Foundation

http://www.nbscf.org

This foundation, chaired in part by Denise Brown and Christopher Darden, works to fund shelters and organizations that protect victims of domestic violence. At this site you can make a donation in the name of someone you love.

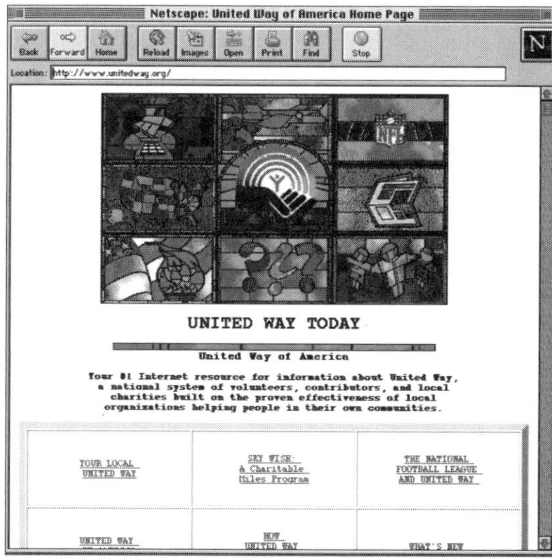

Figure 14.2

United Way Online, *http://www.unitedway.org*

ACTIVISM, ADVOCACY, AND SUPPORT

National Coalition for the Homeless

http://nch.ari.net

This organization can offer what many organizations only strive for—a true "home" on the Web. Read the story of one family who were about to be evicted from their home, but then found this page, sent an e-mail, and received help. Twenty percent of the Coalition's board members are or have been homeless, making this a truly grass-roots organization.

The League of Women Voters

http://www.lwv.org/~lwvus/index.html

Although somewhat buried under several layers of links, this site contains useful political information for women. Among the things to look for are statements and testimony from the LWV President that help clarify important issues, a section on how to contact Washington, and links to local chapters.

Global Fund for Women

http://www.igc.apc.org/gfw

This nonprofit organization is an important resource for international women's organizations and female human rights advocates in that it offers financial support to women's groups in developing countries. The GFW site outlines its programs and features important world news. Come here to find out how you can help sister organizations get off the ground.

The National Breast Cancer Coalition

http://www.natlbcc.org

Learn how to play a part in the fight against breast cancer. This site provides straightforward information on the NBCC's political campaign, goals, and accomplishments. Sign up to become a member of the Coalition, or plan a trip to the Annual Advocacy Conference.

National Women's Political Caucus

http://www.feminist.com/nwpc.htm

Are you interested in running for office? This Web site can offer some advice. NWPC is a nonprofit group that campaigns to get more women into political office. It provides campaign support to women, as well as free campaign training. The caucus also strives to get women appointed to office, regularly offering names and credentials of women to the Administration.

Women for Women in Bosnia

INTERNATIONAL APPEAL

http://www.embassy.org/wwbosnia/wwbosnia.html

At this site, you can sponsor a Bosnian woman trying to rebuild her life after the war by lending emotional support via letter exchanges, or by giving your financial support of $22 a month for food and clothing. This nonprofit resource works to help the victims of war crimes in Bosnia.

Save a Female Through Education

INTERNATIONAL APPEAL

http://www.cs.duke.edu/~surendar/safe

This one-track site pertains to the issue of gender inequality in Indian education. Through the site, you can donate money that will be put toward books and scholarships for girls. Just one of many discriminations against women in India, lack of education is a problem that this group of U.S. college students is trying to correct. According to them, less that 40 percent of women in India are literate, as opposed to 64 percent of men.

Amnesty International

INTERNATIONAL APPEAL

http://www.io.org/amnesty

AI is the largest international group that fights for human rights. Their site is basic and not very pretty, though clean and easy to navigate. You can join Amnesty's appeals to help prisoners of conscience and victims of torture, and to combat unfair trials, disappearances, unfounded executions, and the death penalty.

Coalition of Silicone Survivors

INTERNATIONAL APPEAL

http://bcn.boulder.co.us/health/silicone/sshead.html

Although scanty in the design department, this barebones guide provides a necessary service to women who have had silicone and saline breast implants. The nonprofit organization offers an educational newsletter, support groups, and contact information to help you find attorneys specializing in these cases.

Guerrilla Girls

http://www.voyagerco.com/gg/gg.html

The Guerrilla Girls site adds a sense of humor to traditional feminist issues. This group of anonymous female artists creates posters about sexual discrimination in the art world. The site displays their witty work and will make you smile.

Human Rights Web

INTERNATIONAL APPEAL

http://www.traveller.com/~hrweb/hrweb.html

Simple in layout and design, this site will help you determine what a human rights emergency is. Complete with guidelines and contacts, this page can help you save people who you know are in trouble. Or, help people who you don't already know—read through the biographies of current Prisoners of Conscience.

Your Say

http://www.world.net/yoursay/home.html

Your Say is an easy-to-use virtual protest site. Every week, a new topic appears. You have the option of protesting to the appropriate world leaders via fax, regular mail, or e-mail. Contact information and a sample letter are provided.

National Organization for Women

http://www.now.org

NOW's site addresses women with the thought, "Your Life Has Changed; The World Hasn't Caught Up." Whether you're experiencing sexual discrimination on the job, having trouble being a single mom, or are a lesbian worried about losing custody of your children, NOW urges you to take action. Link to your local chapter for more information.

Feminist Majority Foundation

100 BEST SITES

http://www.feminist.org

You can show your support for women's rights—officially—by filling out the National Feminist Census. This well-designed site (see Figure 14.3) focuses

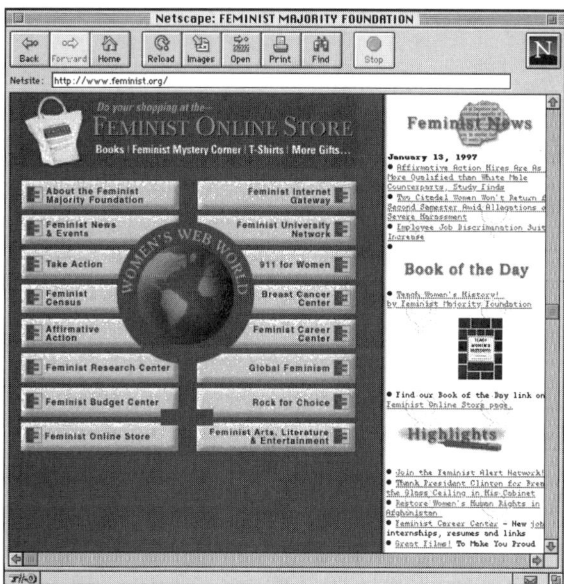

Figure 14.3
Feminist Majority Foundation,
http://www.feminist.org

on equality through a variety of projects including Rock for Choice, an organization that stages benefit concerts funding pro-choice; and the Task Force on Women and Girls in Sports, who battle still-prevalent discrimination in sports.

Action on Smoking and Health

http://www.ash.org

Did you know that being subject to second-hand smoke as little as one hour a day can triple your chances of developing breast cancer? This fact is just one example of the extensive collection of smoking information you'll find on the ASH site. Petitioning for the rights of non-smokers, the ASH site beckons you to get involved.

Child Quest International

http://www.childquest.org

The heavy graphics on this well-designed site are the only barrier to its many benefits. The site allows you to report sightings of missing children and get tips on how to keep your own children safe. It also tracks missing children through a searchable database that includes photos of the children and abduction information.

The National Center for Missing and Exploited Children

http://www.missingkids.org

If your child uses e-mail or surfs the Web, be sure to read this site's section on Child Safety and the Information Superhighway. This national organization also works to find missing children. Their site allows you to report sightings, and also contains a comprehensive list of missing children as well as ways to protect your own child from joining the list.

Mothers' Voices

http://www.mvoices.org

This is a grass-roots group of mothers that have come together to help fight AIDS. Join in the campaign to help lower the cost of drugs that fight AIDS, brush up on your HIV protection tips, and learn how to approach your children to teach them about this deadly disease.

National Abortion Rights Action League

http://www.naral.org/home.html

Pro-choice activists will find NARAL to be a great resource on the Web. The Act Now section details immediate actions you can take to help support a woman's right to choose, and to prevent anti-choice violence. Navigation is a breeze with the site's organization and clean look.

National Right to Life

http://www.nrlc.org

From the other side of the "choice" debate, covering euthanasia, RU486, abortion, and assisted suicide, this site is really a listing of related news articles. All of the information has a Right to Life spin on it, although it is presented as news flashes and medical facts. The site also includes Supreme Court updates and encourages you to "urge your congressman."

The National Rifle Association Women's Issues

http://www.nra.org/wi/wips2.html

This site works to limit the number of female victims of violent crimes. It offers a mix of topics, with an agenda—including "women and shooting" and "women against gun control" illustrated with large stars—but its resources for women are useful: The NRA offers a three-hour seminar in cities throughout the country, taught by women, titled "Refuse to Be a Victim." Also, read through the list of 42 strategies for personal safety.

Virtual Sisterhood

http://www.igc.apc.org/vsister/vsister.html

This nonprofit group wants to help women get on line to network, publish, and support women's issues. The site contains a global listing of women's groups, broken down by region and by organization. Already listed in seven languages, the Sisterhood site invites you to add to the resource by translating the information into your own language.

HungerWeb

http://www.brown.edu/Departments/World_Hunger_Program

If you are a researcher, advocate, educator, or field worker interested in hunger issues, this site is a good resource. Researchers will find study results and bibliographies; advocates and field workers will find organizations and legislation; and educators will find syllabi, ideas for teaching children about hunger, and listings of undergraduate courses.

The Ada Project (TAP)

http://www.cs.yale.edu/HTML/YALE/CS/HyPlans/tap

Paying homage to Ada Bryon King, a computing pioneer, as well as to all women in the field of computer science, TAP is a resource worth bookmarking. TAP reports the latest progress of women in the computer industry, along with job resources, grant information, and a photo gallery of women and computers. Be sure to send young women you know to TAP Junior, geared for the K-12 computer enthusiasts.

Foundation for Women's Health

http://gnomes.org/forward/index.html

This pro-active site contains straightforward information about victims of female genital mutilation. According to them, there are 128 million women throughout the world who fall into this category. Find out more about this crime and how you can help to put an end to it. The site also offers information about the Foundation for Women's Health and legislative updates in the U.S. and abroad.

54 Ways to Help the Homeless

http://ecosys.drdr.virginia.edu/ways/54.html

Do you feel helpless when approached on the street by a homeless person? This online book will teach you who the homeless are and how to offer help. Your response can be as simple as a kind word or an extra sandwich, or as involved as volunteering at a local shelter.

The Family Violence Prevention Fund

http://www.igc.apc.org/fund

Take a domestic violence quiz at this site to find out how much you really know on the subject. Find out simple things that you can do at work, at the doctor's office, and while talking with men to help put an end to domestic violence. The site also offers advice on how to speak directly with a victim of domestic violence.

Project America

http://project.org

Have you always wanted to volunteer but have never gotten around to it? This site's action guide provides local, state, and national resource guides of organizations that always need volunteers. If you are a leader, find ideas and tips on how to organize your own volunteer project.

Avon's Breast Cancer Awareness Crusade

http://www.pmedia.com/Avon/avon.html

This resource will give you all of the basic facts on breast cancer and mammograms. Learn prevention and diagnosis strategies and read true stories of survivors in the online conference transcripts. The site also lists local breast cancer support groups.

Girl Power

http://www.health.org/gpower/index.htm

Girl Power is a Department of Health and Human services campaign to help better shape the lives of girls ages 9 to 14. According to the site, this period of time in a girl's life is often marked by lost self-confidence and feelings of self worth. The site's colorful pages include tips on empowerment, a diary, and profiles of strong female role models.

Survivors of Stalking

http://www.gate.net/~soshelp

This is an extensive compilation of resources for preventing and stopping stalking, as well as a site that offers counseling and support, legal advice, and personal stories. Help protect yourself by learning the warning signs, discover local groups and volunteer options, or find out what action to take if you or a friend becomes a victim.

INTERNATIONAL APPEAL

Children's Defense Fund

http://www.tmn.com/cdf/index.html

This group helps children by working to prevent sickness, school dropout, family breakdown, or any trouble. For starters, the site provides a list of ten simple things you can do to help children get a healthy start in life. If you would like to do more, start a Child Watch program, observe a children's Sabbath, or make a donation.

Fem*Mass

http://users.aimnet.com/~mijo/Femmass.html

This site has an incredible personal touch—it is a list of women's home pages. You'll find it's not just a collection of home pages designed by women, but a collection of personalities. The well-chosen pages are indexed by pictures of the women who "own" the pages and by their philosophies on life.

Tenant Net

http://tenant.net

This site covers the basics of residential landlord/tenant law, organized by state. If you are a renter, it's important to know your rights so that a landlord cannot take advantage of you. Find out what you should know before you rent and how to handle problems after the move-in. Topics covered include leases, discrimination, rent control, landlord access, noisy neighbors, and more.

where they surf

Surfer: Karen Coyle

Chair of the Berkeley, California chapter of Computer Professionals for Social Responsibility (**http://www.cpsr.org**) and frequent Web contributor.

Her favorite Web sites of the moment:

The Ada Project

http://www.cs.yale.edu/HTML/YALE/CS/HyPlans/tap

"I especially like their history pages about women working on the earliest computers. Every woman who programs should learn about Admiral Grace Hopper, the woman who decided that UNIVAC I should be a little friendlier, and, thus, the first compiler came into being. The year was 1949."

The Progressive Directory

http://www.igc.org/igc

"A great gathering of socially-oriented nonprofit groups. WomensNet has links to the less flashy but hard-working Web pages of organizations working for women's rights all over the world. They can renew your faith, and give you hope."

DEBORAH RUSSELL, EDITOR

Impact Online

http://www.impactonline.org

With the lofty ideal of turning good intentions into action, this nonprofit group pairs people that have similar concerns. This site (see Figure 14.4) features a searchable database that will match you with a volunteer organization in your area by taking your talents and interests into consideration. Before you begin, talk with others about their experiences in the Impact chat room.

Figure 14.4
Impact Online, *http://www.impactonline.org*

National Child Rights Alliance

http://www.ai.mit.edu/people/ellens/NCRA/ncra.html

A pure advocacy organization for children, the NCRA acts to ensure that children are not treated as property. The site details the legal actions taken by children in order to divorce their parents, as well as the emotional, physical, and political implications of such actions. Learn about the steps being taken to insure a child's protection and read the Youth Bill of Rights.

Club Girl Tech

http://www.girltech.com

A good environment for girls on the Web, Club Girl Tech is full of free resources and colorful, animated graphics. Girls can talk to one another through the Chick Chat area or play interactive games in the Game Cafe. But most important is Girl's World, where visitors can read about successful women throughout history.

Network of East-West Women

http://www.igc.apc.org/neww

Have you stopped to think about how the drastic political changes in Eastern Europe and the former Soviet Union may be affecting women? NEWW's site (see Figure 14.5) provides a forum for Eastern and Western women's rights advocates to stay in touch and to discuss both unique and universal gender issues.

Mothers Against Drunk Driving

http://www.gran-net.com/madd/madd.htm

This site gives tips on how to change drunk driving statistics. It focuses on public awareness, citizen services, and

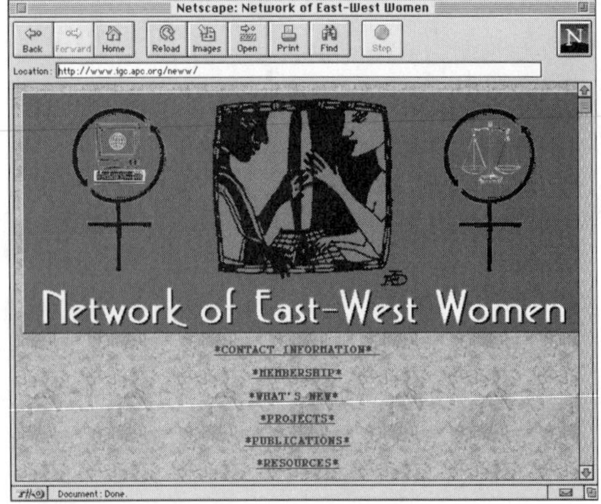

Figure 14.5
Network of East-West Women, *http://www.igc.apc.org/neww*

legislative measures. The site encourages you to join a local chapter, contribute, write your local newspaper, or contact elected officials with your concerns.

United Nations Division for the Advancement of Women

http://www.un.org/dpcsd/daw

The Women's Division site focuses on the making of women's policy and the struggle to end sexism. Find the latest report from the Commission of the Status of Women. Also find out what was done at the Beijing Conference on Women in 1995, and what has been done since the conference.

Parents Against Speeding Teens

http://www.nh.ultranet.com/~gweety/past.htm

Did you know that car accidents are the number one killer of teens? Advertising that "Speed Kills," this organization educates high school kids about speeding. Sit down with your teen to print out and sign the site's "Contract for Teenagers and Parents," designed to make your teen comfortable asking you for a ride in a potentially dangerous situation.

GENERAL NONPROFITS

Pacific News Service

http://www.pacificnews.org/jinn/index.html

Pacific News Service is an organization that brings together journalists with perspectives that are not traditionally covered in mainstream periodicals, including those of teenagers, immigrants, and expatriates. Their Web site reflects this philosophy, and includes Yo!, their youth magazine, and Jinn, an online publication that serves as a forum for alternative journalists and youth. Topics include a variety of culturally and politically important issues, from guerrillas in Peru to teenage street life in Oakland. A fascinating read.

Consumer World

http://www.consumerworld.org

Ralph Nader didn't create this index, but his spirit fuels its pointers to "over 1,400 of the most useful consumer resources on the Internet." We're talking about all sorts of info a buyer needs to make wise decisions in the post-modern marketplace, as well as the means for faulty business practice victims to fight back. All that's missing from

[OVERHEARD ON WOMEN'S WIRE]

http://chat.women.com

ON SURFING THE WEB:

"I love talking on line... We have a lot of public health sites at the Centers for Disease Control, so I always try to surf those sites."

ABOUT HER JOB:

"You meet interesting people. You work on important issues. And you get to play golf with the president. He always wins. He gets to because he's the president."

—U.S. Secretary of Health and Human Services Donna Shalala in a live chat on Women's Wire.

Consumer World's vivid interface are audio clips of shysters muttering, "Curses, foiled again!"

National Institute for Literacy
http://novel.nifl.gov

This site provides basic information on adult literacy and adult education in general. While it doesn't have any bells and whistles, the calendar of events will at least keep you up-to-date on special programs, such as National Family Literacy Day, Walk for Literacy, and NetDay.

National Association for Women in Science
http://www.awis.org

Created 25 years ago to promote equal opportunities for women in science careers, the NAWIS provides free mentoring programs around the country. Career options, research opportunities, and balancing work and family are a few of the issues covered. Link to your local chapter for details.

Parents Helping Parents: The Family Resource Center
http://www.php.com

PHP Online is a free service for families who have children with special needs. An online resource directory database allows you to search for medical care by diagnosis, language, service, city, or state. In addition to family members, PHP is useful to teachers, nurses, and physicians.

Experts.Com
http://www.experts.com/engine.html

This free, searchable database will help you to find an expert in any professional field. You may search by name, company, topic, or location, and discover experts in your area or on line. The database includes everything from lawyers to business consultants.

Nolo Press Self-Help Law Center
http://www.nolo.com

Are you aware that in some cases, your boss may legally read your e-mail? Find out exactly what is and is not legal without paying a lawyer's consultation fee. This site offers features on hot legal issues, including how to rebuild your credit, how to get out of default on your student loan payments, how to get the most out of your lawyer, and more. Also contains legal and structure advice for businesses.

LaborWeb
http://www.aflcio.org

The home page of the AFL-CIO is another that recommends the boycott of particular companies and goods. The list is comprised of companies in violation of union standards. Visit the Stand Up Online Center, where you may send e-mail to your congressman regarding jobs, wages, or worker protection.

KID Appeal

Al-Anon and Alateen
http://solar.rtd.utk.edu/~al-anon

Al-Anon and Alateen are recovery groups for friends and families of alcoholics. The site includes questions to help you decide whether or not you need a recovery group and to determine whether alcoholism has affected your childhood or present life. Learn the groups' traditions or search the directory for a group near you or one on the Internet.

Legal Aid for Abused Women
http://ourworld.compuserve.com/homepages/laaw

Despite the name of the organization, LAAW provides support to both women and men trying to remove themselves from abusive situations. The site provides information on the cost of legal necessities such as restraining orders, custody battles, separation, and divorce. A legal aide offers help in paying for these services.

National Parent Information Network
http://ericps.ed.uiuc.edu/npin/npinhome.html

This site is a free resource for parents and parent educators. In the Resources for Parents section, "Parents Ask Eric" will answer parenting questions with articles and contacts to relevant organizations. In addition, you may subscribe to the electronic mailing list to participate in discussions on child development, education, and care.

The National Federation of the Blind

http://www.nfb.org/default.htm

Describing blindness as "only a physical nuisance," this upbeat site focuses on educating and training the blind. Resources include a list of Frequently Asked Questions about being blind and a job listing for the blind. How do the blind access this site? Go to the Technology for the Blind section to find out.

Deaf World Web

http://deafworldweb.org/dww

Deaf-owned and deaf-run, this site provides information on deaf resources throughout the world. Find local and national resources listed by country. You'll find a parents' guide for deaf children and an Online Deaf Encyclopedia, defining most everything in the deaf community. For kids, the Deaf CyberKids section will put you in touch with a pen pal.

Planned Parenthood Federation of America

http://www.igc.apc.org/ppfa

The largest source of reproductive health information in the country, Planned Parenthood offers online information regarding contraception, pregnancy, STDs, sex education, abortion, reproductive rights, and more. You can also find contact information for the clinic nearest you.

American Medical Womens' Association

http://www.amwa-doc.org/index.html

The AMWA is for female physicians, female medical students, and members of the general public who are concerned with female health issues. Find out how to become a member and how to get the AMWA resource book, "The Women's Complete Healthbook," written entirely by women physicians.

American Association of University Women

http://www.aauw.org

The AAUW promotes the education of women and girls by lobbying congress for gender equity and working with educators to achieve gender-fair education programs in schools. Resources include grants, fellowships, and a legal fund. Because the site (see Figure 14.6) is somewhat cluttered in organization, it is best navigated using the site directory.

Computer Professionals For Social Responsibility

http://www.cpsr.org/dox

With technology developing so fast, someone needs to stop and take a look at how it is impacting society. CPSR is a group of computer scientists and concerned individuals that come together to do just that. Studies include Women and Computing, Education, Ethics, and Privacy. The site also includes articles on the "Millennium Problem," and legislation regarding online censorship and privacy.

The Arc

http://TheArc.org/welcome.html

Formerly the Association for Retarded Citizens of the United States, the Arc is the largest national voluntary organization for the welfare of children, adults, and family members affected by mental retardation. The site's primary focus is on advocacy, posting political positions and

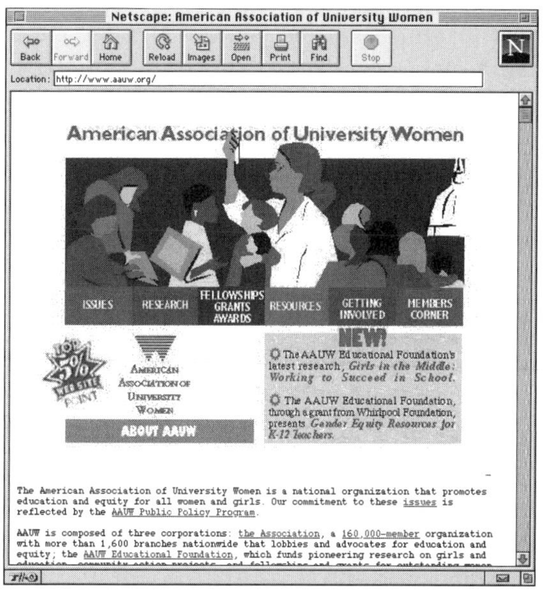

Figure 14.6

American Association of University Women, *http://www.aauw.org*

government reports. Fact sheets on mental retardation and local chapter links are available.

Online Intergroup of Alchoholics Anonymous

http://aa-intergroup.org

Most AA Intergroups are designed to serve particular geographic regions of the world. The Online Intergroup's region is cyberspace. Whether you prefer an e-mail group or one that meets in a chat room, you'll be able to find one that suits your needs in the site's directory.

Bereavment and Hospice Support Netline

http://www.ubalt.edu/www/bereavement

This site deals with the delicate issues of loss and grief. A good resource for you or those you care about, the Netline offers support group listings by state. Groups deal with issues including pregnancy/infant loss, suicide, homicide/murder, AIDS, cancer, and more.

INTERNATIONAL APPEAL

The World Health Network

http://www.worldhealth.net

Want to slow the aging process? Once only wishful thinking, Anti-Aging Medicine is now a science. Find the latest information on this nonprofit site. Link to the Chicago Tribune's Longevity Test, which may determine where you stand and where you are going in the aging process by your current lifestyle.

The Virtual Memorial Garden

http://catless.ncl.ac.uk/Obituary/memorial.html

Honor a loved one or a pet who died by creating a memorial for them here. The service is free. The poetry or message you write to/about your loved one will appear under their name on the pages of this electronic monument. You can direct far-away family members to the memorial and visit as often as you like.

The Lost Friends Center

http://www.lost-and-found.com/lfc/locate.html

Do you have a friend or loved one that you can't seem to locate? This free service allows you to post a listing and description of your loved one. But be warned—the lost entries list is very large. It may take a while to download.

ReuNet: The Reunion Network

http://reunion.com

This site offers you a number of unique ways in which to find your missing loved one. You may enter a mutual consent registry, post a permanent online advertisement, post on the adoption or missing person bulletin boards, or register for a free television reunion.

Internet NonProfit Center

http://www.nonprofits.org

If you're looking for a specific way to volunteer your time or a specific organization to receive your donation, this site's Nonprofit Locator will find virtually any charity in the U.S. If you're not sure where to start, try the site's Top 40 Charities list. You can even find information on how to start your own nonprofit group.

The Financial Aid Information Page

http://www.finaid.org

This site will be invaluable to anyone looking for virtually any kind of financial aid. Research scholarships, fellowships, contests, grants, loans, study abroad programs, exchange programs, and different payment plans are covered. The site includes special pages for women and other special interest students. There's even an Aid Advisor who will answer your questions.

KID APPEAL

The Life Education Network

http://www.lec.org

The nonprofit LEN works to educate people, especially children, on the dangers of drug abuse. Along with a colorful education page for your children, the most useful part of the site is a drug database. Here you will find a list of the most abused drugs, their side effects, and the clues that may indicate that someone you know is using.

MINORITIES

Asiannet

http://www.asiannet.com

One of the most comprehensive Asian-oriented sites on the Net, the home pages on this site are broken into countries—from Japan to Thailand. From there they are divided by topic—from education to business. The site is both fun and informative, with coverage of celebrities, kids' sites, and an extensive link section.

Asian-American Resources

http://www.mit.edu:8001/afs/athena.mit.edu/user/i/r/irie/www/aar.html

A compilation of clubs, organizations, media links, and home pages relevant to Asian-American lifestyles. Look here for information services, events, and news in a format that is easy to use.

INTERNATIONAL APPEAL

Asia OnLine

http://www.asia-online.com

This graphically energetic online magazine covers international news and culture with an Asian perspective. Calling itself the new medium for the new Asian, this is an interesting site if you are loking for culturally interesting features full of attitude.

INTERNATIONAL APPEAL

Democracy and Human Rights in the Americas

http://worldpolicy.org/americas/index.html

With coverage of Latin American countries, as well as the U.S. and Canada, this informative site particularly discusses human rights action, violations, and legislation. It is also a great place for links to networks in specific countries, or if you are looking to find up-to-date news from all of the Americas.

Latino Link

http://www.latinolink.com

Latino Link is a very extensive online magazine with easy-to-navigate graphics. The site covers news and politics, and also provides a forum for discussion topics on everything from U.S.-Cuban relations to Latin stars. Sections also include career resources, book reviews, and cultural phenomena (most recently, Chupacabras). Latino Link has an incredible list of links with mini-reviews to help you streamline your searches.

Latin World

http://www.latinworld.com

This is a simple but helpful site that serves as a forum for Latinos in the U.S., particularly focusing on thought and culture, recent news, and important upcoming events.

LatinoWeb

http://www.latinoweb.com/favision

LatinoWeb is a practical site which includes a search engine to facilitate your browsing. Latino coverage is extensive, with features varying from Radio Latino and history, to job links and classifieds. One bonus to take a look at is the What's New section, which profiles weekly new sites of interest.

Diversity Links for Women and Minorities

http://www.careermosaic.com/cm/cm33.html

More than just a database of job listings, this site is also an online career resource guide. It can assist you in deciding on a career, getting the education you need and finding available work. You can ask questions here, as well as browse through the resume helper.

INTERNATIONAL APPEAL

MiraeNet

http://www.mirae.com

The nonprofit Mirae Foundation sponsors this site as a national forum for the Korean-American community. Although very basic, the site offers pages with information on career opportunities, corporate internships, community service, and conferences for Korean-Americans.

Melanet—African-American Business Directory

http://www.melanet.com/melanet

Melanet offers an online African-America experience through a marketplace, a Kwanzaa bazaar, and a chat series with prominent leaders in the African-American community. You'll also find a listing of African-American-owned businesses throughout the world. And the Universal Afrocentric calendar will keep you in touch with African-American events both on and off the Web.

National Urban League

http://www.nul.org

The NUL is a nonprofit organization designed to help African-Americans achieve social and economic equality. Most helpful in the site is the job bank, which allows you to search by location, job description, or company. Place yourself on the Urban Leaders list to join a virtual community of problem-solvers.

AfriNet

http://www.afrinet.net

AfriNet is looking for African-Americans to join an electronic community that includes an African and Caribbean art gallery, event listings, a business directory, and a searchable database. Although still being developed, the site has some nice features and design.

The Chicana Feminist Home Page

http://www-leland.stanford.edu/~slg

Created by a Chicana Studies professor in California, this page is an all-encompassing resource. You'll find information on Chicana leaders, literature and art, plus links to many other Chicana, Chicano, and women's sites.

South Asian Women's Net

http://www.umiacs.umd.edu/users/sawweb/sawnet

This site covers a variety of resources for and about South Asian women, which includes those from Bangladesh, Bhutan, Burma, India, Nepal, Pakistan, and Sri Lanka. Visit the home pages of South Asian women and find information on related grants, charities, and news.

National Association for the Advancement of Colored People

http://www.naacp.org

This well-designed site urges visitors to read the latest issue alert and take action. Whether the latest concern happens to be state elections or the boycott of a leading oil company, the NAACP is always in the forefront of action. Find out how you can join the action in your own community by using a clickable map.

Minority Affairs Forum

ftp://heather.cs.ucdavis.edu/pub/README.html

If you're interested in issues including immigration, affirmative action, bilingual education, or race relations, this forum is for you. Designed to cover the intricacies that mainstream print and electronic media miss, you can receive your information via articles, mailing lists, or organizations.

NetNoir

http://www.netnoir.com

An entertainment site and online community about Afrocentric culture (see Figure 14.7), this is the companion site of NetNoir's online community on America Online (AOL). In the Lifestyle department, you can find articles about the world of hip hop, profiles of musicians and album reviews, as well as the latest on

where they surf

Surfer: E. David Ellington

President and CEO of NetNoir (http://www.netnoir.com)

Favorite Web sites of the moment:

Shareware.com

http://www.shareware.com

"This product of CNET is great and has a lot of FREE downloads."

Africa Online

http://www.AfricaOnline.com

"A really cool way to learn about Africa and keep up with football (soccer) on the continent."

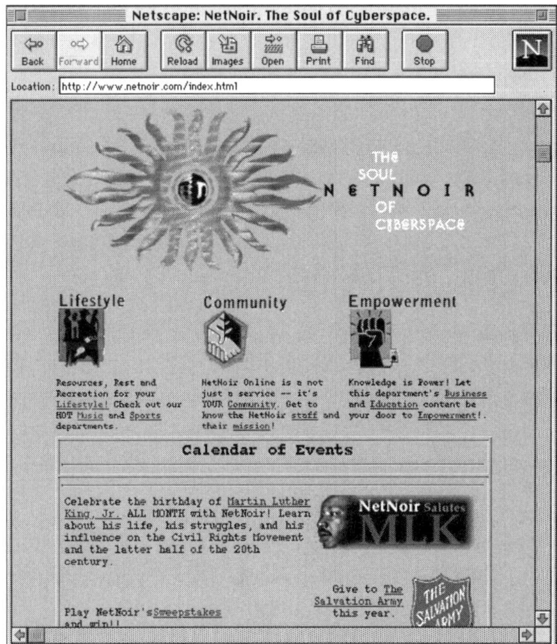

Figure 14.7

NetNoir, *http://www.netnoir.com*

sporting events and celebs. The spotlight section features a different topic monthly. Past months have included celebrations of Martin Luther King, Jr., Kwanzaa, and Women's History Month. The Empowerment department will lead you to useful resources as well as an impressive presentation of interactive African folktales.

GAY AND LESBIAN RIGHTS

Gay and Lesbian Alliance Against Defamation

http://www.glaad.org/glaad

This national watchdog organization works to improve public attitude towards homosexuality through careful monitoring of the media. Read the GLAAD news on their site to find out how mass media portrays gays and lesbians. You can also report defamation by e-mailing the Alert line.

OutRage!

http://www.OutRage.cygnet.co.uk

OutRage! is a gay advocacy group in England that believes in direct action. They work to eliminate discrimination by exposing, confronting, and embarrassing homophobic individuals. Read about the latest antics, browse the "I Can See Queerly Now" photo gallery, and pledge your allegiance.

Parents, Families, and Friends of Lesbians and Gays

http://www.pflag.org

Through this site (see Figure 14.8), find a local affiliate and attend a meeting of PFLAG, a nonprofit group that supports family and friends and works to eliminate homophobia. If you have a friend or family member who is gay, lesbian, or bisexual, you may want to stop by this site and help them with their goal of eliminating discrimination.

Lesbian Mothers Support Society

http://www.lesbian.org/lesbian-moms

This site pays attention to the issues unique to lesbian families, including access to insemination, the rights of non-biological parents, and custody issues in lesbian family

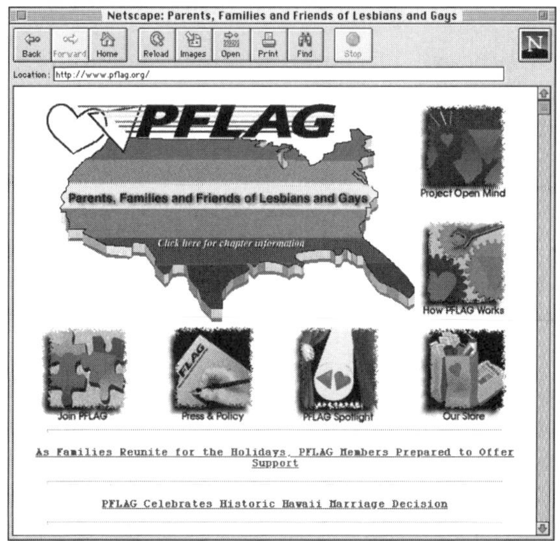

Figure 14.8

Parents, Families and Friends of Lesbians and Gays, *http://www.pflag.org*

breakups. Mothers are encouraged to give and receive peer support by exchanging stories and experiences with other lesbian mothers.

Human Rights Campaign
http://www.hrcusa.org

This lesbian and gay equal rights group lobbies Congress for issues important to the gay community, especially AIDS research funding and health issues. The site explains HRC's platforms and suggests what you can do to help as an individual. Become a citizen advocate, find out about local HRC events, and pledge your membership on line.

SENIORS

SenioriNet
http://seniornet.org

This site (see Figure 14.9) is a comprehensive resource for seniors on the Net, with features like an interview with Rosalyn Carter and discussions about Medicare. It is also a social and interactive forum, with ongoing round table discussions that you can contribute to, not to mention a mystery novel that you can add to.

Figure 14.9
SeniorNet, *http://seniornet.org*

The Older Women's League
http://www.scn.org/scripts/menus/o/owl/menu

At a time when women still retire on less income than men do, and quite possibly without health insurance, this Web site's support network is much needed. Aimed at mid-life to older women, OWL is a national organization that offers support through educational publications and forums.

Seniors-Site
http://seniors-site.com

This catch-all senior resource includes free information for seniors on retirement, education, finances, nursing homes, and legal issues. One especially useful service is a bulletin board that lists warnings of scams aimed at seniors, including Social Security Disability Fraud and Medicare Fraud.

GeroWeb
http://www.iog.wayne.edu/GeroWeb.html

The home of the Virtual Library on Aging, this site is a good bookmark for researchers, practitioners, or anyone interested in aging. The library includes searchable listings of universities, government agencies, and private organizations with an interest in Gerontology.

Elderhostel Home Page
http://www.elderhostel.org

Do you wish you could go back to college to learn something new? Age has its benefits: If you're at least 55 years old, you can take advantage of short-term liberal arts adventures at universities around the world, without homework and exams.

Eldercare Help Page
http://www.mindspring.com/~eldrcare/elderweb.htm

If you're a caregiver for an older parent, grandparent, or any senior citizen, bookmark this site. You'll use it over and over again, with local resources on personal care, nursing homes, senior sitters, retirement communities, and transportation. Arrange for your loved one to receive a daily phone call or ask the Eldercare Lady a pertinent question.

ENVIRONMENTAL AND ANIMAL RIGHTS

Animal Rights Resource Site

http://envirolink.org/arrs/index.html

At this site, get some insight on where to draw the line in the heated debate on preventing animal abuse. Learn what it really means to be a vegan and how you can avoid using products packaged in boxes made with glue which contains animal products.

The Rainforest Action Network

http://www.igc.apc.org/ran

Chock full of rainforest photos and colorful graphics, RAN is one of the best environmental sites on the Web (see Figure 14.10). On the "Seven Things You Can Do to Save The Rainforest" page, you'll find that you can make a difference without spending a cent. Discover and boycott large companies that destroy rainforests.

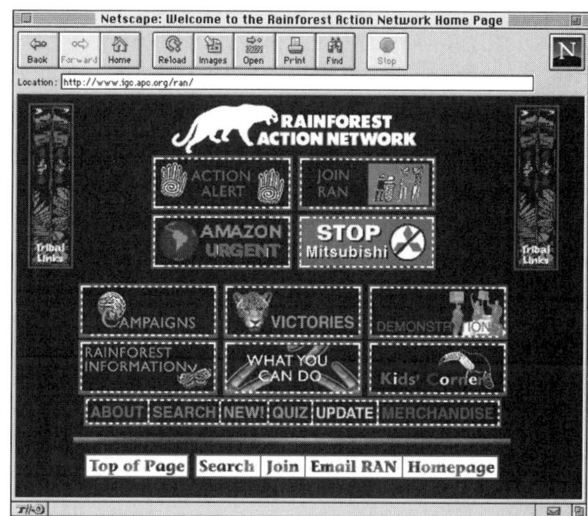

Figure 14.10
The Rainforest Action Network,
http://www.igc.apc.org/ran

Adopt A Gorilla

http://voyager.paramount.com/CAdopt.html

Do you want a gorilla of your very own? Visit this site and, as part of the Dian Fossey Gorilla Fund, you may adopt Amy, one of seven endangered mountain gorillas born recently in the Virungas. For $30, you'll get an adoption certificate, a T-shirt, Amy's photo and reports from field researchers—not to mention the satisfaction of knowing you've helped a furry friend.

Conservation International

http://www.conservation.org

Keep abreast of the latest statistics while CI keeps watch over the world's ecosystems. According to the CI site, one-fourth of all known mammals are at risk of extinction. You can contribute to CI by shopping in the online marketplace, featuring products made by locals in the rainforests. Also learn about Ecotourism, the environmentally conscious vacations that are growing in popularity.

The Sierra Club

http://www.sierraclub.org

This conservation group and their site focus on protecting the environment through public policy and promoting stewardship through outdoor trips that are open to the public. Sign up for trips including the following: activism, backpacking, biking, canoeing, family, international, rafting, and skiing.

Greenpeace International

http://www.greenpeace.org

Easy to navigate with simple icons, this site is a well of information on environmental threats to the earth. Find the specifics on how Greenpeace is trying to protect biodiversity, prevent pollution, and promote peace through projects and campaigns. Find the nearest office and get involved locally, or find out how to take action on line.

World Wildlife Fund

http://www.wwf.org

Check in with this nonprofit group's online wildlife reports (see Figure 14.11) to find out about the most threatened marine animals, insects, and flowers, then help them save the natural habitats of these endangered animals. You can join the group for as little as $15, or show your support by using products that help the WWF.

EnviroLink Network

http://www.envirolink.org/envirohome.html

With a textured, earthy theme, this nonprofit site (see Figure 14.12) makes you want to poke around, if only to check out the ancient art and symbols that adorn the site. The environmental library is broken down in the most elemental fashion, with the categories being earth, air, fire, and water. Speak up in the Envirochat area or shop in the Green marketplace.

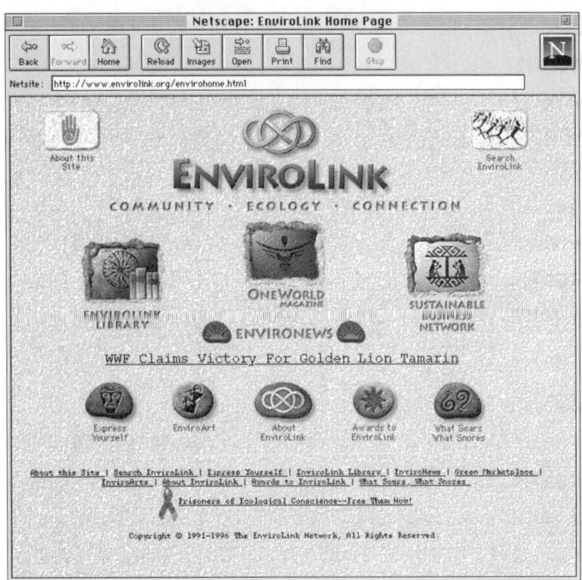

Figure 14.12
EnviroLink Network,
http://www.envirolink.org/envirohome.html

National Parks and Conservation Association

http://www.npca.org/home/npca

This nonprofit citizens group works to bring attention and protection to the overused, yet financially neglected National Parks. This well-organized site details how you can get involved in a grass-roots letter-writing campaign. No time? Find out how you can make the most out of your financial donation to the Parks.

Figure 14.11
World Wildlife Fund, *http://www.wwf.org*

EarthWatch

http://gaia.earthwatch.org

Unlike other environmental groups, EarthWatch has a primary objective to sponsor field scientific research projects. Whether you're a scientist or citizen, you can become involved in the projects. Students can even receive college credit by being a member of an EarthWatch team. Check the site for details on participating in an existing project or proposing your own.

Veggies Unite!

http://www.vegweb.com

This site not only advocates vegetarianism, but shows you exactly how to do it. A huge recipe database gives you tasty meals for holidays and every day. The Green Grocery Shoppe allows you to buy many of your ingredients on line. And the VegWeb Chat is a real-time forum for vegetarian discussion and friendship.

League of Conservation Voters

http://www.lcv.org

Visit this site for, among other things, the online version of the National Environmental Scorecard, an annual report which shows how Congress has voted on the environment. In contrast to most of the grass-roots environmental groups, LCV concentrates solely on legislation and environmental policy. This bipartisan group works to save the earth through voter education.

U.S.D.A. Forest Service Home Page

http://www.fs.fed.us

This site will help you to take advantage of a lesser-known resource, the National Forests. Maps and recreation information are available on the site, along with instructions on how to make campground reservations. But more importantly, a Forest Health report may just inspire you to volunteer for the forests or to take part in an ecological stewardship program.

SPOTLIGHT ON THE ENVIRONMENT

With most of the world's endangered species and threatened rainforests located at least one continent away, in the past it might have seemed difficult to find correct information and ways to help. Now, environmental Web sites bring environmental issues to your computer screen, along with situations in your home or a neighboring state.

Five Facts

1. One-fourth of all known mammals are at risk of extinction, according to Conservation International.
2. An average of 137 species of life are driven into extinction every day, according to the Rainforest Action Network (RAN).
3. Also every day, 214,000 acres of rainforest—an area larger than New York City—are destroyed.
4. International illegal wildlife trade (including that of endangered species) is estimated at $2 to $3 million per year, according to the World Wildlife Foundation.
5. The U.S. National Park Service has documented over $8 billion worth of needed repairs not funded by this year's budget, according to the National Parks and Conservation Association.

Five Sites

Get to know the outdoors a little better (though virtually) on the Sierra Clubs site. Sign up for backpacking, hiking, biking, rafting, or skiing trips.

http://www.sierraclub.org

Join Greenpeace in the fight to prevent pollution and right environmental wrongs.

http://www.greenpeace.org

Learn which animals are the most endangered on earth at the site of the World Wildlife Fund. By joining the WWF, you can help to protect the natural habitats of these animals.

http://www.wwf.org

At this site from the Rainforest Action Network, learn seven things that you can do to save the rainforest, from changing your buying habits to writing a few e-mails.

http://www.igc.apc.org/ran

At this site of the League of Conservation Voters you can see how Congressmembers have been voting on environmental issues.

http://www.lcv.org

GOVERNMENT RELATED

Federal Emergency Management Agency

http://www.fema.gov

Although FEMA's site offers safety tips and a Tropical Storm Watch, the most useful section of the site is titled "Help After a Disaster." Here disaster victims will find the important basics—where to stay, how to find food and water, how to contact family members, and how to apply for Federal Assistance.

Consumer Products Safety Commission

http://www.cpsc.gov

The information on this site is easy to find and downloads quickly. This government organization is a product watchdog, striving to reduce the risk of injuries and death from consumer products. Find how to report safety problems and product-related injuries through the site.

U.S. Department of Labor Women's Bureau

http://www.dol.gov/dol/wb

The Women's Bureau was created to help level the "paying" field among the sexes. Use the Fair Pay Clearinghouse hotline to find how employees and employers can prevent discrimination in the workplace. Also, read about the first National Girls' Conference.

Find Your Rep

http://www.georgemag.com/hfm/resources/index.html

From George Magazine, this colorful, user-friendly site is an image map of the U.S. Click on a state to find the representatives' and senators' snailmail and e-mail addresses, phone numbers, fax numbers, and URLs.

World Health Organization

INTERNATIONAL APPEAL

http://www.who.ch

The WHO works to eliminate worldwide disease through education, vaccination, and proper treatment. Here, you can view a summary of the latest World Health Report, an international health census. Also find out about the latest disease outbreaks. Plan to participate in the next World Health Day and World No-Tobacco Day.

U.S. Dept. of Health and Human Services

http://odphp2.osophs.dhhs.gov/consumer.htm

The HHS site is a resource that will provide you with information on an endless number of subjects, from birth defects to social security. Many other resources are also available, including a catalog of Federal Domestic Assistance Programs, and the Consumer Information Center Catalog.

where they surf

Surfer: Ida Castro

Director designate of the Department of Labor's Women's Bureau, **http://www.dol.gov/dol/wb**

Her favorite Web sites of the moment:

Women's Web Magazine

http://www.womenswebmagazine.com

"This is a look and learn Website. When I log on here, I get a spectrum of topics about women—both domestic and international."

Voices of Women

http://www.voiceofwomen.com

"It's like being part of a roundtable discussion, with a panoply of ideas and information, without ever leaving your desk."

Cizitens Against Government Waste (Spending)

http://www.govt-waste.org/mf.main/welcome.html

Dubbing themselves "The Government Waste Watchers," this group of citizens prods visitors of their site to get angry over government overspending. Go to the research portion of the site regularly to find the current national debt and what your share of it is. Despite the seriousness of this site, the group maintains a sense of humor, shown in the site's political cartoons.

The United States Securities and Exchange Commission

http://www.sec.gov

If you are a small business owner or an investor of any kind, the SEC has important information for you. With pages on what questions you should ask about your investments, how to choose a broker and an investment, and how to look out for trouble, you will be better prepared after perusing this site.

Federal Trade Commission

http://point.lycos.com/reviews/database/9_08_003.html

Similar to the Better Business Bureau but not as comprehensive, the FTC's charge is to protect the consumer. Briefs on the site tell tales of potential consumer pitfalls, such as "get-rich-quick" schemes, electric checkout scanners, and scholarship scams. Find out what the government is doing and what you can do to prevent such unethical practices.

The Consumer Information Center

http://www.pueblo.gsa.gov

What are the least crowded National Parks to visit? How can you appeal an IRS audit? How do you protect your family from Carbon Monoxide? This site has a comprehensive listing of federal consumer publications, ranging in topics from health to finance and more. Most of the publications are either free or very inexpensive.

Electronic Privacy Information Center

http://epic.org

This site has formerly secret documents released now under the Freedom of Information Act. Want to find out what kind of technology is hampering FBI wiretapping? EPIC is a research center designed to inform and to protect the public from electronic civil liberties issues, including the Clipper Chip, the Communications Decency Act, and encryption export.

CRIME AND FRAUD PREVENTION

The Better Business Bureau

http://www.bbb.org/council/main/index.html

The ultimate consumer advocate, the Better Business Bureau works to resolve disputes between consumers and businesses. If you have a complaint with a business regarding their advertising, selling practices, credit, or billing, you can file it on line.

Fearless

http://www.math.grin.edu/~moilanen

This site concentrates on preventing gender-based violence and promoting highway safety. Ever fear you would get stranded on a lonely highway without a phone nearby? Here you'll find a list of items to carry in your car at all times, and what to do if you have a highway emergency.

National Fraud Information Center

http://www.fraud.org

This government site works to keep you alert to scams and fraud that have entrapped many others. The site hosts a daily report, a means of reporting suspected fraud, and tips on how to protect yourself and your finances. Special sections are included on Internet fraud and that aimed at senior citizens.

Taxpayers Against Fraud

http://www.taf.org/taf

As opposed to the NFI, which protects citizens against direct cases of fraud, the TAF site works to protect the

Federal Government against fraud. Through the provisions of the federal False Claims Act and the filing of whistleblower lawsuits, this nonprofit group protects tax dollars from your greedy fellow taxpayers.

Fight Crime: Invest in Kids!

http://www.fightcrime.org

This nonprofit group fights crimes of the future, instead of existing problems. By devoting attention and time to the care and development of children, the group hopes to cut crimes by as much as 50 percent. At the site you can read the 24-year study that supports the group's philosophy.

CyberAngels

http://www.cyberangels.org

The CyberAngels are an outcropping of the grass-roots urban protection group, the Guardian Angels. But rather than patrolling the city streets, the CyberAngels patrol the Internet. Their site is shown in Figure 14.13. They work to deter online harassment, hate mail, stalking, and child pornography. If you are subject to any of these abuses, this group will help you to file complaints on line and trace the source.

I·N·T·E·R·N·E·T M·I·N·U·T·E

NEWSGROUPS

The concept of a newsgroup is hardly new; they're really a version of a radio talk show. Usenet newsgroups focus on specified subjects for users to hash out and mull over. From agroforestry to atheism, from windsurfing to woodworking, if someone has an interest, a newsgroup exists. Where a newsgroup differs from a radio show, however, is that individuals contribute to a discussion by posting messages and responses. The benefit of this is that the reader may consider these messages and responses on his/her own time. Also, while some newsgroups have a moderator (a host), many are unmoderated.

Usenet newsgroups are similar to electronic bulletin boards, another online info-swapping mechanism, except newsgroups speed information between numerous modems and are not centered around a particular site.

To join a newsgroup, individuals use client software to subscribe and read the automatically sent messages. For basic information see:

http://www.jmas.co.jp/FAQs/usenet/what-is/part1

and

http://scwww.ucs.indiana.edu/NetRsc/usenet.html

To find a listing of newsgroups, try using a search engine and searching in "Usenet" instead of the Web. Some sites on the Web have compiled indexes of several newgroups, such as:

http://www.du.edu/newsgroups

There is even a newsgroup discussing newsgroups. If interested in the baptism-by-fire approach, subscribe to news.groups. Other sites exclusively archive old newsgroup postings for reference. Online researchers should take a look at:

http://index.opentext.net/search/newsearch.html

New members may be unsure if they're posting to the online equivalent of NPR's Talk of the Nation or a Howard Stern-style discussion, so it's recommended that you do some research to avoid disappointment. Be sure to read the FAQ that accompanies a newsgroup (often one of the first messages listed) before jumping in.

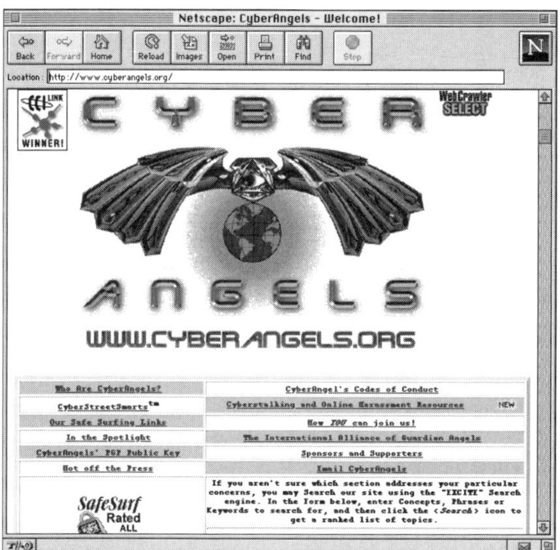

Figure 14.13

CyberAngels, *http://www.cyberangels.org*

Measure your political views against the majority by trying the "Family Values Flow Chart," a humorous political choose-your-own adventure.
http://www.wlo.org/gazette/values

Gallery hop at the online art show of the Guerrilla Girls, a group of female activists who have created delightfully witty posters.
http://www.voyagerco.com/gg/mainposter.html

Measure how crime-proof your home is with this home security quiz.
http://www.protect-mgmt.com/expert/library/hometst.html

Social Security Frequently Asked Questions

http://www.cpsr.org/cpsr/privacy/ssn/ssn.faq.html

Almost everyone asks for your social security number these days. The question is, should you give it to them? Is it an invasion of your privacy? Can it be used fraudulently? This incredibly useful site explains why you should NOT give out your number and how to protect that freedom.

KEYWORDS

For more information on topics in this chapter, start your Web search with these keywords.

Social Services and Community Affairs: nonprofit organizations, advocacy, activism, environment, adoption, crime, government, community organization, charitable organizations, seniors, minorities

Chapter 15

Search and Reference

- SEARCH ENGINES, DIRECTORIES, AND GUIDES
- PEOPLE AND BUSINESS DIRECTORIES
- DICTIONARIES, TRANSLATORS, AND GRAMMAR REFERENCE
- ENCYCLOPEDIAS AND QUOTATIONS
- MISCELLANEOUS REFERENCE
- CALENDAR AND TIME REFERENCE
- GOVERNMENT REFERENCES AND STATISTICS
- PROFESSIONAL REFERENCE
- LIBRARIES
- STATISTICS
- POSTAL AND GEOGRAPHIC REFERENCE
- GENEALOGICAL REFERENCE

10
USEFUL THINGS YOU CAN DO *RIGHT NOW*

1 Use BigFoot to track down a long lost friend.

http://bigfoot.com

2 Choose a restaurant to dine in this weekend by typing your zip code and criteria, then receive a map and directions to a recommended location.

http://www.bigbook.com

3 Visit the World Wide Holiday and Festival page to discover where the best party in the world is happening.

http://www.smiley.cy.net/bdecie/index.html

4 Use the Kelley Blue Book site to find out how much your car is worth before you sell it or trade it in.

http://www.kbb.com

5 Synchronize all your clocks with the absolutely correct time, to the nanosecond.

http://tycho.usno.navy.mil/time.html

6 Make sure you've got the right zip code for the next package you send at the U.S. Postal Service Site.

http://www.usps.gov/postofc/pstoffc.htm

7 Plan your next ride on a subway, in any city, using the Subway Navigator.

http://metro.jussieu.fr:10001/bin/cities/english

8 Send a letter to your Congressperson via the Congressional E-mail Directory.

http://www.webslingerz.com/jhoffman/congress-email.html

9 Find out how to discover where your ancestors came from and when they lived using the Genealogy Home Page.

http://www.genhomepage.com

10 Look up the unfamiliar words you hear at the doctor's office using the MedicineNet Medical Dictionary.

http://www.medicinenet.com/MAINMENU/GLOSSARY/Gloss_A.htm

We live in an information age. Service—especially information service—is displacing manufacturing as the backbone of our economy, yet only recently have these services begun to enter the home. Since the advent of the now antiquated 300 baud modem in the early '80s, companies have been looking for ways to bring the information revolution into consumers' homes. Finally, a successful delivery device has been found in the World Wide Web.

From a profile of the Swallow Bellied Mangalitza pig to Supreme Court decisions and Post Office rates, volumes of information await your perusal on the Web. However, having this information available is futile if it can't be searched in an efficient way. Search tools and contextual hyperlinks help make the Web accessible and useful to the public.

In addition to leading you to pragmatic data, the search and reference sites on the Web can bring you to businesses and people. They are giving us a taste of the futuristic luxury of having vast sums of knowledge at our fingertips. The spectrum is by far incomplete, but the swaths that have been filled in so far are useful, and give us a glimmer of what's to come.

SEARCH ENGINES, DIRECTORIES, AND GUIDES

AltaVista

100 BEST SITES

http://altavista.digital.com

AltaVista is a search engine that employs a software "robot" called Scooter to traverse the Web and Usenet and send everything it finds back to AltaVista's Web index. Scooter works 24 hours a day just so you'll have a complete, timely index of the Web at your fingertips. This is the place to go to search for Web sites that contain specific words or phrases somewhere in their text.

Lycos

100 BEST SITES

http://www.lycos.com

Lycos is a complete reference service for the Web, letting you search the Web for text, sounds, or pictures. Lycos boasts services including news coverage, a people locator, maps, and reviews of what they consider the top five percent of Web sites in any given subject area. One of those categories is Women's Resources, and Lycos does a fine job of listing sites of special interest to women.

Deja News

http://www.dejanews.com

If the Web sometimes seems like a giant collection of tacky billboards, drop by Deja News to find real people. Deja News is a search engine for Usenet, which is the collection of newsgroups on the Web. It searches places where people actually interact with each other, on topics that range from arguing politics to exchanging recipes.

Excite

http://www.excite.com

Excite offers a complete set of tools to help you find things on the Web. It includes a search engine, categorized Web site reviews, and a service called city.net that helps you find geographical locations, provides details and tips about any spot, and can help you plan trips. City.net's interactive maps of places all over the world make you feel like you've got your own spy satellite.

Galaxy

http://galaxy.einet.net

The Galaxy is a search engine and taxonomy of the Web. Its engine has some cool features, one of which allows you to search for text only within the titles or links of Web pages.

HotBot

INTERNATIONAL APPEAL

http://www.hotbot.com

HotBot, a Wired Magazine affiliate, is a pure search engine. It makes no attempt to do anything intellectual like categorize the Web; it just relies on sheer power to give you what you want. It uses a software Web crawler called "Slurp the Web Hound" to constantly peruse all of the Web and Usenet. "Slurp" visits roughly ten million pages per day and sends them back to HotBot's database for your power searching pleasure. Good dog.

Beatrice's Web Guide

http://bguide.com

Beatrice's Web Guide, produced by Women's Wire and Yahoo!, is a practical guide to the best of the Web, especially for women. Its Web-savvy host, Beatrice, recommends the most useful and interactive sites to save people time. Don't miss her "fab" features and weekly tech tips, and, if you can't find what you're looking for, go to the Cafe chat area to ask other surfers for advice. Or just "Ask Beatrice."

Infoseek

http://www.infoseek.com

Infoseek offers a search engine and categorizes the Web by topics for people who prefer browsing. It also provides a free personalized news service that will gather and present stories based upon a profile you provide. Infoseek puts the world back into World Wide Web by offering versions of itself in four different languages: German, French, Spanish, and Japanese.

MetaCrawler

http://metacrawler.cs.washington.edu/index.html

This site is a search engine of search engines. It will send your query to nine different search engines including AltaVista, Yahoo!, and Excite, and then return the results to you in a uniform format. This site, a student project of two computer science students at the University of Washington, is simple and powerful.

Open Text

http://index.opentext.net

Open Text stores every word of every Web page in its database and provides a search engine to rifle through it all. The engine is fast and offers advanced searching capabilities that let you search for words, phrases, or complex combinations of text.

Yahoo!

http://www.yahoo.com

The best-known site of its kind, Yahoo! is like the card catalog of the Web. This site offers a search engine, for power searches, but also has humans who categorize Web sites into topical areas (such as art, entertainment, and health) so that you can find pages easily. Check out the sites with "cool shades" for their top picks. "My Yahoo!" lets you create your own page that matches your interests with personalized news, Web sites, sports, stock quotes, and other services. Also, Yahoo! Net Events features a daily schedule of live chats across the Web. Plus Yahoo! is branching out to other parts of the world with Yahoo! Japan and Yahoo! Canada; as well as to other regions with localized search sites such as Los Angeles, San Francisco, and other major urban centers.

SavvySearch

http://guaraldi.cs.colostate.edu:2000

Looking for a search engine that provides an interface in Polish? This site is a search engine of search engines that uses 28 engines including AltaVista, Yahoo!, Excite, Inktomi, and others. As a bonus you can choose to interact with the site in one of 23 languages. This site is a student project at Colorado State University.

Cybergrrl

http://www.cybergrrl.com

Real-life Cybergrrl Aliza Sherman provides net-chicks on the cutting edge—or those who wanna get there—with link lists and a networking group for women in new media. The site is home to directory FeMiNa, femzine WomenSpace, and the Webgrrl network, which provides a forum for women to exchange information, find job and business leads, learn about new technologies,

I·N·T·E·R·N·E·T M·I·N·U·T·E

SEARCHING THE WEB

Imagine trying to find information in a library by strolling down each row and thumbing through every page of every book until you found what you needed. Pretty inefficient? A library without a card catalog would be like the Web without its search sites. There are two basic kinds of search tools on the Web to help you find what you seek: search engines and directories.

Search engines send out "webcrawlers" that search every single Web page and send back all the text to a database made available for your searches. Directories are taxonomic sites, which classify Web sites into subject catagories much like a card catalog at the library. To save you time, many of the large search sites house both types of search tools under one site.

If you know exactly what you're looking for, and if it is perhaps not so easy to classify, then head straight for one of the power search engines. For example, if you want information on the duck-billed platypus (Is it a mammal? Is it a reptile? Is it a bird?) go to HotBot or AltaVista and type in, "Platypus." Other places to try would be Open Text or WebCrawler.

The drawback of these kinds of sites is that you will get all kinds of references to the "Platypus," including cartoon characters or nicknames that might appear on someone's personal home page.

If you're looking for, say, "Missouri politics," a classification-style site is the place to start. The premier examples of directory sites are Excite, InfoSeek, Lycos, and Yahoo!. Each of these search sites group sites into broad categories, but also provide a power search engine in case you're not sure which category you should be looking in. The advantage of directory sites is that, usually, a human has actually classified everything, saving you the time of looking at sites that contain a reference to your search item but are not really about the subject you are looking for.

The ideal strategy for searching is to use both types of sites: search engines and directories.

Some Well-Known Directories

Excite
http://www.excite.com

Infoseek
http://www.yahoo.com

Yahoo!
http://www.yahoo.com

Examples of Search Engines

AltaVista
http://altavista.digital.com

Lycos
http://www.lycos.com

HotBot
http://www.hotbot.com

Open Text
http://index.opentext.net

The WebCrawle:
http://www.webcrawler.com

mentor, intern, train, and more. FeMiNa lists sites of interest to women in subject categories. You can e-mail your URL to be included in the directory.

The WebCrawler

http://www.webcrawler.com

The WebCrawler features an indexed database of the Web assembled by its Web crawling software program called, cleverly enough, Spidey. It also offers reviews of selected sites and such silliness as WebRoulette, a game where Spidey randomly selects ten sites for your review. WebCrawler even lets you surf the Web backwards allowing you to find out who links to your Web page.

WWWomen

http://www.wwwomen.com

A search engine for all things female on the Internet. Well organized by subject, and information packed, WWWomen, according to co-founder Sue Levin, "...gets you to women-related sites and topics faster than any other resource on the Web." From networking resources to popular 'zines, if you're looking for women's resources the Net, look no further.

Garriga's WWWorld... Beyond the Black Stump

http://werple.mira.net.au/~lions/index.html

This is a grab bag of links to just about everything on the Net, direct from an Australian Web junkie who even has time to post a puzzle of the week. There are other pointers to riddles, puzzles, daily horoscopes, and Aussie info, as well as links to Reuters News, software libraries, television shows, and lots, lots more. Check out the Girl's Guide to find sites especially useful to women.

Accurate Eye

http://www.ozemail.com.au/~acceye

Information specialist Jane Ponting created Accurate Eye "to provide quick access to ready-reference sources for people who are looking for information." Indeed, she has accomplished her goal. This is one of the best reference work indices on line (see Figure 15.1). It moves far beyond the standard English language and quotations links, offering lengthy listings of resources in myriad categories, including Biographies, Geographic Data, Directories, Documents & Speeches, and Yearbooks & Almanacs.

Figure 15.1
Accurate Eye, *http://www.ozemail.com.au/~acceye*

Research-It!

http://www.itools.com/research-it/research-it.html

Whether you're searching for a zip code or tracking a Fed-Ex package, translating English to German or converting yen to drachma, Research-It! is an all-in-one reference toolbox for you. Its multiple resources are organized in a single-page, form-based collection of search engines that lets you reel around the Internet hunting down all sorts of info. Organized by categories, the resources gathered are impressive, from the encyclopedias and translators in the Language section to the GNN/Koblas Currency Exchange program and stock quote finders in the financial section.

Barbara's News Researcher Graffiti Page

http://www.gate.net/~library/index.html

Fresh from an actual newspaper librarian and researcher, Barbara Gellis Shapiro of Florida's Palm Beach Post, comes this extensive listing of the most useful Internet reference works. Whether it's banned books available on line or the Divorce Home Page you want, the links are here. Shapiro's idea was to take the most useful links for news researchers and put them together in a convenient listing, so don't expect this to be everything about anything.

Yahooligans!

http://www.yahooligans.com

The people who brought you the amazingly popular Yahoo! Web directory are pointing out sites for the eight to 14-year-old set. If Yahoo!'s popularity is any indication, this kids-only Web index (see Figure 15.2) has a lot going for it. It's designed almost exactly like the regular site, but adapted to appeal to the Net's youngest surfers.

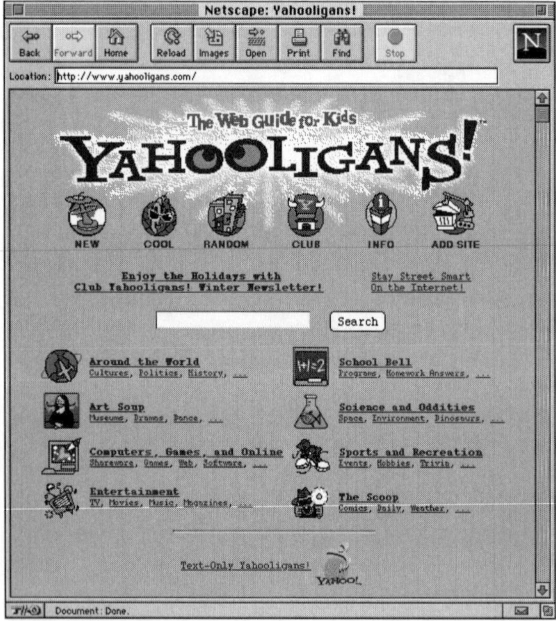

Figure 15.2

Yahooligans!, *http://www.yahooligans.com*

PEOPLE AND BUSINESS DIRECTORIES

Switchboard

http://www.switchboard.com

This site (see Figure 15.3) helps you find people or businesses in North America whether they're on the Web or not. You give Switchboard a name of a person or business and it will return the address and phone number of that entity, if it knows it. Switchboard's information is compiled from published white pages and other sources. This utilitarian site is fast and easy to use.

World Pages

http://www.worldpages.com

World Pages has 170 million people and businesses from 57 countries in their database. It's a little more demanding than Switchboard in what it requires you to enter—you must provide a state or province along with a name. But, you get the world; and in case you don't quite remember all your geography, World Pages will also try to provide the latitude and longitude of the address it finds for you.

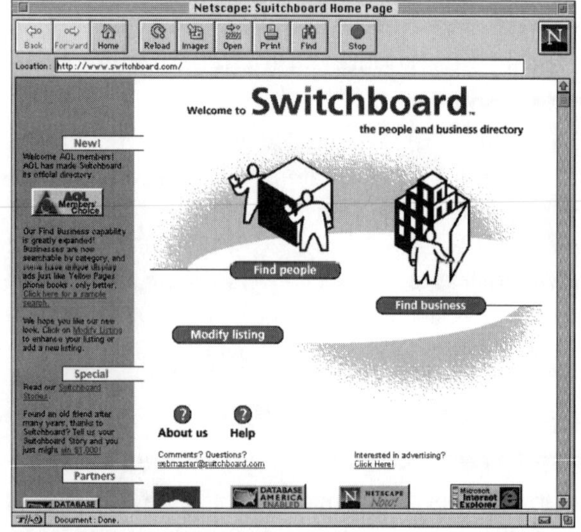

Figure 15.3

Switchboard, *http://www.switchboard.com*

InfoSpace

http://www.infospace.com

This complete directory service offers phone and address listings for the U.S. and Canada as well as for several other countries. Once you've found a name, it has a silly but fun gizmo that will dial the number for you if you hold your touch-tone phone to your computer speaker. Thumb your nose at your phone company with the Internet phones you can download from InfoSpace. Also check out the extensive government and company information. Use My Town to look up the town you grew up in and find out if it's changed since you left.

Four11

http://www.four11.com

Four11 has the complete U.S. white pages in their database for your perusal. The site is well-designed, fast, and offers an e-mail directory. It provides the same links to Internet phone providers as InfoSpace. What sets this site apart is its celebrity directory. It's a directory of the stars, and you don't even have to go to Beverly Hills to get it.

Yahoo! People Search

http://www.yahoo.com/search/people

This is about the only online phone directory that offers reverse searches. That is, you can enter a phone number and find out whom it belongs to. Yahoo! also lets you search for people by name and provides an e-mail directory.

PeopleFinder

http://www.stokesworld.com/peoplefinder/index.html

This site is a bulletin board for people looking for lost friends, relatives, or loves. You can enter a name of a person you're trying to locate as well as a message. There are lots of notes there already, so take a look, maybe that long forgotten blind date is wondering where you are.

Where Did They Go?

http://www.semaphorecorp.com

This site lets you search the address change records of the U.S. Postal Service to find people or companies that have moved. Nothing flashy about the layout or the search engine, but it's fast and effective. You can also enter old phone numbers and find new numbers to which they might have been changed. This site also happens to have a list of the zip codes of U.S. Navy vessels. Did you know ships had zip codes?

Internet @ddress.finder

http://www.iaf.net

This e-mail address directory has over five million listings, most of which have been gleaned from Usenet. This site is speedy and easy-to-use, but if you're looking for someone who's never posted something to a newsgroup, you probably won't find them here.

Bigfoot

http://bigfoot.com

Bigfoot will help you find people's e-mail or physical addresses, and also offers a unique free service to keep people from getting lost in the first place. You can register for a free e-mail address with Bigfoot, which will then forward all your e-mail to you at whatever e-mail address you might have in the future. If you're one of those people that keeps changing Internet service providers or jobs, Bigfoot can help you stay in touch.

Classmates

http://www.classmates.com

If you look at old high school yearbooks and wonder what happened to that skinny guy with the funny hair, this site may be for you. You have to submit a free registration form to use this site that focuses on reuniting classmates. It gets all of its data from people voluntarily registering, so don't expect to find a majority of your old pals listed.

ESP

http://www.esp.co.uk

This is another site that culls Usenet for e-mail addresses and adds them to its database for your perusal. This British-based site is planning to add a feature that will allow the site to figure out what country you're in to customize its interface in your language. But for now, it doesn't set itself apart from the many e-mail search engines on the Web.

Places to Stay

http://www.placestostay.com

Places to Stay offers a directory of hotels, inns, and resorts, as well as an online reservation service that can make your travel planning easier and more affordable. Registration is free, and qualifies you for various discounts and off-season rates. Choose from bed & breakfasts, inns, resorts, and vacation homes around the world, and confirm your registration on line. The service gets their goodies from travel industry sources as well as from popular guidebooks like AAA and Guide Michelin, among others.

ISO Country Codes

http://world.std.com/~walthowe/country.htm

This page simply lists the International Standards Organization's two-letter country codes for Internet addresses—all 238 of 'em. Most are easy, of course: Japan is "JP" and the United Kingdom is "UK." But did you know that Algeria is "DZ," Croatia is "HR" (for the local name "Hravatska"), and South Africa is "ZA"? Sure you did. This is bland, but it's an essential site for budding Net detectives.

Big Yellow

http://s13.bigyellow.com

Big Yellow is simply a yellow pages on the Web. You can search for businesses by category or by

SPOTLIGHT ON ONLINE PRIVACY

While the Internet has introduced a whole new world to us, it has also introduced us to the world at large. Information on who we are, where we live, and where we surf is now just a mouse click away from inquiring minds. Until the Internet came along, anyone interested in finding personal information might have had to brave the DMV or comparable bureaucracy. Not so anymore. Databases and tracking software make it easier for people and organizations to access this information. Take note: The courts have generally upheld employers' rights to read employees' e-mail.

Keep in mind that with countless numbers of e-mail messages being sent and Web pages being surfed, chances are no one is going to pay too much attention to one individual. If you are worried, here are some steps you can take to protect your privacy:

Unlist your phone number—Web-based people directories get their information from phone books which include only listed numbers. Also, be careful when filling out online surveys to only include information you don't mind passing along.

Take your name off of databases. For example, to remove your name from Lexis-Nexis's P-trak database that allows people to look up information about you, go to:

http://www.lexis-nexis.com/lncc

Encrypt your e-mail. Software called Pretty Good Privacy scrambles your message so only people who have been issued a special key can decode it:

http://world.std.com/franl/pgp/where-to-get-pgp.html

You can also get an e-mail pseudonym with something called a remailer. Keep in mind that the companies providing the anonymous addresses must keep a record of your true identity:

www.labyrinth.net.au/pirovich/remail.html

Check out the Center for Democracy and Technology's Privacy Demonstration Page. It has more information on who can watch you and what you can do about it:

http://www.13x.com/cgi-bin/cdt/snoop.pl

name. This site is simple, fast, and useful. It also offers an e-mail directory and residential listings.

The ElectraPages

http://electrapages.com

This directory of women's resources boasts 7,000 listings from Women in Electronics of Duluth, GA, to Aunt Violet's Bookbin in Seattle, WA, to the Planned Parenthood clinic in Phoenix, AZ. Search buttons seem to be placed at random on the screen, but what this site lacks in aesthetics and ergonomics, it makes up for in effectiveness.

BigBook

http://www.bigbook.com

This yellow-pages-style site (see Figure 15.4) will help you find any business in the United States and draw you a map of how to get there. It will also let you set up a home page for your business free of charge. But the coolest thing about BigBook is their appreciation for special effects. You can try out a Beta version of BigBook3D which will let you "fly" through a 3D map of a city, showing you locations of businesses on the 3D model.

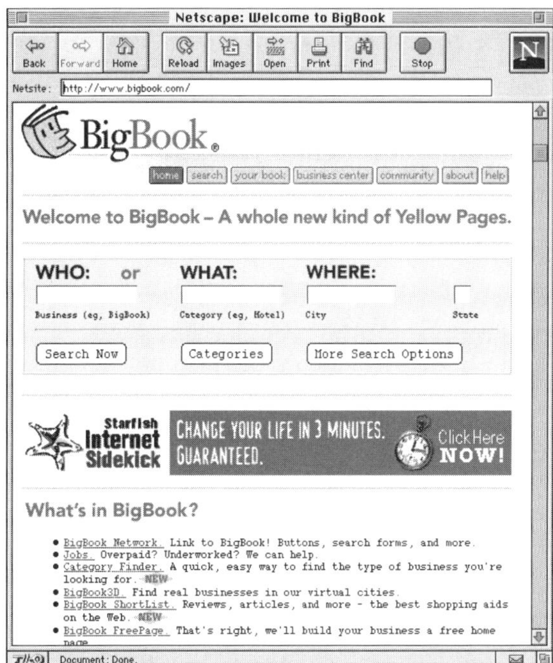

Figure 15.4

BigBook, *http://www.bigbook.com*

Commercial Site Index

http://www.directory.net

Want to go shopping on the Web? This site is a directory of sites that would love to lighten your pocketbook. It offers a search engine and an alphabetical listing of companies selling their wares on the Web. Unfortunately, it doesn't include a directory of the companies so you have to know who you're looking for.

BizWeb

http://www.bizweb.com

This site lists businesses by category and sub-category, and offers a search engine in case you know exactly what business you're looking for. BizWeb has about 7,700 companies in its database. If you're really in a compulsive shopping sort of mood, you might like BizWeb in that it has a nifty graphic placed next to each company's listing that will let you order on line.

Ethicalbusiness

http://www.bath.ac.uk/Centres/Ethical

Ever think half the people on the Web are trying to rip you off? This site lists groups trying to do something about that. EthicalBusiness lists organizations and businesses who make a business of ethics, like the Better Business Bureau, ecofriendly retailers, and even a site called McSpotlight that is conducting a lonely campaign against the Golden Arches.

The Minority Business and Professional Directory

http://www.minbizdir.com

This specialty business directory provides a search engine and alphabetical listing of minority- and woman-owned businesses either on or off the Web. It's an effective, no frills site that doesn't monkey around with flashy gizmos or graphics. It just provides the info.

ComFind

INTERNATIONAL APPEAL

http://comfind.com

ComFind has millions of listings of companies in 150 different countries. You can drill the listings down by category or location to find the companies you want. The layout is a bit sloppy, but they give you lots of searching options and the information is there.

Central Source Yellow Pages

http://www.telephonebook.com

This is a useful tool for finding the names and locations of businesses around the U.S. It operates much like a telephone book, except that you enter the business name and state (or phone number or even category) and then see if anything matches. The results include the full name, address, and phone number of the particular company. Interested businesses can submit information to the index. Now under construction, but growing, is a listing of Internet service providers for the U.S. and Canada.

Canada NetPages

INTERNATIONAL APPEAL

http://www.visions.com/netpages

This is a "north of the border only" collection of goods and services. For a fee, Web-friendly businesses can be listed here, with a link to their own informational page. The founders hope to become a clearinghouse for Net commerce. So far, the neatly organized Canada Net Trade Show is the main highlight. Other features look promising, but are still somewhat thin on resources.

GTE SuperPages

http://yp.gte.net

Use this site to search over 11 million business listings by products and services offered, brands carried, the hours they're open, or the methods of payment they accept (Visa, Amex, and others). Never show up with the wrong credit card again. If you like, you can add your business to their listings for free.

LookupUSA

http://www.lookupusa.com/lookupusa/index.htm

This business and people directory lets you search for companies or individuals much like other directory sites. The unusual thing about this site is that it provides credit ratings of companies. For example, it'll tell you that one Microsoft Corporation of Redmond, WA, has a credit rating of "very good" (LookupUSA's highest rating).

where they surf

Surfers: Sue Levin and Kathleen McMahon

Co-founders of WWWomen, at **http://www.wwwomen.com**

Sue's favorite site of the moment:

Girls on Film

http://www.girlsonfilm.com

"If you like movie reviews that are well-written and really funny, tune into Girls on Film. They also have great features on film-related topics. Where else could you see a forum called 'Keanu-A-Go-Go'?"

Kathleen's favorite site of the moment:

Movie Link

http://www.MovieLink.com

"For time away from business, I like to peruse MovieLink to see what movies are playing locally and join in chat groups about the latest movies. I definitely find movies and showtimes faster than in the newspaper, and you can even purchase tickets via credit card over the Net."

DICTIONARIES, TRANSLATORS, AND GRAMMAR REFERENCES

Ethnologue Database

http://www-ala.doc.ic.ac.uk:80/~rap/ Ethnologue

This database version of the "Ethnologue" cross-references 6,500 languages with their nations, demographic, and ethnic groups. The Ethnologue is a primary resource for serious linguists, though search results are often as dry as a dusty book. Yet the database is amazing for its laundry list of tongues, from Abnaki-Penobscot to Zuni, many of which are still alive around the world today.

United Kingdom English for the American Novice

http://www.hps.com/~tpg/ukdict

If you think the British and the Americans speak the same language, think again. Terry Gliedt's United Kingdom English for the American Novice eases the confusion of the mother tongue. This lexicon of more than 600 terms is a doozy of a collection of UKisms, organized into rather cheeky alphabetical letter groupings such as "abattoir through aunt sally" (ick!).

Grammar and Style Notes

http://www.english.upenn.edu/~jlynch/ Grammar

For those who might be wondering about the true definition of a gerund, it can be found at this site, along with everything else your 6th grade English teacher tried to teach you. Maintained by a graduate student in English at the University of Pennsylvania, this site will help you mind your dangling participles and your prepositional phrases, as well as teach you a thing or two about writing style.

Rivendell Dictionaries and Translators

http://rivendel.com/~ric/resources/ dictionary.html

Want to become part of the global village? Need help with your Swahili homework? This site (see Figure 15.5)

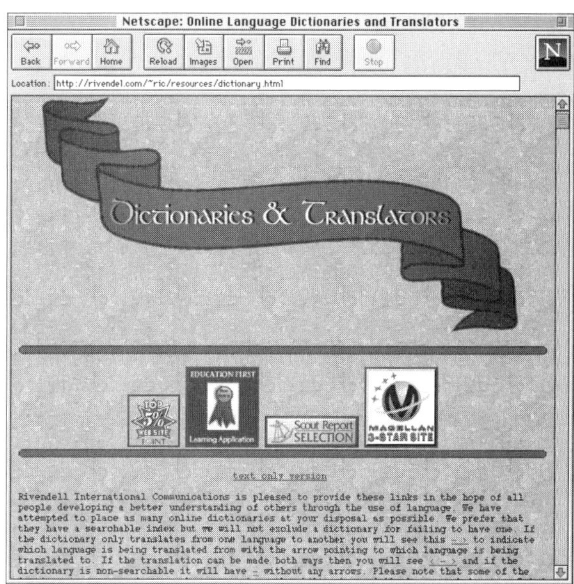

Figure 15.5
Rivendell Dictionaries and Translators,
http://rivendel.com/~ric/resources/dictionary.html

lists many of the language dictionary sites on the Web and offers its own translation tool. It was created in an effort to help Web users chat with each other no matter what languages they speak.

The Oxford English Dictionary

http://www.oed.com

This site is still under construction, but it shows promise. Someday it will allow you to search the Oxford English Dictionary on line, giving not just all the shades of meaning for any word, but the history of the word as well, in obsessive completeness. Not surprisingly, they plan to charge fees for usage.

Webster's Dictionary

http://c.gp.cs.cmu.edu:5103/prog/webster

This search engine of Webster's dictionary was written by a computer science professor at the University of California, San Diego. It'll look up any word you desire and return to you a complete definition from Webster's dictionary with each word in the definition linked to its own definition. Real hypertext.

The Dorktionary

http://www.latech.edu/~jlk/jwz/dorktionary/index.shtml

Ever wanted to make up a word, but weren't sure how to spell it? The Dorktionary could, conceivably, help. Then again, maybe not. It's a loony collection of word wannabes and daffy definitions for existing words. The prevailing theme throughout is that these are terms commonly used, mangled, or made up by cyberites. Some are here because they have a different meaning in the e-world. "Apple" is not defined as a fruit but as a computer company. And "Tandy" isn't an Oscar-winning actress but rather, "any computer hardware or software that's lame, outdated or otherwise undesirable."

Roget's Thesaurus

http://www2.thesaurus.com/thesaurus

What's another word for thesaurus? Find out here. Roget provides this extremely useful site free of charge, no promotions, just words, words, words. It's another example of hypertext at its best. Each word that comes back as a synonym of your search word is linked to its synonyms, and so on, and so on.

WordNet

http://vancouver-webpages.com/wordnet

This site is an interface to a Princeton University linguistics project. It is basically a thesaurus, but unlike the Roget's site, it will allow you to search for antonyms of your word as well as synonyms.

NASA Thesaurus

http://www.sti.nasa.gov/nasa-thesaurus.html

The thesaurus for the rocket scientist in all of us, this site will tell you all the synonyms for terms such as oblate spheroids. As you can see by the URL, it is a product of our friends at NASA.

The Alternative Dictionaries

http://www.notam.uio.no/~hcholm/altlang

Ever been called a mrsulko (mr-soul-ko) in Macedonian? Well, it wasn't a compliment—The Alternative Dictionaries, an international slanguage collection, defines "mrsulko" as a "snotty person, crybaby, coward; It means that the person to whom it is intended is very immature in his actions." But you coulda been called much worse; most of the other Macedonian terms listed have unprintable definitions.

Devil's Dictionary by Ambrose Bierce

http://www.specbench.org/~aca/bierce/devilsabr.html

This is a humorous site of word definitions, based on newspaper articles written between 1881 and 1906. The concept spawned the Cynic's Word Book and was commercialized by imitators who helped form the current negative definition of the word "cynic." Often offensive, but with illustrative quotations, this site is more interesting than useful.

The Totally Unofficial Rap Dictionary

http://www.sci.kun.nl/thalia/rapdict

Yo, yo, yo homeboy, where's the best 411 on rap lingo? Uh, the Netherlands, actually. Believe it or not, "Jax," a Dutchman, has a complete, often-amusing dictionary of rap and hip-hop slang, which designates parts of speech, proper usage, and original sources for words, Webster's style. "Fade," for example, means "to not listen to, erase, or get rid of," derived from "the fader on a mixer," a music instrumentation panel. Parents be warned: This site (see Figure 15.6) does contain vulgarities, but it's in the context of the culture.

The Skeptic's Dictionary

http://wheel.ucdavis.edu/~btcarrol/skeptic/dictcont.html

Doubting Thomases will have fun scrolling through these entries debunking the existence of Bigfoot, God, and the lost city of Atlantis. Noting that "the only thing infinite is our capacity for self-deception," the Skeptic's Dictionary offers serious arguments against alien abductions and psychology, then turns playful by including "The Contract With America." The dictionary's author is Robert Carroll, who has a Ph.D from the University of California, San Diego and teaches philosophy at Sacramento City College. Or so he says.

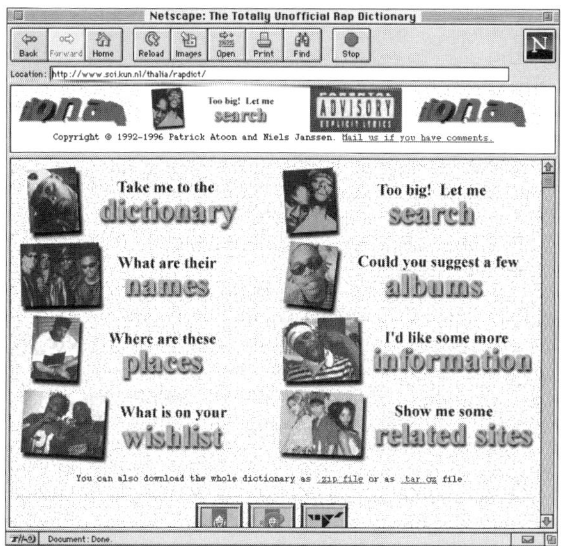

Figure 15.6
The Totally Unofficial Rap Dictionary,
http://www.sci.kun.nl/thalia/rapdict

Casey's Snow Day Reverse Dictionary (and Guru)

http://www.c3.lanl.gov:8064

What's a reverse dictionary? Instead of knowing the word and needing the definition, you need to find the word. Typing in a phrase (say, "one who rides on horseback") gets you a list of matching possibilities (for our example, "equestrian"). The fun is that you get others, too. Typing "what is the meaning of life," for instance, produces a list topped by the words "bloodshed" and "deathbed." Even the creators can't explain this. We're not sure how useful it is, but it can sure be fun.

The Elements of Style

http://www.columbia.edu/acis/bartleby/strunk

Here is perhaps the best book ever written about writing, presented in a simple manner William Strunk would no doubt approve of. (Actually, according to Strunk, that should read "doubtless." Elementary Principles of Composition rule #13 reads, "Omit needless words.") The page is all text and nothing flashy, but that's the book's style. This is just the best advice on improving your writing, from one of the most popular texts of all time

Dan's Poker Dictionary

http://www.universe.digex.net/~kimberg/pokerdict.html

Unless you're an ace at poker, you've probably got a lot to learn about this seemingly simple card game. Dan's Poker Dictionary shuffles you through the intricacies of play, from "Ace to Five," to "Weak," the later term characterizing an easily beat table, a poor player, or one who exhibits "a readiness to fold and a reluctance to raise."

HSTM Biographical Dictionary

http://www.asap.unimelb.edu.au/hstm/hstm_ove.htm

Here, the famous people of science and medicine are immortalized—or at least their biographical data is on hand. From Ptolemy to Edwin P. Hubble, the links here lead to biographies and even pictures of scientists and inventors—perfect for the kids' school reports. Visitors can learn that Hubble, for instance, was a law student and a boxer before he became a major figure in modern astronomy.

The Human Languages Page

http://www.hardlink.com/~chambers/HLP

Let's chatter in Arabic! Or Spanish, Japanese, or even Lojban, a language created by researchers to avoid cultural references (we're not kidding). This page offers the most comprehensive set of links on languages around. Some sites are just dictionaries, others offer tutorials or computer software (like "Tibetan Tools for Windows"). It's all put together by Tyler Jones, an Oregon resident who's hoping to attend grad school and major in computer science.

Interactive ASL & Braille Guide

http://www.disserv.stu.umn.edu/AltForm

The Interactive ASL & Braille Guide is a basic online reference to American Sign Language (ASL) and braille alphabets. Created by the University of Minnesota's Disability Services WWW Server, the site is simple and to the point: Choose a letter from the alphabet, and see it illustrated as either an ASL hand sign or braille dot configuration. This is a work in progress, so some areas, notably the Finger Spelling Quiz (where visitors will be shown an ASL letter and asked to identify it) are still being developed.

The Internet Braille Wizard Access 20/20

http://www.access2020.com

Those searching for Braille tools will find a dynamic duo at the Access 20/20 site. The company, a "world leader in braille transcription and production of audio tapes for the blind and visually-impaired," offers visitors to its site the Internet Braille Wizard, a form-based translator. Type in a word or phrase and the system translates it into Braille dots. Also, part of the site is the English Braille Alphabet page, which diagrams the A through Z of Braille.

LingWhat?

http://idris.com/lingwhat/lingwhat.html

Ever find yourself staring at a foreign document, trying to figure out just which language it's written in? LingWhat? rides to the rescue—it's a funky little language deciphering tool brought to you by IDRIS, developers of knowledge discovery programming. LingWhat? guides you through a series of questions about the document ("Does the language use the latin alphabet?" and "Does the word `od' occur?") until it identifies the language for you. It can't actually do the translation, but at least you know which dictionary or linguistics program to turn to next.

List of Dictionaries

http://math-www.uni-paderborn.de/HTML/Dictionaries.html

Herein lies a dictionary for everybody, a virtual lexicon for legions. Sure, it's got the familiar German to English and English to French varieties, but it's the out-of-the-ordinary entries that make this special. Browse the English to Slovene dictionary. For non-Americans (and parents of American teenagers), the American English dictionary will help you decipher the lingo.

Jellinek's Baby Name Chooser

http://www.jellinek.com/baby

Ever wonder how your parents came up with your name? If you'd prefer a different one, just be thankful Jellinek's Baby Name Chooser (see Figure 15.7) wasn't around. You might have ended up with Ximenes, Wandie, or Anatol. On the other hand, if you think those are great names, maybe you should give this site a lookover if you're ever blessed with giving a little one a moniker.

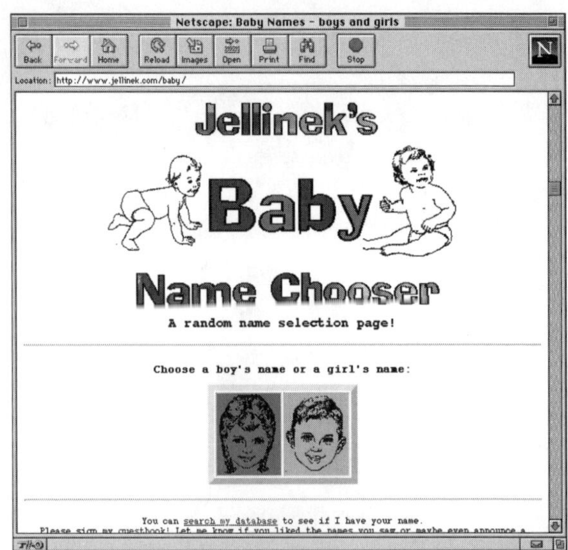

Figure 15.7
Jellinek's Baby Name Chooser,
http://www.jellinek.com/baby

The Acronym and Abbreviations List

http://www.ucc.ie/info/net/acronyms/index.html

Love 'em or hate 'em, acronyms are HTS (here to stay), and the Acronym and Abbreviations List is the perfect place to ponder these alphabetical atrocities. Search tools let you type in an acronym and find out what it means. And if you think they're all just stodgy chunks of official jargon such as DACOWITS (Defense Advisory Committee on Women in the Service), think again: Type in IACOCCA and you get "I Am Chairman Of the Chrysler Corporation of America." (No longer true, but cute.)

Acronyms

http://www.chemie.fu-berlin.de/cgi-bin/acronym

This page from the Free University of Berlin contains more than 12,000 acronyms from the worlds of science and government. Many lean toward chemistry (the page is from the FUB chemistry department), but you'll also find an interesting mix of German and American terms. A search for "EPA," for instance, turns up four definitions, including both "Environmental Protection Agency" and "Europaeisches PatentAmt." Still, some famous acronyms don't make the cut: regrettably, the file has no definition for "IHOP."

ENCYCLOPEDIAS AND QUOTATIONS

Britannica Online

http://www.eb.com

This expansive reference site abounds with beautiful graphics, but be prepared to wait. All those pretty pictures from Aardvark to Zebra can take a while to download. Britannica offers a limited amount of tantalizing free information, a free 7-day trial to use the whole service, but then charges $14.95 per month or $150 per year with a $25 initial charge for use of their online encyclopedia.

Knowledge Adventure Encyclopedia

http://www.adventure.com/library/encyclopedia

This site is aimed at young kids. Besides its encyclopedia, it has a library, a coloring area, a science lab, and a gaming section. It's definitely aimed at the Nintendo generation. The encyclopedia is a bit sparse and lacks pictures, but the layout is simple and fast. The games are fun, sort of educational, and also a marketing tool for Knowledge Adventure's CD-Roms.

The Volume Library

http://www.digicity.com/vlibrary/tablecon.htm

If you were schooled at home in the '40s or '50s you might have used this reference book. For some reason, someone has decided to transcribe it onto the Web, illustrations and all. As you might expect, it's a bit dated but good for some kitchey graphics.

The Smithsonian Institution

http://www.si.edu/newstart.htm

The Smithsonian isn't just 18 incredible museums in Washington—it's a cottage industry. This Web site proves it, with layers and layers of information on the famous museums (including the National Zoo), membership, D.C. sightseeing, policy statements on pets and strollers, and, inevitably, an online shopping mall. Among the museums available for electronic exploration are the Cooper-Hewitt National Design Museum, the National Museum of American History, and the National Air & Space Museum.

The International Finance Encyclopaedia

http://www.euro.net/innovation/Finance_Base/Fin_encyc.html

If you stocked up on ear candy when your parents suggested you invest in CDs, perhaps a trip to the International Finance Encyclopaedia is in order. It's an exhaustive glossary of banking and investment terms, from the familiar (ATM) to the foreign ("Saitori" is "a Japanese term for members of the Tokyo, Nagoya, and Osaka stock exchanges who specialise in buying and selling securities on behalf of brokers").

Quotations from Hell

http://www.concentric.net/~cynicus/QuotationsFromHell.html

Tired of rose-colored glasses and cockeyed optimists? Quotations from Hell is a barbed-wired Bartlett's for diehard cranks. Super-cynic Ezra Libowsky created this companion volume to Ambrose Bierce's "The Devil's Dictionary" with bitter bits of wit and wisdom from such silver-tongued spoil-sports as Albert Camus and Oscar Wilde. Charlie Chaplin is quoted as saying, "Man as an individual is a genius. But men in the mass form the Headless Monster, a great, brutish idiot that goes where prodded."

Bartlett's Familiar Quotations

http://www.columbia.edu/acis/bartleby/bartlett

O, what is so rare as a quote on line? Shakespeare said that. Or was it Keats? Hey, look it up on line in Bartlett's Familiar Quotations. Don't expect Neil Armstrong or Dr. Seuss here: this is Bartlett's 1901 edition (now in the public domain). It was brought on line in March 1995 thanks to Columbia University's Project Bartleby, which aims to build a cyber-library of great books. This edition is fairly slow and clumsy to use, but hopefully it'll improve with age.

The Quotation Page
http://www.starlingtech.com/quotes

Michael Moncur's Quotation Page is not your father's Bartlett's. Moncur is a quote-crazy collector who's been gathering sayings from famous people and unknowns alike for more than a decade, and he's put them in this funny and fresh database of bon mots. You can also search other people's quote collections here: The system lets you pan for literal gold among sources ranging from the Devil's Dictionary to the works of humorist Dave Barry.

Poor Richard's Quotation Collection
http://www.tiac.net/users/poorrich/quotations.html

Some of the best quotes at this site come from celebrities like W.C. Fields ("Start every day off with a smile and get it over with"), Woody Allen ("It's not that I'm afraid to die, I just don't want to be there when it happens"), and Mae West ("Too much of a good thing is wonderful"). In addition to the collected wisdom of celebs, you'll find quotable quotes on marriage, learning, and cats. (According to Jeff Valdez, "Cats are smarter than dogs. You can't get eight cats to pull a sled through snow.")

MISCELLANEOUS REFERENCE

The Almanac of American Politics
http://politicsusa.com/PoliticsUSA/resources/almanac

Tucked away inside the PoliticsUSA site is this online version of the popular political reference. The Almanac is written by two senior editors, one at U.S. News & World Report and the other at Reader's Digest. This site provides detailed background information on each state. (Oregon, for example, is America's "most unchurched state," the authors say.) Each entry includes the state's congressional districts and demographic statistics.

Americans with Disabilities Act Document Center
http://janweb.icdi.wvu.edu/kinder

The Americans with Disabilities Act gets its share of praise and condemnation. Some restaurants and private establishments think it's too restrictive. Advocates for the disabled say it's absolutely necessary. Visit this site to see for yourself exactly what the law requires and how it came about. Attorney Duncan C. Kinder, who survived a bout with cancer in his youth, has created an index of federal documents (including the ADA itself) and legal guides for preparing a workplace for disabled employees.

The Association of Brewers Glossary
http://www.csn.net/aob/glossary.html

This glossary, from the Association of Brewers, offers a healthy gulp of excerpts from Carl Forget's "Dictionary of Beer and Brewing," an A-to-Z lexicon of thirst-quenching terms. The site is light on graphics, but offers plenty of full-bodied descriptions for such lesser-known words as "Reinheitsgebot," a German law that signifies "pledge of purity or order of purity."

INTERNATIONAL APPEAL

Foreign Exchange Rates
http://www.dna.lth.se/cgi-bin/kurt/rates

Got a yen for a drachma? Hey, you just got ripped off—at least according to this currency exchange site. (One yen was equal to .37 drachma at press time.) Created by Swedish computer science student Kurt Swanson, the page has exchange rates for more than 35 important billfolds, updated daily at 22:00 Swedish time. This quick and easy site is on the mark.

INTERNATIONAL APPEAL

Currency Converter
http://www.olsen.ch/cgi-bin/exmenu

Maybe you know how to find out what your money is worth today in the U.S. But do you know what your dough was worth, say, five years ago somewhere else? Here at Olsen & Associates, a Switzerland firm, interested travelers or traders can check to see how much foreign currency their money would have brought yesterday, last week, or last year. So while U.S. $100 may be worth 254.20 Malaysian ringgit now, in 1992 that amount fetched 253.15 Malaysian ringgit.

Butterfly Glossary

http://www.rirr.cnuce.cnr.it/Glossario/glhpage.html

This glossary of Net and data communications terms takes a natural approach to linguistics—the fonts heading each section of the glossary are "nature's own alphabet, etched in gossamer hues on the wings of butterflies" (created by Kjell B. Sandved). Sounds a lot more poetic than the reality of this useful site, which is actually version 2.0 of the CNUCE ZC-235 user's manual published by CNUCE Institute of the Italian National Research Council (CNR).

CIA Publications

http://www.odci.gov/cia/publications/pubs.html

The Central Intelligence Agency receives billions of dollars to keep tabs on other nations. The factbook at this site is one grand example of that work, with political, social, and economic information on places you may not have known existed. For instance, are you familiar with the Ashmore and Cartier Islands, located between Australia and Indonesia? Together, the factbook says, they are about the size of the Washington DC mall.

The Better Business Bureau Web Server

http://www.bbb.org/council/main/index.html

The BBB is the place for information on everything from "work-at-home" schemes to complaint reports on businesses in your area. And the BBB's Internet presence is growing. Plans are in the works for individual bureaus to offer "reliability reports" on area businesses.

University Wire

http://www.mainquad.com/uwire.html

University Wire serves up an array of references databases (for example, "Bureau of Justice Statistics"). The site's Kopyedit Korner is good for the likes of a "College Slang Dictionary," and the latest "World Fact Book." Having originated at Northwestern University's Medill School of Journalism, this virtual newsroom has stylishly kept pace with Web technology. Stay in touch with collegiate colleagues via pointers to university newspaper sites throughout the U.S.

Congressional E-mail Directory

http://www.webslingerz.com/jhoffman/congress-email.html

This address collection makes it easy to e-mail your representatives in the U.S. Congress. As long as your browser preferences are set for the "mailto" function, you can simply click on an e-mail address and type away. Various congressional home pages are also available for your viewing pleasure.

Jane's Information Group

http://www.thomson.com/janes/default.html

This source for "accurate and impartial" defense, weaponry, civil aviation, and transportation information is somewhat hard to fathom, but no less intriguing. In "Who's Jane?" you can read that founder Fred T. helped start the British security service MI5. ("A well-known hoaxer, he made something of a hobby of 'kidnapping' people.") World leaders such as USAF Chief of Staff, Gen. Ronald R. Fogleman, are featured in the "Jane's Interview of the Week" archive. Lots here to interest industrial-military aficionados, and those who would keep tabs on them.

The Jargon File 3.2.0

http://www.cnam.fr/Jargon

This handy online dictionary has a world of Net definitions at the ready. A ten-finger interface is not a one-two punch to the head of your opponent, but rather "the interface between two networks that cannot be directly connected for security reasons." Pascal Courtois and Pierre-Yves Lochou designed this site in France. Courtois is at Paris's Conservatoire National des Arts et Métiers.

Knight-Ridder Information Services

http://www.dialog.com

Researchers and information brokers will cherish this online guide to Knight-Ridder's commercial information services. The biggies here are DIALOG and DataStar, online services that offer archives from hundreds of newspapers and wire services from around the world, charging you $60 an hour or more to search them. You can also buy a service that automatically sends you information updates on a particular subject. You could save tedious hours at the microfilm machine at the public library... just make sure your boss is paying the bill.

The Media History Project
http://www.mediahistory.com

This site (see Figure 15.8) is an index of resources for those interested in the history of communication, from petroglyphs to pixels. If most history sites could be compared to dingy bus stations, this is the spanking-new, light-rail platform. Besides links to related sites, a list of "keywords" can help sort out some of the issues and theories in the study of media history. Professional historians and students can benefit from the "Courseware" and syllabi offerings, or dig into the issues on the future of the Net.

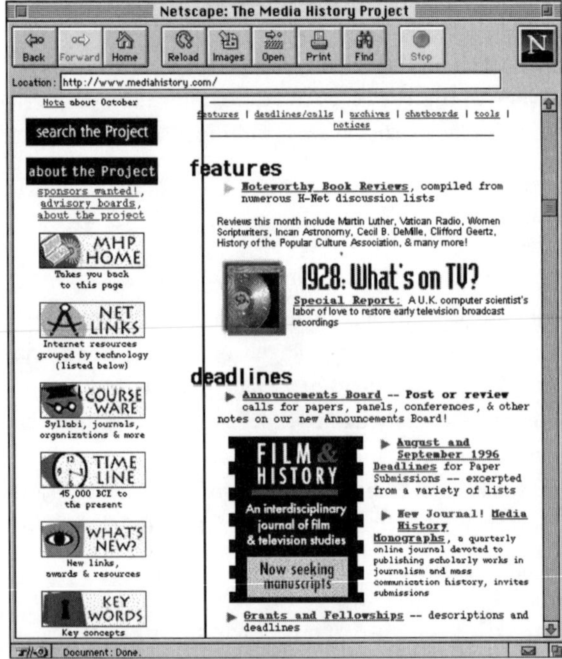

Figure 15.8
The Media History Project,
http://www.mediahistory.com

The Reference Desk
http://www-sci.lib.uci.edu/~martindale/Ref.html

This page at the University of California Irvine library has plenty of reference links, especially for health and medicine centers. It also includes an unusual number of links to the time: at least four links to clocks, plus a page that tells the time on the seven continents. And there's more. Want to know which movies Denzel Washington has appeared in? Looking for a site on line that can perform Chi-square statistical tests? You'll find them here.

The Stolen Bike Registry
http://www.nashville.net/cycling/stolen.html

"The chances of getting back a stolen bike are slightly greater than being hit by lightning, but less than the chance you might win the lottery." So announces this Registry, which aims to improve those odds by allowing folks to register (via forms) their stolen bicycles, and browse stolen bike listings. The server is based in Nashville, Tennessee, yet the listings already boast entries from all over the United States.

Rulers
http://www.geocities.com/Athens/1058/rulers.html

Let's say you're watching Final Jeopardy and you need to know who was Prime Minister of Gabon in 1980. While the music plays, dash to your computer and dial up this page where you'll find the name of Leon Mebiame, who served from 1976-1990. Basically, this is a huge list of kings, presidents, and heads of state for just about any country on Earth, dating back centuries in some cases.

The Nobel Prize Archive
http://www.almaz.com/nobel

The Nobel Foundation recently announced its 1996 prize recipients, and this is the page with all the background. Naturally, past winners are lodged here also, but what makes this site a worthy stop is its easily accessible explanations of why these individuals are winners of such big chunks of change. Another treat is the section devoted to Women Nobel Laureates.

NlightN

http://www.nlightn.com

Partly a Lycos-style Web index and partly a proprietary database, NlightN's pay-as-you-go policies will come as a mild shock to Net surfers used to seeing information as a free commodity. NlightN serves up a unified search engine that covers not just the Web and Usenet, but also the commercial databases of newspapers, trade journals, and magazines. Web links are free, but to get at the commercial databases expect to pony up some cash via a transfer from your credit card to your account at NlightN.

Pulitzer Prizes

http://www.pulitzer.org

You'll find the best of the news here. The Pulitzers are given in more than a dozen categories to the best examples of journalism, photography, literature, and music each year. But don't just take the Pulitzer committee's word for it, you can personally peruse the winning articles and photos yourself at this site. From the commentary of the New York *Daily News*'s E.R. Shipp to the editorial cartoons of Jim Morin of the *Miami Herald*, here's the best of the best.

INTERNATIONAL APPEAL

TallWeb II

http://www.bluplanet.com/tallweb

TallWeb II is a site for people who rise above the crowd. (Bada-boom!) Seriously, this is a genuine resource for people who are taller than average. For instance, it lists places to buy specialized furniture and clothing. Also featured is a list of the year's events sponsored by the Tall Club International in North America, and contact information for other "tall clubs" in the U.S., Canada, and Europe. All it's missing is a sign reading "You Must Be Taller Than This Line To View This Site."

Taglines Galore!

http://www.brandonu.ca/~ennsnr/Tags

Taglines. Taglines. Taglines. More than 59,000 taglines to be exact. Click on Full Deck-isms at this site and you're rewarded with old favorites that range from "Body by Fisher—Brains by Mattel" to "As Smart as Christie Brinkley is ugly" to "Parked his head and forgot where he left it." Just as fun is the daily list of 100 Random Taglines ("If corn oil is made from corn, what's baby oil made from?") and Book Titles ("Clothes for Germ Kings" by Mike Robes).

The Nizkor Project

http://remember.org

"...truth is far more fragile than fiction ... reason alone cannot protect it"—Deborah Lipstadt, Denying the Holocaust. This site denies those who would deny Adolf Hitler's holocaust. It fights the untruths of holocaust "revisionists" with a collection of factual references about the holocaust. It also provides examples of racist charges that deny the occurrence of the holocaust, just to give you a taste of the ignorance that's out there.

where they surf

Surfer: Howard Rheingold

Author of "The Virtual Community" and founder of online community Electric Minds located at **http://www.minds.com**

His favorite sites of the moment:

Justin's Links from the Underground

http://www.links.net

"I love this site because Justin puts his entire life, in painfully candid detail, on line, on a daily basis. He really is living on the Web."

Feed

http://www.feedmag.com

"It's great to see real editors and real writers in a context that encourages conversation by readers. Feed is a site that does this well."

Breeds of Livestock

http://www.ansi.okstate.edu/breeds

From the Swallow Belied Mangalitza pig to the Chincoteague Pony, this site is literally a zoo. Here, you can find out more about what's on your table, and what you'll likely never find on your table, than you ever wanted to know. And the Oklahoma State Univesity designers of this site are no country bumpkins either; their intelligent use of frames and graphics will make you happier than a pig in the poke.

From Primitives to Zen

http://www.enteract.com/~jwalz/Eliade

You probably didn't think you could find Zen on the Web, but here it is, along with Raluvhimba, the High God of the Venda, and Tirawa, the Supreme God of the Pawnee. Dr. Mircea Eliade, of the University of Chicago, compiled this religious reference work to aid his students in their studies. Now, it's available to you on line for just a bit less money than tuition at the august University of Chicago.

CALENDAR AND TIME REFERENCE

The World Wide Holiday and Festival Page

http://www.smiley.cy.net/bdecie/index.html

Need to know if you'll be able to find a hotel room in Brazil on March 25 of next year? Consult this site. You'll find a calendar of the major holidays and festivals for most countries. It also includes links to other sites that will calculate moveable holidays, such as Easter and Ramadhan.

Calendar Conversions

http://genealogy.org/~scottlee/calconvert.cgi

Wondering what today is on the Jewish calendar? Need to convert some Gregorian dates to Julian dates? This simple site will do the math for you.

Calendar

http://www.stud.unit.no/USERBIN/steffent/kalender.pl

This site is for people who love to plan in advance, way in advance. It'll give you the entire calendar year, not just for the next few years, but for any four digit year you enter. Wondering what day of the week your birthday will be on in the year 4523? Now you'll know.

Today's Calendar and Clock Page

http://www.panix.com/~wlinden/calendar.shtml

This site will tell you more than you ever wanted to know about today, whatever today might be. For example, if you want to know what year of American independence today happens to be a part of, you can find the answer here. This site also has links to many other calendar sites.

Home Page for Calendar Reform

http://ecuvax.cis.ecu.edu/~pymccart/calendar-reform.html

If you hate Mondays, check out this site. It's devoted to calendar reform. This site provides a bunch of background on various calendar systems and reform proposals. It also has many links to other sites that delineate new ideas about how to keep time.

NetCal!

http://www.itribe.net/netcal

The purpose of this site is to provide a common area on the Web where people can post dates for events. Of course, to be useful it needs to gain a critical mass of event postings. The information is sparse at the moment. The frame-based interface is cool, though.

Today-in-History

http://www.scopesys.com/today

Drop by this site to find out what happened on the present day. It'll let you know who was born, who died, and what historical events occurred throughout history on the current day, as well as other things. The most interesting feature is a list of soldiers reported MIA on that day and a synopsis of their cases.

Directorate of Time

http://tycho.usno.navy.mil/time.html

Clock watchers will enjoy every second at the Directorate of Time (see Figure 15.9), a service of the U.S. Naval Observatory in Washington, D.C. Not only can you get the exact time accurate to the nanosecond, but you'll be amazed to read just how much trouble it takes to keep the entire civilized world from losing a tick here and there. Of course, everyone knows it takes 50 cesium beam frequency standards and ten hydrogen masers to keep a master clock like theirs from missing a beat, but it's nice to be reminded.

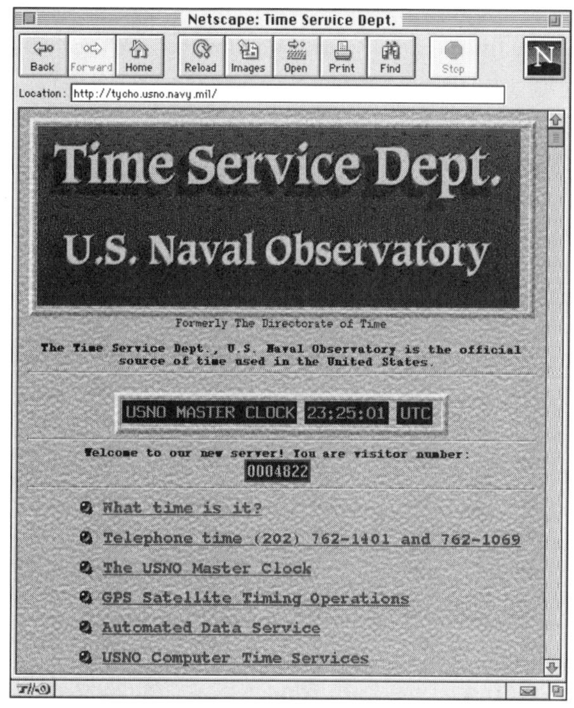

Figure 15.9

Directorate of Time,

http://tycho.usno.navy.mil/time.html

GOVERNMENT REFERENCES AND STATISTICS

GPO Access on the Web

http://thorplus.lib.purdue.edu:8100/gpo

Purdue University ought to get a medal for this site, which allows users to search through over a dozen Government Printing Office databases, including the Congressional Record, the Federal Register, and much more. For instance: the General Accounting Office, the research arm of Congress, produces hundreds of "blue book" reports a year on major legislative issues like health care and federal funding of education, and visitors can find them here.

Government Information Sharing Project

http://govinfo.kerr.orst.edu

This Oregon State University project enables users to access data and tables from several government resources that haven't been on line. An example is the economic

[OVERHEARD ON WOMEN'S WIRE]

http://chat.women.com

"I have great hopes for cyberlife. It's low-energy, nonpolluting, and can potentially make sure that no one is ever lonely."

—Barbara Ehrenreich, Time magazine columnist and Zeitgeist watcher, in a live chat.

census report on minority- and women-owned businesses. Or the Export-Import page, which can tell you how many agricultural machinery products were shipped to Portland, ME, from, say, France in 1991 (just one, but it was worth $23,000). Other databases contain census, agriculture, and economic data. A gold mine of information.

U.S. Census Bureau

http://www.census.gov

If you need to know exactly how many people are living in the United States *right now*, get an educated here. This effective site (see Figure 15.10) also lets you search for all sorts of census documents, from reports on the fertility of U.S. women to the Farm and Ranch Irrigation Survey. Check out the map section to find out how many people live in your neighborhood.

Government Printing Office Access—UCSD

http://ssdc.ucsd.edu/gpo

Like its counterpart at Purdue University, this site allows users to search through Congressional bills, the Federal Register, and plenty of other enormous federal documents. The advantage of this site is that it has deeper data, including House and Senate calendars, economic indicators, and Congressional reports. Want to find out what Newt Gingrich really said on the House floor? How

Figure 15.10

U.S. Census Bureau, *http://www.census.gov*

did that parakeet tariff bill become law? It's all here, along with a simple search mechanism, too.

Energy Information Administration

http://www.eia.doe.gov/index.html

For flat-out consumption, it's hard to beat American citizens. According to the U.S. Department of Energy, consumption of fossil fuels jumped from 29 quadrillion BTUs in 1949 to more than 75 quadrillion BTUs in 1994. Scientists and energy-types can access all sorts of figures here, including something called the Coal Transportation Rate Data Base. It would help if you actually understand this stuff before visiting, but it's also aesthetically pleasing for anyone who can't comprehend "end use consumption."

Bureau of Economic Analysis

http://www.bea.doc.gov

The BEA calls itself the "Nation's accountant." This Department of Commerce agency serves up dozens of reports and tables on America's economic health, including the monthly Survey of Current Business, which costs dough to get. Most of the information is free, though, and there's plenty of it: charts on price indexes and other indicators since 1960, plus quarterly data summarizing personal income and corporate profits.

Statistical Reports on U.S. Science and Engineering

http://www.nsf.gov/sbe/srs/stats.htm

Ah, the magic of government statistics! Visitors here will find a wealth of surveys, reports, and statistics on the sciences. Examples include a 1994 report on women and minorities in the sciences and a survey on science degrees from 1966-1993, available in ASCII, WordPerfect, or even Lotus Worksheet formats. A tremendous resource for educators and researchers, this site is a good example of what bureaucrats do so well: gather and crunch numbers.

FAA Office of System Safety

http://nasdac.faa.gov

The Federal Aviation Administration meticulously records every crash it can find. From this site visitors can get brief accident reports from the National Transportation Safety

Board. You can, for example, find out how many planes have crashed in Rhode Island since 1983 (the answer? 82).

National Archives and Records Administration

http://www.nara.gov

Archives are tricky things on the Web. Most of America's vital documents are just that: pieces of paper. Trying to work around that is the U.S. NARA, which handles everything from the Al Capone tax evasion trial files to a searchable database of material related to the assassination of John F. Kennedy. It's also the home of the daily table of contents for the Federal Register and a nifty exhibit on the American West.

The National Clearinghouse for Criminal Justice Information Systems

http://www.ch.search.org

Visitors will find Supreme Court opinions, back issues of the FBI Law Enforcement Bulletin, and much more at this occasionally clumsy site. The good stuff is here—like a directory of online criminal justice resources—though let's just say that it's not as easy as it could be to get around. But with a growing set of databases (including lists of criminal justice training programs and job opportunities), this site is a keeper.

PROFESSIONAL REFERENCE

LAWLinks

http://www.counsel.com

LAWLinks is a service of the Lexis Counsel Connect, which bills itself as the largest online communications and information network for lawyers. What makes this site more than just another list of legal links is the LCC Spotlight. The Spotlight shines on legal documents which explain the news of the day, with cases like U.S. vs. Microsoft and Ewing vs. NBA. In short, LAWLinks offers the law behind the news.

Meta-Index for Legal Research

http://gsulaw.gsu.edu/metaindex

Inspired by CUI's Internet Meta-Index, this site is an excellent tool for finding that elusive piece of legal information on the Web. The Meta-Index lets you search judicial sources (such as U.S. Supreme Court Syllabi) and legislative sources (such as the Thomas site at the Library of Congress). Visitors can also search non-legal sites such as Harvest and Lycos. It may not be very pretty, but it works well.

The 'Lectric Law Library

http://www.lectlaw.com

You have to take a quick tour of this site before you can use it, but your time will be well spent. We all, one way or another, must deal with the well-developed legal system of our country and the 'Lectric Law Library will help you out forthwith. Whether you need a template for a will or contract, or advice about negotiating a divorce without a lawyer, turn here for some pro bono help.

LIBRARIES

100 BEST SITES

Library of Congress

http://www.loc.gov

If the question is reference, here's the answer. The Library of Congress site (see Figure 15.11) is the mother lode of information that goes far beyond library paste. It affirms the core democratic value of open access to information with special displays like the hitherto top-secret Revelations from the Russian Archives. Every month the server is updated with new exhibits, new prints, and photographs.

INTERNATIONAL APPEAL

CARRIE: An Electronic Library

http://www.ukans.edu/carrie/carrie_main.html

CARRIE (a cryptic acronym never explained) is the name of a library at the University of Kansas. All the materials here are available on line, from Vatican documents dating back centuries, to American author William Faulkner's Nobel Prize acceptance speech. Plenty of authors are

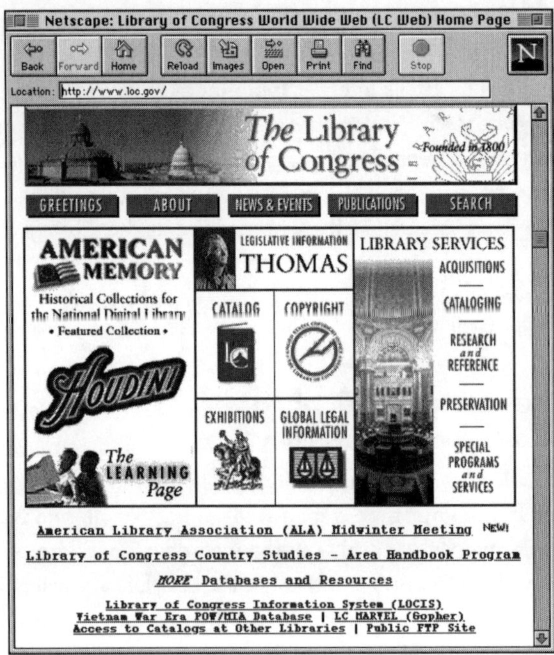

Figure 15.11
Library of Congress, *http://www.loc.gov*

represented and the collection includes foreign texts in Spanish, Latin, and Scandanavian, among other languages.

The Electric Library
http://www2.elibrary.com/search.cgi

Infonautics, the folks who gave Prodigy users Homework Helper, has developed The Electric Library for Web users seeking information on any and every topic. This plugged-in, souped-up media database lets you run keyword searches for related articles, excerpts, transcripts, and photos from thousands of newspapers, magazines, broadcasts, books, and other resources. Type in your word or phrase and the program brings home the full-text bacon. The catch? A $9.95 monthly fee, though there's a free trial period before you sign on the dotted line.

Electronic Library: University of Waterloo
http://www.lib.uwaterloo.ca

This site began as a service to actual visitors and the U. of Waterloo (Ontario, Canada) community. But now this electronic library offers access to information resources from all over. Those include the types of indexes, references volumes, and collections one would expect to find at a college library, such as a biographical dictionary, and scores of e-journals and e-texts. We were forbidden access to some features like the Oxford English Dictionary. For serious Net researchers, however, it doesn't get much better on line than this.

TSU Folklore Collection
http://harpo.tnstate.edu/~folklore

Sure, you've heard the old proverb, "Absence makes the heart grow fonder"—but have you heard that "If you throw a brick into a pack of dogs, the one that screams is the one you hit"? If not, high-tail your mouse over to the delightful TSU Folklore Collection site. Here, Dr. Lucas Powers's students at Tennessee State University are assembling an online assortment of proverbs both well-known and not. They've also got a collection of folk superstitions, from such nearly mundane concepts as "knock on wood," to some downright weird beliefs, such as "When your finger nails start growing, you're pregnant."

Bill's Library
http://www.io.org/~jgcom/library.htm

Now here's a library and a half—at least. Bill Henderson, who lives in Toronto, Canada, and has a cool homepage in his own right, has amassed an eminently readable collection of online magazines, literature, and the like. "'Twas brillig, and the slithy toves..." from Lewis Carroll's "Jabberwocky" is among the many delights to be found in the Poet's Corner. You may not know what "The Morpo Review" is, but you sure can find out (It's an electronic magazine published by creative college students around the U.S.).

Newsletter Library
http://pub.savvy.com

Maybe, just maybe, your favorite topic isn't well-represented on the Internet (although that's doubtful). Well, the chances are good that somebody is publishing a newsletter about the subject, and here's a giant listing for you to check. Maybe it's banking (ten subject headings), women's rights, or telecommunications (15 different subjects). Perhaps bilingual education is your cup of tea.

Whichever it is, just fill out the handy form here, send it in, and you'll get sample copies of newsletters pertaining to the issues you request. For Free!

Project Bartleby

http://www.cc.columbia.edu/acis/bartleby

This site bills itself, not incorrectly, as the "public library of the Internet." Named after a Herman Melville book ("Bartleby, the Scrivener"), this resource provides online access to out-of-print classics and poetry. Bartlett's Familiar Quotations has several Internet homes, most of them unofficial (for that matter, illegal) but can the same be said of Walt Whitman's "Leaves of Grass" or Mary Wollstonecraft's "A Vindication Of The Rights Of Woman: With Strictures On Political And Moral Subjects"? Probably not.

INTERNATIONAL APPEAL

World Library

http://lanic.utexas.edu/world/library

An international flavor makes this collection of reference links different. While it includes many of the useful American reference links—the National Archives and major university libraries, for example—this site also features the national libraries of the Netherlands and of Australia. South American libraries, from the University of Buenos Aires to the Monterrey Institute of Technology, are a big part of this list.

STATISTICS

INTERNATIONAL APPEAL

Demography & Population Studies from the Virtual Library

http://coombs.anu.edu.au/ResFacilities/DemographyPage.html

This number-filled page has far-ranging links to demographic resources in places like Thailand and Norway. Visitors can browse abstracts from the Australian National University's demography program (with titles like "Growing up in Melbourne") or Princeton University's Office of Population Research. Data is the key word here, as these sites have lots of it, or will tell you how to get it.

Consumer Prices and Price Indexes

http://stats.bls.gov/cpihome.htm

The answer to the popular question, "What is a consumer price index?" can be found here. This site is chock-full of statistics—some available by gopher—on the prices of food, clothing, and pretty much anything. And get this: the Bureau of Labor, which compiles the data, gets most of the information through personal interviews. Yet another labor-saving device for those of us who can be called "comparison shoppers."

Bureau of Labor Statistics

http://stats.bls.gov/blshome.html

Politicians love to run around quoting statistics about how good, or how bad, the economy is doing. Ever wonder if they're being completely truthful? You can find out by visiting this site. It'll give you all the statistics on the employment situation.

American Demographics

http://www.marketingtools.com

The publisher of American Demographics and Marketing Tools magazines has created a Web site loaded with information for people who need to know stuff like how much money the average person in Suffolk, N.Y., spends on books and magazines ($249.72 a year). Most of the information is drawn from this Dow Jones company's publications, but the site includes a search engine to help you find the demographic factoid you need.

The Gallup Organization

http://www.gallup.com

Two out of three people say this site is cool. Okay, that was made up. But the Gallup Organization's site is the place when it comes to opinion surveys and polls. A June 1995 survey reported that "a significant number of people in the world today appear to be generally satisfied with their personal lives" (in Iceland, 87 percent were satisfied, while in Hungary the number was just 21 percent).

FECInfo

http://www.tray.com/fecinfo

Tony Raymond and Robyn Jimeson both left the Federal Election Commission—and the general public is much better off—because there's more information on federal campaign contributions here than at the FEC's fine site. Try searching for "tobacco" and you'll get the list of contributions made by, among others, Brown & Williamson. Perhaps you'd like to see the financial reports of North Dakota's Congressional candidates—no problem there, either. This is both staggeringly easy and staggeringly informative for anyone chasing the money trail.

USADATA

http://www.usadata.com

If you're selling the perfect product for American tennis-playing singles who drink Mountain Dew and keep a pet bird, the people at USADATA can tell you exactly how big your market is. And now the company's Web site makes it possible for subscribers to request reports on such arcane information on line. The key word is "subscribers," because custom analysis or access to all of the company's 60,000 reports on American market demographics and shopping habits costs money.

National Crash Analysis Center

http://gwuva.gwu.edu/ncac

Based at George Washington University, the U.S. National Crash Analysis Center does federally funded research on automobile "crashworthiness." They smash 'em up, look over the mess, and try to figure out exactly what happened. Laid out in efficient frames, their home page is a rich repository for research results, and quite fascinating. That is, if you're into comparing the "gross vehicle deformation" of a 35 mph Taurus to Taurus head-on at 50 percent offset, say, to one at 30 percent offset. Yes, rubber-neckers, a few crash test MPEGs are available.

Office of Population Research

http://opr.princeton.edu

Princeton University is the home of this gentle-looking site (although the building pictured here has a rather large cannon in front of it). The OPR is filled with people who love demographics (you know, like how many left-handed people over 30 live in Akron, Ohio). One major work: fertility studies which chart the growth of American families since the 1950s. The OPR's data archive contains the results of these and other studies, which can be downloaded by other researchers for their own use.

POSTAL AND GEOGRAPHIC REFERENCE

United States Postal Service

http://www.usps.gov/postofc/pstoffc.htm

This is a truly useful site if, like most people, you still send an occasional package or letter in the actual, physical, real world. You can come here to find out things like postage rates, zip codes for addresses, and much more. You can

where they surf

Surfer: Aliza Sherman (a.k.a. Cybergrrl)

Founder of Cybergrrl Internet Media, at **http://www.cybergrrl.com**

Favorite Web sites of the moment:

Newspage

http://www.newspage.com

"All your headline news served up in one place, by category—who has time to read the newspaper anymore? I have this set up as the homepage on my Netscape browser so I can start the day with my tea and news."

WomenSpace

http://www.womenspace.com

"I wish there was a resource like this when I was growing up. Health and sexuality issues for young women in an honest, fresh, straightforward manner—a very personable and informative site."

even submit a change of address notice on line. Ever wonder what the post office does with unclaimed mail? They sell it. Find out where the auctions are at this site.

ZipFind

http://link-usa.com/zipcode

This is an interface to a database than can tell you the distance between any two zip codes. Also, if you enter a zip code and a radius, it'll tell you how many people live in the circle centered upon that zip code.

Color Landform Atlas of the United States

http://fermi.jhuapl.edu/states/states.html

If you've ever seen a good relief map on line, you probably can thank this page's creator, Ray Sterner. This Johns Hopkins mathematician first posted his colorized maps of the United States in a newsgroup in 1994. This site (see Figure 15.12), with maps and links for all 50 states, is an extension of that work.

Geographic Nameserver

http://www.mit.edu:8001/geo

To call this just a geography site isn't fair; hey, geography should always be this fun. Visitors can enter a name (even their own) and seconds later receive a listing of all cities and towns in the United States with that name. For example, ten towns named "Elmer" exist in the U.S., two in Louisiana alone. This simply designed site also generates the county, zip code, area code, and latitude/longitude coordinates for each result, which makes it (would you believe) useful, too.

The Great Globe Gallery

http://hum.amu.edu.pl/~zbzw/glob/glob1.htm

The Great Globe Gallery puts a global spin on geographic visualization with its assortment of swirling globes and other Earthy depictions. Though hardly a substitute for the real thing (you can't put a pin on your screen), this Polish site (see Figure 15.13) is as cool a way as you'll find to virtually see the world.

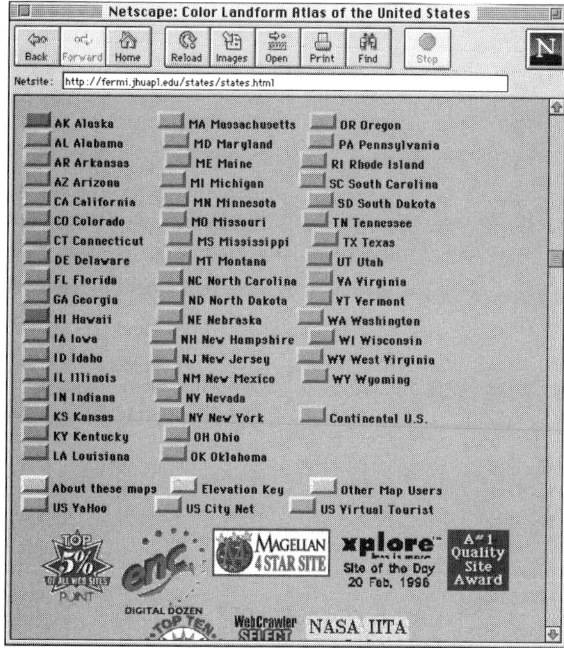

Figure 15.12
Color Landform Atlas of the United States, *http://fermi.jhuapl.edu/states/states.html*

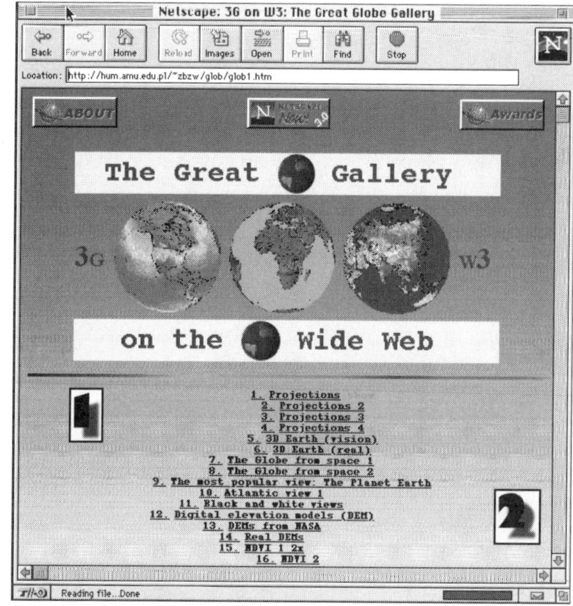

Figure 15.13
The Great Globe Gallery, *http://hum.amu.edu.pl/~zbzw/glob/glob1.htm*

How Far Is It?

http://www.indo.com/distance

This nifty little mileage marker maker figures out the distance between two cities. It's simple: just type in point A and point B, then let the system do its thing (it draws on geographical name servers in several locations). Plus, its resources are amusingly deep. Request the distance between Tel Aviv and Budapest, and the program will innocently ask whether you mean Budapest, Hungary or Budapest, Georgia.

Gary-Chicago-Milwaukee Corridor Transportation Information Center

http://www.ai.eecs.uic.edu/GCM/GCM.html

Anyone who's tried driving through Chicagoland at a time other than 2:00 a.m. will appreciate this Department of Transportation sponsored site, intended to improve mobility via better management of existing Gary-Chicago-Milwaukee Corridor highways. It features a color-coded road map, updated by the minute, indicating present congestion. This is a nice idea, and surely beats radio traffic reports for those millions with Web access in their car.

Subway Navigator

http://metro.jussieu.fr:10001/bin/cities/english

The Subway Navigator makes instant public transportation "triptiks" for travelers between any two points in a given city's metropolitan area. This service, provided by an anonymous Frenchman, is available in a remarkable 61 cities in 29 countries (see Figure 15.14). For example, if you're starting out in Tuckahoe, New York and want to end up in Sheepshead Bay, Brooklyn, the Subway Navigator can tell you which trains to take, and estimate that your trip will take 95 minutes.

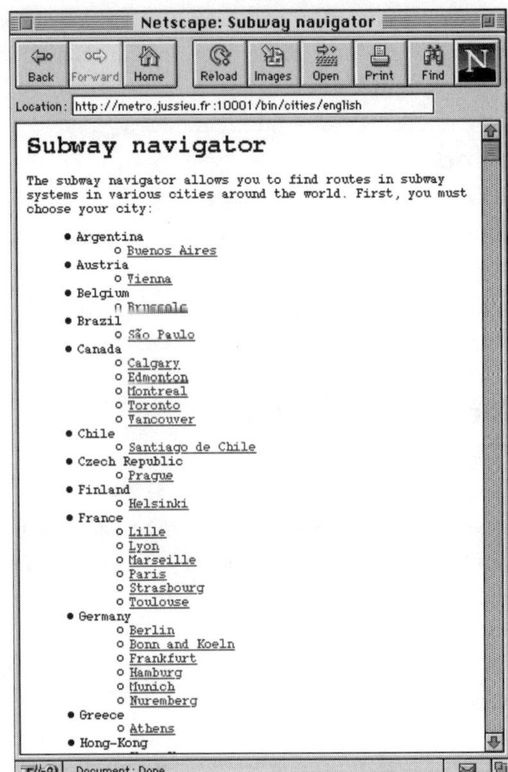

Figure 15.14
Subway Navigator,
http://metro.jussieu.fr:10001/bin/cities/english

NAISMap

http://ellesmere.ccm.emr.ca/naismap/naismap.html

This handy Web gadget by Glen Newton at the National Atlas Information Service in Canada gives you views into different geographic aspects of that country. The program generates a color-coded map based on your specifications, and there's a number of data layers for you to choose from: typical ones like lakes, streams, and railways, and not-so-typical ones like low streamflow and the range of the striped chorus frog.

U.S. Gazetteer

http://www.census.gov/cgi-bin/gazetteer

The grand-daddy of geographic name servers, the Census Bureau's U.S. Gazetteer lets you find almost anywhere in the U.S. by its name. Type in the key word "love," for instance, and it calls up every place name with "love" in the title (from Cloverdale, Indiana to Loveland, Ohio). You get the basics (population and zip code), and can link over to the 1990 Census Lookup site for deeper statistical info. The top dog here is the Tiger Map Server (TMS): once you've identified your place, click over to TMS and it'll create, on the fly, a full-color map of the location.

MapQuest

http://www.mapquest.com

This extensive mapping site doesn't just provide you detailed color maps of the whole world, it also gives you specific directions for driving between any of 150,000 cities in North America. This fast site has groovy graphics and an intelligent interface. Too bad you can't install it on your dash.

GENEALOGICAL REFERENCE

The Genealogy Toolbox

http://genealogy.tbox.com/genealogy/guides/guidintr.html

Want to find out how you turned out the way you did? This introduction to genealogy will get you started on the path to your ancestry. Find out how to focus your search, where to look for records, how to interpret the records, and how to begin writing your family history.

National Genealogical Society

http://www.genealogy.org/~ngs

So you've decided to research your family's history. How do you deal with name changes? How about burned courthouses? Or (gasp!) even illegitimacy? This national organization's site offers resources that deal with the practicalities of genealogical research. Find out how to become a member, join, and then gain access to journals, periodicals, and a genealogical newsgroup.

Genealogy's Most Wanted

http://www.cityet.net/mostwanted

It was inevitable: the marriage of the *Most Wanted* TV craze and a Web site. Here it's being applied to genealogy with some interesting results. Are you looking for a lost relative? Search through almost 4,000 names and leave them a note. Or, you might find out that you are the one they want. The only catch: you have to keep checking in.

Everton's Guide to Genealogy on the World Wide Web

http://www.everton.com/a1.htm

If you've ever wanted to trace your family's roots, this comprehensive site is the place to start your search. The publisher of one of geneaology's oldest magazines, *Everton's Genealogical Helper* brings its considerable know-how to the Web. Learn all the basics on how to get started, and review resources that professional genealogists use. There's even a checklist for the "20 Ways to Avoid Grief in Your Research."

Genealogy Dictionary

http://www.electriciti.com/~dotts/diction.html#DICT

Looking for your roots but can't find the words? The Genealogy Dictionary, created by Dorothy E. Stanley as part of her Dott's Genealogy Home Page, is an online family tree lexicon that defines all those confusing genealogical terms and Latin phrases that can get in the way of historical research. Ever heard of "Ahnentafel"? No, it's not a Greek sandwich. Dott's dictionary says it's "a table of one's ancestors, from the German *Ahnen* (ancestor) and *Tafel* (table or list)."

The Genealogy Home Page

http://www.genhomepage.com

If you're stumped about your family roots, this page (the result of combined efforts by several genealogy buffs) may help you get the real story. For example, if you know that a great-uncle emigrated from Leningrad, but was born in Berlin, the German-Russian genealogical library is a logical next step. Only a few genealogical libraries let you do online searching so far, but the site suggests other ways you can trace the names of your ancestors using the Net's growing resources.

Genealogy on the World Wide Web

http://www.everton.com

Genealogy on the World Wide Web is a service of Everton Publishers (serving family historians for over 45 years). They've packed this site with information about the art of searching your family tree, via entries like 20 Ways to Avoid Grief in Your Genealogical Research.

Everton also offers its magazine and commercial services, including research-for-hire and a tote bag reading, "To a genealogist, everything is relative." A great spot for beginners and veterans alike.

☞ KEYWORDS

For more information on topics in this chapter, start your Web search with these keywords.

Search and Reference: search engines, encyclopedias, directories, dictionaries, calendars, white pages, yellow pages, mailing list directories, newsgroup directories, people directories, facts and figures, date and time, translators, postal directories, phone directories.

Use Casey's Snow Day Reverse Dictionary to look up words that go with definitions of your own making.
http://www.c3.lanl.gov.8064

Brush up on your poker game using Dan's Poker Dictionary.
http://www.universe.digex.net/~kimberg/pokerdict.html

Learn Braille and American Sign Language at the Interactive ASL & Braille Guide.
http://www.disserv.stu.umn.edu/AltForm

Learn a new tongue using the translator tool of Rivendell's Dictionaries and Translators site.
http://rivendel.com/~ric/resources/dictionary.html

Look up current statistics about any country in the world at the CIA factbook site.
http://www.odci.gov/cia/publications/pubs.html

Appendix A

Tips for Using Lycos to Search the Web

To search the Lycos catalog, just enter one or more words (better known as a "search query") in the text entry box on the Lycos home page or search results page. Next, press the Enter key (or click the Go Get It button). Lycos will display the results. If you need to customize or refine your search, however, Lycos provides an easy way for you to "fine-tune" your search.

The Customize Your Search form is a tool that Lycos provides to make searching its index easy for you to do. It's especially helpful if you need to do any of the following:

- Make your search wider or more narrow
- Have the search match ALL words in a query rather than ANY single word (which is the default setting)
- Search for special variations of a given term (for example, to search for several possible spellings of a word AND some other word)

Most of the time you won't need to use this search form at all if you only want to perform "wide" searches of the Web. However, Lycos gives you other Search options, which you can change if you want to search for different types of information, such as pictures, sounds, and sites that have been categorized by subject.

You can also "refine" your search by making it more narrow or wide. You can have the search match ALL words in your query rather than the default ANY word. You can also search for a number of terms which are DIFFERENT from the number you entered (for example, to search for several possible spellings of a word AND some other word).

The search form gives you two ways to control your search: *Search Options* and *Display Options.* You'll notice that both Search Options and Display Options are pull-down menus. Simply click the down-arrow in each of these pull-down menus and look at the selections that are available.

USING SEARCH OPTIONS TO SET TERMS TO MATCH (BOOLEAN)

You might wonder why you can't do Boolean searches on Lycos. You might also want to know what exactly a Boolean search is. *Boolean searches* are those queries that let you search the Web for very specific combinations of words. For example, you might want to see all instances of peanut and butter together, but only where they appear without jelly.

Although you can't perform true Boolean searches on Lycos, you can come very close by using the Search Options features. Just keep these simple guidelines in mind:

- AND searches are possible by selecting the match all terms (AND) option and then entering whatever words you want in the search box. In the above example, you'd simply enter peanut butter.

- NOT searches are a bit trickier. You may currently prepend (that is, begin) a term with a hyphen to make it a negative indicator, like this: -jelly. This will only reduce the score for sites containing the word jelly, not remove them entirely. The good news is that the first set of results you get will most likely give you what you want: peanut butter without jelly.

By default, Lycos will find all documents matching any word you type in your query (except for certain words like "a" and "the" which are generally not meaningful in a search). If you type "jeep cherokee" as your query, Lycos will find all documents containing either "jeep" OR "cherokee." This is the match any term (OR) Search Option, and is what you get when you type a query into the form on the home page, or if you select the match any term (OR) option on the Customize Your Search form.

Sometimes you might want to find only documents that match ALL the words in your query. This is the match all terms (AND) option. Try it on the form and then see what Lycos returns for "jeep cherokee" when you use the "OR" option and when you use the "AND" option.

SYMBOLS YOU CAN'T USE IN YOUR SEARCHES

You can't use + in search terms. A common instance of this is the term C++, which gets stripped down to c. Unfortunately, this leaves a single letter which, being shorter than three characters, is ignored. This behavior can be annoying, but Lycos is in the process of choosing the best solution to solve it (and related problems) without affecting the speed and performance of conducting searches. For now we suggest you search for related terms: Instead of C++, for instance, you might try programming languages. Hopefully, Lycos will fix this soon.

You also cannot search for numbers. The current version of Lycos strips out all numbers at the beginning of words. This causes problems if you search for 3DO, 4AD Records, or any other letter-number combination.

The problem is that numbers are a whole different breed of cat from letters. Lycos is trying to teach its retrieval engine to determine for itself which sequences of letters are words and which are not; once they do, you'll be able to make these searches.

SYMBOLS YOU CAN USE IN YOUR SEARCHES

At the present time, you can use the following symbols in your search queries:

- (-) As we mentioned earlier, you can use the - symbol to help narrow down your search. For example, to search for bank, but without river turning up in the search, you would type bank -river in your search query. This is similar to the NOT Boolean search term.

- (.) Use a period at the end of the keyword to limit it with no expansions. Bank. will bring up only results with the keyword "bank" and ignore expansions like "bankers" and "banking."

- ($) Put this symbol after the keyword to make the search engine expand it. The search term "gard$" will bring up results like "garden" and "gardenias." This feature is great if you don't know how to spell a word, or if you aren't sure what you're looking for.

LIMITING YOUR SEARCH TO A SPECIFIED NUMBER OF TERMS

You might also be wondering why you need "match 2 terms," "match 3 terms," and so on. These options give you more flexibility in your search. Suppose you wanted to find references to Sarajevo and Yugoslavia. But you're not sure whether Sarajevo is spelled "Sarajevo" or "Sarayevo." So you enter your query

"Sarajevo Sarayevo Yugoslavia." To get the best results, you can use the Search Options.

You can't use match all terms (AND) because that would give you only documents which contain both spellings of "Sarajevo" AND Yugoslavia, and there probably aren't any of those. You could use match any terms (OR), because that would return all documents that contain any of these three terms, but you would also get lots of documents you don't want in the list.

Here's what you do: Enter "Sarajevo Sarayevo Yugoslavia" as your query, and choose match 2 terms. This selection will match at least two terms in each document. Since it's quite unlikely Sarajevo will be spelled two different ways in the same document, the results returned will have references to BOTH one of the two spellings of Sarajevo AND Yugoslavia.

USING THE SEARCH OPTIONS TO SET THE SELECTIVITY OF THE SEARCH

You can change the Search Options to adjust the selectivity of the Lycos search engine. When set to "loose match," you will get more documents, but they will tend to be less relevant to the query you've made. Often, particularly when you are beginning a search and wish to cast the widest possible net, this is exactly what you want.

If you want the Lycos search engine to be more selective, change the Search Option from loose match to "strong match." Lycos will return only documents which have a very high relevance to your query. If you are on a slow dial-up connection, setting the selectivity to "strong match" can save you time by reducing the number of irrelevant hits downloaded to you.

You should try out the effect of changing various selectivity settings on the form. Try some searches with various selectivity settings to get a feel for how it affects your results.

SETTING THE DISPLAY OF THE RESULTS PAGE SIZE

Lycos always gives you all the results or "hits" matching your query, even if there are hundreds or thousands of documents. If the number of hits is large, however, Lycos does not display them all at once, so you don't need to wait a long time for the whole page to come to you. By default, Lycos displays 10 hits on each results page. Once you've looked at those 10, you click on the "Next 10 hits" link at the bottom of the page to get the next 10 hits, and so on until all the hits are displayed.

To change the default from 10 hits displayed on each page, you can set the number in the Display Options pull-down menu. Simply choose another value from 10 to 40 results per page.

SETTING THE AMOUNT OF RESULTS DETAIL YOU WANT DISPLAYED

You can also control the amount of information you want Lycos to display about each result. There are three levels of detail you can choose from:

- Standard (the default)
- Detailed (all information displayed)
- Summary (the minimum amount of information is displayed)

INTERPRETING THE RESULTS OF A SEARCH

The percentage numbers are simply Lycos's way of showing you how close it thinks each site will match what you're looking for, based on the words you asked Lycos to search for.

When the Lycos search engine compares each page to your query, it gives higher scores to pages that contain the words as you typed them in. It also looks for pages that mention these words early on, rather than far down in some sub-section of the site. The page with the combination most like the words you typed in is ranked at the top and assigned the number 1.000. Other sites are ranked below and assigned numbers based on how much or how little they resemble your search terms.

This means that if you asked for Hungarian goulash, then a site titled The Hungarian Goulash Recipe Page will end up above sites that mention Carpathian goulash, salad, and Hungarian bread, or some less precise combination.

The percentages are in no way a rating of how good Lycos thinks any page is. They're simply a tool to help you narrow down your choices.

Appendix B

Using the CD-ROM

The CD-ROM that's packaged with this book includes software for you to use. The software will not only allow you to explore the Internet and search the Web, but will also allow you to view a fully hyperlinked HTML version of the printed book, also contained on the CD-ROM. Before you can use the software, you will need to install it on the hard drive of your computer. This is a simple procedure that will take only a few minutes.

WHAT'S ON THE CD-ROM?

The CD-ROM includes the following software and other items that can be installed on your computer:

- Microsoft Internet Explorer Web browser for PCs and Macs
- Earthlink Internet connection software for PCs and Macs
- A fully hyperlinked HTML version of the book for PCs and Macs, which you can view using your Web browser

Viewing the Hyperlinked HTML Version of the Book

The CD-ROM contains the fully hyperlinked text of the book, which lists thousands of Web sites and Internet addresses, including live links to Women's Wire and Lycos, the search engine. Although you can use the CD and view the HTML book version without a live Internet connection, every section of the CD allows you to select an Internet address and instantly connect to the actual site. To connect directly to these Web sites, however, you'll need an Internet connection.

Using the CD-ROM

To view the hyperlinked version of the book, you will need to use a Web browser. Simply follow the steps below.

Running Most Web Browsers (Including Netscape Navigator)

1. Place the CD-ROM in your CD-ROM drive.
2. Launch your Web browser.
3. Choose **Open File** from the File menu.
4. Select your CD-ROM drive. For PC users, this is usually drive **D**. Mac users, this is on your desktop.
5. Open the file named **Welcome.htm**.

Running Microsoft Internet Explorer

1. Place the CD-ROM in your CD-ROM drive.
2. Launch **Internet Explorer**.
3. Choose **Open** from the File menu.
4. Click the **Browse** button.

5 Select your CD-ROM drive. For PC users, this is usually drive **D**. Mac users, this is on your desktop.

6 Open the file named **Welcome.htm**.

7 Click on **OK**.

Installing Web Browser Software

If you do not have a Web browser currently installed on your computer, we have included Microsoft's Internet Explorer on this CD. The steps for installing Internet Explorer are described below.

Recommended PC System

- 486 Processor (Pentium Processor preferred)
- Windows OS (3.x or 95)
- 8MB of RAM (16MB preferred)
- 8MB free space on your hard drive (15MB preferred)
- 2x CD-ROM drive (4x recommended)

Macintosh System Requirements

- Apple Macintosh or Power Macintosh (or clone) running System 7.0.1 or later
- 8MB of RAM (16MB preferred)
- 8MB of free space on your hard drive (16MB preferred)
- 2x CD-ROM drive (4x preferred)

Installing Internet Explorer

Internet Explorer Version 3.01 for Windows 95

You must be using Microsoft Windows 95 to run Microsoft Internet Explorer 3.01. Locate the IE-Win95 folder in the MS-IE directory on the CD.

Double-click on the IE301M95.EXE file. Follow the instructions that appear on your screen to complete the installation.

Internet Explorer Version 2.1 for Windows 3.1

You must be using Microsoft Windows 3.1 to run Microsoft Internet Explorer 2.1. Locate the IE_WIN31 folder in the MS-IE directory on the CD.

Double-click on the DLMINI21.EXE file. Follow the instructions that appear on your screen to complete the installation.

Internet Explorer Version 2.0 for the Macintosh

Double-click the Internet Explorer installer icon, located in the MS Internet Explorer Folder, to install. Follow the prompts that appear on your screen to complete the installation.

Note: Eudora Light is an Internet Mail client application that is included in Microsoft Internet Explorer 2.0 for the Macintosh. Documentation for Eudora Light is not included. To download the Eudora Light Manual separately, visit the Microsoft Internet Explorer Web site at: http://www.microsoft.com/ie/iedl.htm#mac.

Installing Earthlink Internet Connection Software (for Macs and PCs)

To install Earthlink as your Internet service provider, follow these steps:

For PC's

1 From the Earthlink Folder on the CD-ROM open the Win31 or Win95 directory (depending on your system).

2 Run the Setup.exe file appropriate for your system and follow the on screen setup instructions.

For the Mac

1 From the Earthlink Folder on the CD double-click on the TotalAccess Installer.

2 Follow the onscreen instructions to load Earthlink as your Internet Service Provider.

Glossary of Internet Lingo

While the Web is user-friendly, sometimes the vocabulary can seem off-putting. Here are some easy-to-understand definitions of commonly used terms that will help you get the most from your Web travels.

Access Provider (also Internet Service Provider). A company that provides consumers and businesses with a connection to the Internet via local telephone lines (for example, CompuServe, America Online, Netcom, Earthlink, and Microsoft Network).

Avatar. A three-dimensional representation of yourself used for communicating with other people online. A cartoon-like character that you can select from a gallery of available images on Web sites that feature avatars (usually chat sites and virtual world sites).

Bandwidth. The speed of the connection between your computer and the Internet dictating how much information can pass through the connection, usually measured in bits-per-second. The higher the bandwidth, the faster the connection, the more quickly the content (text, graphics, video) will appear on your screen.

Baud. A measurement of the speed of a modem—the number of bits per second it can transfer. The higher the baud rate, the faster the modem, and the faster you can send and receive data over the Net.

Bookmark. A tool provided with Internet browsers that allows users to save favorite Web addresses (URLs) in an easy-to-access list for future reference.

Browser. Software that allows you to navigate ("browse") the Web. The most popular brand names are Netscape Navigator and Microsoft Internet Explorer. Other browsers include Mosaic and Netcruiser.

Bulletin Board. See Forum.

Chat (also Live Chat). Text-based online conversations that take place in real time in chat rooms on the Internet. Participants must be online at the same time and in the same chat room to chat with each other. Chats can be free-form or moderated by a host and featuring celebrity guests.

Cyberspace. A phrase coined by author William Gibson in his 1984 novel *Neuromancer*. The term is now generally used to describe all of the information available online.

Directories. Web sites designed to help you find other sites of interest on the Web (for example, Lycos, Yahoo, Excite). They organize Web sites into categories for quick and easy browsing.

Domain Name. The Internet address of a computer on the Internet used in Web site and e-mail addresses. Think of it as a phone number—each computer on the Internet has a unique domain name (for example, www.womenswire.com). Domain names have two or more parts, separated by dots (".").

DNS. The Internet's Domain Name System, a standard which makes it easy to find a particular site if you have its Uniform Resource Locator (URL) or address.

Download. A way to transfer a file from a remote computer to your own computer.

E-Mail (also Electronic Mail). A text mail message that is sent from one Internet user to another. You can attach documents, for example audio and video files, to e-mail messages.

E-Mail Address. When you set up an Internet access account, you receive an e-mail account and a unique e-mail address. You can send and receive e-mail using this account. An e-mail address looks like this: yourname@msn.com.

Emoticon (also Smiley). A group of letters or symbols that form a picture when you look at them with your head turned sideways. These pictures are usually faces used for expressing feeling in an otherwise emotion-free zone : ^). Tilt your head to the side to view.

E-Zine. See Zine.

FAQ. Pronounced "fak," FAQ is an acronym for Frequently Asked Questions, a document that provides answers to commonly asked questions.

File Transfer. The transfer of an electronic file from one computer to another. Files can be transferred using e-mail, floppy disks, or by downloading or uploading.

Flame. A nasty online message.

Forum (also Bulletin Board). A public, text-based conversation area on a Web site or online service where you can post and read messages on a variety of topics. Forums are asynchronous, which means they take place over time, and conversation participants do not have to be at the same place at the same time to engage in conversation.

FTP. File Transfer Protocol is the traditional Internet application for sending or receiving (uploading or downloading) files from your computer to another computer. On the Web, you can just click on a file name to automatically transfer it to your computer.

Home Page. The primary page or entry point of a Web site. The home page usually provides an index or pointers to the information provided on the Web site.

HTML. Hypertext Markup Language is the fundamental programming language of the Web. Web pages are created and designed using HTML.

HTTP. Hypertext Transfer Protocol is the protocol that transports HTML. It's usually seen at the beginning of Web addresses (for example, http://www.women.com), but the most popular Web browsers are set up so that you do not have to type "http://" each time. If you want to go to Women's Wire, you can just type in "women.com".

Hyperlink (also Link or Hot Link). A point-and-click button, icon, or text link that allows surfers to click and link to another page on the same or different Web site anywhere in the world.

Interface. The text, menus, or graphics a computer or online service uses to organize information or communicate.

Internet (also the Net). A network of millions of computers at businesses, universities, government agencies, homes, and libraries connected via phone lines. Individuals hook up to the Internet by making a connection with a computer system that's on the Net—either through an online service, their work or school, a local Internet service provider, or a library or government agency that offers connections.

Internet Service Provider. See Access Provider.

ISDN. Integrated Service Digital Network is a high-bandwidth digital network that moves data over a dial-up digital phone line. A special phone line has to be installed in your home or office for ISDN.

Java. A programming language used to create interactive multimedia content on the Web. You will need to have a Java-capable browser, such as Netscape 3.0 or Internet Explorer 3.0 or a newer version, in order to see Java applications. If you have a Java-enabled browser, the Web comes alive with fun, and sometimes frivolous, animations and interactivity.

Modem. A device that converts computer data into sounds that can be transmitted over telephone lines. Modems can be external (a small box that connects to your computer) or internal (circuitry that is inside your computer).

Multimedia. A catch-all phrase that mainly means the convergence of many kinds of media, including sound, video, text, graphics, and animation.

Newsgroup (also Usenet Newsgroup). A discussion group or forum devoted to talking about a specific topic. Currently there are over 9,000 Usenet newsgroups on the Internet.

Online Service. A proprietary (meaning they develop their own unique software interface) service that offers e-mail accounts, a variety of content, and Internet access for a monthly subscription fee (examples are America Online and CompuServe).

Plug-in. Programs running inside your browser that help you view multimedia files or run special programs. Plug-ins are not built into browsers, so you must download them.

Protocol. Communications rules that help different kinds of computers communicate with each other and share data.

QuickTime. A program developed by Apple Computer that allows you to view video clips on the Web. Built into most Macintosh computers, QuickTime can be downloaded and used to play movies on PCs, too.

Search Engines. Online search tools designed to help you find sites of interest on the Web (for example, Alta Vista and Hot Bot). These sites offer keyword searching of the entire Web.

Shareware. Software provided free on the Internet. You need to download it to your computer in order to use it.

Smiley. See Emoticon.

Snail Mail. A humorous term used by people online to refer to the U.S. postal mail because it is so much slower than e-mail.

Spam. An unsolicited sales pitch posted to an online forum or sent via e-mail to many people at the same time.

T1. A high-speed (1.54 megabits/second) connection to the Internet that stays live all the time so that you don't have to dial in to use it. A type of connection provided by some workplaces to connect employees to the Internet.

TCP/IP. Transmission Control Protocol/Internet Protocol, the common platform or language of the Internet, which allows computers on the Internet to communicate with each other.

Upload. To transfer a file from your computer to a remote computer. For example, you can send someone a picture by uploading it to their server or attaching it to an e-mail you are sending to them.

URL (also Web Address). Uniform Resource Locator is a unique online address that allows Internet users to access a Web site by entering the address. A URL looks like this: http://www.women.com.

Usenet Newsgroup. See Newsgroup.

Web Site. A place or stop on the World Wide Web where a company, individual, or organization posts information.

World Wide Web (also the Net, the Web, WWW). The multimedia portion of the Internet. Technically speaking, a protocol to present information through the Internet in a graphical format. The Web is composed of thousands of unique Web sites that have text, graphic, audio, video, and computer programming capabilities.

Yahoo. A popular online search engine and directory on the World Wide Web.

Zine (also E-Zine). Short for "fanzine" or "magazine," e-zines are online magazines produced by an individual or small group of people, often done for fun or personal reasons rather than to make a profit. Zines tend to be irreverent, bizarre, or esoteric.

Credits

Index

A

A&E Classroom 155
Abacab 329
Abbington Village 358
ABC Radio Net 122
Aboriculture Trees & Timber 314
Abortion & Reproductive Rights Internet Resources 43
About Work 69
Above & Beyond—The Tall and All Mall 358
Above the Unicorn 96
Academic Careers Information Database 69
Access Market Square 358
Accurate Eye 413
Achoo 21
ACLU 140
ACME Pet 167
Acme Pet 318
Acronym and Abbreviations List 422
Acronyms 422
Action Girl's Guide to Female Figures 102, 315
Action on Smoking and Health 389
Acupuncture.com 39
Ada Project 78, 391
Addicted to Noise 107
Addicted to Stuff 111
Adidas Webzine 210
Adolescence Directory Online 166
Adopt A Gorilla 401
Adoptees Mailing List 169
Adoption: Assistance, Information, Support 169
Adoption Network 169
Adult Distance Education Internet Surf Shack 255
Advancing Women 68
Adventures in Education 239
Advertising and Media Jobs Page 61
Advocat 125
Aerobics! 35
Aesop's Fables 154
Affairs of the Net 97
AFL-CIO 66
Africa News Service 125
Africa Online 398
AfriNet 398
After the Affair 194
Agenda Online 190
Aging and Aging Parents Index 171
AGropolis 314
AIDS in Mexico 28
Airwalk Online 210
Aisle Say 89
AJR JobLink 62
Al-Anon and Alateen 394
Aldo Negri Fashion 206

Alert-IPO 267
All About Health Magazine 17
All About Kids 149
All Business Network 283
All-Internet Shopping Directory 358
All Politics 139
All Things Automotive Directory 366
Almanac of American Politics 424
alt.culture 87
ALT.DAYS 97
Alt.Spam FAQ 335
Altamira Investment Services 274
AltaVista 410, 412
Alternative Dictionaries 420
Alzheimer Page 29
Amateur Radio 317
Amazing Story of Kudzu 313
Amazon Books 90
Amazon City Professional District 80
Amazon.Com 183
Amazon.com Books 369
American Academy of Child & Adolescent Psychiatry 46, 148
American Association of Botanical Gardens and Arboreta 311
American Association of Individual Investors (AAII) 273
American Association of Pediatrics 147
American Association of University Women 241, 395
American Bar Association 132
American Cancer Society 26
American Childcare Solutions 151
American Demographics 433
American Horticultural Society 311
American Humanist Association-Wedding Section 193
American Individual Magazine and Coffeehouse 284
American Institute for Cancer Research 38
American Kennel Club 320
American Library Association 248
American Medical Womens' Association 395
American Physiological Society Job Listings 63
American Red Cross 167, 386
American Savings Education Center (ASEC) 280
American Singles 187
American Society of Interior Designers 296
American Stock Exchange 268
American War Library 246
Americans with Disabilities Act Document Center 424
America's Best! 358
America's Employers 53
America's Job Bank 53
AMMA Therapy 40
Amnesty International 388
Amoreee! 183
Andersen Consulting 346, 361
Andrew and Jackie's Koi and Pond Page 314
Andromeda Books and Gifts 369
ANGLE 337
Angelnet 40
Angel of Fashion 219
Animal Rights Resource Site 401
Ansel Adams: Fait Lux 296
Answers 171
Antique Alley's Dealers 298
Antique Gallery 297
A.P.C. 354
Apparel and Textile Network 222
ApparelNet 219
Apple Education 252
Apple User Groups 327

Appraisal Institute 281
AquaLink 315
Arbor Communications—Guide to Nutrition Resources 36
Arc 44, 152, 395
Archeus-Work search resources 54
Architecture and Building Net Resources 297
Arent Fox 131
Arlene Wilson Models 214
Armani Exchange 209
Art Crimes 86
ArtNet 295
ArtSource 297
Asahi Shimbun 125
Asia, Inc. 287
Asian Arts 86
Asian-American Resources 397
Asiannet 397
Asia One 120
Asia OnLine 397
Ask an Oral Maxillofacial Surgeon 17
Ask CoverGirl 218
Ask Dr. Math 231
Ask Dr. Tracy 178
AskERIC Virtual Library 232
Ask NOAH About Health 17
ASPCA/NAPCC 319
Asperger's Syndrome Resources 25
Associated Press Wire Service 124
Association for Support of Graduate Students 240
Association of Brewers Glossary 424
Association of Computer User Groups (APCUG) Home Page 329
Association of Women Industrial Designers 78
As the Web Turns 97
Astrology Zone by Susan Miller 110
Astronomy and Space on the Internet 101
Atlanta Journal-Constitution 126
Atlanta Reproductive Health Center 42, 276
Atlantic Monthly 103, 120
@mode 200
Attorney Net 136
Audiobooks.com 370
AudioNet 124
Aunt Annie's Craft page 163
Auntie Lois 110
Aupair JobMatch Service 63
Australian National Botanic Gardens 312
Authoritative Matchmaker 185
Autism Society of America 152
Auto-By-Tel 366
AutoMall 366
Automobile Leasing 277
AutoNetwork 366
Autorow 367
AutoSite 367
AutoWeb Interactive 367
Avant Garde: A Virtual Marketplace 358
Aveda 217
Avon 217
Avon's Breast Cancer Awareness Crusade 390
A.Word.A.Day 156

B

Babyonline 147
Baker Institute for Public Policy 142
Balance Fitness Magazine 34
Balducci's 372
BAMTA Job Bank 53
Banca della Svizzera Italiana 278
BangkokNet-Thai Models and Celebrities 212
Bank of Montreal 282
Barbara's News Researcher Graffiti Page 414
Barbizon International Schools of Modeling 212

Barnard College 241
Barneys New York 356
Barra 263
Barron's Online 286
Bartlett's Familiar Quotations 423
Basic Rules for Cats Who Have a House to Run 320
Bay's Auction Web 365
BBC 123
Beakman's Electric Motor 156, 231
Beatrice's Web Guide 411
BeautyLink 214
BeautyNet 215
Beautyspot 215
BeautyTech 215
BeautyWorks 215
Beertown 299
Beginner's Guide to HTML 339
BeHome 295
Bereavment and Hospice Support Netline 396
Bergen Record 128
Berkeley Earth Sciences & Map Libraries 246
Berkshire Online 266
Bermuda Weather Page 129
BERNSHAW 204
Berskerkistan 122
Best Bets from the Net 54
Best Jobs USA 56
Best Video 375
Better Business Bureau 373, 405
Better Business Bureau Web Server 276, 425
Bibliographic Formats for Citing Electronic Information 254
BigBook 417
Big Brothers and Sisters of America 387
Big Busy House 153
Bigfoot 415
Big Top Productions 254
Big Yellow 416
Bill's Library 432
Biographies of Women Mathematicians 243
BioTech 238
Bipolar Disorders: Pendulum Resources 44
Bird Dog News 318
Bitch 106
BitStreet Internet 337
BitWitch Oracle 335
Biz 93
BizCom '96 Love and Relationship Resources 178
BizWeb 358, 417
BizWomen 78, 287
Bjorn's Guide to Philosophy 87
Black & Decker 294
Black Enterprise 284
Blind Children's Center 231
Blind Date on the Net 184
Blind Links 30
Bloomberg News 285
Bloomberg News Radio 286
blue dot 87
Blue Highway 108
Blue Note 108
BMUG Online 327
Bobbi Brown Cosmetics Online 218
Bobbin Blenheim Online 222
Body Electric 29
Body Project 34
Body Shop 218
BodyFX 215
Bonsai 311
Book of Bitterness 111, 177
Book Stacks 370
Book Stacks Unlimited 296
Book Stacks Unlimited, Inc. 90
Books That Work 292

BookWire 90, 370
Borders on the Web 370
Boss Models 212
Boston Globe 125
Branch Mall 358
Brazzil 103
Breast Cancer Information Clearinghouse 27
Breast Cancer Roundtable 26
Breastfeeding Page 147
Breeders Guide 320
Breeds of Livestock 428
Breed Specifics FAQ 321
Brentwood 96
Brian's Harley-Davidson/Buell 367
Bridal Mag 190
BridalNet 191
Bride Wore 193
Briefing 285
Britannica Online 423
Brooklyn Botanical Garden 312
Brookstone 376
Browse the Federal Tax Code 272
BrowserCaps 342
BSA CareerMart 56
Buckingham Greenery, Inc. 313
Buffalo Boots 210
Building Blocks to Reading 228
Build Your Own PC 324
Bureau of Economic Analysis 430
Bureau of Labor Statistics 433
Bureau of Labor Statistics home page 66
Burrito Page 305
Busch Gardens/Sea World Animal Resource Information 159
Business and Workplace Briefs—Nolo Press 67
Business Incorporating Guide 77
Business Job Finder 64
Business Page 282
Business Plan 77
Business Questions and Answers 70
Business Resource Center 283
BusinessWeek 286
Business Wire 286
Business Women's Network 79
Busy Teachers' Web Site K-12 232
Butterfly Glossary 334
Buzz Online 103

C

Cafe Los Negroes 299
Calendar 428
Calendar Conversions 428
California Culinary Academy's Online SPICE 308
California School-to-Career Information System 68
CaliforniaMart 222
Calvin and Hobbes Gallery 110
Camera Nazionale della Moda Italiana 223
Campus Travel 380
Campus Voice: The College Site 240
Canada NetPages 418
Canada/British Columbia Business Service Centre 283
Canadian Broadcasting Corporation (CBC) 123
Canadian Press 118
CancerGuide 28
Cape Breton Pictorial Cookbook 309
CAPEX Capital Exchange, Inc. 282
Captain Morgan CyberShip 301
Career Alternatives for Art Historians 71
Career and Resume Management for the 21st Century 55
Career Atlas for the Road 74
Careerfile 61
Career Mosaic 52

CareerNet's Career Resource Center 55
Careers On Line 59
CareerPath 57
Career Plan for Fiction Writers 71
Career Search-Jobs Online 54
Careers in Architecture 70
Career Toolbox 60
CareerWeb 57
Careers—Where to Go to Make Your Dough 56
Caregiver Survivor Resources 29
Carlos' Coloring Book 161
Carol Hurst's Children Literature 155
CARRIE: An Electronic Library 431
Cars @ Cost 367
Cartoon Network 161
Casey's Snow Day Reverse Dictionary (and Guru) 421
CASO 255
Catapult 54
Cat Fanciers 317
Cato Institute 141
Cats, Cats, & More Cats 318
Caviar & Caviar, Ltd. 304
CBS News 122
CD Now 375
CDworld 375
CEA Science Education Home Page 236
CEARCH: Cisco Educational Archive 250
Celebration of Women Writers 241
Celestial Seasonings 372
Center for Democracy and Technology 136
Center for Financial Well-Being 277
Center for Labor Research and Education Gopher Menu 65
Center for the American Woman and Politics 141
Center on Education and Work 72
Centers for Disease Control National AIDS Clearinghouse 26
Central Source Yellow Pages 418
Centre for the Easily Amused 111
Centripedus Center 341
Challenger Center for Space Science Education 233
Chanel 205
Charles Schwab Online 265
Charlotte.com 126
Chase Tavern Farm Alpacas 356
Cheesenet 304
Chicago Board of Trade 266
Chicago Board Options Exchange 262
Chicago-Kent College of Law 133
Chicago Mercantile Exchange 266
Chicago Tribune 126
Chicana Feminist Home Page 398
Child Quest International 169
Childbirth.org 146
Children and Adults with Attention Deficit Disorders 25
Children with Diabetes 153
Children's Defense Fund 391
Children's Literature Web Guide 154
Children's Literature-Fairrosa Cyber-Library 155
Children's Museum of Indianapolis 158
Children's Software Company 330
Chilegod 305
China the Beautiful 88
Chiphead Harry Daily Soap 97
Chiropractic Online Today 39
Christian Coalition 142
Christian Science Monitor 125
Chronic Illnet 29
CIA Publications 425
CIA World Fact Book 131
Cigar Journal 180

Citation Guide 137
Cizitens Against Government Waste (Spending) 405
Clambake Celebrations 300
ClariNet News 125
Classic Automobiles, Inc. 368
Classic Car Source 367
Classical Net 107
Classique Image 301
Classmates 415
Cliff's Notes 252
Clinique 218
Clock Chipping 327
Clothestime 356
Club Girl Tech 392
c|net 269
CNN 122
CNN Style 203
CNNfn 285
Coalition for Positive Sexuality 43
Coalition for Positive Sexuality—Sex-Education for Teens 42
Coalition of Silicone Survivors 388
Cockroach World 320
Cocktail 301
Coffee a GoGo 301
Cold Fusion 344
Collaborative Bibliography of Women in Philosophy 243
Collector Link 316
Collector's Coin Universe 315
College and Career Programs for Deaf Students 30
College and University Home Pages 237
College Board Online 239
College Grad Job Hunter 72
College Guides and Aid Home Page 244
CollegeNet 240
Collegian Fashionable Decor 296
Color Landform Atlas of the United States 435
ComFind 418
Commercial Site Index 417
Common Gateway Interface 344
Compaq Computer Corp. 325
Complete Works of William Shakespeare 92
Computer Currents Interactive 351
Computer Professionals For Social Responsibility 395
Concord Coalition 142
Conde Nast Publications, Ltd. 198
Congenital Heart Disease Resource Page 28
Congressional E-mail Directory 425
Conscious Singles Connection and The Single Life 187
Conservation International 313
Consortium 119
Consumer Information Catalog: Money 274
Consumer Information Center 405
Consumer Law Page 133
Consumer Mortgage Information Network 281
Consumer Prices and Price Indexes 279
Consumer Products Safety Commission 404
Consumer World 275
Container Store 293
Contract Employment Weekly 63
Cook's Garden 311
Cookin With Frito-Lay 308
Cool Central 337
Cool School Tools 232
Cool Site of the Day 338
Cool Works 62
CoolSchool 337
Copycat Recipes 304
Copyright and Netiquette Primer 336
Copyright Web Site 133
Corey's MacOS Page 326

Cornell Theory Math and Science Gateway 233
Cornucopia! 302
Corporate Financials Online 269
Corporation for Public Broadcasting 122
Cosmo 198
Cosmopolitan (Italian edition) 198
Couch 177
Counterpoint 248
Court Locator Service 133
Court TV 133
Cow Sounds 103
Cracks in the Web 96
CraftNet Village 316
Crayola 162
Crayon 299
CreatAbiliTOYS 114
Creative Investment Research 261
Credit Card Network 276
Crescendo Cove 97
Crestar Student Lending 276
Cretins, Inc. 96
Crisp 104
Cruel Site of the Day 111
C-Span 139
Cult of Macintosh 327
Culture Zone 200
Cupcake 104
Cupid's Cove CityLink 180
Cupid's Network, Inc. 187
Currency Converter 424
CU-SeeMe Event Guide 189
CyberAngels 406
Cybercash 361
CyberDance: Ballet on the Net 89
Cyberdiet 36
CyberDyne CS Limited 63
Cybergrass 108
Cybergrrl 411
Cyberhomes 281
CyberKids 164
Cybermad 113
CyberMom 150
Cyber Patrol 163
Cyber Psychic 48
Cyber-Romance 101 175
Cyberschool Magazine 233
CyberShop 359
Cybersitter 163
Cyberspace Field of Dreams 81
Cyberspace Hospital 18
Cyberspace Middle School 233
Cyberspace TeleMedical Office 21
Cyberteens 165
CyberTown 359
Cyndi's Catalog of Gardening Catalogs 310
Cyrano server 181

D

Daily Buzz 338
Daily Muse 121
Daily Record 127
Dallas Morning News 128
Dan's Poker Dictionary 421
Dance Online 89
DanceScape 89
Dast Library of Photography 102
Date Net 184
DaveNet: 24 Hours of Democracy 350
Dave's Web of Lies 111
David Baldwin's Trauma Info Pages 45
David Slack's Automatic Wedding Speech Writer 190
Daycare page 151
Dead Beat Victims Voice 170

Deaf World Web 152
DealerNet 368
Dear Doc… 22
Definitive Guide to Relationships 175
Deja News 410
Deloitte & Touche Online 277
DeltaPoint 344
DeMOCKracy 138
Democracy and Human Rights in the Americas 397
Democratic Party 140
Democratic Socialists of America Home Page 142
Demography & Population Studies from the Virtual Library 433
Depression 46
Depression FAQ 47
Derek's Free Stuff Page 378
Designercity 200
Detroit News 204
Devil's Dictionary by Ambrose Bierce 420
Diabetes Homepage 24
Diary of a Madwoman in the Attic 97
Diesel Jeans 208
DigiCrime 346
Dilbert Zone 110
Dimension X, Inc. 341
Dinner Co-Op 303
Diner's Grapevine 106
Diotima 88
Diotima: Materials for the Study of Women and Gender in the Ancient World 242
Directorate of Time 429
Disability Resources from Evan Kemp Associates 30
Dischord 113
Discovery Channel Online 98
Diseases & Disorders 24
Disney 160
Disney World 160
Disney.com 115
Diversity Links for Women and Minorities 397
Divorce Helpline Webworks 169
Divorce home page 169
Divorce Online 170
Divorce Page 136
Docent's Tour of Salvador Dali Resources 86
Doc Love 178
Dr. Bob's Virtual En-psych-lopedia 45
Dr. Frank Boehm's Essays 18
Dr. Grohol's Mental Health Page 44
Dr. Pribut's Running Injuries Page 35
Dr. Ruth's SexNet 42
Dog Fanciers 317
Dog-Play: Dog Links to Dog Links 276
Dolce Vita 201
Dollar Stretcher 278
Dollhouse 205
Donna Karan 205
Don't Miss Out: A Student's Guide to Financial Aid 244
Doonesbury Electronic Town Hall 108
Dorktionary 420
Dorothy Parker Page 91
Douglas Gerlach's Invest-o-rama 262
Dow Jones Business Information Services 288
Dragonfly Toy Company 253
Dreamers Hobbies 317
DreamLink 47
duJour.com 112
Duke University Healthy Devil On-Line 22
D.Y.K.E. 186
Dyke Street: A Soap 95
Dyke's World 186

E

Eagle Express Flowers 376

Earth Watch Weather On Demand 130
EarthWatch 402
East Village 95
Easter Egg Archive 329
easySABRE 380
Eating Disorders Shared Awareness 38
eBay Auction Web 298
ecash 373
Economic Conversion Information Exchange 68
Economist 120
Eco-Rating International 265
Eddie Bauer 357
Edelbrock Performance Products 368
Editor & Publisher 128
EdLinks 233
Education Place 233
Educational Marketing International 255
Educational Policy Analysis Archives 249
Educational Software Institute 253
Educom 250
EdWeb 250
Edwin Jeans 357
EE-Link 251
EFFWeb 345
80s Server 114
Eldercare and the Modem-Two Frontiers 171
ElderCare Help page 171
Eldercare Help Page 400
Eldercare Locator 170
Eldercare Web 170
Elderhostel Home Page 400
ElectraPages 417
Electric Library 432
Electronic Archives for Teaching the American Literatures 251
Electronic Library: University of Waterloo 432
Electronic Orchid Greenhouse 311
Electronic Privacy Information Center 133
Electronics Manufacturers on the Net 329
Elements of Style 102
Elite Models 212
Elle 198
Elle International 199
eMall 359
EMILY's List 141
Empire Mall 359
Employee Relations Web Picks 65
Employment Opportunities in Wildlife and Fisheries Science 63
Empowerment Zones and Enterprise Communities 284
Emusic 375
Encyclopedia of Women's History 241
Endometriosis Information and Links 29
Energy Information Administration 430
English Server 88
Enterprise Profit Ability 77
Entertainment Recruiting Network 65
Entertainment Weekly 105
Entrepreneurial Edge Online 283
Entrepreneurs on the Web 284
EnviroLink Network 402
Environment Canada 130
Environmental Careers Organization 71
Environmental Education Network 236
Epicurious 356
Epicurious Food 302
Erick's Guide to Medical School Admissions 238
eShop Plaza 359
ESP 415
E-Span 56
Esperfonto 341
Esprit 208
Esquire 199

Ethical Business 264
ethicalBusiness 417
Ethnologue Database 419
E-TRADE 267
E-Trust 373
European Travel Network 381
Everton's Guide to Genealogy on the World Wide Web 437
Excite 410
Exec-u-Net 59
Exotic Automobile Showroom 368
Experts.Com 394
Exploratorium 158
Exploring Your Future in Math & Science 231
Express 356
Extreme Resume Drop 60

F

FAA Office of System Safety 430
Faces 94
FAD Megazine 201
Fairview Health System 171
Fake Out! 158
Families-Priority 1 166
Family Channel: FamFun 161
Family.com 151
Family Law News 170
Family Planet 149
Family Violence Prevention Fund 390
Famous Marriages 194
Farm Direct Marketplace 372
Fashion Beauty Internet Association—FBIA 223
Fashion Biz 219
Fashion Careers of California College 219
Fashion Group International 223
Fashion Icon 201
Fashion Institute of Design & Merchandising 220
Fashion Institute of Technology 220
Fashion Internet 201
Fashion Live 201
Fashion Net 201
Fashion Online 202
Fashion TV 204
Fashion UK 202
fashionfirst 201
FashionLink Hong Kong 219
Fashionmall.com 211
FashionWeb UK 202
fastWEB 244
Fatfree: The Low Fat Vegetarian Archive 305
Fathering Magazine 149
FatherNet 150
Fearless 405
FECInfo 433
Federal Election Commission 143
Federal Emergency Management Agency 404
Federal Trade Commission 405
FedWorld via Telnet 60
Feed 427
Fem*Mass 391
Female Bodybuilders 33
Feminist Career Center 58
Feminist Majority Foundation 141
Feminist.com career page 77
Ferndale 97
Ferret Central 318
FERTILITEXT 43
Fidelity Investments 270
Field Museum of Natural History 158
50 Greatest Conspiracies of All Time—Online 114
54 Ways to Help the Homeless 390
Fight Crime: Invest in Kids! 406
FILL: Financial Information Link Library 264
Film.com 93

Film Festivals Server 94
FilmZone 93
FinanCenter 275
FinanceHub 282
Finance Wat.ch 261
Financial Aid Information 246
Financial Aid Information Page 396
Financial News Center 285
Financial Players Center 273
Financial Scandals 287
Financial Services Technology Consortium 278
Financial Times 128
Financial Times Group 286
FINdex 263
Find Your Rep 404
First Aid Online 167
1st in Flowers! 313
First Lesbian Marriage in Latvia 185
First Union Corp. 278
First Virtual 373
firstVIEW 206
FishNet 160
Fitness Partner Connection Jumpsite 34
Flea News 318
Flora of Europe 313
Floriculture and Ornamental Horticulture 311
Florida Wildflower Page 312
Flower Stop 181
Flying Solo 169
Fodor's 106
FollyWorld 97
Food and Nutrition Information Center 37
FOODplex! 303
Food Tales 97
Food TV 308
FoodWine.Com 303
Foolproof Guide to Making Any Woman Your Platonic Friend 176
Forbes Magazine 288
Foreign Affairs 121
Foreign Exchange Rates 424
Foreign Report 139
Fortune 286
Foundation for Women's Health 390
Four 11 76
475 Madison Avenue 96
Foxy 104
Franchise Handbook 77
Franchise Source 284
Frank Lloyd Wright Page 294
Frank Potter's Science Gems 231
Franklin Institute of Science Museum 158
Free Burma 121
Freedom Forum First Amendment Center 136
Freelance On-line 62
Freezone 164
French Elle 199
Friends & Lovers 174
Friends and Partners 189
From Now On 251
From Primitives to Zen 428
From the Heart 179
FTD Online 376
Fuji Publishing Group Cigar Page 379
Fulbright Scholar Program 243
Fun Stuff 157
Fund Library 271
Furniture Direct 296
Fur Online 219
Futures Magazine 267

G

Galactic User Group 331

Galaxy 410
Gallery of Interactive Geometry 236
Gallup Organization 433
Games at Road to Nowhere 112
Games Domain 157
Games Kids Play 157
Gard's Laws on Love 176
Garden Escapes 310
Garden Gate 310
Gardening Web Directory 101
GardenNet 310
Garriga's WWWorld... Beyond the Black Stump 413
Gary-Chicago-Milwaukee Corridor Transportation Information Center 436
Gate 127
Gay and Lesbian Alliance Against Defamation 399
Gay Daze 95
gay.guide New York 186
GaySource 185
Geek Cereal 95
Gender Issues at Work: Office Romance 175
Gender-Free Pronoun FAQ 256
Genealogy Dictionary 437
Genealogy Home Page 437
Genealogy on the World Wide Web 437
Genealogy Toolbox 437
Genealogy's Most Wanted 437
Generation War 96
Geoffrey B. Small 207
Geographic Nameserver 435
George Magazine 139
George Smith 295
GeroWeb 31
Get a Job! 64
Get Met on the Net 183
Getting Past Go: A Survival Guide for College Graduates 58
Gianni Versace 207
Giesswein 208
Gigaplex! 359
GI Joe—Action Soldier 316
Gingerbread House 307
Girl Power 391
Girl's World 189
Girls on Film 331
GlamOrama Wedding Chapel 192
Glaucoma Research Foundation 29
Global Campus 255
Global Fund for Women 387
Global Internet News Agency (GINA) 349
Global Law Net 135
GlobalMedic 17
GlobalNet's Latin American Career Center 60
Global SchoolNet Foundation 249
Global Vision, Africa News 123
Godiva 307
Golf Online 32
Good Health Web 16
Good Stuff Cheap 360
Good Works—A Guide to Social Change Careers 63
Gourmet Connection E-Zine 302
Gourmet Today 372
Government Documents 247
Government Information Sharing Project 429
Government Printing Office Access—UCSD 430
GPO Access on the Web 429
Grammar and Style Notes 419
GrantsWeb 244
GrapeJam 97
Grapes 372
Great American Beer Club 301
Great Globe Gallery 435
Greek Pages 240
Green Market 360

GreenMoney Online Guide 261
Greenpeace International 401
Greyhound Friends 319
Grimm's Fairy Tales 154
Grouchy Cafe 302
Gryphon House Books, Inc. 253
GTE SuperPages 418
Guerrilla Girls 388
Guess? 208
Gumbo Pages 304
gURL 104
Gymn Forum 32

H

Habitat for Humanity 386
HairNet 216
Hall of Malls 360
Ham Radio Outlet 317
Hands on Children Museum 159
Handyman Hints 293
Hanen Early Language Program 231
Hangman 157
Happy Household Pet Club 317
Happy Puppy 157
Hard@Work 65
Harmony Central 102
HarperCollins Publishers 370
Hartford Courant Daily Horoscopes 110
Harvard AIDS Institute 26
Harvard Business School 70
Harvard Espresso Company 372
Harvard Medical School Department of Radiology 27
Haunted Home Page 165
Hawaii Visitor Bureau 191
Headbooks Online 212
Health and Retirement Study (HRS) 30
HealthAtoZ 19
HealthCraze! 39
Health Ink 20
Healthline Publishing, Inc. 17
Healthtouch 20
Health Trek 360
Healthwise 18
Healthy Choice Home Page 307
Healthy Flying with Diana Fairechild 19
Healthy Office 293
Heart 58
Heart Hotel 96
Heart Information Network 25
HearthNet 294
Hedgehog's Classroom Resources 230
Help Wanted 60
Henry Neeman's Dance Hotlist 88
HEPROC 249
Herbed Cheese Pretzels 304
HerbNET 39
Heritage Foundation 143
Herring.com 73
High Technology Careers Magazine 62
Highway One Classic Autos 368
Hiking and Walking Homepage 34
Hispanic Magazine 121
History Buff's Reference Library 247
History Channel Classroom 234
HIV InfoWeb 26
H-Net: Humanities Online 249
Hobby Stores on the Net 379
Hobby World of Montreal 379
Holistic Internet Resources 40
Hollywood Online 93
Holt Report Index 266
HomeArts 294
HomeArts, Network—Runway 199

Home Business Solutions 284
Homebuyers Fair 298
Home Education Resource Center 253
Home Furnishing Netquarters 296
Home of the H$H Investment Club 268
HomeNet 298
Home Office Design 294
Homeopathy Home Page 38
Homeowner's Finance Center 280
Home Page for Calendar Reform 428
Homes and Land Electronic Magazine 281
HomeScout 281
HomeSell 298
Hometimes 292
Honeymoon Magazine 193
Honeymoons.com 193
Hoover's Online 265
Horse Country 318
Hospitality Net Virtual Job Exchange 80
Hot Rods Worldwide 368
Hot Wired 103
HotBot 410
Hotflash Jobs! 63
Hotwired 356
HotWired Network 347
Hound Dog Fashions 320
Housepainting FAQ 309
How Do They Do That With HTML? 342
How Far Is It? 436
How to Date a Millionaire 184
How to Select An Internet Service Provider 332
How to Talk New Age 41
How to Toilet Train Your Cat FAQs 317
Howard Rheingold's Brainstorms 347
HR Headquarters 77
HSTM Biographical Dictionary 421
HTML Bad Style Pages 343
HTMLscript 342
HTML Validation Service 340
HTML: Working and Background Materials 344
Hugh's Mortgage and Financial Calculators 274
Human Languages Page 421
Human Rights Campaign 400
Human Rights Web 388
HumorNet UK 111
HungerWeb 390
Hurricane Home Page 130
Hypermode 202
Hyperstand 339
Hypnotica Home Page 48

I

ICA Gem Site 223
I Ching 40
ICLnet: Institute for Christian Leadership 256
Ida Ferri (Italy) 221
Idea Cafe 73
IEEE Computer Society 328
Igloo 186
IMAGE 212
iMall 360
Impact Online 392
I Need My Chocolate 307
In, Around and Online 350
In Loving Memory 46
Inc. Online 282
InContext Systems 342
Incredible Art Department 235
Indesign 297
Indian River Gift Fruit Company 372
Indiana University School of Law 131
Infinite Ink's Directory 335
infoPost 360
InforM Women's Studies Database 241

Information Collection 164
Information on Academic Careers and Academic Life 249
Infoseek 411
InfoSpace 415
Inkspot 102
Innovation Network 351
Innovations Gift Point 360
Insider Watch 262
Institute of Chinese Medicine 40
In-StyleWorks Online 223
Insurance Career Center 71
Intel Corporation 324
Intellicast Weather 128
IntelliMatch Online Career Services 57
Interactive Age 349
Interactive ASL & Braille Guide 421
Interactive Creativity: Funny People Puppets 164
Interactive Ego Booster 179
Interactive Frog Dissection 234
Interactive Gourmet 374
Interactive Media Association 339
Interactive Pregnancy Calendar 146
Interbiznet 54
Intercamp: Internet Summer Camp Directory and Resource 160
InterFace 328
InterGo and KinderGuard 163
Interleaf, Inc. 344
Internal Revenue Service Digital Daily 272
International Association for Financial Planning (IAFP) 280
International Directory of Women Web Designers 78
International Finance Encyclopaedia 266
International Hearts Club 184
International Herald Tribune 128
International Myeloma Foundation 28
International Paralympic Committee 32
International Real Estate Directory and News 280
International Small Business Consortium 282
Internet @ddress.finder 415
Internet Antique Shop 309
Internet Audit Bureau 342
Internet Bankruptcy Library 276
Internet Book Shop 370
Internet Braille Wizard Access 20/20 422
Internet Chef 303
Internet Cigar Group 316
Internet College Exchange 240
Internet Conservative Network 139
Internet Crime Archives 95
Internet for Kids 153
Internet for the Fine Arts 297
Internet Guide to Hostelling 100
Internet Headquarters for Student Governments 237
Internet Help Desk 334
Internet Herald—The Generation X Webzine 351
Internet Magazine 349
Internet Mall 362
Internet Movie Database 92
Internet NonProfit Center 396
Internet Personals 183
Internet Resource Center 332
Internet Resources for Women's Legal and Public Policy Information 243
Internet Securities 266
Internet Shopping Network 362
Internet Shopping Outlet 362
Internet Shortcuts by CRE8 326
Internet Travel Network 381
Internet Underground Music Archive 107
Internet Underground Online 105

Inter-Quote 269
Intertain.com Internet Bookstore 371
Invention Dimension 234
Investigative Reporters & Editors 118
Investment Brokerages Guide 265
Investment Research 270
Investment Wizard from Online Intelligence 261
Investor Channel 269
Investor's Network 260
Investors Edge 262
IPL Youth Division 155
Isis 87
ISO Country Codes 416
Italian Greyhound Club of America 318
I Thee Web 192
i3 297
It's My Future 72

J

Jackpot! What to Do Before and After You Win Lottery 278
Jane Austen Information Page 91
Janell Beals Design 354
Jane's Brain Page 48
Jane's Information Group 425
Japanese Green Tea 301
Jargon File 3.2.0 425
JASON Project 156
Java Jabber 96
Java: Programming for the Internet 341
JavaWorld 341
Jazz Central Station 108
J.C. Penney 354
Jellinek's Baby Name Chooser 147
Jerusalem Post 126
jhanebarnes.com 204
Jimbo's Big Book of Dating 175
Jim Brain's Commodore Home Page 324
Job-Banker 60
JobCenter 57
Jobs.cz 65
JobHunt 53
Job Search Process 55
Job Seekers Go Online for an Edge on the Competition 59
Jobs in Academe 61
JobSmart 59
Jobtrak 55
Job Web 69
Joe Boxer 208
Joe's Amazing Relationship Problem Solver 111
Jogle's Favorite Theatre Related Resources 90
John Casablancas Modeling and Career Centers 212
John Labovitz's e-zine list 105
John's Word Search Puzzles 158
Jonah Weiland's Comic Book Resources 109
Joseph Wu's Origami page 102
Journal of a Short-Timer 96
Journals and Newspapers 120
Journey to Love 178
J.P. Morgan 263
Jumbo! 329
Juno—Free Internet E-mail 332
Justin's Links from the Underground 427

K

Kabbalah Now 40
Kabuki for Everyone 90
Kakasarian: Queer Resources for Filipinos 186
Kansas Mentor Project 70
Kanter Auto Products 369
Kaplan Educational Centers 252
Kaplan's Muskrat Love 181
Kapow 96

Kassandra Project 243
Keepers of Lists 111
Keirsey Temperament Sorter 112
Keypals International 235
K-5 Cybertrail 231
KidLink 166
Kid Safety 148
Kid Source OnLine 168
KidsCom 153
Kids Crafts 162
Kids Health-Children's Health and Parenting Info 167
Kid World 164
KinderGarden 156
Kiplinger Online 263
Kneenbec River Company 318
Knight-Ridder Information Services 425
Knowledge Adventure 253
Knowledge Adventure Encyclopedia 423
KOOKAI 208
Kristen's Unofficial Play-Doh Page 162

L

LaborWeb 394
La Leche League International Home Page 43
Lamb Chop's Play Along 162
LA Models 213
Lancôme 218
Land of Oz 110
Language and Culture Center 254
Language in the Judicial Process 135
Largest Pet Related Link Spots 319
Latino Link 397
Latino Web 119
Latin World 397
Laughingbirds Mega Tips: Cleaning Tips 294
Law Employment Center 72
LawInfo 135
Law Journal EXTRA! 137
LAWLinks 431
Law School Dot Com 238
Law Student Web 131
Law Talk 131
Lawyers Cooperative Publishing 136
LDS Friends Worldwide 184
League of Conservation Voters 403
League of Women Voters 140
'Lectric Law Library 133, 431
Lee Jeans 209
Legal Aid for Abused Women 394
Legal Information Institute 66
LeisureWeb 381
Lesbian Mothers Support Society 399
Le Tip 80
Letter of the Law 135
Letters from Abroad 96
Levi's 208
Library of Congress 246
LibraryWeb: Columbia University Libraries WWW Information System 247
Life 121
Life Education Network 396
LifeMatters 194
LifeNet 274
Lifetime Online 98
Lighthouse Depot 317
LingWhat? 422
Lipstick Page 218
List 332
List of Dictionaries 422
Literal Lies 177
Literary Kicks 92
Living Home 309
L. L. Bean 355

Local Times Around the World—Asia & Australia 130
Loci 237
LOLU 255
Lombard Institutional Brokerage 269
London College of Fashion 221
London Mall 362
Lonely Planet 100
Longevity Game 22
Look On-Line 202
LookupUSA 418
L'Oreal 218
Loser Living Upstairs 97
Los Negroes Café 113
Lost Friends Center 396
Louis Vuitton 211
Love and Relationships 181
Love Blender 179
Loveplex 179
LoveSearch 184
Lovesongs 180
Love Test 179
Lowe's Home Improvement Page 309
Lucidcafe 341
Lucy Lipps 178
Lumiere 202
Lurker Files 96
Lycos 410
Lycos Top 5% 336

M

Mac Central 327
Mac Internet Helpers 334
Macmillan Publishing USA Information SuperLibrary 371
Macromedia, Inc. 339
Mac Today Online 327
MacWeek Online 328
Macy's 355
Madeleine Vionnet 207
Mad Libs 158
Magazine: Inside Asian America 120
Magical World of Fisher-Price 379
Main Floor 216
Main Quad 237
Maintenance Men's Lounge 97
M&M's Chocolate Mini Baking Bits 307
Man's Life 188
MapQuest 100
MAPS 24
Margapita 210
Mark Twain Bank 265
Mark's Apology Note Generator 175
Marriage 194
Marriage and Relationships 194
Marriage Toolbox 194
Mart 223
Mary Kay, Inc. 218
Massimo Osti Production 206
Mastercard 373
Match.com 182
Matchmaking Game 184
Matrix Space 110
Matzah Market 374
Maui Island Computing-Customer Support 329
MBA Page 239
MBA Style Magazine 202
MCA/Universal Home Video Kid's page 157
McCall's Patterns 199
McDonald's 106
MCI 362
Media History Project 426
Media Secrets 96
Medical Mall 147

Medicine Box 22
MedicineNet 23
MedicineNet Medical Dictionary 21
Medsearch America 63
MedSurf 21
Megabyte Mall 362
MegaMall 362
Melanet—African-American Business Directory 397
MelrosEast 95
Menopause: Another Change in Life 31
Mental Health Net 44
Mesh Mart 340
MetaCrawler 411
Meta-Index for Legal Research 431
Metropolis Online 293
MexPlaza 363
Miami Herald 126
Michael Jackson's Beer Hunter Online 300
Microquest 275
Microsoft Kids 253
Microsoft NBC 123
Middle Eastern Dance Reference Guide 89
Midlink Magazine 153
Minnesota Zoo 159
Minnetonka Moccasins 210
Minority Affairs Forum 398
Minority Business and Professional Directory 417
MiraeNet 397
Mirkin Report 35
Mirsky's Worst of the Web 337
Mission Critical 250
Missouri Botanical Garden 312
Mister Rogers' Neighborhood 228
MMWire Classifieds 65
MMWire Weekly 347
Moan and Groan Page 328
Model's Lynk 214
Models Online 214
Modenet 363
Moms' Night Out 97
MonasteryNET 175
MoneyHunter 284
Money Manager Review Page 272
Money Online 275
Money Talks Magazine 260
Monster Board 52
Monterey Bay Aquarium 160
Montessori for Moms 229
Montessori Network 236
Mother Jones 138
Mother Nature's General Store 374
Mothers Against Drunk Driving 392
Mothers' Voices 389
Motley Fool 262
Motorcycle Shopper Online 369
Movie Link 418
MovieLink and Moviefone 94
Movie Poster Page 379
Mr. Edible Starchy Tuber Head home page 157
Mr. Showbiz 93
MTV 216
MTV Online 99
Mudcat Cafe Presents Deltablues.com 108
Mudders 97
Multimedia Exhibits in Women's History 242
Multimedia Mom 150
Municipal Bond Scandals—The Web Site 285
Municipal Resource Center 262
MU Online Writery 256
Museum of Science and Industry of Chicago 158
Music Boulevard 107
Mutual Funds Interactive 272
Mutual Funds Magazine Online 271

My Boss Is a 68
My Yahoo 183
Mysticism in World Religions 41

N

NAFTAnet 287
NAISMap 436
Names! 147
Names Project 28
Nando Times 131
NASA Thesaurus 420
Natalie Engel's Chest of Lust, Longing and Obsession 181
National Abortion Rights Action League 389
National Agricultural Library 247
National Alliance of Breast Cancer Organizations 26
National Archives and Records Administration 431
National Association for the Advancement of Colored People 398
National Association for the Education of Young Children (NAEYC) 230
National Association for Women in Science 394
National Association of Female Executives 79
National Association of Investors Corporation 265
National Breast Cancer Coalition 27
National Center for Employee Ownership 66
National Center for Fathering 150
National Center for Missing and Exploited Children 169
National Center to Improve Practice 256
National Child Rights Alliance 392
National Clearinghouse for Criminal Justice Information Systems 431
National Coalition for the Homeless 167
National Computer Security Association (NCSA) 346
National Crash Analysis Center 434
National Decorating Products Association 296
National Defense University 255
National Earthquake Information Center 130
National Federation of the Blind 152
National Food Safety Database (NFSD) 308
National Fraud Information Center 405
National Genealogical Society 437
National Geographic 154
National Gothic Singles Network 187
National Institute for Literacy 394
National Journal of Sexual Orientation Law 135
National Law Journal 135
National Library of Education 246
National Oceanic and Atmospheric Administration 129
National Opinion Registry 139
National Organization for Rare Disorders 28
National Organization for Women 388
National Organization of Women 141
National Parent Information Network 148
National Parenting Center 148
National Parks and Conservation Association 402
National Park Service 100
National Political Index 137
National Psoriasis Foundation 25
National Public Radio 122
National Public Telecomputing Network 333
National Research Council Fellowship Office 244
National Rifle Association 142
National Rifle Association Women's Issues 389
National Right to Life 389
National Stroke Association 29
National Tourette's Syndrome 152
National Urban League 398
National Weather Service 129
National Wildflower Research Center 312
National Women's Political Caucus 387
National Women's Resource Center 32

Native Sources 87
Natural History Museum of Los Angeles County 87
NBC News 123
NBC Online 98
NCS Career Magazine 56
Neiman Marcus 355
Nest Egg Magazine 276
Netamorphix 341
Net as a Telephone FAQ 334
NetCal! 428
Netcash 373
NetEx Unofficial Windows95 Software Archive 325
Netiquette 336
Netiquette Comic Strip 335
Netizen 143
Net Law News 348
Netly News 349
NetMall 363
NetNanny 163
NetNoir 123
Net Profit Private Investor Service 266
Net Radio 124
Netscape's Creating Net Sites 339
NetShare 276
Netsurfer Digest 337
NetTax '96 272
Net Tips 293
Net: User Guidelines and Netiquette 335
Network of East-West Women 392
NETworth 270
New Age Journal Online 40
New Century Network 119
New England Journal of Medicine 121
News Alert 288
News from Around the World 122
Newsletter Library 432
NewsPage 287
Newspapers/Media 119
Newsroom 120
New Tools for Teaching 251
New York Botanical Garden 312
New York Post 128
New York Times 126
NewView's Specs 163
NewWork News 66
NeWWW 350
NEXT Online 214
Nicole Brown Simpson Charitable Foundation 387
Nicole Miller 205
Nine Lives 361
Nine Lives Clothing Consignment Store 357
1996-97 Occupational Outlook Handbook 70
19th Century American Women Writers Web 91
9to5: What every woman needs to know about sexual harassment 66
Nizkor Project 427
NlightN 427
Nobel Prize Archive 426
Nolo Press Self-Help Law Center 394
Non-Stick Looney Page 110
Noodles' Panic-Anxiety Page 47
Norma Kamali 205
Notebooks.com 330
Nrv8 106
N-touch Magazine 203
NumaWeb 261
Nutri Link 37
Nutrition Pages 38
Nutritionist's ToolBox 37
NYStyle 202

O

Oakdale 2 97
Oasis 193

Objectivism (and Ayn Rand) Web Service 91
O'Brien's Cafe 97
Obsolete Computer Museum 330
Obstetric Ultrasound 42
Odyssey of the Mind 235
Office of Population Research 434
Official Hopeless Romantics page 178
Off the Net 346
Oilily 211
Older Women's League 400
Once Upon a Time in the Eighties 238
OncoLink: U. of Pennsylvania Cancer Resource 24
One Day at a Time: Survival Guide for Relationships 179
One-and-Only Internet Personals 182
1-800-Dedicate 177
1-800-Flowers 313
1-800-TAX-LAWS 273
1-800-USA-GIFT 377
101 Easy Ways to Say No 177
101 Hollywood Blvd. 95
1040.com 273
1World Plaza 363
Online Birth Center 43
Online Career Center 53
Online Health Network 19
Online Intelligence Project 118
Online Intergroup of Alchoholics Anonymous 396
Online PC Review 347
Online Sports 65
Onsale 378
Onsale Steals and Deals 361
Open Prairie Syndicate 186
Open Text 411
Operabase 108
OperaWeb 107
Orchid House 312
Orchid Mall 377
O'Reilly and Associates 328
Oscar-Mayer Cyber Cinema 304
Our Honeymoon: Two City Slickers in the Middle of Nowhere 194
Out.com 185
Outdoor Action 160
Outlet Bound 378
OutRage! 399
Over the Coffee 301
Owens Corning 294
Oxford English Dictionary 419

P

Pacific News Service 393
Page at Pooh Corner 154
Paint It Yourself: Faux Finish Instructions 292
Pantheon.org 88
Paper Magazine 206
Papermag 377
Papermag's Stylin Section 199
Parade Fashion Consulate 203
Paramount 115
Parenthood Web 149
Parenting Twins or Other Multiples 151
Parent News 151
Parents Against Speeding Teens 393
Parents, Families, and Friends of Lesbians and Gays 399
Parents Helping Parents: The Family Resource Center 394
Parents of Preschoolers Resource Page 229
Parent Soup 148
Parents Place 149
Parkinson's Web 25
Parsons School of Design 222
Patent Law 132
Pathfinder 53

Pathfinder's DreamShop 363
Pathfinder Travel 99
Pathways to School Improvement 250
Paul Smith 207
PAWWS: Wall Street on the Internet 270
PBS Online 98
PC/Computing Online 324
PC Flowers and Gifts 377
PC LapTop Magazine 326
PC Lube and Tune 325
PC Magazine Online 326
PCTravel 381
PC Week Online 326
Peace Net 142
Peace Page 110
Peachpit Press 328
Pediatric Points of Interest 23
PEDINFO Home Page 22
Pencom Interactive Salary Survey 74
Penguin Books 371
Pennsylvania Dutch Marketplace 363
PeopleFinder 415
People Magazine Online 94
Perfect Present Picker 377
Perry-Casta-eda Library Map Collection 130
Perry Ellis 365
Persfin Digest/Personal Finance Web Sites 277
Personal Finance Network 273
Pet Bird Page 318
Peter Schmidt, CTA 277
Pete's Pond Page 314
Pet Hotline 321
Pet Loss & Grieving Resource Pages 321
Pet Phocus 319
Pharmaceutical Information Network Home Page 23
Pharmacy Week 80
Philadelphia Online 127
Philatelists Online 380
Philippa's Problem Page 178
Phoebus Action Gallery Online Auction 298
PhotArchipelago 87
Photodisc, Inc. 340
Piano Education Page 254
Pillow Talk's Stork Site 146
Pitsco Technology Education 253
Pixelsight 340
Places to Stay 416
Planned Parenthood Federation 166
Planned Parenthood National Site 44
Planning a Cocktail Party 300
Planning Your Future 74
Plastic Princess page 103
Plastic Princess Collector's Page 315
Playbill 89
P-Link, The Plastic Surgery Link 29
PointCast Network 269
PoliticsNow 138
Polynesian Cultural Center 159
Poor Richard's Quotation Collection 424
Poot! 209
Post 127
Power Computing Corporation 327
PowerPC 328
PowerSurge 31
Pratt Institute 222
Preschool Page 229
Presidential Libraries IDEA Network 248
Preview Travel 100
Preview Vacations 381
Primarily A Cappella 108
Princeton Review 252
Prints Plus 296
Prison Legal News 137

PR Newswire 124
Prodigy Shopping Net 364
Prodigy Web Personals 182
Product 354
Professional Organizations in the Information Sciences 248
Progress of Nations 1996 22
Progressive Directory 391
Project America 390
Project Bartleby 91
Project Cool 338
Project Vote Smart 141
Prostate Cancer InfoLink 25
PSI Interramp 331
Psychiatry & the Law 132
Psychology.Com 66
Pukeiti Rhododendron Trust 313
Pulitzer Prizes 427
Purchase Agenda: The Computer Buyer's URL 326
Purina Pet Care 317

Q

Queer Resources Directory 167
Quest: NASA K-12 Internet Initiative 235
Quick Guide to Resume Writing 58
Quicken Financial Networks 275
QuickTime Continuum 327
Quotation Page 424
Quotations from Hell 423
Quotations Page 131
QuoteCom 267
Qworld 186

R

Rachel's Wedding Frugality Page 190
RAGS Magazine 200
Ragu Presents: Mama's Cucina 305
Rainforest Action Network 401
Rare Genetic Diseases in Children 153
ReadyWeb 228
Real Audio 340
Really Useful Company Presents… 90
Real World: Suicide 46
Recipe Archive Index 304
Recovery Home Page 46
Recruiters OnLine Network 58
Rec.Travel Library 100
Reebok 210
Reference Desk 426
Reform Party 140
Relationship Game 181
RenalNet Information Service 29
Rent Net 281
Repetitive Strain Injury Page 24
Republican National Committee 140
Research-It! 413
Retro 113
ReuNet: The Reunion Network 396
Reuters 124
Reuters Business Alert 288
Reverse Link 165
Revlon 218
Rhino Beach 97
Richard's Restaurant Ranking 106
Richmond Journal of Law & Technology 132
Riddler 112
Riley Guide 52
RINACO Plus 266
Rivendell Dictionaries and Translators 419
Roald Dahl Index 154
Rocky Mountain Cyber Mall 364
Rocky Mountain News 127
Roe v. Wade, 410 U.S. 113 (1973) 243
Roget's Thesaurus 420
Rolling Your Own Sushi 300

Romance Novel Database 179
Romance Web 175
Romantic Rendezvous 184
Romeo Gigli 205
Roommate Bulletin Board 189
Roommates From Hell 189
Root 96
Royal Cashmere 357
Rubbermaid Site 294
Rulers 426
Runner's World 33
RuPaul's House of Love 94
Rutgers University Law School 131
RxList—The Internet Drug Index 23

S

Safari Splash home page 155
Safe Surf 148
Safer Sex Page 42
Safer Sex Pages 336
SafeSurf 149
Safety Link 21
SafetyNet Domestic Violence Resources 31
Saint Louis University School of Law 132
Sally's Place 304
Salon 104
Salon Magazine 139
Salons USA 216
Saludos Web 69
SampleSale 378
Sam's Interactive Cable Guide 349
Sandwich Generation 170
San Jose Mercury News 127
Santa's Home Page 165
Satore Township (a Retreat on the Shores of the Internet…) 66
Sausage Software 344
Save a Female Through Education 388
Save-A-Pet 319
SavvySearch 411
SBA's Women's Business Ownership Page 73
Schneid's Volleyball Page 32
Scholarly Journals Distributed Via the World-Wide Web 249
Scholarly Societies Project 251
Scholarship Foundation of America 246
School House Rock page 161
Schoolhouse Videos and CDs 254
Science of Obesity and Weight Control 36
Science's Next Wave 72
Sci-Fi Channel: The Dominion 98
SCORE home page 81
Screaming Capitalist 274
Screen Savers for Windows From A-Z and WindowsWallpaper 325
Scrivenery: A Writer's Journal 71
Scrolling Mystery Theater 96
Sea Ray Boats 369
Sea World/Busch Gardens Animal Information Database 236
Season's Greetings 165
SEC EDGAR Database 262
Secrets and Whispers: Daughters of the Dust home page 93
Securities Law Home Page 263
Security APL Stock Quote Server 270
Self-Help Psychology Magazine 47
SeniorNet 400
Seniors-Site 400
Sensible Saver 280
7Avenue 203
770 Oceanwalk 95
7th on Sixth 223
Sexual Assault Information Page 32

Sexuality Bytes 43
Shakespeare's Diary 98
Shareware.com 398
Sharper Image 293
Sharp Placement Professionals Inc. 58
Shenkar College (Israel) 222
Shiseido 219
ShoeInfoNet 211
Shoes on the Net 211
Shoeworld 211
ShopSite Marketplace 364
Sidney Herald Online 126
Sierra Club 401
Sierra Club Books 371
Signet Bank College Money Matters 244
Silicon Investor 36
Simply Easter 165
Single Life Institute 187
Singles Web 188
Sisley 209
Skaff's Oriental Rugs 295
Skeptic's Dictionary 420
SkillSearch 60
Sleep Medicine Home Page 25
Small- and Home-Based Business Links 283
Small Business Journal 284
Smart Valley Inc.'s Telecommuting Web Pages 72
Smith Barney Wall Street Watch 267
Smithsonian Institute 86
Smithsonian Institutions Libraries 247
Snakebite Emergency Web Page 315
Snax.com 304
So@pNet 96
Soap Links 95
Social Security Frequently Asked Questions 407
Society for Human Resource Management 81
Software for the Macintosh 334
SOHO Central 75
SonicNet 107
Sony Online 114
Soundbite Kiss 180
South Asian Women's Net 398
South Florida Magazine 200
Southerners 97
Southern Living 299
Speak to Me 364
Special Car Journal 369
Specifica 46
Spencer Gifts 377
Spiegel Directions 355
Spirit-WWW 41
Sports Illustrated for Kids 164
Sportszone 36
Spot 95
SPRYNET 331
Squat 98
St. Cyberburg 97
St. Petersburg Times 127
Stan's Place 177
Star and SA Times 128
Star Child 235
Star Child…Astronomy for Kids 156
Star-Brite Learning Program 252
StarNine: WebStar 344
Statistical Reports on U.S. Science and Engineering 430
Stepstones 97
Steve Jackson Games vs. The Secret Service 347
Stitcher's Source 380
Stock Club 268
StockDeck 268
Stock Master at MIT 268
Stock Research Group 267
Stolen Bike Registry 426

Straight Spouse Support Network 186
Strange Case of the Lost Elvis Diaries, The 96
StreetNet 270
StreetStyle 203
Strong Funds 270
Student Guide: Financial Aid from the U.S. Department of Education 246
Student Services 244
Students for a Democratic Society 142
StudioNet 216
Style by Suzy Menkes 204
Style Front 203
Sub Pop Online 107
Subway Navigator 436
Suck 106
Sudden Infant Death Syndrome Network 147
Sumac Ridge Estate Winery 374
Sunergy 349
Super 70s 114
SUPERMODEL.COM 214
Supermodel.com 95
Support for Stepfamilies 167
Supreme Court Decisions 135
Surf News 348
SurfWatch 163
Survey of Men: Sex, Virginity, Dating, Commitment, Marriage 182
Survey.net 350
Survivors, In Search of a Voice 27
Survivors of Stalking 391
Suzi Saint Tropez 357
Swatch 211
Sweet Seductions 374
Switchboard 76
Swoon 174
Syndicate 262
System Optimization 325

T

Taglines Galore! 427
Tales of Wonder 155
Talk Shop 74
TallWeb II 427
Tarheel Mall 364
t@ponline.com 113
t@p Style 203
Taxi's Newspaper List 120
Taxing Times 272
Taxpayers Against Fraud 405
Tax Prophet 273
TBS Kids Disaster Area 161
TD Bank 261
TeachNet: The Teachers Network 251
Tea Man 301
Techno3 96
Techno Weenie 330
TechWeb 347
Telecommuting and Telework Resource Page 72
Telecommuting Jobs 63
Telecom Information Resources 331
Telegarden 313
Tenant Net 391
Tennis Warehouse 380
Terra IncogNeta 341
Theatre Central (International) 90
Thierry Mugler 206
This Old House 309
Thomas 140
Thrive 19
Ticketmaster 216
Ticketmaster Online 376
Tic-Tac-Toe 157
Time Out 121
Time Out Net 100
Timecast 124

TIPnet 265
Today-in-History 428
Today's Calendar and Clock Page 428
Tom's Guide to Good Livin' 17
Ton Cremers and Marian Beereboom's Book Information Web site 92
Totally Unofficial Rap Dictionary 420
Tourette Syndrome Home Page 24
Toys R' Us 164
Tradeline Investor Center 270
Trade Mission, Inc. 378
Trade Point USA 282
Training.net 81
Training-Nutrition Home Page 36
Travel Discounts 381
Travel Health Online 18
TravelNow 381
Travelocity 99
TravelShop 364
Travlang 99
Tree Doctor 314
Tripod 75
Troma 180
Trusts and Estate 135
TSU Folklore Collection 432
Tucows 329
Tuppertime 302
Turbo-Charge Your Job Search 56
TV Guide Online 99
TV Tonight 99
Tweak 336
Twentieth Century Fox 114
24 Hours in Cyberspace 113
Twinless Twins 151
Twins Book Research 152
2B! 206

U

U.C. Berkeley Libraries 248
Ultimate Band List 107
Ultimate Restaurant Guide 106
Ultimate Television List 95
UnCover 252
Unicef 386
UniSci 249
United Colors of Benetton 208
United Homeowners Association 310
United Kingdom English for the American Novice 419
United Media 127
United Nations 140
United Nations Division for the Advancement of Women 393
U.S. Census Bureau 430
U.S.D.A. Forest Service Home Page 403
U.S. Deptartment of Health and Human Services 404
U.S. Department of Justice 135
U.S. Department of Labor Women's Bureau 404
U.S. Gazetteer 436
U.S. House of Representaties Internet Law Library 132
U.S. News & World Report 121
U.S. Patent Office 132
U. S. Postal Service 434
U. S. Securities and Exchange Commission 405
U. S. Swimming 33
U.S. Two-Year Colleges 238
United Way 167
United Way Online 387
Universal Studios 115
University Financing Foundation 252
University of Cincinnati College of Law 133
University of Washington Medicinal Herb Garden 314

University of Waterloo Career Development Manual 57
University Wire 425
Unofficial Martha Stewart Home Page 299
Unsolved Mysteries 123
Upjohn Institute for Employment Research 67
Upside 288
Urban Decay 219
Urban Desires 106
USADATA 434
USA Recovery from debt home page 274
USA Today 125
USA Track & Field 33
Used Software Exchange 328
Usenet Info Center Launch Pad 334
USGS Learning Web 236
Utilities Design Match 356

V

Van DerGrift's Children's Literature Page 154
Vegas.COM presents Las Vegas 193
Veggies Unite! 305
Ventana Online 371
Versions 331
ViaBazaar 200
Viamall 365
Vibe Online 103
Vidal Sassoon Academy 216
VINE™ Entrepreneur Mall 74
Virtual Background Museum 343
Virtual Flyshop 316
Virtual Garden 310
Virtual Garment Center 224
Virtual Headbook 62
Virtual Health 305
Virtual Job Fair 57
Virtual Kissing Booth 180
Virtual LEGO 162
Virtually React 165
Virtual MeetMarket 183
Virtual Memorial Garden 396
Virtual Online University 255
Virtual Pet Cemetery 320
Virtual Press Job Information 54
Virtual Sisterhood 390
Virtual Society on the Web 340
Virtual Software Library 330
Virtual Toystore 380
Virtual Vineyards 300
VirtuaLynx 365
Visa 373
Visibilities 187
Visible Embryo 44
Vivarin Date-Ability Index 175
Vodoun (Voodoo) Information Pages 41
Voices of Women 404
Voices of Youth: World Summit 166
Volcano World 156
Volume Library 423
Vox Pop 142

W

W.&L.T. 207
WAHM—The Online Magazine for Work-At-Home Moms 79
Wall Street Direct 265
Wall Street Journal 286
Wall Street Online 269
Walter Moszel 205
Warner Bros. 115
Warner Bros. Animation 161
Washington Post 125
Washington Weekly 137
WealthWEB 267

Weather Channel 128
WebActive 137
Web-A-Sketch 112
WebCrawle: 412
Web Designer 343
Web Developer's Virtual Library 340
Web-grrl 78
Web Master Magazine 340
Web Multimedia Tour 339
WebMuseum 86
Web of Addictions 31
WEB Personals 182
Web Poetry Kit 112
Webreference.com 339
Web Servers Comparison Chart 344
WEBster 348
Webster's Dictionary 419
Web-sters' Net-Work: Women in Info Technology 81
Web Toolz Magazine 339
Web Warehouse 365
Web Week 351
Web Wise 338
Wedding Bells 191
Wedding Circle 190
WeddingLine 192
Wedding Source 192
Wedding Web 190
WedNet 191
Weekend a Firenze 365
Weekend City Press 285
Weight Watchers 307
Welcome to @WWWiz 347
Wellesley College 241
WellnessWeb 17
Wellness World 40
Wells Fargo 278
WFMU's Catalog of Curiosities 378
Whale Adoption Project 320
What's Newt: Keeping Track of Newt Gingrich 139
Where Did They Go? 415
Where It's @ 349
Where to Buy Model Railroad Supplies in the 1990s 316
White House for Kids 159
Whitehouse.Net 143
Whoopie! 336
WhoWhere 76
Why Cats Paint 320
Why? The Failed Marriages of Generation X 194
Wildlife Conservation Society 159
Wimmer Companies 309
Windows95.com 325
Wine.com 375
Wine Making Pages 300
Wines on the Internet 375
Womanist 242
Women & Family Law 133
WomenBiz 274
Women for Women in Bosnia 388
Women in Higher Education 79
Women in Politics 138
Women in Technology International (WITI) 78
Women of Marvel Comics 109
Women of 1970s Punk 107
Women of Star Trek 99
Women's Business Resource Site 69
Women's Campaign School 242
Women's Edge 17
Women's Health Hot Line 23
Women's International Center 242
Women's Link by Bristol Myers 215
WomenSpace 434
Women's Rugby 34

Women's Sports Page 32
Women's Studies 242
Women's Studies on Disc: The Women's Studies Index on CD-ROM 254
Women's Studies Research Guide 242
Women's Studio Workshop 79
Women's Web/BizNet 69
Women's Web Magazine 404
Women's Wire Body Channel 16
Women's Wire Buzz Channel 113
Women's Wire Cash Channel 277
Women's Wire Chat 74
Women's Wire News Channel 119
Women's Wire Shopping Channel 356
Women's Wire Style Channel 198
Women's Wire Work Channel 68
Wonderful Stitches 102
Wool Home 209
Word 105
Word Mill 371
WordNet 420
Working Solo 76
Working Together Listserv (mailing list) 67
Worklife 67
Workplace at Galaxy 58
World Book of Holiday Traditions 165
Worldclass 287
World Guide to Vegetarianism 37
World Health Network 30
World Health Organization 404
World Hug Week 179
World Lecture Hall 239
World Liberalism 142
World Library 433
WorldNews Online 120
World of Macanudo and Partagas 299
World of Multiple Sclerosis 26
World of Tea 301
World Pages 414
Worldport Personals 183
Worldshop 365
World Singles 184
WorldVillage 330
World Wide Arts Resources 297
WorldWide Classifieds 298
World-Wide Collectors Digest 380
World Wide Holiday and Festival Page 428
World Wide Magic 366
World Wide Mall 366
World Wide Wanderer Cyberian Bucket Shop Guide 361
WorldWideWeb Consortium 350
World Wildlife Fund 402
Wounded Healer Journal 31
Writer's Edge 71
Writers Resource Center 71
WWD (Womens Wear Daily) 204
WWWMall 366
WWW Virtual Library: Cryptography, PGP, and Your Privacy 345
WWWomen 413

X

X Avenue 366
Xplore 338

Y

Yahoo! 53
Yahooligans! 162
Yahoo Net Events 74
Yahoo! People Search 415
Yale C/AIM WWW Style Manual 342
Yecch! 111
Yenta—The Student.Net Matchmaker 185
Y-ME National Breast Cancer Organization 27

Yoga Paths 41
Your Health Daily 21
Your Personal Salon 216
Your Say 388
Youth Action Online 185
YPN Net News and Money 275
Yum Yum 303
Yush Ponline 103
Yves Saint Laurent 206

Z

Zac Attac 357
Zack's Investor's Window 263
ZDNet 346
ZD Net Software Library 330
Zenith Data Systems 325
ZipFind 435
Z Magazine 137
Zora Neale Hurston Home Page 91
Zuzu's Petals Literary Resource 88

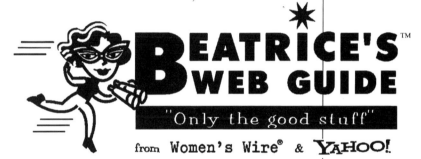

■ END-USER LICENSE AGREEMENT

READ THIS AGREEMENT CAREFULLY BEFORE BUYING THIS BOOK. BY BUYING THE BOOK AND USING THE PROGRAM LISTINGS, CD-ROM, AND PROGRAMS REFERRED TO BELOW, YOU ACCEPT THE TERMS OF THIS AGREEMENT.

The program listings included in this book and the programs included on the CD-ROM contained in the package on the opposite page ("CD-ROM") are proprietary products of Macmillan Computer Publishing USA and/or third party suppliers ("Suppliers"). The program listings and programs are hereinafter collectively referred to as the "Programs." Macmillan Computer Publishing USA and the Suppliers retain ownership of the CD-ROM and copyright to the Programs, as their respective interests may appear. The Programs and the copy of the CD-ROM provided are licensed (not sold) to you under the conditions set forth herein.

License. You may use the CD-ROM on any compatible computer, provided that the CD-ROM is used on only one computer and by one user at a time.

Restrictions. You may not commercially distribute the CD-ROM or the Programs or otherwise reproduce, publish, or distribute or otherwise use the CD-ROM or the Programs in any manner that may infringe any copyright or other proprietary right of Macmillan Computer Publishing USA, the Suppliers, or any other party or assign, sublicense, or otherwise transfer the CD-ROM or this agreement to any other party unless such party agrees to accept the terms and conditions of this agreement. This license and your right to use the CD-ROM and the Programs automatically terminates if you fail to comply with any provision of this agreement.

U.S. GOVERNMENT RESTRICTED RIGHTS. The CD-ROM and the programs are provided with **RESTRICTED RIGHTS**. Use, duplication, or disclosure by the Government is subject to restrictions as set forth in subparagraph (c)(1)(ii) of the Rights in Technical Data and Computer Software Clause at DFARS (48 CFR 252.277-7013). The Proprietor of the compilation of the Programs and the CD ROM is Macmillan Computer Publishing USA, 5903 Christie Avenue, Emeryville, CA 94608.

Limited Warranty. Macmillan Computer Publishing USA warrants the physical CD-ROM to be free of defects in materials and workmanship under normal use for a period of 30 days from the purchase date. If Macmillan Computer Publishing USA receives written notification within the warranty period of defects in materials or workmanship in the physical CD-ROM, and such notification is determined by Macmillan Computer Publishing USA to be correct, Macmillan Computer Publishing USA will, at its option, replace the defective CD-ROM or refund a prorata portion of the purchase price of the book. **THESE ARE YOUR SOLE REMEDIES FOR ANY BREACH OF WARRANTY.**

EXCEPT AS SPECIFICALLY PROVIDED ABOVE, THE CD-ROM AND THE PROGRAMS ARE PROVIDED "AS IS" WITHOUT ANY WARRANTY OF ANY KIND. NEITHER MACMILLAN COMPUTER PUBLISHING USA NOR THE SUPPLIERS MAKE ANY WARRANTY OF ANY KIND AS TO THE ACCURACY OR COMPLETENESS OF THE CD-ROM OR THE PROGRAMS OR THE RESULTS TO BE OBTAINED FROM USING THE CD-ROM OR THE PROGRAMS AND NEITHER MACMILLAN COMPUTER PUBLISHING USA NOR THE SUPPLIERS SHALL BE RESPONSIBLE FOR ANY CLAIMS ATTRIBUTABLE TO ERRORS, OMISSIONS, OR OTHER INACCURACIES IN THE CD-ROM OR THE PROGRAMS. THE ENTIRE RISK AS TO THE RESULTS AND PERFORMANCE OF THE CD-ROM AND THE PROGRAMS IS ASSUMED BY THE USER. FURTHER, NEITHER MACMILLAN COMPUTER PUBLISHING USA NOR THE SUPPLIERS MAKE ANY REPRESENTATIONS OR WARRANTIES, EITHER EXPRESS OR IMPLIED, WITH RESPECT TO THE CD-ROM OR THE PROGRAMS, INCLUDING BUT NOT LIMITED TO, THE QUALITY, PERFORMANCE, MERCHANTABILITY, OR FITNESS FOR A PARTICULAR PURPOSE OF THE CD-ROM OR THE PROGRAMS. IN NO EVENT SHALL MACMILLAN COMPUTER PUBLISHING USA OR THE SUPPLIERS BE LIABLE FOR DIRECT, INDIRECT, SPECIAL, INCIDENTAL, OR CONSEQUENTIAL DAMAGES ARISING OUT THE USE OF OR INABILITY TO USE THE CD-ROM OR THE PROGRAMS OR FOR ANY LOSS OR DAMAGE OF ANY NATURE CAUSED TO ANY PERSON OR PROPERTY AS A RESULT OF THE USE OF THE CD-ROM OR THE PROGRAMS, EVEN IF MACMILLAN COMPUTER PUBLISHING USA OR THE SUPPLIERS HAVE BEEN SPECIFICALLY ADVISED OF THE POSSIBILITY OF SUCH DAMAGES. NEITHER MACMILLAN COMPUTER PUBLISHING USA NOR THE SUPPLIERS ARE RESPONSIBLE FOR ANY COSTS INCLUDING, BUT NOT LIMITED TO, THOSE INCURRED AS A RESULT OF LOST PROFITS OR REVENUE, LOSS OF USE OF THE CD-ROM OR THE PROGRAMS, LOSS OF DATA, THE COSTS OF RECOVERING SOFTWARE OR DATA, OR THIRD-PARTY CLAIMS. IN NO EVENT WILL MACMILLAN COMPUTER PUBLISHING USA'S OR THE SUPPLIERS' LIABILITY FOR ANY DAMAGES TO YOU OR ANY OTHER PARTY EVER EXCEED THE PRICE OF THIS BOOK. NO SALES PERSON OR OTHER REPRESENTATIVE OF ANY PARTY INVOLVED IN THE DISTRIBUTION OF THE CD-ROM IS AUTHORIZED TO MAKE ANY MODIFICATIONS OR ADDITIONS TO THIS LIMITED WARRANTY.

MACMILLAN COMPUTER PUBLISHING USA'S LICENSOR(S) MAKES NO WARRANTIES, EXPRESS OR IMPLIED, INCLUDING WITHOUT LIMITATION THE IMPLIED WARRANTIES OF MERCHANTABILITY AND FITNESS FOR A PARTICULAR PURPOSE, REGARDING THE SOFTWARE. MACMILLAN COMPUTER PUBLISHING USA'S LICENSOR(S) DOES NOT WARRANT, GUARANTEE OR MAKE ANY REPRESENTATIONS REGARDING THE USE OR THE RESULTS OF THE USE OF THE SOFTWARE IN TERMS OF ITS CORRECTNESS, ACCURACY, RELIABILITY, CURRENTNESS OR OTHERWISE. THE ENTIRE RISK AS TO THE RESULTS AND PERFORMANCE OF THE SOFTWARE IS ASSUMED BY YOU. THE EXCLUSION OF IMPLIED WARRANTIES IS NOT PERMITTED BY SOME JURISDICTIONS. THE ABOVE EXCLUSION MAY NOT APPLY TO YOU.

IN NO EVENT WILL MACMILLAN COMPUTER PUBLISHING USA'S LICENSOR(S), AND THEIR DIRECTORS, OFFICERS, EMPLOYEES OR AGENTS (COLLECTIVELY MACMILLAN COMPUTER PUBLISHING USA'S LICENSOR) BE LIABLE TO YOU FOR ANY CONSEQUENTIAL, INCIDENTAL OR INDIRECT DAMAGES (INCLUDING DAMAGES FOR LOSS OF BUSINESS PROFITS, BUSINESS INTERRUPTION, LOSS OF BUSINESS INFORMATION, AND THE LIKE) ARISING OUT OF THE USE OR INABILITY TO USE THE SOFTWARE EVEN IF MACMILLAN COMPUTER PUBLISHING USA'S LICENSOR HAS BEEN ADVISED OF THE POSSIBILITY OF SUCH DAMAGES. BECAUSE SOME JURISDICTIONS DO NOT ALLOW THE EXCLUSION OR LIMITATION OF LIABILITY FOR CONSEQUENTIAL OR INCIDENTAL DAMAGES, THE ABOVE LIMITATIONS MAY NOT APPLY TO YOU.

Some states do not allow the exclusion or limitation of implied warranties or limitation of liability for incidental or consequential damages, so the above limitation or exclusion may not apply to you.

General. Macmillan Computer Publishing USA and the Suppliers retain all rights not expressly granted. Nothing in this license constitutes a waiver of the rights of Macmillan Computer Publishing USA or the Suppliers under the U.S. Copyright Act or any other Federal or State Law, international treaty, or foreign law.